ADAPTIVE PERSPECTIVES *on* Human–Technology Interaction

SERIES IN HUMAN–TECHNOLOGY INTERACTION

SERIES EDITOR

Alex Kirlik

Adaptive Perspectives on Human–Technology Interaction: Methods and Models for Cognitive Engineering and Human–Computer Interaction
Edited by Alex Kirlik

PCs, Phones, and the Internet: The Social Impact of Information Technology
Edited by Robert Kraut, Malcolm Brynin, and Sara Kiesler

ADAPTIVE
PERSPECTIVES
on

Human–Technology Interaction

Methods and Models for Cognitive Engineering and Human–Computer Interaction

EDITED BY

Alex Kirlik

OXFORD

UNIVERSITY PRESS

2006

OXFORD
UNIVERSITY PRESS

Oxford University Press, Inc., publishes works that further
Oxford University's objective of excellence
in research, scholarship, and education.

Oxford   New York
Auckland   Cape Town   Dar es Salaam   Hong Kong   Karachi
Kuala Lumpur   Madrid   Melbourne   Mexico City   Nairobi
New Delhi   Shanghai   Taipei   Toronto

With offices in
Argentina   Austria   Brazil   Chile   Czech Republic   France   Greece
Guatemala   Hungary   Italy   Japan   Poland   Portugal   Singapore
South Korea   Switzerland   Thailand   Turkey   Ukraine   Vietnam

Published by Oxford University Press, Inc.
198 Madison Avenue, New York, New York 10016

www.oup.com

Oxford is a registered trademark of Oxford University Press

Library of Congress Cataloging-in-Publication Data
Adaptive perspectives on human-technology interaction : methods and models for cognitive
engineering and human-computer interaction / edited by Alex Kirlik.
    p. cm. — (Human-technology interaction)
Includes bibliographical references and indexes.
ISBN-13 978-0-19-517182-2
ISBN 0-19-517182-9
1. Human-computer interaction.   2. Human-machine systems.   I. Kirlik, Alex.   II. Series.
QA76.9.H85A34 2005
004'.01'9—dc22   2005009304

9 8 7 6 5 4 3 2 1

Printed in the United States of America
on acid-free paper

To Egon Brunswik and Kenneth R. Hammond

Kenneth R. Hammond

Foreword

This book will no doubt stand as an advance for cognitive engineering, but it will also stand as an affirmation of Egon Brunswik's claims for the significant change he claimed was necessary for the advancement of psychology. His claims—put forward in very scholarly yet unusually bold terms —were that behaviorism built on narrow, deterministic, stimulus-response theory, and its accompanying methodology (the rule of one variable) derived from a physicalistic theme that should be given up in favor a theme almost exactly opposite to that. It has taken over a half century for change in that direction to reach this point, but as the many contributors to this volume show, a firm step in the direction Brunswik advocated has now been taken.

Although Brunswik's book *Perception and the Representative Design of Psychological Experiments* (1956) presented his arguments in a coherent and substantive fashion, it could not have appeared at a worse time for his thesis to be considered. The methods of analysis of variance (ANOVA) introduced by Fisher some 30 years earlier had by then been discovered by psychologists and found to be an answer to their dreams. No longer would they be restricted to Woodworth's 1938 dictum about the "rule of one variable" that exhausted the experimental methodology of the day, and once multiple variables could be employed (as in factorial design), they were required, and research blossomed, along with scientific prestige—well, a little, anyway. And you better not try to publish in a major journal without a prominent use of ANOVA. Yet it was this very technique—this goose that was laying the golden egg of scientific respectability—and research money—that Brunswik was trying to kill. Of course, his challenge didn't stand a chance, and it didn't get one.

In 1941, however, Brunswik got his chance to go head to head with Clark Hull and Kurt Lewin, the leaders of the conventional approaches to psychology. In his presentation Brunswik made this statement:

> The point I should like to emphasize is . . .
> the necessary imperfection, inflicted upon
> achievements . . . by the ambiguity in the
> causal texture of the environment. . . . Because
> of this environmental ambiguity, no matter
> how smoothly the organismic instruments and
> mechanisms may function, relationships cannot
> be foolproof, at least as far as those connecting
> with the vitally relevant more remote distal
> regions of the environment are concerned.
> (Hammond & Stewart, 2001, p. 59)

Now, to be frank, in 1941 no psychologist but Brunswik spoke like this: "causal texture?" "Environmental ambiguity?" "Vitally relevant more remote distal regions of the environment?" None of these terms were part of a psychologist's vocabulary in the 1940s. As a result, many simply refused to try to understand what he was saying and rejected everything with scornful remarks about Brunswik's inability to write. Although it is probably true that some readers even today won't be familiar with those words and what they signify, they will come much closer than Hull and Lewin did to understanding that Brunswik was saying a great deal, albeit in unfamiliar language applicable to a bold new conception of psychology.

Today's cognitive engineers, however, won't be afraid of that sentence because the ideas in it—wholly mystifying to mid-century learning theorists—are now common. Brunswik was pointing out that human beings were going to make inaccurate empirical judgments ("the necessary imperfection, inflicted upon achievements") and these will occur not through any fault of their own ("no matter how smoothly the organismic instruments and mechanisms may function") but instead because of "environmental ambiguity," and that this was particularly true of the more important ("vitally relevant more remote distal regions of the environment") judgments we make, about other people, for example. Thus he prepared the way for differentiating among various cognitive goals (ranging from accurate proximal judgments close to the skin along a continuum to accurate judgments about covert distal personal or meteorological variables). Communication failed not because he was poor writer (he was highly precise), but because in calling attention to environmental ambiguity, no one knew or was interested in what he was talking about, and that was because no one was then giving any consideration to the environment. The organism and its "instruments and mechanisms" dominated everything; all that was needed was a stimulus to get it going and produce a response. But not for cognitive engineers: Given the goals of their profession—and these include the design of the environment, and the design of technical displays—cognitive engineers know exactly what Brunswik was saying to psychologists, and that was: Consider the informational characteristics of the environment and how these affect the judgments of individuals.

Brunswik was fully aware of the hard road he faced in trying to direct the attention of the psychologists of the mid-twentieth century to the role of the causal texture of the environment, and in 1955 he made his final effort with the publication of *Perception and the Representative Design of Psychological Experiments* (published posthumously in 1956). In the preface of that book he stated: "This book has been written with two major purposes in mind. One is the exposition of the more complex attainments of perception, those attainments that help stabilize our grasp of the relevant features of the physical and social environment. The other purpose is the development of the only methodology by which the [aforesaid goal] can be reached, that is, representative design" (Brunswik, 1956, p. vii). Those complex attainments will be exactly those that interest cognitive engineers, and the methodology of representative design will be one that they will struggle with for some time; their results need to generalize to the environment of interest. In short, it is essential to their purposes.

The reader will see some of those struggles in the following chapters, for it is no accident that Kirlik chose to collate these chapters within the Brunswikian framework. He chose them because no paradigm is more conducive to the goals of cognitive engineering than the Brunswikian one, and that is because no other paradigm so clearly differentiates proximal and distal environmental material both theoretically and methodologically (even historically). Whereas Brunswik focused his work on the natural environment to speak to the academic psychologists of the day, he was mindful of the strong implications his paradigm held for the artificial, or "engineered," environment. Those implications can be reduced to one: The environment toward which the researcher intends to generalize should be specified in advance of the design of the experiment. That (a priori) specification should include theory as well as method. Conventional academic psychology ignored both requirements throughout the twentieth century and suffered the consequences of producing floating results; "floating" because the simple logic of generalization was applied only to subject populations; environmental generalization was ignored; consequently, the implications of the results were left unanchored. The studies Kirlik chose to include here may not meet Brunswikian ecological criteria in every way in every case, yet they will illustrate the need for meeting them and will bring us closer to our goal of understanding the problems of cognitive engineering.

It would be hard to find a field that will evoke a greater fit for the Brunswikian paradigm than cognitive engineering, for here the distinctions between natural environments and engineered environments arise immediately. An organism in a natural environment is required to cope with what Brunswik called an "uncertainty-geared" environment; probabilism is at its core. (This was an idea neither Hull and Lewin could stomach in that symposium in 1941, and they made their revulsion known to Brunswik.) But accepting that contrast between uncertainty-geared and certainty-geared environments made clear exactly what the goal of cognitive engineering would be, namely, replacing the uncertainty-geared natural environment with a certainty-geared environment; the optimal replacement created by cognitive engineers.

Indeed, one might say that such replacement defines the field of cognitive engineering. Why? Because uncertainty in the environment means error in judgment, errors of judgment can be extraordinarily costly, therefore in situations in which errors are costly, cognitive engineers should drive out or at least reduce to a minimum environmental uncertainty.

Possibly the best and most successful example of meeting the challenge to cognitive engineering to reduce environmental uncertainty is illustrated in aviation psychology. Aviation is an example of a trade or profession that began with its practitioners—the pilots—utterly dependent on information provided by perceptual (including kinesthetic) cues afforded by the uncertainty-geared natural environment. But aviation engineering has now moved to the point where information from this environment is ignored in favor of information from an artificial certainty-geared, wholly engineered environment. Uncertainty has been driven out of the flight deck to a degree unimaginable when aviation began. That change made commercial airline travel practical and saved countless lives. Exactly how much the study of cognition contributed to that engineering achievement is unclear, but history is not likely to give it much credit. We are now at a point, however, where cognitive engineering of information for the pilot is indispensable, as several

chapters in this volume show (see especially chapter 12 and chapter 18).

If the cognitive engineering of information is now indispensable, it is also highly varied and complex. A glance at the table of contents of this book will be sufficient to grasp that it involves an astonishingly wide range of topics. This can also be seen in the editor's introductions to the various parts; they offer an education in the struggle to make psychological knowledge useful. This broad vision works to the reader's advantage, for it removes cognitive engineering from mere application of knowledge already at hand to the forefront of knowledge acquisition, which was surely the editor's intention. This sophisticated consideration of theory and method together with the pursuit of utilization led to the conclusion that representing the environment was essential; theory and method would have to be adjusted accordingly. Thus cognitive engineering is changing not only applied psychology but psychology itself.

Therefore this book does more than just affirm, it points to the future. The down-to-Earth characteristics of its contents will show how the recognition of the duality of error increased the research sophistication of its authors, thanks largely to the fruitfulness of the application of such techniques as signal detection theory (SDT) and the Taylor-Russell (T-R) diagram. Although introduced roughly a decade earlier than SDT, it was not applied in the field of cognitive science until much later (see Hammond, 1966, for a brief history of both). Both techniques are directed toward the idea of separating false positive errors and false negative errors and that separation immediately made apparent the critical role of cost, benefits, and, most important, values and trade-offs among them. SDT and the T-R diagram offered valuable quantitative means of clarification of these relationships in a manner not seen before. The future will bring these ideas to a new prominence, and in doing so new distinctions will appear that will advance theory and research. For example, it will become obviously necessary to distinguish between environments of reducible and irreducible uncertainty both theoretically and methodologically.

Environments that permit reducible uncertainty will be targets of opportunity for cognitive engineers—provided other engineers haven't already exploited them. The aviation industry was already exploited because the essentially uncluttered nature of the sky invited exploitation, and the necessary technology fit with the rapid development of electronics. The navigational (and traffic) uncertainties of the uncluttered sky were steadily reducible by electronic means of measurement and communication. Allow me a brief anecdote to show how recent that was. In 1941 I was an observer in the Weather Bureau at the San Francisco Airport. On the night shift I often talked with the janitor, a bent-over old man who had been a sky-writer pilot in the early days of such stunts. His stories were fascinating; he often mentioned lack of instruments ("we had almost nothing") and what that meant (attacks of the "bends") due to a too-rapid descent. Thus, in less than a century aviation engineering went from almost nothing to the glass cockpit in which information from inside the cockpit means more than information from without. That uncluttered environment was successfully exploited by conventional, largely electronic engineering and remains now only to be tidied up by cognitive engineers. There remain many other environments that offer reducible uncertainty that cognitive engineers will exploit to the benefit of all of us.

Fortunately, Brunswikian theory and method provides a big tent; it is inclusive rather than exclusive. By virtue of its demand that the study must be designed to justify generalization to the environment of interest, it permits the use of any design that meets that criterion. That means that when generalization can be met by factorial or other forms of ANOVA, then these designs will be appropriate. When, however, the situation toward which the generalization is intended involves interdependent variables and other features not represented by factorial and similar designs, then they should not be used because the generalization will not be justified. Representation, whatever its form, is key to generalization.

But contrast that virgin—"blue sky"—territory with its reducible uncertainty with the murky territories, such as social policy formation, that entail irreducible uncertainty. Such "territories" offer the best example of requiring humans to cope with environments of irreducible uncertainty. Here is the strong future challenge to cognitive engineers; they need not and should not restrict themselves to situations involving gauges and electronics and mechanical artifacts. Their knowledge and skills are badly needed in areas where disputes remain largely at the level of primitive people past and still in modern times regularly leading to mayhem, murder, and wholesale slaughter, not to mention degradation and poverty. But cognitive engineers are accustomed to work at abstract systems levels; therefore their theories and methods should be applicable, albeit at a level of complexity that will demand innovation in theory and method and thought because of the shift to environments characterized by irreducible uncertainty.

At the level of irreducible uncertainty the Brunswikian approach will be of considerable assistance to cognitive engineers because it will allow the broadest range of theories and methods to be included. Domains of reducible uncertainty will be conquered with and without the aid of cognitive engineers, as indeed the domain of aviation psychology already has. But the domains of irreducible uncertainty will demand all the knowledge and skills and ingenuity of the modern cognitive engineer to cope with the consequences of the duality of error that follow from irreducible uncertainty. That demand will surely include the newfound knowledge of Brunswikian psychology that includes cognitive theory and the methodology appropriate to it.

References

Brunswik, E. (1956) *Perception and the representative design of psychological experiments.* Berkeley, CA: University of California Press.

Hammond, K. R. & Stewart, T. R. (2001) *The essential Brunswik: Beginnings, explications, applications.* New York: Oxford University Press.

Contents

Contributors

Leonard Adelman
Department of Systems Engineering and
 Operations Research
George Mason University

Ellen J. Bass
Department of Systems and Information
 Engineering
University of Virginia

Ann M. Bisantz
Department of Industrial Engineering
University at Buffalo, State University of
 New York

Amy E. Bolton
Training Systems Division
U.S. Naval Air Warfare Center

Michael D. Byrne
Psychology Department
Rice University

Gwendolyn E. Campbell
Training Systems Division
U.S. Naval Air Warfare Center

Stephen M. Casner
Human Factors Research and Technology
 Division
NASA Ames Research Center

Terry Connolly
Department of Management and Policy
University of Arizona

Asaf Degani
Computational Sciences Division
NASA Ames Research Center

Chris S. Fick
Department of Psychology
Rice University

Arthur D. Fisk
School of Psychology
Georgia Institute of Technology

Gordon J. Gattie
Department of Industrial Engineering
University at Buffalo, State University
 of New York

Paul Gay
Delta Airlines

William M. Goldstein
Department of Psychology
University of Chicago

Wayne D. Gray
Department of Cognitive Science
Rensselaer Polytechnic Institute

Kenneth R. Hammond
Department of Psychology
University of Colorado

William J. Horrey
Liberty Mutual Research Institute for Safety

Pratik D. Jha
Titan Corporation

Alex Kirlik
Human Factors Division and Beckman
    Institute
University of Illinois at Urbana-Champaign

Shane T. McCauley
Department of Psychology
San Francisco State University

Sheryl L. Miller
Department of Systems Engineering and
    Operations Research
George Mason University

Kathleen L. Mosier
Department of Psychology
San Francisco State University

Donita Phipps
Department of Psychology
Georgia Institute of Technology

Peter Pirolli
User Interface Research
PARC

Amy R. Pritchett
School of Industrial and Systems
    Engineering
Georgia Institute of Technology

Ling Rothrock
The Harold and Inge Marcus Department of
    Industrial and Manufacturing Engineering
Pennsylvania State University

Michael G. Shafto
Exploration Systems Mission Directorate
NASA Headquarters

Younho Seong
Department of Industrial & Systems
    Engineering
North Carolina A&T State University

Thomas R. Stewart
Center for Policy Research
University at Albany, State University of
    New York

Richard Strauss
Fatwire Software

Wendi L. Van Buskirk
Training Systems Division
U.S. Naval Air Warfare Center

Kim J. Vicente
Department of Mechanical and Industrial
    Engineering
University of Toronto

Neff Walker
UNAIDS

Christopher D. Wickens
Human Factors Division and Department of
    Psychology
University of Illinois at Urbana-Champaign

Cedric Yeo
Department of Systems Engineering and
    Operations Research
George Mason University

Background and Motivation

Alex Kirlik

Cognitive Engineering: Toward a Workable Concept of Mind

It seems plain to me now that the "cognitive revolution" . . . was a response to the technological demands of the Post-Industrial Revolution. You cannot properly conceive of managing a complex world of information without a workable concept of mind.

—Bruner (1983, p. 63)

Perhaps no one has understood the depth to which the ever-increasing technological nature of the human ecology has shaped psychological theory better than Jerome Bruner. In his memoir *In Search of Mind* (1983), Bruner shared his reflections on the origins of the cognitive revolution. Although a great many factors may have played a role (e.g., Chomsky, 1959; Miller, 1956; Newell & Simon, 1972), Bruner turns much conventional thinking on its head, implying that scientists had to invent a theory of mind in response to the practical demands of finding coherent ways of understanding and coordinating a largely invented world of people engaged with post–Industrial Revolution technologies. The seeds of this scientific revolution, it seems, were not so much "in the air" as in the digital circuitry and in the need to understand and manage "a complex world of information."

A Workable Concept of Mind

The purpose of this book is to take additional steps toward building what Bruner referred to as a "workable concept of mind." Special emphasis is given here to the word *workable*. The central goal is to

provide methods and models that can be fruitfully applied to solving practically relevant problems in human–technology interaction. These problems include designing and evaluating technological interfaces, decision aids, alerting systems, and training technology, as well as supporting human–automation interaction and human–computer interaction. In short, the aim of this book is to provide practical resources for addressing the menagerie of problems making up *cognitive engineering* (Hollnagel & Woods, 1983; Kirlik & Bisantz, 1999; Norman, 1986; Rasmussen, 1986). Along the way, many contributors to this volume also present insights and approaches that may shed light on fundamental problems in the science of adaptive cognition and behavior. This may be especially true when it comes to the challenge of understanding and formally articulating the role of the environment in cognitive theory.

Six themes unite the contributors' orientation toward developing a concept of mind that is both workable and valuable from a cognitive engineering perspective. These themes are illustrated in the selection of research problems, methods, and analysis and modeling techniques presented in the following chapters.

1. An Ecological or Systems Perspective

Pioneers of the cognitive engineering discipline, such as Rasmussen (1990) and Woods (1995), have emphasized the essential *ecological* character of the cognitive engineering enterprise. What does this mean, and why is it the case? The answers to these questions lie in the nature of the systems studied and the practical problems associated with their analysis and design. Cognitive engineering research is largely concerned with the analysis and design of human–technology systems and the role of technology as a mediator between humans and the external objects and events comprising a work domain. As such, cognitive engineering is fundamentally concerned with systems composed of humans, mediating technologies and task environments, as well as the interactions among these system components. Of all the schools or approaches to psychology relevant to cognitive engineering (and there are many), both the theoretical orientation and unit of analysis presumed by ecological psychology are perhaps best aligned with the task of understanding and supporting the mediated coupling between humans and their environments. By reviewing the Instructions for Authors appearing in each issue of *Ecological Psychology*, one learns that the focus of the discipline is a broad range of psychological problems (perception, cognition, communication, development, learning, etc.), but with one noteworthy constraint. In particular, ecological psychology is concerned with those problems only "to the extent that those problems derive from a consideration of whole animal-environmental systems, rather than animals or environments in isolation from each other."

This broad and inclusive perspective on what it means to take an ecological approach to cognitive engineering is the one presumed in this book. As such, the approach is much in the spirit of the Joint Cognitive Systems tradition in cognitive systems engineering (Hollnagel, Mancini, & Woods, 1986). It is inherently a systems approach in which each element of the human–technology–environment unit of analysis receives attention and treatment during analysis and design and where each element is considered in light of its functional role within the overall human–technology–environment system. Although some authors in this book use the phrase "ecological analysis" to highlight the study of the environmental components of these systems and "cognitive analysis" to highlight the study of the internal or mental activities of their human components, the intended meaning of each term will be clear from context. At this point, suffice it to say that the perspective taken in this book is that a *psychological* theory or model, especially one capable of providing cognitive engineering with a workable concept of mind, should include a description of the "whole" human–technology–environment system and not merely internal cognition.

This systems or ecological orientation toward cognitive engineering has long roots in human factors, and especially within the field of "human–machine systems." As noted by Sheridan (2002, p. 5), shortly after World War II human factors researchers increasingly began to borrow modeling techniques from engineering, such as mathematical theories of estimation, information, decision, and control. They did so "to look at information, control, and decision making as a continuous process within a closed loop that also included physical subsystems—more than just sets of independent stimulus-response relations" (Sheridan, 2002, p. 4). The rationale for including a description of physical subsystems within such models, that is, descriptions of the task environment and any mediating technology, was well expressed by Baron, a human–machine systems engineer: "Human behavior, either cognitive or psychomotor, is too diverse to model unless it is sufficiently constrained by the situation or environment; however, when these environmental constraints exist, to model behavior adequately, one must include a model for that environment" (Baron, 1984, p. 6).

Exactly this point, the need for a psychological model to include an environmental model, was one of the defining features of the theory and method developed by one of ecological psychology's pioneers, Egon Brunswik (1903–1955). As will be discussed in greater detail by Goldstein in the following chapter, Brunswik is perhaps best known for his lens model, whose ecological nature is directly apparent in its symmetrical arrangement as a pair of joined human and environmental models (Brunswik, 1952, 1956; also see Hammond & Stewart, 2001). The pervasive influence of Brunswik's theory of probabilistic functionalism and experimental methodology of representative design is evident throughout this volume.

This is not to imply, of course, that only Brunswik's ecological theory is capable of giving rise to workable resources for cognitive engineering. For example, Vicente (1999) has drawn heavily and profitably on the ecological theory of James J. Gibson (1979/1986) in the development of his Cognitive Work Analysis and Ecological Interface Design (also see Burns & Hajdukiewicz, 2004) cognitive engineering techniques. As both Vicente (2003) and Kirlik (1995, 2001) have observed, it is possible to view the ecological theories of Brunswik and Gibson to be complementary rather than conflicting, despite what much of the psychological research conducted in each of the two traditions may lead one to believe. As such, one should view the research presented in the current volume, largely grounded in Brunswikian theory, and the research program of Vicente and his colleagues, influenced by Gibsonian theory, as similarly complementary rather than conflicting. Neither subsumes the other with respect to the central problems addressed or the techniques provided. The same could also be said of the distributed cognition approach (e.g., Hollan, Hutchins, & Kirsh, 2000; Hutchins, 1995) and any other framework embodying the ecological notion that the unit of psychological analysis and modeling must span the human–environment boundary if it is to provide cognitive engineering with a workable concept of mind (also see Clark, 2003; Dourish, 2001; Kirlik, 1998; Kirsh, 1996; Olson & Olson, 1991; Zhang & Norman, 1997).

2. An Adaptive, Functional Perspective

Anyone who has ever read (or even better, taught from) Donald Norman's (1988) insightful book *The Psychology of Everyday Things* will almost certainly recognize his characterization of the problems faced by a technology user in terms of bridging a "gulf of execution" and a "gulf of evaluation." How do I get it to work? What is it doing? These are questions we find ourselves asking all to often in our interactions with technology. As one who has graded over a thousand students' answers to "define and give an everyday example" exam questions about these gulfs, I have found that if a student is going to get anything correct on an exam it is likely to be these questions. These concepts are immediately intuitive to anyone who has ever experienced difficulty or frustration when using technology, whether in pro-

gramming a VCR or the flight control automation in a modern glass cockpit airliner (Degani, Shafto, & Kirlik, 1999; Sarter & Woods, 1992).

One reason the authors of this volume have become attracted to Brunswik's functionalist theory of cognition and behavior is its grounding in exactly these gulfs. In particular, and as explained in greater detail by Goldstein in chapter 2, Brunswik's theory is founded in an examination of the proximal–distal relationships characterizing a person's encounter with the world (also see Tolman & Brunswik, 1935). A technological interface provides us with both proximal, or directly available, information sources and proximal opportunities for action. The intended target of our interaction, however, is all too often distal, or not so directly available to us: a goal state to be achieved by taking a correct sequence of proximal actions, and an understanding of whether we have achieved our goal, which can often be gained only by correctly integrating proximally available information.

In 1972, Newell and Simon began their seminal book, *General Problem Solving,* with an expression of debt to Tolman & Brunswik's (1935) *Psychological Review* article emphasizing the necessity of a detailed analysis of these proximal–distal relations to understand goal-directed behavior. Newell and Simon appreciated the insight that such behavior is typically directed toward distal objects or ends that can be achieved only by the adaptive use of proximal information and action resources. One result was Newell and Simon's characterization of problem solving as a search through a "problem space" to find a series of proximal actions that would lead to distal goals. A problem space is a model of a problem solver's environment.

Every chapter in this volume deals in one way or another with an examination of the proximal–distal relations characterizing or mediating one's encounter with the environment and a parallel examination of the degree to which humans are well adapted to these relations. This is what is meant here by an adaptive, functional perspective on cognition and behavior. There is no initial assumption that people are either well or poorly adapted to the demands and opportunities of any particular situation. Instead, the approach taken in the following chapters is to perform detailed functional analyses of task environments and then empirically measure the degree of adaptivity attained in light of both the cognitive and environmental resources available.

Various chapters in parts IV, V, and VI of this book also examine the relationship between Brunswik's original approach to these problems and more recent yet related adaptive approaches to cognition such as Anderson's (1990) Rational Analysis and ACT-R model (Anderson & Lebiere, 1998), and the Ecological Rationality approach developed by Gigerenzer, Todd, and their colleagues (Gigerenzer, Todd, & the ABC Research Group 1999).

3. Embracing Uncertainty

Another aspect of Brunswik's thinking adopted by the authors in this volume is the idea that the relationship between the human and environment must often be characterized in probabilistic terms. Note, however, that this does not reflect an a priori commitment to probabilism but instead the need to have conceptual and technical resources available for measuring and modeling uncertainty where it is found to exist. Having techniques available to represent the possible probabilistic structure both within a task environment and within the operations of inner cognitive processes is especially important for the purpose of evaluating the adaptivity of behavior, and also when motivating interventions aimed at enhancing it. Why?

First, environmental uncertainty places a ceiling on the accuracy of adaptive behavior in any given instance. As Lipshitz et al. (2001a) have (qualitatively) put it, "Uncertainty is intimately linked with error: the greater the uncertainty, the greater the probability of making an error" (p. 339). As such, it is important to recognize the existence of environmental uncertainty from a forensic perspective because human "error" must always be expected when people are performing in environments with irreducible uncertainty (Hammond, 1996). Second, the possible presence of uncertainty suggests that questions about adaptive cognition be addressed and answered at the level of how well tailored or calibrated a performer's judgments or actions are to the environment on average, or at a distributional level of analysis, rather than on an instance-by-instance basis.

4. Embracing Representativeness

The research presented in this book shares with the Naturalistic Decision Making (NDM) paradigm the goal of "conducting one's study with representative samples of subjects, tasks, and contexts to which one wishes to generalize" (Lipshitz et al., 2001b, p. 386). This is illustrated in this volume by the complete reliance on either field observation or the use of dynamic and interactive simulations modeled after the target context of scientific generalization. As will be described by Goldstein in more detail in chapter 2, this methodological commitment is consistent with Brunswik's methodology of representative design. However, as will be illustrated in nearly all of the chapters that follow, this orientation does not preclude the use of systematically designed interventions in representatively designed experiments. This book is filled with examples of investigators using hybrid representative/systematic experimental designs to both foster the generalization of results to a target context and also to test various hypotheses regarding the efficacy of design, training, or aiding interventions and to examine how adaptivity may be influenced by factors such as time stress.

5. A Formal Perspective

The research presented in this volume displays a commitment to abstraction and formalization in the creation of modeling and measurement techniques (also see Byrne & Gray, 2003). The contributors to this volume, as illustrated by their demonstrated commitment to study cognition and behavior in context *and* to perform formal (mathematical or computational) modeling, agree with Todd and Gigerenzer (2001) in noting that the alternatives for describing context-sensitive, adaptive cognition "are not context-free formal modeling versus context-bound informal modeling" (p. 382).

Instead, I hope that the chapters that follow illustrate that it is quite possible to have a deep appreciation for the role of the environmental context in cognition and behavior, yet also to have an appreciation for and ability to formally model the essential aspects of this context. As I have pointed out elsewhere (Kirlik, 2003), research in fields such as human factors and cognitive engineering nearly always begins (or should begin) with a qualitative, naturalistic phase to identify and distill the central features of a target problem to be solved or phenomena to be investigated. Yet if attention then turns directly to creating an intuitive solution or qualitative account (regardless of how well received by stakeholders), without bringing these central features to an abstract level, it is often impossible to know the conditions in which that same solution will prove useful. As such, each cognitive engineering problem will have to be solved largely from scratch. A workable concept of mind useful for cognitive engineering should be one that is fertile in giving rise to a toolbox of formal analysis and modeling techniques, as scientific generalization rides chiefly on the winds of abstraction.

6. A Problem-Solving Perspective

The problem-solving orientation displayed in the research presented herein will be immediately apparent. What might be less obvious in these pages is that in virtually every case researchers had to work with the behavioral situation given to them, and this required them to invent a wide variety of novel extensions and improvisations on the general theoretical perspective uniting these studies within a common intellectual and historical perspective. It is likely that the more important contributions within these chapters lie in the development of these extensions to current theory and method, rather than in any particular empirical findings presented. It may be useful to highlight this aspect of the book at the outset.

To explain, the study of human–technology interaction and the disciplines of cognitive engineering, human factors, and human–computer interaction are changing so rapidly that the practically relevant lifetime of any particular empirical effect or finding is likely to be quite short. In a world continually undergoing reinvention, the specific barriers to adaptive cognition and behavior are likely to change as rapidly as the ecology itself (Kirlik, 2005). As is often the case with the workers and performers cognitive engineers intend to support, our own work as researchers, practitioners, and students of human–technology interaction is one of almost continuous adaptation to novel problems and opportunities. As such, a useful method, model, or measurement technique is likely to have a longer shelf life, as measured by its duration of practical relevance, than any particular experimental result or field observation.

As such, one can only hope that those who might embrace the perspectives on which this book is based and those who might use the methods and models presented here appreciate that these techniques are all works in progress, and additional progress depends on extending and elaborating these tools and techniques. Only then will cognitive engineering come to possess the kind of diverse and reusable toolbox of measurement, analysis, and modeling techniques characteristic of other engineering disciplines.

Conclusion

After the immediately following chapter on theory and method, this volume consists of a set of chapters presenting research adhering to each of the six general themes or perspectives outlined in this chapter. Although it is traditional in a volume such as this to provide an introductory overview and roadmap of the chapters that follow, this is unnecessary for two reasons. First, in chapter 2 Goldstein provides an introduction and tutorial that explicitly situates each chapter by name within its intellectual and historical place in Brunswik's thought and scholarship. Second, I have provided introductory overviews prefacing each of the volume's subsequent sections. Should one desire to gain a quick overview of the substantive contents of the volume, reading Goldstein's chapter and/or reading through each of these brief section introductions should serve this purpose well.

References

Anderson, J. R. (1990). *The adaptive character of thought*. Hillsdale, N.J.: Erlbaum.

Anderson, J. R., & Lebiere, C. (1998). *The atomic components of thought*. Mahwah, N.J.: Lawrence Erlbaum.

Baron, S. (1984). A control theoretic approach to modeling human supervisory control of dynamic systems. In W. B. Rouse (Ed.), *Advances in human-machine systems research*, vol. 1. (pp. 1–48). Greenwich, Conn: JAI Press.

Bruner, J. (1983). *In search of mind*. New York: Harper & Row.

Brunswik, E. (1952). The conceptual framework of psychology. In *International Encyclopedia of Unified Science*, vol. 1, no. 10. (pp. 1–102) Chicago: University of Chicago Press.

Brunswik, E. (1956). *Perception and the representative design of psychological experiments*. Berkeley: University of California Press.

Burns, C. M., & Hajdukiewicz, J. R. (2004). *Ecological interface design.* Boca Raton, Fla.: CRC Press.

Byrne, M. D., & Gray, W. D. (2003). Returning human factors to an engineering discipline: Expanding the science base through a new generation of quantitative methods—preface to the special section. *Human Factors, 45,* 1–4.

Chomsky, N. (1959). A review of Skinner's *Verbal Behavior. Language, 35,* 26–38.

Clark, A. (2003). *Natural-born cyborgs.* New York: Cambridge University Press.

Degani, A., Shafto, M., & Kirlik, A. (1999). Modes in human-machine systems: Review, classification, and application. *International Journal of Aviation Psychology, 9*(2), 125–138.

Dourish, P. (2001). *Where the action is: The foundations of embodied interaction.* Cambridge, Mass.: MIT Press.

Gibson, J. J. (1979/1986). *The ecological approach to visual perception.* Hillsdale, NJ: Erlbaum.

Gigerenzer, G., Todd, P. M., & the ABC Research Group. (1999). *Simple heuristics that make us smart.* New York: Oxford University Press.

Hammond, K. R. (1996). *Human judgment and social policy: Irreducible uncertainty, inevitable error, unavoidable injustice.* New York: Oxford University Press.

Hammond, K. R., & Stewart, T. R. (Eds.). (2001). *The essential Brunswik.* New York: Oxford University Press.

Hollan, J., Hutchins, E., & Kirsh, D. (2000). Distributed cognition: Toward a new foundation for human-computer interaction research. *ACM Transactions on Human-Computer Interaction, 7*(2), 174–196.

Hollnagel, E., Mancini, G., & Woods, D. D. (1986). *Intelligent decision support in process environments.* New York: Springer-Verlag.

Hollnagel, E., & Woods, D. D. (1983). Cognitive systems engineering: New wine in new bottles. *International Journal of Man-Machine Studies, 18,* 583–600.

Hutchins, E. (1995). *Cognition in the wild.* Cambridge, Mass.: MIT Press.

Kirlik, A. (1995). Requirements for psychological models to support design: Toward ecological task analysis. In J. Flach, P. Hancock, J. Caird, and K. J. Vicente (Eds.), *Global perspectives on the ecology of human-machine systems* (pp. 68–120). Mawhah, N.J.: LEA.

Kirlik, A. (1998). The design of everyday life environments. In W. Bechtel and G. Graham (Eds.), *A companion to cognitive science.*(pp. 702–712). Oxford: Blackwell.

Kirlik, A. (2001). On Gibson's review of Brunswik. In K. R. Hammond and T. R. Stewart (Eds.), *The essential Brunswik* (pp. 238–242). New York: Oxford University Press.

Kirlik, A. (2003). Human factors distributes its workload. Review of E. Salas (Ed.), *Advances in human performance and cognitive engineering research. Contemporary Psychology, 48*(6).

Kirlik, A. (2005). Work in progress: Reinventing intelligence for a reinvented world. In R. J. Sternberg & D. Preiss (Eds.), *Intelligence and technology* (pp. 105–134). Mahwah, N.J.: Erlbaum.

Kirlik, A., & Bisantz, A. M. (1999). Cognition in human-machine systems: Experiential and environmental aspects of adaptation. In P. A. Hancock (Ed.), *Handbook of perception and cognition* (2nd ed.): *Human performance and ergonomics* (pp. 47–68). New York: Academic Press.

Kirsh, D. (1996). Adapting the environment instead of oneself. *Adaptive Behavior, 4*(3/4), 415–452.

Lipshitz, R., Klein, G., Orasanu, J., and Salas, E. (2001a). Focus article: Taking stock of naturalistic decision making. *Journal of Behavioral Decision Making, 14,* 331–352.

Lipshitz, R., Klein, G., Orasanu, J., and Salas, E. (2001b) Rejoinder: A welcome dialogue—and the need to continue. *Journal of Behavioral Decision Making, 14,* 385–389.

Miller, G. A. (1956). The magical number seven, plus or minus two: Some limits on our capacity for processing information. *Psychological Review, 63,* 81–97.

Newell, A., & Simon, H. A. (1972). *Human problem solving.* New York: Prentice Hall.

Norman, D. A. (1986). Cognitive engineering. In D. A. Norman & S. W. Draper (Eds.), *User centered system design: New perspectives in human-computer interaction* (pp. 31–61). Mawhah, N.J.: LEA.

Norman, D. A. (1988). *The psychology of everyday things.* New York: Basic Books.

Olson, G. M., & Olson, J. S. (1991). User-centered design of collaboration technology. *Journal of Organizational Computing, 1,* 61–83.

Rasmussen, J. (1986). *Information processing and human-machine interaction: An approach to cognitive engineering.* New York: North-Holland.

Rasmussen, J. (1990). Cognitive engineering, a new profession? In L. P. Goodstein, S. E. Olsen, & H. B. Anderson (Eds.), *Tasks, errors and mental models* (pp. 325–334). New York: Taylor & Francis.

Sarter, N., & Woods, D. D. (1992). Pilot interaction with cockpit automation. I. Operational experiences with the Flight Management System. *International Journal of Aviation Psychology, 2,* 303–321.

Sheridan, T. B. (2002). *Humans and automation: system design and research issues.* Santa Monica, Calif.: Human Factors and Ergonomics Society and John Wiley & Sons.

Todd, P., & Gigerenzer, G. (2001). Putting naturalistic decision making into the adaptive toolbox. *Journal of Behavioral Decision Making, 14,* 381–382.

Tolman, E.C., & Brunswik, E. (1935). The organism and the causal texture of the environment. *Psychological Review, 42,* 43–77.

Vicente, K. J. (1999). *Cognitive work analysis.* Mahwah, N.J.: Erlbaum.

Vicente, K. J. (2003). Beyond the lens model and direct perception: Toward a broader view of ecological psychology. *Ecological Psychology, 15*(3), 241–267.

Woods, D. D. (1995). Toward a theoretical base for representation design in the computer medium: Ecological perception and aiding human cognition. In J. Flach, P. Hancock, J. Caird, and K. J. Vicente (Eds.), *Global perspectives on the ecology of human-machine systems* (pp. 157–188). Mawhah, N.J.: LEA.

Zhang, J., & Norman, D. A. (1997). The nature of external representations in problem solving. *Cognitive Science, 21*(2), 179–217.

William M. Goldstein

Introduction to Brunswikian Theory and Method

Egon Brunswik (1903–1955) was a perceptual psychologist with deep interests in the history and philosophy of science. His work on perception led him to develop a general vision for psychology called probabilistic functionalism (Brunswik, 1952, 1956; Hammond, 1966; Hammond & Stewart, 2001). Brunswik's thinking had a systemic integrity with interwoven perspectives on the nature of psychology, its definitive problems, and proper methodology. Unfortunately, some of Brunswik's positions were out of step with the mainstream psychology of his day, and his work was not well received at the time (Gigerenzer, 1987; Kurz & Tweney, 1997; Leary, 1987). Even today, although a number of Brunswik's ideas are widely employed by psychologists who may be unaware of their origins, Brunswikian thinking is represented mainly by a vocal minority of researchers who study judgment and decision making (Goldstein, 2004). However, Brunswik's probabilistic functionalism has been receiving increasing attention from researchers in cognitive engineering (see chapter 1), and one purpose of this book is to announce, explain, and promote that trend. The purpose of this chapter is to acquaint readers with the basics of probabilistic functionalism so that they can see its appeal for cognitive engineering and evaluate the contri-

butions it has facilitated in the remaining chapters of this book.

It might help to introduce Brunswik's thinking by outlining the kind of research problem that inspired it. Brunswik's early research, conducted during the 1920s and 1930s when he was a member of the Vienna Psychological Institute, concentrated on various perceptual constancies. Size constancy, for example, is demonstrated by the fact that the apparent (e.g., estimated) size of an object tends to remain more or less constant at various distances from an observer, even though the object's projection on the retina differs. Other features, such as shape and color, similarly tend to be perceived as relatively constant despite changes in the proximal information available to the observer. The issue of perceptual constancy, stated this way, contains the seeds of some enduring concerns for Brunswik: (1) the relationship between the proximal information available to the observer and the distal state of affairs, emphasizing the ambiguous or even misleading implications of individual items of proximal information taken in isolation; (2) the establishment of a stable percept despite (or perhaps because of) variability and interrelationships among the items of proximal information; and (3) the accuracy of the stabilized percept. Briefly,

Brunswik highlighted the importance of the individual's adjustment to the world (i.e., not just inner perceptual processes), and he portrayed the individual's understanding of the world as *mediated* by proximal information that could be unreliable. Although Brunswik continued to emphasize perceptual examples, he extended his thinking to overt action after a visit from Edward Chase Tolman resulted in collaboration (Tolman & Brunswik, 1935). For overt action, Brunswik again emphasized the individual's adjustment to the world (i.e., the ability to bring about distal states of affairs that match one's internal desires) and the unreliable mediation of that adjustment (i.e., by proximal actions that may or may not have the desired distal effects).

The highlighting of (1) adjustment to the world and (2) the mediated nature of that adjustment are exactly the features of probabilistic functionalism that make it attractive to cognitive engineering. As stressed by Alex Kirlik (chapter 1), cognitive engineering is a problem-centered field where the goal is to develop and use technology that will help people accomplish tasks more effectively. It is not a field that can be content to study only the inner psychological processes underlying people's interactions with technology; the ultimate goal is to improve people's adjustment to the world. Moreover, that adjustment is increasingly mediated by complex technology whose connection to the world may be less than obvious to the user. Technology augments and/or replaces components of a perception- or evaluation-like process when it is used (1) to sense and collect information, (2) to display information, or (3) to suggest inferences. Technology augments and/or replaces components of overt action when it is used to respond with great speed, strength, or precision; across great distances; or with any type of performance that humans themselves cannot execute. Technology may also combine the processes of perception/evaluation and overt action in various forms of automation (e.g., flying on autopilot). A source of theoretical and methodological ideas for studying such technologically mediated relationships with the world is surely worth the consideration of cognitive engineers.

This is where probabilistic functionalism and its extensions come in. The contributors to this volume apply or extend Brunswik's ideas to the technological mediation of perception/evaluation and overt action in many substantive domains, including aviation (piloting and pilot–automation interaction: Bass & Pritchett, chapter 9; Byrne, Kirlik, & Fick, chapter 18; Casner, chapter 14; Degani, Shafto, & Kirlik, chapter 13; Mosier & McCauley, chapter 12; Pritchett & Bisantz, chapter 7), military applications (threat assessment, resource allocation, identification of unknown craft, and other aspects of command and control: Bisantz, Kirlik, Walker, Fisk, Gay & Phipps, chapter 3; Campbell, Van Buskirk , & Bolton, chapter 11; Gray, chapter 16; Horrey, Wickens, Strauss, Kirlik, & Stewart, chapter 5, Seong, Bisantz, & Gattie, chapter 8; Rothrock & Kirlik, chapter 10), dynamic system or process control (fault diagnosis, worker-tool-environment interaction: Jha & Bisantz, chapter 6; Kirlik, chapter 15), team performance (Adelman, Yeo, & Miller, chapter 4), and human-computer interaction (Gray, chapter 16; Pirolli, chapter 17).

In this chapter, I introduce Brunswik's ideas in a way that will illuminate their use in these many applications. In the first section, I review some of the core principles of Brunswik's probabilistic functionalism, concentrating on: (1) functionalism, (2) vicarious functioning, (3) probabilism, and (4) representative design. In the second section, I outline some theoretical extensions and lines of empirical research that have led to social judgment theory, a Brunswikian approach to the study of judgment. In the third section, I draw connections between chapters in this book and aspects either of Brunswik's original theory or its subsequent extension in the form of social judgment theory.

Fundamentals of Brunswik's Probabilistic Functionalism

Functionalism

Adjustment to the World

The term *functionalism* refers to too many schools and movements in psychology (and other disciplines) for it to be meaningful without elaboration. Brunswik was a functionalist in at least two senses. First, he considered psychology to be "concerned with the interrelationships between organism and environment" (Brunswik, 1957, p. 5), with special emphasis on the interrelationships by which organisms manage to perform important tasks (i.e., to "function") in their environments. This sense of functionalism has Darwinian connotations and can be linked to the functionalist movement of early twentieth-century American psychology (e.g., Angell, 1907). Second, Brunswik also had ties to the nineteenth-century European functionalism (also known as act psychology) of Franz Brentano (1874/1973). Act psychology was known for its insistence that mental states have the quality of being "about" something (e.g., about the outside world). Mental states are said to be "intentional," in the technical sense that philosophers give to this term. That is, they point to or "intend toward" something outside themselves. Both senses of functionalism direct attention to people's adjustment to the world, and both are reflected in Brunswik's emphasis on central–distal (cognition–world) relationships.

Central–Distal Correspondence

Brunswik (1957, p. 5) considered the organism and environment to be distinct systems, each with its own "surface and depth, or overt and covert regions," and he argued that the "coming to terms" of these "equal partners" most crucially involved the development of "rapport between the central, covert layers of the two systems." The central, covert layer of the environment contains the distal variables the organism cares about, all of which are objects, events, or properties that are remote from the organism in space and/or time. The organism's own central, covert variables include especially its perceptions, understandings, and motivational states. (In what follows, the term "central" will be restricted somewhat to refer to the covert layer of the organism only.) Brunswik's emphasis on the correspondence between covert distal and central variables followed from his functionalist orientation, in both of the senses discussed earlier. Adequate adjustment to the world requires accurate perception and effective actions, and these are matters of central–distal correspondence: (1) bringing one's (central) perceptions into line with (distal) objects and (2) bringing about (distal) states of affairs that coincide with one's (central) desires. Brunswik referred to central–distal correspondence as "achievement," "attainment," or "functional validity." In today's parlance, this correspondence is perhaps most frequently discussed in terms of the "adaptive" character of behavior or cognition (e.g., Anderson, 1990).

It is important to note that by emphasizing the rapport between the central and distal layers, Brunswik was *de*emphasizing the proximal/peripheral layer that is the interface between the organis-mic and environmental systems. Brunswik explicitly recognized that whatever degree of central–distal correspondence the organism managed to achieve, it brought it about by the *mediation* of proximal events and processes. Moreover, these mediating processes drew a great deal of Brunswik's theoretical attention. However, as we will see shortly, Brunswik thought they should be regarded as secondary in empirical investigations.

Vicarious Functioning

Stabilization of Central–Distal Relationships via Adaptable Mediation

"Vicarious functioning" is a phrase that Brunswik borrowed from Hunter (1932) to refer to a critical property of mediating processes. Hunter was attempting to distinguish the subject matter of psychology from that of physiology. He indicated that whereas the physiological functions of one organ are rarely carried out by another organ, it is typical of the behavior studied by psychologists that if the parts of the body normally used in a performance are impaired, other parts of the body can function "vicariously" to perform the behavior. Generalizing from Hunter's examples, Brunswik used the phrase "vicarious functioning" to refer more broadly to exchangeability of means to an end. He emphasized that through the flexible adaptation of means to an end the observable hallmark of *purposive* behavior is achieved: the " 'stabilization' of the end stage" and the "diversity of preceding stages" (Brunswik, 1952, p. 17). That is, overt behavior mediates the relationship between organisms' (central) desires and the (distal) state of affairs, and vicarious functioning in their overt behavior enables organisms to stabilize this relationship, helping them reach their goals even if different means must be employed on different occasions. (In the tradition of Gibsonian, rather than Brunswikian, ecological psychology, vicarious functioning is more commonly discussed in terms of the "context-conditioned variability" of behavior, e.g., Turvey, Fitch, & Tuller, 1982.)

Brunswik extended this line of thought by applying a similar analysis to perception. In this case the "end stage" refers to the formation of a (central) percept rather than the reaching of a goal, and the (mediating) "preceding stages" refer to the organism's collection and use of sensory information rather than its overt behavior. It is not obvious that perception requires the same adaptable mediation as goal pursuit. However, Brunswik saw (1) that percepts must be inferred or constructed from proximal sensory "cues" to the distal object's properties and (2) that proximal cues must be selected and used differently to perceive objects under different environmental conditions. For example, concerning proximal cues to the distance between oneself and an object (e.g., binocular parallax, convergence of the eye axes, etc.), Brunswik wrote:

> [N]one of these proximal variables can be considered to be *the* distance cue in the sense of an effect which would be present without exception whenever the distal condition should obtain. Some of the cues will more often, others less often, be present, depending on circumstances, and occasionally all of them may be cut off (so that the fact of a certain distance relationship must remain unrecognized by the organism in question). (Brunswik, 1943, p. 256, emphasis in original)

Thus, adaptable mediation again enables organisms to stabilize the relationship between their (central) percepts and (distal) objects, thereby producing the perceptual constancies that initially attracted Brunswik's attention. Brunswik referred to multiplicity and flexibility in the use of both cues and means to an end as vicarious functioning, and he took vicarious functioning (broadly construed to include multiplicity, flexibility, intersubstitutability, and combination of both cues and means) to be the core feature that makes behavior interesting to psychologists.

The Lens Model

Brunswik's lens model derives its name from the fact that a pictorial representation of vicarious functioning resembles a diagram of a convex lens. Figure 2.1 shows the lens model as it appeared in Brunswik's (1952, p. 20) book, where he referred to it as a "composite picture of the functional unit of behavior." The figure is shown in a general form that is applicable to both perception and overt behavior. Interpreted in terms of perception, the image is one in which a distal stimulus at one focus (i.e., the "initial focal variable") emits a scatter of rays, representing proximal cues, from among which the organism selects a subset to be recombined into the central perception at the other focus (i.e., the "terminal focal variable"). For overt behavior, a central motivational state is pictured as the

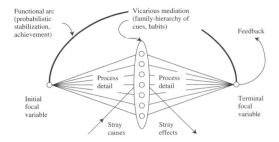

Figure 2.1. The lens model: Composite picture of the functional unit of behavior. Reprinted by permission of University of Chicago Press from Brunswik, 1952, p. 20.

initial focal variable, and the scatter of rays represents a set of proximal means among which the organism selects, all of which lead to the same distal end shown as the terminal focal variable. In different contexts, organisms select different subsets of cues or means to achieve similar ends, and the composite picture shows the collection of cues or means that are used over a large number of contexts.

On Research in Psychology

When Brunswik referred to particular variables as focal, in Figure 2.1, he was not merely alluding to the picture's resemblance to a convex lens. Rather, he was distinguishing between variables that can and cannot be brought into stable relationships with each other. Relationships between focal variables are stabilized by the adaptable mediation of vicarious functioning. The fact that it is central and distal variables that turn out to be focal, on Brunswik's analysis, reinforced his emphasis on functional achievement (i.e., central–distal correspondence) as the proper subject matter of psychology. As argued earlier, functionalism identifies central–distal relationships as the ones of primary importance to the organism. In addition, the lens model indicates that these are the relationships that will be stable enough to bear scientific investigation.

By contrast with his support for studying central–distal relationships, Brunswik was wary of research on mediating processes, especially the mediating internal processes that occupy the majority of attention of today's cognitive scientists. Vicarious functioning is a stabilizing process (i.e., it produces stable relationships between central and distal variables) but is itself unstable (i.e., it exhibits flexibility and variability), producing "relative chaos in the regions intervening between focal variables"

(Brunswik, 1952, p. 20). Therefore, Brunswik thought mediating processes to be a difficult and unpromising area for research. In his early writings, he suggested that a classification of the kinds of distal objects "attained" by an organism would provide a description of its abilities and performance, and he favored the pursuit of such inventories over the investigation of mediating processes. Brunswik's later writings, on the other hand, did acknowledge the study of mediating processes as important, but his enthusiasm for the subject remained restrained, and he urged psychologists to keep research problems in perspective. Specifically, he warned against replacing the functionalist study of organisms' adjustment to the world with a focus on quasi-solipsistic "encapsulated" organisms in isolation. Indeed, Brunswik implied that such a trend had already gone too far when he wrote, "Psychology has forgotten that it is a science of organism-environment relationships, and has become a science of the organism" (Brunswik, 1957, p. 6). In this comment he presaged the critique of cognitive science to be leveled some 35 years later by Donald Norman (1993), who caricatured its nearly sole focus on internal processes as resulting in a theory of cognition as "disembodied" and cut off from the world in which it is embedded.

Consequently, Brunswik addressed the study of mediating processes with caution and circumspection. In particular, he distinguished between studies of "macromediation" and "micromediation." The former examine "the gross characteristics or macrostructure of the pattern of proximal and peripheral mediation between the distal and central foci," and thereby address "the problem of the grand strategy of mediation" (Brunswik, 1957, p. 8). The latter "attempt to break down the cognitive process further into its component parts" and thus concern "mediational tactics" (p. 9). As he (p. 9) put it, "Achievement and its strategy are molar problems; tactics is a molecular problem," and clearly he felt the former problems should precede and inform the latter.

The lens model helps clarify what is involved in elucidating the (macromediational) "grand strategy" by which an organism achieves a stable central–distal relationship. Specifically, beyond assessing the degree of achievement that the organism actually reaches, the organismic (for the purposes of this book, human) and environmental systems must be analyzed separately and compared. Expressed in terms of perception (with a comparable statement applying to action), this means the following. First, the environment must be studied to determine what Brunswik called the "ecological texture." That is, one must (1) identify the features that correlate with the distal object (and are therefore candidates for being used by the organism as proximal/peripheral cues), (2) ascertain the strengths of the relationships between the distal object and the (potential) proximal/peripheral cues (i.e., the "ecological validities" of the cues), and (3) assess the interrelationships among the cues (for this is part of what permits the cues to function vicariously for one another). Second, one must study the organismic system to determine which of the (potential) proximal/peripheral cues are actually used and in what strengths. Finally, the environmental and organismic systems must be compared to see if the organism's utilization of cues is appropriate, where "[w]e may call it appropriate in a generalized sense if the strength of utilization of a cue is in line with the degree of its ecological validity" (Brunswik, 1957, p. 11).

In sum, Brunswik's theoretical ideas about functionalism and vicarious processing lead to a general outline for investigations of human–environment relations, an outline that continues to apply when these relations involve mediation by technologies of various sorts. This is part of Brunswik's appeal for cognitive engineers, and further details that elaborate this outline will be given in what follows. First, however, some of Brunswik's other theoretical ideas that also have implications for methodological practice will be discussed in the next two subsections.

Probabilism

Although in principle the relationship between proximal/peripheral and distal variables must be determined in studies of ecological texture, Brunswik was convinced that these relationships would virtually always prove to be somewhat unreliable, ambiguous, or "equivocal." At least, this was the argument for individual cues and means. The extent to which an organism could combine cues and select means to overcome their limitations when taken singly is, of course, the problem of achievement—the main subject of research in Brunswik's functionalist view.

The equivocality of means may be more readily apparent than that of cues. A proverb reminds us that the best-laid plans of mice and men oft go awry, and it is easy to see that failure is possible even in simple cases. Regarding perception, Brunswik gave numerous examples of proximal cues that were ambiguous, and he suggested that this would be typical. A trapezoidally shaped retinal image may be due to a rectangular object seen at an angle, or the object may actually be trapezoidal. Of two objects, the one with the larger retinal projection may be the closer, or its larger image may be due to its great physical size. These examples are telling because they indicate a pattern: In both cases the cue is ambiguous not because of an inherently probabilistic environment but because of incompleteness of the information. Without challenging determinism, Brunswik argued that organisms usually have access to sets of proximal cues that are incomplete or otherwise inadequate for applying the laws that govern distal objects and distal–proximal relationships. He wrote, "The universal lawfulness of the world is of limited comfort to the perceiver or behaver not in a position to apply these laws. . . ," and that "ordinarily organisms must behave as if in a semierratic ecology" (Brunswik, 1955, p. 209). That is, the environment must appear to organisms to be probabilistic, even if in a philosophical sense it is deterministic. To emphasize the organism's predicament, Brunswik coined the metaphor that the perceptual system must act as an "intuitive statistician" (e.g., Brunswik, 1956, p. 80).

From these observations, Brunswik drew an important implication for both theory and method. Specifically, certain parts of the project to explicate achievement and its strategy must be expressed in probabilistic terms. First, as just argued, the environment or that part of it accessible to an organism must appear to it to be probabilistic. Therefore, studies of ecological texture, which aim to describe the relationships between distal variables and the *accessible* proximal/peripheral cues and means, must describe a set of probabilistic relationships. For example, although the relationship between size of retinal projection and size of distal object is deterministic for objects at a fixed distance from the organism, the relationship is probabilistic when it must be taken over objects at the various distances the organism encounters in its environment. Second, in addition to ecological texture, achievement itself must be described in probabilistic terms. The reason is that, faced with ambiguous, apparently probabilistic cues, "[a]ll a finite, sub-divine individual can do when acting [or perceiving] is . . . to

make a posit, or wager" (Brunswik, 1943, p. 259), and wagers are occasionally lost (e.g., see Byrne, Kirlik & Fick, chapter 18; Rothrock & Kirlik, chapter 10). Brunswik (1943, p. 270) concluded that "there can be no truly molar psychology dealing with the physical relationships of the organism with its environment unless it gives up the nomothetic [universal, lawlike] ideal in favor of a thoroughly statistical conception."

An implication for cognitive engineers is that they should expect technological aids to produce no more than a probabilistic relationship between a person and the environment (also see Kirlik, 2005; Vicente, 1999). Even when technology is designed specifically to reduce the uncertainty in this relationship (e.g., by responding with greater precision than people are capable of), a person's central goals or judgments might fail to correspond with the distal environment because of conditions the technology was not designed to handle. Although these situations don't reflect a failure of the technological aid, they nonetheless render the central–distal relationship uncertain.

Representative Design

The last aspect of Brunswikian theory to be discussed here was and remains one of the most controversial. By the 1950s, it was commonly appreciated that participants in psychological investigations must be sampled at random from a specified population for the findings to generalize beyond the participants themselves. Brunswik argued similarly that for findings to generalize beyond the particular stimuli and conditions employed in a study, they also must be sampled to be representative of the ecology. Such experiments had what Brunswik called a "representative design," in contrast to the more typical "systematic design" where experimenters manipulate the stimuli and conditions to produce orthogonal independent variables that are convenient to analyze yet often uncharacteristic of the ecology.

Recall that Brunswik's project to study achievement and its strategy decomposed into four parts: (1) the study of achievement itself, (2) the study of ecological texture, (3) the study of the organism's utilization of cues, and (4) a comparison of the ecological and organismic systems. It is relatively easy to see the importance of representative design for the first two of these four parts. Clearly achievement can be made excellent or poor by the use of stimuli that in the appropriate sense are easy or hard. Little is revealed about achievement in a target environment unless the stimuli and conditions are representative of those that occur in that target environment. Even more clearly, the ecological texture of relationships among distal and proximal/peripheral variables cannot be studied adequately in a set of stimuli that distorts the relationships to be studied. The real controversy surrounding the use of representative design centers on its application to studies of cue utilization, and only a sketch of the issues can be given here, stated in terms of the sampling of stimuli.

One argument for representative design, even in studies of cue utilization, holds that the logic of statistical inference requires the probability sampling of units from populations. Generalizing beyond the specific stimuli employed in the study requires this no less than generalizing beyond the specific participants. Some might find this argument unconvincing, either because there are other, nonstatistical bases for generalization (e.g., theory-guided inference) or because they are not convinced that organisms are sufficiently sensitive to their task environments for the orthogonalization of stimulus properties to affect their cue utilization. One might reply, however, that sensitivity to the task environment is itself a matter for empirical investigation.

A second argument for representative design meets a similar objection, and one might give a similar reply. Specifically, the heart of cue utilization—and from a Brunswikian perspective the main interest in a study of cue utilization—is vicarious functioning. Therefore, organisms should be given full scope to display the vicarious functioning they normally employ in their environment. Moreover, vicarious functioning includes the flexible selection of cues, that is, allowing some cues on occasion to substitute for other cues, on the basis of prior learning of cue intercorrelations in the environment. Deliberately destroying these cue intercorrelations in an orthogonal design could easily produce "intercombinations of variates [that] may be incompatible in nature or otherwise grossly unrealistic" (Brunswik, 1955, p. 205). Encountering such strange stimuli might confuse the participants, prevent them from taking the task seriously, or at least make them wary of relying on the intersubstitutability of cues that would normally characterize their vicarious functioning. As before, a critic might suggest that participants are not so sensitive to their task environments, and

one might reply that sensitivity to task environment is an empirical question. The frequency with which cognitive engineers have heard experienced performers (e.g., pilots) complain about even minor issues associated with the lack of complete representativeness of a research environment (e.g., a flight simulator) should bring this point home.

As indicated, the need for representative design remains a controversial issue, turning in large part on empirical questions about people's sensitivity to task environments (see Goldstein, 2004, for further comments). At the very least, an implication for cognitive engineers is that they should be wary of assessing technological aids in test environments that depart from the settings in which they are intended to be used. Such a sentiment is reflected in attempts to study or simulate field conditions rather than use abstract laboratory tasks (as demonstrated in nearly all of the chapters of this volume).

Development of Social Judgment Theory

As mentioned earlier, Brunswikian research in psychology has been pursued most vigorously by a group of researchers who study judgment and decision making (Goldstein, 2004). The point of departure for these researchers was a paper by Hammond (1955), in which he drew an analogy between Brunswik's analysis of perception and the problem of clinical judgment. Specifically, just as people must infer or construct a percept from a collection of sensory cues that provide only incomplete and fallible information, Hammond argued that a patient's behaviors, expressions, and test scores provide ambiguous cues to the patient's personality and diagnosis. In both cases the clinician/perceiver must use multiple cues and indicators to infer something that goes beyond the cues themselves.

Subsequent work by Hammond and colleagues produced a voluminous literature of empirical findings, as well as theoretical and methodological extensions of Brunswik's approach. The work evolved into an approach called social judgment theory (Brehmer, 1988; Brehmer & Joyce, 1988; Doherty, 1996; Hammond et al., 1975, 1977; see also Hammond, 1996, 2000; Hammond & Joyce, 1975; Hammond & Stewart, 2001; Hammond & Wascoe, 1980; Juslin & Montgomery, 1999; Rappoport & Summers, 1973). In this section, I selectively review some of the developments that are of particular relevance to cognitive engineers and/or connect to the contributions in this book.

The Lens Model Equation

Figure 2.2 shows the lens model as it was adapted (Hammond, 1955; Hammond et al. 1975) for the study of judgment. Modeled on the case of perception, rather than action, the to-be-judged criterion variable Y_e plays the role of the distal stimulus at the initial focus, whereas the person's judgments Y_s play the role of central perceptions at the terminal focus. The proximal cues $X_1, X_2, \ldots, X_n$ constitute the information available to the judge and are related to the criterion by ecological validities (i.e., cue–criterion correlations) and to the judgments by cue utilization coefficients (i.e., cue–judgment correlations). Judgmental accuracy or achievement is assessed by the correlation between judgment and criterion values.

At the time of Brunswik's death, the environmental and organismic systems could be modeled separately (e.g., by linear regression), but only a qualitative and impressionistic comparison of the two systems could be offered. That situation was changed by the development of the lens model equation (Hursch, Hammond, & Hursch, 1964;

Tucker, 1964). The lens model equation (LME) is a formula for decomposing the achievement coefficient, that is, the correlation between criterion and judgment, for a given set of proximal cues:

$$r_a = GR_eR_s + C\sqrt{(1 - R^2_e)}\sqrt{(1 - R^2_s)},$$

where (see Figure 2.2):

r_a is the achievement coefficient, that is, the correlation between the criterion variable Y_e and the judgment variable Y_s;

R_e is the multiple correlation of the criterion variable with the proximal cues;

R_s is the multiple correlation of the judgments with the proximal cues;

G is the correlation between the linear components of the criterion and judgment variables, that is, the correlation between the values Y'_e that are predicted by linear regression of the criterion variable on the proximal cues and the values Y'_s that are predicted by linear regression of the judgments on the proximal cues; and

C is the correlation between the nonlinear components of the criterion and judgment variables, that is, the correlation between the residuals $Y_e - Y'_e$ and the residuals $Y_s - Y'_s$.

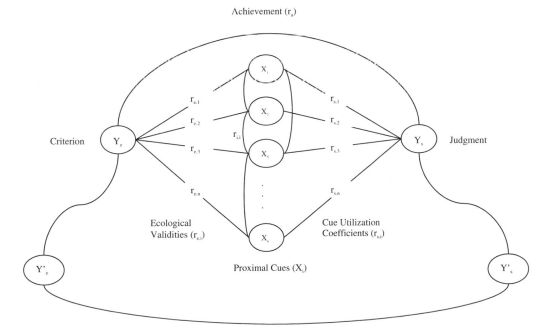

Figure 2.2. Brunswik's lens model as modified for social judgment theory, shown together with components of the lens model equation. See text for details.

The LME has become a standard tool of Brunswikian research because it allows the investigator to decompose performance in a meaningful way and to see which component(s) of performance are affected by various manipulations (e.g., different kinds of feedback about one's task performance, introduction of a technological aid). The indices R_e and R_s indicate the linear predictability of the two systems, environmental (criterion) and organismic (judgment), respectively, based on a particular set of proximal cues. The indices G and C indicate the extent to which the judge has succeeded in matching his or her own systematic use of the proximal cues (linear/additive and nonlinear/configural, respectively) with the criterion variable's systematic dependence (linear/additive and nonlinear/configural) on the proximal cues. In a sense, then, G and C assess the judge's knowledge of the task.

It is relatively common to find that neither the criterion variable nor the judge has any consistent nonlinear or configural dependence on the proximal cues, and this situation simplifies both the LME itself and the interpretations of the indices. In this case, the LME reduces to the following approximation:

$$r_a \approx GR_eR_s$$

because in the absence of systematic nonlinear variance the expected value of C equals zero. The indices R_e and R_s, then, indicate the total predictability of the environmental and organismic systems, respectively (i.e., linear/additive predictability is all there is, apart from sampling fluctuations). The index R_s indicates the consistency with which the judge executes the (only) systematic component of his or her judgment, and therefore the index is called cognitive control (Hammond & Summers, 1972). The index G indicates the extent to which the (only) systematic component of the judge's performance is related to the (only) systematic component of the task environment and therefore is called knowledge. The LME reveals the fact that even when knowledge is perfect ($G = 1$), achievement is limited by the consistency with which this knowledge is executed (R_s) and the consistency of the task environment (R_e).

Many of the chapters in this volume either employ the LME as a tool for analyzing the impact of technological aids or address the LME itself by proposing modifications and extensions. For example, cognitive control figures importantly in chapter 3 by Bisantz, Kirlik, Walker, Fisk, Gay, and Phipps, where it is found to explain individual differences in performance in a combat information center environment, and in chapter 4 by Adelman, Yeo, and Miller, where it is used to explain group achievement with different computer displays under time pressure. A number of chapters (to be discussed shortly in a somewhat different context) suggest alternatives to the LME's implicit linear and static modeling of both the environment and the organism. Still others consider various mathematical extensions or embeddings of the LME in other decompositions of performance (chapter 5; chapter 6; also see Stewart, 2001).

Individual Learning

Brunswik portrayed organisms as having to adapt to environments whose distal properties were indicated only probabilistically by proximal cues. This raises the question of how organisms learn probabilistic relationships, and Brunswikian researchers have produced a large body of literature on the subject using a paradigm called multiple-cue probability learning (MCPL). On each trial of an MCPL study, the respondent examines a profile of cue values and predicts the value of a criterion variable. In a study using outcome feedback, the respondent is then told the correct criterion value and must learn the cue–criterion relationships over many trials (for a review, see Klayman, 1988). In general, learning from outcome feedback tends to be surprisingly slow and limited. Todd and Hammond (1965) introduced the notion of cognitive feedback, where respondents are shown statistical properties over blocks of trials rather than the outcomes of single trials. The result is that learning is generally faster and better than with outcome feedback. (See Balzer, Doherty, & O'Connor, 1989, for a decomposition of cognitive feedback into components that are differentially responsible for the improved performance.)

A number of the chapters in this book touch on issues of feedback and training, sometimes in the context of other concerns. For example, Seong, Bisantz, and Gattie (chapter 8) discuss the use of cognitive feedback, although their main interest has to do with human trust of automated systems, and Bass and Pritchett (chapter 9) provide a feedback-based technique for improving the correspondence between human and automated judgments. Chapters by Rothrock and Kirlik (chapter 10) and

Campbell, Van Buskirk, and Bolton (chapter 11) also address issues of training, although they are mainly concerned with using nonlinear models to represent human performance.

Interpersonal Conflict and Interpersonal Learning

The LME was described earlier as applying to the correlation between judgments and criterion values. However, the LME applies to the correlation between any two variables that are each in turn related to the same set of cues. Therefore, one can use it to decompose the correlation between two people's judgments. Indeed, one can decompose the correlation between any pair of variables in a group of variables. In such a case, the model is referred to as the N-system lens model. If one of the N systems is a criterion variable and there are $N - 1$ judges, then $N - 1$ of the correlations will refer to judges' achievement and the remaining $(N - 1)(N - 2)/2$ correlations will refer to agreement between pairs of judges. Changes in the LME components of each correlation, over blocks of trials, indicate the results of the interactions taking place among the people in addition to any other feedback that might be available.

Social judgment theory has generated a large number of experiments that examine the resolution of conflicts between people who must reach consensus judgments despite their (initial) differences in the use of proximal cues (Hammond, 1965, 1973). In addition, social judgment theory has addressed two different kinds of interpersonal learning. First, there is the case in which one person learns from another about the skillful performance of the task (Earle, 1973). A second kind of interpersonal learning can be studied in a procedure that adds a phase to the experiment, after the interaction between people, where the participants are separated and each is asked to judge new cases as well as to predict the other participant's judgments of these cases. Using this procedure (Hammond, Wilkins, & Todd, 1966), one can study what participants learn *about* each other (i.e., what they learn about the judgmental systems of their partners) as well as what they learn *from* each other (i.e., how their own judgmental systems are changed due to exposure to their partners). (It is the social nature of these lines of research that gave social judgment theory its name.) Many of the same factors that have been manipulated in MCPL studies have also been examined in investigations of interpersonal learning and conflict. Hammond et al. (1975) review the effects of task consistency, ecological validity of cues, cue-criterion function forms, and cue intercorrelations. (For other reviews and discussions, including extensions to negotiations and small-group processes, see Adelman, Henderson, & Miller, 2001; Brehmer, 1976; Cooksey, 1996; Mumpower, 2001; Rohrbaugh, 2001.)

The relevance of these studies and these sorts of analyses for cognitive engineering is that the various judges in an N-system lens model may be provided with different kinds of displays of the cues, so that (dis)agreement between judges reflects the impact of display conditions. Pritchett and Bisantz (chapter 7) present just such an analysis of judges employing different cockpit display designs in a simulated conflict detection task. They also apply the N-system lens model to assess the agreement between human judges and automated systems that are designed to produce suggested judgments. Comparable issues are examined by Horrey, Wickens, Strauss, Kirlik, and Stewart (chapter 5) in a simulation of military threat assessments and resource allocation decisions. These investigators evaluate people's performance with and without display conditions that highlight the most threatening enemy units and with and without the use of an automated display enhancement that suggests an appropriate allocation of resources. The contributions by Seong, Bisantz, and Gattie (chapter 8) and by Bass and Pritchett (chapter 9) further examine the interactions between humans and automated systems for suggesting judgments and decisions, the latter chapter explicitly drawing on social judgment theory research on interpersonal learning.

Further Applications and Extensions of Brunswikian Principles

The areas of research reviewed in the previous section are the classic ones that contributed directly to the development of social judgment theory. However, this brief review cannot begin to convey the range of theoretical issues and domains of application where Brunswikian-inspired research on judgment has been fruitful. In this section, I touch on some of the applications and extensions of social judgment theory to which the chapters in this volume make contributions.

Dynamic Tasks and Time Stress

Because many tasks involve time as a key element in one form or another, a number of researchers have been interested in tasks that go beyond that of static judgment or the one-shot choice of an action. For example, information may be accrued over time, judgments or actions may be required under time pressure, actions may need to be adjusted as their results unfold over time, and so on. Researchers working within the context of individual learning (see previous discussion) have studied dynamic environments in which the validity of cues can change (Dudycha, Dumoff, & Dudycha, 1973; Peterson, Hammond, & Summers, 1965; Summers, 1969) or where the value of the criterion variable is affected by the respondent's predictions or actions (Camerer, 1981; Kleinmuntz, 1985; Kleinmuntz & Thomas, 1987; Mackinnon & Wearing, 1985; for research on learning in even more complex dynamic environments, see Brehmer, 1992, 1995, 1996).

Several of the contributions to this volume share this concern with dynamic aspects of task environments and performance (chapter 4; chapter 18; chapter 16; chapter 6; chapter 10). The chapter by Bisantz, Kirlik, Walker, Fisk, Gay and Phipps (chapter 3) in particular extends the lens model approach by developing time-stamped, idiographic (individualized) models of the task environment, which is necessary for examining judgment in dynamic tasks. The chapter by Kirlik (chapter 15) provides a technique for formalizing both perception and action cue-criterion relationships in a unified environmental model, which is necessary for studying interactive tasks where the performer has some control over available stimulation. These contributions complement the work described next, in which researchers extend the other (internal) "half" of the lens model by proposing nonlinear models of the organism.

Macromediation: Gross Characteristics of the Pattern of Proximal and Peripheral Mediation between Distal and Central Foci

As discussed earlier, Brunswik's project to illuminate achievement and its "grand strategy" requires separate models of the environment and the organism and a comparison of those models. Phrased in terms of judgment, that means that separate models are needed to describe (1) criterion–cue relationships and (2) cue–judgment relationships. Studies that focus on the latter type of model are often referred to in social judgment theory as efforts in "policy capturing" (referring to the judge's "policy" for using the cues; see Brehmer & Brehmer, 1988). Moreover, in keeping with Brunswik's advice to study macromediation before micromediation (see previous discussion), researchers frequently fit models to people's judgments without much concern for the model's fidelity to the "process detail" (using Brunswik's expression as it is reproduced in Figure 2.1) by which people are "actually" using the cues. Models that describe criterion–cue relationships while remaining uncommitted about the detailed time course of the underlying cognitive processes are often called paramorphic (Hoffman, 1960; see Doherty & Brehmer, 1997, for a different view of paramorphic models).

Some of the contributions to this volume involve efforts in this spirit. That is, models are fit to capture the structure and predictability of people's behavior, but the authors refrain from making strong claims that the models describe underlying processes. All of the chapters presenting applications of the linear-additive formulation of the lens model are of this type. In addition, the canonical correlation analysis by Degani, Shafto, and Kirlik (chapter 13) and Casner's analysis of adaptation (chapter 14) are concerned with determining the task demands and environmental conditions to which aircraft pilots are sensitive in deciding where to set the aircraft's mode of control on a continuum between fully manual and fully automatic. In both cases, the goal of describing the internal details of the pilot's decision process is deferred.

In other chapters, the authors depart more radically from the use of linear models and techniques (see Dawes, 1979; Dawes & Corrigan, 1974) to describe people's judgment policies. Instead, the authors employ models that are thought by some to be more consistent with cognitive theory and with people's verbal reports of their processes. In particular, Rothrock and Kirlik (chapter 10) present a method for inferring rule-based heuristics from people's judgments. These simplified, noncompensatory strategies are more plausible descriptions of people's judgment processes, especially when people are time-stressed or otherwise facing cognitive limitations. Similarly, Campbell, Van Buskirk, and Bolton (chapter 11) investigate the use of fuzzy logic for modeling people's judgments and decisions.

Micromediation: Breaking Down the Cognitive Process into Its Component Parts

Still other chapters are more explicit in attempting to flesh out the process detail of people's adaptation to the environment. Recall that it was late in Brunswik's career before he explicitly incorporated the study of inner psychological processes into his framework (but see Goldstein & Wright, 2001). As noted earlier, Brunswik was restrained about studies of cognitive processes for two reasons. He thought that researchers might tend to study cognitive processes apart from the task environments in which they occurred, abandoning the study of functional adaptation. Also, he thought that the flexibility of vicarious functioning might produce "relative chaos in the regions intervening between focal variables" (Brunswik, 1952, p. 20), making it difficult and unrewarding to study cognitive processes in detail. Although Brunswik's concerns on the first point may have been valid, the cognitive revolution in psychology has shown the study of cognitive processes to be eminently feasible and amply rewarding.

Some of the chapters in this volume have taken up the challenge of integrating detailed models of cognitive processes into Brunswik's framework. Whereas organisms' sensitivity to their task environments was offered earlier as an argument for representative design and a matter for empirical study, Gray (chapter 16) uses a current cognitive theory (ACT-R) and related computational techniques to consider how even minor changes in task environments can affect cognitive processes and influence overt performance. He goes even further to sketch out his vision more generally of a "rapprochement" between cognitive and ecological analyses. In a study of airline pilots' performance in landing and taxiing to gate under foggy conditions, Byrne, Kirlik, and Fick (chapter 18) combine detailed cognitive models with ecological analyses. In particular, they model pilots' taxi route decisions as heavily involving the use of two simple heuristics (see also chapter 10), and they find that the model is predictive of decision errors in ecologically atypical situations that short-circuit these heuristics' efficacy. Pirolli (chapter 17) investigates people's navigation among pages on the Web. Part of his approach involves portraying people as using proximal cues (provided by the current Web page) to predict the utility of distal pages, and this predictive activity is modeled with spreading activation in a network of nodes that represent the person's understanding of the search domain.

Degani, Shafto, and Kirlik (chapter 13) do not so much attempt to contribute to theory of cognitive processes but instead to draw on recent cognitive theory to address fundamental questions in Brunswik's probabilistic functionalism. In particular, they ask the question "What makes vicarious functioning work?" They are motivated to ask this question by their observation that many largely digital, technological interfaces seem to defeat vicarious functioning and thus adaptive behavior itself. Degani and colleagues conclude that the discrete, technological ecology often does not support the approximation and convergence (learning) operations supported by continuous ecologies. These learning operations are claimed to be crucial to the development of robust and adaptive "intuitive" (Hammond, 2000) or "System I" (Kahneman, 2003) cognition.

Revisiting the Fundamentals

A number of researchers have urged that some of the principles of Brunswik's program be revisited and possibly reinterpreted. Two of these lines of thought will be mentioned here, concerning (1) the appropriate meaning (and measure) of functional adaptation and (2) the adequacy of studying perception/judgment and overt action separately.

Regarding adaptation, Gigerenzer and his colleagues (Gigerenzer & Kurz, 2001; Gigerenzer, Todd, & the ABC Research Group, 1999) note that Brunswik's functionalist perspective led him to emphasize the adaptiveness of an organism's behavior in specific environments, but that accuracy of judgment is only one facet of its adaptiveness. Speed and the ability to make use of limited information are also important features. Similar reasoning has prompted Rothrock and Kirlik (chapter 10) and Byrne, Kirlik, and Fick (chapter 18) to suggest that researchers reconsider the task criterion that is analyzed, especially in studies of time-stressed tasks. Both chapters attend to the observation that approximate yet fast (rather than accurate yet slow) judgment and decision strategies may be favored in dynamic tasks. Mosier and McCauley (chapter 12) elaborate on a distinction emphasized by Hammond (1996) between a focus on correspondence with the environment (e.g., accuracy of judgment) versus coherence of judgments and/or actions (e.g., logical consistency). Mosier and McCauley draw attention to the fact that technology has transformed a number of tasks so that human operators must assess the coherence of information and, if necessary, take steps to reestablish coherence. The cognitive processes underlying these tasks and the standards of adaptiveness for evaluating them must be considered carefully.

Finally, Kirlik (chapter 15) reconsiders the separate application of Brunswik's lens model to matters of perception or judgment versus matters of overt action. Although Brunswik recognized and discussed the applicability of his approach to both sets of issues (compare Tolman & Brunswik, 1935), his own substantive interest concerned problems of perception, and most of his followers have been interested in judgment. The implicit assumption is that perception/judgment and action can be studied independently without serious loss. Kirlik demonstrates that the simultaneous analysis of perception/judgment and action in a specific task environment constrains theories of the underlying cognitive processes much more adequately than modeling them in isolation. Casner (chapter 14), Gray (chapter 16), Kirlik, Byrne, and Fick (chapter 18), and Pirolli (chapter 17) also demonstrate benefits from an integrated analysis of perception/judgment and overt action.

Conclusion

Brunswik's probabilistic functionalism emphasizes (1) adjustment to the world and (2) the mediated nature of that adjustment. It is becoming increasingly clear that cognitive engineering must do so as well. Brunswik's approach leads to important theoretical and methodological implications, and his original formulation has been amplified and extended by social judgment theory and other lines of research. This volume attempts to explain the applicability of Brunswik's ideas to cognitive engineering and demonstrate some of its potential contributions. Those who would like a more substantial historical presentation of Brunswik's ideas and the manner in which they have been applied and extended should see Hammond and Stewart (2001).

Acknowledgments.   Parts of this chapter have been adapted from Goldstein (2004).

References

Adelman, L., Henderson, D., & Miller, S. (2001). Vicarious functioning in teams. In K. R. Hammond & T. R. Stewart (Eds.), *The essential Brunswik: Beginnings, explications, applications* (pp. 416–423). Oxford: Oxford University Press.

Anderson, J. R. (1990). *The adaptive character of thought.* Hillsdale, N.J.: Lawrence Erlbaum Associates.

Angell, J. R. (1907). The province of functional psychology. *Psychological Review, 14,* 61–91.

Balzer, W. K., Doherty, M. E., & O'Connor, R., Jr. (1989). Effects of cognitive feedback on performance. *Psychological Bulletin, 106,* 410–433.

Brehmer, A., & Brehmer, B. (1988). What have we learned about human judgment from thirty years of policy capturing? In B. Brehmer & C. R. B. Joyce (Eds.), *Human judgment: The SJT view* (pp. 75–114). Amsterdam: Elsevier Science Publishers B.V. (North-Holland).

Brehmer, B. (1976). Social judgment theory and the analysis of interpersonal conflict. *Psychological Bulletin, 83,* 985–1003.

Brehmer, B. (1988). The development of social judgment theory. In B. Brehmer & C. R. B. Joyce (Eds.), *Human judgment: The SJT view* (pp. 13–40). Amsterdam: Elsevier Science Publishers B.V. (North-Holland).

Brehmer, B. (1992). Dynamic decision making: Human control of complex systems. *Acta Psychologica, 81,* 211–241.

Brehmer, B. (1995). Feedback delays in complex dynamic decision tasks. In P. A. Frensch & J. Funke (Eds.), *Complex problem solving: The European perspective.* Hillsdale, N.J.: Erlbaum.

Brehmer, B. (1996). Man as a stabiliser of systems: From static snapshots of judgement processes to dynamic decision making. In M. E. Doherty (Ed.), *Social judgement theory* [Special issue of *Thinking and Reasoning,* 2(2/3), 225–238]. East Sussex, UK: Psychology Press.

Brehmer, B., & Joyce, C. R. B. (Eds.). (1988). *Human judgment: The SJT view.* Amsterdam: Elsevier Science Publishers B.V. (North-Holland).

Brentano, F. (1874/1973). *Psychology from an empirical standpoint.* L. L. McAlister, Ed.; A. C. Rancurello, D. B. Terrell, & L. L. McAlister, Trans. London: Routledge.

Brunswik, E. (1943). Organismic achievement and

environmental probability. *Psychological Review, 50*, 255–272.

Brunswik, E. (1952). *The conceptual framework of psychology*. Chicago: University of Chicago Press. (*International Encyclopedia of Unified Science*, vol. I, no. 10.)

Brunswik, E. (1955). Representative design and probabilistic theory in a functional psychology. *Psychological Review, 62*, 193–217.

Brunswik, E. (1956). *Perception and the representative design of psychological experiments* (2nd ed.). Berkeley: University of California Press.

Brunswik, E. (1957). Scope and aspects of the cognitive problem. In H. E. Gruber, K. R. Hammond, & R. Jessor (Eds.), *Contemporary approaches to cognition: A symposium held at the University of Colorado* (pp. 5–31). Cambridge, MA: Harvard University Press.

Camerer, C. F. (1981). The validity and utility of expert judgment. Unpublished doctoral dissertation, Graduate School of Business, University of Chicago.

Cooksey, R. W. (1996). *Judgment analysis: Theory, methods, and applications*. San Diego, CA: Academic Press.

Dawes, R. M. (1979). The robust beauty of improper linear models in decision making. *American Psychologist, 34*, 571–582.

Dawes, R. M., & Corrigan, B. (1974). Linear models in decision making. *Psychological Bulletin, 81*, 95–106.

Doherty, M. E. (Ed.). (1996). *Social judgement theory* [Special issue of *Thinking and Reasoning, 2*(2/3)]. East Sussex, UK: Psychology Press.

Doherty, M. E., & Brehmer, B. (1997). The paramorphic representation of clinical judgment: A thirty-year retrospective. In W. M. Goldstein & R. M. Hogarth (Eds.), *Research on judgment and decision making: Currents, connections, and controversies* (pp. 537–551). Cambridge: Cambridge University Press.

Dudycha, A. L., Dumoff, M. G., & Dudycha, L. W. (1973). Choice behavior in dynamic environments. *Organizational Behavior and Human Performance, 9*, 323–338.

Earle, T. C. (1973). Interpersonal learning. In L. Rappoport & D. A. Summers (Eds.), *Human judgment and social interaction* (pp. 240–266). New York: Holt, Rinehart & Winston.

Gigerenzer, G. (1987). Survival of the fittest probabilist: Brunswik, Thurstone, and the two disciplines of psychology. In L. Kruger, G. Gigerenzer, & M. S. Morgan (Eds.), *The probabilistic revolution: Volume 2. Ideas in the sciences* (pp. 49–72). Cambridge, MA: MIT Press.

Gigerenzer, G., & Kurz, E. M. (2001). Vicarious functioning reconsidered: A fast and frugal lens model. In K. R. Hammond & T. R. Stewart (Eds.), *The essential Brunswik: Beginnings, explications, applications* (pp. 342–347). Oxford: Oxford University Press.

Gigerenzer, G., Todd, P. M., & the ABC Research Group (Eds). (1999). *Simple heuristics that make us smart*. New York: Oxford University Press.

Goldstein, W. M. (2004). Social judgment theory: Applying and extending Brunswik's probabilistic functionalism. In D. J. Koehler & N. Harvey (Eds.), *Blackwell handbook of judgment and decision making* (pp. 37–61). Oxford: Blackwell.

Goldstein, W. M., & Wright, J. H. (2001). "Perception" versus "thinking": Brunswikian thought on central responses and processes. In K. R. Hammond & T. R. Stewart (Eds.), *The essential Brunswik: Beginnings, explications, applications* (pp. 249–256). Oxford: Oxford University Press.

Hammond, K. R. (1955). Probabilistic functionalism and the clinical method. *Psychological Review, 62*, 255–262.

Hammond, K. R. (1965). New directions in research on conflict resolution. *Journal of Social Issues, 21*, 44–66.

Hammond, K. R. (Ed.). (1966). *The psychology of Egon Brunswik*. New York: Holt, Rinehart & Winston.

Hammond, K. R. (1973). The cognitive conflict paradigm. In L. Rappoport & D. A. Summers, (Eds.), *Human judgment and social interaction* (pp. 188–205). New York: Holt, Rinehart & Winston.

Hammond, K. R. (1996). *Human judgment and social policy: Irreducible uncertainty, inevitable error, unavoidable injustice*. New York: Oxford University Press.

Hammond, K. R. (2000). *Judgments under stress*. New York: Oxford University Press.

Hammond, K. R., & Joyce, C. R. B. (Eds.). (1975). *Psychoactive drugs and social judgment: Theory and research*. New York: Wiley.

Hammond, K. R., Rohrbaugh, J., Mumpower, J., & Adelman, L. (1977). Social judgment theory: Applications in policy formation. In M. Kaplan & S. Schwartz (Eds.), *Human judgment and decision processes in applied settings* (pp. 1–30). New York: Academic Press.

Hammond, K. R., & Stewart, T. R. (Eds.). (2001). *The essential Brunswik: Beginnings, explications, applications*. Oxford: Oxford University Press.

Hammond, K. R., Stewart, T. R., Brehmer, B., & Steinmann, D. (1975). Social judgment theory. In M. F. Kaplan & S. Schwartz (Eds.), *Human judgment and decision processes* (pp. 271–312). New York: Academic Press.

Hammond, K. R., & Summers, D. A. (1972). Cognitive control. *Psychological Review, 79,* 58–67.

Hammond, K. R., & Wascoe, N. E. (Eds.). (1980). *Realizations of Brunswik's representative design.* San Francisco: Jossey-Bass.

Hammond, K. R., Wilkins, M. M., & Todd, F. J. (1966). A research paradigm for the study of interpersonal learning. *Psychological Bulletin, 65,* 221–232.

Hoffman, P. J. (1960). The paramorphic representation of clinical judgment. *Psychological Bulletin, 57,* 116–131.

Hunter, W. S. (1932). The psychological study of behavior. *Psychological Review, 39,* 1–24.

Hursch, C. J., Hammond, K. R., & Hursch, J. L. (1964). Some methodological considerations in multiple-cue probability studies. *Psychological Review, 71,* 42–60.

Juslin, P., & Montgomery, H. (Eds.). (1999). *Judgment and decision making: Neo-Brunswikian and process-tracing approaches.* Mahwah, N.J.: Erlbaum.

Kahneman, D. (2003). A perspective on judgment and choice: Mapping bounded rationality. *American Psychologist, 58*(9), 697–720.

Kirlik, A. (2005). Work in progress: Reinventing intelligence for an invented world. In R. J. Sternberg & D. Preiss (Eds.), *Intelligence and technology; The impact of tools on the nature and development of human abilities* (pp. 105–133). Mahwah, N.J.: Lawrence Erlbaum & Associates.

Klayman, J. (1988). On the how and why (not) of learning from outcomes. In B. Brehmer & C. R. B. Joyce (Eds.), *Human judgment: The SJT view* (pp. 115–162). Elsevier Science Publishers B.V. (North-Holland).

Kleinmuntz, D. N. (1985). Cognitive heuristics and feedback in a dynamic decision environment. *Management Science, 31,* 680–702.

Kleinmuntz, D. N., & Thomas, J. B. (1987). The value of action and inference in dynamic decision making. *Organizational Behavior and Human Decision Processes, 39,* 341–364.

Kurz, E. M., & Tweney, R. D. (1997). The heretical psychology of Egon Brunswik. In W. G. Bringmann, H. E. Lück, R. Miller, & C. E. Early (Eds.), *A pictorial history of psychology* (pp. 221–232). Chicago: Quintessence Books.

Leary, D. E. (1987). From act psychology to probabilistic functionalism: The place of Egon Brunswik in the history of psychology. In M. G. Ash & W. R. Woodward (Eds.), *Psychology in twentieth-century thought and society* (pp. 115–142). Cambridge: Cambridge University Press.

Mackinnon, A. J., & Wearing, A. J. (1985). Systems analysis and dynamic decision making. *Acta Psychologica, 58,* 159–172.

Mumpower, J. L. (2001). Brunswikian research on social perception, interpersonal learning and conflict, and negotiation. In K. R. Hammond & T. R. Stewart (Eds.), *The essential Brunswik: Beginnings, explications, applications* (pp. 388–393). Oxford: Oxford University Press.

Norman, D. (1993). *Things that make us smart* (pp. 139–153). Cambridge: Perseus Books.

Peterson, C. R., Hammond, K. R., & Summers, D. A. (1965). Multiple probability learning with shifting cue weights. *American Journal of Psychology, 78,* 660–663.

Rappoport, L., & Summers, D. A. (Eds.). (1973). *Human judgment and social interaction.* New York: Holt, Rinehart & Winston.

Rohrbaugh, J. (2001). The relationship between strategy and achievement as the basic unit of group functioning. In K. R. Hammond & T. R. Stewart (Eds.) *The essential Brunswik: Beginnings, explications, applications* (pp. 384–387). Oxford: Oxford University Press.

Stewart, T. R. (2001). The lens model equation. In K. R. Hammond & T. R. Stewart (Eds.) *The essential Brunswik: Beginnings, explications, applications* (pp. 357–362). Oxford: Oxford University Press.

Summers, D. A. (1969). Adaptation to change in multiple probability tasks. *American Journal of Psychology, 82,* 235–240.

Todd, F. J., & Hammond, K. R. (1965). Differential feedback in two multiple-cue probability learning tasks. *Behavioral Science, 10,* 429–435.

Tolman, E. C., & Brunswik, E. C. (1935). The organism and the causal texture of the environment. *Psychological Review, 42,* 43–77.

Tucker, L. (1964). A suggested alternative formulation in the developments by Hursch, Hammond, and Hursch, and by Hammond, Hursch, and Todd. *Psychological Review, 71,* 528–530.

Turvey, M. T., Fitch, H. L. & Tuller, B. (1982). The Bernstein perspective: I. The problems of degrees of freedom and context-conditioned variability. In J. A. S. Kelso (Ed.), *Human motor behavior: An introduction* (pp. 239–252). Mahwah, N.J.: Lawrence Erlbaum Associates.

Vicente, K. J. (1999). *Cognitive work analysis.* Mahwah, N.J.: Lawrence Erlbaum Associates.

Technological Interfaces

Alex Kirlik

Introduction

As described by Goldstein in chapter 2, Brunswik's approach to the study of perception drew heavily on the distinction between proximal cues, and the distal environmental objects and events associated with those cues. The chapters in this section demonstrate how this same distinction can be usefully coopted to shed light on a quite different unit of cognitive analysis: human interaction with an environment mediated by a technological interface. In particular, the authors of the following chapters use the proximal-distal distinction to distinguish between the sources of information proximally available from an information display (e.g., a blip on a radar screen) and a distal environmental object or event represented by that information (e.g., an aircraft that may be beyond the bounds of normal perception).

Although this analogy between the two situations (perception versus technologically mediated cognition) seems direct enough, the following chapters reveal that the dynamism and complexity of today's technological work environments often require that investigators seeking to use Brunswikian theory and methods must augment their analysis and modeling in a variety of ways. In chapter 3, for example, Bisantz and colleagues had to deal with two features of dynamic, interactive environments

that make a standard application of the lens model problematic. Because people often have at least some freedom to determine when they will make judgments, in a dynamic environment it is unlikely that any two participants in a study will make their judgments on the basis of identical cue sets, because the latter are perpetually and autonomously changing. Additionally, in interactive environments, people may also have the opportunity to seek out information actively. Because people may differ in this regard as well, interactivity again increases the possibility that cue sets will be specific to the individual studied. A central contribution of their work is the development of a technique to create idiographic (performer-specific) models to use as the basis for lens model analysis in dynamic tasks.

In chapter 4, Adelman and coauthors present a study of how distributed teams respond to time pressure. Their research demonstrated how the lens model could be extended to a multilevel form using path modeling to describe flows of information among team members and how the team responded to time stress. Adelman and colleagues found that as the tempo of the dynamic task increased, the effectiveness of information flow among team members suffered, with measurable (and independent) effects on both knowledge and consistency of performance.

As Adelman and colleagues note in their chapter, the "achievement" performance measure presumed by the standard lens model, being a correlation, may be insensitive to aspects of performance concerning the mean and standard deviation of judgments. A more demanding measure, such as mean squared error, or MSE (the absolute Euclidean distance between two data sets, rather than merely their correlation), would also capture these potential base rate and regression biases. Although Adelman and colleagues reported that their results did not change when they analyzed MSE rather than solely achievement, in chapter 5 Horrey and coauthors present a study that demonstrates the utility of complementing a lens model analysis with an examination of a more demanding, MSE-based measure. In particular, their research on the use of automation to enhance visual displays revealed that the most pronounced effects of automation were associated with regression biases to which lens model analysis is insensitive. An intriguing result was that their most sophisticated form of automation, which actually displayed a suggested judgment to performers, appeared to have its main benefit in allowing performers to better adapt the range or severity of their judgments to the range of their task criterion. The reason why Adelman and colleagues found effects solely within lens model measures, whereas Horrey and his co-workers found effects solely within regression biases almost surely lies in finely grained differences between the tasks studied. Fortunately, the techniques presented by these authors provide exactly the resources necessary for a sustained series of investigations to provide a more complete understanding of the relationship between task features (e.g., time pressure, type of display intervention) and their cognitive consequences.

In chapter 6, Jha and Bisantz present a study of fault diagnosis in which they varied both visual presentation format (graphical displays of only the values of physical system variables versus this information supplemented with functional information) and also fault severity. The complexity of the task required them to use a multivariate formulation of the lens model and canonical correlation techniques for data analysis. The patterns found through canonical correlation, like those reported by Degani, Shafto, and Kirlik (this volume) in an aviation context, proved quite useful in making sense of the effects of their display design and severity manipulations on problem-solving performance. Collectively, these chapters portray a promising future for looking at the problems of information display design and understanding technologically mediated interaction through a Brunswikian lens.

Ann M. Bisantz, Alex Kirlik, Neff Walker,

Arthur D. Fisk, Paul Gay, and Donita Phipps

Knowledge versus Execution in Dynamic Judgment Tasks

Introduction

Two-hundred ninety people were killed on July 3, 1988, when the USS *Vincennes* mistakenly shot down an Iran Air commercial jetliner over the Persian Gulf (Fogarty, 1988). As a result of this tragedy, the U.S. Office of Naval Research established a research program called Tactical Decision Making Under Stress, or TADMUS (Collyer & Malecki, 1998). A central goal of the 7-year TADMUS program was to better understand human strengths and limitations in coping with time stress, technological complexity, and situational ambiguity while performing judgment and decision-making tasks. The TADMUS program spawned a wide range of empirical and theoretical research, characterized by close involvement among researchers at universities, government laboratories, and the naval operational community. These investigators were united by a shared vision that an improved understanding of human performance in dynamic, uncertain, technological environments could better support the design of future military training, aiding, and display systems and thus hopefully reduce the likelihood of future incidents like the *Vincennes* tragedy.

The research presented in this chapter was one of the many efforts initiated and supported under the TADMUS program (for a comprehensive account of TADMUS research products see Cannon-Bowers & Salas, 1998). As described in a chapter written with our colleagues in that volume (Kirlik et al., 1998), one of the initial steps in our own research was to visit a naval precommissioning team training site, consisting of a full-scale hardware and software simulation of a ship-based Combat Information Center (CIC). At this site, entire CIC teams received tactical decision-making and crew coordination training just prior to taking to sea and conducting active operations. We focused our observations and subsequent research on the task of the Anti-Air Warfare Coordinator (AAWC), who was responsible for using a computer workstation containing a radar display and a wide variety of other information sources to make identification judgments of initially unknown objects, called tracks, in the environment of his or her ship.

During these visits we were impressed by the significant amount of time and resources devoted to realism in both simulator and scenario design. At the same time, however, we were distressed by the comparatively little time and few resources devoted to providing individuals and teams with diagnostic and timely feedback on the positive and negative aspects of their judgment performance.

Because there is currently a strong movement toward computer-based and embedded training systems in technological contexts (e.g., Kozlowski et al., 2001), we saw an opportunity to guide the future design of such systems by creating techniques for identifying a trainee's performance strategy (and its potential limitations) directly from a trainee's history of behavioral data collected during simulation or training exercises. With such techniques available, it would then become feasible to either guide the selection of training interventions toward remedying any strategic, knowledge-based deficiencies reflected by a trainee's strategy or focus training on mastering the skills required to consistently execute judgment strategies under time stress.

Selecting a Modeling Approach

Through field observations, interviewing performers and trainers, preliminary task analysis and a review of the literature, we determined that the central task of the AAWC was largely consistent with the image of judgment portrayed by Brunswik's lens model (Brunswik, 1955; Cooksey, 1996; Hammond et al., 1975; also see Goldstein, this volume). A primary challenge faced by this performer was to use multiple, proximally displayed information sources (or cues) of various degrees of reliability (or ecological validity) to identify remote (or distal) environmental objects, in this case, the identities of a tracks presented on a radar display.

This characterization of the AAWC task is consistent with many aspects of another decision-making paradigm, naturalistic decision making (NDM) (Klein, 1993; 1999). NDM focuses on studying "how people use their experience to make decisions in field settings" (p. 97). Like lens modeling, NDM does not have its basis in either the classical decision theory (CDT) or behavioral decision making (BDM) approaches to the study of cognition. Both of those approaches have their foundation in models based on the internal *coherence* of cognition, typically by appeal to one theory of normative rationality or another (e.g., expected utility theory, Bayes theorem, etc.). The view of performance portrayed by the lens model, like that of NDM, is instead based on a *correspondence-based* approach, where the primary yardstick for evaluating cognition and behavior is its empirical success in terms of adaptive fit to environmental structure (for a discussion of the contrast

between coherence- and correspondence-based approaches, see Gigerenzer & Todd, 1999; Hammond, 1999; Mosier & McCauley, this volume).

There are substantive ties between the two approaches as well. First, both the lens model and NDM acknowledge that environmental uncertainty places a ceiling on human achievement (Hammond, 1996). As Lipshitz and others (2001a) have (qualitatively) put it, "Uncertainty is intimately linked with error: the greater the uncertainty, the greater the probability of making an error" (p. 339). Second, NDM, due to its historical roots in Klein's recognition-primed decision (RPD) model, places a heavy emphasis on the identification and use of perhaps subtle environmental cues supporting inference (e.g., Crandall and Getchell-Reiter, 1993) —the aspect of judgment behavior that is captured in the lens model. Third, like the lens model, NDM provides a view of judgment and decision making in terms of "situation-action matching decision rules" as opposed to concurrent choice (Lipshitz et al., 2001a, p. 334; also see Kirlik et al., 1996). Finally, owing to the methodological roots of lens modeling in Brunswik's (1955) probabilistic functionalism, our research approach shares with NDM the goal of "conducting one's study with representative samples of subjects, tasks, and contexts to which one wishes to generalize" (Lipshitz et al., 2001b, p. 386). Each of these features characterizes the empirical and theoretical research presented in the study described in this chapter.

Our research goals did, however, require us to restrict our aims to a different, narrower set of activities than is often associated with the NDM approach. Unlike NDM, we did not attempt to create qualitative, conceptual accounts of the very broad range of cognitive activities that may accompany judgment in operational settings. We have no doubt that judgment and decision making in complex, technological contexts is likely to involve cognitive activities that are currently beyond the reach of formal modeling (e.g., metacognition, mental simulation, and assumption-based reasoning, to name a few; see Lipshitz et al., 2001a). It remains the case, however, that a necessary step toward improving judgment in operational environments through computer-based or embedded training interventions is to be able to provide automated techniques for diagnosing the sources of observed performance limitations. Creating such techniques necessarily requires abstraction and formal modeling.

As such, the research presented here is narrower in scope than NDM or other, less formal approaches to analyzing technological work (e.g., cognitive task analysis [CTA], see Gordon & Gill, 1997 and Militello & Hutton, 1998; or cognitive work analysis [CWA], see Vicente, 1999). At the same time, however, our research demonstrates that important, if selective, aspects of experienced performance in naturalistic settings and tasks can indeed be abstractly modeled and also that it is worthwhile and enlightening to attempt to do so (also see Todd & Gigerenzer, 2001).

In their introduction to the fifth volume in a series of books on NDM, Montgomery, Lipshitz, and Brehmer (2005) reflected on its current status, noting: "The challenge of demonstrating that NDM methodologies can produce general and testable models in addition to valuable insights on how decisions are actually made looms as large today as it was a decade ago" (Montgomery, Lipshitz, & Brehmer, 2005, p. 10). We hope that the methodology presented in this chapter takes at least one step toward the development of such general and testable models.

Knowledge versus Execution

A common distinction is made between two factors limiting performance in cognitive tasks, especially those performed in dynamic environments under time stress: the content knowledge required for high levels of accuracy, and the efficiency or consistency with which knowledge-based performance strategies can be executed. Ideally, technological design and training interventions should selectively address whether observed human performance limitations are due primarily to deficits in task knowledge or instead due primarily to the demands of applying what is known to the task at hand in a timely and consistent fashion. Of course, it may be the case in any particular instance that both factors may play a role.

To illustrate this distinction, which plays a fundamental role in the analysis and modeling that follows, consider the task of performing a series of 100 two-digit multiplication problems (e.g., 12 × 35, 91 × 11) using pencil and paper. Imagine that two groups of subjects in a laboratory experiment were asked to perform this task: elementary schoolchildren who had only recently learned multiplication and college seniors. Also imagine that each group was asked to perform this task under two conditions: In the first, one hour was allotted for the task, whereas in the second, only five minutes was allotted. What results would we expect to see? For the purpose of this example, assume that task knowledge corresponds to knowledge of how to multiply any two single digits along with a strategy for correctly performing two-digit multiplication (carrying, and so forth). What might one expect the results of such an experiment be?

First, one would (hopefully) expect that college seniors would perform this task nearly flawlessly when given one hour to do so, indicating that they not only possessed the necessary task knowledge but were also able to execute their knowledge-based strategies in a nearly perfect manner. In contrast, we may expect a higher proportion of errors in the elementary student group. A detailed analysis of these latter errors could be used to reveal whether, for any particular student, the errors were systematic in some fashion (e.g., forgetting to carry, erroneous knowledge of what 7 times X equals, and so on). Any such systematic errors would likely signal knowledge deficits (Anderson et al., 1995), as opposed to error patterns appearing unsystematic or random (e.g., a child who got the same problem right twice but erred the third time), more likely signaling deficits of execution.

Now consider the results one might expect to see in the five-minute condition. Almost certainly, we would expect both groups to make more errors. But consider the college student group. Does this result indicate that they somehow lost some of their knowledge of multiplication? Unlikely. Instead, it is more likely that their errors would be largely nonsystematic; that is, slips rather than mistakes (Norman, 1981), because they had previously demonstrated complete knowledge required for the multiplication task. As a result, a training intervention designed to improve this group's performance at the speeded version of the task based on further educating them on the single-digit multiplication table and a correct strategy for two-digit multiplication would be quite unlikely to improve subsequent performance. Instead, what seems to be called for is for additional training focused on their abilities to *execute* their knowledge-based strategies under the target conditions of speeded performance (e.g., Fisk, Ackerman, & Schneider, 1987).

Turning back now to the dynamic CIC context and the AAWC judgment task that motivated the present research, we realized that important implications for training could result if we could tease apart whether observed judgment performance limitations were due largely to knowledge deficits or instead to failures to successfully execute judgment strategies using this knowledge in a highly time-stressed context. As demonstrated in the following, the lens model is potentially quite useful in this regard because it provides a means for decomposing the quality of a performer's task-relevant knowledge in judgment tasks and the quality of a performer's ability to make consistent judgments on the basis of this knowledge. This may be an especially useful distinction to make when studying judgment under conditions of high information load, time stress, and uncertainty characteristic of many technological, operational contexts.

In the context of the lens model, "knowledge" is taken to mean knowing which of the many candidate judgment cues or information sources are useful, their relative reliability or ecological validity, and how they should be weighted and combined to arrive at a judgment. Providing feedback guided by the results of lens model analysis (called "cognitive" and "task" feedback) has been shown to be an effective technique in a range of behavioral situations (Balzer, Doherty, & O'Connor, 1989; Balzer et al., 1992; 1994). It is also important to mention that lens model analysis also allows one to diagnose the extent to which observed performance limitations are not due to knowledge or execution limitations on the part of the human at all but are instead due to inherent uncertainty in the performer's task environment. In such cases, training is insufficient to improve judgment performance. Here, performance can be improved only by enhancing the overall reliability of the proximally displayed information (e.g., by improving or adding sensor or display technology).

Experiment

Representative Design

We designed a laboratory simulation modeled on the naval CIC environment and the task of the AAWC observed in our fieldwork. Although we naturally had to limit the fidelity of our simulation due to time

and resource constraints, the simulation captured many of the central aspects of both the surface (proximal) appearance of the AAWC's workstation as well as the depth, or formal properties of the judgment task (cue ecological validities that were at least ordinally similar to those present in the operational environment). In addition, the dynamic scenarios presented to participants were designed with substantial guidance from a subject matter expert who was a highly experienced former naval officer.

Laboratory Simulation

The Georgia Tech-Aegis Simulation Platform (GT-ASP), a real-time, dynamic, and interactive simulation of the AAWC position in an Aegis CIC (Rothrock, 1995), was used in this experiment to study judgment in a dynamic task. The AAWC, in actuality a naval officer, is responsible for making judgments regarding the identity of unidentified tracks in the vicinity of the officer's ship or other ships in the area. The AAWC must gather information about each track and use that information to determine the type of aircraft (e.g., a helicopter or an electronic surveillance aircraft) and its intent (hostile, friendly). After making an identification judgment, the AAWC enters data using a computer console regarding the identity of aircraft and coordinates possible actions against aircraft that are identified as a threat. These actions include sending a warning to the aircraft, sending patrol aircraft to intercept a threatening aircraft, or engaging the aircraft.

To ensure that hostile aircraft do not threaten friendly forces, judgments of track identity must be made quickly with information that may be incomplete or uncertain. For example, it may not be possible to obtain certain identifying electronic profiles (e.g., radar emissions) from a track if the aircraft represented by the track does not have its own radar turned on. Other characteristics, such as the speed and altitude of a track, were always available for all aircraft represented by tracks in the GT-ASP simulation, whether they were commercial airliners or friendly or hostile military aircraft.

GT-ASP provided a graphical radar display, shown in Figure 3.1, which showed reported radar contacts (tracks) and textual and verbal information describing any selected track. Participants selected aircraft, requested information, and engaged hostile aircraft using a keyboard and trackball. To simulate verbal interactions with other CIC team members,

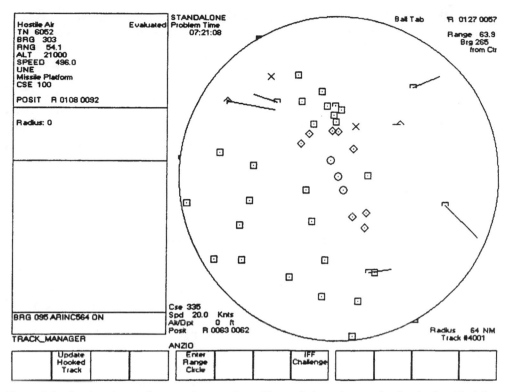

Figure 3.1. The GT-ASP interface. Tracks are indicated by symbols on the round radar display. The left text window provides detailed state and identity information on any selected track.

three rule-based modules representing these team members were constructed within GT-ASP. These modules were both autonomous, verbally alerting the AAWC each time a specified event occurred, and also reactive, responding to AAWC queries for information. Participants received prerecorded verbal information from these simulated team members through headphones. Participants could obtain information about a track's radar signature and Identification Friend or Foe (IFF) status from the simulated team members by selecting the aircraft with the trackball and issuing a series of keystroke commands. Dynamic flight characteristics (e.g., altitude, airspeed, range, heading) could be obtained by either observing the track's movements (e.g., to assess heading) or by viewing textual information provided on the screen when the track was selected.

Procedure

Eight male, Naval ROTC undergraduates participated in the study. Each participant performed eight 30-minute simulated sessions over five days.

In each session, participants were presented with a different tactical scenario modeled after a realistic hypothetical situation in the Arabian Gulf. Topography, commercial airports and flight patterns, and the existence of naval, air, and ground forces were consistent with the actualities of that region. The scenarios were presented in sequence to represent a tactical situation unfolding over time.

Prior to the experiment, participants were given a one-hour briefing describing the task and a packet of information they could refer to during the scenarios. The packet included a briefing on the geopolitical situation, information about various aircraft and their properties (e.g., radar signatures, weapons capabilities, flight schedules of commercial aircraft), information about the GT-ASP displays, and the rules of engagement (ROE), which described the AAWC's responsibilities and actions. The ROE essentially served as the participants' task instructions.

The experiment then consisted of participants performing the scenarios. Time stress was induced by the ROE, which instructed participants that they were required to make identifications of unknown tracks before they approached within 50 nautical miles (nm) of the ship and to take action (by warning, illuminating, and/or engaging) any tracks identified as hostile that threatened the ship. Immediately after each scenario, participants were provided with graphical and textual feedback regarding their performance at identifying aircraft as hostile or friendly, as well as the timeliness with which these judgments were made.

Data Collection

GT-ASP automatically logged all participant actions to query information and identify aircraft, as well as the time of those actions. Additionally, track parameters (e.g., range, altitude, status of radar as on or off) were recorded at every simulation update (every six seconds).

Modeling and Analysis

Goldstein (this volume) provides a general introduction and overview of the generic lens model and its statistical formulation. Figure 3.2 provides a graphical depiction of the lens model we created specifically for describing participant–environment interaction in the GT-ASP track identification task. The left side of the figure depicts the model of the environment, which describes the relationship between the judgment criterion value (e.g., friendly, hostile, commercial airliner) and the cue values available at the time a judgment was made. The model of the human, shown on the right side of Figure 3.2 represents the relationship between the cue values and a participant's judgments (the *judged* criterion value) and represents the participant's

policy or strategy. In these two models, the actual criterion value and the judged criterion value are represented as linear combinations of the cue values. Thus, these two models are linear regression models of participant judgments and the environmental criterion.

By comparing aspects of these two linear models, the relationship between human judgment policies and the structure of the environment can be characterized. As described by Goldstein (this volume), the lens model equation (LME) provides a formal means for comparing the two models:

$$r_a = GR_sR_e + C\sqrt{(1 - R_s^2)}\sqrt{(1 - R_e^2)},$$

In this equation, r_a, known as achievement, measures how well human judgments correspond to the actual values of the environmental criterion to be judged. Achievement is shown in Figure 3.2 as a line linking judgments to criterion values. In the track identification task, achievement corresponds to how well participants judged the actual identity of the aircraft. This measure (r_a) is calculated as the correlation between the participants' judgments and the values of the (actual) environmental criterion.

Lens model parameter G, often called knowledge, measures how well the predictions of the *model* of the human judge match predictions of the *model* of the environment. G, shown in Figure 3.2 as a line linking predicted judgments to predicted criterion values, measures how well the linear model of the judge matches the linear model of the environment: If the models are similar, they will make the same predictions. Thus, it reflects how well a modeled judgment policy captures the linear structure in the environment and can be seen as measuring a judge's knowledge of or adaptation to the environment's cue-criterion structure. G is calculated as the correlation between the *predictions* of the participant model (predicted judgments) given a set of cue values, and the *predictions* of the environmental model (predicted criterion value) given the same set of cue values.

R_e, shown as a line in Figure 3.2 linking actual to estimated criterion values, measures how well the value of the environmental criterion can be predicted with a linear model of the cues. That is, it measures the adequacy of a linear model of the environment. Thus, the value of R_e for the track identification task measures how linearly predictable a track's identity was given its cue values and is considered a measure of environmental predict-

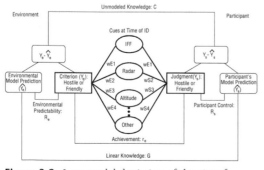

Figure 3.2. Lens model depiction of the aircraft identification task. Adapted from Cooksey, 1996.

ability. R_e is computed as the correlation between the predictions of a linear model of the environment (e.g., predicted criterion values) given a set of cue values and the actual criterion values.

R_s, shown in Figure 3.2 linking human to predicted judgments, is a parallel measure to R_e and measures how well a participant's judgments can be predicted with a linear combination of the cue values. For the track identification task, R_s describes how well a participant's identifications of a track could be predicted given a linear combination of the track's cue values. A higher R_s indicates that a participant is making judgments more consistently with respect to a linear model. R_s is considered a measure of cognitive control or the consistency with which a judgment strategy is executed by a performer (Cooksey, 1996). If a performer's behavior is not well predicted by a linear model of the participant's own judgments in tasks such as this one, where task structure and previous research provide strong evidence that a linear-additive model should be descriptive (e.g., Brehmer & Joyce, 1988; Goldberg, 1968; Hammond et al., 1975), then a low value for R_s suggests that a participant is not consistently executing the strategy represented by that model. R_s is computed as the correlation between the outputs of a linear model of a participant (e.g., predicted judgments) given a set of cue values, and the actual judgment.

Finally, C, shown in Figure 3.2 linking the differences between predicted and judged or actual criterion values, measures the extent to which participant's judgment strategy and the environmental structure share the same unmodeled (in this case, nonlinear) components. A high value of C indicates that these differences, or linear model residuals, are related. For the track identification task, a high value of C would indicate a nonlinear relationship between cue values and a track's identity, and that participants' judgment behavior also reflected that nonlinear relationship. However, one can see from the form of the LME that the total contribution of any such unmodeled knowledge to overall achievement is mediated by the magnitude of both the R_e and R_s terms, so one should consider the magnitude of the entire second term of the LME to determine the relative contribution of modeled (term 1) and unmodeled (term 2) knowledge to achievement, as opposed to examining only the magnitude of C itself. C is computed as the correlation between two vectors of residuals: those of the linear models of the participant and the environment.

The LME indicates that each of these factors (environmental predictability: R_e, cognitive control or consistency of strategy execution: R_s, and modeled knowledge: G, along with unmodeled knowledge, C) contributes to overall task achievement (r_a), and each of these factors can be individually measured in the analysis of judgment performance.

Dynamism and Interactivity: Modeling Considerations

Applying the lens model to our laboratory simulation of the CIC context and the AAWC task was complicated by the dynamic nature of the task and environment. The lens model has not typically been applied to dynamic judgment environments (Cooksey, 1996), and for this reason application to our task required novel methodological problems to be addressed. Most important, a model of judgment in dynamic environments must account for differences in the cue values available at the time performers made identification judgments, because they were not constrained to make their identification judgments at the same times in the experimental scenarios. Therefore, a secondary objective of this research was to develop and demonstrate a method for applying the lens model to dynamic tasks.

In addition to the problems associated with dealing with the time dependency of the cue values available to participants when they chose to make their judgments, other psychological issues may arise in interactive (as opposed to merely dynamic) judgment tasks as opposed to single-shot, noninteractive tasks. For example, several researchers, such as Brehmer (1990; Brehmer & Allard, 1991), Connolly (1988), and Hogarth (1981) have noted that dynamic and interactive tasks provide for an iterative, cyclical interleaving of judgment and action. In these conditions, feedback (especially if it is immediate) regarding the effects of judgment-guided actions can make it possible for people to act without making highly accurate initial judgments because they may be able take a series of successive, feedback-guided, remedial actions (but see Brehmer, 1990; Brehmer & Allard, 1991, on the potentially disruptive effects of delayed feedback).

Interactive tasks may also allow the performer to query the environment for information sources beyond those immediately available, which was the case here. Participants had discretion over the time at which they made identifications of tracks. During the scenario, characteristics of the aircraft changed (e.g., changing altitude or speed), and certain information became available or unavailable as a function of the participants' own activities (e.g., turning radar and IFF on and off). Additionally, IFF information was only available if participants requested it. Thus, participants could change the information available to them. In this way, participants' actions, coupled with the dynamic characteristics of the tracks themselves, shaped the characteristics of the environment in which they individually made judgments. A single environmental model for all participants, which is typically used in lens model applications, would therefore be inappropriate.

To deal with these issues, a time-slice approach to modeling was employed. This approach is illustrated in Figure 3.3. Track state, in terms of the cue values, was documented for each track the participants judged over the duration of each experimental scenario. This resulted in multiple time-indexed state descriptions for each track, as its associated cue values changed over time. Then, for each participant, the state description corresponding to the time of track identification by that participant was determined. The cue values from this description were selected for inclusion in the participant model based on information about participants' actions (e.g., asking for IFF) and were then combined with participants' judgments of aircraft intent (e.g., hostile or friendly) to create the entire set of cue values and judgments, which were subsequently used to generate models of each participant's judgment strategy.

The set of cue values and actual aircraft intents used to create the eight environmental models (one per participant, according to the idiographic approach discussed by Goldstein, this volume) was generated in a similar manner. For each aircraft, the state description corresponding to the time of identification was obtained and combined with information about participants' actions. Thus the cue values were identical to those used to generate the participant models. However, the actual intent of the aircraft was used rather than the participants' judgments for the environmental model.

Regression Modeling

To create the linear regression models of participants and their environments, a judgment or actual status of a hostile track was coded as a 1, whereas a judgment or actual status of a friendly track was coded as 5. Cue variables were coded as follows:

- *Radar*: Radar was coded as −1, 0, or 1 depending on whether the aircraft had a definitely hostile, ambiguous, or definitely friendly radar signature. If a track's radar was not turned on, or if participants did not request radar emission information,[1] radar was coded as 0.
- *IFF*: The IFF signal was also coded as −1, 0, or 1 depending on whether the track had a definitely hostile, ambiguous, or definitely friendly IFF signal. IFF was coded as 0 if the participant did not request an IFF or made an identification while a track was farther than

Time Indexed State Description of Track

Time1	Time2	Scenario	Aircraft	Altitude	Speed	Radar Type	Radar-ON	IFFType	IFF-On	ID
0	32	9	52	26481	458	1	0	1	1	1
32	693	9	52	26481	458	1	1	1	1	1
693	1374	9	52	9474	227	1	1	1	1	1
1374	1794	9	52	1000	210	1	1		1	1

Participant Log

Scenario 9, Track 52
ID = Hostile (5)
IFF not

Data to Create Participant Model

Time1	Time2	Scenario	Aircraft	Altitude	Speed	Radar	IFF	ID
693	1374	9	52	9474	227	1	0	5

Data To Create Environmental Model

Time1	Time2	Scenario	Aircraft	Altitude	Speed	Radar	IFF	ID
693	1374	9	52	9474	227	1	0	1

Figure 3.3. Modeling approach: The time indexed description of aircraft states was combined with information from log files of participants' actions to create parallel data sets for use in the construction of participant and environmental models.

150 nm from the ship, when IFF was unavailable. IFF was coded as −1 if a requested IFF was not turned on when the track was within 150 nm of the ship, because all aircraft exhibiting this behavior were hostile.

- *Range*: Range was coded as 0 if the aircraft was within 150 miles of the ship, and 1 if the track was farther than 150 miles from the ship. This variable was included because if a track was within 150 miles of the ship and did not have an IFF turned on, the track was definitely hostile.
- *Speed*: Speed was coded as 0 if the aircraft had a speed of more than 600 knots, and 1 if the aircraft had a speed of less than 600 knots. Aircraft that flew at speeds of less than 600 knots were typically commercial airliners and therefore friendly (although helicopters, which could be hostile or friendly, also flew at low speeds). Aircraft that flew at speeds of more than 600 knots were military aircraft and therefore could be hostile.
- *Altitude*: Altitude was coded as 0 if the aircraft was flying at 27,000 feet or higher, and 1 if the aircraft was flying at an altitude of less than 27,000 feet. Higher-flying aircraft were typically commercial airliners and

therefore friendly, whereas lower-flying aircraft could be military aircraft and therefore potentially hostile.

After cue, criterion, and judgment coding, linear regression was used to identify optimal cue weights associating the cues with the judged or actual track intent. The inputs to this process were the cue values determined by the time-slice approach, and the judgments or actual intents at the time at which each track identification was made. A total of 16 regression models were created: 8 models represented each of the eight participants' judgment strategies, and 8 models represented the participant-specific environments in which each of the participants made judgments.

Results

Examination of the Linear Models

As a first step in identifying factors contributing to judgment performance, we examined the individual linear models of participants' judgments. Figure 3.4 depicts the (normalized) computed weights for each cue in the eight participants' judgment models. The

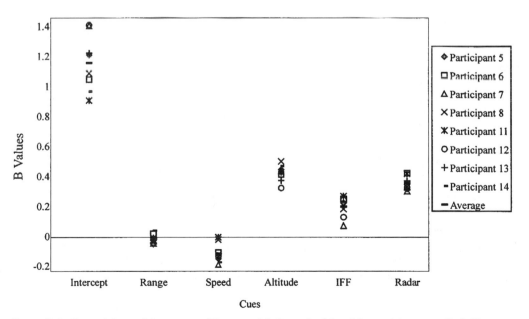

Figure 3.4. Cue weights and intercepts of linear models for each of the eight participants studied. The participant numbers are nonconsecutive because they were performers in a baseline version of the task that was part of a larger experiment incorporating various training interventions.

figure indicates that participants generally weighted the multiple cues in very similar ways. First, the absolute weights of the cues were similar across participants. Additionally, the relative ordering of cue weights was similar across participants: They appeared to weight, or rely on, altitude and radar most heavily, followed by IFF and speed. It is important to note that participants were *not* informed of the relative importance of these cues. The only information they received on their performance was outcome-based feedback (the accuracy and timeliness of their identification judgments) at the end of each experimental session. The general agreement among participants indicates that they all used similar strategies reflecting what they apparently believed to be the relationship between the cue values and the identity of tracks in the GT-ASP task environment.

In addition to examining the relative cue weights among participants, it is illustrative to compare the participant models to their respective environmental models. Figures 3.5 and 3.6 present the participant and environmental model cue weights for the participant with the highest performance (115 correct judgments out of 115 attempts) and the participant with the lowest performance (10 errors out of 110 judgments). Examination of Figure 3.5 shows that the linear model of the best performer had identical cue weights to his corresponding environmental model (due to his perfect performance), whereas, as seen in Figure 3.6, there was slightly less agreement between participant and environmental cue weights for the lower performer.

These comparisons illustrate the concept of adaptivity, or how well participants have adapted to the characteristics of the particular environment in which they make judgments. The extent to which the participants' models mirror their corresponding environmental models is indicative of the ex-

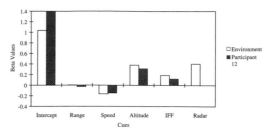

Figure 3.6. Environment and operator cue weights for low scorer.

tent of adaptation. In this case, it appears that the poorer performer showed somewhat (though hardly profound) less successful adaptation than did the better performer. However, it is still not clear, given the overall similarity of the strategies shown in Figure 3.4, if this difference was the major factor in understanding their difference in performance. The LME provides the analytical resources to address this question.

Lens Modeling Results

A lens model analysis was performed for each participant, using each participant model-environment model pair, as illustrated in Figure 3.2. Predicted criterion ($\hat{Y}_E$) and judgment ($\hat{Y}_S$) values, actual criterion (Y_E) and judgment (Y_S) values, and the residuals ($[\hat{Y} - Y_E]$, $[\hat{Y}_S - Y_S]$) were obtained from the regression analysis and then used to calculate LME parameters. Standard multiple regression is not typically applied when either the independent or dependent regression variables are discrete, as in the case described here. Assumptions of the standard multiple regression method normally require these values to be continuous, and other regression methods may be recommended. However, if the goal of the analysis is to examine lens model parameters, Cooksey (1996) suggests that standard multiple regression methods are acceptable.

Values for the lens model parameters for the highest scoring participant, the lowest scoring participant, and for the average of all participants are shown in Figure 3.7. As before, the high and low scorers were selected on the basis of the number of correct identifications. This performance measure roughly corresponds to the value of r_a (achievement). The best performer had a perfect match between judgments and the environmental criterion, indicating that he made no incorrect identifi-

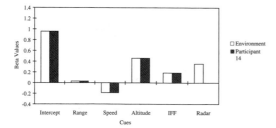

Figure 3.5. Environment and operator cue weights for highest scorer.

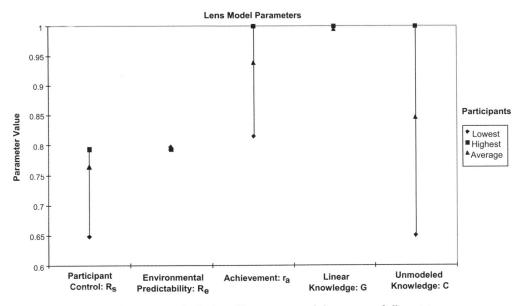

Figure 3.7. Lens model parameters for high and low scorers, and the average of all participants.

cations, and the worst performer had a lower r_a, due to some incorrect identification judgments.

From the LME, achievement (r_a) is dependent on linear knowledge (G), consistency of strategy execution (R_s), environmental predictability (R_e), and unmodeled knowledge (C). Examination of Figure 3.7 provides insight into how each of these different components affected achievement. First, recall that the environmental model for the identification of any particular track could vary across participants based on when participants made their identification judgments and by any actively sought information they obtained. It is possible that some participants may have made identifications at a time when a track had exhibited some behavior highly predictive of a hostile or friendly aircraft (e.g., a very high speed), or after obtaining a highly predictive cue value (e.g., hostile IFF), whereas other participants may have perhaps made identification judgments with less predictive information.

However, the consistent value for R_e across all participants shown in Figure 3.7 indicates that the environmental criterion was similarly predictable for both the best and worst performers and the average of the other participants. Thus, participants did not tend to identify tracks at times when the environment was differentially predictable, nor did they appear to differ in their success at information search. Therefore differences in environmental predictability cannot account for differences in perfor-

mance (however see Rothrock & Kirlik, this volume, for evidence of such differences using a complementary modeling approach in the GT-ASP task with a different group of participants).

Additionally, achievement also depends on the extent to which participants could be modeled with judgment policies that accurately reflected the linear relationship between cue values and aircraft identities in the environment. Good performers could have had "better" judgment policies than poor performers (i.e., more adaptively mirroring external cue ecological validities in their internal cue utilization patterns). However, the high value of G in Figure 3.7 for all participants indicates that the best, worst, and average performers were all quite similar in this regard. Thus differences in good and poor performance could not be explained by differences in participants' linear or modeled knowledge of the cue-criterion structure of the task environment. As such, the differences between environmental and participant model weights shown previously in Figures 3.5 and 3.6 were not the primary cause of differences in performance.

Instead, and as can be seen from Figure 3.7, the major difference between the high and low performers was due to both consistency of strategy execution (R_s) and to unmodeled knowledge (C). The high performer had a value for R_s extremely close to his value for R_e, indicating that his judgments were as consistent with a linear model as the environment was linearly predictable. In contrast, the poor performer was less consistent (had a lower R_s). Thus, the high performer appeared to be better able to consistently execute his judgment strategy incorporating knowledge of the linear-additive cue-criterion environmental structure than was the poor performer. Additionally, the high performer had a high (unity) value for C, indicating that he made good use of the nonlinear relationships between cue values and actual track identities. An examination of the cue coding scheme used for regression modeling is informative as to what types of knowledge this was likely to have been.

For example, we previously noted that the speed cue was coded in such a way that if a track was moving at less than 600 knots it was most likely to be friendly, because most tracks moving at less than that speed in GT-ASP tended to be commercial airliners, and most enemy aircraft flew faster than 600 knots. However, we noted that a few friendly and hostile helicopters also flew below this speed. As such, one can see that a solely linear-additive regression model would likely lead to error in the correct identification of these slow flying helicopters if they were enemy helicopters. The reason for this is that the many commercial (friendly) aircraft and all friendly helicopters flew below 600 knots, whereas the majority of enemy tracks were aircraft flying above this speed. As such, linear regression would tend to individually weight the speed cue in such a way that lower speed would be indicative of friendly intent, and higher speed would be indicative of enemy intent.

Correctly discriminating between commercial airliners, enemy helicopters, and friendly helicopters would therefore require one to view the speed cue conditionally, or interactively, in combination with other cues. Although the highest (perfect) scoring participant was apparently able to perform this type of conditional inference, describing this ability would likely require introducing an interaction term into regression for the resulting model to do likewise. Because our environmental modeling was restricted to a simple linear-additive form, it is understandable that the highest value of for R_e observed in this experiment was approximately 0.80 rather than 1.0. As demonstrated by his perfect performance, the high performer apparently was able to overcome this less than ideal linear predictability with knowledge of environmental cue–criterion relationships that could not be captured in a simple linear-additive form.

Interestingly, Rothrock and Kirlik (this volume) provide converging evidence regarding this challenging aspect of the GT-ASP task. In particular, they found that the lowest performer in their experiment made errors in misidentifying enemy helicopters as "assumed friendly" commercial airliners but that their best performer was able to correctly identify these helicopters as having enemy intent despite having a friendly speed signature.

Summary

The lens model analysis indicated that in this task, the differences between high and low performers could be explained in part by the consistency with which participants executed their judgment strategies and in part by task knowledge. Importantly, however, both high and low performers were equally able to acquire knowledge of the linear structure of the ecology, as indicated by both performers demonstrating a G, or linear knowledge, value near unity. What set them apart, in addition to consistency of strategy execution, was the ability to acquire knowledge of the cue-criterion environmental relations that could not be captured in a simple linear form.

These findings are in accord with the large body of previous research indicating that people have relatively little trouble in adapting to the linear-additive aspects of judgment ecologies but typically have more difficulty in adapting to nonlinear (configural or curvilinear) cue-criterion relations (e.g., Brehmer & Joyce, 1988; Goldberg, 1968; Hammond et al., 1975). Additionally, our findings indicating that the time-stressed naval CIC ecology might require performers to make judgments based on configural or conditional cue usage (e.g., maximum R_e and R_s values of only 0.80 and a near-unity C value for the highest performer) suggested that we should pursue complementary forms of both environmental and participant judgment modeling in this task environment (Rothrock & Kirlik, this volume). The present study, however, served a necessary and indispensable role in guiding these further investigations (also see Campbell et al., this volume).

Discussion

The present need and opportunity to enhance training using feedback embedded within training simulations (e.g., Kozlowski et al., 2001) requires the development of formal techniques for diagnosing the underlying causes of observed performance limitations in dynamic judgment tasks. We have shown how lens model analysis can be tailored to the specific requirements imposed by dynamic judgment tasks by the use of idiographic environmental models that take into account when a performer made a judgment and the active search for judgment cues. We demonstrated how this technique could be used to analyze an individual performer's judgment history to diagnose the sources of observed performance limitations. This technique opens the door for targeting feedback, or the nature of a training intervention itself, toward the particular needs of an individual trainee.

Importantly, we have demonstrated that this technique is able to discriminate between situations in which a performer would benefit from training focused on providing more accurate knowledge of a task environment and those situations in which training should instead be focused on providing additional practice in consistently executing a knowledge-based strategy. Like many of the other measurement, analysis, and modeling techniques presented in this book, we hope that the technique presented in this chapter will become a useful addition to the toolbox of those involved with supporting adaptive cognition and behavior in human–technology interaction.

Acknowledgments. Portions of this chapter are taken from Bisantz et al. (2000) and reprinted with permission. The authors thank the U.S. Naval Air Warfare Center for support.

Notes

1. Although participants' heard radar information along with the aircraft identification number, whenever an aircraft turned on its radar, it was impossible to tell if a participant linked the audible radar signature to the aircraft visible on the screen. Therefore, we took a conservative approach by coding radar only when participants actively selected it.

References

Anderson, J. R., Corbett, A. T., Koedinger, K., & Pelletier, R. (1995). Cognitive tutors: Lessons learned. *Journal of Learning Sciences, 4,* 167–207.

Balzer, W. K., Doherty, M. E., & O'Connor, R. (1989). Effects of cognitive feedback on performance. *Psychological Bulletin, 106,* 410–433.

Balzer, W. K., Hammer, L. B., Sumner, K. E., Birchenough, T. R., Parham Martens, S., & Raymark, P. H. (1994). Effects of cognitive feedback components, display format, and elaboration on performance. *Organizational Behavior and Human Decision Processes, 58,* 369–385.

Balzer, W. K., Sulsky, L. M., Hammer, L. B., & Sumner, K. E. (1992). Task information, cognitive information, or functional validity information: Which components of cognitive feedback affect performance? *Organizational Behavior and Human Decision Processes, 53,* 35–54.

Bisantz, A., Kirlik, A., Gay, P., Phipps, D., Walker, N., and Fisk, A.D., (2000). Modeling and analysis of a dynamic judgment task using a lens model approach. *IEEE Transactions on Systems, Man, and Cybernetics, 30*(6), 605–616.

Brehmer, B. (1990). Strategies in real-time, dynamic decision making. In R. M. Hogarth (Ed.), *Insights in decision making* (pp. 262–279). Chicago: University of Chicago Press.

Brehmer, B., & Allard, R. (1991). Dynamic decision making: The effects of task complexity and feedback delay. In J. Rasmussen, B. Brehmer, & J. Leplat (Eds.), *Distributed decision making: Cognitive models for cooperative work* (pp. 319–334). New York: Wiley.

Brehmer, B., & Joyce, C. R. B. (1988). *Human judgment: The SJT view.* Amsterdam, Netherlands: North-Holland.

Brunswik, E. (1955). Representative design and probabilistic theory in a functional psychology. *Psychological Review, 62,* 193–217.

Cannon-Bowers, J. A., & Salas, E. (1998). *Making decision under stress: Implications for individual and team training.* Washington, D.C.: American Psychological Association.

Collyer, S. C., & Malecki, G. S. (1998). Tactical decision making under stress: History and overview. In J. Cannon-Bowers & E. Salas (Eds.), *Decision making under stress: Implications for individual and team training* (pp. 3–15). Washington, D.C.: American Psychological Association Press.

Connolly, T. (1988). Hedge-clipping, tree-felling, and the management of ambiguity: The need for new images of decision-making. In L. R. Pondy, R. J. Boland, & H. Thomas (Eds.), *Managing ambiguity and change* (pp. 37–50). New York: Wiley.

Cooksey, R. W. (1996). *Judgment analysis: Theory, methods, and applications.* New York: Academic Press.

Crandall, B., & Getchell-Reiter, K. (1993). Critical decision method: A technique for eliciting concrete assessment indicators from the intuition of NICU nurses. *Advances in Nursing Science, 16*(1), 42–51.

Fisk, A. D., Ackerman, P. L., & Schneider, W. (1987). Automatic and controlled processing theory and its application to human factors problems. In P. A. Hancock (Ed.), *Human factors psychology* (pp. 159–197). New York: North-Holland.

Fogarty, W. M. (1988). *Formal investigation into the circumstances surrounding the downing of a commercial airliner by the U.S.S.* Vincennes *(CG 49) on 3 July 1988.* Unclassified letter to Commander in Chief, U.S. Central Command Ser. 1320.

Gigerenzer, G. & Todd, P. M. (1999). Fast and frugal heuristics: The adaptive toolbox. In G. Gigerenzer, P. M. Todd, and the ABC Research Group (Eds.), *Simple heuristics that make us smart* (pp. 3–34). New York: Oxford University Press.

Goldberg, L. R. (1968). Simple models or simple processes? Some research on clinical judgments. *American Psychologist, 23,* 483–496.

Gordon, S. E., & Gill, R. T. (1997). Cognitive task analysis. In C. E. Zsambok & G. Klein (Eds.), *Naturalistic decision making* (pp. 131–140). Mahwah, N.J.: Lawrence Erlbaum.

Hammond, K. R. (1996). *Human judgment and social policy.* New York: Oxford University Press.

Hammond, K. R. (1999). Coherence and correspondence theories of judgment and decision making. In T. Connolly, H. R. Arkes, and K. R. Hammond (Eds.), *Judgment and decision making: An interdisciplinary reader* (pp. 53–65). New York: Cambridge University Press.

Hammond, K. R., Stewart, T. R., Brehmer, B., & Steinmann, D. O. (1975). Social judgment theory. In M. F. Kaplan & S. Schwartz (Eds.), *Human judgment and decision processes.* New York: Academic Press.

Hogarth, R. M. (1981). Beyond discrete biases: Functional and dysfunctional aspects of judgmental heuristics. *Psychological Bulletin, 90,* 197–217.

Kirlik, A., Fisk, A. D., Walker, N., & Rothrock, L. (1998). Feedback augmentation and part-task practice in training dynamic decision-making skills. In J. A. Cannon-Bowers & E. Salas (Eds.), *Making decisions under stress: Implications for individual and team training* (pp. 91–113). Washington, D.C.: American Psychological Association.

Kirlik, A., Walker, N., Fisk, A. D., & Nagel, K. (1996). Supporting perception in the service of dynamic decision making. *Human Factors, 38,* 288–299.

Klein, G. A. (1993). A recognition-primed decision (RPD) model of rapid decision making. In G. A. Klein, J. Orasanu, R. Calderwood, & C. E. Zsambok (Eds.), *Decision making in action: Models and methods* (pp. 138–147). Norwood, N.J.: Ablex.

Klein, G. A. (1999). Applied decision making. In P. A. Hancock (Ed.), *Handbook of perception and cognition: Human performance and ergonomics* (pp. 87–108). New York: Academic Press.

Kozlowski, S., Toney, R. J., Mullins, M. E., Weissbein, D. A., Brown, K. G., & Bell, B. S. (2001). Developing adaptability: A theory for the design of integrated-embedded training systems. In E. Salas (Ed.), *Advances in human performance and cognitive engineering research* (vol. 1, pp. 59–124). New York: Elsevier Science.

Lipshitz, R., Klein, G., Orasanu, J. and Salas, E. (2001a). Focus article: Taking stock of naturalistic decision making. *Journal of Behavioral Decision Making, 14,* 331–352.

Lipshitz, R., Klein, G., Orasanu, J. and Salas, E. (2001b) Rejoinder: A welcome dialogue—and the need to continue. *Journal of Behavioral Decision Making, 14,* 385–389.

Militello, L. G., & Hutton, R. J. B. (1998). Applied cognitive task analysis (ACTA): A practitioner's toolkit for understanding cognitive task demands. *Ergonomics, 41*(11), 1618–1641.

Montgomery, H., Lipshitz, R., & Brehmer, B. (2005). *How professionals make decisions* (pp. 1–11). Mahwah, N.J.: Lawrence Erlbaum Associates.

Norman, D. A. (1981). Categorization of action slips. *Psychological Review, 88*(1), 1–15.

Rothrock, L. R. (1995). Performance measures and outcome analyzes of dynamic decision making in real-time supervisory control. Ph.D. dissertation, School of Industrial & Systems Engineering, Georgia Institute of Technology, Atlanta, Ga.

Todd, P., & Gigerenzer, G. (2001). Putting naturalistic decision making into the adaptive toolbox. *Journal of Behavioral Decision Making, 14,* 381–382.

Vicente, K. J. (1999). *Cognitive work analysis: Toward safe, productive, and healthy computer-based work.* Mahwah, N.J.: Lawrence Erlbaum Associates.

Leonard Adelman, Cedric Yeo,

and Sheryl L. Miller

Understanding the Effects of Computer Displays and Time Pressure on the Performance of Distributed Teams

Introduction

Some studies (e.g., Urban et al., 1996) have shown that time pressure degrades team decision-making performance. In contrast, other studies have shown process changes but no effect on performance (e.g., Hollenbeck et al., 1997b). Using a longitudinal design, Adelman and colleagues (2003) found that teams adapted their processes in different ways, all of which were effective in maintaining high and constant performance until almost twice the initial time pressure level. Then different teams lost performance constancy as time pressure increased, depending on their process adaptations. The findings suggest that one should not necessarily expect to find a process–performance relationship with increasing time pressure; team processes change early and in different ways, but performance can be maintained under high time pressure levels depending on the effectiveness of the team's process adaptations. These findings are consistent with Entin and Serfaty's (1999) team adaptation model and, as discussed in Adelman, Henderson, and Miller (2001), Brunswik's (1952) concepts of vicarious functioning (process intersubstitutability) and performance constancy.

Also consistent with Brunswikian theory (Hammond & Stewart, 2001), one can argue that one's results depend on the task, and in the case of Adelman et al. (2003), the features of the human–computer interface. In a follow-up study, Miller and colleagues (2000) demonstrated this point, but only to a limited extent. They found that a "perceptual" interface designed to make it easier for team members to see what decisions they had made permitted teams to maintain the percentage of decisions they made as time pressure increased. However, contrary to prediction based on previous research (e.g., Balzer, Doherty, & O'Connor, 1989), a "cognitive" interface designed to provide feedback on team members' decision processes had no effect on decision accuracy. As time pressure increased, team decision accuracy declined regardless of the type of human-computer interface.

We were unable to explain this finding fully at the time of the study. We can now do so using a Brunswikian theory of team decision making and the lens model equation. The next section presents the relevant theoretical concepts; then we describe the experiment and new analyses. The final section discusses the strength and limitations of the research.

Brunswikian Theory and Lens Model Equation

Brehmer and Hagafors (1986) extended Brunswik's lens model to a "multilevel lens model" to represent staff functioning. Figure 4.1 shows the multilevel lens model for our aircraft identification task. The "outcome" (correct answer) is an aircraft's true hostility level, which two subordinates and a leader are trying to judge using six pieces of information ("cues"), such as how the aircraft responded to an Identification Friend or Foe (IFF) query. All three team members received the three cues represented by the solid lines, plus one other cue. The unique cues are represented in Figure 4.1 by the dashed lines at the top, middle, and bottom of the figure. Conceptually, one subordinate received the cue shown at the top; the other subordinate received the cue shown at the bottom. Only the leader received the IFF cue, which was the most important and is shown in the middle of the figure. Team members had to send their unique cue information to each other to have all the information about an aircraft. The heavy, dotted lines going only from the subordinates to the leader represent the process of them sending their judgments ("recommendations") to the leader.

Using the multilevel lens model, Hollenbeck et al. (1995) and Ilgen et al. (1995) developed the multilevel theory of team decision making. They showed that team decision accuracy depends on the effective distribution of information among the team (team informity), the accuracy of subordinates' recommendations (staff validity), and the leader's ability to rely on the recommendations of the more accurate subordinates (hierarchical sensitivity). Team informity, staff validity, and hierarchical sensitivity have been called "core constructs." Multilevel theory has predicted that the effect of noncore variables, such as team members' experience or system feedback, on leaders' decision accuracy should be fully mediated by the core constructs.

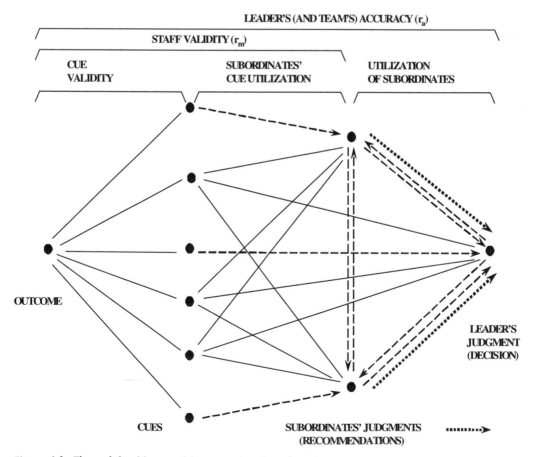

Figure 4.1. The multilevel lens model representing the task.

Research (e.g., Hollenbeck et al., 1995, 1998) has shown this to be largely the case with minimal variance in the leaders' decision accuracy being attributable to noncore variables.

If team members sent their unique cues to each other all the time in our task, then team informity would be perfect because all team members would always have all six cues prior to the subordinates and leader making their recommendations and decision. If the leader also has the subordinates' recommendations, then his or her decision can be based on the cues and/or recommendations. By correlating each subordinate's recommendations with the outcomes, one can calculate the accuracy of each staff member (staff validity, r_m), as shown pictorially in Figure 4.1. Similarly, by correlating the leader's decisions with the outcomes, one can calculate the leader's (and team's) level of accuracy (r_a). Using hierarchical regression, one can assess the extent to which the leader is using the cues and recommendations. If the leader is using the recommendations of the more accurate staff member, his or her "hierarchical sensitivity" will be high.

Multilevel theory has not, however, used the lens model equation (LME) developed by Hursch et al., (1964) to decompose the leader's accuracy into its distinct conceptual components. This omission may have occurred because multilevel theorists (e.g., Hollenbeck et al., 1995) usually defined accuracy as the mean absolute error of the team's decision. However, Brehmer and Hagafors's (1986) original formulation of the multilevel lens model defined the leader's accuracy in terms of the achievement correlation, typically used in Brunswikian social judgment theory research (e.g., Brehmer & Joyce, 1988; Cooksey, 1996; Hammond et al., 1975). Although Hollenbeck et al. (1997a) used the achievement correlation, they did not decompose it into its component parts using the LME. Bisantz and coauthors (2000) did so using a dynamic aircraft identification task, but they focused on individual not team decision making.

Because both the correct answers and decisions were predicted by a linear equation in the current study, we adopted Tucker's (1964) version of the LME, presented in Equation 4.1:

(4.1) $r_a = GR_sR_e$

where

  r_a = decision accuracy or "achievement," defined operationally as the correlation

(Pearson product-moment) between a person's judgments and the correct answers;

G = model similarity or "knowledge," defined operationally as the correlation between the predictions of two models, the best-fitting (least-square) linear model predicting the person's judgments and the best-fitting (least-square) linear model predicting the correct answer, which the participants were trained to use;

R_s = judgment model predictability or "cognitive control," defined operationally as the correlation between a person's actual judgments and their predicted judgments based on the best-fitting, linear model; and

R_e = task model predictability, defined operationally as the correlation between correct answers and the predicted correct answers based on the best linear model.

This chapter shows how Brunswikian theory and the LME can explain the previously unexplained effects of computer displays and time pressure on the achievement (r_a) of distributed teams reported in Miller et al's. (2000) experiment. For by using the LME and holding task predictability (R_e) constant, one can determine whether changes in leaders' achievement (r_a) was caused, on average, by corresponding changes in their knowledge of what to do (G) or their cognitive control in applying their knowledge (R_s). By using a path model to operationally define multilevel theory, one can determine mediating pathways between noncore variables (e.g., time pressure), core construct variables (e.g., informity), and the LME parameters (G and R_s) comprising leaders' achievement (r_a). An initial effort by Henderson (1999) suggested the potential viability of this approach but was limited by not using the steps described next to calculate G and R_s under the range of conditions of cue and recommendation availability.

Experiment

Hypotheses

The effectiveness of different human–computer interfaces was studied under increasing levels of time pressure. Because previous research (Adelman et al., 2003) found a main effect for time pressure, we again predicted a time pressure main effect. In addition, we predicted an interface main effect and a time pressure by interface interaction. Previous research (e.g., Balzer, Doherty, & O'Connor, 1989; Hammond, 1971) showed that cognitive feedback about how one made judgments and about how one should according to task characteristics, improved achievement (r_a) because it improved knowledge (G) and cognitive control (R_s). Therefore, we predicted that teams using such an interface would have higher r_a, G, and R_s when averaged over all time pressure levels and be able to maintain higher achievement at higher time pressure than teams using other interfaces. (As noted earlier, Miller et al. [2000] found that teams using the perceptual interface described herein maintained decision quantity longer than teams using the cognitive interface. These results are not considered here. We only consider r_a.)

Participants

Twenty-four Army Reserve Officer Training Corps (ROTC) cadets from a suburban university volunteered to participate for seven two-hour sessions. The cadets were placed in eight three-person teams based on availability. An effort was made to equate teams by gender and cadet rank. By default, the highest-ranking cadet was the team leader. All team leaders were male because there were few female cadets in the ROTC program. Teams competed for prize money donated to the cadet's fund-raising mission. (A ninth team was dropped when the leader was hospitalized due to an extended illness.)

Task

The task was a simulated air defense task representative of that by Hollenbeck et al. (1995), and modeled after the task of AWACS and Patriot air defense teams. It was designed for a leader and two subordinates dispersed geographically who communicate with each other only through their computer system. The leader and subordinates tracked multiple aircraft (called targets) on their radar screens, shared unique information about the target, and made decisions about targets' threat level, as described generally in Figure 4.1. Although team members could request information, it was almost always sent without being requested. Therefore, information passing represented a "voluntary, cooperative act" (Adelman et al., 1986, p. 799) and a form of "implicit coordination" (e.g., Entin & Serfaty, 1999, p. 313). Although interaction was only possible through the system during the identification task, team members could talk face to face between trials.

Apparatus

The task was implemented using the Argus synthetic task environment (Schoelles & Gray, 2001). Figure 4.2 shows the basic interface. The first component is the radar screen on which aircraft appeared in different segments represented by concentric circles (left). The second component is the data display window, where cue values and recommendations appeared (upper right). The third and fourth components are the message inbox (middle right) and email system (lower right).

An ideal interaction involved the participant first "hooking" a target by clicking on its icon on the radar screen. The data associated with that target would appear in the upper right section of the display. All participants received the bearing and three cues (airspeed, course, and range) about each target. They also received a unique cue. Leaders received IFF; one subordinate received altitude, the other radar. Ideally, participants would send the unique cue to their teammates and receive cue information in return. Received information was presented in red in the data display window. Participants made a decision about the target's threat level on a 1–7 (increasing threat) scale. For example, a 7 meant the target is certainly hostile; fire a missile to shoot it down.

The environmental model was determined by Equation 4.2, which participants were trained to use to calculate a target's threat level. Participants were given target cue information in the appropriate metric and then transformed it into a three-point hostility-indicator scale (from 0 to 2) used for each of the cues in Equation 4.2. Participants then transformed the overall threat level, which could go from 0 to 14 using Equation 4.2, into the final seven-point decision scale. The task required two to three hours of training before reaching criterion, which was an achievement correlation (r_a) of 0.80 between a participant's threat recommendations/decisions and the true threat levels for a set of targets.

(4.2)   Threat = (2*IFF) + (1*Speed) +
                  (1*Course) + (1*Range) +
                  (1*Altitude) + (1*Radar)

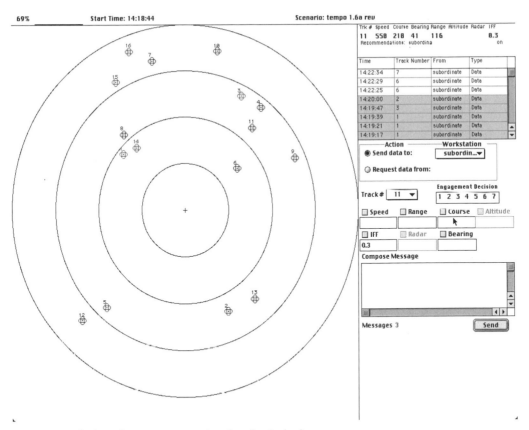

Figure 4.2. The basic human–computer interface for the leader.

Experimental Conditions

Time Pressure ("Tempo")

Time pressure was manipulated by increasing the tempo level, defined operationally as the number of new targets per minute appearing on the radar screen during a 15-minute scenario. Tempo was a within-subject variable; each team performed all seven tempo levels (0.8, 1.2, 1.6, 2.0, 2.4, 2.8, and 3.2). Only three levels (1.2, 2.4, and 3.2) were used in the analysis presented herein because of the slow, laborious effort required to develop the judgment models for calculating G and R_s, as will be described. Tempo 1.2 had 18 targets, tempo 2.4 had 36 targets, and tempo 3.2 had 48 targets. Two judgments were required per target, so the number of required judgments ranged from 36 to 96. (Note: There were two runs at each tempo level using isomorphs of the basic scenario. The analysis reported herein is always for the second run. Analysis of variance [ANOVA] results reported replicated those using both runs for all tempo levels.)

Interface

There were three human-computer interface conditions

- Original: Targets always appeared as yellow circles on the radar screen.
- Perceptual: Used color to indicate a target's status and shape to indicate remaining time. Each target initially appeared on the screen in red. When the target was hooked, it turned yellow, and when a recommendation/decision was made, it turned blue. Thus, color enabled operators to determine which targets had been dealt with without having to rely on memory. Also, targets changed shape when they approached the concentric circles to visually indicate that a judgment was required before the target moved into the next sector. Targets turned into a rectangle when there was 30 seconds remaining for a judgment; they turned into a triangle when there were only 15 seconds left. Thus, shape

served as a cue to help operators determine which targets to prioritize.

- Original plus cognitive feedback: Teams used the original interface to make judgments during each trial, and received cognitive feedback after it. The leaders' feedback included the number of decisions and recommendations made by them and each of the two subordinates, and their (and subordinates') decision accuracy (achievement correlations, r_a) and performance. (Note: The analysis reported herein only focused on decision accuracy, r_a. We note here for completeness that performance was defined as {[7 − Absolute Value (Truth − Decision)] / 7}, with Decision = 0.0 for all decision opportunities for which no decision was made, averaged over all decision opportunities.)

Leaders also were shown their relative agreement with (or dependency on) each subordinate's recommendations. This was calculated by simultaneously regressing their decisions on each subordinate's recommendations, and then dividing the absolute value of each beta weight by the sum of the absolute values of the two beta weights. Last, leaders were shown their relative cue weights, which was the ratio of the beta weight on each cue based on the best fitting judgment model for all six cues divided by the beta weight based on the task model they should have used. The ratio was 1.0 if they weighted a cue correctly, greater than 1.0 if they overweighted it, and less than 1.0 if they underweighted it. Except for learning the team's overall performance, subordinates only received feedback about themselves. Teams usually finished examining their cognitive feedback within five minutes. (Note: Feedback assumed that team members had all six cues when they made their judgments. The analysis presented herein will indicate that was a mistake.)

Two teams used the original interface, three teams used the perceptual interface, and three teams used the original interface with cognitive feedback. (The team dropped from the study because of the leader's illness used the original interface.)

Experimental Design

The experimental design was 3 Interface (Original, Perceptual, and Original + Cognitive Feedback) × 3 Time Pressure (1.2, 2.4, and 3.2 tempo levels) fac-

torial design. Interface was a between-subject variable; time pressure was a within-subject variable.

Procedures

Training was incremental over a two-week period. During the first week, the participants read a detailed task outline that described the aircraft cues and rules for making recommendations and decisions. Written instructions were supplemented with verbal instruction. Quizzes were administered at appropriate intervals to assess task learning; the participants were required to memorize all task cues and rules. When sufficient task proficiency was achieved, teams were shown a computer demonstration of the task.

Participants refamiliarized themselves with the instructions and interface during the second week of training. Each one sat at an individual workstation and practiced performing the task. They were seated in separate rooms and instructed not to talk during the task to simulate a distributed team. After individuals were sufficiently trained, teams were presented with low tempo scenarios (e.g., tempo 0.4 = 6 targets/15 minutes). Teams were required to achieve an achievement (r_a) level of 0.80 on these scenarios before they were allowed to proceed to the experimental trials.

Teams performed the experimental trials over the following five weeks. Tempos progressed each week, beginning with tempo 0.80 on the first week and concluding with tempo 3.2 on the last. Teams performed two scenarios at each tempo, each of which presented the same aircraft and flight paths, but in different ordered sequences so participants could not remember them. Teams could not talk during a scenario, but they could talk after them. They knew tempo would be increased, but they did not know future levels. Teams also knew they were working with different interfaces but not the differences and were not shown the three interfaces until after the study. Last, consistent with what they were told at the outset, the three best teams (one for each interface) were identified for commendation at the year-end military ball, which clearly motivated them.

Dependent Variables

There were two sets of dependent variables: those defined by multilevel theory, which are presented first, and those defined by the LME.

- Informity: Team Informity was the average amount of unique cue information (sent via email messages) to the three teammates. For example, if the three teammates always sent their unique cue to each other, then team informity would be 100%; if they sent two messages, on average, it would be 66%; and so forth. We also calculated the Leaders Informity, which was the average amount of information sent to the leader, and Staff Informity, which was the average amount of information sent to the two subordinates.

- Staff Validity: The achievement (or validity) of each subordinate's (or staff member's) recommendations was illustrated in Figure 4.1 and defined as the Pearson product-moment correlation between their recommendations and the correct answers (r_m). Fisher z-transforms are routinely taken in lens model research to normalize the correlation distribution, which is skewed at its upper end. Consequently, (overall) staff validity was defined operationally as the mean Fisher z-transforms of the r_m coefficients for the two subordinates.

- Hierarchical Sensitivity: measures how effectively leaders weight the recommendations of their more valid staff members. Hierarchical sensitivity was calculated using a six-step process. First, using an ordinary least squares regression, we separately regressed the leader's decisions on each subordinate's recommendations to obtain the beta weights indicating how much the leader weighted each subordinate's recommendations. Second, we regressed the correct answers on the recommendations to obtain the beta weights indicating how much they should have weighted each subordinate's recommendations. Third, we calculated the absolute value of the difference between the leader's and the correct answer's beta weights for each subordinate. Fourth, we multiplied this difference by the number of recommendations made by each subordinate to ensure that the more active subordinate received more weight in the measure. Fifth, we summed the weighted differences for the two subordinates and divided it by the total number of recommendations to obtain the hierarchical sensitivity score. Sixth, we took

the logarithm of the hierarchical sensitivities because they were heavily skewed. (The skewness value was 2.62 times its standard error [1.259/0.481].) Lower values meant greater hierarchical sensitivity because there was less difference between the leader's and the task's beta weights.

The three terms of the LME used in the data analysis were achievement (r_a), knowledge (G), and control (R_s). Task predictability (R_e) was constant, approaching 1.0, except for rounding error. It is important to note here that the procedure used to calculate the best-fitting judgment models had to account for the fact that the leaders and subordinates did not always have all the information that was to be sent to them when they made their judgments. This was accomplished in three steps.

The *first step* was to determine what information each participant had when they made a judgment. For example, when a leader made each of his decisions, did he have a recommendation from each of the two staff members? Did he have six, five, or four cue values for that target? (They would have six if both staff members sent the values for their unique cues.)

The *second step* was to perform a simultaneous regression for each data set to calculate the best-fitting judgment model for that data set. Depending on the team, tempo, and the amount of data per partition, a leader might have two or more best-fitting models. For example, a leader might have a best-fitting judgment model for cases (i.e., targets) where there were two recommendations and six cue values (i.e., eight independent variables), and another model for cases where there were no recommendations and only four cue values (i.e., four independent variables). Subordinates only had models based on six, five, or four cues.

The *third step* was to calculate G and R_s. G was calculated by correlating the predictions of the task model with the predictions for the best-fitting judgment model for all cases for which there was a judgment. The task model was always based on the six cues. The judgment model was the one appropriate for a particular case (i.e., target). So, for example, a leader might have made decisions for some cases when he had two recommendations and six cues, other decisions when he only had four cues and no recommendations, and so forth. Consequently, in the first example, we used the best-fitting judgment model based on two recommendations and six cues; in the second example, we used the best-fitting model based on only four cues, and so on. R_s was calculated by correlating all the predicted judgments (regardless of the model used to generate them) with the person's actual judgments for those cases. Fisher z-transforms were taken of G and R_s to normalize both correlation coefficients. (It is important to again note that r_a [for the leader] and r_m for each subordinate is fully decomposed into G and R_s given that R_e approached one.)

Results

First, we present the ANOVA results for leader achievement (r_{az}) and multilevel theory core constructs. Then, we present the ANOVA results for the leaders' LME parameters (G_z and R_{sz}) and the path model linking them to the multilevel theory variables and the independent variables.

Achievement and Multilevel Theory Core Constructs

A 3 Interface (Original, Perceptual, Original + Cognitive Feedback) 3 Tempo (1.2, 2.4, 3.2) ANOVA was performed for each dependent variable. Interface was a between-subject factor and Tempo was a within-subject factor.

- Leader Achievement (r_{az}): The only significant effect was a Tempo main effect [$F(2, 10)$ = 8.07, p = 0.008]. Mean r_{az} values were 1.22, 0.92, and 0.82 for Tempos 1.2, 2.4, and 3.2, respectively.
- Hierarchical Sensitivity (log): There were no significant main effects, although the main effect for Tempo approached the traditional p = 0.05 level [$F(2, 10)$ = 3.29, p = 0.09], with poorer hierarchical sensitivity with increasing tempo.
- Staff Validity (r_{mz}): There was a significant main effect for Tempo [$F(2, 10)$ = 9.80, p = 0.006]. As tempo increased, staff validity (r_{mz}) decreased (1.22, 0.91, and 0.87).
- Informity: Results for team, leader, and staff informity are presented, in turn.
- Team Informity: There were significant main effects for Tempo [$F(2, 10)$ = 14.90, p = 0.002] and Interface [$F(2, 5)$ = 26.45, p = 0.002]. As tempo increased, mean team informity decreased (0.89, 0.70, and 0.51).

Mean team informity was highest for the original interface (0.87), and then the perceptual (0.74), and cognitive feedback (and original) interfaces (0.50).
- Leaders' Informity: There was only a significant Tempo main effect [$F(2, 10)$ = 4.96, p = 0.032, means were 0.87, 0.71, and 0.56].
- Staff Informity: There were significant main effects for Tempo [$F(2, 10)$ = 11.05, p = 0.007] and Interface [$F(2, 5)$ = 23.15, p = 0.003]. Mean values for tempo were 0.89, 0.70, and 0.50, respectively. The mean was highest for the original interface (0.88), then the perceptual (0.76), and finally the cognitive feedback interface (0.45).

Lens Model Equation Parameters

We first present the results of the 3 Interfaces (3 Tempo ANOVAs for leaders' G_z and R_{sz} values). The ANOVA results for the subordinates were almost identical to those of the leaders' and are not presented here.

The only significant ANOVA effects were Tempo main effects. The mean values for Tempos 1.2, 2.4, and 3.2, respectively, and the ANOVA statistics for the leaders' G_z and R_{sz} parameters were:

- Mean G_z: 1.30, 0.96, and 0.86, F(2, 10) = 5.883, p = 0.02.
- Mean R_{sz}: 3.24, 2.33, and 2.17, F(2, 10) = 8.65, p = 0.007.

Figure 4.3 presents the path model for core and noncore variables and the leaders' G_z and R_{sz} values. (Because subordinates' ANOVA results for G_z and R_{sz} were almost identical to the leaders', they were not added to provide the most parsimonious model [fewest variables] predicting leader achievement given the small sample size.) The model was created by performing a series of hierarchical regressions predicting the leaders' achievement (r_{az}) by moving from the figure's right to left-hand side, consistent with the causal pathways proposed by multilevel theory (Hollenbeck et al., 1995). In particular, we first regressed r_{az} on all eight variables shown in Figure 4.3, but only leader knowledge (G_z) and cognitive control (R_{sz}) significantly predicted r_{az}. We then regressed G_z on the remaining seven variables, but only leader informity, hierarchical sensitivity, and staff validity significantly predicted G_z. Then we regressed the remaining six

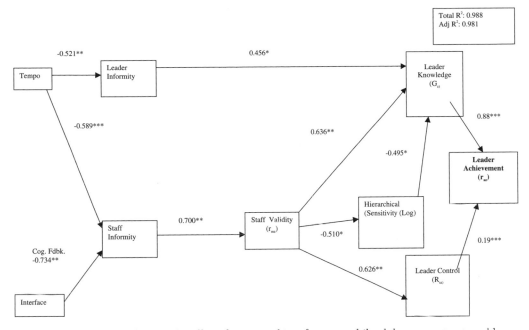

Figure 4.3. Path model showing the effect of tempo and interface on multilevel theory constructs and lens model equation parameters. (The numbers are beta weights. The number of asterisks refers to whether the weights were significant at $p < 0.05$, 0.01, or 0.001.)

variables on R_{sz}, and so forth. Only significant relationships ($p < 0.05$) and beta weights are shown in Figure 4.3. The total R^2 was 0.988 (adjusted R^2 was 0.981). This occurred because r_a is fully decomposable into G and R_s when R_e is held constant and approaches 1.0, as in our study.

We make five points. First, the effect of all noncore and core constructs' on leader achievement (r_a) is mediated through its effect on leaders' knowledge (G_z) and cognitive control (R_{sz}). One needs these LME parameters to understand why time pressure (tempo) affected leader achievement, and why cognitive feedback did not.

Second, leaders' informity affected leaders' knowledge (G_z), their ability to use the judgment model they were trained to use Equation 4.2. Achievement (r_a) for targets without staff recommendations appears to have decreased with increasing tempo because of a decrease in the amount of information sent to the leaders, which caused them to adopt less accurate judgment strategies for combining information, as shown by the decrease in G_z.

In contrast, cognitive feedback had no affect on leader informity; consequently, it had no affect on their knowledge (G_z) or achievement (r_{az}) without staff recommendations. Cognitive feedback did af-

fect staff informity and, in turn, leader achievement through the relationships shown in Figure 4.3, but these mediated effects were not sufficient to result in a significant interface main effect or interface by tempo interaction on leader achievement.

Fourth, as tempo increased, staff informity decreased, which decreased staff validity. Decreased staff validity caused a decrease in the leaders' knowledge of what to do (G_z), their sensitivity to their subordinates' accuracy (hierarchical sensitivity), and their control of the judgment strategies they tried to use (R_{sz}).

Fifth, decreased hierarchical sensitivity only affected G_z, not R_{sz}. Leaders' decreased sensitivity to the validity of their subordinates' recommendations significantly caused them to modify their judgment strategies. It had no effect on their ability to apply whatever strategies they chose.

Discussion

Brunswikian multilevel theory, as operationally defined by the LME and path modeling, showed that the decrease in leader achievement with increasing time pressure (tempo) was caused by a breakdown in the flow of information among team members. Once informity fell, all the other constructs fell like dominos. As tempo increased, the amount of information passed among the team decreased, as did staff validity. With less information and less accurate recommendations, leaders were less able to use the decision model they were trained to use (G_z), less sensitive to which staff member was more accurate (hierarchical sensitivity), and less consistent (R_{sz}) when making their decisions.

The provided cognitive feedback could not compensate for this domino effect, because it was not designed to support information flow. Moreover, it was not as accurate as it should have been, for the regression equation showing team members the weights they placed on the cues assumed that they had all six cues when they made their decisions and therefore did not account for the breakdown in information flow.

There are ways to maintain information flow. For example, Hedlund, Ilgen, and Hollenbeck (1998) showed that face-to-face teams have higher informity levels than computer-mediated teams like those in our study. Hollenbeck et al. (1998) and Adelman et al. (2004) have demonstrated that information flow can be maintained by providing informity feedback or implementing a simple modification to the human–computer interface, respectively. However, providing rapid and accurate cognitive feedback may be more difficult because of the complexity of the steps to calculate judgment models accurately when all the cue information and subordinates' recommendations are not available. Of course, that is an issue for future research. Nevertheless, the presented analysis indicates that cognitive feedback will not matter much if the flow of information is not maintained.

It is important to emphasize that knowledge (G) and control (R_s) are conceptually independent (Hammond & Summers, 1972). Noncore and core constructs can affect one without affecting the other. For example, tempo's negative effect on leader informity only affected their knowledge (G), not their control (R_s) in applying it. In contrast, tempo's negative effect on staff informity negatively affected staff validity, which negatively affected leaders' knowledge and control, as well as their hierarchical sensitivity.

The path analysis was post hoc, because the experiment was not designed to manipulate specific pathways. However, the results fulfilled all three conditions for establishing mediation between tempo and achievement (Hedlund, Ilgen, & Hollenbeck, 1998). First, tempo (a noncore, independent variable) had an effect ($p < 0.05$) on the mediating, core variables (leader informity, staff informity, staff validity, and hierarchical sensitivity, $p = 0.09$), and leader knowledge and cognitive control. Second, tempo significantly affected leader achievement (r_a), the dependent variable. Third, all mediating variables had a significant relationship with r_a, although informity dropped out of the regression when staff validity and hierarchical sensitivity entered it. Given the small sample size (8 teams by 3 tempos for 24 data points), the effect size was large for all variables in the path model. Nevertheless, the post hoc nature of the analysis and the small sample size are limitations. Although the obtained pathways have substantial face validity in explaining the results in Miller et al. (2000) and meet the conditions for mediation, research needs to test them versus other pathways (Hollenbeck et al., 1998) to assess their generality.

Gigone and Hastie (1997) argued that mean square error (MSE) is the best measure of group accuracy because it not only incorporates r_a, but measures of mean bias and standard deviation bias in one's decisions. In an analysis not reported here, ANOVAs generated the same results for MSE as for r_a because there were no effects for mean or standard deviation bias for either the leaders' or subordinates' decisions. Consequently, we used r_a in the path modeling, not MSE, to have fewer variables given the small sample size.

In closing, the research showed how Brunswikian theory and the LME can be used to study the effect of computer displays on team (or individual) decision making. Moreover, we have built on this initial study. Adelman, Miller, and Yeo (2004) used the same task as the one described herein, but they controlled the flow and therefore amount and type of information received by individuals. They found that an icon telling individuals when they had received information from their (simulated) teammates about a target led to higher achievement under low tempo. However, achievement with the icon significantly decreased as tempo increased, in part, because of a significant decrease in cognitive control, not knowledge. In contrast, they found that individuals with higher working memory capacity had higher achievement, whether or not they had the icon, because they had higher knowledge (ability to use Equation 4.2) with more information, not because of any effect on their cognitive control (or consistency) in doing so. That research, like the one described here, shows that the sensitivity provided by the LME and scope of the Brunswikian theory in which it is embedded has substantial power to improve our ability to understand the effect of technology on the user's mind.

Acknowledgments.   We thank Michael Schoelles for modifying the Team Argus interface for the study and for implementing the data collection scheme required for data analysis. The research was supported under Grant no. F49620-97-1-0353 from the Air Force Office of Scientific Research to George Mason University. The views, opinions, and findings herein are those of the authors and not a Department of the Air Force position.

References

Adelman, L., Henderson, E. D., & Miller, S. L. (2001). Vicarious functioning in teams. In K. R. Hammond and T. R. Stewart (Eds.), *The essential Brunswik: Beginnings, explications, and applications* (pp. 416–423). New York: Oxford University Press.

Adelman, L., Miller, S. L., Henderson, D., & Schoelles, M. (2003). Using Brunswikian theory and a longitudinal design to study how hierarchical teams adapt to increasing levels of time pressure. *Acta Psychologica, 112*(2), 181–206.

Adelman, L., Miller, S. L., & Yeo, C. (2004). Testing the effectiveness of perceptual interface components for supporting distributed team decision making. *IEEE Transactions on Systems, Man, and Cybernetics Part A: Systems and Humans, 34*(2), 179–189.

Adelman, L., Zirk, D. A., Lehner, P. E., Moffett, R. J., & Hall, R. (1986). Distributed tactical decision-making: Conceptual framework and empirical results. *IEEE Transactions on Systems, Man, and Cybernetics, SMC-16*, 794–805.

Balzer, W. K., Doherty, M. E., & O'Connor, R. O. Jr. (1989). Effects of cognitive feedback on performance. *Psychological Bulletin, 106*, 410–433.

Bisantz, A. M., Kirlik, A., Gay, P., Phipps, D. A., Walker, N., & Fisk, A. D. (2000). Modeling and analysis of a dynamic judgment task using a lens model approach. *IEEE Transactions on Systems, Man, and Cybernetics Part A: Systems and Humans, 30*, 605–616.

Brehmer, B., & Hagafors, R. (1986). Use of experts in complex judgment making: A paradigm for the study of staff work. *Organizational Behavior and Human Decision Processes, 38*, 181–195.

Brehmer, B., & Joyce, C. R. B. (Eds.) (1988). *Human judgment: The SJT view.* New York: North-Holland.

Brunswik, E. (1952). *The conceptual framework of psychology.* Chicago: University of Chicago.

Cooksey, R. W. (1996). *Judgment analysis: Theory, methods, and applications.* New York: Academic Press.

Entin, E. E., & Serfaty, D. (1999). Adaptive team coordination. *Human Factors, 41*, 312–325.

Gigone, D., & Hastie, R. (1997). Proper analysis of group judgments. *Psychological Bulletin, 121*, 149–176.

Hammond, K. R. (1971). Computer graphics as an aid to learning. *Science, 172*, 903–908.

Hammond, K. R., & Stewart, T. R. (Eds.). (2001). *The essential Brunswik: Beginnings, explications, and applications.* New York: Oxford University Press.

Hammond, K. R., Stewart, T. R., Brehmer, B., & Steinmann, D. O. (1975). Social judgment theory. In M. Kaplan & S. Schwartz (Eds.), *Human judgment and decision processes* (pp. 271–312). New York: Academic Press.

Hammond, K. R., & Summers, D. A. (1972). Cognitive control. *Psychological Review, 79*, 58–67.

Hedlund, J., Ilgen, D. R., & Hollenbeck, J. R. (1998). Decision accuracy in computer-mediated versus face-to-face decision making teams. *Organizational Behavior and Human Decision Processes, 76*, 30–47.

Henderson, E. D. (1999). *Model for adaptive decision-making behavior of distributed hierarchical teams under high temporal workload.* Ph.D. dissertation. Fairfax, Va.: George Mason University.

Hollenbeck, J. R., Ilgen, D. R., Colquitt, J. A., LePine, J. A., & Hedlund, J. (1997a). The multilevel theory of team decision making: Testing theoretical boundary conditions. *Proceedings of the Third International Command and Control Research and Technology Symposium*, 328–346.

Hollenbeck, J. R., Ilgen, D. R., LePine, J. A., Colquitt, J. A., & Hedlund, J. (1998). Extending them multilevel theory of team decision making: Effects of feedback and experience in hierarchical teams. *Academy of Management Journal, 41*, 269–282.

Hollenbeck, J. R., Ilgen, D. R., Sego, D. J., Hedlund, J., Major, D. A., & Phillips, J. (1995). Multilevel theory of team judgment making: Judgment performance in teams incorporating distributed expertise. *Journal of Applied Psychology, 80*, 292–316.

Hollenbeck, J. R., Sego, D. J., Ilgen, D. R., Major, D. A., Hedlund, J., & Phillips, J. (1997b). Team judgment-making accuracy under difficult conditions: Construct validation of potential manipulations using the TIDE[2] simulation. In T. Brannick, E. Salas, & C. Prince (Eds.), *Team performance assessment and measurement: Theory, methods, and applications* (pp. 111–136). Malwah, N.J.: Lawrence Erlbaum and Associates.

Hursch, C. J., Hammond, K. R., & Hursch, J. L. (1964). Some methodological considerations in multiple-cue probability studies. *Psychological Review, 71,* 42–60.

Ilgen, D. R., Major, D. A., Hollenbeck, J. R., & Sego, D. J. (1995). Raising an individual decision-making model to the team level: A new research model and paradigm. In R. A. Guzzo & E. Salas (Ed.), *Team effectiveness and decision making in organizations* (pp. 113–148). San Francisco: Jossey-Bass.

Miller, S. L., Adelman, L., Henderson, E. D., Schoelles, M., & Yeo, C. (2000). Team decision making strategies: Implications for designing the interface in complex tasks. *Proceedings of the 44th Annual Meeting of the Human Factors and Ergonomics Society.* Santa Monica, Calif.: Human Factors and Ergonomics Society.

Schoelles, M. J., & Gray, W. D. (2001). Argus: A suite of tools for research in complex cognition. *Behavior Research Methods, Instruments, & Computers, 33,* 130–140.

Tucker, L. R. (1964). A suggested alternative formulation in the developments by Hursch, Hammond, and Hursch and by Hammond, Hursch, & Todd. *Psychological Review, 71,* 528–530.

Urban, J. M., Weaver, J. L., Bowers, C. A., & Rhodenizer, L. (1996). Effects of workload and structure on team processes and performance: Implications for complex team decision making. *Human Factors, 38*(2), 300–310.

William J. Horrey, Christopher D. Wickens,

Richard Strauss, Alex Kirlik,

and Thomas R. Stewart

Supporting Situation Assessment through Attention Guidance and Diagnostic Aiding: The Benefits and Costs of Display Enhancement on Judgment Skill

Introduction

Many operational environments are characterized by large amounts of dynamic and uncertain information presented to performers on technological interfaces. To perform accurately and consistently in such environments, people must manage, integrate, and interpret this information appropriately to formulate an accurate assessment of the current situation. In the battlefield environment, for example, effective commanders must perceive and integrate a wide range of tactical, organizational, and environmental information, information guiding planning (Graham & Matthews, 1999), as well as an array of potentially fallible information from a number of different sources (e.g., Wickens, Pringle, & Merlo, 1999). Regardless of the context, the extent to which performers can successfully integrate these sources of information into a coherent assessment will directly impact their situation awareness as well as their subsequent decisions and actions.

In this chapter, we present a study of human performers' ability to integrate multiple sources of displayed, uncertain information in a laboratory simulation of threat assessment in a battlefield environment. Two different types of automated aids were used to enhance the situation display, the first guiding visual attention to relevant cues, the second recommending an actual judgment. We assessed performance in terms of *skill score* (Murphy, 1988), as well as its decomposition using Stewart's (1990) refinement of Murphy's skill score measure using Brunswik's lens model (see Goldstein, this volume; Cooksey, 1996). Results indicated that the introduction of display enhancement in this task had both benefits and costs to performance. Modeling aided us in providing plausible interpretations of these (in some cases counterintuitive) effects.

Attention guidance automation, for example, actually appeared to decrease performance by narrowing the variance (or range) of aided performers' judgments relative to the variance of unaided judgments. We found, however, that this result would be consistent with the design of automation in this task, to the extent that participants may not have used the attention guidance cue for guidance but rather as a judgment cue itself (the attention guidance cue, too, had lower variance than the task criterion). In contrast, performance did improve when automation instead recommended an actual judgment. By using an automation failure or "catch" trial designed to detect automation overreliance, we found that this automation benefit was due almost exclusively to those participants who used automation as an *additional* information source to be integrated with the raw data, rather than as a *substitute* for making judgments themselves.

Both findings, suggested by post-hoc modeling and thus requiring further study, highlight the need for designers to appreciate both the potential costs and benefits of automation in display design. This may be especially important in uncertain environments and where automation may be imperfect. We are naturally uncertain whether these particular findings will stand the tests of time and generalization to operational contexts. We do, however, believe this research provides a useful demonstration of how additional insights into situation assessment and human–automation interaction can be gained by analysis and modeling that simultaneously describes human judgment, the task environment, and their interaction.

Background: Automation and Human Performance

High levels of performance in complex, operational environments often require performers to integrate multiple, potentially fallible sources of information during situation assessment. Often referred to as situation awareness (SA) (Endsley, 1995), this assessment has been postulated by Endsley to involve the perception of cues pertaining to the current situation (Level 1), the integration and interpretation of this information into a coherent understanding of the current situation (Level 2), as well as the projection of current events into the near future (Level 3). The importance of situation awareness in complex, uncertain environments, such as the battlefield environment, should be readily apparent. However, because operational environments can often be characterized by an abundance of information, and because people have limited perceptual, attentional, and memory capabilities, automated attention guidance and diagnostic aiding systems have been suggested as possible interventions to benefit the management, acquisition, and integration of information to enhance situation awareness.

Automation Taxonomy

Parasuraman, Sheridan, and Wickens (2000) proposed a four-stage taxonomy of human–automation

interaction in which automation can be applied (in varying degrees or levels) to any of the stages: (1) information acquisition (attention guidance), (2) information analysis and integration (diagnosis), (3) selection of decision and action (choice), and (4) action implementation.

Automation in the information acquisition stage (Stage 1) acts to support human sensory and attentional processes (e.g., detection of relevant information). Automation of this sort may guide attention to what the automated agent infers to be the most relevant information, or filter irrelevant information from a display, thereby reducing the cognitive demands of selective attention and visual search. At the next stage (2), information analysis, automation could be potentially designed to reduce cognitive demands by integrating relevant information, drawing inferences, and/or predicting future trends. For Stage 3 (selection of decision and action), automation may provide users with a complete set of decision alternatives or present only a single, recommended action. Finally, Stage 4 automation (action implementation) aids the user in the execution of the selected action (e.g., an autopilot or cruise control).

As shown in Figure 5.1, the model proposed by Parasuraman et al. (2000) maps onto Endsley's (1995) model, with early stages of automation contributing to the establishment and maintenance of SA. It follows that first-level situation awareness (the perception of cues) may benefit from Stage 1 automation that supports the same underlying processes of sensation, perception, and attention allocation. Similarly, Stage 2 automation, which supports such cognitive functions as information integration and working memory, may also enhance situation awareness. Because of the obvious implications for SA, we focus our discussion on these early stages of automation.

Stage 1 Automation

A number of studies have reliably demonstrated the benefits of Stage 1 automation (attention guidance) in target detection tasks, in both basic (e.g., Egeth & Yantis, 1997) and applied settings (e.g., Kirlik et al., 1996; Mosier et al., 1998; Yeh, Wickens, & Seagull, 1999). Although the benefits of Stage 1 automation have been demonstrated, an important consideration is the impact of this automation on the overall breadth of processing of information in

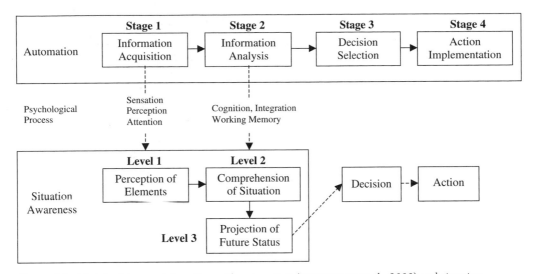

Figure 5.1. Models of human interaction with automation (Parasuraman et al., 2000) and situation awareness (Endsley, 1995).

a display, in particular, the processing of information that is not explicitly highlighted through the automation. In a series of studies that examined the influence of attentional cueing on battlefield target detection, Yeh and colleagues (Yeh et al., 1999, 2003; Yeh & Wickens, 2001) found that cueing narrowed the focus of attention around the cued target such that it reduced the accuracy of detecting more important, but uncued targets that were present in the same scene. This narrowing of attention has important repercussions in situations where uncued information has some bearing on the performed task or in situations where the automation fails or is unreliable (Parasuraman & Riley, 1997). For example, Metzger and Parasuraman (2001) showed that there were slower response times and higher miss rates for air traffic conflicts that an automated agent failed to highlight compared to nonautomated conditions.

Stage 2 Automation

Despite the potential benefits of reduced cognitive load for Stage 2 automation, there are negative implications for human performance when these systems are unreliable. Mosier et al. (1998) examined the effects of Stage 2 automation failure on the automated flight deck through the presentation of automated diagnoses that were inconsistent with the raw data. When this automation failed, pilots showed strong evidence of automation overreliance, failing to utilize all of the available information in

making their judgments, attending instead to the highly salient automated cues. Wickens, Gempler, and Morphew (2000) found similar evidence for overreliance, with pilots allocating more attention to a predicted flight path than to the raw data on the actual aircraft trajectory, especially with increased task complexity. Automation overreliance is likely to most naturally occur with systems that are typically highly reliable.

In general, research has demonstrated that automation failures at later stages (e.g., information analysis, decision making) have more serious repercussions (i.e., greater decrements to performance; Crocoll & Coury, 1990; Sarter & Schroeder, 2001) than early stage automation. However, such research has tended to examine later stages of automation (Stages 2 versus 3). We now consider in more detail the specific manifestation of automation benefits and costs at Stages 1 and 2, which is the focus of the current experiments.

Present Research

The current research examines both Stage 1 attention guidance (Experiment 1) and Stage 2 diagnostic aiding (Experiment 2) in an information integration task where all the raw data are present in a display. In both experiments, the effects of stage of automation were examined in the context of a static battlefield map display through (1) the influence of automation on performers' assessed threat of enemy attack and (2) a potential overreliance on imperfect automation.

Participants used information presented on situation displays to make time-pressured judgments of relative enemy threat from different locations or directions, as expressed in terms of the relative amount of defensive resources allocated to those directions. The information sources varied on a number of attributes, such as reliability of intelligence reports and strength of the enemy unit. These different attributes made the accurate integration of this objective threat value a cognitively challenging task. In Experiment 1 (Stage 1 automation), enemy units that were most relevant (i.e., those that were most dangerous) to the participant's threat assessment were highlighted by the automated aid. An automation failure was said to occur when a highly relevant information cue was not highlighted when it should have been.

In Experiment 2, an automated diagnostic decision aid (Stage 2) replaced the cueing aid that was used in Experiment 1. This decision aid made suggestions regarding the appropriate deployment of defensive resources based directly on the inferred threat level, thus reducing the cognitive load of information integration for the performer. The failure of automation involved the presentation of an inappropriate suggestion for the optimal allocation of resources.

Experiment 1

Participants

Sixteen students from the University of Illinois (ages 20–38 years, $M = 24$ years) volunteered for this study; 11 men and 5 women. All participants had normal or corrected-to-normal vision and were familiar with topographical (contour) maps. All participants were paid US$7 per hour for completing the study.

Materials

Hardware

Battlefield scenarios were presented to participants on a 21-inch Silicon Graphics color monitor (1280 × 1024 resolution) using a Silicon Graphics O2 workstation. Scenarios were created using in-house graphics and development software.

Battlefield Scenarios

Battlefield scenarios were developed using topographical maps of Fort Irwin, CA. Standard military symbols for enemy, neutral, and friendly units were embedded within these map sections (USMC, 1997; Figure 5.2). These units varied in strength (e.g., platoon), type (e.g., enemy combat mechanized), location, and the reliability of the displayed information. Three levels of reliability were used that represented varying degrees of certainty: highly reliable information (confirmed; marked by solid lines), medium reliability (marked by dashed lines), and low reliability (unconfirmed; marked by dotted lines; Figure 5.2). The participant's own unit was always located near the center of the map.

For each scenario, participants deployed a total of 20 defensive resources to the east or west of their unit's position, based on their evaluation of the overall threat of enemies in both directions. For example, a large threat from one direction would optimally receive a larger proportion of the available resources than a lower perceived threat from the opposite direction. The overall threat was the summed threat of each individual unit occupying a particular region. For example, the threat of attack from the east was a function of the additive threat from all units located in the eastern region.

Threat Values

The relative threat of each unit to the participant's own unit was based on weighted evidence from multiple cues: That is, threat was determined by enemy strength, the separation distance (relative to their own position), the difficulty of the terrain between the unit and themselves, and cue reliabilities. Threat values for each unit were calculated using Equation 5.1, which was derived from threat assessments made by independent raters (see Horrey & Wickens, 2001, for more details):

$$(5.1) \qquad \text{Threat}_{unit} = X_{type}(90 + 4\,X_{strength} - 5\,X_{dist} - 14\,X_{diff}) \times R$$

where $X_{strength}$, X_{dist}, and X_{diff} define the unit strength, distance, and difficulty of the terrain, respectively. R, a moderator variable, is the overall reliability of the information (values ranging from 0 to 1, where $R < 1$ denotes degraded levels of reliability), and X_{type} is the type (1 for enemy units, 0 for neutral or friendly).

From Equation 5.1, it follows that only enemy units are perceived as threats, and threat increased

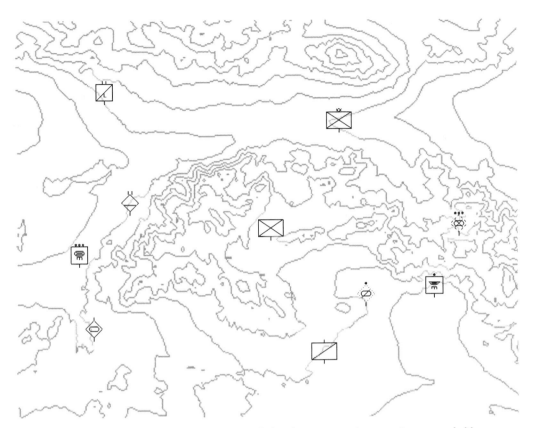

Figure 5.2. Sample battlefield scenario. Central symbol is the participant's own unit, surrounded by enemy, friendly and neutral forces. On average, there were 20 other units of varying composition (from Horrey & Wickens, 2001).

with unit strength, proximity, ease of approach, and reliability of information.

Stage 1 Automation

On some of the trials, an automated highlighting feature guided attention to the most relevant (highest threat) symbols on the map, by displaying them with a highly salient pulse from high to low intensity at a rate of approximately 1 Hz. The automation feature enhanced symbols that had threat values equal to or greater than 30 (based on Equation 5.1), yielding on the average trial, automation highlighting of approximately 22% of the units.

Failure

In one scenario, the automation failed to enhance a highly relevant unit in one direction, yet appropriately highlighted all the relevant units in the opposite direction. This nonhighlighted enemy unit had a substantial impact on the optimal allocation policy for the trial. Accurate performance on this

trial depended on whether participants attended only to the highlighted units or to all of the available information on the display, both highlighted and nonhighlighted.

Procedure

Participants completed an informed consent form and a brief demographic questionnaire at the beginning of the 45-minute session. Participants were then given verbal instructions that familiarized them with the maps and contour lines, military symbology, rules of engagement, automation features, and task demands. Participants were instructed to assume the role of a battlefield commander positioned in a central unit. As the commander, they were asked to make critical decisions for the defense of their position based on information obtained from a map display. Participants were instructed to observe each battlefield scenario carefully and assess the relative threat from forces in the east versus those in the west, based on the unit attributes of strength, distance, terrain difficulty, and reliability of information. Using this situation assessment, they were required to allocate 20 defensive resources to the appropriate east–west positions. Participants were informed that the purpose of the automation was to guide their attention to the most relevant units on the battlefield and that nonhighlighted units were not necessarily irrelevant but rather deemed to be less of a threat than the highlighted units.

Each trial began with a brief instruction screen after which the battlefield scenario appeared (on keystroke). The trial ended when the participant pressed another key or after 25 seconds had elapsed. This time value was chosen (after pilot testing) to impose considerable time stress to perform the task accurately and thereby increase the likelihood that the assistance from the automated highlighting would be used. The map display then disappeared and the response screen appeared. Participants first completed a brief practice block (5 scenarios) followed by the experimental block, which consisted of 51 scenarios. On roughly half of the trials, the automation feature was active. Automation scenarios were randomly selected and counterbalanced across participants. On the *final* trial of the block, participants were presented with the failure trial. The self-paced block was approximately 30 minutes long. Following the experimental block, participants completed a postexperimental questionnaire and were remunerated for their participation.

Experiment 1: Results

Following Strauss (2000), in the following we report the results of an analysis of experimental data using Murphy's (1988) "skill score" (SS) performance measure and Stewart's (1990) extended decomposition of the SS measure using the lens model equation. Other performance measures (e.g., allocation accuracy, response times) are reported elsewhere (Horrey & Wickens, 2001). The present analysis was used to gain insights into how the different stages of display enhancement automation affected performance on the situation assessment task.

Skill Score

Although the correlation coefficient (such as the lens model measure, r_a; see Goldstein, this volume)

provides a useful measure of the correspondence between human judgments and an environmental criterion, its properties limit its sensitivity, and thus utility, for measuring judgment quality (Cronbach & Gleser, 1953). More specifically, correlation captures only *shape* differences between two sets of variables, that is, their shared pattern of ups and downs, without distinguishing differences in either their *magnitude* or *scale*. These deficiencies of the correlation coefficient have motivated several researchers to look for more sensitive measurements of judgment correspondence. One alternative has been to look at the distance between data sets rather than their shared shape, a strategy often found in studies of meteorological forecasting (e.g., Murphy, 1988). Mean square error (MSE), a measure of the squared Euclidean distance between two data sets (Cooksey, 1996), has been regularly adopted for this purpose (e.g., Lee & Yates, 1992). Distance using MSE is calculated using the following equation:

$$(5.2) \qquad MSE_Y = (1/n)\Sigma(Y_i - O_i)^2$$

Here, the two data sets are the judgments of the human (Y_i) and the corresponding true environmental states (O_i). These two sets are used to form n pairs, where one element of the pair comes from each set. When the human judgments are perfect, MSE is equal to zero. As a replacement for the correlation coefficient, MSE would be unremarkable except that it can be partitioned into three distinct components representing shape (correlation), scale, and magnitude. Here, we present the decomposition proposed by Murphy (1988), introducing first, however, his SS measure of judgment quality.

Skill Score as a Measurement of Judgment Quality

To develop his decomposition of MSE, Murphy (1988) used the concept of *skill*, which he defined as judgment performance relative to a reference judgment. A commonly used reference is a constant judgment based on the average, or base rate, value of the criterion being judged. As shown in Equation 5.3, the MSE for such a judgment is termed MSE_R (R stands for the "reference" value against which actual human judgment performance is measured):

$$(5.3) \qquad MSE_R = (1/n)\Sigma(O_i - \bar{O})^2$$

Deriving the skill score requires measuring the ratio between the MSE of the human's judgments (Equation 5.2) and the MSE of the reference (Equation 5.3). This ratio is then subtracted from unity to create the skill score (SS). This relationship is shown in Equation 5.4. In this basic form, the SS provides an overall evaluation of the quality of a performer's judgments scaled to the judgment performance that would achieved by making a judgment equal to the base rate in each instance.

(5.4) $SS = 1 - [MSE_Y/MSE_R]$

When SS is positive, the human's judgments are better than chance ($MSE_Y < MSF_R$); when it is zero, the human's judgments are at chance performance ($MSE_R = MSE_Y$); and when SS is negative, the human's judgments are worse than chance ($MSE_Y > MSE_R$).

Murphy's Decomposition of the Skill Score

Murphy (1988) developed the SS to enable the MSE to be decomposed. By substituting the equations for MSE_Y (Equation 5.1) and MSF_R (Equation 5.2) into the form of the skill score (Equation 5.3), Murphy (1988) showed how to derive the desired decomposition. A conceptual representation of his decomposition is presented in Equation 5.5:

(5.5)   Judgment Skill (SS) = [Shape
                (correlation) – Scale Error
                – Magnitude Error]

Here, SS is partitioned into three components, and thus shape (correlation) is separated from errors associated with differences in magnitude and scale. The result is a more sensitive and diagnostic measurement than correlation alone (which measures only shape similarity, as in the standard lens model's measure of achievement, r_a). The scale error component has been called *Regression Bias* (RB), because it measures whether the performer has appropriately scaled judgmental variability to situational variability and the level of judgmental achievement (r_a) demonstrated. More specifically, the value of RB vanishes only when the standard deviation of human judgments is equal to the product of the standard deviation of the task criterion and the judge's achievement. When achievement (r_a) is perfect (unity), then the dispersion or standard deviation of human judgments should be identical to the dispersion or standard deviation of the task criterion. As the judge demonstates lower levels of achieve-

ment, the dispersion or standard deviation of human judgments should reduce proportionally (e.g., if human judgments have no correlation with the criterion at all, then there is no good reason for the judge to demonstrate any variance in his or her judgments).

Finally, the magnitude error component of Murphy's Equation 5.5 has been called *Base Rate Bias* or BRB (Stewart, 1990). It measures the overall (unconditional) bias in the operator's judgments, thus diagnosing a tendency to over- or underestimate the judged situation. This bias equals zero only when the mean of the operator's judgments equals the mean of the judged criterion (i.e., the objective base rate), and is nonzero when the mean of the human's judgments is either too high or low relative to the criterion mean.

Murphy's decomposition of the skill score provides a sensitive measure of the judgmental components of situation assessment, as it disentangles the joint contributions of shape, scale, and magnitude in the measurement of judgment quality. The mathematical decomposition is presented below in Equation 5.5, and a summary of each term is presented in Table 5.1.

(5.6) $SS = (r_{YO})^2 - [r_{YO} - (s_Y/s_O)]^2$
                $- [(\bar{Y} - \bar{O}/s_O]^2$

In Equation 5.6, r_{YO} is the correlation between human judgment and the criterion, which is identical to the lens model achievement measure r_a. The s terms in Equation 5.6 are standard deviations of either the set of human judgments (Y) or the true state or task criterion (O). Finally, the barred terms are the means of either the set of human judgments or the true state or task criterion. Stewart (1990) took Murphy's decomposition presented in Equation 5.6 above one step further by noting that the first term in the equation is the squared value of the lens model's achievement measure. As such, a more elaborate decomposition of SS is possible. By combining the lens model equation (see chapter 2; Cooksey, 1996) with Equation 5.6, Stewart (1990) derived the decomposition of SS shown in Equation 5.7:

(5.7) $SS = (R_{O.X}GR_{Y.X})^2 - [r_{YO} - (s_Y/s_O)]^2$
                $- [(\bar{Y} - \bar{O}/s_O]^2$

In this equation, X is used to indicate the cue set against which human judgments are regressed to create the model of human judgments and against which the criterion vector is regressed to create the

Table 5.1. Components of Murphy's (1988) decomposition of the skill score (SS) (after Kirlik & Strauss, 2003).

Component	Name	Description
SS	Skill Score	A relative measure of "actual" judgment quality.
r_{YO}	Correlation Coefficient	**Shape**—degree of linear association between judgments and situation. "Potential" skill in judgment.
$\left[r_{YO} - \left(s_Y \big/ s_O \right) \right]^2$	Conditional/ Regression Bias (RB)	**Scale**—degree that standard deviation of judgments accounts for imperfect correlation; for the bias to vanish, sY must be adjusted to equal $r_{YO}(s_O)$.
$\left[\left(\overline{Y} - \overline{O} \right) \big/ s_O \right]^2$	Unconditional/ Base Rate Bias (BRB)	**Magnitude**—degree that average judgment equals the base rate of occurrence in the situation.

model of the task environment. As such, $R_{O.X}$ in Equation 5.7 is identical to the lens model term R_e and $R_{Y.X}$ is identical to the lens model term R_s. As such, Stewart's decomposition of SS represented in Equation 5.7 demonstrates that perfect judgment performance requires each of the following:

1. An $r_{YO} = r_a$ correlation between judgments and criterion value of unity. Assuming a linear-additive task ecology, by the lens model equation this requires:
   1.1 A G or linear knowledge value of unity;
   1.2 An R_e or environmental predictability value of unity;
   1.3 An R_s or cognitive control value of unity.
2. A BRB of zero; and
3. An RB of zero.

For the current analyses, these parameters were derived through statistical modeling of both the task environment and participants' judgment strategies. We discuss these models next.

Modeling

For environmental modeling, we used an optimal allocation score as the criterion variable in a multiple regression. This score was based on the ratio of threats from units in the east versus those in the west. For each displayed unit, the threat value was calculated and summed for each direction (i.e., the overall threat from that direction). For example, the summed threat of 40 from the west and 60 from the east would yield a ratio of 2:3, such that the optimal distribution of the 20 defensive resources from west to east would be 8 to 12.

For each trial, the predictor variables of unit strength, distance, terrain, and reliability of infor-

mation were entered into a multiple regression. These variables were transformed so that the values were bounded between 0 and 1. Because Equation 5.1 was not strictly linear , we first attempted to model the environment with a nonlinear regression of the form: $Y = b_0 + (b_1X_1 + b_2X_2 + b_3X_3) * b_4X_4$ (which follows the same form as Equation 5.1). This model yielded a reasonably good fit ($R^2 = 0.93$). However, we determined that a more parsimonious, linear model of the environment ($Y = b_0 + b_1X_1 + b_2X_2 + b_3X_3 + b_4X_4$) performed equally well ($R^2 = 0.95$). We therefore elected to use the simpler (yet robust) linear model for the purpose of this study.

Similar linear models were created for each participant, based on their own allocation behavior. As with the environmental model, the linear models of participants explained as much variance as nonlinear models (linear, $R^2 = 0.91$; nonlinear, $R^2 = 0.88$; averaged across all participant models). Therefore, the lens model parameters for each participant are derived from their own best fitting linear model.

Skill Score Analysis

For the following analyses, we removed one participant as an outlier. This participant scored below chance performance and well below the mean score (> 2 SD below).

Figure 5.3 plots the participants' skill scores as well as the associated lens model parameters for the (a) No Automation and (b) Automation conditions (we also plot achievement, r_a, and potentially unmodeled cue usage, C). To examine the impact of automation on skill score, we compared participant performance across these two groups. As shown by Figure 5.3, there was a marginally significant *decrease* in SS in the Automation condition ($M = 0.52$)

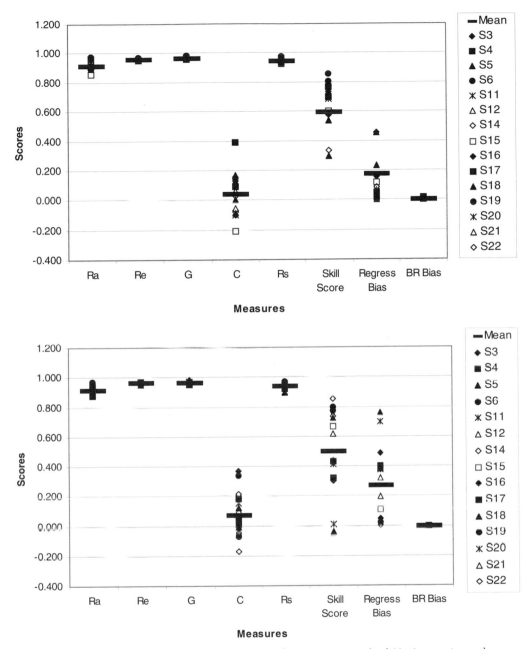

Figure 5.3. Skill scores and lens model subcomponents for participants in (top) No Automation and (bottom) Automation conditions.

compared to the No Automation condition ($M = 0.66$; $t_{(14)} = 1.9$, $p = 0.08$). We further note that the variability of SS in the Automation condition ($M = 0.08$) was greater than in the No Automation condition ($M = 0.03$), such that the presence of automation spread individuals apart (approaching significance, the 90% CI for the ratio of the two variances was [1.2, 7.4], $H_0 = 1.0$ – equal vari-

ances—is excluded by this interval; the actual measured ratio of estimated variances, Ratio$_{Var} = 2.67$).

Given that SS is made up of several components, an increase or a decrease in SS must be associated with a respective change in one or more of these subcomponents. In general, there were no differences in the (R_s, G, R_e, or BRB) parameters across automation condition ($p = 0.20$ to 0.53).

However, an analysis of RB did indeed reveal marginally significant differences, with higher (worse) RB scores in the Automation condition ($M = 0.26$) than the No Automation condition ($M = 0.12$; $t_{(14)} = 1.9$, $p = 0.08$). This finding suggests that the presence of automated display enhancement caused a moderate increase in RB, which in turn could account for the moderate decrease in observed SS. The regression bias was manifest in a *reduction* in response variability, such that the standard deviations of participants' judgment distributions were less than the product of their achievement (r_a) levels and the standard deviation of the task criterion distribution. As was the case with SS, automation appeared to spread individuals apart, with an increase in the overall variability in RB scores ($M = 0.07$) compared to the No Automation condition ($M = 0.02$; 90% CI [1.2, 7.4], the actual ratio of estimated variances, Ratio$_{Var}$ = 3.5).

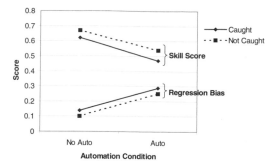

Figure 5.4. Skill score and regression bias by automation condition and performance on failure trial.

Failure Trial

On the failure trial, automation did not cue a highly relevant target that was intended to have a significant impact on the allocation of defensive resources. Thus, whether or not a participant noticed the unit was inferred from their allocation score for this trial. These results suggested that roughly half of the participants (7 of 15) failed to notice and integrate the uncued, high-relevance unit. We refer to these individuals as those "Caught" by the failure of automation, and the others "Not Caught."

We compared these two groups of performers on measures of SS and RB across the automation conditions to determine whether this categorization could shed additional insight into the observed effects. As shown in Figure 5.4, the introduction of the failure trial in an attempt to diagnose possible automation over-reliance did not result in any enlightening results in this analysis. Both the Caught and Not Caught groups showed trends toward decreased SS and increased RB in the Automation condition compared to the No Automation condition, mirroring the overall findings reported previously.

Experiment 1: Discussion

Our goal in Experiment 1 was to examine the impact of Stage 1 attention guidance display enhancement on human judgment in a battlefield assessment task. Most prior research on early stage automation has focused on the *detection* of highlighted targets (as a primary task), but the current study highlighted targets of relevance to be *integrated* in forming a situation assessment.

The results from this study suggested a decline in performance for users of reliable Stage 1 automation, which was attributed to an increase in regression bias. As noted previously, regression bias measures whether the performer has appropriately scaled judgmental variability to achievement and situational variability (Stewart, 1990; Stewart & Lusk, 1994). In the current study, the presence of automation resulted in a reduction in the variance of judgments made by the participants relative to the optimal variance (the product of achievement and actual situational variability).

One possible explanation of this finding is that participants did not process the raw data in the display broadly when provided with automated cueing. That is, the experimental results are consistent with the interpretation that participants may have attended more (or perhaps only) to the automation cues themselves (e.g., a "beta" strategy; Yeh & Wickens, 2001), rather than to the entire set of both automated and preexisting cues regarding every unit's attributes (see Mosier et al., 1998, on "automation bias"). For example, participants may have adopted a strategy by which they used the number of highlighted objects in either direction as an indicator of the appropriate distribution of defensive resources—a strategy that would be largely ineffective. A judgment model based on this single automated cue (i.e., the ratio of the number of highlighted objects in each direction) yielded very poor predictions of optimal allocation scores: $r^2 < 0.20$.)

We speculate that the observed regression bias reflecting a *narrowing* of the distribution of participants' judgments may have arisen due of the thresholding logic used in the automation algorithm. This logic, by highlighting only the most threatening units, resulted in the existence of a novel judgment cue with *far less variance* than the task criterion itself. If participants were using this automated cue as either an additional judgment cue or as a crutch, they, too, would have then exhibited a decrease in the variance of their judgment distributions. For example, for a given series of trials, the ratio of *highlighted* units from west to east ranged from 1:1 to 1:3 to 2:3 and the like. As such, there were relatively small differences in this ratio across trials (i.e., participants did not encounter trials where the ratio was 1:10). The reduced variance of the automation highlighting relative to the criterion variance, coupled with the assumption that the highlighting provided a salient judgment cue, possibly accounted for the moderately reduced variance, and thus moderately reduced performance, associated with automation in this task.

Although certain costs of Stage 1 automation (Parasuraman et al., 2000) were found in this experiment, it is less clear how higher stages of automation involving automatic diagnosis might affect performance in the battlefield scenario. The second study examined Stage 2 automation (diagnosis) in the same experimental paradigm.

Experiment 2

Participants

Twelve students at the University of Illinois volunteered for this second study (ages 22–33 years, M = 26 years). Six men and six women made up this group. All participants had normal or corrected-to-normal vision and were familiar with topographical (contour) maps. All participants were paid $7 per hour for completing the study.

Materials

Automation

The experimental set up and battlefield scenarios were the same as those used in Experiment 1. However, in contrast to the attention guidance automation used in Experiment 1, this experiment used Stage 2 automation exclusively, which integrated the threat values and suggested an appropriate resource allocation. On a given trial, display enhancement in the form of two red boxes containing a suggested allocation of resources appeared to the east and west of the participant's unit (see Figure 5.5). This suggestion was based on the optimal allocation as determined by Equation 1.

Failure Trial

The failure scenario differed from that used in Experiment 1. In this study, automation suggested an inappropriate allocation for the displayed units. Specifically, this suggestion failed to consider a very important unit in one direction. The purpose of this trial was to determine whether participants were attending to all of the raw data on automated trials or instead perhaps overrelying on the automated display aiding.

Procedure

Experiment 2 followed the same general procedure described in Experiment 1. Participants were instructed that the automation's assessment was only a suggestion and that the final allocation decision would be theirs to make. Furthermore, they were informed that the automation was highly reliable but not perfect. Scenarios in which displayed units overlapped with the automated aid's displayed advice were excluded from this experiment. The experimental block consisted of 43 trials, including the failure trial.

Experiment 2: Results

Skill Score Analysis

Following the same protocol as in Experiment 1, we examined participants' SS across automation conditions. As shown in Figure 5.6, skill scores were higher in the Automation condition (M = 0.82) compared to No Automation (M = 0.68; $t_{(11)}$ = 2.62, p = 0.02). Unlike Stage 1 automation examined in the first experiment, Stage 2 automation increased participants' SS. Additionally, there was reduced variance in SS across participants in the automation condition (M = 0.005) compared to the No Automation condition (M = 0.02; 90% CI [0.11, 0.88], the actual of estimated variances, $Ratio_{Var}$ = 0.25).

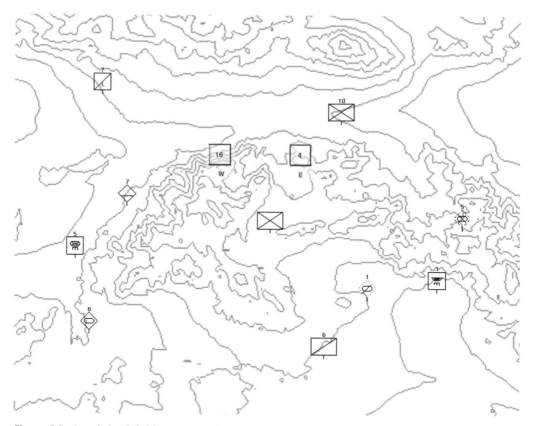

Figure 5.5. Sample battlefield scenario with Stage 2 automation. Center symbol represents participant's own unit. Allocation recommendations are presented in the two boxes above own unit (in actual display, these were red). Typical scenarios included 20 surrounding units comprising enemy, friendly, and neutral forces (from Horrey & Wickens, 2001).

Although this reduction in variance may have been largely attributable to the automated aid, it may also have been due in part to a ceiling effect (with more performers nearing peak performance).

We examined the components of the SS to determine the source of the observed differences. A comparison of lens model parameters did not reveal any differences across automation condition for R_s, G, R_e, and BRB ($p = 0.18$ to 1.0). There was, however, a significant reduction in RB in the Automation conditions ($M = 0.03$) relative to the No Automation ($M = 0.13$; $t_{(11)} = 2.27$, $p = 0.04$). This reduction is a likely explanation for the observed differences in SS. The tendency was for participants to make judgments in a range that was too *narrow* in the nonautomated condition. The Stage 2 automation, apparently, helped participants calibrate the range or variance of their judgments to the criterion variance or range given their demonstrated levels of achievement (r_a).

Failure Trial

On the failure trial, the Stage 2 automation failed to integrate the displayed information accurately, such that an important cue was not weighed in the threat assessment. As in Experiment 1, we inferred whether a participant noticed the automation discrepancy from his or her allocation score (i.e., whether they based their allocations on the automated suggestion or on the raw data). Results suggested that roughly half of the participants (5 of 11) failed to notice the highly relevant unit or noticed it but opted to allocate their resources according to the automation's suggestion (i.e., those "Caught" by the failure).

A comparison of SS and RB across the automation conditions and two groups of performers (Caught, Not Caught) revealed some interesting findings. As shown in Figure 5.7, there were no differences in SS for the Caught group across the

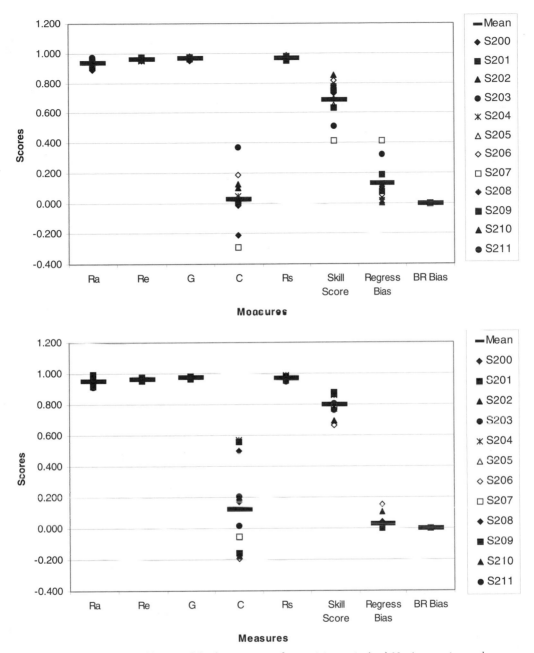

Figure 5.6. Skill scores and lens model subcomponents for participants in (top) No Automation and (bottom) Automation conditions.

automation conditions (No Auto: $M = 0.74$; Auto: $M = 0.79$; $t_{(4)} = 0.79$, $p = 0.47$), nor were there differences in RB (No Auto: $M = 0.10$; Auto: $M = 0.06$; $t_{(4)} = 0.88$, $p = 0.43$) for the Caught group. In contrast, the Not Caught group showed significantly higher levels of SS in the Automation condition ($M = 0.82$) compared to the No Automation condition ($M = 0.61$; $t_{(5)} = 4.09$, $p = 0.009$). There was

also a marginally significant lower level of RB for the Not Caught group in the Automation condition ($M = 0.01$) compared to the No Automation condition ($M = 0.18$; $t_{(5)} = 2.30$, $p = 0.07$).

Interestingly, then, it was the Not Caught group of individuals who accounted for the overall improvement in performance observed in this experiment. That is, the Caught group did not show any

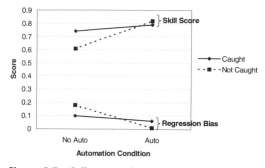

Figure 5.7. Skill score and regression bias by automation condition and performance on failure trial.

improvement in SS with the addition of Stage 2 automation. Furthermore, the mechanism by which the Not Caught group was able to improve their performance was through the reduction of regression bias, such that they were able to use automation to better calibrate their judgments to their own levels of achievement and the variance of the task criterion.

Experiment 2: Discussion

The results of Experiment 2 revealed that participants' skill scores with reliable Stage 2 automation were superior to unaided performance. The overall increase in SS was associated with a reduction in RB, such that participants were better calibrated to the appropriate distribution of judgments than when performing the task unaided. Interestingly, this improvement in performance was *not* simply due to reliance on the automated agent (which typically gave accurate recommendations). Instead, it was the participants who were not overly reliant on the automation who showed a significant improvement in SS. That is, the Caught group (who, by definition, overused the automated aid when it was present) did not show any improvements in judgment performance in the automated condition. The overall improvements in SS, instead, were attributable to the Not Caught group, who may have used the automated aid as an additional information cue to integrate with the raw data in their assessment of the situation (rather than relying exclusively on the automated assessment). As shown in Figure 5.6, the improvement in SS was largely due to a decrease

in RB, suggesting that the Not Caught group was able to use the information displayed by the automation to better calibrate their judgments to the criterion distribution as a whole.

General Discussion

In two experiments we explored performance on a military situation assessment task using two different types of automated display enhancement. In Experiment 1, automation highlighted those enemy units inferred to be the greatest threat to each performer's unit. In terms of skill score, Stage 1 automation, as implemented here, actually reduced performance by introducing regression biases into participants' judgment processes. In general, the judgments of participants who were provided with automation were distributed over a range that was narrower than was appropriate. It is possible that this reduced variability was due to an inappropriate strategy for automation use in which participants used the highlighting not merely as an attention aid, but also as a judgment cue itself. This pattern of results suggests that the implementation of Stage 1 automation may require caution with respect to operator training and design. To be of benefit, the logic underlying such automation needs to be well understood by performers, so that they do not adopt improper procedures for using attention guidance information.

In contrast, the participants in Experiment 2 showed marked improvements while using a Stage 2 automated aid, suggesting that this type of automation was of greater value to participants. The overall improvement in performance was diagnosed as a decrease in regression bias that was present in the Not Caught group of participants, but not in the Caught group. This finding suggests that the former group was able to use the automation effectively as an additional information source rather than a crutch.

We should explicitly note that the costs and benefits of automation found here, all apparently revolving around the need to tailor the *distribution* of one's judgments to the *distribution* of a task criterion, appeared to reflect an important task demand in this particular task and environment. As such, these specific findings are not intended, as is the modeling and analysis approach itself, to be generalized to tasks with different key demands.

Why, for example, were participants so well adapted to base rates both with and without automation (as indicated by negligible base rate biases in all cases), whereas in contrast relatively less able to adapt the *range* of their judgments to the criterion distribution? We note that base rate information could be simply communicated during instructions (i.e., there was no tendency for greater threats to come more frequently from either direction), the particular value of the base rate (1/2) is intuitive (e.g., a coin flip), and base rate, as an empirical frequency, is relatively easily learned through experience (e.g. Sedlmeier & Betsch, 2002).

The *distribution* of the task criterion or appropriate response, however, is a more abstract concept. No explicit instructions were given on this task demand, and without feedback or other information specifying this distribution (which is indeed a plausible interpretation of the functional role played by the suggestions provided by Stage 2 automation in Experiment 2), this information is more difficult to learn through experience.

In other task environments it may well be that BRB (rather than RB) is the primary limiting factor, or that achieving knowledge of cue weighting patterns (G) or consistency (R_s) is the most difficult task demand for performers to overcome (e.g., see contributions by Adelman et al. and Bisantz et al. in this volume). As such, we encourage researchers who, like us, often find it difficult to integrate findings on complex task performance to provide equally detailed descriptions of both their empirical findings and the detailed structure of their tasks. We believe that both descriptions are essential in enabling research on adaptive behavior, an inherently context-sensitive phenomenon, to progress in a cumulative and integrated fashion.

In summary, across the two experiments reported here, we note that the skill score decomposition augmented with lens model analysis allowed us to discover results that would not be readily apparent using more traditional measures of performance such as percent correct or reaction time. Most notably, we identified the source of the divergent results with respect to automated aids: Increased regression bias in Experiment 1 lead to a reduction in performance, whereas reduced regression bias improved performance in Experiment 2 for those participants who used automation as an additional information source rather than as a crutch. We believe that the style of analysis and modeling presented here may provide an important tool for continued research on both display design and human-automation interaction.

Acknowledgments. The authors thank Sharon Yeakel and LTC Keith Beurskens for their assistance. Research funding for this project was provided through a grant from the U.S. Army Research Laboratory under the Federated Laboratory Program, Cooperative Agreement DAAL0196-2-0003. Mr. Bernie Corona and Dr. Michael Barnes were scientific technical monitors. Any opinions, findings, and conclusions or recommendations expressed in this document are those of the authors and do not necessarily reflect the views of the U.S. Army Research Laboratory.

References

Cooksey, R. W. (1996). *Judgment analysis: Theory, methods, and applications.* San Diego, Calif.: Academic Press.

Crocoll, W. M., & Coury, B. G. (1990). Status or recommendation: Selecting the type of information for decision aiding. *Proceedings of the 34th Annual Meeting of the Human Factors Society* (pp. 1524–1528). Santa Monica, Calif.: Human Factors Society.

Cronbach, L. J., & Gleser, G. C. (1953). Assessing similarity between profiles. *Psychological Bulletin, 50*(6), 456–473.

Egeth, H. E. & Yantis, S. (1997). Visual attention: Control, representation, and time course. *Annual Review of Psychology, 48,* 269–297.

Endsley, M. R. (1995). Toward a theory of situation awareness in dynamic systems. *Human Factors, 37*(1), 32–64.

Graham, S. E., & Matthews, M. D. (1999). *Infantry situation awareness: Papers from the 1998 Infantry Situation Awareness Workshop.* Alexandria, Va.: U.S. Army Research Institute.

Horrey, W. J., & Wickens, C. D. (2001). *Supporting situation assessment through attention guidance: A cost-benefit and depth of processing analysis.* (Tech Report ARL-01-16/FED-LAB-01-1). Savoy: University of Illinois, Aviation Research Laboratory.

Kirlik, A., & Strauss, R. (2003). A systems perspective on situation awareness I: Conceptual framework, modeling, and quantitative measurement. (Tech Report AHFD-03-12/NTSC-03-0). Savoy:

University of Illinois, Aviation Human Factors Division.

Kirlik, A., Walker, N., Fisk, A. D., & Nagel, K. (1996). Supporting perception in the service of dynamic decision making. *Human Factors, 38*(2), 288–299.

Lee, J. W., & Yates, J. F. (1992). How quantity judgment changes as the number of cues increases: An analytical framework and review. *Psychological Bulletin, 112*(2), 363–377.

Metzger, U., & Parasuraman, R. (2001). Conflict detection aids for air traffic controllers in free flight: Effects of reliable and failure modes on performance and eye movements. *Proceedings of the 11th International Symposium on Aviation Psychology*. Columbus: Ohio State University.

Mosier, K. L., Skitka, L. J., Heers, S., & Burdick, M. (1998). Automation bias: Decision making and performance in high-tech cockpits. *International Journal of Aviation Psychology, 8*(1), 47–63.

Murphy, A. H. (1988). Skill scores based on the mean square error and their relationship to the correlation coefficient. *Monthly Weather Review, 166*, 2417–2424.

Parasuraman, R., & Riley, V. (1997). Humans and automation: Use, misuse, disuse, and abuse. *Human Factors, 39*(2), 230–253.

Parasuraman, R., Sheridan, T. B., & Wickens, C. D. (2000). A model for types and levels of human interaction with automation. *IEEE Transactions on Systems, Man, and Cybernetics Part A: Systems and Humans, 30*(3), 286–297.

Sarter, N. B., & Schroeder, B. (2001). Supporting decision-making and action selection under time pressure and uncertainty: The case of inflight icing. *Proceedings of the 11th International Symposium on Aviation Psychology*. Columbus: Ohio State University.

Sedlmeier, P., & Betsch, T. (2002). *Etc. frequency processing and cognition*. Oxford: Oxford University Press.

Stewart, T. R. (1990). A decomposition of the correlation coefficient and its use in analyzing forecasting skill. *Weather and Forecasting, 5*, 661–666.

Stewart, T. R., and Lusk, C. M. (1994). Seven components of judgmental forecasting skill: Implications for research and improvement of forecasts. *Journal of Forecasting, 13*, 579–599.

Strauss, R. (2000). A methodology for measuring the judgmental components of situation awareness. Unpublished doctoral dissertation, School of Industrial & Systems Engineering, Georgia Institute of Technology, Atlanta, GA.

USMC. (1997). *Operational terms and graphics* (Field Manual 101-5-1). Washington, D.C.: Department of the Army.

Wickens, C. D., Gempler, K., & Morphew, M. E. (2000). Workload and reliability of predictor displays in aircraft traffic avoidance. *Transportation Human Factors, 2*(2), 99–126.

Wickens, C. D., Pringle, H. L., & Merlo, J. (1999). *Integration of information sources of varying weights: The effect of display features and attention cueing* (Tech Report ARL-99-2/FED-LAB-99-1). Savoy: University of Illinois, Aviation Research Laboratory.

Yeh, M., Merlo, J. L., Wickens, C. D., & Brandenburg, D. L. (2003). Head up versus head down: The costs of imprecision, unreliability, and visual clutter on cue effectiveness for display signaling. *Human Factors, 45*(3), 390–407.

Yeh, M., & Wickens, C. D. (2001). Explicit and implicit display signaling in augmented reality: The effects of cue reliability, image realism, and interactivity on attention allocation and trust calibration. *Human Factors, 43*(3), 355–365.

Yeh, M., Wickens, C. D., & Seagull, F. J. (1999). Target cueing in visual search: The effects of conformality and display location on the allocation of visual attention. *Human Factors, 41*(4), 524–542.

6

Pratik D. Jha and Ann M. Bisantz

Applying the Multivariate Lens Model to Fault Diagnosis

Introduction

Overview

This study investigates the application of a multivariate lens model to judgments of fault diagnosis in a dynamic, process control system. Although there are documented examples of the univariate lens model across numerous domains, applications of the multivariate model are more limited and have not been extended to judgments in more complex, human–machine systems. Such extensions may prove valuable, because many judgments in such systems, such as those concerning fault diagnosis and recovery, are multivariate or categorical in nature. To investigate the utility of the multivariate lens model for this application, a sensitivity analysis was conducted on simulated fault diagnosis data at three levels of performance, within the context of a dynamic process control simulation. Additionally, experimental results were collected and modeled from 16 participants under two interface and two fault severity conditions using the same simulation. The sensitivity analysis showed that parameters of the multivariate model were in fact sensitive to changes in fault diagnosis performance. However, multivariate parameters showed less sensitiv-

ity to performance changes in the experimental results because of the nature of the faults that were made and the canonical correlation procedures used to compute the parameters. Further investigation of the canonical correlation outputs was useful in identifying participants' judgment strategies.

Background

In many decision-making situations, important aspects of the environment, such as the values of informative variables or the relationships between variable values, change over time. Feedback about results of actions is typically available, and it may be necessary to make decisions quickly (Cannon-Bowers, Salas, & Pruitt, 1996; Zsambok 1997). In these situations, decisions are often composed of series of smaller decisions and actions, decision choices are impacted by feedback about the results of just-prior actions, and decision makers must identify the state of the situation to act (Brehmer, 1990; Hogarth, 1981). The remainder of this section discusses models of such dynamic decision making, particularly as applied to fault diagnosis, and relate judgments regarding situation state to the lens model formalism.

Models of dynamic or naturalistic decision making in the real world emphasize the cyclical nature of decision making already noted. For example, because of the continuous, cyclical nature of judgment and action in the natural environment, Hogarth (1981) claims that people can reduce effort and risk by making locally sound choices, and then adjusting their actions over time based both on feedback and the new state of the world. Similarly, Connolly (1988) proposed a goal directed model for studying dynamic decision tasks. He proposed a decision cycle analogous to "perceptual cycle" used by Neisser (1976) to demonstrate how individuals acquire knowledge in the environment. His cyclical model suggests that decision making proceeds by assessing the state of environment relative to the goal state and consequently taking the actions based on the values, purpose, and intentions. The consequences of action in turn impact the state of the environment and its relationship to the goal state. Brehmer and Allard (1991) describe dynamic decision making using a control theory model, in which decisions result in actions that affect the environment (the controlled system). Then, feedback about the effects of the actions allows decision makers to adjust their actions.

Recognition or judgments of the state of the environment are a critical component of these models and of theories of decision making in naturalistic environments (Cannon-Bowers, Salas, & Pruitt, 1996, Zsambok 1997). For example, Cannon-Bowers, Salas, and Pruitt (1996) claim that it is necessary to focus on situation assessment as a crucial part of the decision-making process in natural environments. This focus stems from Klein's (1993; Klein and Calderwood, 1991) process model of naturalistic decision making, recognition primed decision making. In this model, decision makers attempt to recognize the current situation and identify actions based on their past experience with the situation. They mentally simulate how the actions would work in the current situation and modify them if necessary.

Research on decision making in human–machine systems has been shaped by this approach. For example, Cohen, Freeman, and Wolf (1996) describe a recognition/meta-recognition model of decision making and use their model to describe the process by which people monitor the stages of decision making. The model qualitatively describes how a decision maker verifies the results of a recognition process or recognizes the need to search for more information. Kaempf et al. (1996) stud-

ied descriptions of decision-making incidents collected during semi-structured interviews and found that naval officers typically identified situations by comparing features of the situation with those they had previously experienced. Also, they recognized the course of action to take based on experience, instead of generating new course of actions or comparing various courses of action.

One domain that has long served as the focus for research on decision making in complex dynamic setting is process control (Bainbridge, 1979; Rasmussen, 1976). In particular, processes of fault detection, diagnosis, and recovery have been studied by a number of researchers (Rouse, 1983; Hunt and Rouse, 1984; Knaeuper and Rouse, 1985; Rasmussen, 1980). Problem solving in process control environments is essentially a multilevel problem that proceeds from detection to diagnosis and finally to compensation of faults. Detection proceeds by recognizing that a state exists that is not normal (Vicente, 1999) and consequently diagnosing the nature of fault proceeds by mapping existing symptoms depicted by the system to an existing mental model (Rouse, 1983; Rasmussen, 1980). Like more general models of naturalistic and dynamic decision making, research on fault detection and diagnosis has emphasized the role of situation assessment, based on experience, in determining the nature of a fault.

For example, Rasmussen and Jensen (1974) and Rasmussen, Pejtersen, and Goodstein (1994) point out that pattern recognition can play an important role in the diagnosis process. To diagnose faults, operators may rely one of several symptomatic search strategies based on the observation of symptoms exhibited by the system. Rasmussen et al. describe three different symptomatic search strategies: pattern recognition, decision table, and hypothesis testing. Pattern recognition is essentially a data-driven strategy and proceeds by a parallel recognition of the pattern of symptoms generated by a fault. The decision table strategy is a rule-based strategy and relies on serial comparison of the pattern of symptoms to those known to match a particular fault. In both cases, the process of fault diagnosis relies on the recognition of the system state.

Other pattern recognition models (Greenstein & Rouse, 1982) are based on production system models, which view human behavior in terms of how situations or patterns of events evoke actions.

For instance, Knaeuper and Rouse (1985) presented a rule-based model of human problem solving in which human behavior controlling a dynamic process was represented by a set of rules. Fault detection and diagnosis behavior was modeled by rules, including those representing the mapping of observed states to known fault categories. Hunt and Rouse (1984) developed a fuzzy rule-based model to describe fault diagnosis in a simulated process control task. Rules in the model included those consistent with the symptomatic search strategies identified (Rasmussen et al., 1994; Rasmussen & Jensen, 1974), in which patterns of symptoms were mapped directly to failure modes. Results of their study showed that the fit of the model to participant data during diagnosis of a more familiar system was degraded when the symptomatic rules (as opposed to other rule types included in the model) were removed, indicating the primacy of such strategies in diagnosing faults.

If in fact judgments of situation state play a critical role in dynamic decision making in general, and fault diagnosis in particular, then an important aspect of modeling these processes includes modeling the state recognition process. Whereas other theories, including the recognition primed decision model (Klein, 1993), include descriptions of the state recognition process, these descriptions do not provide a direct means for measuring aspects of state recognition behavior. Such measurements may be valuable, for instance, in determining interventions for aiding diagnosis performance.

The Lens Model: A Candidate for Modeling Judgments of State Recognition

A candidate model for use in representing judgments of the system state is the lens model (Brunswik, 1955; Cooksey, 1996). Because the lens model can be used to describe judgments, including those of the system state, and provides a means to quantify aspects of judgment performance, it has potential value in modeling the components of dynamic decision making, including fault diagnosis, that involve recognition of the situation.

Although there has been extensive application of the univariate lens model, which relates single judgments to a single environmental criterion, many judgments of interest are multivariate or categorical in nature. For instance, one may want to

determine how a situation rates on each of several variables or judge which of several situations are occurring. This would be the case, for example, in fault diagnosis, when it is necessary to determine which of many possible faults has occurred. To address such situations, including complex judgment-task ecologies that had multiple criteria over which the judgments have to be made, a multivariate extension of the lens model, relying on canonical correlation techniques, was developed (Castellan, 1972; Cooksey & Freebody, 1985).

Moray (1980) provides a description of the characteristics of fault diagnosis, which include the fact that there are multiple sources of information (values of state variables); that values of variables in different parts of the system are often highly correlated, so that knowledge of one provides information about the values of others; and that information regarding one state variable is often not sufficient to support fault diagnosis. This description is consistent with the use of the lens model to describe fault diagnosis, because the model explicitly includes available cues, which may be correlated.

Additionally, the multivariate lens model, and the lens model in general, is used to describe performance of judges at an individual level, rather than modeling performance of group characteristics. Thus, individual models may reflect the fact that different judges may rely on different cues, or patterns of symptoms, in diagnosing faults, due to the fact that cue values are correlated. Researchers have noted individual differences in fault diagnosis (Christoffersen, Hunter, & Vicente, 1997), and Sheridan (1980) has suggested that because it is difficult to eliminate individual differences in fault diagnosis performance, detection and diagnosis aids should account for them. Thus, a focus on such idiographic, or individual modeling may be valuable in modeling an individual's fault diagnosis performance to better understand how to provide training or displays to aid individuals.

In contrast to the univariate lens model that compares judgments of a single criterion value to the true criterion value, the multivariate lens model, shown in Figure 6.1, allows simultaneous analysis of judgments of multiple criteria. In this figure, Y_{ei} represent the multiple judgment criteria, Y_{si} represent the multiple judgments, and x_i represents the cue values. V_e and V_s represent canonical variates stemming from the weighting and combination of the environmental criteria and judgments, respectively.

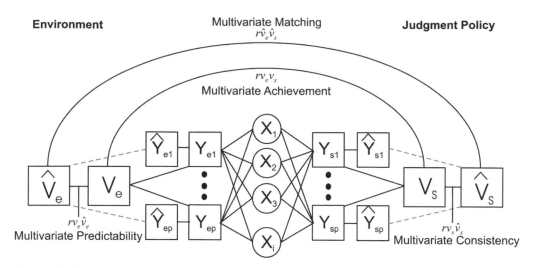

Figure 6.1. Depiction of the multivariate lens model, showing multiple judgments ($Y_{S1} \ldots Y_{Sp}$) of multiple criteria ($Y_{E1} \ldots Y_{Ep}$), and illustrating the parameters used to assess judgment performance.

For example, Cooksey and Freebody (1985) applied the multivariate approach to a social judgment domain for analyzing teacher's predictions of multiple aspects of children's reading achievement. The multivariate lens model can also be directly applied to the analysis of categorical (rather than ordinal or interval) judgments where there are multiple possible categories. Like the univariate case, parameters reflecting multivariate achievement (the correspondence between the multivariate criteria, and judgments; indicated on Figure 6.1 as r_{VeVs}); predictability of the criteria based on the cue values (indicated by $r_{Ve\hat{v}e}$), consistency of judgments made (indicated by $r_{Vs\hat{v}s}$), and the match between judgment policies and the environmental structure (indicated by $r_{Ve\hat{v}s}$) can be computed. The computations are based on canonical correlation procedures rather than multiple regression as in the univariate case (for details on these procedures, see Castellen, 1972; Cooksey, 1996). Canonical correlation is a technique to analyze the relationship between two sets of variables. The technique is similar to multiple regression in which the value of the dependent variable is predicted based on a number of independent variables. However in the case of canonical correlation there exists a set of dependent variables as well as a set of independent variables. The multivariate lens model parameters, derived from the canonical correlation procedures, are analogous to those in univariate case and yield an measurement of overall performance across the

multiple categories. The multivariate lens model equation is depicted below:

$$rv_evs = rv_e\hat{v}_e * rv_s\hat{v}_s * r\hat{v}_e\hat{v}_s + ru_eu_s * rv_ev_s * rv_su_s$$

In this case $rv_e\hat{v}_e * rv_s\hat{v}_s * r\hat{v}_e\hat{v}_s$ (ecological predictability * judgment consistency * linear matching) constitutes the multivariate linear component of the equation and is analogous to the term in the univariate lens model equation in which knowledge, ecological predictability, and consistency are combined.. The multivariate ecological predictability, $rv_e\hat{v}_e$, in this case is a measure of overall strength of association between the values predicted by the canonical estimation and the observed values over the p criteria. A similar explanation holds for the rest of the lens model parameters obtained by multivariate technique. The term $r_{UeUs} * r_{VeUe} * r_{VsUs}$ represents the residual component of the lens model equation, and r_{UeUs} is analogous to C (nonlinear matching) as defined in univariate case.

Study Goals

Although the univariate lens model has been applied in numerous contexts (see Cooksey, 1996) such as medical decision making and social policy judgments, the multivariate lens model has few demonstrated applications (see Cooksey & Freebody, 1985, for an example in a social judgment domain), and none known for a dynamic situation, such as fault diagnosis in process control. The motivation of the present study was to investigate the effectiveness and applicability of the multivariate lens model for describing human judgment in a complex, dynamic task—fault diagnosis in process control—and to investigate the sensitivity of this modeling technique in capturing variations in performance across participants. The remainder of the chapter describes the process by which this modeling technique was applied to describe both simulated fault diagnosis data and data collected in an experimental setting. As is described in the final sections of the chapter, results of such modeling could be used to evaluate the effectiveness of displays and, through an assessment of operator performance, provide information regarding training needs. Further details regarding this study can be found in Jha (2001).

Judgment Environment

Process Control Environment

The approach taken for this research was to first conduct a sensitivity analysis to determine model responses to simulated fault diagnosis data and subsequently collect and model experimental data. DURESS (Dual Reservoir System Simulator) II (Vicente, 1999), a real-time interactive simulator of thermohydraulic process control was used in this study. The DURESS-II simulator consists of two redundant feed water streams (FWS), which include pumps, pipes, valves, reservoirs, and heaters and can be configured to supply water at a particular rate and temperature. The simulation provides two choices of graphical user interfaces to display the state of the dynamic processes and to support control over system components. The Physical (P) interface is similar to a typical industrial display, showing settings and values associated with the system components (e.g., valve settings, heater settings), whereas the Physical and Functional (P+F) interface is an enhanced graphical display that provides higher-level functional information based on an analysis of system goals and operating constraints. DURESS-II and earlier simulation versions have been used in a substantial body of research (Bisantz & Vicente, 1994; Vicente, 1999; Vicente & Rasmussen, 1992). It can be configured to produce a number of faults and thus provides a test-bed for the analysis of fault diagnosis performance (Christoffersen, Hunter, & Vicente, 1996, 1997).

Fault Trial Development

To conduct the experiment and sensitivity analyses, 24 fault situations were created, which varied based on the component which was faulty (e.g., a pump, valve, reservoir, or heater) and the direction of the fault in terms of a negative or positive offset from steady state. Faults were categorized both in terms of the specific component that was faulty, as well as whether the component was related primarily to water transport (e.g., a pump) or energy flow (e.g., a heater). Twenty-four configuration sets specifying initial reservoir volumes, mass demand levels, and temperature demands were randomly assigned to each trial. Trials started with the DURESS system at steady state, which was computed based on the configuration set assigned to the trial and indicated that the system is in energy and mass balance. The 24 fault situations were created at four percentage levels. For "low extent" faults, the percentage of failure was either 15% or 20%, and for "high extent" faults the percentage of failure was either 25% or 30% (yielding 48 total fault trials in both the low and high extent conditions). Fault extents overall were selected at these relatively low levels to maintain a challenging fault diagnosis task. Within each trial, failures occurred randomly at 1 of 24 possible times between 30 seconds and 4 minutes, 30 seconds after the start of the scenario.

Judgment Modeling

Both simulated (for the sensitivity analysis) and experimental fault diagnosis data were modeled as follows. Judgments about the fault type were formalized as cue-criterion judgments, in which participants made judgments about the value of the criteria (the fault) based on the value of cues in the environment and were modeled using the multivariate lens model. Input to the models included, for each trial, the cue values at the time that the fault diagnosis was made and an indication of the actual nature of the fault, and the fault judgment that was made.

Cue Selection

Cues used for modeling were dependent on the information that was available visually on the interface and included features such as values of valve settings, flow meters, heater settings, reservoir levels, and parameters (such as angle size) describing graphical elements specific to the interface. There were 4 cues identified for the P interface, and 20 for the P+F interface. In each trial, a fault occurred in only one of the two symmetric feed water streams, so we incorporated cues only for the part of the system in which the fault occurred (for example, if the fault occurred in the upper feed water stream, only variables that were related to the upper stream changed, and only they were incorporated as cues for modeling). For each trial, cue values were automatically recorded at the time that the fault judgment was made.

Fault and Judgment Representation

Faults were categorized as one of nine types: pump fault, primary valve fault, secondary valve fault, output valve fault, leak in reservoir, extra source of water into the reservoir, an unexpected rise in the inlet water temperature, a hidden heat source, and heater malfunction. Eight dummy coded criteria and judgment variables were created to code these categorical criteria and judgments.

Sensitivity Analyses

Prior to collecting and analyzing the experimental data, we conducted a simulated test to explore the sensitivity of the multivariate lens model parameters to overall differences in fault diagnosis performance. Three sets of simulated fault trial data were created using the 48 fault trials at the low level of fault extent. For each trial, a diagnosis was simulated one minute into the trial. At this point, cue values were recorded. For purposes of this sensitivity analysis, the P+F interface and associated cues were used. A simulated judgment was created which corresponded either to a correct judgment or to a randomly selected incorrect judgment (i.e., a component that was not faulty was randomly selected to be identified as faulty). The percent of incorrect diagnoses was set at 25%, 50%, or 75% percent incorrect across the three fault sets.

Multivariate lens models were created for each of the three simulated data sets. Multivariate lens model parameters (as seen in Figure 6.1 and described previously) are shown in Table 6.1.

The parameters in Table 6.1 show the sensitivity of the multivariate lens model in capturing the

differences in judgment performance. The values of achievement are reflective of the performance in each of the conditions. In particular, poor performance in the condition where only 25% of the judgments were coded correctly is indicated by the low achievement of 0.69 as compared to 0.94 in the condition where 75% of the judgments were correct. The value of Rs for the 25% condition was 0.73, indicating that poor performance is in part due to a failure to make judgments consistently. The lower value for G reflects a lesser degree of policy matching between the model linking judgments to available cues and the model linking true fault categories to those same cues.

As reflected by the multivariate estimate of ecological predictability (Re), the ecology system was not perfectly predictable from the cue set. This indicates that the task was uncertain—that is, faults could not be diagnosed perfectly based on the available environmental cues. Although the environment for each trial was the same across the three data sets, it should be noted that there are slight differences in Re, due to the nature of the canonical correlations procedures used for the multivariate parameter estimation (Cooksey et al., 1986).

Experimental Results

Data Collection

Sixteen participants performed the fault diagnosis task using DURESS-II in one of four conditions. They watched the simulation display, indicated when a fault occurred, and identified the nature of the fault. Both interface (P or P+F) and fault extent (low or high percentage change in variable value) were manipulated. All participants were university graduate students with a background in chemical or mechanical engineering. Thus, participants, though novices with the particular experimental task, had some expertise in the task domain. After training (which involved instructions, a short written test about the system, trials in which faults were identified, and trials in which the participant could control the system) each participant performed 48 trials in blocks of 12, across 4 days.

Because the focus of this chapter is on the application of the multivariate lens model, the results described next focus primarily on issues surrounding the modeling, rather than performance on

Table 6.1. Multivariate lens model parameters computed for the sensitivity analysis. Multivariate as well as univariate labels for the parameters are indicated for clarity

Condition	Achievement $rv_e v_s$ (r_a)	Ecological Predictability $rv_e \hat{v}_e$ (RE)	Policy Consistency $rv_s \hat{v}_s$ (R_S)	Policy Matching $r\hat{v}_e \hat{v}_s$ (G)	Residual Matching C	Linear Component	Residual Component
75% correct	0.94	0.87	0.86	0.96	0.88	0.72	0.21
50% correct	0.85	0.80	0.75	0.89	0.79	0.54	0.30
25% correct	0.69	0.89	0.73	0.83	0.48	0.54	0.14

the fault diagnosis task itself. Other researchers (Christoffersen, Hunter, & Vicente, 1997) have provided detailed results regarding fault diagnosis performance in this experimental setting.

Diagnosis Performance

A two-way analysis of variance (ANOVA) was performed to investigate the impacts of interface type and fault extent on the percentage of correct fault diagnoses. There was a significant effect of interface ($F_{1, 12} = 39.11$, $p <= 0.000$), and a significant interface by fault extent interaction ($F_{1, 12} = 4.87$, $p = 0.048$), but no main effect of fault extent ($F_{1,12} = 1.82$, $p = 0.202$). Diagnosis in the P condition was slightly greater than 40%, whereas in the P+F condition, diagnosis performance was close to 65% in the high extent condition and near 80% in the low extent condition.

Lens Model Analysis

Table 6.2 summarizes the lens model parameters (corresponding to those labeled on Figure 6.1) obtained for participants in the experimental conditions. Because there were few differences among participants in the different fault extent conditions, likely due to the small differences in fault extent across these conditions, our comparisons focused on differences between the display conditions.

In contrast to the results from the sensitivity analysis, it can be seen that the values of achievement (the index which measures overall performance, across all of the fault categories) indicate values that are not reflective of performance as measured by the percent correct, as seen in Table 6.2.

Results from the experiment (refer to Table 6.2) show that the ecological predictability (R_e) varied as expected. A high value of R_e was expected for the

Table 6.2. Multivariate lens model parameters computed based on experimental data. Results in bold are example good and poor performers for each interface, determined based on the percentage correct of correct diagnoses (rightmost column)

Participant	Interface	Fault	ra	Re	Rs	G	C	Linear	Residual	% Correct
1	P+F	Low	0.96	0.81	0.79	0.97	0.94	0.62	0.34	67
2	P+F	Low	0.99	0.82	0.82	1.00	0.97	0.67	0.32	75.5
3	P+F	Low	0.98	0.84	0.85	0.98	0.98	0.70	0.28	64
4	P+F	Low	0.98	0.96	0.95	0.99	0.83	0.90	0.08	78
5	P+F	High	1.00	1.00	1.00	1.00	1.00	1.00	0.00	71
6	P+F	High	0.98	0.89	0.87	0.99	0.94	0.76	0.21	62
7	P+F	High	0.94	0.86	0.81	0.96	0.91	0.67	0.28	62
8	**P+F**	**High**	**0.99**	**0.92**	**0.91**	**0.91**	**0.95**	**0.83**	**0.15**	**58**
9	P	Low	0.98	0.30	0.29	0.97	0.98	0.08	0.90	43
10	P	Low	**0.93**	**0.41**	**0.39**	**0.98**	**0.92**	**0.15**	**0.77**	**59**
11	P	Low	**0.95**	**0.20**	**0.45**	**−0.10**	**1.00**	**−0.01**	**0.96**	**38**
12	P	Low	0.94	0.14	0.14	0.74	0.94	0.01	0.92	38
13	P	High	0.96	0.22	0.21	0.98	0.96	0.04	0.91	37.5
14	P	High	0.91	0.47	0.39	0.99	0.89	0.18	0.72	41
15	P	High	0.94	0.22	0.28	0.99	0.94	0.06	0.88	46
16	P	High	0.96	0.31	0.32	0.98	0.96	0.10	0.87	48.9

P+F interface as it has significantly greater number of cues to predict the ecology. The P+F interface provided 20 cues for the purpose of fault diagnosis and could be better represented with a linear model than the P interface, which provided only 4 cues for the purpose of diagnosis and could not be adequately modeled with a linear model. The decomposition of achievement into linear and residual component indicates that high achievement in the case of P interface was essentially due to the residual component. This indicates that participants could well use the nonlinear relationship of the environment at least for one of the fault type.

As with the sensitivity analysis, R_e varied somewhat from participant to participant, in this case both because of the canonical correlation procedures and the fact that participants could make their detection diagnosis at different points in time, resulting in different cue values. Variations in R_e due to the dynamic nature of the environment have been noted in a previous study that applied univariate lens models to judgments in a dynamic environment (Bisantz et al., 2000).

Additionally, a high value of policy matching (G) for participants in the P+F condition can be seen in Table 6.2, reflecting the fact that participants adapted well to the environment. Likewise, high values for C indicated that residuals from the participant models were similar to those of the environment models, indicating that participants were adapted to any nonlinear components as well. It should be noted that Participant 11 (P interface and low fault extent group) had the worst performance as measured by percent accuracy in fault diagnosis. His poor performance can be explained by the negative value of G obtained for this participant, indicating that he did not have sufficient knowledge about the environment.

However, comparison of achievement values with percent correct indicates that the overall best performer (Participant 2, low extent, P+F condition) had 75.5% correct fault diagnoses and had an Ra value of 0.99. Participant 5, who had maximal values for the lens model parameters derived from the canonical analysis, had less than perfect accuracy. The overall worst performer (Participant 11) was successful in identifying only 38% of faults but had a lens model achievement parameter of 0.95. Thus, it appears that the lens model parameter derived from the canonical correlation analysis, which is intended to reflect overall judgment achievement,

was not sensitive to differences in diagnosis performance. This result is unexpected, particularly given the results of the sensitivity analysis.

Further Analysis

To further understand these results, more detailed analyses of the output of the canonical correlation procedures used in generating the lens model parameters, for both the sensitivity analysis and experimental analysis, were conducted. For brevity, a description of these analyses for the experimental results will focus on representative good and poor performers with the P+F interface.

To understand the apparent discrepancy in results, it is necessary to consider the canonical correlation techniques used to create the multivariate lens models. As noted, canonical correlation is a technique to analyze the relationship between two sets of variables. Canonical correlation measures the strengths of relationships between subsets of variables within these two sets of interest. In this case, the two sets of interest were judgments and actual faults. The process of canonical correlation identifies canonical variate pairs (paired subsets of judgments and actual faults) in a way that maximizes the linear relationship between the subsets in the pairs. The strength of these linear relationships is measured by the canonical correlation associated with each canonical variate pair. The number of pairs, or roots, obtained by this process equals the number of variables in one of the sets (or the number of variables in the smaller set, if the sets are unequal). In this case, eight such roots were identified because there were eight coded judgment and environment variables. These roots are arranged in descending order so that the first root represents the variables that have maximum linear relationship. For a detailed discussion on the topic of canonical correlation, readers are advised to refer to Tabachnick and Fidell (2001) or Monge and Cappella (1980).

For the purpose of computing the lens model parameters, only the correlation related to the first root (the maximum correlation) is used. In the study here, this single root describes performance on only a subset of fault categories and does not incorporate performance across all of the ecological criteria. Thus, it is possible that all of the participants could successfully diagnose at least one of the types of faults and make consistent identifications of that fault across the trials.

To illustrate, consider the following example. Suppose when the ecological criterion is a primary valve fault, a participant consistently judged the fault to be primary or secondary valve fault. This behavior would produce at least one canonical variate pair (linking the primary valve on the environment side to the primary valve and secondary valve on the judgment side) with a high canonical correlation. However, overall multivariate achievement, which is based on the highest canonical correlation, could be reflective only of this behavior and not on any other fault diagnosis performance. Thus, even poorly performing participants in the experiment may have been diagnosing some faults in a consistent manner. In contrast, the errors introduced into the simulated performance data in the sensitivity analysis were random. Thus, no strong relationships between judged faults and actual faults would be expected in the condition where only 25% of the faults were diagnosed correctly.

Further inspection of the details of the canonical correlation outputs for each of the participants confirms this interpretation of the results. Figure 6.2 shows the canonical correlations associated with each canonical variate pair, for a good and poor performer using the P+F interface (participants in bold from Table 6.2). The canonical correlations associated with each canonical variate are ordered in descending order. As seen in Figure 6.2, both the good and poor performers had at least one highly

significant root, with similar values for the canonical correlation. Looking across all of the roots, however, it is apparent that the better performer had larger canonical correlations across all of the roots, compared to the poorer performer. One interpretation of these results is that better participants could establish stronger relationships between the variables for more type of faults.

In contrast, inspection of Figure 6.3 showing canonical correlations for the sensitivity analysis data sets shows that as the simulated data sets contained more errors, the values of the maximum canonical correlations (corresponding to the first root) became smaller. These changes were reflected in the changing values for the achievement parameter. Also, as performance decreased with the simulated data sets, fewer roots had significant correlation values.

More detailed inspection of the matrices of canonical loadings associated with participant performance and the sensitivity data sets provides additional insights into the differences in model results across the two cases. Canonical loadings can be used to interpret the patterns of judgments made by the participant in response to different faults. In addition to canonical correlations, matrices of canonical loadings are produced that indicate the weight associated with each variable in a particular canonical variate pair. Canonical loadings that have a positive or negative value higher than 0.3 are typically considered strong enough to be of interest (refer to Tabachnick & Fidell, 2001). Table 6.3

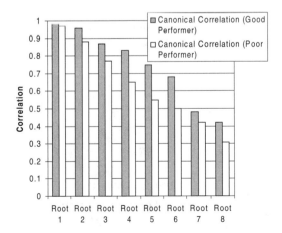

Figure 6.2. Canonical correlations for an example good and poor performer. All correlations except the last (root 8) value for the poor performer were significant at the $p = 0.05$ level.

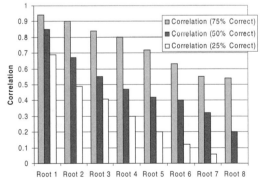

Figure 6.3. Canonical correlations for the three conditions investigated for the sensitivity analysis. All correlations for the 75% correct condition were significant ($p \leq 0.00$); the first two correlations for the 50% correct condition were significant ($p = 0.05$); and no correlations for the 25% correct condition were significant ($p > 0.9$ for all).

Table 6.3. Canonical loading of roots for participant 8 in P + F interface.
Boldface numbers indicate loadings greater than 0.3

Criteria	Fault category	Canonical Variate Pair							
		Root 1	Root 2	Root 3	Root 4	Root 5	Root 6	Root 7	Root 8
Environment	Inlet water	**−0.497**	−0.300	**0.570**	**−0.540**	0.204	0.061	−0.001	0.025
	Primary valve	**0.386**	**−0.323**	0.071	0.137	0.209	0.244	**−0.787**	−0.100
	Secondary valve	**0.582**	**−0.442**	0.059	−0.158	0.046	0.022	**0.672**	0.010
	Reservoir leak	0.196	0.076	−0.158	**−0.362**	**−0.601**	**−0.613**	−0.249	−0.013
	Reservoir extra water	**−0.322**	−0.087	**−0.306**	0.290	0.071	−0.139	−0.021	**0.828**
	Heater	**−0.492**	−0.233	−0.156	**0.429**	**−0.459**	0.237	0.014	**−0.478**
	Hidden Heat	−0.117	0.173	**−0.480**	−0.041	**0.653**	**−0.356**	0.002	**−0.414**
	Outlet valve	0.081	**0.587**	−0.180	**−0.396**	−0.084	**0.659**	0.074	0.114
Judgment	Inlet water	**−0.446**	−0.275	**0.577**	**−0.571**	0.239	−0.079	−0.002	0.052
	Primary valve	**0.565**	**−0.461**	0.092	0.17	0.234	0.248	**−0.561**	−0.006
	Secondary valve	**0.371**	−0.288	0.043	0.065	0.038	−0.020	**0.878**	0.015
	Reservoir leak	0.242	−0.013	−0.125	**−0.308**	**−0.588**	**−0.675**	−0.168	−0.019
	Reservoir extra water	−0.158	−0.044	−0.169	0.168	0.046	−0.098	−0.021	**0.951**
	Heater	**−0.616**	−0.285	−0.173	**0.456**	**−0.440**	0.207	0.008	−0.256
	Hidden heat	−0.171	0.112	**−0.500**	0.050	**0.673**	**−0.440**	−0.007	−0.244
	Outlet valve	0.083	**0.563**	**−0.301**	**−0.486**	−0.083	**0.580**	0.045	0.060

shows the canonical loadings associated with the canonical variate pairs for a good participant in the P+F interface condition. Canonical loadings can be used to interpret the patterns of judgments made by the participant in response to different faults. Figure 6.4 illustrates the canonical loadings and subsequent relationships between faults and judgments found from the first canonical variate pair (the numeric loadings in Figure 6.4 correspond to those found in Table 6.3.) As seen in Figure 6.4, the first pair consists of six variables on the environment side and four variables on the judgment side.

Variables on the environment side of the pair show high negative loadings on inlet water, reservoir extra water, heater and hidden heat, and high positive loadings on the primary valve and secondary valve. On the judgment side, the inlet water and heater have high negative loadings, whereas the primary valve and secondary valve have high positive loadings. This situation indicates that when the ecological criterion was the primary valve or the secondary valve, the participants judged it as primary or secondary valve. Similarly, faults of inlet water temperature, reservoir (extra water) and heater (all faults which can affect the energy balance of the system) tended to be judged as faults with the inlet water temperature or the heater. Simi-

lar analyses can be performed by inspecting patterns of loadings for the other canonical variate pairs shown in Table 6.3. For example, for the second pair it can be seen that on the ecological side the only variable having a significantly high positive weight is output valve. A high weight on the same variable can be seen on the judgment side, indicating that when the criteria had an output valve as a failure, the judgment was likely to be the output valve. Similar to the first root, there was a relationship between primary and secondary valve faults and judgments of primary valve. Other relationships that can be observed in the canonical loadings include those of inlet fault and inlet judgment

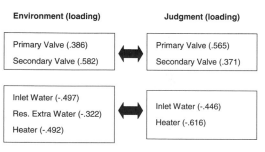

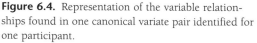

Figure 6.4. Representation of the variable relationships found in one canonical variate pair identified for one participant.

(root 3), reservoir leak and heater or hidden heat fault and judgments of the same (roots 5 and 6), and an extra water source or source of hidden heat and judgment of an extra source (root 8).

Inspection of patterns of judgments and faults provides confirmation of these analyses. Table 6.4 shows the correspondence between actual faults (across the columns) and judgments made (down the rows) for the same participant, across all trials. Cell entries indicate the number of trials resulting in the fault–judgment pair that define the cell. Perfect judgment performance would be indicated by entries only along the diagonal. Judgment errors made included identifying some secondary valve failures as primary valve failures (as captured in root 1, shown in Table 6.3) and extra water sources as hidden heat sources (root 8, shown in Table 6.3). (These errors are highlighted in bold in the Table 6.4).

Further exploration of the results of the multivariate lens model analysis can provide additional insight into the judgments of each fault category individually. Intermediate computational products in the multivariate analysis procedures can be used to provide lens model parameters associated with each of the judgment or fault categories (see Cooksey, 1996, for details). Table 6.5 shows the results of one such analysis, the univariate lens model parameters associated with diagnosis of the inlet water temperature fault for all 16 participants.

In contrast to the parameters shown in Table 6.2, inspection of the parameter Ra in Table 6.5 does indicate variability across participants. This variability was reflective of differences in performance diagnosing this fault. For instance, participants with

relatively high levels of Ra (participants 1, 2, and 4) had diagnosis performance of 80% on this fault, whereas participants with relatively low levels of Ra (participants 5 and 13) had diagnosis performance of 20% on this fault. Inspection of additional parameters reveals other information about performance on this fault category. For instance, the ecological predictability varied according to the type of interface, with the P+F interface having higher values, indicating that the faults were more linearly predictable given the information available with the P+F interface than the P interface. Additionally, there were large differences in Re for the P interface. The best performer for that interface also had the largest value for ecological predictability, indicating that this participant made diagnosis decisions when the environment was more predictable. Additionally, in cases where the values of G were small, the corresponding achievement values were also small, indicating poor matching between participants judgment policies and the nature of the cue-criterion relationships in the environment may have led to poor performance diagnosing this fault.

Discussion and Conclusions

In summary, a multivariate lens model analysis was performed on simulated and actual fault diagnosis data in a dynamic, process control task. Sensitivity analysis results of the multivariate lens model parameters indicated that model parameters were sensitive to simulated performance differences. However, this result was not supported by analysis of the experi-

Table 6.4. Fault judgments compared to actual faults for a participant 8 in P + F interface. The number in each cell corresponds to the number of trials where that pattern of results occurred.

Judgment	Fault Criteria								
	Inlet Water	Primary Valve	Secondary Valve	Reservoir Leak	Reservoir Extra Water	Heater	Hidden Heat	Output Valve	Pump
Inlet water	4								
Primary valve		4	**4**						
Secondary valve			4						
Reservoir leak			1	2					
Reservoir extra water					1				
Heater	1				2	6			
Hidden heat					1		3		
Output valve				1			1	8	
Pump								1	4

Table 6.5. Univariate lens model parameters associated
with the inlet water temperature fault category

Interface	Fault	Part.	Ra	Re	Rs	G	C	Linear	Residual
P+F	1	1	0.88	0.74	0.73	0.93	0.83	0.50	0.38
P+F	1	2	0.89	0.76	0.72	0.93	0.83	0.51	0.37
P+F	1	3	0.76	0.76	0.77	0.93	0.52	0.55	0.21
P+F	1	4	0.88	0.74	0.71	0.92	0.85	0.48	0.40
P+F	2	5	0.48	0.77	0.75	0.27	0.78	0.15	0.33
P+F	2	6	0.69	0.80	0.99	0.81	0.70	0.64	0.05
P+F	2	7	0.54	0.77	0.59	0.29	0.79	0.13	0.41
P+F	2	8	0.81	0.86	0.99	0.87	0.86	0.74	0.07
P	1	9	0.86	0.15	0.32	0.53	0.89	0.03	0.83
P	1	10	0.72	0.14	0.33	0.64	0.75	0.03	0.70
P	1	11	0.69	0.29	0.70	0.00	1.00	0.00	0.69
P	1	12	0.43	0.25	0.50	0.89	0.37	0.11	0.31
P	2	13	0.48	0.10	0.50	0.35	0.54	0.02	0.47
P	2	14	0.86	0.56	0.32	0.99	0.86	0.18	0.68
P	2	15	0.84	0.31	0.33	0.97	0.87	0.10	0.79
P	2	16	0.84	0.25	0.12	0.36	0.91	0.01	0.87

mental results. This result appeared to be due to the nature of the canonical correlation procedure. Further inspection of the canonical outputs showed that better performing participants had more sets of more strongly related variables than poorer performing participants. Inspection of matrices of canonical weights allowed an interpretation of diagnosis performance in terms of which judgment categories were associated with which actual fault categories. These interpretations were consistent with the patterns of judgments and faults. In contrast, the data sets created for the sensitivity analysis exhibited random patterns of errors and (for the poorest performing case) no strong judgment–fault pairing. Thus, for poorer performing simulated data, there were no strong associations and no significant roots. Further inspection of outputs of canonical correlation procedures allowed identification of these systematic strategies.

However, as noted by Cooksey et al. (1986) the multivariate lens model parameters provide a general depiction of performance. Subsequent analysis can be performed to extract univariate lens model parameters from the multivariate analysis, allowing descriptions of performance on each criterion. As illustrated by the inlet water temperature fault, although there are concerns regarding sensitivity of overall multivariate parameters, the univariate parameters are sensitive to performance on individual faults and can provide information about participant performance on a fault-by-fault basis. The combination of the application of a multivariate analysis with the subsequent extraction of the univariate models is valuable because it allows computation of these models through a single set of analyses and based on a smaller number of faults in each category than would be used to construct models of each fault type individually. Thus the study demonstrated the potential applicability of the multivariate lens model to a reasonably complex, dynamic environment. Because of the fact that the models represent individual performance, applications of these techniques may provide information relevant to the design of individualized training programs.

Modeling Limitations and Further Research

As one of the few studies that have attempted to apply the multivariate lens model, and the only example we could find of its application in a complex and dynamic experimental environment, some features of the work were necessarily exploratory and illuminated some limitations of the research and opportunities for future work, stemming from the modeling approach and computation framework, as well as the particular study reported here.

First, the theoretical foundation of the lens model focuses on describing the relationship between people and the environment in which they make judgments (Cooksey, 1996) and as such is less of a model of the particular cognitive processes by which humans produce judgments. Instead, the lens model postulates that a relatively simple linkage between environmental cues and judgment outcomes is sufficient to describe judgment performance. Other research regarding human performance has indicated that models directly linking functional-level descriptions of the environment to selection of action are sufficient to explain performance in a complex dynamic environment. For instance, Kirlik, Miller, and Jagacinski (1993) showed that a model that selected actions based on the opportunities for action, or affordances, provided by different environmental conditions was sufficient to predict performance in a multivehicle supervisory control task.

Additionally, the computational frameworks that have been instantiated for univariate as well as multivariate lens model focus on modeling and decomposing linear components of the environmental structure and judgment processes and therefore may be less successful capturing performance situations with significant nonlinear relationships. However, past research has indicated that linear models can be successful in capturing human judgment behavior, even when there is evidence that more complex, nonlinear strategies are being used. For example, Goldberg (1968) described how linear models reliably predicted clinical judgments such as psychological diagnoses, even when judges reported using more complex, nonlinear strategies. He concluded that linear models were powerful enough to reproduce most judgments. Dawes (1979) described how even nonoptimal linear models (e.g., with nonoptimal weights) can successfully predict judgments. Additionally, Einhorn, Kleinmuntz, and Kleinmuntz (1979) showed how linear models could successfully replicate seemingly more cognitively representative, process tracing, or rule-based models of judgment. In the case of the multivariate models created here, there were aspects of judgment behavior and the environment that could be modeled linearly, as indicated by the fact that even the poorer performer had some significant canonical roots.

Finally, few studies have applied lens model frameworks to dynamic environments, and this is the first to do so in case of multivariate judgments. The approach taken here, as in previous studies (Bisantz et al., 2000) is to capture cue values at the point in time that the judgment was made. However, this approach does not capture information that judges may have relied on about dynamic aspects of the cue values. Some past research from a normative, control theoretic tradition investigated models for fault detection that incorporated aspects of information change over time. For instance, Gai and Curry (1976) modeled fault detection behavior as a two stage process, relying on Kalman filters and observations of state variable residual values over time. Future research regarding lens models of judgment behavior should similarly expand the use of dynamic cue information. For instance, models could incorporate multiple values for each cue, showing change over time, cue values indicating the direction of change, or derivative values indicating rates of change. A potential concern with these techniques, however, is the need to add additional cues to capture such information, which in experimental settings may lead to requirements for additional trials to create stable lens model equations.

Other limitations apply more particularly to this study. For instance, the study used relatively small sample size ($n = 8$ for each display condition), which reduces our abilities to make statistical comparisons across the display groups. However, because the lens model is idiographic in nature (that is, computes parameters for judges on an individual basis, rather than across a group of individuals), this limitation did not affect the reliability of the individual models. The number of judgments made per participant was also limited by the complexity of the scenarios, and the dynamic nature of the process being judged, both of which led to relatively lengthy judgment trial times. This limitation, however, would be a problem in similarly complex experimental settings more generally.

One difficulty that arose in modeling the experimental data was that in some cases participants' performance was perfect (i.e., they identified all the faults correctly), or alternatively, they did not identify a single fault in any given category. Under these conditions there was no variability within that particular fault category, leading to the generation of singular matrices in the analysis, which precluded further canonical analysis. To solve this problem, we created pseudo-trials as needed for fault categories in which either no judgment was made or all judgments were correct. To create the necessary variability, one of the judgments in the category was randomly coded as a different judgment. The cue values remained the same. Pseudo-trials were created for 12 out of 16 participants and averaged 1.93 per each of the 12 participants (with a mode of 2).

With increased experimental trials, or if data could be captured in real-world settings, perhaps leading to additional variability in judgments made, it may have been possible to compute the multivariate analysis without the use of pseudo-trials, which slightly affected judgment results for some participants. The subsequent analysis and evaluation of the modeling technique that was performed comparing better and worse participants, however, was internally consistent and based on the adjusted data.

Other future work involves the exploration of the use of this modeling technique for multiple faults. Other researchers (Holtzblatt, 1988; Reising, 1993) have pointed out that although nonroutine faults (simultaneous multiple faults) pose a unique modeling challenge, these situations been researched only rarely. The multivariate lens model could be applied in this regard, because it can capture simultaneous judgments of multiple criteria—in this case, the presence or absence of multiple types of faults. Similarly, this work modeled judgments of fault diagnosis, rather than judgments regarding courses of action with respect to fault recovery, which are also critical fault related judgments.

Implications for Training and Design

Prior work on the application of lens models to dynamic decision making (Bisantz et al., 2000) indicated how the computation of lens model parameter for individual judges could have implications for training. In particular, because the parameters differentiate between consistency of performance and knowledge of how environmental information indicates appropriate judgments, the analysis can provide input to the design of interventions during training that targets potential performance problems in these areas. Similar application could be made of parameters from the univariate models, generated for each fault category, which result from the multivariate analysis. For instance, there is an extensive body of research indicating that feedback (graphical and numeric) based on the lens model parameters, known as cognitive feedback, may improve judgment performance in a wide range of situations (primarily involving laboratory judgment experiments) particularly when compared to outcome feedback, in which participants are only provided with feedback regarding the correct judgment (Adelman 1981; Balzer et al., 1992, 1994; Lindell, 1976; Steinmann, 1974; and see Balzer, Doherty,

& O'Connor (1989) for an extensive review). Outputs from the analysis described here could be used to produce such feedback during training.

Additionally, it may be possible to use aspects of this analysis for the evaluation of interfaces. For instance, one could make a comparison of two interfaces regarding whether there was enough information, as measured by Re, to allow someone to make correct fault diagnoses. If not, it may point to the need for additional cues, in the form of information sources, on the display. For instance, from Table 6.5 one can make a comparison of Re values for the inlet water temperature fault across the P+F and P interfaces used in this study. The considerably lower values for the P interface indicate that the interface is less successful in providing diagnostic information. Additionally, parameters measuring judgment performance (e.g., consistency and knowledge) could be compared across interfaces to investigate the impact of different interfaces on components of performance. Thus, these models could be used to explicitly compare the degree to which interfaces allow participants to make judgments with differing levels of consistency or the degree to which the interface is providing information to allow simple identification of faults.

Acknowledgment.   The authors acknowledge the National Science Foundation under grant number IIS9984079 to the second author for their support of this work.

References

Adelman, L. (1981). The influence of formal, substantive and contextual task properties on the relative effectiveness of different forms of feedback in multiple-cue probability learning tasks. *Organization Behavior and Human Performance, 27,* 423–442.

Bainbridge, L. (1979). Verbal reports as evidence of the process operators knowledge. *International Journal of Man Machine Studies, 11,* 411–436.

Balzer, W. K., Doherty, M. E., & O'Connor, R. (1989). Effects of cognitive feedback on performance. *Psychological Bulletin, 106*(3), 410–433.

Balzer, W. K., Hammer, L. B., Sumner, K. E., Birchenough, T. R., Parham Martens, S., & Raymark, P. H. (1994). Effects of cognitive feedback components, display format, and elaboration on performance. *Organizational Behavior and Human Decision Processes, 58*, 369–85.

Balzer, W. K., Sulsky, L. M., Hammer, L. B., & Sumner, K. E. (1992). Task information, cognitive information, or functional validity information: Which components of cognitive feedback affect performance? *Organizational Behavior and Human Decision Processes, 53*, 35–54.

Bisantz, A.M., Kirlik, A., Gay, P., Phipps, D., Walker, N., & Fisk, A. (2000). Modeling and analysis of dynamic judgment task using a lens model approach. *IEEE Transaction on System, Man and Cybernetics, 30*(6), 1–12.

Bisantz, A. M., and Vicente, K. (1994). Making the abstraction hierarchy concrete. *International Journal of Human-Computer Studies, 40*, 83 – 117.

Brehmer, B. (1990). Strategies in real-time, dynamic decision-making. In R. M. Hogarth (Ed.), *Insights in decision making*. Chicago: University of Chicago.

Brehmer, B., & Allard R. (1991). Dynamic decision-making: The effects of task complexity and feedback delay. In J. Rasmussen, B Brehmer, & J. Leplat, (Eds.), *Distributed decision-making: Cognitive models for cooperative work* (pp. 319–334). New York: Wiley.

Brunswik, E. (1955). Representative design and probabilistic theory in a functional psychology. *Psychological Review, 62*, 193 – 217.

Cannon-Bowers, J. A., Salas, E., & Pruitt, J. S. (1996). Establishing the boundaries of a paradigm for decision-making research. *Human Factors, 38*(2), 193–205.

Castellan, N. J. (1972). The analysis of multiple criteria in multiple-cue judgment tasks. *Organizational Behavior and Human Performance, 8*, 242–261.

Christoffersen, K., Hunter, C. N., & Vicente, K. J. (1996). A longitudinal study of the effects of ecological interface design on skill acquisition. *Human Factors, 38*, 3, 523–541.

Christoffersen, K., Hunter, C. N., & Vicente, K. J. (1997). A longitudinal study of the effects of ecological interface design on fault management performance. *International Journal of Cognitive Ergonomics, 1*(1), 1–24.

Cohen, M. S., Freeman, J. T., & Wolf, S. (1996). Metarecognition in time-stressed decision making: Recognizing, critiquing, and correcting. *Human Factors, 38*(2), 206–219.

Connolly, T. (1988). Hedge-clipping, tree-felling and the management of ambiguity: the needs for new images of decision making. In R. Louis and R.J.Pondy (Eds.), *Managing ambiguity and change* (pp. 37–50). New York: Wiley.

Cooksey, R. W. (1996). *Judgment analysis: Theory, methods and applications*. New York: Academic Press

Cooksey, R. W., & Freebody, P. (1985). Generalized multivariate lens model analysis for complex human inference tasks. *Organizational Behavior and Human Decision Processes, 35*, 46–72.

Cooksey, R. W., Freebody, P., & Davidson G. (1986). Teachers' predictions of children's early reading achievement: An application of social judgment theory. *American Educational Research Journal, 23*(1), 41–64.

Dawes, R. M. (1979). The robust beauty of improper linear models in decision making. *American Psychologist, 34*, 571–582.

Einhorn, H. J., Kleinmuntz, D. N., & Kleinmuntz, B. (1979). Linear regression and process-tracing models of judgment. *Psychological Review, 86*, 465–485.

Gai, E. G., & Curry R. E. (1976). A model of the human observer in failure detection tasks. *IEEE Transactions on Systems, Science and Cybernetics, SMC-6*, 85.

Goldberg, L. R. (1968). Simple models or simple processes? Some research on clinical judgments. *American Psychologist, 23*, 483–496.

Greenstein, J. S., & Rouse, W. B. (1982). A model of human decision making in multiple process monitoring situations. *IEEE Transactions on Systems, Science and Cybernetics, SMC-12*, 182.

Hogarth, R. M. (1981). Beyond discrete biases: functional and dysfunctional aspect of judgment heuristics. *Psychological Bulletin, 90*(2), 197–217.

Holtzblatt, L. J. (1988). Diagnosing multiple failure using knowledge of component states. *Proceedings of 4th IEEE conference on AI application*, San Diego, Calif., pp. 165–169.

Hunt, R. M., & Rouse, W. B. (1984). A fuzzy rule-based model of human problem solving. *IEEE Transactions on Systems, Science and Cybernetics, SMC 14*(1), 112–120.

Jha, P. (2001). *Modeling human performance in dynamic process control task using lens model*. Unpublished master's thesis, University at Buffalo, New York.

Kaempf, G. L., Klein, G. A., Thordsen, M. L., & Wolf, S. (1996). Decision making in complex naval command-and-control environments. *Human Factors, 38*(2), 220–231.

Kirlik, A., Miller, R. A., & Jagacinski, R. J. (1993). Supervisory control in a dynamic and uncertain environment: A process model of skilled human-environment interaction. *IEEE Transactions on Systems, Man, and Cybernetics, 23*, 929–952.

Klein, G. A. (1993). A recognition-primed decision (RPD) model of rapid decision making. In G. A. Klein, J. Orasanu, R. Calderwood, & C. E.

Zsambok (Eds.), *Decision making in action: Models and methods* (pp. 138–147). Norwood, N.J.: Ablex.

Klein, G. A., & Calderwood, R. (1991). Decision models: some lessons from the field. *IEEE Transactions on Systems, Science and Cybernetics, 21*(5), 1018–1026.

Knaeuper, A., & Rouse, W. B. (1985). A rule-based model of human problem-solving behavior in dynamic environments. *IEEE Transactions on Systems, Science and Cybernetics, SMC-15*(6), 708–719.

Lindell, M. K. (1976). Cognitive and outcome feedback in multiple-cue probability learning tasks. *Journal of Experimental Psychology: Human Learning and Memory, 2*, 739–745.

Monge, P. R., & Cappella, J.N. (1980). *Multivariate techniques in human communication research.* New York: Academic Press.

Moray, N. (1980). The role of attention in the detection of errors and the diagnosis of failure in man-machine systems. In J. Rasmussen and W. Rouse (Eds.), *Human detection and diagnosis of system failures* (pp. 185–197). New York: Plenum.

Neisser, U. (1976). *Cognition and reality.* San Francisco: Freeman, 1976.

Rasmussen, J. (1976). Outlines of hybrid model of the process plant operator. In T. B. Sheridan and G. Johannsen (Eds.), *Monitoring behavior and supervisory control* (pp. 371–383). New York: Plenum.

Rasmussen, J. (1980). Models of mental strategies in process plant diagnosis. In J. Rasmussen and W. Rouse (Eds.), *Human detection and diagnosis of system failures* (pp. 241–258). New York: Plenum.

Rasmussen, J., & Jensen A. (1974). Mental procedures in real life tasks: A case study of electronic troubleshooting. *Ergonomics, 17*(3), 293–307

Rasmussen, J., Pejtersen, A. L. and Goodstein, L. P. (1994). *Cognitive Systems Engineering.* New York, Wiley and Sons.

Reising, D. V. (1993). Diagnosing multiple simultaneous faults. In. *Proceeding of the Human Factors and Ergonomic Society 37th Annual Meeting* (pp. 524–528). Santa Monica, Calif.

Rouse, W. B. (1983). Models of human problem solving: detection, diagnosis and compensation for system failures. *Automatica, 19*(6), 613–625.

Sheridan, T. B. (1980). Computer control and human alienation. *Technology Review,* October, 61–73.

Steinmann, D. O. (1974). Transfer of lens model training. *Organizational Behavior and Human Performance, 15*, 168–179.

Tabachnick, B. G., & Fidell, L.S. (2001). *Using multivariate statistics,* 4th ed. Needham Heights, Mass.: Allyn & Bacon.

Vicente, K. J. (1999). *Cognitive work analysis: Towards safe, productive, and healthy computer-based work.* Hillsdale, N.J. : Lawrence Erlbaum.

Vicente, K. J., & Rasmussen, J. (1992). Ecological interface design: theoretical foundations. *IEEE Transactions on Systems, Science and Cybernetics, 22*(4), 589–606.

Zsambok, C. E. (1997). Naturalistic decision making: Where are we now? In C. E. Zsambok & G. Klein (Eds.), *Naturalistic decision making* (pp. 3–16). Mahwah, N.J.: Lawrence Erlbaum.

Automation and Decision Aiding

Alex Kirlik

Introduction

The introduction of technology into modern work settings is quickly moving well beyond computer interfaces to include various forms of automation geared to gain people's attention, help them make decisions, and so on. The three chapters in this section present studies addressing these issues from the perspective of the lens model, its extensions, and empirical findings on the effects of feedback on human learning and performance. In chapter 7, Pritchett and Bisantz present a study of human interaction with alerting automation in an aviation collision detection task. As was the case with the chapters in the previous section, a more sophisticated than typical version of the lens model had to be created for analysis and modeling, due to the desire to capture the relationships not only between human judgments and a task ecology but also relationships between these entities and a variety of automated alerting algorithms. Using such an n-system lens model, Pritchett and Bisantz were able to identify the information used (and, just as important, unused) by their participants in making collision detection judgments, and they examine the coherence and lack of coherence between the judgment strategies used by their human participants and those embedded within alerting automation. Their technique has potential applications beyond

aviation to include alerting systems in human–computer interaction, automobiles, health care, and the like.

In chapter 8 Seong and colleagues take the matter one step further and consider the situation in which human judgments are not only made in concert with automation but also in part on the basis of the information provided by an automated decision aid. This added layer of complexity leads them to develop a framework using both n-system lens modeling and also hierarchical lens modeling. Of particular interest to Seong and his coauthors is how feedback information (informed by hybrid n-system/hierarchical lens model analysis) might be used to influence and perhaps calibrate an appropriate level of human trust in decision aids. Factors known to influence trust, such as aid reliability and validity, were manipulated where these measures were grounded in the values of various lens model parameters. In this way they were able to determine that poor aid validity had more severe detrimental effects on human judgments than did poor aid reliability. Interestingly, however, providing participants using aids with poor reliability and/or validity with cognitive feedback (or instruction) on the manner in which the aid functioned (e.g., cue weights, etc.) allowed participants in their poor aid group to perform at the level of participants using their better aid. Because any actually fielded decision aid will always be fallible in one situation or another, these methods and findings may have important implications for future decision aid design and training for effective use.

In chapter 9, Bass and Pritchett draw on the interpersonal learning (IPL) paradigm originally developed by Hammond and colleagues to investigate conflict and possibly promote compromise or agreement among multiple human judges. Coopting this paradigm for the purposes of enhancing human interaction with judgment or alerting automation, Bass and Pritchett present a multistage training framework. A human judge is first trained on a task, then the judge is trained to make judgments in concert with automation, and in the final stage the judge is required to predict the behavior of automation. This approach was used to train participants in a conflict detection task in which both display design and task uncertainty were manipulated. Bass and Pritchett's analysis demonstrated that a lens model analysis using a sophisticated representation of this training framework was useful for precisely characterizing the strong individual differences observed in their study.

Amy R. Pritchett and Ann M. Bisantz

Measuring the Fit between Human Judgments and Alerting Systems: A Study of Collision Detection in Aviation

Introduction

Methodologies for assessing human judgment in complex domains are important for both the design of displays that inform judgment and automated systems that suggest judgments. This chapter describes a use of the n-system lens model to evaluate the impact of displays on human judgment and to explicitly assess the similarity between human judgments and a set of potential judgment algorithms for use in automated systems. Specifically, the n-system model was used to examine a previously conducted study of aircraft collision detection that had been analyzed using standard analysis of variance (ANOVA) methods. Our analysis found the same main effects as the earlier analysis. However, the lens model analysis was able to provide greater insight into the information relied on for judgments and the impact of displays on judgment. Additionally, the analysis was able to identify attributes of human judgments that were—and were not—similar to judgments produced by automated alerting systems.

Motivation

A common paradigm in human–automation interaction requires a human to make a judgment in parallel with an automated system and then to consider, accept, or reject the automated output as appropriate. Such judgments are normally made in concert with displays relaying important aspects of environmental conditions. Designing such automated systems and displays requires understanding the attributes of judgment that they are to support and the impact of their design on human judgment.

Methodologies for assessing and capturing judgments in complex, uncertain domains are therefore important for several reasons. First, these methodologies can allow us to understand the information sought by a human judge about the environment and how this information is used to form judgments. Second, this understanding can be used to drive the design of displays that inform judgment. Third, understanding the degree to which human judgments are similar to the processes and outputs of automated decision support systems is necessary for the design of displays and training such that human operators understand, trust, and appropriately rely on such automated systems.

This research details a methodology for measuring human judgment in general and the fit between human judgment and the output of alerting algorithms (a type of automated decision aid) in particular. Building on judgment analysis methods, the utility of using n-system lens modeling to directly compare the judgment correspondence between human judgments and those provided by automated systems is demonstrated. Specifically, this method can highlight the degree of agreement between human judgment and automated system judgments, thereby predicting situations where the human may disagree with and potentially not rely on an automated system. To demonstrate this methodology, we used an n-system lens model to examine results from a study previously analyzed using nomothetic methods.

Required Capabilities in a Measurement Methodology

Studies of human judgment must consider both human behavior and the ecology in which the judgments are made. For example, take the case of a pilot judging whether an aircraft on a parallel approach is deviating from its approach path to a collision course with the pilot's own aircraft. As shown schematically in Figure 7.1a, the important entities in such judgment processes involve both the environmental criterion (in this example, whether a conflict is actually developing) and the human's judgments (in this example, whether the pilot judges a conflict to be developing) and available information by which the human makes the judgment. This view of decision-making has its basis in the lens model of Brunswik (Brunswik, 1955; Cooksey, 1996; Hammond, 1996), in which humans make judgments of a *distal* (unknown or hidden) criterion, based on proximal (known) cues that are probabilistically related to the criterion. The extent to which a judgment corresponds to the environmental criterion reflects the degree of success of the decision maker. Using the lens model suggested by Figure 7.1 (top), we see that the relationship between judgment and criterion is mediated by the information available to the judge about the environment (shown here as *cues*). The human's judgment policy is defined by which cues are considered and how those cues are combined to result in a judgment. An equivalent definition can be created for the relationship between the cues and the environmental criterion. A methodology for assessing judgment, then, should be able to capture these elements of judgment strategy.

Some studies of human judgment focus primarily on the relationship between criterion, cues, and judgment; these studies can provide insight into

expert behavior, inform display design, and assess system performance. An additional requirement for a methodology is the ability to also compare observed human behavior with the judgments that may be formed in parallel by other judges such as automated systems. As viewed by the n-system lens model (shown schematically in Figure 7.1 [bottom] all of the judgment agents reference the same cues, which are then assembled by different policies; the amount of agreement between the different judgment agents provides a measure of *correspondence*.

An additional consideration in the study of judgment similarity is the need to assess the *consistency* of judgments; that is, the extent to which actual judgments are consistent with a given policy. Inconsistency can occur not only within human judgments but also in the judgments made by other systems and in the environmental criterion's relationship to cues because of environmental uncertainty. As such, comparing two judges should consider whether *judgment correspondence* is degraded by poor consistency in applying a judgment policy.

In summary, a suitable methodology for analyzing judgment in complex, uncertain domains should have the capability to:

1. capture and describe the policy of a human judge;
2. compare humans' judgments to an environmental criterion when assessments of achievement are desired;
3. compare humans' judgments to those formed by other policies, such as those implicit in automated systems, when assessments of policy similarity and actual similarity are desired; and
4. distinguish between the impact of policy similarity and consistency on achievement (relative to the environment) or similarity in judgments to those of other judgment agents.

However, common methodologies for assessing human judgment do not meet the needs of designers of automated systems. Some focus exclusively on the human judge; for example, policy capture methods can generate a model of how judgments are formed but typically contrast them neither with the ecology to measure achievement nor with other policies to measure similarity. Likewise, common experimental methods rely on nomothetic analysis across subjects to infer policy from ob-

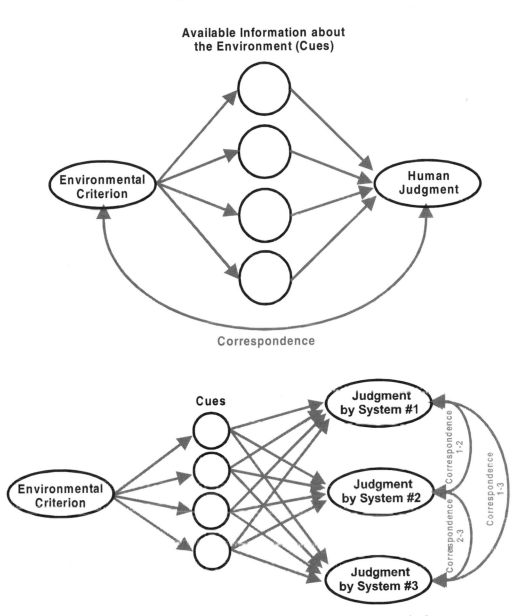

Figure 7.1. Lens model description of relationship between judgment, environment, and achievement. top: single judge; bottom: multiple judges.

served patterns of behavior. For example, a recent study of collision detection found the results summarized in Table 7.1. These results infer judgment policy from consistencies in observed behavior across conditions without constructing a more descriptive policy model. Also, the results did not allow a direct comparison of the human's policy to other policies, such as those employed by collision alerting systems (Pritchett, 2000).

Background: *n*-System Lens Model Analysis

To meet the requirements for studying judgment in complex, uncertain domains, we propose applying the *n*-system lens model.

Like the single-system lens model, the *n*-system model allows judgment performance to be understood in terms of characteristics of both judgments

Table 7.1.

In a low-fidelity flight simulator, participants were asked to monitor a cockpit traffic display during approach in case an aircraft on a parallel approach should blunder towards them. Displays, scenarios (i.e., collision trajectories) and side-task workload were varied. Conditions were recorded at the instant participants indicated the need to maneuver to avoid a collision. The condition measures included: lateral and longitudinal separation from the other aircraft, range from the other aircraft, speed of each aircraft, convergence angle, time to conflict, etc. Each condition measure was analyzed for display, scenario, workload and participant characteristics effects.

Workload effects	None
Scenario Effects	Most condition measures varied significantly between scenarios. However, lateral separation (distance of the other aircraft to the side of the participant's aircraft) was largely invariant to scenario: i.e., participants' judgments of a conflict tended to occur at the same lateral separation. Because the scenarios were dramatically different, this consistency was inferred to arise from the participants' judgment policy relying heavily on lateral separation.
Display effects	Weak display effects were found that suggest participants may have been more conservative with certain displays.
Display-scenario interactions	None, suggesting that no traffic display encouraged reactions tailored to the demands of specific scenarios.
Participant effects	No significant differences were found between pilots and nonpilots.

agents and the environment in which the judgments are being made. The use of an n-system lens model additionally enables comparisons between multiple judgment agents, such as comparisons between a human judge and the algorithms used by an automated system, as shown schematically in Figure 7.1 (bottom). Figure 7.2 shows a single-system lens model (for comparison) along with an n-system lens model, annotated with the lens model parameters. Each of the three systems shown in Figure 7.2 represents a judgment agent with its own judgment policy. If desired, any of these agents' algorithms can be compared to the environment in the same manner that the single system lens model relates judgments from a single system to the environmental criterion. Additionally, each judgment system has its own measure of consistency (R_i, where i serves as an identifier for each system). These policies can be also compared between judges through measurements of judgment correspondence (r_{ai-j}, calculated in the same manner as achievement), policy similarity (G_i, calculated in the same manner as knowledge), and unmodeled agreement (C_i, calculated in the same manner as in the single-system lens model).

Aircraft Conflict Detection during Closely Spaced Parallel Approaches

Subsequent sections of this chapter describe how the n-system lens model was used to analyze colli-

sion detection judgments that were made during a previous study on closely spaced parallel approaches (CSPA). This study has been documented previously, as noted in Table 7.1 (Pritchett, 2000); however, its results had not previously been examined using lens modeling techniques.

The task of collision detection during CSPA has unique qualities. The aircraft are closer together than during any other airborne phase of flight. Because the aircraft are "low, slow, and dirty," collision avoidance maneuvers are limited in their severity and therefore need to be initiated well before a potential collision; however, false alarms will require missed approaches of aircraft in close proximity to each other and will reduce landing capacity. In addition, unlike many en route environments, the future trajectory of the aircraft cannot be extrapolated by a simple straight flight path. Instead, collision trajectories are more likely to occur when aircraft are continuously maneuvering (Pritchett, 1999).

In this task, a judgment is a binary value that switches from "not alerted" to "alerted" at the point of detection. Several alerting algorithms may be used by automatic conflict detection systems, including:

- *Approach Nonconformance (ANC):* This alerting algorithm switches should the other aircraft depart its approach, mimicking an automated system capable of monitoring for conformance to an assigned flight path. This algorithm is very conservative (i.e., has a high

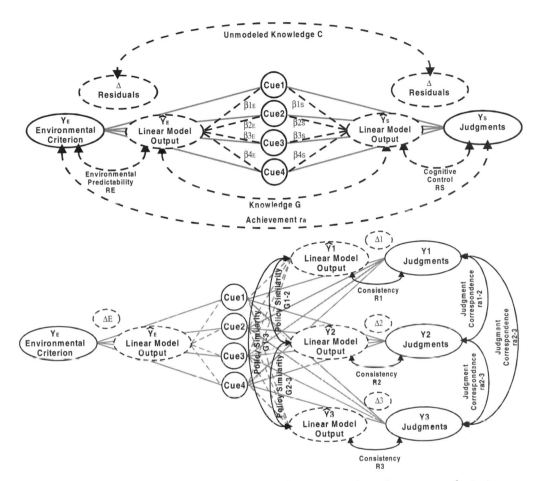

Figure 7.2. Lens model parameters. Top: Parameters within a single judge and environmental criterion; bottom: parameters between multiple judges.

probability of correct detection with a reasonable threshold). It is also very prone to false alarms when the departure of the other aircraft from its approach path will not cause a collision.

- *Nontransgression Zone (NTZ):* This alerting algorithm triggers if the other aircraft enters into an NTZ located at a lateral separation of 1,350 feet to the left or right of the participants' aircraft. Similar algorithms have been proposed for parallel approaches (e.g., Wong, 1993); in addition, the original analysis of this study's results hypothesized that this algorithm best matched the apparent strategy of the participants (see Table 7.1 and Pritchett, 2000).

- *MIT:* This alerting algorithm was generated by Kuchar and Carpenter (1997) for cockpit alerting systems using extensive simulations

of collision trajectories during CSPA. It combines several measures of the environment, including lateral separation, longitudinal separation, other aircraft velocity, convergence angle, and other aircraft heading rate. It switches to an alert only once the probability of collision (if no avoidance maneuver is initiated) reaches a threshold of unacceptable risk. Therefore, it has significantly fewer false alarms than the other algorithms, because it generates alarms only when the aircraft is threatened and immediate action is required.

Method

A part-task, desktop flight simulator experiment was conducted with the following objectives:

- Examine participants' judgments in a collision detection task during CSPA; and
- Evaluate the impact of differing traffic situation display semantic content on participants' behavior.

The experimental study examined in this chapter has been previously documented in full (Pritchett, 2000). The following sections outline those elements of the experiment design relevant to *n*-system lens model analysis of its results.

Experimental Task

Participants were told they were flying an approach. Their declared primary task was to keep their wings level, referenced to an artificial horizon, through the use of a sidestick. Their declared secondary task was to press a button on the sidestick as soon as they thought the aircraft on a parallel approach was deviating from its approach, as evidenced by the traffic display; no automatic alerts were provided.

Participants

Nineteen people participated in the experiment. Two were current airline flight crew, 4 were current Certified Flight Instructors (CFIs) in general aviation aircraft (1 with jet fighter experience), 2 held private pilot licenses, and the remaining 11 were undergraduate or graduate students without piloting experience.

Experimental Design

Five traffic displays were tested. All were based on the moving map presentation common to air transport navigation displays, and the displays varied only in terms of the amount of semantic content explicitly representing the other aircraft's flight path, as follows.

- *Display 1:* This display presented information about the other aircraft's position, with a top-down view, track-up orientation, iconic presentation of the other aircraft's horizontal position and a text presentation of the other aircraft's altitude.
- *Display 2:* This display added a cue indicating the distance of the other aircraft from its own approach path.

- *Display 3:* This display added an indication of the other aircraft's heading (which is equivalent to convergence angle in this specific phase of flight).
- *Display 4:* This display added a graphic indication of heading rate and projected position within the next 15 seconds as an indication of convergence angle and projected position. The position projection used exact foreknowledge of future aircraft behavior to give a smooth projection; as such, this display would be not be physically realizable in actual operations.
- *Display 5:* This display used the same position projection symbol as used in Display 4. This position projection was based on a noisy measurement of the other aircraft's current bank and had no predictive capability for adjusting for the other aircraft's future intent.

To create a variety of conditions in which to test participants' judgments, several different scenarios were created. Each started with the participant's aircraft established on the approach course and with the other aircraft following an intercept angle to reach its own approach course 2,000 feet to the left or right. The scenario types were:

- *Missed Intercept:* The other aircraft did not capture its parallel approach course but continued on a straight-line collision course. As such, the other aircraft never turned.
- *Hazardous Blunder:* The other aircraft turned at the appropriate time to join its own approach course, but at a random time later in the approach, turned to establish a collision trajectory.
- *Less Hazardous Blunder:* The other aircraft joined its approach course, but at a random later time established a trajectory passing at least 1,000 feet in front of the participant's aircraft.
- *Safe Approach (Placebo):* The other aircraft turned at the appropriate time to join its own approach course and then followed this course down to land without deviating.

Two scenario factors were varied to create four different conditions within the blunder scenario types. The convergence angle of the other aircraft was picked to be high in one half of the runs (45°) and to be low in the remaining runs (15°). Likewise, the turn rate of the other aircraft was set to a high value in one half of the runs (4.5°/s) and low in the remaining half (1.5°/s). For the Missed Intercept scenarios, the convergence angle was set to be high in half of the runs with each display (45°) and to be low in the remaining half of the runs (15°). Additionally, the difficulty of the wings-leveling task was set to either High or Low, creating different workloads for the participants.

The display variable combined with the scenario and workload variations were fully crossed, creating 40 experimental runs. Most participants completed 40 experimental runs, allowing for within-subject comparisons; four participants did not have runs with the smooth predictor display (Display 4) due to problems with the simulator.

Dependent Measures

The measurements of interest to this chapter are those describing the state of the environment at the time of the participants' reactions. As shown in Figure 7.3, these measurements identify the temporal and spatial cues available to the subject explicitly on the displays or implicitly through spatial relationships and the movement of the other aircraft's symbol across the screen. Additional measurements that could be inferred from the display were the other aircraft's rate of change of heading, the dis-

tance of each aircraft from their runway, and the other aircraft's ground speed and vertical speed.

Results

Three steps were followed in the lens model analysis:

1. Creation of linear models of participant and alerting algorithm judgments from the experiment data;
2. Computation of the lens model parameters from the linear models; and
3. Analysis of the lens model parameters for participant, display, and alerting algorithm effects.

The following sections describe the data collected from the experiment and then detail these three analysis steps.

Data Collected

In generating the n-system lens model, the environmental cues were originally recorded as a static picture of situation state at the point of the participants' reactions. However, judging the proper time for a reaction to a possible impending collision occurs in a very dynamic environment created by constantly maneuvering aircraft. Therefore, a time slice approach was used in creating the lens mod-

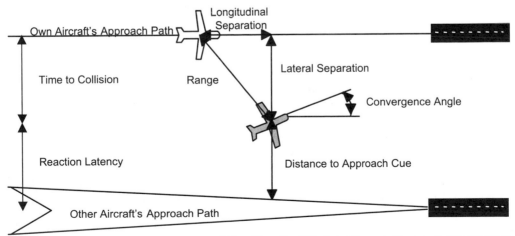

(Other Aircraft's Altitude Is Shown in Text on Traffic Displays)

Figure 7.3. Schematic of collision detection cues recorded at time of participants' reactions.

els (Bisantz et al., 2000) so that we could not only examine the environment at participant reactions but also analyze the conditions that did not cause the participants to issue an "alert" judgment. Specifically, each experimental trial was numerically simulated using the same dynamic models used in the experiment's flight simulator, and situation state was recorded in one-second slices. Participants' judgments were then identified and coded for each time slice: If a participant reacted at or before the time slice, the judgment was coded as 1 (alert); if they had not reacted, the judgment was coded as −1 (no alert). We also labeled each time slice according to whether its conditions would trigger an alert from each of the alerting algorithms for CSPA described earlier: ANC, NTZ, and MIT. As with participants, judgments of the algorithms were coded 1 (alert) or −1 (no alert) in each time slice.

The complete data set available for this analysis comprised all time slices in all of the data runs requiring a judgment; because the placebo scenario did not provide a comparative assessment of conditions with and without participant reactions, it was not included. In addition, the ability of some of the simulated data runs to re-create the environment viewed by the participants could not be verified and were therefore disregarded. Altogether, 14,361 time slices were included in the data set, an average of 758 per participant.

Creation of Linear Models of Participant and Policy Judgments

Separate linear models relating judgments to available cues were constructed for each participant within each display condition; in addition, a single linear model was developed for each participant across all display conditions. Likewise, associated with each participant linear model, linear models were created of each of the three alerting algorithm's output resulting from the same conditions experienced by the participant. These linear models were constructed using standard multiple regression techniques. Although these methods are not typically applied when some of the regression variables are discrete (as is the case here with the alert/no alert judgments), if the goal of the analysis is primarily to examine lens model parameters, Cooksey (1996) suggests that these methods are acceptable.

Although the discrete indicator of the judgment limits their efficacy, the regression weights calculated for the linear models retain some ability for suggesting the cues on which the participants and alerting algorithms tended to rely. These weights are shown in Figure 7.4. A dominant cue for the participants appears to be lateral separation—as the value of the cue became smaller, participants were more likely to react, switching the value of their judgment from not alerted (−1) to alerted (+1). Despite its comparative importance, only the MIT alerting algorithm appears to use range as a dominant cue.

The regression weights were also calculated for each participant's data runs within the five display conditions, as shown in Figure 7.5. These weights are notable in that they do not show any clear indication of participants relying on the extra cues explicitly provided by the more informative traffic displays. For example, the explicit presentation of neither convergence angle nor the other aircraft's heading rate appears to have a corresponding increased reliance on those cues. These findings may explain the lack of difference in overall performance across the different display conditions.

Analysis of Lens Model Parameters

An n-system lens model was created for each participant across all five display conditions, which compared participants' judgments with those made by each of the three alerting algorithms. The corresponding parameters are shown in Figure 7.6. At one extreme, participants' judgments were the most similar to the NTZ algorithm's judgments, with a very high measure of policy similarity G_{NTZ} for all participants (between 0.955 and 0.998). The judgment correspondence r_{aNTZ} is somewhat lower (between 0.813 and 0.942) due to inconsistencies in the NTZ judgments compared to their linear model (i.e., R_{NTZ} between 0.817 and 0.864) and in the participants' reactions compared to their linear model (i.e., R_S between 0.767 and 0.867). These results are consonant with the results in Table 7.1, obtained by ANOVA of the same raw data across scenario types (Pritchett, 2000).

At the other extreme, participants' judgments were often different from the MIT algorithm's judgments, as shown by judgment correspondence overall and by the greater variance in this measure between participants than for other alerting algorithms (i.e., r_{aMIT} between 0.367 and 0.733). This lower and more varied judgment correspondence

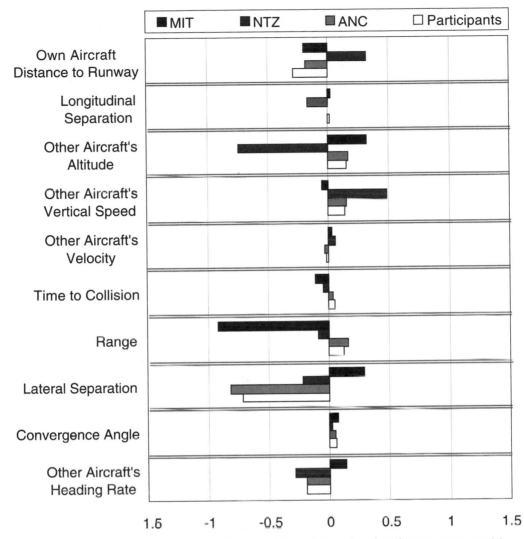

Figure 7.4. Regression weights for the participants and three alerting algorithms (average, across participants). Weights are shown for each cue (indicated on the left side of the figure); within each cue, weights are shown for each of the three alerting algorithms, and the participant model. Of particular interest is the relatively large weight placed by both the participants, and the ANC algorithm, on lateral separation, and the overall dissimilarity in weights between the participants and the MIT algorithm.

appears to be partly due to inconsistencies in the MIT algorithm's judgments (i.e., R_{MIT} between 0.624 and 0.832), in addition to inconsistencies in the participants' reactions (i.e., R_S between 0.767 and 0.867). However, unlike the NTZ algorithm, the lower judgment correspondence is also partly due to lower and more varied measures of policy similarity (i.e., G_{MIT} between 0.537 and 0.889). This discrepancy between participant judgments and the MIT algorithm was suggested by an ANOVA of the raw data across scenario types

but could not be tested directly using those methods (Pritchett, 2000).

Analysis for Alerting Algorithm, Display, and Participant Effects

Additionally, the n-system lens model parameters comparing participants' judgments to the three alerting algorithms were generated for each participant for each display condition. ANOVA was used to test for effects of display condition and alerting

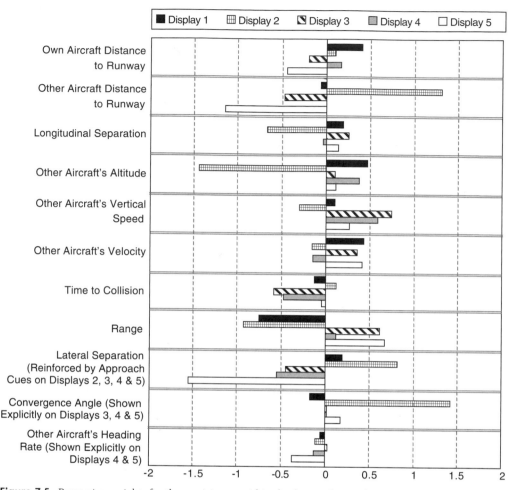

Figure 7.5. Regression weights for the participants within display conditions (average, across participants). Weights are shown for each cue (indicated on the left side of the figure); within each cue, weights are shown for each of the five display conditions. Of particular interest is the fact that there appears to be little correspondence between cues provided explicitly in the more advanced displays, and participants' reliance on those cues.

algorithm on the n-system lens model parameters. Displays and alerting algorithms were treated as within-subject variables. Because the parameters are correlations, before performing the ANOVA, the parameters were transformed using Fisher's r to z transformation (Cooksey, 1996), where r corresponds to the parameter, and z the transformed parameter:

$$z_r = (1/2)\log_e[(1 + r)/(1 - r)]$$

The ANOVA results are summarized in Table 7.2. There were significant effects of alerting algorithm on all lens model parameters with the exception of R_S (which is a measure of participant

behavior only and therefore cannot vary with alerting algorithm), indicating that the relationship between participants' judgments and the alerting algorithms' judgments differed among algorithms.

There were neither display effects nor any significant interactions between displays and alerting algorithms significant at the $p < 0.05$ level, suggesting that none of the displays encouraged participants to react more similarly to any of the alerting algorithms. The n-system lens model parameters comparing participant judgments to the three algorithms in each of the five display conditions are shown in Figure 7.7. A marginally statistically significant display effect ($p = 0.076$) was

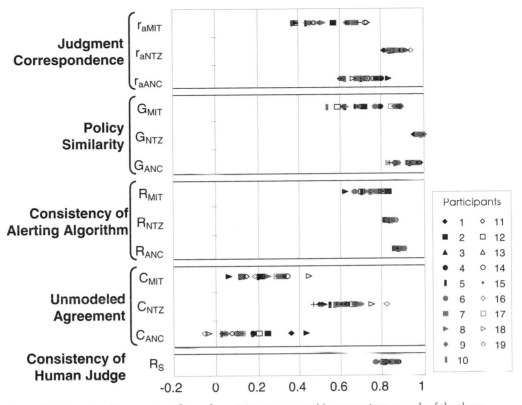

Figure 7.6. Lens model parameters for each participant, measured in comparison to each of the three alerting algorithms. Results are organized by parameter, as indicated on the left side of the figure. Within each parameter, values are shown for each of the three alerting algorithms.

found in the measures of judgment correspondence, which likely corresponds to the slight increase in correspondence between participant's judgments and the MIT and ANC algorithms in conditions with the more informative displays. These results are consonant with the results described in Table 7.1, obtained by ANOVA of the same raw data (Pritchett, 2000).

To examine any effects caused by inclusion of both pilots and nonpilots as participants, n-system lens model parameters were compared between pilots and nonpilots and algorithms. Because displays were not found to have an effect, parameters from the n-system lens models collapsed across display conditions were used, thus providing a greater sample of judgments on which to base the lens model parameters. Pilot or nonpilot status was treated as a between-subjects factor, and alerting algorithm was treated as a within-subjects factor. Results, given in Table 7.3, indicate no significant differences in lens model parameters between pilot and nonpilot par-

ticipants for any of the parameters. This result is consonant with the results described in Table 7.1, obtained by ANOVA of the same raw data across scenario types (Pritchett, 2000).

Discussion

This study provides an illustrative application of the lens model in general and the n-system lens model in particular. Although this model has been widely demonstrated in static situations, there are few examples of its application to a complex, dynamic judgment task (but see Bisantz et al., 2000). Specifically, this chapter described a lens model analysis of aircraft collision detection during closely spaced parallel approaches. As with the initial analysis, the n-system lens model analysis found weak display effects and no effect due to participants' status as a pilot. The equivalence of our analysis here with analysis conducted using more common

Table 7.2.

Effect	Judgment Correspondence r_a	Policy Similarity G	Consistency of Alerting Algorithm R	Consistency of Human R_S	Un-modeled Agreement C
Alerting algorithm	$F_{2,52} = 122.4,$ $p < .001$	$F_{2,52} = 120.5,$ $p < .001$	$F_{2,52} = 77.83,$ $p < .001$	NA	$F_{2,56} = 143.0,$ $p < .001$
Display	$F_{2,52} = 2.245,$ $p = 0.076$	$F_{4,52} = 1.515,$ $p = 0.211$	$F_{4,56} = 0.169,$ $p = 0.953$	$F_{4,56} = 0.671,$ $p = 0.615$	$F_{4,56} = 1.807,$ $p = 0.372$
Alerting algorithm x display	$F_{8,104} = 0.613,$ $p = 0.765$	$F_{8,104} = 0.434,$ $p < 0.898$	$F_{8,104} = 1.385,$ $p = 0.212$	NA	$F_{8,112} = 1.291,$ $p = 0.225$

nomothetic methods supports the assertion that the *n*-system lens model parameters are suitable for testing the main effects typically investigated in many experimental studies.

Unlike other methods of examining judgment, the *n*-system lens model parameters provided additional insight by directly measuring the policy similarity and judgment correspondence of participants' judgments compared to alerting algorithms for automated systems. Because the lens model allows the direct comparison of human performance to the behavior of other judgment agents such as decision aids, the degree of agreement between human judgment behavior and automated system judgment behavior can be directly assessed. For example, both the consistently high judgment correspondence and policy similarity of the participants' judgments compared to the NTZ alerting

algorithm, and the consistently low judgment correspondence and policy similarity of the participants' judgments compared to the MIT alerting algorithm, have implications for the design of alerting systems for CSPA. Specifically, these results suggest that pilots in actual CSPA operations will tend to make conflict detection judgments consonant with an NTZ algorithm and dissonant with an MIT algorithm. Given that the MIT algorithm is our best estimate of an environmental criterion at this time, the actual detection performance of pilots (measured by false alarms and late alerts) may not always be at the high level desirable in such a safety-critical task. Likewise, the MIT algorithm has been proposed as the basis for conflict alerting systems (Kuchar & Carpenter, 1997); these results suggest that such an alerting system could frequently be dissonant with pilots' assessments of their immediate traffic situation.

This analysis also constructed linear models of the participants' and alerting algorithms' judgment behavior. Although their associated regression weights are limited in efficacy due to the discrete nature of the judgment indication, they can provide insight into the dominant cues used in forming judgments. In this case, these weights suggest that participants relied heavily on the cue Lateral Separation between Aircraft, whereas the MIT algorithm weighted heavily the cue Range; this discrepancy may have contributed to their low judgment correspondence and policy similarity between participants and the MIT alerting algorithm. However, no consistent changes in cue utilization were observed across the displays tested in this study, suggesting that encouraging pilots to use different cues may not be as simple as varying the semantic content of the displays.

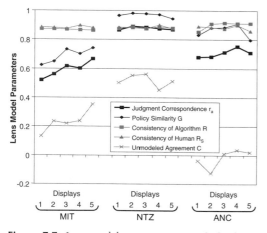

Figure 7.7. Lens model parameters in each display condition averaged over participants, measured in comparison to each of the three alerting algorithms.

Table 7.3.

Effect	Judgment Correspondence r_a	Policy Similarity G	Consistency of Alerting Algorithm R	Consistency of Human R_S	Un-modeled Agreement C
Pilot/ nonpilot	$F_{1,17} = 1.99$, $p = 0.176$	$F_{1,17} = 1.701$, $p = 0.210$	$F_{1,17} = 0.705$, $p = 0.413$	$F_{117} = 0.016$, $p = 0.9$	$F_{1,17} = 1.88$, $p = 0.188$
Alerting algorithm	$F_{2,34} = 117.83$, $p < 0.001$	$F_{2,34} = 110.4$, $p < 0.001$	$F_{2,34} = 161.69$, $p < 0.001$	NA	$F_{2,34} = 103.58$, $p < 0.001$
Pilot x algorithm	$F_{2,34} = 1.923$, $p = 0.162$	$F_{2,34} = 0.927$, $p = .406$	$F_{2,34} = 1.381$, $p = 0.265$	NA	$F_{1,34} = 2.790$, $p = 0.075$

Implications for Practice and Design

Applications from this work include those related to the specific collision detection problem analyzed as well as more general implications. First, as noted in the preceding section, use of the lens model revealed important similarities and differences between human judgment behavior and that of three alerting algorithms. The participants tested were most similar to the alerting algorithm that was based on a relatively simply heuristic (which relied on lateral separation between the aircraft), and were most dissimilar from the more complex (albeit higher performance) MIT algorithm. This finding has implications for the design of displays and training for any collision avoidance systems that implement this MIT algorithm. Other studies have indicated negative impacts on acceptance and trust for alerting systems that are contrary to operator's expectations or produce alerts that are interpreted as false alarms (Gupta, Bisantz, & Singh, 2002; Pritchett, 2000), whereas research on trust in decision aids has indicated that meta-information about how the aid is performing can allow better calibration of trust and judgment performance (Seong, 2002; Seong & Bisantz, 2002). To support pilot acceptance of and trust in the alerting system, pilots may need additional training and/or displays that make the computation of the alerting algorithm transparent and understandable.

Additionally, this research demonstrated how the lens model can be used as part of a methodology that compares human judgments to that of automated agents to identify correspondences and potential conflicts that would need to be remedied with training, displays, or other techniques, such as on-demand explanations of agent reasoning. Also, the methodology can be used to measure how differences in contextual factors, such as the displays tested here, along with other factors such as type of training, situation, or experience level affected the human–agent judgment correspondence.

Conclusions

The ability to develop detailed models of human judgment in complex, uncertain environments is valuable. Knowledge of the information sought by a human judge can be used to determine the information content of displays. Likewise, given the increasing prevalence of automated alerting systems to support attention and judgment, it is also important that these models enable comparison of human judgments with the output of automated systems. A low level of observed correspondence between human judgments and automated system output can suggest the potential for disagreement between a human and automation in operations, suggesting ineffective human–automation interaction as manifested in the human judge's reliance on and trust in the automated system.

In this chapter, we applied the n-system lens model to generate these insights regarding a previous study of collision avoidance. Our analysis identified the same main effects as the previous nomothetic analysis. More important, the analysis identified the cues tied closely with judgments, enabled direct assessment of display impact on judgment, and measured the coherence of participants' judgments and their actual and policy similarity to judgment policies used by automated systems.

These results highlight the utility of the n-system lens model for analyzing human interaction with automated systems. Our analysis examined pilots and conflict-alerting systems; however, it is reasonable to expect that the utility of this analysis method will extend beyond aviation to other complex environments, given the range of domains in which the underlying methods associated with lens models have proven effective. Likewise, it is reasonable to expect that these methods will also be beneficial in designing other types of automated systems than the alerting system judgment policies tested here, such as decision aids that make continuously scaled judgments instead of the binary, alert/no alert judgment in this study.

Acknowledgment. Portions of this chapter are drawn from Bisantz & Pritchett (2003) and reprinted by permission. The second author was supported by the National Science Foundation under grant number IIS9984079 during the conduct of this work.

References

Bisantz, A. M., Kirlik, A., Gay, P., Phipps, D., Walker, N., & Fisk, A. D. (2000). Modeling and analysis of a dynamic judgment task using a lens model approach. *IEEE Transactions on Systems, Man, and Cybernetics: Part A: Systems and Humans, 30*(6), 1–12.

Bisantz, A. M. & Pritchett, A. R. (2003). Measuring the fit between human judgments and automated alerting algorithms: A study of collision detection. *Human Factors, 45*(2), 266–280.

Brunswik, E. (1955). Representative design and probabilistic theory in a functional psychology. *Psychological Review, 62*, 193–217.

Cooksey, R. W. (1996). *Judgment analysis: Theory, methods, and applications.* San Diego: Academic Press.

Gupta, N., Bisantz, A. M., & Singh, T. (2002). The effects of adverse condition warning system characteristics on driver performance: An investigation of alarm signal type and threshold level. *Behaviour and Information Technology, 21*, 235–248.

Hammond, K. R. (1996). *Human judgment and social policy.* New York: Oxford University Press.

Kuchar, J. K., & Carpenter, B. D. (1997). Airborne collision alerting logic for closely-spaced parallel approach. *Air Traffic Control Quarterly, 5*(2), 111–127.

Pritchett, A. (1999). Pilot performance at collision avoidance during closely-spaced parallel approaches. *Air Traffic Quarterly, 7*(1), 47–75.

Pritchett, A. (2000). Display effects on shaping apparent strategy: A case study in collision detection and avoidance. *International Journal of Aviation Psychology, 10*(1), 59–83.

Seong, Y. (2002). Modeling human operator's judgment and trust in conjunction with automated decision aids. Unpublished doctoral dissertation. University at Buffalo, State University of New York, Amherst, N.Y.

Seong, Y., & Bisantz, A. M. (2002). Judgment and trust in conjunction with automated decision aids: A theoretical model and empirical investigation. *Proceedings of the Human Factors and Ergonomics Society's 46th Annual Meeting.*

Wong, G. A. (1993). Development of precision runway monitor system for increasing capacity of parallel runway operations. Paper presented at the AGARD meeting on machine intelligence in air traffic management.

Younho Seong, Ann M. Bisantz,

and Gordon J. Gattie

Trust, Automation, and Feedback: An Integrated Approach

Introduction

A large body of research exists that uses lens modeling outcomes to provide cognitive feedback to a human judge to improve the judge's own policies and performance. Our research extends this work by using modeling outcomes to provide assessments of one agent's judgment performance to other agents in a multiagent judgment system. More specifically, meta-information about an automated decision aid, which comprised parameters measuring the aid's performance, was developed based on concepts of cognitive feedback. In such systems, trust serves as an important intervening variable in decisions on the part of the human agent to use outputs from automation. Problems of miscalibration of trust can lead to both underuse of good-quality automated systems as well as overuse of poor-quality systems (Parasuraman & Riley, 1997). Providing operators with information to enhance their understanding of the quality of the automation's outputs and its processes may provide a means of improving trust calibration. This chapter reviews research in which an integrative framework, based on the lens model, was developed to address these issues. The framework characterizes aspects of automated systems that affect human trust in those systems and allows

assessment of aspects of human trust through the application of lens modeling outcomes. Implications are drawn from an empirical study that relied on this integrative framework and are provided for the design of training systems and displays.

Cognitive Feedback: An Application of Lens Model Outcomes

One application of outcomes from the lens model has been in the area of cognitive feedback. Human judges may be viewed as information processors that can change their judgment strategies based on evaluations provided from previous judgments. The lens model equation can generate useful feedback information to provide these evaluations. Cognitive feedback based on the lens model equation includes information about the properties of and relations between an individual's judgment policy and the environmental structure. Because feedback information can be delivered before future judgments are made, it may be considered both feedback and feedforward information (Cooksey, 1996). Although feedback provides information about the "correctness" of prior judgments made compared to the truthful states of the environment, cognitive feedback can also be used in a feedforward manner, allowing human operators to use the information in making future judgments. This distinction is important for identifying information that not only summarizes judgment performance but provides judges with information to enhance their understanding of the task environment and their own judgments.

Feedback regarding judgment quality can be readily obtained from lens model parameters. This type of detailed feedback, called cognitive feedback, has been shown to improve judgment performance, particularly compared to outcome feedback, in which participants are only provided with the correct judgment (Adelman, 1981; Balzer, Doherty, & O'Connor, 1989; Balzer et al., 1992; Lindell, 1976; Steinmann et al., 1977). Cognitive feedback can include information about the task environment (e.g., ecological predictability—R_e, ecological validities, or the relationship forms linking cue values to criterion values), cognitive information about the judge's policy (e.g., cognitive consistency—R_S, cue utilization validities, or the relationship forms linking cue values to judged criterion values), or functional validity information, which shows the relationship between the task environment and actions of the judge (e.g., overall achievement—r_a, linear knowledge—G, or degree of nonlinear knowledge—C; Doherty & Balzer, 1988).

Cognitive feedback can also include comparative information, such as the relative size of environmental cue weights compared to a judge's cue weights. Feedback can be presented verbally, in terms of textual descriptions of the forms of the cue-criterion relationships (e.g., the criterion value increases linearly as the cue value increases); numerically, in terms of correlations for R_e and R_S, or numeric cue weights; or graphically, using bar graphs to show sizes of cue weights or line graphs to depict cue-criterion function forms. Typically, cognitive feedback is provided by first collecting data on several participant judgments and then computing lens model parameters based on those values. Participants are then either provided with the information immediately (e.g., after a block of 20 judgments) or after some time period has passed (e.g., before the next experimental session). Gattie and Bisantz (2002) performed an experiment in a dental training domain to investigate the effects of different types of cognitive feedback under different environmental and expertise conditions. Specifically, the task environments (consisting of cases drawn from actual patients) were either well represented by a linear model or not, as measured by R_e; and participants were either medical trainees, primarily in dental medicine, or medical novices. Feedback was provided after each case decision. Results indicated that performance and consistency initially declined with the introduction of cognitive feedback but recovered after some experience with interpreting the detailed feedback. Overall, medically trained participants performed better with task information, and the presence of cognitive information allowed untrained participants to perform at similar levels to trainee participants.

Multiagent Judgment Systems and Trust

As discussed, cognitive feedback has generally been used to provide information to a judge regarding his or her own judgment policy, the environmental structure, and the individual–environment relationship to improve judgment performance. Additionally, information drawn from the lens model, analogous to cognitive feedback, may prove to be useful as a diagnostic tool to help individuals understand the behavior of other judgment systems with which they interact. These systems could include automated as well as human agents. Collaboration among such systems of judges may be made more effective and efficient if judges have an understanding of each others' judgment policies. In particular, two types of information regarding a judgment agent—cognitive information and functional validity information—may provide critical information in understanding the behavior of the agent by providing an indication of both the quality of judgments produced by the agent (i.e., his or her functional validity) and the reliability with which they are produced (i.e., through the cognitive information, specifically R_s, regarding the agent).

Many complex work environments involve multijudge systems in which human operators must assess and choose whether to rely on the outputs from one type of judgment agent: automated decision aids. Such aids provide estimates and information that support situation assessment judgments and choices made by the human operator. Bass and Pritchett (chapter 9) present a methodology that explicitly addresses the measurement of human interaction with an automated judge.

Issues regarding human judgments in conjunction with such decision aids include the following.

1. Because of the inherent uncertainty residing within the environment, judgment and decision-making tasks challenge human information processing capabilities. Furthermore, the environmental uncertainty is transferred to the situational estimates generated by automated decision aids, which subsequently places the human operator in the difficult position of determining whether they should rely on the decision aid. Such decisions are related to the circumstances and the level of automation autonomy that has been selected (Endsley & Kaber, 1999; Parasuraman, Sheridan, & Wickens, 2000).

2. Automated decision aids are subject to multiple types of failures, such as simple mechanical malfunctions, environmental disturbances, and intentional attacks, which can make decisions to rely on the aid difficult (Bisantz & Seong, 2001).

In systems with automated judgment agents, questions of human operators' trust in those agents become important. Empirical studies have shown that operators' trust in automated controllers is a critical intervening component affecting operators' performance in controlling the systems as well as using the automated controllers (Lee & Moray, 1992; Muir & Moray, 1996). Many characteristics that influence the level of individual's trust in automated systems have been suggested by researchers (Lee & Moray, 1992; Lee & See, 2004; Muir & Moray, 1996; Sheridan, 1988), including reliability, validity, transparency, utility, and robustness. Among these, an understanding of the reliability of an automated system (i.e., the consistency with which it performs) has been suggested as critical in allowing humans to correctly calibrate their trust in and subsequently use the automated system. Interestingly, one component of cognitive feedback, as applied within a multiagent judgment framework, represents information regarding the reliability of the other judgment agents: the R_s of other judgment systems. In this sense, cognitive feedback can be used to diagnose the reliability of automated systems, which in turn may affect the level of an individual's trust in such systems.

There are other important characteristics that play important roles in determining the level of trustworthiness of automated decision aids. For instance, Sheridan (1988) discussed validity as an important characteristic. Within a framework in which the automation is providing situational estimates, such a characteristic corresponds to the validity (or correctness) of the estimates provided. Again, the functional validity information provided by the lens model can serve as a measure of this validity.

Additionally, Sheridan (1988) suggested that the understandability and transparency of a system plays an important role in determining the level of trust in an automated system. If operators can better understand and evaluate the actions or judgments provided by an automated system, they may be better able to calibrate their trust in and reliance on such systems. Providing information in the form of reliability and functional validity information as described above may enhance the human judge's understandability of an automation system.

Theoretical Model

The lens model with its extensions (Brunswik, 1952; Cooksey, 1996) can provide a framework within which aspects of human interaction with an automated judgment agent, such as that already described, can be modeled. In particular, the n-system design (in which multiple agents make judgments about the same environmental criterion) provides a framework to represent a situation where the human judge is supported by automated technology. In this case, a human operator and an automated system are making judgments about the same environmental state (see chapter 7 for a more extensive description of the n-system Lens Model). However, in contrast to a standard n-system model, these judgments are not separate: the human judgment is based not only on the cues themselves, but also on the output of the decision aid. Thus, the hierarchical lens modeling framework also has applicability, in that the cues are used by the automated decision aid, which subsequently provides a situational estimate to the human judge, who partially bases his or her judgment on the decision aid's judgment. However, the hierarchical framework does not capture the fact that the human judge may have access to the same cues as the automated decision aids. To address this modeling need, a hybrid approach was taken, combining elements of both the n-system and hierarchical models.

Figure 8.1 depicts the components of this n-system/hierarchical hybrid Lens Model. Judgments of some environmental criterion (e.g., the intent of a hostile aircraft) are made, based on a set of cues, by both an automated decision aid (ADA) and the human operator without the decision aid (HO) (the top and bottom agents in the figure, respectively). In a system where the human operator has access to the outputs from the aid (shown as the second judgment agent), the judgment made by the aid serves as an input—essentially another cue—to the human's judgment (note the link from the aid's judgment to the human + aid agent). As with the standard single-system lens model, the degree of judgment competence of all three of these systems (the ADA, the human judge acting alone, or the human judge acting with aid input—HO + ADA) can be assessed by measuring the correspondence between the environmental criterion and the output of the system (i.e., using the standard measure of achievement). Additionally, one can compare the judgment outputs across systems (as shown by the links on the right side of the figure), to evaluate the degree to which the human and ADA correspond (see chapter 7 for an elaboration of this comparison); the degree to which the judgment from an unaided human is similar to that with the aid (to understand the impact of the aid on the human's judgment) and the similarity of the aided human judgment with the output from the aid itself (to assess the degree to which the human mimics the output from the aid).

The parameters identified within this modeling framework may be able to illuminate important characteristics of human operators' trust in the decision aid and their resulting strategies in considering the decision aid's estimates. For example, assume that the ADA produces accurate estimates of the environmental states. If the human judge is well calibrated to the performance of the aid, this should result in a high performance level of the human operator in combination with the decision aid and will also result in a high degree of correspondence between the ADA and HO + ADA estimates. The extent to which the aid is having an influence, over and above the human operator, would be reflected in the level of correspondence between the unaided HO and the HO + ADA. In contrast, if the aid is not performing well but the operator is able to compensate (i.e., still maintain a high degree of judgment performance), there should be a low degree of correspondence between the HO + ADA and the aid alone, but a high degree of correspondence between the HO and the HO + ADA.

One can also consider the lens model outcomes from each of the judgment systems independently. For instance, consider the lens model associated with the first judgment agent: the automated aid (Figure 8.2). Lens model parameters or outcomes associated with this model are provided in Table 8.1. Here, the lens model parameters (shown in the leftmost column) can be used to assess the performance of the automated aid, including its consistency in producing estimates, the policy it uses to provide estimates (as assessed through its weighting scheme), and the degree to which the aid's policy matches the environmental criterion (i.e., the competence of the aid). The knowledge parameter (G) reflects the degree to which the designers of the aid have captured the linear aspects of the environment as part of the aid's judgment algorithms.

Such an analysis can serve several purposes. For instance (as is demonstrated in chapter 7), when these parameters are compared against those of human operators, similarities and differences in judgment policies can be assessed. This comparison can be useful in such cases where conflicts or similarities can hinder or support human judgment performance in concert with automated systems. Additionally, however, these parameters can provide important information regarding the functioning of the automated aid. Lens model outcomes in this case are not providing "cognitive" feedback (about the functioning of a human judge) but rather *meta-information* about the performance and functioning of the aid.

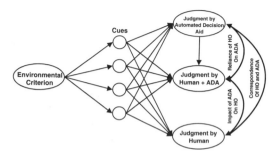

Figure 8.1. Hybrid *n*-system/hierarchical lens model. Three judgment agents (an automated decision aid [ADA], a human acting alone, and a human acting in concert with the automated aid) are shown. Note that the output from the ADA acts as an addition cue for the human + ADA system.

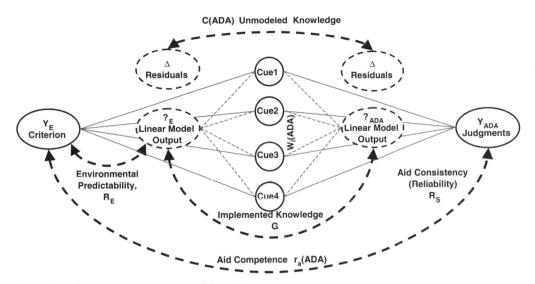

Figure 8.2. Single-system lens model of the ADA.

Model Application and Empirical Findings

An important outcome of the model is that it can be applied as a methodological framework within which research questions regarding human interaction with automation can be both instantiated and measured. Measures to evaluate the automated decision aid's performance can be selected from the parameters provided by the hybrid lens model, which in turn provides a cornerstone for investigating the issues of operator's trust (and trust calibration) in such systems. This section of the chapter reports an empirical study designed to measure issues of judgment performance and trust related to using a decision aid with varying levels of reliability and validity, and the impact of meta-information about the decision aid's functioning (computed

based on lens model outcomes) on human judgment performance and trust (Seong & Bisantz, 2002).

Within the modeling framework presented here, several factors previously hypothesized to affect trust can be systematically measured and experimentally manipulated, including system reliability, validity, and understandability.

First, the reliability of an ADA can be measured by the regression model indicating the consistency with which the decision aid makes judgments (e.g., $R_{s(ADA)}$). Second, the validity of the automated decision aid can be measured by $r_{a(ADA)}$, labeled in Figure 8.2 as Aid Competence. Third, the understandability of an automated system, or the degree to which human operators understand why and how the system is behaving, has been identified as a contributing factor to human operator's trust. Within this modeling framework, providing an operator with information on a decision aid's functioning (e.g., parameters reflecting validity, consistency or reliability, or the judgment policies in terms of the weighting scheme) may positively contribute to understandability. Note that these types of information concern the relationship between the environment, the informational cues, and the automated decision aid's estimates. This is important because such information is identical to some forms of cognitive feedback that have been shown in previous studies to increase the level of operator's judgment performance.

Table 8.1. Lens model parameters associated with a model of an automated decision aid, and the associated interpretations

Parameter	Description
$W_{i(ADA)}$	ADA's weighting scheme
$r_{a(ADA)}$	ADA's achievement; ADA's competence
G_{ADA}	Knowledge that is implemented in the ADA
C_{ADA}	Knowledge that is not considered in the ADA
$\hat{Y}_{env}$	Predicted environment
R_e	Environmental predictability
$R_{s(ADA)}$	Cognitive control (Consistency*)

In this way, the model provides an experimental framework that can explore and validate the theoretical model in a specific task situation in which the human operator's task is to identify the environmental criterion based both on available cues and an automated decision aid producing situational estimates. This framework and the three independent variables related to trust and performance are represented in Figure 8.3. On a judgment case–by–judgment case basis, validity measures the match between the decision and the environmental state, reliability measures consistency in estimates across (similar) judgment cases, and understandability reflects the degree that a human operator has access to information about how the aid is functioning (e.g., its judgment policies, validity, and reliability).

In the study, 56 participants performed an aircraft identification task in which they identified aircraft as friendly or hostile based on a set of four cues, both with and without the support of an automated decision aid. The aid provided an estimate regarding the status of the aircraft in the form of a probabilistic range (e.g., the probability that the aircraft is friendly ranges from 0.1 to 0.4). All participants performed the task without the automated aid on the first day. On the second day, there were seven between-participant experimental conditions: one control condition in which participants made judgments without the decision aid; three conditions across which the reliability and the validity of the aid (as measured by $R_{s(ADA)}$ and $r_{a(ADA)}$, respectively) were varied; and three corresponding conditions in which meta-information was provided, based on the lens model parameters about the functioning of the decision aid.

Across the three conditions, the reliability and validity of the estimates provided by the decision aid were manipulated to create conditions with either high reliability and high validity, high reliability and low validity, or low reliability and low validity. Reliability corresponded to the consistency with which the aid provided estimates and was manipulated by including aircraft with identical parameters within the trials and varying whether the aid provided the same or different estimates about those aircraft. Validity corresponded to the degree to which the aid's estimates corresponded to the "true" nature of the criterion. The meta-information (i.e., cognitive feedback) that was provided consisted of the cue utilizations, or weights, used by the decision aid along with the consistency with which the aid made judgments ($R_{s(ADA)}$).

Results are reported in more detail elsewhere (Seong & Bisantz, 2002) and thus will be only summarized here. Generally, results showed that participants in conditions with a "poor" quality decision aid (either the high reliability and low validity or low reliability and low validity conditions) were adversely impacted by quality of the decision aid. Specifically, participants performed worse, in terms of identification accuracy, on the second day with the "poor" decision aid than they did on the first day without the help from the decision aid. This is consistent with what others (Lee & Moray, 1992; Lerch & Prietula, 1989; Muir & Moray, 1996) have found in terms of the effects of poorly performing automated control systems on operator's performance. Furthermore, results suggested that poor validity had greater impact on judgment performance than poor reliability did. Most important, participants who received the meta-information performed better on the second day than those with the decision aid only, even in conditions with the poorly performing aid. In fact, the levels of performance of participants in the two poor-quality aid conditions, who received the meta-information, approached that of participants with the "better" quality decision aid.

Thus, the analysis of the correspondence between the judgments over two days within each experimental condition revealed that those with the meta-information were able to adjust their judg-

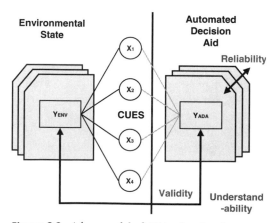

Figure 8.3. A lens model of ADAs showing three independent variables.

ment strategies to perform the task at a similar level to those with better decision aid, compensating for the decision aid's performance. Additional analyses indicated that the correspondence between the judgments made by participants on the second day and the estimates provided by the decision aid (as shown in Figure 8.1) varied based both on the quality of the decision aid and the presence of feedback. Correspondence was less for the poorer-performing aids, particularly when participants were provided with the meta-information. These results indicate that participants who were provided with the feedback regarding the decision aid were able to use this information to form a better understanding of the decision aid's behavior, and appropriately calibrate their use of the decision aid.

These results were consistent with subjective ratings of trust in the decision aid, which were provided by participants at three points during the task on day 2. Ratings were obtained using a 12-item questionnaire that has been previously documented (Jian, Bisantz, & Drury, 2000). Generally, the ratings regarding trust indicated that participants had more negative feelings of trust toward the poorer-performing aids and that this effect was strengthened when meta-information was provided. Positive feelings of trust were lower for the poorer aids than the good aid, but were higher when meta-information was provided about the poorer aids. Interestingly, negative perceptions of trust were higher and positive perceptions were slightly lower for the good aid when meta-information was provided—perhaps because even the good-performing aid did not provide "perfect" estimates. Thus, there is evidence that participants were able to calibrate their perceptions of trust in the aid, that meta-information based on lens model parameters influenced that calibration, and the judgment performance and participants' reliance on the aid were also appropriately affected by the meta-information.

The presence of the decision aid as well as the meta-information, had additional impacts on the measures of cognitive control and linear knowledge for each participant. Significant differences were found between the "good" decision aid and the two "poor" decision aids on levels of cognitive control (with improved cognitive control associated with the good aid), indicating that characteristics of the automated decision aid may be reflected in measures of individual judgment characteristics. Also,

within each pair of conditions with the poor-quality aid (either with or without the meta-information) significant differences in terms of cognitive control and linear knowledge were found only for the low validity–high reliability condition, and no differences were seen across the low validity–low reliability pair. That is, participants were able to perform the identification task better when they were provided with the additional meta-information, in the condition where the ADA generated consistently invalid environmental estimates. This indicates that the meta-information was used to identify the reliability or consistency of the ADA.

Additionally, participants in both poor decision aid groups showed a significant decrement in the levels of linear knowledge in the absence of meta-information, whereas participants in the rest of the conditions showed similar levels of linear knowledge across both days of the tasks (i.e., with and without the meta-information). In fact, the two groups with the poor decision aid with the meta-information showed increases in linear knowledge from already relatively high levels (around 0.9) on the first day, and the rest of the groups showed decreases (although these were not significant). This indicates that the meta-information was particularly valuable in the case of the poor-quality decision aids, providing the support necessary for participants to adapt to the structure of the task. Taken together, results were encouraging that participants provided with the additional lens model–based feedback information together with the ADA's estimates performed the task significantly better than those without the information.

Conclusions and Implications

There is a large body of research indicating that judgment feedback based on lens model parameters—cognitive feedback—is superior to simple outcome feedback. Cognitive feedback provides detailed information regarding relationships in the environment, the manner in which the judge is performing, and the relationship between these two entities, whereas outcome feedback only provides information regarding judgment correctness. Additionally, cognitive feedback can be considered a type of feedforward information when it is provided dynamically to a judgment agent to affect future judgment strategies. The framework developed here along with the companion experiment demonstrate both theoretically and empirically how outcomes from the lens model can be expanded beyond their traditional applications toward improving judgment performance in a single-judge system. Specifically, meta-information based on concepts of cognitive feedback can be used in a feedforward manner to provide information about an agent's judgment policies and performance to other agents in a multiagent judgment system.

This framework has particular implications for systems composed of humans and automated judgment agents. Such systems, in which human judges take input and advice from other agents (automated or human) to support situation assessment and response selection activities, have been recognized as one model for human–automation interaction—for instance, in the human centered automation levels of Endsley and Kaber (1999), or Parasuraman, Sheridan, and Wickens (2000). Trust in the automated components of such hybrid environments has been recognized for many years as an important intervening variable in decisions on the part of the human agent to use outputs from automation. Problems of miscalibration of trust can lead to both underuse of good-quality automated systems as well as overuse of poor-quality systems (Parasuraman & Riley, 1997). Providing operators with information to enhance their understanding the quality of the automation's outputs is a means of improving trust calibration. Such information could be displayed in near real time to an operator, especially if the true state of the ecological criterion could be computed during real-time operations. Alternatively, meta-information could be provided during training scenarios, when lens model parameters could be computed based on known environmental states, to allow operators to become sensitive to situations when the automated aid performed better or worse.

The lens model–based framework presented herein provides a means for both providing that understanding as well as measuring the degree of calibration of the operators' reliance on the automation. Empirical evidence supports the conclusion that providing lens model–based meta-information regarding the quality of judgments made by an ADA enhances judgment performance—particularly when the aid is of poor quality—and allows

users to better calibrate their use of the aid based on its performance.

References

Adelman, L. (1981). The influence of formal, substantive, and contextual task properties on the relative effectiveness of different forms of feedback in multiple-cue probability learning tasks. *Organizational Behavior and Human Performance, 27,* 423–442.

Balzer, W. K., Doherty, M. E., & O'Connor, R. O. J. (1989). Effects of cognitive feedback on performance. *Psychological Bulletin, 106,* 410–433.

Balzer, W. K., Sulsky, L. M., Hammer, L. B., & Sumner, K. E. (1992). Task information, cognitive information, or functional validity information: Which components of cognitive feedback affect performance? *Organizational Behavior and Human Decision Processes, 53,* 35–54.

Bisantz, A. M., & Seong, Y. (2001). Assessment of operator trust in and utilization of automated decision-aids under different framing conditions. *International Journal of Industrial Ergonomics, 28*(2), 85–97.

Brunswik, E. (1952). *The conceptual framework of psychology.* Chicago: University of Chicago Press.

Cooksey, R. W. (1996). *Judgment analysis: Theory, methods, and applications.* New York: Academic Press.

Doherty, M. E., & Balzer, W. K. (1988). Cognitive feedback. In C. R. B. Joyce (Ed.), *Human Judgment: The SJT approach.* Amsterdam: North-Holland.

Endsley, M. R., & Kaber, D. B. (1999). Level of automation effects on performance, situation awareness and workload in a dynamic control task. *Ergonomics, 42*(3), 462–492.

Gattie, G. J., & Bisantz, A. M. (2002). Utilizing dynamic cognitive feedback to facilitate learning on diagnostic tasks. *Proceedings of the Human Factors and Ergonomics Society 46th Annual Meeting.* Santa Monica, Calif.: Human Factors and Ergonomics Society.

Jian, J., Bisantz, A. M., & Drury, C. G. (2000). Foundations for an empirically determined scale of trust in automated systems. *International Journal of Cognitive Ergonomics, 4*(1), 53–71.

Lee, J. D., & Moray, N. (1992). Trust, control strategies, and allocation of functions in human–machine systems. *Ergonomics, 35*(10), 1243–1270.

Lee, J. D., & See, K. A. (2004). Trust in automation:

Designing for appropriate reliance. *Human Factors, 46*(1), 50–80.

Lerch, F. J., & Prietula, M. J. (1989). How do we trust machine advice? In M. J. Smith (Ed.), *Designing and using human–computer interface and knowledge based systems* (pp. 410–419). Amsterdam: Elsevier Science.

Lindell, M. K. (1976). Cognitive and outcome feedback in multiple-cue probability learning tasks. *Journal of Experimental Psychology: Human Learning and Memory, 2*, 739–745.

Muir, B. M., & Moray, N. (1996). Trust in automation. Part II Experimental studies of trust and human intervention in a process control simulation. *Ergonomics, 39*(3), 429–460.

Parasuraman, R., & Riley, V. (1997). Humans and automation: Use, misuse, disuse, abuse. *Human Factors, 39*, 230–253.

Parasuraman, R., Sheridan, T. B., & Wickens, C. D. (2000). A model for types and levels of human interaction with automation. *IEEE Transactions on Systems, Man, and Cybernetics, 30*(3), 269–296.

Seong, Y., & Bisantz, A. M. (2002). Judgment and trust in conjunction with automated decision aids: A theoretical model and empirical investigation. *Proceedings of the Human Factors and Ergonomics Society 46th Annual Meeting*. Santa Monica, Calif.: Human Factors and Ergonomics Society.

Sheridan, T. B. (1988). Trustworthiness of command and control systems. Paper presented in the IFAC Man-Machine Systems.

Steinmann, D. O., Smith, T. H., Jurdem, L. G., & Hammond, K. R. (1977). Application of social judgment theory in policy formation: An example. *Journal of Applied Behavioral Science, 13*, 69–88.

Ellen J. Bass and Amy R. Pritchett

Human–Automated Judgment Learning: Enhancing Interaction with Automated Judgment Systems

Introduction

Judgment is a critical component of many human activities, and technology to aid judgment is proliferating. Effectively coupling human and such automated judges involves more than merely providing the output of the automated judge to the human. Because automated judges are not perfect, human judges may face difficulties in understanding how to combine their own judgments with those of the automated judges.

Improved theoretical constructs are necessary for explaining (and quantitative methodologies for analyzing) human–automated judge interaction. Measures of interaction have been inferred from fitting observed behavior to models of judgment. For example, interaction between automated and human judges has been modeled using signal detection theory (SDT) (Robinson & Sorkin, 1985; Sorkin & Woods, 1985). This model implicitly views automated and human judgments as serial processes, each with their own sensitivity and response bias (Wickens & Flach, 1988). However, it can neither measure continuous valued judgments nor provide detailed insight into the causes of poor judgment. Fuzzy SDT (Parasuraman, Masalonis, & Hancock, 2000) can help overcome the

former limitation but is still susceptible to the latter.

Pritchett and Bisantz (this volume) used judgment analysis (Cooksey, 1996) to examine human and automated judges, demonstrating the ability of the n-system lens model to assess conflict between a human judge and what an automated judge would have said and to decompose the contributions of their knowledge and cognitive control. However, this study examined only human and automated judgments made individually without any interaction.

Seong and colleagues (this volume) combined an n-system lens model approach with subjective estimates of trust in the automated judge to model human–automated judge interaction. They manipulated the automated judge's quality and the display of its feedback. Results showed that performance and assessments of trust were impacted by the decision aid's quality, and that participants used the feedback effectively to compensate for a poor-performing aid. Although they explicitly measured trust and manipulated feedback about the automated judge, they did not measure the human judge's ability to predict the aid.

A comprehensive method should be capable of many measures of human interaction with automated judgments, including:

- Cues used by each judge in rendering judgments;
- Uncertainty in the relationship between the cues and the task environment;
- Judgment strategies by which the judges combine cues;
- The consistency with which these judgment strategies are applied;
- The amount of conflict between the judges;
- Whether the human judge compromises with the automated judge and how;
- Whether the human judge adapts to the automated judge and how; and
- The ability of the human judge to predict the automated judge and the human's perceived similarity between their judgments.

To address these requirements, this chapter presents a methodology for investigating human interaction with automated judges capable of informing training and design: human–automated judgment learning (HAJL) (Bass, 2002; Bass & Pritchett, accepted for publication). After introducing HAJL, the chapter describes the experimental task and experimental design used as a test case for investigating HAJL's utility. Then idiographic results representative of the insights that HAJL can bring and a nomothetic analysis of the experimental manipulations are presented. The chapter ends with conclusions surrounding HAJL's utility.

Human–Automated Judge Learning

HAJL builds on research from interpersonal learning (IPL) (Earle, 1973; Hammond, 1973; Hammond, Wilkins, & Todd, 1966) and sociotechnical systems frameworks (e.g., Lee & Moray, 1992, 1994; Muir, 1987, 1994). IPL's general concepts include the ideas that human judges may conflict with, compromise toward, and adapt to another judge. However, unlike human judges who can negotiate, the automated judge is assumed here to be capable only of providing judgments. HAJL adapted the three phases used in IPL to capture different types of interaction with the automated judge, detailed in the following subsections.

First Phase: Training

As with IPL, HAJL first focuses on training the individual judge. In this case, only the human judge

participates. The IPL paradigm often intentionally creates conflict between judges by training them in different environments or to use different judgment strategies; the resulting cognitive conflict is often the desired subject of study. In contrast, HAJL trains the human to make individual judgments in a realistic environment; rather than artificially create conflict, HAJL serves to later examine whether conflict between a well-trained human and an automated judge will occur. This training may be conducted in any of several ways as suited to the situation, including being fit into an established training program. In addition to its utility in training the human judge, this phase also captures her or his individual judgment policy at the end of training for comparison with judgments in the subsequent phases.

Second Phase: Interactive Learning

In interactive learning (IL), the human and automated judges first make independent initial judgments. The correspondence between their initial judgments measures their (lack of) conflict (Figure 9.1). Each trial continues by having the human create a second "joint" judgment once shown the automated judgment as an additional cue. Unlike the human judges tested in IPL, the automated judge cannot fully negotiate; however, if it can highlight the cues it relies on or otherwise portray its judgment policy, this information can also be provided to the human. Correspondence between the human's initial and joint judgments provides a measure of (lack of) compromise, correspondence between the automated judge's judgment and the joint judgment

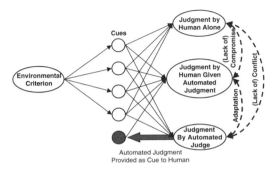

Figure 9.1. Interactive learning phase lens model of independent human and automated judgments, and human judgment given automated judgment: (lack of) conflict, (lack of) compromise, and adaptation.

measures the extent to which the human adapts to the automated judgment (Figure 9.1).

Third Phase: Prediction

In the prediction phase, the human judge makes a judgment independent of the automated judge. Also, she or he predicts the automated judgment. Three comparisons can be made: predictive accuracy of the human (i.e., correspondence between the automated judgment and her or his prediction of it), assumed similarity (i.e., correspondence between the human's judgment and her or his prediction of the automated judgment), and actual similarity (i.e., correspondence between the human and automated judgments) (Figure 9.2).

HAJL Measures

Each phase provides measures of human judgment and interaction with an automated judge (Table 1). These measures can be examined directly, and they can also be decomposed via the lens model equation (LME) (Hursch, Hammond, & Hursch, 1964) to identify which underlying aspects of judgment behavior are causing the differences in judgment performance.

The training phase, beyond its utility in training the human judge, establishes the ability in later phases to predict what the human judgment would have been without the automated judge. In addition, it provides an assessment of the (lack of) conflict between human and automated judgments formed independently.

The interactive learning phase provides direct measures of human reliance on the automated judge,

including the (lack of) conflict between their independent judgments, and the compromise with and adaptation to the automated judgments in forming a joint judgment. Their linear models and lens model parameters may also be examined. For example, high cue utilization by the human on the automated judge's judgments when forming a joint judgment may suggest that the human is using the automated judgment as a heuristic replacement for other cues, indicative of automation bias (Mosier et al., 1998). Beyond these direct measures of interaction, comparisons between the measures can illustrate whether the human's reliance on the automated judge enhances performance (Table 9.2). Underreliance would be indicated by a lack of compromise toward a reliable automated judge when the human's initial judgment achievement is low; overreliance would be indicated by a high degree of compromise toward the automated judge when its achievement is relatively low. The best interaction would result in a joint judgment higher than either individual initial judgment.

The prediction phase measures the human's ability to predict the automated judge (Table 9.1). An ability to predict the automated judge can provide a basis for the human to trust it (e.g., Lee & Moray, 1992; Muir, 1994) and can also suggest the extent to which the human's interaction with the automated judge is based on accurate understanding.

Method

Experimental Task: Aircraft Conflict Prediction

Under many of the concepts for aviation, such as "free flight" (RTCA, 1995), pilots will be expected to maintain safe separation from other aircraft, rather than relying on air traffic controllers. Cockpit displays of traffic information (CDTI) and automated judges such as conflict alerting systems are being investigated to support pilot judgment and decision making at this task (e.g., Yang & Kuchar, 1997). However, pilot interaction with automated judges must be effective and safe, requiring careful analysis such as HAJL is intended to provide.

Using a cockpit simulator in straight-and-level cruise flight, participants monitored the progress of their own aircraft flown by an autopilot (the "own-

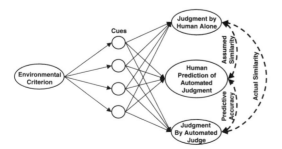

Figure 9.2. Prediction phase lens model of independent human and automated judgments, and human prediction of automated judgment: actual similarity, assumed similarity, and predictive accuracy.

Table 9.1. Summary of HAJL measures by phase

Measure	Description
Training Phase: Independent Judgments Made by Human and Automated Judge	
Human judgment characteristics	LME parameters describing human judgment: Achievement relative to criterion, knowledge, cognitive control, unmodeled agreement, environmental unpredictability
Automated judgment characteristics	LME parameters describing automated judgment: Achievement relative to criterion, knowledge, cognitive control, unmodeled agreement, environmental unpredictability
(Lack of) Conflict	Correspondence between independent human and automated judgments
Interactive Learning Phase: Independent Judgments Made by Human and Automated Judge, Then Joint Judgment Made by Human Once Given the Automated Judgment	
Human (Initial) Judgment Characteristics	LME parameters describing initial human judgment: Achievement relative to criterion, knowledge, cognitive control, unmodeled agreement, environmental unpredictability
Automated Judgment Characteristics	LME parameters describing automated judgment: Achievement relative to criterion, knowledge, cognitive control, unmodeled agreement, environmental unpredictability
Joint judgment characteristics	LME parameters describing joint judgment made by human once provided by the automated judgment: Achievement relative to criterion, knowledge, cognitive control, unmodeled agreement
(Lack of) Conflict	Correspondence between initial human and automated judgments
(Lack of) Compromise	Correspondence between initial human and joint judgments
Adaptation	Correspondence between joint and automated judgments
Prediction Phase: Independent Judgments Made by Human and Automated Judge, Human Also Predicts the Automated Judgment	
Human judgment characteristics	LME parameters describing human judgment: Achievement relative to criterion, knowledge, cognitive control, unmodeled agreement, environmental unpredictability
Automated judgment characteristics	LME parameters describing automated judgment: Achievement relative to criterion, knowledge, cognitive control, unmodeled agreement, environmental unpredictability
Prediction characteristics	LME parameters describing prediction: Achievement relative to the automated judgments, knowledge, cognitive control, un-modeled agreement, environmental unpredictability
Actual similarity	Correspondence between human and automated judgments
Assumed similarity	Correspondence between human judgment and prediction
Predictive accuracy	Correspondence between prediction and automated judgment

ship") relative to traffic. White noise was added to the traffic information: its standard deviation was 19 knots for the traffic's indicated airspeed, 3.8° for its heading, and 0.11 NMI for its horizontal position. This uncertainty degraded environmental predictability to 0.886, which was perceptually apparent on the CDTI.

Experimental Procedure

This experiment included the three HAJL phases. In each phase, each trial ran for a random preview time uniformly distributed between 15 and 30 seconds before participants made judgments. Then, the participants were asked to provide judgments

Table 9.2. Summary of inferences from comparing HAJL measures, by phase

Measures	Description
Interactive Learning Phase: Independent Judgments Made by Human and Automated Judge, Then Joint Judgment Made by Human Once Given the Automated Judgment	
Achievements of initial and joint judgments	Comparison can reveal whether or not human correctly adapts to automated judgments. Incorrect adaptations can include not adapting, adaptations that lower achievement, or possible overreliance on automated judge.
Achievement of initial judgment and compromise	Comparison can reveal whether or not human compromises appropriately given his individual judgment achievement.
Achievement of joint judgment and adaptation	Comparison can reveal whether or not joint judgment is appropriately adapted to the automated judgment.
Prediction Phase: Independent Judgments Made by Human and Automated Judge, Human Also Predicts the Automated Judgment	
Assumed and actual similarity	Comparison can reveal calibration of human judge's understanding of the automated judge.

about the risk of losing safe separation, that is, the probability that the traffic will be closer than 5 NMI. In the training phase, participants made individual judgments without the automated judge. In the IL phase, participants formed an initial judgment independently, and then, once shown the automated judgment, a second "joint" judgment. In these two phases, once judgments were entered, participants could then view the remainder of the flight in faster-than-real time to assess the actual outcome. In the prediction phase, participants provided an individual judgment and a prediction of the automated judgment with no outcome feedback provided. In the training phase, each participant judged 180 trials, distributed in four sessions over the first two days; in the IL phase, each judged 180 trials, distributed in four sessions over the third and fourth days; and, in the prediction phase, each participant judged 45 trials in one session on the fifth day.

Participants and Apparatus

Sixteen paid undergraduate engineering student volunteers, eight male and eight female, participated. The experimental apparatus used a tailorable part-task aviation software suite (Pritchett & Ippolito, 2000; Bass, 2002) with three display areas: the primary flight display (PFD), the CDTI, and the data entry area. Because ownship was in straight-and-level cruise flight controlled by an autopilot, it maintained a constant heading (174°), airspeed (400 KIAS), and altitude (30,000 feet); therefore the information on the PFD never changed substantially.

The egocentric CDTI updated once a second. Ownship position was depicted by a white airplane. A compass with tick marks every 5° appeared 40 NMI from ownship. Five other white-dashed range circles at 5, 10, 20, 30, and 50 NMI indicated distance from ownship. Traffic was depicted by a green triangle pointing in the direction of track heading, with a text depiction of the traffic's indicated airspeed in knots. All aircraft were at the same altitude as ownship so altitude was not displayed. Simulated noise was manifested by the traffic symbols moving with lateral position error, the orientation of the symbol changing with course error, and the displayed indicated airspeed fluctuating with airspeed error.

The data entry area collected the judgments and provided trial control. To enter a judgment, a participant entered the probability by using a slide bar. In the IL phase, the automated judgments were also shown in this area at the appropriate time.

The automated judge estimated the probability of losing safe separation based on current aircraft states and the uncertainty in the environment. This probability was calculated as the cumulative distribution function around the 5 NMI safe separation boundary accounting for the variance in the predicted horizontal miss distance ($\hat{h}_{miss}$), created by extrapolating the independent errors in current aircraft position, velocity, and heading.

Scenarios

Scenarios were designed based on conflict geometries known to affect human judgment performance (e.g., Smith, Ellis, & Lee, 1984). Six relative headings (+/– 45°, +/– 90°, and +/– 135°) and five indicated airspeeds (300, 350, 400, 450, and 500 knots) were selected to create the traffic encounter geometries. For each of the 30 heading-speed combinations, 6 trials were created with bearings selected to create conflict probability frequency distributions matching those created by aircraft distributed uniformly in horizontal space. The time to point of closest approach was selected randomly from a uniform distribution between 20 and 340 seconds.

Independent Variables and Experiment Design

The first between-subjects experimental manipulation investigated HAJL's ability to assess a training phase intervention. Simplification, the notion that a task should be simplified so that the trainee can develop skills (for example, see Wightman & Lintern, 1985), was implemented by increasing the environmental predictability in the training phase. In the "high noise" training condition, the environmental predictability was 0.886, as described earlier. In the "low noise" training condition, the noise in traffic state variables was halved, increasing the environmental predictability to 0.941. Regardless of their training condition, all participants experienced the same high noise condition in the subsequent IL and prediction phases.

The second between-subjects experimental manipulation was in the feedback provided by the automated judge to test HAJL's ability to measure a display design intervention. Although the automated judge's judgment strategy is fixed, there is flexibility in how it represents its judgments to the participant (e.g., Adelman et al., 1998; Pritchett & Vándor, 2001; Seong et al., this volume). In the "outcome only" condition, the automated judgment was available as a number. In the "strategy display" condition, two additional elements were added to the CDTI (Figure 9.3): future positions at the point

of closest approach and probability contours. The automated judge's estimate of the ownship's and traffic's future position were represented directly on the CDTI. Color-coded probability contours also shown on the CDTI represented the distribution through horizontal space of the automated judge's estimated probability of conflict. For more detail, see Bass (2002). This intervention was used in the IL phase while the participants made joint judgments with the automated judge.

These two manipulations were crossed to create four experimental conditions. Two male and two female participants were assigned to each condition, creating a nested-factorial design with participants nested within gender, training noise level, and display design in the IL phase.

Dependent Variables and Judgment Analysis Methods

All the measures in Table 9.1 were obtained. Participants judgments were recorded, including their individual judgments (all phases), their joint judgment formed with reference to the automated judgment (the IL phase), and their prediction of the automated judgment (prediction phase). In addition, the automated judgments were recorded in all phases, whether or not they were shown to the participants. The achievement of these judgments were assessed and decomposed using the LME using $\hat{h}_{miss}$ and the signed reciprocal of the standard deviation of the horizontal position error as cues. Because the sign of the error from a regression model fitted using $\hat{h}_{miss}$ changes depending on whether the miss distance is greater or less than 5 NMI, the cue value is negated when the miss distance is less than this amount. The reciprocal is used as smaller variances require the probability value to diverge further from the line fitted using $\hat{h}_{miss}$ alone. For more detail, see Bass (2002).

Results

Representative Results of the Idiographic Analyses

To illustrate the insight provided by idiographic HAJL analyses, the following highlight the results of three participants with different judgment behaviors.

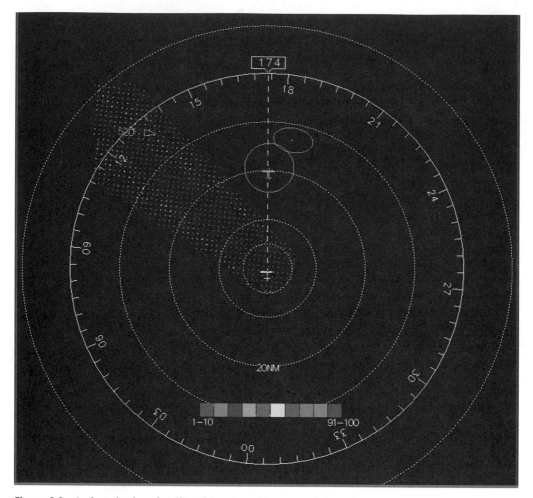

Figure 9.3. Cockpit display of traffic information with strategy information.

Participant 6: Poor Judgment Achievement Performance

Participant 6 trained without simplification and viewed the strategy display during the IL phase. Her initial judgment achievement was low, in some sessions near zero or negative (Figure 9.4a). Low linear knowledge contributed to her poor performance; given its fluctuations between the nine sessions, her judgment strategy apparently never stabilized. Low cognitive control also limited her individual judgment achievement.

In the IL phase, the automated judgments conflicted with her judgments, as shown by the low values of the (lack of) conflict measure. By compromising progressively more with the automated

judge, her joint judgment achievement approached that of the automated judge. However, her interaction with the automated judge did not noticeably improve either her linear knowledge or her initial judgment achievement; her joint judgment achievement may reflect reliance on the automated judge more than learning from and about it.

Low individual initial judgment achievement was again found in the prediction phase. She also scored with low predictive accuracy; her predictions of the automated judge were very close to her initial judgments, suggesting an incorrect belief that her judgments were similar to the automated judgments as shown by an assumed similarity of 0.981. In reality, the differences between them were significant, as reflected by a low actual similarity of 0.155.

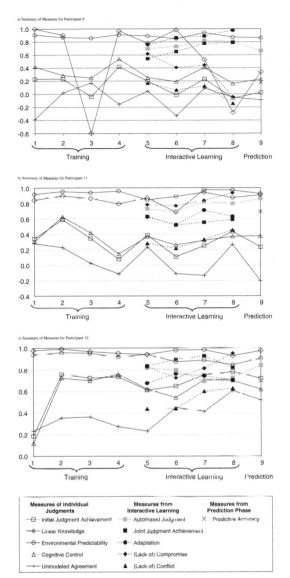

Figure 9.4. Idiographic analyses of individual participants. (a) Summary of measures for Participant 6; (b) summary of measures for Participant 11; (c) summary of measures for Participant 12.

Participant 11: Better at Predicting the Automated Judgments than Judging Traffic Conflicts

Participant 11 trained in the "simplification" condition and viewed the outcome-only display in the IL phase. He exhibited a high level of linear knowledge; however, his low cognitive control often bounded his individual judgment achievement (Figure 9.4b).

In the IL phase, as with other participants, Participant 11's joint judgments were better than his initial judgments; however, his patterns of compromise and adaptation to the automated judge were quite different in that he only partially adapted and partially compromised with the automated judgments, thus establishing joint judgments with achievement partway between those of his own individual judgments and the automated judgments. Given his relatively low initial judgment achievement, this was not the most performance-enhancing strategy.

In the prediction phase, Participant 11 exhibited another unique pattern of behavior. Unlike any other participant, Participant 11's achievement was low (0.201), but his predictive accuracy was quite high (0.699), showing him better at predicting the automated judgments than at his individual judgments. The result was surprising given the fact that he had had more motivation, experience, and feedback with the latter type of judgment. Participant 11 still assumed that his judgments were more similar to the automated judgments than they really were (assumed similarity of 0.47 compared to an actual similarity of 0.27).

A comparison of the lens model parameters for his probability of conflict judgments and for his predictions of the automated judge identifies the source of the behavior pattern. At both tasks, he had a high value of linear knowledge (0.973 for his individual judgments; 0.977 for his prediction of automated judgments). However, although his cognitive control measure at his primary judgment task was low (0.375), his cognitive control measure when predicting the automated judgments was significantly higher (0.689); this increase in cognitive control enabled his higher achievement in the prediction task. If this insight were identified as part of a training program, his conflict prediction performance would not necessarily be improved by encouraging him to replace his current judgment strategy with that used in predicting the automated judge. Instead his achievement would be improved by focusing on his cognitive control.

Participant 12: Highest Performing Joint Judgments

Participant 12 trained in the simplification condition and viewed the outcome-only display when interacting with the automated judge during the IL phase. His individual judgments had the highest achievement of all the participants. He developed linear knowledge quickly. After the first session, he also maintained a relatively high level of cognitive control (Figure 9.4c).

In the IL phase, with the change in environmental predictability (experienced in the first session without the simplification training condition), Participant 12 appeared to have some difficulty maintaining his cognitive control, but he improved with practice. In contrast with all other participants, Participant 12's initial judgment achievement improved in successive sessions, to the point where his initial judgment achievement and joint judgment achievement was higher than that of the automated judgments. These results suggest that he may have been not only learning from the automated judge but also exploiting it in a sophisticated manner: considering it when it was of more value and ignoring it otherwise. Through successive sessions, the value of unmodeled agreement rose progressively, suggesting that Participant 12 may have evolved to a more sophisticated use of the cues than captured in the linear model used in this analysis; this effect was also suggested in his debriefing where he described considering the magnitude of the noise-generated error in his judgment.

As with many participants, Participant 12's ability to predict the automated judgments was as good as his individual judgment ability. Likewise, his predictions suggest that he thought his individual judgments were more similar to the automated judge than they really were (assumed similarity of 0.891 versus actual similarity of 0.547).

Results of Nomothetic Analysis

To demonstrate the sensitivity of the HAJL parameters in identifying significant aggregate effects, two conditions were tested here: a simplification training intervention and a display design intervention. In addition, this analysis examined a demographic effect (gender). All results are reported as significant at the 0.05 level. Trends are reported at the 0.10 level. Linear mixed models with repeated measures analysis of variance (ANOVA) analyses were conducted where the repeated measurements were within the sessions. The fixed effects included gender, session, display condition, and training condition. Participants, nested within gender, training, and display condition, were modeled as random effects. The Wald test, calculated as the ratio

of the parameter estimate to its standard error, was used to analyze the random effects' covariance matrices (Jennrich & Schluchter, 1986).

For the probability of conflict measures, a transformation was used to stabilize the variance before performing analyses (Box, Hunter, & Hunter, 1978):

$$(9.1) \qquad y = \sin^{-1}(\sqrt{x})$$

As suggested by Cooksey (1996), before performing the analyses of correlations, the parameters were transformed using Fisher's r to z_r transformation.

Training Phase

The participants' individual judgment achievement was in general quite low; even by the fourth session the mean was only 0.31. None of the fixed effects were significant at the 0.05 level. Common in judgment analysis studies (Brehmer, 1994), participants were found to be a significant source of variation (Wald $Z = 2.013$, $p = 0.044$).

IL Phase

In this phase, the participants' initial and joint judgments were compared with each other, with the automated judgment, and with the environmental criterion (Figure 9.5). Overall, initial judgment achievement was quite low (mean = 0.208), and the achievement of the joint judgments was much higher (mean = 0.672). The (lack of) conflict between the initial and automated judgments was very low, illustrating how different the participants' and automated judgments were. The (lack of) compromise between the initial and subsequent joint judgments and high adaptation to the automated judgments demonstrated that the participants' judgments did change after seeing the automated judgments.

No fixed effects were found in the achievement of either the initial or the joint judgments. A significant display effect was found in the (lack of) conflict measure ($F_{1,9.094} = 5.719$, $p = 0.040$); less conflict was found with the outcome-only display. Likewise, a significant display effect was found in the (lack of) compromise measure ($F_{1,9.315} = 5.611$, $p = 0.041$), with less compromise shown in the outcome-only display condition. In the adaptation measure, a significant session effect was found ($F_{3,12.767} = 6.063$, $p = 0.008$), identifying greater adaptation over time.

In all five measures, a trend was found toward participants being a significant source of variation:

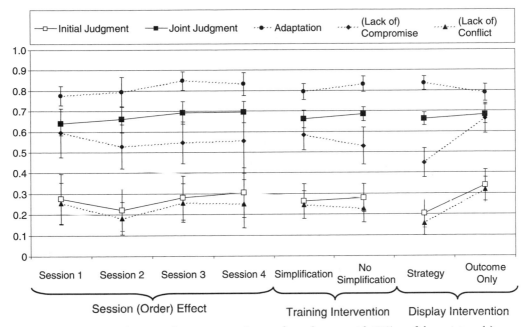

Figure 9.5. Interactive learning phase measures (untransformed, mean with 95% confidence intervals).

for initial judgments (Wald Z = 1.754, p = 0.079), joint judgments (Wald Z = 1.713, p = 0.087), (lack of) conflict (Wald Z = 1.667, p = 0.093), (lack of) compromise (Wald Z = 1.919, p = 0.055), and adaptation (Wald Z = 1.732, p = 0.083).

Prediction Phase

In each trial in this phase, participants provided their individual initial judgment and a prediction of the automated judgment. Their predictive accuracy is the correspondence between their prediction and the automated judgment; in general, the achievement of participants' initial judgments tracked their predictive accuracy closely (Figure 9.6). Assumed similarity is the correspondence between their initial judgment and their prediction of the automated judgment; in general, participants assumed that their judgments were similar to the automated judgments (mean = 0.779). Actual similarity is the correspondence between their prediction and the actual automated judgment; in contrast to their assumed similarity, actual similarity measured tended to be quite low (mean = 0.144). This result demonstrates that the participants were not well calibrated with respect to the automated judgments.

In this phase, the participants completed one session of trials, establishing only one correlation measure per participant. Therefore, a simplified

general linear model ANOVA analysis of the transformed achievement values was completed without examining for a participant effect. A main effect in the initial judgment achievement was found between the display conditions ($F_{1,9}$ = 5.106, p = 0.050); participants experiencing the outcome-only display group in the previous IL phase performed better than the group with the strategy display. The same display effect was found in the predictive accuracy measure ($F_{1,9}$ = 12.37, p = 0.007). No main effects were found in the assumed similarity measure. In the actual similarity measure, there was a trend for a display effect ($F_{1,9}$ = 4.95, p = 0.053) with the outcome-only display corresponding to higher actual similarity.

Conclusions

To fully validate the HAJL methodology would require several demonstrations spanning several domains, types of automated judges, and types of judgments. This experiment has provided a first step by fully exercising HAJL in a judgment task representative of future air traffic control environments and requiring interaction with an automated judge. The results of this experiment demonstrate HAJL's ability to not only capture individual judg-

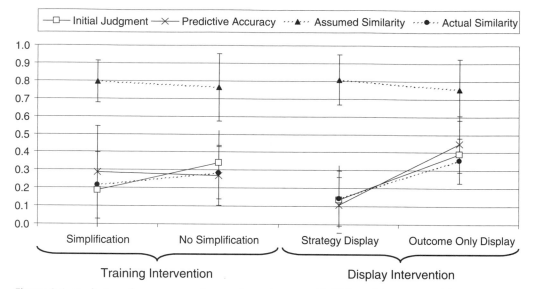

Figure 9.6. Prediction phase measures (untransformed, mean with 95% confidence intervals).

ment achievement, interaction with an automated judge, and understanding of an automated judge but also identify the mechanisms underlying these performance measures, including cognitive control, knowledge, conflict, compromise, adaptation, and actual and assumed similarity.

Analysis of HAJL's measures starts with an idiographic analysis of each participant's judgments. In this experiment, this idiographic assessment found substantially different patterns of behavior, ranging from very poor individual judgment masked by reliance on the automated judge (Participant 6) to very good individual judgment achievement complemented by a strategy for recognizing the value of an automated judgment and incorporating it accordingly (Participant 12). HAJL's measures also allow for analysis of the contributors to participants' achievement, including their reliance on the automated judge, their understanding of it, their levels of cognitive control and linear knowledge, and the cues on which they appear to base their judgments.

For example, interventions specific to each participant can be identified that address their individual weaknesses (e.g., the poor individual judgment performance of Participant 6), or that help capture their specific expertise (e.g., Participant 12's strategy for accounting for noise in the automated judgment). Not only can the judgment achievement of participants be assessed at the end of every session but also the extent to which poor cognitive control or knowledge may have limited it. Similar

calculations can also provide measures of a participant's interaction with an automated judge during the IL phase and of a participant's understanding of an automated judge during the prediction phase. These measures may potentially be shown directly to the participants, or they may be the basis for selecting or creating training interventions tailored to each participant's needs (see Strauss, 2000, for such model-based interventions).

When using HAJL for idiographic analysis, a number of process variants may be imagined. For example, participants may continue until their respective measures of performance (individual judgment achievement in the training phase; joint judgment achievement in the IL phase; and predictive accuracy in the prediction phase) have stabilized or meet some minimum criteria. Ultimately, many of the HAJL phases may be conducted (and many of the HAJL measures may be collected) as part of larger training programs or during real operations, and analyzed automatically for problematic behaviors requiring intervention.

HAJL may also serve as a methodology helping guide research and design of training programs, automated judges, and displays intended to inform judgment. HAJL provides direct measures of judgment and interaction with an automated judge with sufficient sensitivity to discern differences between participants and between main effects and changes over time; given a representative sample of participants, nomothetic analysis of these measures can provide assessments of the overall effect of interventions on a population.

For example, HAJL did identify several patterns of judgment behavior of interest to designers. First, participants with higher individual judgment achievement tended to have higher predictive accuracy when estimating automated judgments. Second, participants generally thought that their individual judgments were closer to the automated judgments than they really were, as shown by the often substantial differences between assumed and actual similarity. These patterns may share an underlying cause: if participants predicted the automated judgments to be close to their own, then higher-performing individual judgments would result in predictions closer to the high achievement automated judgments.

Nomothetic analysis of participant behavior in this experiment, with large individual differences identified between the participants, found few statistically significant effects due to the training and display interventions. Of note, strategy display participants did not adapt to the automated judgments more, learn to improve their individual judgment achievement over time, and predict the automated judgments; instead, they showed more conflict between their individual judgments and the automated judgments and had poorer individual judgment achievement and predictive accuracy in the prediction phase. The strategy display was intended to provide participants of equal motivation with better information; these results instead suggest that participants may have used the display passively, that is, as an aid that justified greater compromise to the automated judge rather than for learning from and about the automated judge. These results, therefore, highlight the number of factors that go into designing effective human–automated judge interaction, which require detailed methods for measurement and analysis.

Acknowledgment.   This work was supported in part by the Navy Air Warfare Center Training Systems Division contract N611339-99-C-0105 (Gwen Campbell, technical monitor).

References

Adelman, L., Christian, M., Gualtieri, J., & Johnson, K. L. (1998). Examining the effects of cognitive consistency between training and displays. *IEEE Transactions on Systems, Man and Cybernetics, 28*(1), 1–16.

Bass, E. J. (2002). Human-automated judgment learning: A research paradigm based on Interpersonal Learning to investigate human interaction with automated judgments of hazards. *Dissertation Abstracts International, 63*(03) B, (UMI no. 3046873).

Bass, E.J. & Pritchett, A. R. (accepted). Human-Automated Judgment Learning: A methodology for examining human interaction with information analysis automation. *IEEE Transaction on Systems, Man, and Cybernetics, Part A.*

Box, G. E. P., Hunter, W. G., & Hunter, J. S. (1978). *Statistics for experiments.* New York: Wiley.

Brehmer, B. (1994). The psychology of linear judgment models. *Acta Psychologica, 87,* 137–154.

Cooksey, R. W. (1996). *Judgment analysis: Theory, methods, and application.* New York: Academic Press.

Earle, T. C. (1973). Interpersonal learning. In L. Rappoport & D. A. Summers (Eds.), *Human Judgment and Social Interaction* (pp. 240–266). New York: Holt, Rinehart & Winston.

Hammond, K. R. (1973). The cognitive conflict paradigm. In L. Rappoport & D. A. Summers (Eds.), *Human judgment and social interaction* (pp. 188–205). New York: Holt, Rinehart & Winston.

Hammond, K. R., Wilkins, M., & Todd, F. J. (1966). A research paradigm for the study of interpersonal learning. *Psychological Bulletin, 65,* 221–232.

Hursch, C. J., Hammond, K. R., & Hursch, J. L. (1964). Some methodological considerations in multiple-cue probability. *Psychological Review, 71,* 42–60.

Jennrich, R. I., & Schluchter, M. D. (1986). Unbalanced repeated-measures models with structured covariance matrices. *Biometrics, 42,* 805–820.

Lee, J. D., & Moray, N. (1992). Trust, control strategies and allocation of function in human–machine systems. *Ergonomics, 35,* 1243–1270.

Lee, J. D., & Moray, N. (1994). Trust, self-confidence, and operators' adaptation to automation. *International Journal of Human-Computer Studies, 40,* 153–184.

Mosier, K. L., Skitka, L. J., Heers, S., & Burdick, M. (1998). Automation bias: Decision making and performance in high-tech cockpits. *International Journal of Aviation Psychology, 8*(1), 47–63.

Muir, B. M. (1987). Trust between humans and machines, and the design of decision aids. *International Journal of Man-Machine Studies, 27,* 527–539.

Muir, B. M. (1994). Trust in automation: Part I. Theoretical issues in the study of trust and human intervention in automated systems. *Ergonomics, 37,* 1905–1922.

Parasuraman, R., Masalonis, A. J., & Hancock, P. A. (2000). Fuzzy signal detection theory: Basic postulates and formulas for analyzing human and machine performance. *Human Factors*, 42(4), 636–659.

Pritchett, A. R., & Ippolito, C. (2000). Software architecture for a reconfigurable flight simulator. *AIAA Modeling and Simulation Technologies Conference*. Denver, Colo.

Pritchett, A. R., & Vándor, B. (2001). Designing situation displays to promote conformance to automatic alerts/ *Proceedings of the Annual Meeting of the Human Factors and Ergonomics Society*. Minneapolis, Minn.

Robinson, D. E., & Sorkin, R. D. (1985). A contingent criterion model of computer assisted detection. In R. E. Eberts & C. G. Eberts (Eds.) *Trends in ergonomics/human factors II* (pp. 75–82). Amsterdam: Elsevier Science.

RTCA (1995). *Final report of RTCA task force 3: Free flight implementation*. Washington, D.C.: RTCA.

Smith, J.D., Ellis, S. R., & Lee, E.C. (1984). Perceived threat and avoidance maneuvers in response to cockpit traffic displays. *Human Factors*, 26, 33–48.

Sorkin, R. D., & Woods, D. D. (1985). Systems with human monitors: A signal detection analysis. *Human-Computer Interaction*, 1, 49–75.

Strauss, R. (2000). A methodology for measuring the judgmental components of situation awareness. Unpublished doctoral dissertation, Georgia Institute of Technology.

Wickens, C. D., & Flach, J. M. (1988). Information processing. In E. L Wiener & D. C. Nagel (Eds.), *Human factors in aviation* (pp. 111–155). San Diego, Calif.: Academic Press.

Wightman, D. C., & Lintern, G. (1985). Part-task training for tracking and manual control. *Human Factors*, 27, 267–283.

Yang, L., & Kuchar, J. (1997). *Prototype conflict alerting logic for free flight*. AIAA 97–0220. Reston, Va.: American Institute of Aeronautics and Astronautics.

IV

Alternatives to Compensatory Modeling

Alex Kirlik

Introduction

A recent research trend following in the footsteps of Brunswik's probabilistic functionalism has been to entertain and evaluate whether human judgment and decision strategies may, in some contexts, make even fewer demands on cognition than the linear-additive (compensatory) rules presumed by the standard lens model (Dhami & Ayton, 2001; Dhami & Harries, 2001; Gigerenzer & Goldstein, 1996; Gigerenzer et al , 1999). This trend is readily apparent in the "ecological rationality" paradigm of Gigerenzer and colleagues, which portrays cognition as an "adaptive toolbox" of "fast and frugal" heuristics (for more detail, see especially chapters 10, 12, and 18 and the introduction to part VI). This paradigm shares with Brunswik the view that cognitive strategies should be evaluated according to their adaptive mesh with both environmental demands (e.g., time and accuracy constraints) and resources (e.g., available information sources and their statistical texture).

At present, however, it is premature to estimate what impact the ecological rationality approach will have in the area of human–technology interaction. Looking at the temporal aspects of the situation, there are ample reasons to believe that its impact will be significant. Technological work contexts often require working under high levels of time pressure, in which quick yet approximate solutions

are likely to earn more favor than slow yet precise ones (e.g., chapter 18). To date, however, those who have adopted the ecological rationality perspective have chiefly focused on informing cognitive theory, rather than on studying and supporting behavior in the types of dynamic, interactive, technological ecologies that are the focus of this book.

As such, the first chapter in this section represents one of the first attempts to view technology interaction from the perspective of ecological rationality. In Chapter 10, Rothrock and Kirlik revisit the dynamic judgment task studied in chapter 3 by Bisantz and colleagues but from the perspective of heuristic- or rule-based (noncompensatory) rather than linear-additive (compensatory) modeling. Rothrock and Kirlik note that the ecological rationality approach currently lacks techniques for inferring rule-based heuristics directly from behavioral data (the purpose served by linear regression in compensatory lens modeling and policy capturing). To address this need, they present a study in which they developed a technique using a genetic algorithm to infer candidate noncompensatory descriptions of the logical (if/and/or/not/then) rules that best described the behavior of participants in their experiment. Notably, their findings shed additional light on the relatively high use of unmodeled knowledge demonstrated by the highest performer in the Bisantz et al. study. If high performance in this dynamic judgment task indeed did require the use of a noncompensatory strategy, as Rothrock and Kirlik's analysis suggests, then it should not come as a surprise that Bisantz and colleagues found that they could not model a significant portion of their highest-performing participant's knowledge using the compensatory lens model.

In chapter 11, Campbell and colleagues also pursue a noncompensatory alternative to linear-additive modeling, again using a variant of the dynamic judgment task discussed in both chapters 3 and 10. Specifically, a fuzzy set approach is used to model participants in their study and to compare the resulting fits of both the fuzzy and linear-additive rules to behavioral data. The fuzzy models achieved comparable but not significantly superior fits. Interestingly, however, a training intervention that provided initially low-scoring participants with feedback derived from fuzzy rules was shown to be superior to one where feedback was derived from linear-additive rules.

In chapter 12, Mosier and McCauley bring a welcome new dimension to the discussion of technology-mediated interaction, drawing on Kenneth Hammond's distinction between correspondence- and coherence-based cognition. The former, which involves the need to achieve a high level of adaptive fit or coupling with the external environment, has nearly been the sole focus of the book to this point. Mosier and McCauley suggest that the prevalence of ever more powerful technologies is promoting an increasing reliance on the latter, coherence-based form of cognition (e.g., the ability to create an internally consistent representation of a situation). Mosier and McCauley base their claim on the observation that "in the world characterized by advanced technology, the environment is more deterministic than probabilistic in that the uncertainty has, for most practical purposes, been engineered out through technical reliability." Although the level of irreducible uncertainty faced by a performer in any given system and environment is certainly an empirical question, the need to support both coherence- and correspondence-based cognition in system design certainly merits additional attention from both the research and design communities (see chapter 13 for more on this issue).

References

Dhami, M. K. & Ayton, P. (2001). Bailing and jailing the fast and frugal way. *Journal of Behavioral Decision Making, 14*, 141–168.

Dhami, M. K. & Harries, C. (2001). Fast and frugal version regression models of human judgment. *Thinking & Reasoning, 7*, 5–27.

Gigerenzer, G. & Goldstein, D. G. (1996). Reasoning the fast and frugal way: Models of bounded rationality. *Psychological Review, 103*, 650–669.

Gigerenzer, G., Todd, P.M. & the ABC Research Group (Eds.). (1999). *Simple heuristics that make us smart*. New York: Oxford University Press.

10

Ling Rothrock and Alex Kirlik

Inferring Fast and Frugal Heuristics from Human Judgment Data

Introduction

Much late twentieth-century literature on the judgment and decision making of experienced performers, especially those working in technological settings, suggests that decisions are rarely made according to the prescriptions of highly enumerative strategies such as utility maximization (Savage, 1972) or its multiattribute variant (Edwards & Newman, 1982). Instead, performers seem to rely heavily on one type of heuristic shortcut or another to meet the demands of time stress, uncertainty, information load, and the often abstract manner in which information is displayed in technological contexts. Researchers have proposed various accounts of these shortcuts. The most notable of these, at least in the human factors and cognitive engineering disciplines, has emerged from the naturalistic decision making (NDM) paradigm (Klein, 1999; Klein et al., 1993). From this perspective, the apparent cognitive efficiency of judgment and decision making in these contexts arises from experience providing the performer with a vast storehouse of cases, often allowing a performer to quickly recognize a good solution rather than having to comparatively evaluate a long list of options.

Additionally, heuristic strategies that may initially appear to be vastly oversimplified for meeting the demands of a particular task often yield surprisingly good and robust performance when compared against the performance of more cognitively demanding, enumerative strategies (Connoll, 1988; Gigerenzer & Kurz, 2001; Hogarth, 1981, Kirlik, Miller, & Jagacinski, 1993; Kirlik et al., 1996a, 1996b). A combination of factors is likely to account for this counterintuitive result. Gigerenzer and colleagues (e.g., Gigerenzer & Selten, 2001; Gigerenzer & Goldstein, 1996, Gigerenzer, Todd, & The ABC Research Group, 1999), following Brunswik's lead, have focused on the role of the statistical structure or "causal texture" of the task environment as playing an important role. For example, they have noted that many judgment or decision ecologies have cue-criterion structures that allow few or perhaps even one cue to provide the basis for sound judgment (see chapter 18 for a concrete example). For instance, knowing that a particular U.S. city has a major league baseball team and another one does not is a highly reliable predictor of relative city population. In addition, one might think that by taking more cues into account one would successively improve the quality of a prediction such as this, but as the work of Gigerenzer and colleagues has demonstrated, this is not always the case. As in linear regression, increasing the number of cues or predictor coefficients may increase the total variance explained, but it may also lead to overfitting the data, yielding a judgment or decision rule that is actually *less* robust to new cases than are simpler versions (the raison d'être for the development and use of the R^2_{adj} statistic in the evaluation of the quality of a regression model).

Additionally, researchers such as Hogarth (1981) and Connolly (1988) have pointed out that dynamic and particularly interactive task environments may actually both reward more highly and provide additional resources to support cognitively efficient heuristic strategies as opposed to highly enumerative ones. These authors point to issues such as the fact that roughly accurate but timely solutions may be more highly rewarded in dynamic contexts than optimal but late solutions and that interactive environments may support cognitively simple and incremental, feedback-guided strategies, among other benefits.

Finally, Kirlik et al. (1996a) have offered the observation that judgment or decision tasks may appear irreducibly complex to a researcher or analyst, who may thereby conclude that a person performing that task successfully must be engaged in complex (even if covert) cognition of some kind. However, this may be fallacious reasoning in cases where the experienced performer has access to or an appreciation for environmental information that the researcher or analyst does not. As Neisser (1976) has persuasively argued, any aspiring predictor of the behavior of a chess master must be able to perceive the many sources of information the board provides at least as well as the chess master him- or herself. Because very few judgment or decision researchers have the time and resources to understand task environments as well as the experienced performers they study, it may come as no surprise that experienced performers report using simpler methods for making decisions and judgments than a researcher or analyst could believe to truly account for the often high levels of performance observed.

Although there is a growing consensus that accounts such as subjective expected utility (SEU) theory and multiattribute utility theory (MAUT) may severely overrationalize the cognitive processes of experienced performers, there is less consensus on whether the heuristic strategies used by these performers are amenable to formal modeling. Advocates of the NDM paradigm, for example, are

highly skeptical of the possibility of formal modeling, indicating that a commitment to "informal modeling" is an "essential characteristic" of the NDM approach (Lipshitz et al., 2001, pp. 334–335). Others disagree about the prospects for modeling naturalistic judgments and decisions. For example, in response to the Lipshitz et al. (2001) article, Todd and Gigerenzer (2001) have gone on record that they believe that "natural decision making can be formally modeled" (p. 381). Todd and Gigerenzer offer up their program on "ecological rationality" and an "adaptive toolbox" of fast and frugal heuristics as an approach useful for developing formal models of cognition in the types of naturalistic and often technological contexts of interest to NDM researchers.

Clearly, many of the contributors to the present volume would likely agree with Todd and Gigerenzer in this regard, as evidenced by their desire (and achievements) to date to put forward formal models of judgment and decision making in complex technological systems. On the other hand, these authors, in most if not all cases, have also been forthcoming about the limitations of their techniques. Judged collectively, it is probably fair to say that we are still quite some time from the point at which all of the behaviors of interest to the NDM community will admit to formal modeling, if that goal is even possible to reach. Until such a time, we embrace the need for naturalistic studies such as those performed by many NDM researchers as necessary to ensure that scientific research contexts are representative of the target contexts toward which research results are intended to apply.

However, we, like Todd and Gigerenzer, believe that a commitment to abstraction and thus formal modeling should remain a guiding light in the study of human–technology interaction and decision making (also see Byrne & Gray, 2003, on this point). Abstraction is not only a crucial requirement for scientific generalization, it has practical benefits as well. Specifically, it allows for the development of modeling tools and techniques enabling those who are not themselves experts in a particular area of scientific research to still benefit by the outcomes of that research. If we do not continue to pursue the path toward abstraction and formalization, we are destined to a future in which it will be impossible to educate competent professionals in cognitive engineering, human factors, and related fields by equipping them with tools and techniques, as do all other successful branches of applied science and engineering.

For this reason, in this chapter we present a formal technique developed to enable an analyst to infer heuristic judgment or strategies directly from behavioral data on human judgment. Although the technique is not yet fully mature, we present it to provide at least one step toward the day when formal modeling of judgment and decision making in naturalistic or technological contexts may possibly become one useful item in the toolbox of a practitioner in cognitive engineering, human factors, and applied psychology.

Compensatory versus Noncompensatory Judgment Strategies

Especially when used for practical purposes such as guiding interface design or training, it is important to keep in mind that the linear regression approach for inferring judgment strategies from behavioral data (see chapter 2) makes specific assumptions about the cognitive processes that underlie judgment behavior. First, regression assumes that the judge has available a set of cues that he or she is able to measure. This measurement can either be binary (i.e., a cue is either absent or present) or in terms of the magnitude of a cue value. In addition, the performer is assumed to use some form of cue-weighting policy, which is correspondingly modeled by the set of weights resulting from the regression model that best fits the judge's behavioral data. Finally, a regression model assumes that the judge then integrates (the possibly differently weighted) cue values into a summary judgment.

This type of weighting and summing judgment process, as represented by a linear-additive rule, has an important property: it reflects a *compensatory* strategy for integrating cue information. These strategies are compensatory in the sense that the presence of a cue with a high value, or a high positive weighting can compensate for an absence of cues with moderate or low weighting. Similarly, cues with high negative weights compensate for cues with high positive weights, reflecting the manner in which a person might differentially weight or trade off evidence for and against a particular judgment.

A *noncompensatory* strategy, on the other hand, is one in which this "trading off" property is absent

(Dawes, 1964; Einhorn, 1970; Gigerenzer & Goldstein, 1996). Einhorn (1970) discussed two noncompensatory judgment rules: a conjunctive rule and a disjunctive rule. A conjunctive rule describes a strategy in which every cue considered in the judgment must have a high value (or exceed some threshold) for the overall judgment to have high value. People being evaluated on their job performance by a conjunctive strategy, for example, are being subjected to a demanding criterion because they will not receive a high evaluation or job promotion unless they perform at a high level on every single dimension of evaluation. Note the noncompensatory nature of this strategy: no cue value, however highly weighted, can compensate for a low value on any one of the other cues.

The second type of noncompensatory strategy discussed by Einhorn (1970) is a disjunctive rule. A disjunctive strategy is one in which only one cue must have a high value or exceed some threshold for the overall judgment to have high value. A good example of a disjunctive strategy might be the evaluation of athletes in a professional (U.S.) football draft: a player might be highly rated if he has high value on any one of the set of relevant, evaluative dimensions (e.g., speed, place-kicking ability, punting ability, passing ability, etc.). Note that this strategy is noncompensatory, in the sense that a low value on a particular cue or set of cues does not detract from a high overall rating, given the presence of at least one cue with high value.

Many simple behavioral rules have a noncompensatory nature. In fact, any set of logical rules for making judgments that is inconsistent with a weighting and summing formula is likely to have a noncompensatory nature. In some cases, linear regression may provide an approximate fit to behavioral data generated by noncompensatory strategies. However, differences may exist between the predictions of a compensatory, linear-additive model and the predictions of a noncompensatory, rule-based model in particular portions of the cue space (For a discussion and graphical depiction, see Einhorn, 1970).

In the present context, it is important to note that many if not most noncompensatory judgment strategies make lower information search and integration demands than do compensatory, linear-additive strategies. The latter require every cue to be assessed, weighted, and combined to yield an overall judgment. Noncompensatory strategies, on the other hand, typically require fewer judgment cues to be considered, weighted, and combined to make a judgment (for a discussion of this issue, see Gigerenzer & Goldstein, 1996). Importantly, psychologists studying judgment have found that two particular task conditions are crucial in prompting people to shift from elaborate and exhaustive, compensatory judgment strategies to less demanding, noncompensatory strategies.

These two conditions are task complexity (Payne, 1976) and time stress (Payne, Bettman, & Johnson, 1988; Wright 1974). Increased task complexity (e.g., the number of cues, the number of possible alternatives), and time stress both tend to increase the likelihood that people will adopt cognitively less demanding, noncompensatory strategies for making judgments. Given that both empirical research and psychological theory suggest that performers in complex, dynamic environments will develop and use noncompensatory judgment strategies, linear regression approaches for inferring these strategies from behavioral data in these contexts may be inappropriate and may lead to misleading accounts of the behavior of these performers. As a result, a need exists to develop techniques for reliably inferring noncompensatory judgment heuristics from behavioral data. The following section describes one candidate technique developed for this purpose.

Induction: A Noncompensatory Approach

As observed by 18th-century philosopher David Hume, any knowledge derived from induction cannot in principle be taken as certain. The purpose of induction in the context of the present research is to generate plausible hypotheses relevant to a person's goals—admittedly a less ambitious goal than, for example, Pearl's causal modeling framework (Pearl, 2000, p. 43). This weaker interpretation of the purpose of induction is drawn from the machine learning literature (Holland et al., 1986; Michalski, 1983; Quinlan, 1986), and serves as the basis for the noncompensatory policy-capturing technique presented in this chapter.

Based on our research experiences and reviews of the NDM literature, we first identified four constraints that informed our selection and develop-

ment of a technique for the induction of judgment strategies in technological, operational contexts:

1. Judgments are made in a dynamic environment in which multiple events are not necessarily independent of one another and human actions may influence future decisions (Klein et al., 1993).
2. No clear distinction between positive and negative examples of concepts or judgments can be assumed. In fact, the only data available are the judgments made by the human and the values of the available cues.
3. Judgments are made in a probabilistic environment in which cues are sometimes (but not always) available and sometimes (but not always) attended to by the decision maker (Gigerenzer & Kurz, 2001).
4. Judgment strategies, consistent with the research of Gigerenzer and his colleagues (Gigerenzer, Todd, & The ABC Research Group, 1999), are fast and frugal, or in the terminology we have used, are based on noncompensatory heuristics.

We now consider our research goals and these constraints in light of available inferential approaches presented in the literature on machine learning, each providing a possible alternative to the compensatory, linear regression approach to judgment strategy induction.

Approaches to Noncompensatory Inductive Learning

Three machine learning approaches to induction dominate the literature: concept-based, instance-based, and evolutionary-based techniques. Concept-based learning techniques are based on forming a class definition by constructing a concept that covers positive and negative examples. Concepts are represented as either decision trees or rules. Decision trees (Quinlan, 1986, 1993) provide a representation of propositional knowledge by using descriptions of situations or objects as inputs to generate a yes-or-no decision as to whether a situation or object is a member of the class represented by the concept. Rules take the form of antecedent-consequent pairs. A rule is said to *cover* an example if all conditions for the rule are true for the example. Rule induction algorithms (Clark & Niblett, 1989; Michalski, 1983;

Michalski & Chilausky, 1999) generally use a set covering approach based on a training set of positive and negative examples.

In contrast to concept-based methods, instance-based learning methods (Aha, Kibler, & Albert, 1991; Cost & Salzberg, 1993; Duda & Hart, 1973) use a quantitative similarity or distance metric to classify examples (e.g., a k nearest neighbors algorithm) as an approach to the problem of induction. However, as emphasized by Degani, Shafto, and Kirlik (chapter 13), many technological ecologies have largely discrete rather than continuous state spaces. As such, an induction approach based on the types of similarity or distance metrics used in instance-based learning techniques are likely to be inapplicable for inferring human judgment strategies in these technological contexts.

Finally, in evolutionary-based approaches (De-Jong, Spears, & Gordon, 1993; Holland, 1975; Holland et al., 2000; Moriarty, Schultz, & Grefenstette, 1999), learning is viewed as a process of ongoing adaptation to a partially unknown environment. Unlike most concept-based or instance based methods, inductive learning is not regarded as an optimization process but as an outcome of the interaction and coordination of a large number of simultaneously active rules.

This brief review of the three dominant machine learning approaches suggests that evolutionary-based methods are perhaps best equipped to meet the requirements for inferring human judgment strategies in dynamic, uncertain, technological contexts in a manner that could best provide useful insights for design or training interventions. First, evolutionary-based methods allow many rules to be active simultaneously, thus allowing the system to consider multiple and even conflicting hypotheses to be considered simultaneously. Because certainty can never be reached via induction, we believe that the most conservative approach to inferring human judgment strategies from behavioral data should indeed be able to provide the complete set of potential hypotheses about what strategies a performer may be using based solely on the performer's history of judgment performance. From the perspective of training and the design of feedback, we believe that such an approach is consistent with the behavior of a good teacher who considers multiple possible diagnoses of a student's performance. This contrasts with a teacher who may leap to a premature (based on the data available)

diagnosis of performance, running the risk that providing feedback or additional exercises to the student based on this diagnosis may not adequately address the underlying issues at hand.

Second, as will be illustrated in the ensuing description of our own inductive approach, evolutionary-based methods make less restrictive assumptions on modeling input data than traditional instance-based (e.g., Aha, Kibler, & Albert 1991) or concept-based methods (e.g., Michalski, 1983). Our approach accommodates discrete, continuous, and hybrid judgment ecologies (see chapter 13). Third, evolutionary-based methods have the added advantage that search is done on the encoding of the genetic strings and not the strings themselves (Goldberg, 1989). The string representation, in effect, enables the researcher to determine not only the functional simplicity of a heuristic but its simplicity in form as well. Again, these points will be concretely illustrated in the discussion of the inferential technique that follows.

A Genetics-Based Policy Capturing Technique

Holland et al. (1986) suggest that induction is a process of revisiting existing condition-action rule parameters and generating new rules based on knowledge of environmental variability (p. 22). Each rule represents a unit of knowledge, and collections of rules represent internal states of a learning system (p. 15). Analogously, we define induction as a process of modifying a population of rule sets representing candidate judgment strategies. The rule sets are generated and modified on the basis of empirical data representing actual instances of human judgment—which we call exemplars. In the following sections, we introduce and describe the technique we have developed for inducing noncompensatory judgment policies from exemplars, which we call genetics-based policy capturing (GBPC).

Representational Issues

To be consistent with the research of Gigerenzer and Goldstein (1996), the representation of each rule set in GBPC is in disjunctive normal form (DNF). To illustrate the form of a rule set, consider a conjunctive rule as a condition-action rule with N statements where:

IF (statement 1) $\cap$ (statement 2) $\cap$ . . . $\cap$
(statement N) THEN (consequence statement)

A disjunction of M statements is represented as:

(statement I) $\cup$ (statement II)
$\cup$ . . . $\cup$ (statement M)

Each rule set in the population is represented as a disjunctive rule where each individual statement (e.g., *statement II*) is a conjunctive rule. DeJong, Spears, and Gordon (1993) demonstrated that a genetic algorithm (GA) was able to learn condition-action rules such as these based on exemplars and with little a priori knowledge. Moreover, because GBPC rule sets are in DNF, the outcomes can potentially reflect not only fast and frugal heuristics (see the following discussion for additional detail) but also any judgment strategy consisting of IF, AND, OR, or NOT operators (Mendelsohn, 1997).

GBPC maintains a population of rule sets, where each rule set consists of a disjunction of conjunctive rules in DNF. Each rule within the rule set is a similarity template—or schema (Holland, 1975; Goldberg, 1989)—and is covered by the ternary alphabet {0,1,#} where # is a match-all character. The population of rule sets is trained on exemplars representing instances of human judgment. The instances consist not only of the human judgments themselves but also cues available at the time of judgment. As in regression-based judgment modeling, the correct identification of cues that actually support human judgment is crucial to the success and utility of the GBPC technique.

Relation to Fast and Frugal Heuristics

A key characteristic of the class of fast and frugal heuristics developed by Gigerenzer and Goldstein (1996) is that each involves a process of steps. Take, for example, the steps described by Gigerenzer and Goldstein for the *Take-the-Best* heuristic:

1. If only one of two objects is recognized, choose the recognized object. If neither is recognized, choose randomly between them. If both are recognized, go to step 2.
2. Retrieve cue values from the best cue from memory. If no cue remains, take a guess.
3. If one cue has a positive cue value and the other does not, select object with positive cue value.
4. If neither cue has a positive value, go to step 2.

We now map the outcomes of the *Take-the-Best* heuristic to a rule set. Given n known cues, let x_i be the cue value for Object A for $i = 2,3, . . . , n$. Let y_i be the cue value for Object B. Let $x_i \in \{0,1,\#\}$ and $y_i \in \{0,1,\#\}$ where 0 is a negative cue value, 1 is a positive cue value, and # is an uncertain cue value. We reserve x_1 and y_1 to indicate the recognition parameter where 0 represents an unrecognized object and 1 represents a recognized one. Moreover, let z be the judgment (Object A or Object B) where 0 indicates Object A is selected, 1 indicates Object B, and # indicates either. A rule set can then be represented as:

$$(x_1 \cap y_1) \cap (x_2 \cap y_2) \cap . . . \cap (X_n \cap y_n) \cap z$$

$$\cup$$

$$(x_{1'} \cap y_{1'}) \cap (x_{2'} \cap y_{2'}) \cap . . . \cap (X_{n'} \cap y_{n'}) \cap z'$$

$$\cup$$

$$. . .$$

where each row represents an individual rule. We can represent both sets of cues as vectors where $\mathbf{x} = [x_1\ x_2\ x_3]$ are the three cue values associated with Object A and $\mathbf{y} = [y_1\ y_2\ y_3]$ are the cues associated with Object B.

For example, consider a decision to select the city (i.e., an object) with the higher population from a pair of alternatives (City A and City B) using the *Take-the-Best* heuristic. Say that both cities are recognized by the decision maker and that the decision maker does not know if either city has a professional baseball team, but that City B has a professional football team. Therefore, $\mathbf{x} = [0\ \#\ \#]$, $\mathbf{y} = [0\ \#\ 1]$, and $z = 1$. It is interesting to observe that although the outcomes of a decision process can be represented through a rule set in DNF, the process itself is lost in the representation. Nevertheless, we will show that by using the DNF representation it becomes possible to infer decision rules systematically.

Illustrating the Representational Approach

We now use an example of a simple judgment ecology and task to illustrate the concepts underlying our induction approach and to clarify implementation details. Consider the case of a private pilot who is flying near a small airfield. The pilot sees four aircraft during the course of his flight and makes judgments of their identity on the basis of two cues—speed and altitude—which we assume to be perceptually measured or encoded in a binary fashion, to simplify the discussion. The aircraft characteristics and corresponding pilot judgments are shown in Table 10.1. This judgment data will be used to demonstrate components of the GBPC inductive inference model and also the binary representation of candidate rule sets.

Consider a binary string representation for the judgments in the sample domain. Using the coding scheme where 1 = fast, 0 = slow, 1 = high, 0 = low, 1 = racing aircraft, and 0 = transport aircraft, each of the judgments in Table 10.1 can be converted into the four exemplars shown in Table 10.2. For example, Exemplar no. 1 represents the following operator judgment:

$(Speed = Fast) \cap (Altitude = Low) \cap$
$(Judgment = racing \ aircraft)$

For simplicity's sake, the consequence statement is represented as part of the conjunctive statement. In addition, for the sake of illustration, consider the rule sets shown in Table 10.3 as the population used to learn the exemplars in the sample ecology. Each rule set in the population represents data that genetic operators manipulate to form improved rule sets in future generations. For example, Rule Set no. 1 is represented by the following string: 1#10#0. The first three characters of the string (Speed = 1, Altitude = #, Judgment = 1) translate to the first rule:

$(Speed = Fast) \cap (Altitude = anything) \cap$
$(Judgment = racing \ aircraft)$

Similarly, the next three characters of the string (Speed = 0, Altitude = #, Judgment = 0) translate to the second rule:

$(Speed = Slow) \cap (Altitude = anything) \cap$
$(Judgment = transport \ aircraft)$

Table 10.1. Aircraft characteristics and pilot judgments for example ecology

Speed	Altitude	Judgment
Fast	Low	racing aircraft
Fast	High	racing aircraft
Slow	High	transport aircraft
Slow	Low	transport aircraft

Table 10.2. Exemplar representation for sample domain judgments

Exemplar No.	Characteristics Represented	Exemplar Representation
1	Fast, low, racing aircraft	101
2	Fast, high, racing aircraft	111
3	Slow, high, transport aircraft	010
4	Slow, low, transport aircraft	000

The rules combine in disjunctive normal form to create the following disjunctive rule set:

$(Speed = Fast) \cap (Altitude = anything) \cap$
$(Judgment = racing \ aircraft)$

OR

$(Speed = Slow) \cap (Altitude = anything) \cap$
$(Judgment = transport \ aircraft)$

Note that Rule Set no. 1 matches all the exemplars shown in Table 10.2.

Bounded Rationality Considerations

To reflect bounded rationality (Simon, 1956), GBPC uses the Pittsburgh approach (DeJong, Spears, & Gordon 1993; Smith, 1983) to learn. In the Pittsburgh approach, each rule set is a candidate judgment strategy and each strategy has a variable number of rules—hence strategies with a few simpler and effective rules reflect a satisficing mode of interaction. Learning consists of applying genetic operators in the order outlined by Goldberg (1989). That is, each learning cycle,

Table 10.3. Sample domain rule sets

Rule Set No.	Rule Set Representation
1	1#10#0
2	1#1
3	0#0
4	###
5	101111010000
6	11#100001000
7	000
8	001
9	010
10	011
11	100
12	101
13	110
14	111

also known as a generation, consists of (1) fitness evaluation, (2) reproduction, (3) crossover, and (4) mutation. The multiobjective fitness evaluation process will be presented in detail in the following sections. Reproduction is achieved through use of a roulette wheel where rule set slots are apportioned based on fitness (for details, see Goldberg, 1989). Mutation is implemented through random alteration of a bit in a rule set.

GBPC uses the variable-length two-point crossover operator developed by DeJong and Spears (1990). The operator was shown to be effective by DeJong et al. (1993). This crossover operator selects a pair of rule sets and then selects two positions within each rule set to exchange information. The positions are constrained only by the relative distance from the beginning and end of each rule set. For example, given Rule Set nos. 5 and 1 and four randomly selected positions (indicated by |):

Rule Set no. 5: 10 | 11110100 | 00
Rule Set no. 1: 1# | 10 | #0

The resulting rule sets after applying the crossover operator are:

Rule Set no. 5: 10 | 10 | 00
Rule Set no. 1: 1# | 11110100 | #0

Through two-point crossover, information between viable rule sets within GBPC are exchanged.

Fitness Evaluation

A central element of GBPC is the multiobjective fitness evaluation function. As mentioned earlier, search in GBPC is done on the encoding of the strings and not the strings themselves. Hence, the quality of a judgment strategy (i.e., the form of the encoding) can be assessed along a range of dimensions, as will be seen in the following. In the traditional linear regression approach to policy capturing, the best fitting linear-additive judgment strategy is determined by least squares minimization. In moving to a noncompensatory approach to judgment modeling, we must define an alternative to least squares for measuring the goodness or fitness of a rule set. In a subsequent section of this chapter, we provide some evidence for the plausibility of our fitness evaluation measure by showing that the rule sets induced by GBPC in a laboratory simulation of a dynamic naval judgment task were consistent with human judgment data.

We start by considering the fitness of a rule set as the ability to classify a set of exemplars in a manner consistent with the satisfying behavior characteristic of bounded rationality. Therefore, a rule set should not only match a set of exemplars but also resemble the types of noncompensatory judgment strategies performers typically use as heuristics in these tasks. This is done in GBPC through the use of a multiobjective function that evaluates fitness along three dimensions: completeness, specificity, and parsimony.

The completeness dimension is based on work by DeJong et al. (1993), and is a measure of how well a rule set matches the entire set of exemplars (i.e., human judgments in a data set). The specificity dimension was first suggested by Holland et al. (1986), and is a measure of how specific a rule set is with respect to the number of wild cards it contains. Therefore, rule sets with fewer match-all (i.e., #) characters are classified as more specific. The parsimony dimension is a measure of the goodness of a rule set in terms of the necessity of each rule. Hence, in a parsimonious rule set, there are no unnecessary rules. GBPC assumes that the most likely rule set representation of noncompensatory human judgment strategies will be one that matches all human judgments, is maximally specific, and is maximally parsimonious. (One might think that the maximum specificity requirement [the fewest match-all or "don't care" characters] contrasts with the "fast and frugal" assumption, which would indeed favor rule sets having the most # characters [maximally selective attention or economical information use]. But without this assumption we get the result: if # . . . then #. . . . As such we have opted to rely on maximizing parsimony to ensure frugality and let the data be our guide regarding specificity.) The mathematical formulation of each dimension will be discussed in the following section.

Mathematical Development of Fitness Dimensions

Definition 10.1

An exemplar matrix, E, consists of a set of binary variable vectors, called exemplars, whose range is the set $\{0,1\}$. Each exemplar within E is represented as $e_{i\bullet}$, for $i = 1, \ldots, m$, where m is the total number of exemplars. Each binary variable within $e_{i\bullet}$ is represented as $e_{i,j}$ for $j = 1, \ldots, n$, where n is exemplar length. Thus, E is a m by n matrix in the form:

$$E = \begin{bmatrix} e_{1,1} & e_{1,2} & \cdots & e_{1,n} \\ e_{2,1} & e_{2,2} & \cdots & e_{2,n} \\ \vdots & \vdots & & \vdots \\ e_{m,1} & e_{m,2} & \cdots & e_{m,n} \end{bmatrix} \quad (10.1)$$

Definition 10.2

A rule set matrix is a matrix, S, consisting of a set of ternary variable vectors, called a rule set, whose range is the set $\{0,1,\#\}$. Each rule within S is represented as s_{kC} for $k = 1, \ldots, p$, where p is the number of rules in the rule set. Each ternary variable within s_{kC} is represented as $s_{k,j}$, for $j = 1, \ldots, n$ where n is the rule length.

Therefore, S is a p by n matrix in the form:

$$S = \begin{bmatrix} s_{1,1} & s_{1,2} & \cdots & s_{1,n} \\ s_{2,1} & s_{2,2} & \cdots & s_{2,n} \\ \vdots & \vdots & & \vdots \\ s_{p,1} & s_{p,2} & \cdots & s_{p,n} \end{bmatrix} \quad (10.2)$$

Matching an exemplar with a rule set requires an indicator function. Therefore, given that $x \in E$ and $y \in S$, an indicator function is defined as I_A where $A = \{x, \#\}$, so that

$$I_A(y) = \begin{cases} 1 \text{ if } y \in A \\ 0 \text{ if } y \in A \end{cases} \quad (10.3)$$

The results of applying I_A to compare a rule set, S, with the ith exemplar $e_{i\bullet}$, is shown as a "matching matrix", M_i, for exemplar i where

$$M_i = \begin{bmatrix} I_{\{e_{i,1},\#\}}(s_{1,1}) & I_{\{e_{i,2},\#\}}(s_{1,2}) & \cdots & I_{\{e_{i,n},\#\}}(s_{1,n}) \\ I_{\{e_{i,1},\#\}}(s_{2,1}) & I_{\{e_{i,2},\#\}}(s_{2,2}) & \cdots & I_{\{e_{i,n},\#\}}(s_{2,n}) \\ \vdots & \vdots & & \vdots \\ I_{\{e_{i,1},\#\}}(s_{p,1}) & I_{\{e_{i,2},\#\}}(s_{p,2}) & \cdots & I_{\{e_{i,n},\#\}}(s_{p,n}) \end{bmatrix} (10.4)$$

Each row of the matching matrix represents how well an exemplar $e_{i\bullet}$ matches a particular rule, $s_{k\bullet}$, within the rule set. To simplify, rewrite M_i so that each element is represented as a binary variable, $m_{i,k,j}$, such that,

$$m_{i,k,j} = I_{\{ei, j,\#\}}(s_{k,j}) \quad (10.5)$$

Before elements of the matching matrix can be algebraically manipulated, one first needs to show that the matrix is a lattice under conjunction and disjunction.

Theorem 10.1

A matching matrix, M_i, is a Boolean lattice under disjunction, $\cup$, and conjunction, $\cap$.

Proof: First, it is seen that M_i is ordered by the relation $\le$ so that, for each pair a,b of binary variables in M_i, $a \, R \, b \Leftrightarrow a \le b$. It follows that M_i is an ordered set. Second, the supremum and infimum of each pair of binary variables can be readily determined as either 0 or 1. Note that the supremum and infimum are, effectively, the disjunctive and conjunctive operators, respectively. Thus, the proof is complete. $\square$

Given a lattice, a where $a = \{a_1, a_2, \ldots, a_n\}$, the disjunct, $a_1 \cup a_2 \cup \bullet\bullet\bullet \cup (a_n$, and the conjunct, $a_1 \cap a_2 \cap \bullet\bullet\bullet \cap a_n$, are denoted by $\cup^n_{i=1} a_i$ and $\cap^n_{i=1} a_i$, respectively. Thus, by applying the disjunct operator on elements of the matching matrix, we define that an exemplar is matched to a rule if and only if

$$\cap^n_{j=1} m_{i,k,j} = 1 \quad (10.6)$$

That is, for any exemplar i, and any rule k, both having length n, a vector-wise match exists if and only if each exemplar value matches the corresponding rule value. Thus, a matching function, f, between a rule set, S, and an exemplar $e_{i\bullet}$, can be formulated as

$$f(M_i) = \cup^p_{k=1} [\cap^n_{j=1} m_{i,k,j}] \quad (10.7)$$

for p rules in the rule set, each with length n. A match, therefore, between an exemplar $e_{i\bullet}$ and a rule set exists if and only if $f(M_i) = 1$.

Definition 10.3

A rule set is said to be complete if it is able to match all the exemplars in the exemplar set. A scaled function to indicate rule set completeness, c, follows:

$$c(M_1, M_2, \ldots, M_r) = \frac{\sum_{i=1}^{r} f(M_i)}{r} \quad (10.8)$$

For r exemplars. Thus, $0 \le c \le 1$. Completeness values for all rule sets shown in Table 10.3 are listed in Table 10.4.

Therefore, c discriminates between rule sets not matching any exemplars (Rule Set nos. 8, 10, 11, and 13), rule sets matching some exemplars (Rule Set nos. 2, 3, 6, 7, 9, 12, and 14), and rule sets matching all the exemplars (Rule Set nos. 1, 4, and 5). Although three rule sets are able to match all exemplars, the usefulness of each rule set as a judgment strategy varies greatly. Rule Set no. 4 represents an overgeneralized strategy (i.e., if anything do anything). Rule Set no. 5 represents a strategy that relies on memorization of all possible

Table 10.4. Sample domain rule set completeness values. Exemplars (see Table 10.2) consist of {101,111,010,000}

Rule Set No.	Rule Set String	c
1	1#10#0	1
2	1#1	0.5
3	0#0	0.5
4	###	1
5	101111010000	1
6	11#100001000	0.5
7	000	0.25
8	001	0
9	010	0.25
10	011	0
11	100	0
12	101	0.25
13	110	0
14	111	0.25

Table 10.5. Sample domain rule set specificity values

Rule Set No.	Rule Set String	t	c*t
1	1#10#0	0.6667	0.6667
2	1#1	0.6667	0.3334
3	0#0	0.6667	0.3334
4	###	0	0
5	101111010000	1	1
6	11#100001000	0.9167	0.4584
7	000	1	0.25
8	001	1	0
9	010	1	0.25
10	011	1	0
11	100	1	0
12	101	1	0.25
13	110	1	0
14	111	1	0.25

outcomes, which may be theoretically possible though practically prohibitive in a complex, dynamic environment. Rule Set no. 1 represents a simplification strategy consistent with the findings in Kirlik et al. (1996b), Klein (1999), Rasmussen (1983), and Rouse (1983).

Thus, although the completeness function is able to measure the degree to which a rule set matches an exemplar set, a well-matched rule set does not necessarily represent a cognitively plausible judgment strategy. Two other fitness dimensions will now be introduced in an attempt to improve the capability of the fitness function to better achieve psychological plausibility. The specificity dimension addresses the task of eliminating rules within a rule set that are over-generalized (e.g., Rule Set no. 4).

Definition 10.4

A rule set is fully specified if there are no match-all characters in the rule set. A scaled function to show rule specificity, t, follows:

$$t(S) = \frac{\sum_{k=1}^{p}\sum_{j=1}^{n} I_{\{0,1\}}(s_{k,j})}{(p*n)} \quad (10.9)$$

for p rules of length n each. Thus, $0 \le t \le 1$. Specificity values for all rule sets shown in Table 10.3 are listed in Table 10.5.

As a complement dimension to c, t discriminates between rule sets not containing match-all

characters (Rule Set nos. 5, 7–14), and rules sets that do (Rule Set nos. 1–4, 6). Table 10.5 also shows a combined completeness/specificity value (in the form of c*t). An examination of c*t shows that the fitness of the overgeneralized rule (Rule Set no. 4) has been reduced in value. Furthermore, the two highest c*t rule sets (nos. 1 and 5) continue to support possible decision strategies as measured by completeness. However, Rule Set no. 6 presents another difficulty that must be overcome. Although half of the rules in Rule Set no. 6 match exemplars in Table 10.2, the others do not. Nevertheless, the two useless rules contribute to the overall specificity value of the rule set. Therefore, the final fitness dimension, parsimony, will now be introduced to eliminate useless rules from the rule set.

Definition 10.5

A rule set is said to be parsimonious if each rule within the rule set matches at least one exemplar in the exemplar set. A scaled function to indicate rule set parsimony, p, follows:

$$p(M_1, M_2, \ldots, M_r) = \frac{\sum_{k=1}^{q}\left[\bigcup_{k=1}^{r}\left(\bigcap_{j=1}^{n} m_{i,k,j}\right)\right]}{q} \quad (10.10)$$

for r exemplars and q rules of length n each. Thus, $0 \le p \le 1$. Parsimony values for all rule sets shown in Table 10.3 are listed in Table 10.6.

The third fitness dimension, p, provides a means of discriminating between rule sets that are wholly

Table 10.6. Sample domain rule set parsimony values

Rule Set No.	Rule Set String	p	$c*t*p$
1	1#10#0	1	0.6667
2	1#1	1	0.33335
3	0#0	1	0.33335
4	###	1	0
5	101111010000	1	1
6	11#100001000	0.5	0.22918
7	000	1	0.25
8	001	0	0
9	010	1	0.25
10	011	0	0
11	100	0	0
12	101	1	0.25
13	110	0	0
14	111	1	0.25

useful (i.e., each rule matches at least one exemplar) and those that are not. Table 10.6 also shows a combined completeness/specificity/specificity value (in the form of $c*t*p$). Notice that the fitness value of Rule Set no. 6 has been reduced to correspond to the usefulness of each rule within the rule set. Thus, an examination of Table 10.6 shows that the two highest $c*t*p$ rule sets (nos. 1 and 5) represent viable decision strategies to judge the identity of an aircraft based on its speed or altitude attributes as outlined in the sample domain.

Interestingly, the two rule sets (nos. 1 and 5) represent disparate decision strategies. Rule Set no. 1 represents a simplification policy that identifies aircraft based strictly on speed, whereas no. 5 generates a comprehensive set of specific rules to describe each exemplar exactly. Because the multiobjective fitness function in GBPC does not prescribe the number of rules to generate, the maximal number of rules employed by an operator should be empirically determined. Regardless, GBPC provides candidate rule sets that represent plausible strategies based on concepts of completeness, parsimony, and specificity. A global function using all three fitness dimensions will now be discussed.

Definition 10.6

A global fitness function, g, combines all three fitness dimensions, and is defined as

$$g = c^2 * t^2 * p^2 \qquad (10.11)$$

Thus, g provides a nonlinear differential reward system for rule sets within the population. The global maximum of $g = 1$ is achieved when all exemplars are fully contained in a rule set (e.g., Rule Set no. 5). Although g was initially selected for its simplicity, further studies are under way to explore alternative formulations (Rothrock, Ventura, & Park, 2003). For the present purposes, it is important to note that the particular formulation for g used here, in which the values of each of the contributing terms are squared prior to summation, was selected for computational rather than psychological reasons. This choice has implications for how to fairly compare the scalar measure of noncompensatory model fitness as represented by g and analogous scalar measures of regression model fitness, such as multiple correlation, as will be seen in the following section. We next describe an empirical evaluation of GBPC for inferring noncompensatory judgment rules in a dynamic task.

Empirical Evaluation of the GBPC Technique

The GBPC inductive inference technique was applied to human judgment data collected in a dynamic laboratory simulation of a U.S. Navy combat information center (CIC). Detailed information on the simulation and experimentation can be found in Hodge (1997), Rothrock (1995), and Bisantz et al. (chapter 3). The simulation required participants to perform the tasks of an anti–air warfare coordinator (AAWC), responsible for making judgments about the identity of initially unknown vehicles (or tracks) entering his or her geographic area of responsibility. GBPC was used to infer the possible heuristic strategies used by AAWC participants to make these track identification judgments.

Participants consisted of university students who were initially briefed on the role of an AAWC operator, functions of the computer interface, and geopolitical context of the simulation. Participants were given maps and profiles of friendly and hostile aircraft in the area to study and later during the scenario runs. Subjects were also briefed on the relative diagnosticity of each type of cue. For example, subjects were told that visual identification is veridical. They were then trained on 15 30-minute scenarios of comparable difficulty. In the training scenarios, postscenario feedback was provided to each participant in terms of correct assessments and incorrect actions. Participants then ran three additional 30-minute scenarios, during which data for GBPC was collected. The number of identification judgments per scenario ranged from 15 to 34.

Participants were provided with a radar display and a suite of controls for obtaining additional information about tracks in the vicinity of their ship. The following types of information, or judgment cues, were available: (a) Identification Friend or Foe (IFF) status, (b) electronic sensor emissions (friendly or hostile sensor onboard), (c) visual identification by combat air patrol (CAP), (d) range, (e) altitude, (f) speed, (g) course, (h) bearing, (i) location of civilian airports and air corridors, (j) legitimate commercial aircraft flight numbers, and (k) designation of hostile and friendly countries. The participant's goal was to use the available information to identify initially unknown tracks as either friendly, assumed friendly, hostile, or assumed hostile. For the simulation, we intentionally made some of this information more diagnostic than others. For example, visual identifications provided by CAP were perfectly diagnostic, and electronic sensor emissions were highly diagnostic. IFF information, however, was much less reliable. Our experimental purposes did not require that we mimic the actual relative reliability of these information sources in the operational naval environment, because we were not attempting to actually train naval personnel using this simulation. Naturally, however, a training simulation should mimic the reliability of information sources in the target context.

General Issues in the Empirical Evaluation of GBPC

The GBPC technique were used to infer judgment strategies from empirical data from the highest (A) and lowest (B) performing participants in the track identification task in a final experimental session (i.e., after judgment strategies had presumably stabilized). Participant A judged the identity of 20 out of 24 possible tracks, made no errors, and did not judge any track multiple times. Participant B judged only 14 out of the 24 tracks, made 4 errors, and judged 5 tracks twice. In every instance where a track was judged twice, the second judgment was made when visual identification became available. The goal in analyzing the behavior of these two participants using both modeling approaches was

to compare the results of the two methods to see if they revealed similarities or differences in representing judgment strategies as well as in explaining the performance differences between the participants. The bottom line in this investigation was to evaluate the potential utility of GBPC by trying to determine why participant A performed this dynamic judgment task more successfully than participant B.

Due to the large number of information sources available in the laboratory task, we first divided these sources into two categories: *active* and *passive*. Active information sources required the operator to make queries about a track. Active sources included queries of IFF, electronic sensor emissions, and requests for visual identifications of a track, obtained by sending CAP resources to fly to a track's location and make a report (if possible) to the AAWC. All other information sources were considered to be passive, because they did not have to be actively requested but were instead continuously available from the radar display (e.g., track location, bearing, speed, altitude, etc.). The first stage of modeling focused solely on the performers' use of active information. We parsed the data in this fashion due to the limited number of human judgments available (a maximum of 24), which meant that we would have to focus on a relatively small set of cues or information sources to give us the chance to obtain reliable fits for GBPC. A potential for combinatorial explosion exists when representing the laboratory task in the binary format required by GBPC.

We must note that by restricting the cue data set in this way, we did not expect to create complete accounts of our performers' judgment strategies. However, focusing on just the set of active information not only enabled an efficient evaluation of GBPC but also helped address the question of whether the difference between the high and low scoring participants could have been due to their policies for actively searching for judgment cues and how they may have used these cues. As will be described in a following section, however, we did conduct a second stage of GBPC based on the use of both active and passive sources of information. Although that second stage is not the primary focus of this chapter, selected findings from that more comprehensive GBPC analysis will be presented—in particular, those that bear on diagnosing the possible task-simplification heuristics underlying participant B's erroneous judgments. A complete account of both stages of GBPC is provided in Rothrock (1995).

Coding the Active Information Data Set to Support GBPC Analysis

For modeling the use of active information, cues and operator judgments were encoded in GBPC as a 10-bit string. The meaning of each string position is shown in Table 10.7. Note that the first six bits represent actions taken to seek judgment cues (and in some cases, the information gained as a result of these actions), whereas the last four bits represent the four possible AAWC identification judgments themselves. Note that representation provided in Table 10.7 is hardly the most efficient binary coding from an information theoretic perspective. However, alternative, more efficient codings may limit the representational flexibility of the model and thus limit its ability to induce rule sets covering the entire range of exemplars in a data set.

It should be noted that the data set considered in the present chapter, though different from the data used in the Bisantz et al. (2000; chapter 3) study in the same laboratory simulation, differed only in the fact that it reflected behavior from a different set of performers collected at a different time. Both data sets came from control groups performing in a series of experiments evaluating a variety of training interventions for the CIC context.

GBPC Analysis of the Use of Active Information

When the GBPC inferential technique was applied to data from performers A and B rather than linear regression, GBPC produced a rule set for A with an overall fitness value, or $g = 0.5625$, and a rule set for B with $g = 0.3600$. The lack of fit (the difference

Table 10.7. AAWC string big position and representation

Bit	Representation	1	0
#1	IFF queried	yes	no
#2	Friendly emitter response	yes	no
#3	Hostile emitter response	yes	no
#4	Negative emitter response	yes	no
#5	Friendly visual sighting	yes	no
#6	Hostile visual sighting	yes	no
#7	Friendly AAWC judgment	yes	no
#8	Assumed friendly AAWC judgment	yes	no
#9	Assumed hostile AAWC judgment	yes	no
#10	Hostile AAWC judgment	yes	no

between g and unity) for both models was due solely to the *specificity* dimension by which fitness was evaluated. GBPC inferred rule sets for performers A and B that were both fully complete (i.e., covered all judgment instances) and also fully parsimonious (i.e., contained no unnecessary rules). The rule set for A achieved a specificity value of 0.7500 (and thus an overall fitness g value of $\{1.0000^2 * 1.0000^2 * 0.7500^2\} = 0.5625$), and a rule set for B with a specificity value of 0.600 (and thus a g value of $\{1.0000^2 * 1.0000^2 * 0.6000^2\} = 0.3600$). A lack of specificity suggests that both performers relied on abstract heuristics or selective attention in judgment (that is, that some of the rules in their final rule sets referred only to a subset of the three IFF, sensor, and visual identification) cues. Finally, in regard to the numerical measures of fit obtained by GBPC, recall that the equation whereby each of the three contributing fitness measures are squared prior to summation was done purely for mathematical convenience and not for any psychological reasons. Thus, it may be just as plausible to assess the GBPC fits without squaring, resulting in a fit for participant A of 0.750 and a fit for participant B of 0.600).

Given that this first stage of modeling inferred judgment strategies on the basis of a highly restricted set of cues (IFF, sensor emissions, and visual identifications), we were surprised to achieve these high (unity) fitness values on the *completeness* fitness dimension. Recall that A made a total of 20 judgments, and GBPC found a disjunctive normal form (DNF) representation of this performer's strategy as a disjunction of seven conjunctive rules, with one of these rules covering only one judgment instance. The remaining six rules in this set covered between two and eight instances each. Operator B made a total of 19 judgments, and GBPC found a DNF representation of this operator's strategy as a disjunctive collection of 11 rules, with 1 of these rules covering only one judgment instance. The remaining 10 rules for Operator B covered between two and eight instances each.

Analysis of the rule sets with maximum g values (i.e., the winning rule sets) revealed interesting findings regarding the use of active information. Operator A's winning rule set indicated a reliance on querying electronic sensor emissions and visual identifications to make track identification judgments. For example, the following two rules from the winning rule set, which covered eight and nine of A's judgments, respectively, indicate reliance on these highly diagnostic sources of information to make "hostile" and "assumed friendly" judgments.

(friendly emitter response = no) ∩ (emitter response = not negative) ∩ (AAWC judgment = hostile)

OR

(emitter response = not negative) ∩ (hostile visual ID = no) ∩ (AAWC judgment = assumed friendly)

Recall that GBPC represents rule sets as disjunctions of conjunctive rules. The first conjunctive rule states that if a sensor emission is queried and the response is neither friendly nor negative, then judge the associated track to be hostile. For all the tracks in the experimental task, correct sensor assessment yields correct identifications. Hence, the rule is diagnostic of the true identity of the tracks.

Now consider the second conjunctive rule. This rule states that if a sensor is queried and some emission (either friendly or hostile) is detected, and CAP resources do not provide a visual identification of the track as hostile, then assume the track to be friendly. This rule has two interpretations. In the first case, assume that the sensor emission is friendly. In this case, the track should be judged as assumed friendly given that visual identification provided by CAP does not indicate otherwise (i.e., does not indicate that the track is hostile). This rule thus represents a reliance on highly diagnostic emission information unless the (even more diagnostic) visual identification conflicts with emission information, and is thus fully consistent with the relative diagnosticity of these two cues in this task environment.

Now, consider the second interpretation of this rule, namely, that the emission response is hostile. In this case, the track should instead be assumed to be friendly if CAP provides a visual identification to override the judgment that would be made on the emission report alone (e.g., the first of the two disjunctive rules). This second interpretation of this rule can also be seen as a refinement of the first rule, because it indicates that information gained by visual identification, if available, should override any judgments made solely on the basis of electronic sensor emissions. In the experimental task, sensor emissions were highly diagnostic, as already mentioned, but visual identifications were 100% diagnostic. Thus Operator A's second rule reflects an adaptive refinement of his first rule to those cases where CAP resources provide conflicting visual identification information.

Finally, the rule set for A also indicated a generally adaptive lack of reliance on relatively unreliable IFF information in making judgments: the only two rules in his rule set that matched judgments where IFF had been queried also relied on sensor information, visual identification information, or both sources to complement any information obtained from IFF.

When GBPC was applied to participant B's use of active information, on the other hand, it was much more difficult to infer a coherent and efficient judgment strategy on the basis of active information alone. At a general level, however, B did not appear to make effective use of the most highly diagnostic types of active information: electronic sensor emissions and visual identifications. In fact, one rule, covering six instances of B's judgments, indicated a reliance solely on unreliable IFF information, with no accompanying reliance on sensor or visual information to supplement IFF as an information source:

(IFF query status = anything) ∩ (AAWC judgment = assumed friendly)

We emphasize, however, that GBPC was less successful in inferring an efficient judgment strategy for participant B than for A, solely on the basis of their use of active information sources. Other than a general overreliance on relatively unreliable IFF information, the inferred strategy for B was not particularly enlightening as to the possible factors underlying his four judgment errors

Modeling the Use of Passive Information: Inferring Error Tendencies

To gain additional insight into the differences between the judgment strategies that may have been used by performers A and B, a second stage of GBPC was performed that also included the seven dimensions of passive information discussed previously. This was a significantly more elaborate and computationally intensive exercise, due to the need to represent the seven passive information sources in a binary format that was hopefully consistent with how the operators perceived and encoded information obtained from the radar display. We eventually settled on a 40-bit representation of the task environment for this second stage of modeling.

The first 8 bits in the 40-bit string represented the 8 different radar ranges (e.g., 8 nm, 16 nm, etc.)

that could be selected by the operator. The ninth bit represented whether a track was emitting electronic sensor information. Bits 10 through 13 represented a track's altitude, put into equivalence classes that were somewhat relevant to a track's identity in this environment (e.g., less than 5,000 feet, between 5,000 and 18,000 feet, etc.). Bits 14 through 17 represented a track's speed in a similar format. Bits 18 through 21 represented a track's course as one of four compass quadrants. Bits 22 through 25 similarly represented a track's bearing. Bits 26 through 33 represented a track's range as a member of one of eight task-relevant equivalence classes. Bits 34, 35, and 36 represented whether IFF, electronic sensor emission, and visual identification information for a track had been sought by the operator. Finally, the last four bits represented the operator's judgment, in the same manner used in the first modeling stage.

A detailed discussion of the results of this second stage of GBPC modeling can be found in Rothrock (1995). Here, the focus is solely on an analysis of the differences between the ways in which A and B made judgments about the identity of three particular tracks. Each of these three tracks was a hostile helicopter, correctly identified as hostile by A but incorrectly identified by B as assumed friendly. These three misidentifications accounted for three of B's four judgment errors. Based on GBPC results from this second modeling stage, rule sets were found suggesting that A correctly identified all three of these helicopters by sending CAP resources to obtain visual identifications. On the other hand, the rules that covered B's judgments about these helicopters indicated that no active information sources were sought for two of these helicopters, and that the third was queried only by relatively unreliable IFF. Additionally, the rule covering these three helicopter judgments for B contained the following information:

$$(altitude\ not\ \{18,000 < a < 40,000\})\ \cap$$
$$(altitude\ not\ \{a > 40,000\}\ \cap\ (speed < 200)$$
$$\cap\ (range\ not\ \{r < 10\})\ \cap\ (range\ not\ \{40 < r < 50\})$$
$$\cap\ (range\ not\ \{r > 150\})\ \cap\ (assume\ friendly)$$

Of particular interest here are the track conditions described in this rule (speed less than 200 knots, altitude < 18,000 feet). This information was available from the radar display. These track conditions generally reflected the radar signature of commercial airliners taking off from airports in our

simulation. All tracks in our scenarios with this signature were indeed airliners except for the three hostile helicopters misidentified by B. Recall that A did not solely use radar information to identify these tracks as hostile, relying instead on actively sought visual identification. Although one cannot be sure that the rule described actually accounted for B's misidentification of these helicopters as assumed friendly, this case does provide an example suggesting how inferential modeling might provide hypotheses about the nature of the task-simplification heuristics performers might employ and how information gained from inferential modeling might provide an important source of feedback for training.

Discussion

Performers in time-stressed, information-rich environments often develop heuristic task-simplification strategies for coping with the time pressure, information overload, and the abstract manner in which task information is often displayed on technological interfaces. Judgment strategies in these environments may have a noncompensatory nature, which may be adaptive to the time-stressed nature of these tasks, because such heuristics typically make lower demands for information search and integration than do corresponding linear-additive compensatory strategies. As a result, linear regression may be inappropriate for inferring the judgment strategies used by performers in time-stressed environments, assuming, as it does, that these strategies can be usefully described by compensatory linear-additive rules.

An alternative approach for inferring judgment strategies from behavioral data has been presented that does not rely on the compensatory assumptions underlying linear regression. The technique, GBPC, infers noncompensatory judgment strategies under the assumption that these strategies can be described as a disjunctive collection of conjunctive rules. The fitness measure embodied in GBPC evaluates candidate rule sets on three dimensions: (a) *completeness* (the inferred rule base is consistent with all operator judgments), (b) *specificity* (the rule base is maximally concrete), and (c) *parsimony* (the rule base contains no unnecessary rules).

The inferential approach was illustrated using behavioral data from the highest and lowest performing operators of a laboratory simulation of a

CIC task. In this application, the GBPC inferred individually valid yet contrasting rule bases for these two operators. Additionally, the two inferred rule bases were consistent with these operators' patterns of both correct and incorrect judgments.

GBPC holds promise for the design of advanced training technologies that use individual performance histories to target feedback toward eliminating any potential misconceptions or oversimplifications a trainee's behavior might reflect. One can imagine using both lens model analysis and GBPC analysis to capture trainee data in real time, infer judgment strategies as enough data on trainee behavior became available, and then make these strategies explicit to a human trainer or the trainee him- or herself as a form of feedback augmentation.

We also believe the GBPC holds promise for advancing the science of judgment and decision making, at least in the realms of naturalistic decision making (NDM) and ecological rationality. One widely stressed aspect of the NDM approach is that experienced performers rely heavily on perhaps subtle environmental cues that are not apparently available to the less experienced performer. One widely stressed aspect of the ecological rationality approach is the availability of a toolbox of fast and frugal heuristics. We have shown that the general picture of judgment presumed by GBPC is consistent with both the notion of cue-based judgment and also that these cues are used in the noncompensatory forms presumed to underlie the fast and frugal heuristics comprising ecological rationality. As such, we believe GBPC, especially as it matures and receives further empirical testing, may become a useful tool for advancing decision and human–technology interaction research from the perspectives of both of these research traditions.

Acknowledgments. Portions of this chapter are drawn from Rothrock & Kirlik (2003) and reprinted by permission. The authors thank the U.S. Naval Air Warfare Center for support.

References

Aha, D. W., Kibler, D., & Albert, M. K. (1991). Instance-based learning algorithms. *Machine Learning, 6*(1), 37–66.

Bisantz, A. M., Kirlik, A., Gay, P., Phipps, D., Walker, N., & Fisk, A. D. (2000). Modeling and analysis of a dynamic judgment task using a lens model approach. *IEEE Transaction on Systems, Man, and Cybernetics Part A: Systems and Humans, 30*(6), 605–616.

Byrne, M. D., & Gray, W. D. (2003). Returning human factors to an engineering discipline: Expanding the science base through a new generation of quantitative methods—preface to the special section. *Human Factors, 45*, 1–4.

Clark, P., & Niblett, T. (1989). The CN2 induction algorithm. *Machine Learning, 3*, 261–283.

Connolly, T. (1988). Hedge-clipping, tree-felling, and the management of ambiguity. In M. B. McCaskey, L. R. Pondy, & H. Thomas (Eds.), *Decision making: An interdisciplinary inquiry.* New York: Wiley.

Cost, S. & Salzberg, S. (1993). A weighted nearest neighbor algorithm for learning with symbolic features. *Machine Learning, 10*(1), 57–78.

Dawes, R. M. (1964). Social selection based on multidimensional criteria. *Journal of Abnormal and Social Psychology, 68*(1), 104–109.

DeJong, K. A., & Spears, W. M. (1990). *An analysis of the interacting roles of population size and crossover in genetic algorithms.* Paper presented at the First International Conference on Parallel Problem Solving from Nature, Dortmund, Germany.

DeJong, K. A., Spears, W. M., & Gordon, D. F. (1993). Using genetic algorithms for concept learning. *Machine Learning, 13*(2–3), 161–188.

Duda, R. O., & Hart, P. E. (1973). *Pattern classification and scene analysis.* New York: Wiley.

Edwards, W., & Newman, J. R. (1982). *Multiattribute evaluation.* Beverly Hills, Calif.: Sage.

Einhorn, H. J. (1970). The use of nonlinear, noncompensatory models in decision making. *Psychological Bulletin, 73*(3), 221–230.

Gigerenzer, G., & Goldstein, D. G. (1996). Reasoning the fast and frugal way: Models of bounded rationality. *Psychological Review, 103*, 650–669.

Gigerenzer, G., & Kurz, E. M. (2001). Vicarious functioning reconsidered: A fast and frugal lens model. In K. R. Hammond & T. Stewart (Eds.), *The essential Brunswik.* Oxford: Cambridge University Press.

Gigerenzer, G., & Selten, R. (Eds.). (2001). *Bounded rationality. The adaptive toolbox.* Cambridge, Mass.: MIT Press.

Gigerenzer, G., Todd, P. M., & The ABC Research Group. (1999). *Simple heuristics that make us smart.* New York: Oxford University Press.

Goldberg, D. E. (1989). *Genetic algorithms in search, optimization, and machine learning.* New York: Addison-Wesley.

Hodge, K. A. (1997). Training for decision making in a

complex, dynamic task environment: An empirical investigation focusing on part-task training and feedback. Unpublished Ph.D. dissertation, Georgia Institute of Technology, Atlanta.

Hogarth, R. M. (1981). Beyond discrete biases: Functional and dysfunctional aspects of judgmental heuristics. *Psychological Bulletin, 90*, 197–217.

Holland, J. H. (1975). *Adaptation in natural and artificial systems: An introductory analysis with applications to biology, control, and artificial intelligence.* Ann Arbor: University of Michigan Press.

Holland, J. H., Booker, L. B., Colombetti, M., Dorigo, M., Goldberg, D. E., Forrest, S., Riolo, R. L., Smith, R. E., Lanzi, P. L., Stolzmann, W., & Wilson, S. W. (2000). What is a learning classifier system? In P. L. Lanzi, W. Stolzmann, & S. W. Wilson (Eds.), *Learning classifier systems: From foundations to application*(Vol. 1813, pp. 3–32). New York: Springer.

Holland, J. H., Holyoak, K. F., Nisbett, R. E., & Thagard, P. R. (1986). *Induction.* Cambridge, Mass.: MIT Press.

Kirlik, A., Miller, R. A., & Jagacinski, R. J. (1993). Supervisory control in a dynamic uncertain environment: A process model of skilled human–environment interation. *IEEE Transactions on Systems, Man, and Cybernetics, 23*(4), 929–952.

Kirlik, A., Rothrock, L., Walker, N., & Fisk, A. D. (1996a). Simple strategies or simple tasks? Dynamic decision making in complex worlds. *Proceedings of the Human Factors and Ergonomics Society 40ᵗʰ Annual Meeting.* Santa Monica, Calif.: Human Factors & Ergonomics Society.

Kirlik, A., Walker, N., Fisk, A. D., & Nagel, K. (1996b). Supporting perception in the service of dynamic decision making. *Human Factors, 38*(2), 288–299.

Klein, G. A. (1999). Applied decision making. In P. A. Hancock (Ed.), *Handbook of perception and cognition: Human performance and ergonomics* (pp. 87–108). New York: Academic Press.

Klein, G. A., Orasanu, J., Calderwood, R., & Zsambok, C. E. (Eds.). (1993). *Decision making in action: Models and methods.* Norwood, N.J.: Ablex.

Lipshitz, R., Klein, G., Orasanu, J. & Salas, E. (2001). Focus article: Taking stock of naturalistic decision making. *Journal of Behavioral Decision Making, 14*(5), 331–352.

Mendelson, E. (1997). *Introduction to mathematical logic* (4th ed.). London: Chapman & Hall.

Michalski, R. S. (1983). A theory and methodology of inductive learning. In R. S. Michalski, J. G. Carbonell, & T. M. Mitchell (Eds.), *Machine*

learning: An artificial intelligence approach. Palo Alto, Calif.: Tioga Publishing.

Michalski, R. S., & Chilausky, R. L. (1999). Knowledge acquisition by encoding expert rules versus computer induction from examples: A case study involving soybean pathology. *International Journal of Human-Computer Studies, 51*, 239–263.

Moriarty, D. E., Schultz, A. C., & Grefenstette, J. J. (1999). Evolutionary algorithms for reinforcement learning. *Journal of Artificial Intelligence Research, 11*, 241–276.

Neisser, U. (1976). *Cognition and reality: Principles and implications of cognitive psychology.* San Francisco: W. H. Freeman.

Payne, J. W. (1976). Task complexity and contingent processing in decision making: An information search and protocol analysis. *Organizational Behavior and Human Performance, 16*, 366–387.

Payne, J. W., Bettman, J. R., & Johnson, E. J. (1988). Adaptive strategy selection in decision making. *Journal of Experimental Psychology: Learning, Memory, and Cognition, 14*(3), 534–552.

Pearl, J. (2000). *Causality: Models, reasoning, and inference.* New York: Cambridge University Press.

Quinlan, J. R. (1986). Induction of decision trees. *Machine Learning, 1*, 81–106.

Quinlan, J. R. (1993). *C4.5: Programs for machine learning.* San Mateo, Calif.: Morgan Kaufmann.

Rasmussen, J. R. (1983). Skills, rules, and knowledge: Signals, signs, symbols, and other distinctions in human performance models. *IEEE Transactions on Systems, Man, and Cybernetics, 13*(3), 257–266.

Rothrock, L. (1995). Performance measures and outcome analysis of dynamic decision making in real-time supervisory control. Unpublished Ph.D. dissertation, School of Industrial and Systems Engineering, Georgia Institute of Technology, Atlanta.

Rothrock, L. & Kirlik, A. (2003). Inferring rule-based strategies in dynamic judgment tasks. *IEEE Transactions on Systems, Man, and Cybernetics: Part A: Systems and Humans, 33*(1), 58–72.

Rothrock, L., Ventura, J., & Park, S. (2003). *An optimization methodology to investigate operator impact on quality of service.* Paper presented at the Interservice/Industry Training, Simulation, and Education Conference (I/ITSEC), Orlando, Fla.

Rouse, W. B. (1983). Models of human problem solving: Detection, diagnosis, and compensation for system failures. *Automatica, 19*, 613–625.

Savage, L. (1972). *The foundation of statistics.* New York: Dover.

Simon, H. A. (1956). Rational choice and the structure of the environment. *Psychological Review, 63*, 129–138.

Smith, S. F. (1983). *Flexible learning of problem solving heuristics through adaptive search.* Paper presented at the International Joint Conference on Artificial Intelligence, Karlsruhe, Germany.

Todd, P. M., & Gigerenzer, G. (2001). Putting naturalistic decision making into the adaptive toolbox. *Journal of Behavioral Decision Making, 14*(5), 381–382.

Wright, P. (1974). The harassed decision maker: Time pressures, distractions, and the use of evidence. *Journal of Applied Psychology, 59*(5), 555–561.

Gwendolyn E. Campbell, Wendi L.Van Buskirk, and Amy E. Bolton

Viewing Training through a Fuzzy Lens

The essence of training in many domains is to help people establish effective strategies for interpreting and responding to incomplete and uncertain cues in technologically mediated environments. A number of training researchers have seen the utility of the Brunswik lens model (Brunswik, 1952; Goldstein, this volume) in this endeavor, and have applied the model to the tasks of assessing trainee performance and providing trainees with feedback (e.g., Balzer, Doherty, & O'Conner, 1989). The typical approach has been to generate two regression equations: one from the student data and the other, representing the "correct" model, from either the environment (i.e., ground truth) or a set of data generated by an expert. Training feedback may be based on the correct model alone or on a comparison of the similarities and discrepancies between the correct model and the student model. Finally, the effectiveness of this feedback at promoting improved student performance is assessed. For example, Balzer et al. (1992) asked participants to predict the number of wins a baseball team would have based on performance statistics such as earned run average (ERA), errors, and batting average. They used regression-based modeling and the Brunswik lens model to provide feedback to the participants about the relative weights of these cues and the

outcome, and then assessed the extent to which participants improved in their ability to make these predictions. Although linear regression has proven to be effective at predicting both student and expert performance in many domains, feedback based on regression equations has not always led to improved performance in training research (Balzer et al., 1989).

A number of reasons have been hypothesized to explain the mixed results of regression-based feedback. One compelling explanation is that there are a number of characteristics and assumptions inherent in regression that make it unlikely that regression equations are capable of capturing the entire range of reasoning processes that humans employ across all domains (Campbell, Buff, & Bolton, 2000; Dorsey & Coovert, 2003; Rogelberg et al., 1999). Specifically, linear regression equations assume that the relationships between the cues and the final decision are linear and additive. The psychological literature, on the other hand, contains many examples of human reasoning that are noncompensatory and/or based on interactions between cues (Stewart, 1988). For example, when investigating the policies that managers use to distribute merit pay among employees, Dorsey and Coovert (2003) found that some managers reported the noncompensatory strategy of only taking into consideration certain factors, such as length of employment, if an employee's performance was acceptable, but not allowing for even very high levels of those factors to compensate for low performance levels.

There are alternative mathematical modeling techniques to regression, of course. Fuzzy logic, for example, though relatively new to psychologists, has been around for years (Zadeh, 1965) and seems to have several advantages as a modeling technique for human judgment data. Dorsey and Coovert (2003) point out that although both fuzzy logic and regression are capable of representing complex, nonlinear relationships, a regression model requires that the researcher specify the nature of the nonlinearity a priori by adding the appropriate term to the equation, and a fuzzy model does not. This may be an advantage when conducting exploratory modeling of human decision making across a wide variety of domains.

In addition, fuzzy system models appear to represent reasoning strategies in a form that is consistent with certain theories of cognition (Campbell et al., 2000; Dorsey & Coovert, 2003; Smithson, 1988). Fuzzy systems have two major components: fuzzy categories and fuzzy rules. To gain an intuitive understanding of fuzzy categories, imagine taking a variable like air temperature, which is numeric and can take on any one of over 100 discrete integer values (depending on where you live), and overlaying that range with 5 classifications: freezing, cold, comfortable, hot, and miserably hot. Next imagine mapping each temperature value into those categories. Some temperatures, such as $-15°F$, would fit easily into exactly one category, but the classification of other temperatures, such as $92°F$, would be less obvious. Is $92°F$ a member of the "hot" or the "miserably hot" category? This conflict is captured in fuzzy systems by mapping specific instances to categories probabilistically. A temperature like $92°F$ can have a 50% probability of being a member of the "hot" category and a 50% probability of being classified as "miserably hot," whereas $97°F$ could belong to the category "miserably hot" with a probability of 90% and to the category "hot" with a probability of 30%. (Note that the probabilities do not need to sum to 100%.) In other words, fuzzy categories are defined mathematically by probabilistic membership functions. The parallel between this representation and the exemplar

(Medin & Smith, 1984) and prototype (Rosch, 1978) cognitive theories of human categorization is obvious. In both cases, the extent to which a particular item or event is a member of a specific category is defined by a numeric value ranging from 0 to 1, often based on some measure of psychological similarity to some other (real or hypothetical) item or event.

Fuzzy rules, the second component of fuzzy system models, bear a strong similarity to a fundamental component of many theories of cognition, production rules (for an early description of production rules, see Newell, 1973). Each fuzzy rule in a model has an "if" clause that indicates which fuzzy category(ies) need to be present, and a "then" clause, which describes the rule's output or predicted decision. For example, a reasonable strategy for controlling your home temperature could easily be expressed in a fuzzy model with three rules: (a) if it is "too cold" outside, then set your thermostat to $68°F$, (b) if it is "too hot" outside then set your thermostat to $82°F$, and (c) if it is "comfortable" outside then set your thermostat to OFF.

Interestingly enough, the output of a single fuzzy rule can be expressed as a regression equation. The additional computing power in a fuzzy system model comes from the fact that the model consists of several rules, and the final output of the model is a weighted sum of the outputs of all of the rules (see Figure 11.1). The output of each rule is weighted by the extent to which the conditions in its "if" clause are met by the instance under consideration.

This feature allows fuzzy systems models to represent a variety of complex, nonlinear and noncompensatory functions (such as the step function that is described in the home temperature control model described previously) that cannot be represented in any single, linear regression equation.

Although fuzzy logic has been shown to be more predictive of expert performance than regression equations in at least one domain (Dorsey & Coovert, 2003), its capability to support diagnosis of trainee performance and the development of effective feedback has not yet been assessed. The current studies were designed to extend the lens model approach to incorporate this new modeling method by comparing the effectiveness of feedback based on regression and fuzzy logic mathematical modeling techniques. Our basic premise is that if an empirically derived model is actually able to capture the

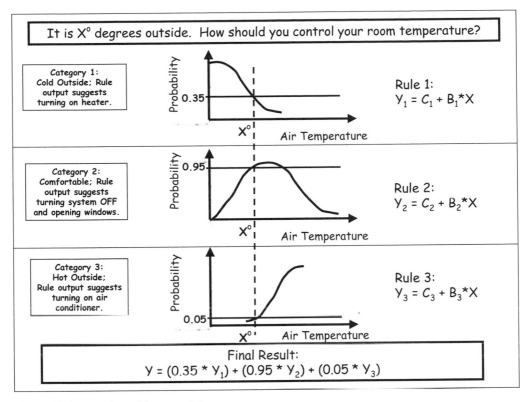

It is X° degrees outside. How should you control your room temperature?

Category 1:
Cold Outside; Rule output suggests turning on heater.

Probability
0.35

$X°$

Air Temperature

Rule 1:
$Y_1 = C_1 + B_1*X$

Category 2:
Comfortable; Rule output suggests turning system OFF and opening windows.

Probability
0.95

$X°$

Air Temperature

Rule 2:
$Y_2 = C_2 + B_2*X$

Category 3:
Hot Outside; Rule output suggests turning on air conditioner.

Probability

0.05

$X°$ Air Temperature

Rule 3:
$Y_3 = C_3 + B_3*X$

Final Result:
$$Y = (0.35 * Y_1) + (0.95 * Y_2) + (0.05 * Y_3)$$

Figure 11.1. Hypothetical fuzzy model.

proximal–distal relationships that form the basis of a person's judgment and behavior, then feedback based on a critique of that model should lead to improved performance. Conversely, if the model is not diagnostic of a person's actual decision-making strategy, then feedback based on that model is not as likely to have much impact on performance.

More specifically, in our first study we attempt to extend the results of the Dorsey and Coovert (2003) research, which were based on experienced decision makers, to novices participating in training. Our hypothesis is that fuzzy logic will be more predictive of trainee behavior than regression. In our second study, we adapt the lens model to incorporate fuzzy logic and test the hypothesis that feedback based on fuzzy logic will lead to more improvement in trainee performance than feedback based on regression equations. We discuss some potential explanations for our mixed findings regarding the usefulness of fuzzy logic in the discussion. This research adds to the body of work illustrating the potential utility a Brunswikian approach can bring to the training research community.

Experiment 1

Materials and Methods

Participants

Twenty undergraduates from the University of Central Florida and two volunteers from the Naval Air Warfare Center Training Systems Division participated in the study. The participants included 14 females and 8 males. None of these participants had prior exposure to the experimental task. Undergraduates received extra credit in psychology courses as compensation. In addition, one of the researchers who had extensive experience with the experimental task also completed the study. This researcher's performance data were used to produce the expert models.

Software and Hardware

The Georgia Tech Anti-Air Warfare Coordinator (GT-AAWC) software suite was used to conduct this research (Gay et al., 1997). GT-AAWC is comprised of seven software programs that run in Windows 3.1 and DOS environments, including a scenario generation program, a part-task trainer, a simulator, and a data conversion program. Two linked personal computers (PCs) are required to run the simulator. The simulation graphics and control functions run on one PC, and the second PC is used to generate and play pre-scripted audio reports through speakers.

Task

The Georgia Tech AEGIS Simulation Platform (GT-ASP), a low-fidelity simulation of the AAWC position in a Navy Combat Information Center (CIC), served as the experimental task. In GT-ASP, participants are responsible for identifying both the type (helicopter, commercial airliner, etc.) and intent (hostile, friendly) of all unknown air tracks (aircraft) in their ship's (called ownship) vicinity, as well as warning or engaging (shooting) hostile aircraft. There are seven cues available in the simulation to support the participant in making these decisions. Four of these cues—an aircraft's altitude, speed, distance from ownship, and direction of flight relative to ownship—are represented in continuous numeric data. Three of these cues—the aircraft's apparent point of origin (hostile or friendly), a radar signal (EWS), and a voluntary identification signal (IFF)—are categorical variables. Certain values of some of these cues immediately and irrefutably identify an aircraft. For example, the altitude and speed of a helicopter are quite distinct, and an EWS signal of ARINC564 is only produced by a commercial airliner. In other cases, the information that these cues provide is at best ambiguous. For example, military aircraft are capable of flying at the same speeds and altitudes as commercial airliners and, whereas an EWS signal of APG71 is emitted by F-14Ds; both sides have this type of military aircraft, so that signal alone does not determine whether it is friendly or hostile. All of this information is made available in either a textual display on the screen or through simulated voice reports over the computer speakers.

For the purposes of this study, we did not inform participants about one component of the testbed: the ability to use friendly military aircraft called Defensive Counter Aircraft to provide (100% accurate) visual identifications of unidentified aircraft. Our rationale was that this activity had the potential to dramatically reduce the participants' reliance on the other available cues and to change the nature of the task from a complex decision making task to a simple reporting task.

Scenarios

Eighteen moderately realistic scenarios, all situated in the Persian Gulf, are provided with the GT-AAWC suite. Unfortunately, certain aspects of these scenarios designed to increase their realism, such as an extremely high ratio of commercial airliners to military aircraft, made them less suitable for modeling purposes. Thus, five of these scenarios were selected and revised before any data collection was conducted. Revisions included increasing the number and variety of available aircraft, to provide the modeling algorithms with a reasonable number of performance observations across all possible classes of objects. Eight pilot participants completed these five scenarios. Their task performance (identification accuracy) was high enough to raise the concern that these scenarios might produce a ceiling effect in a training study. Thus the scenarios were revised again to increase the difficulty, this time by reducing the number of aircraft that were actively producing identifiable radar emissions. Fourteen participants completed the study using the final set of scenarios.

Design

While participants must make many different types of decisions in this task, the decision that was selected to be modeled in Experiment 1 was the determination of an aircraft's *intent* (hostile versus friendly). A within-subjects design was selected. Individual linear regression models and fuzzy logic models were built for each participant.

Procedure

Each participant completed two, 3-hour sessions within one week. During the first session, the participants received training on GT-ASP, which included review of a briefing packet, completion of part-task training exercises and exposure to two shortened and simplified practice scenarios. During these activities, the experimenter provided assistance and coaching. During the second session, participants completed five, 30-minute scenarios in GT-ASP, without any coaching from the experimenter. The simulation software, GT-ASP, maintains a time-stamped log of all relevant data.

Model Development

Separate linear regression and fuzzy models were built in MATLAB (Math Works, 1996) for each participant's performance data from the five 30-minute scenarios in the second session. MATLAB uses matrix algebra to solve a set of simultaneous equations and produce the least squares fit regression model. Our dependent variable was categorical, which theoretically requires specialized regression techniques, however we coded it dichotomously (0 = hostile, 1 = friendly), allowing us to use this approach (see Cohen & Cohen, 1983, pp. 240–241, for a discussion of this issue.)

The genfis2 algorithm provided in MATLAB's fuzzy logic toolbox was used to derive the fuzzy models. This algorithm uses a subtractive clustering routine to identify the number and the nature of clusters in the n-dimensional data space (where n is the number of cues plus the outcome or human judgment) and then creates a fuzzy rule for each of the clusters. Genfis2 is a one-pass method that does not include any iterative process for parameter optimization.

Both types of models were built following the bootstrapping approach described by Dorsey and Coovert (2003). That is, a single participant's data set was input to MATLAB and replicated 100 times, but the replications were not combined. Instead, each replication of the data set was randomly split into two subsets. The training subset (two-thirds of the data) was used to build a model, and the testing subset (the remaining one-third of the data) was used to calculate a correlational measure of the model's predictive validity. Finally, the average of all 100 correlations was calculated. This statistic will be referred to as the cross-validated correlation for that modeling technique when applied to a participant's data set.

Participants did not make enough decisions during the five scenarios to support building a model using all seven of the possible cues as independent variables simultaneously. In addition, the MATLAB (Math Works, 1996) fuzzy modeling algorithms did not produce any statistical measures indicating which cues significantly contributed to the predictive validity of the model. Thus, a jackknifing procedure was followed in which all possible models using anywhere from one to four cues were built. These models were rank-ordered on their cross-validated correlations and the model with the highest cross-validated correlation was identified and selected for further analysis.

Results

Qualitative Assessment of Models

A comparison of the regression and fuzzy models produced for each participant's data showed that the most predictive models did not always include the same set of cues. In fact, as previously reported (Campbell, Rhodenizer, & Buff, 1999), linear regression and fuzzy modeling produced different cues for 12 out of 15 participants (14 trainees and 1 expert) who completed the more difficult set of scenarios. In addition, the fuzzy systems models represented nonlinear cue interactions for all 15 of these participants. For example, the expert's fuzzy model classified low-flying, close aircraft as hostile and all other aircraft (low flying and far; high flying and close; high flying and far) as friendly.

Predictive Validity of Models

We will begin by considering just the expert performance. The expert made 98 decisions in the first (easy) set of scenarios. Linear regression was able to fit these data with a cross-validated correlation of 0.72, and fuzzy logic was able to fit these data with a cross-validated correlation of 0.74. The expert made 125 decisions in the second (difficult) set of scenarios. The cross-validated correlations for linear regression and fuzzy logic on these data were 0.56 and 0.50, respectively.

The average cross-validated correlations across all participants, for each modeling technique within each set of scenarios, are presented in Table 11.1. Modeling techniques were directly compared by applying Fisher's r-to-z transformation to the cross-validated correlations and then performing dependent t-tests. Considering the first nine participants (including the expert) who completed the easier set of scenarios, there were no statistically significant differences between the predictive validities of the two modeling techniques. Considering the remaining 15 participants (including the expert), who completed the more difficult set of scenarios, linear regression models fit the decision-making data significantly better than fuzzy models ($z = 0.605$ versus $z = 0.541$), $t(14) = 5.67$, $p = 0.001$, est. $\eta^2 = 0.70$.

Conclusions

Our first hypothesis, that fuzzy system models would fit our data better than linear regression equations, was not supported. In fact, there was no consistent pattern of statistically significant differences between the predictive validity of regression and fuzzy models across the two sets of scenarios. It may be that these participants, with their minimal experience with this relatively complex task, are

Table 11.1. Predictive validity for experiment 1

	# of Decisions	Linear Regression	Fuzzy Logic
Scenario Set #1 ($n = 8$ + expert)			
Range (Min–Max)	38–98	0.49–0.76	0.40–0.84
Average (SD)	73 (21)	0.64 (0.12)	0.63 (0.15)
Scenario Set #2 ($n = 14$ + expert)			
Range (Min–Max)	52–125	0.32–0.67	0.30–0.71
Average (SD)	81 (25)	0.53 (0.10)	0.48 (0.11)

either not using any particular strategy reliably, or at best only using a simple strategy. This is consistent with the moderate magnitude of our cross-validated correlations, and with the fact that previous research that found fuzzy models to be significantly more predictive than regression (Dorsey & Coovert, 2003) used highly experienced participants who may have developed more reliable and sophisticated reasoning strategies in their domain.

Experiment 2

Although the two modeling techniques could not be distinguished by their ability to predict trainee decision-making performance in this testbed, it was interesting to note that they did not always converge on a single representation of a decision-making strategy. Thus, they may not be equally good at diagnosing underlying decision-making strategies. It is possible for two models with qualitatively different interpretations to fit the same data equally well. From a training perspective, feedback that is based on an accurate diagnosis of underlying reasoning should be most effective. In Experiment 2, we test the hypothesis that feedback based on fuzzy models of decision-making data will lead to more improvement in performance than feedback based on regression equations.

Materials and Methods

Participants

Fifty-one undergraduate students at the University of Central Florida participated in the study. There were 26 female and 25 male participants with a mean age of 20 (ranging from 17 to 29 years). Data from three of these participants are not included in any analyses. These participants did not make enough decisions during the second session to al-

low us to build mathematical models of their data, and they were not invited to return for the third experimental session. This occurred before the treatment was applied, and the three participants who were dropped would have been assigned to different treatment conditions. All participants received extra credit in psychology courses and/or monetary compensation in exchange for their participation. None of the participants had prior exposure to the experimental task. As in Experiment 1, one researcher provided performance data for expert models.

Software, Hardware, and Scenarios

The experimental task from Experiment 1, GT-ASP, was used again in Experiment 2. The final set of five scenarios from Experiment 1 were used for the pre-feedback practice session. Four additional scenarios of similar composition and difficulty were developed to assess trainee performance after the delivery of model-based feedback.

Questionnaire

A subjective strategy questionnaire was designed that asked participants to identify the cues and strategies that they used to make decisions during the scenarios. This questionnaire allowed for comparisons to be made between the decision-making strategies identified by the modeling techniques and the participants' self-reported strategies.

Design

Three decisions that could be modeled to produce feedback were identified in the simulation: (a) which track to hook, (b) the track's intent, and (c) the type of track. Three types of feedback were identified: (a) outcome-based feedback, which focused on the difference between the participant's "score" (percent accuracy) and the expert's "score"; (b) regression-based feedback that highlighted the discrepancies between the participant's and the expert's linear regression models; and (c) fuzzy-based feedback, which described the discrepancies between the participant's and the expert's fuzzy models. In addition, any inconsistency between the number of decisions made by the participant and the number of decisions made by the expert was reported in all three types of feedback.

A partial within-subjects design was used in this study. Each participant received feedback on each decision and each type of feedback. What varied from participant to participant was the pairing between feedback type and decision. A partial Latin square was used to counterbalance the pairings and order of presentation of the feedback across participants (see Figure 11.2). The hook decision feedback was the only exception to a perfectly counterbalanced system. Hook feedback was always presented to participants first, because that is consistent with the way the simulation is played (i.e., a track must be hooked before an assessment of its intent and/or type can be made).

Procedure

Each participant completed three three-hour sessions within one week. During the first session, participants received the same training in GT-ASP that was described in Experiment 1. During the second session, after performing five 30-minute scenarios without any assistance, participants completed the subjective strategy questionnaire.

After completion of the second experimental session, the appropriate mathematical models (depending on the participant's condition) were constructed from the participant's performance data. Each of the participant's models was compared to the

expert model of the same type (regression to regression or fuzzy to fuzzy), and tailored feedback was generated that described both the similarities and the discrepancies between the two models. (More detail is provided on the development of the feedback in the next section.) This process was followed for the two decisions that were assigned to the regression and fuzzy conditions. Feedback was generated for the decision that had been assigned to the outcome condition by comparing the participant's percent accuracy with that of the expert's.

During the third and final session, participants received the feedback based on their performance from the second session. Participants were allowed to take as much time as they wanted to read the feedback, and they were given the opportunity to ask the experimenter questions about the feedback. Then the participants performed four 30-minute scenarios. After the scenarios were completed, all participants were asked to fill out another copy of the subjective strategy questionnaire, reporting the strategies that they used during the third experimental session.

Model and Feedback Development

In between the second and the third experimental sessions, the same bootstrapping and jackknifing procedures used in Experiment 1 were used to build hook, intent, and type models for each participant in Experiment 2. (The one difference was that data from only the last three out of five scenarios from session two were used in this case, as pilot research demonstrated that this subset of data could be modeled with more precision than the entire set of data. We believe that this may be because participant performance was more variable and error-prone during their earliest experiences with the task. Also, to maximize comparability, the expert model was built from the same three scenarios.)

For each decision, the set of jackknifed models containing different subsets of cues (all either regression or fuzzy models) were rank-ordered on their cross-validated correlations, and Fisher's r-to-z transformations and dependent t-tests were used to identify the subset of models with the highest and statistically equivalent cross-validated correlations. If one of the models within that statistically equivalent set contained the exact subset of cues mentioned by the participant on the subjective strategy questionnaire, then that model was used to generate feedback. If not, then the

Presentation Sequences					
First		Second		Third	
Decision	Feedback Type	Decision	Feedback Type	Decision	Feedback Type
Hook	Outcome	Intent	Regression-based	Type	Fuzzy-based
			Fuzzy-based		Regression-based
		Type	Regression-based	Intent	Fuzzy-based
			Fuzzy-based		Regression-based
Hook	Regression-based	Intent	Outcome	Type	Fuzzy-based
			Fuzzy-based		Outcome
		Type	Outcome	Intent	Fuzzy-based
			Fuzzy-based		Outcome
Hook	Fuzzy-based	Intent	Regression-based	Type	Outcome
			Outcome		Regression-based
		Type	Regression-based	Intent	Outcome
			Outcome		Regression-based

Figure 11.2. Twelve conditions generated by partial Latin square.

model with the highest cross-validated correlation was used to generate feedback. This process was followed for both the fuzzy and the regression modeling.

Feedback was generated by comparing the participant's model to an expert model of the same type (regression to regression or fuzzy to fuzzy), and noting the similarities and discrepancies between the two models. Historically, feedback based on regression equations has often been presented in the form of graphical representations of B-weights and/or other statistical parameters (e.g., Balzer et al., 1992). However, the fuzzy models do not easily lend themselves to this type of representation. Thus, to maintain consistency and comparability between the regression-based feedback and the fuzzy-based feedback, we used the following text-based template. First, the cues that appeared in the participant's model were acknowledged. Next, any of these cues that did not also appear in the corresponding expert model were brought to the participant's attention. Third, the similarities and/or differences in usage of the common cues were detailed. Finally, any additional cues that appeared in the expert model were described. See Table 11.2 for an illustration of feedback developed in this format based on fuzzy and regression models of the same data, as well as the outcome-based feedback that would have been produced. (Of course, no participant ever received two types of feedback on the same decision.) When reviewing Table 11.2, it should be noted that the regression and fuzzy analyses identified different sets of cues as being relevant for both the expert's and participant's data sets and this is reflected in the feedback.

More specifically, when regression was the modeling technique, feedback focused on a comparison of the unstandardized regression coefficients (B-weights) in each equation. The 95th percentile confidence interval around the B-weights for each cue in the expert's regression equation was used to identify cases when the participant's B-weights on those same cues were either too high or too low. An example of all possible regression-based feedback statements associated with one cue from the expert's regression equation is provided in Table 11.3.

When fuzzy logic was the modeling technique, generating feedback was a bit more complicated. The first step was to compare the fuzzy categories established on each of the cues that were found in both the expert's and the participant's models. As

can be seen in Figure 11.3, a new set of categories, each of which was completely nested within both the expert's categories and the participant's categories, was established. Verbal labels were assigned to these categories, and the rule sets from each model were rewritten in terms of these new categories. This afforded a direct comparison of the expert's fuzzy rule set to the participant's rules, and feedback was based on the similarities and differences between those rules.

Results

Expert Predictive Validity

The cross-validated correlations for the regression and fuzzy models of the expert data were calculated. Modeling techniques were directly compared by applying Fisher's r-to-z transformation to the cross-validated correlations and then performing dependent t-tests. For each experimental session and for each decision, there was no statistically significant difference between the predictive validity of the regression and fuzzy models of the expert data.

Participant Predictive Validity

Four models were identified for each participant: pre- and postfeedback regression models of data from one decision and pre- and postfeedback fuzzy models of data from another decision. (Recall that the third feedback type was outcome-based, and no mathematical models were built for this condition.) Modeling techniques were directly compared by applying Fisher's r-to-z transformation to the cross-validated correlations and then performing dependent t-tests. There were no statistically significant differences in the predictive validity of regression models and fuzzy models, either when combining all three decision types or when separating decision types.

Diagnostic Utility

To provide a common frame of reference, adjusted accuracy scores were calculated by dividing the number of correct decisions a participant made across a set of scenarios by the number of decisions the expert made across those same scenarios. Each participant received six adjusted accuracy scores: pre- and postfeedback scores on the hook, intent, and type decisions. These adjusted accuracy scores served as dependent variables in all of the following statistical tests of diagnostic utility. Data from

Table 11.2. Comparison of intent feedback that could be generated for one participant

	Linear Regression Feedback	Fuzzy Logic Feedback
Setup	Throughout this task your primary activities include hooking tracks and trying to identify their type and intent. The feedback on this page refers to the characteristics of unknown tracks which may influence your decision to identify them as hostile or friendly. You labeled 61 different unknown tracks as either hostile or friendly, while the expert labeled 70 unknown tracks. A comparison of your data and the expert's suggests that you should be entering more intent identifications into the system.	
Identify cue set participant used	According to your data, it looks as if you considered a track's **relative direction to ownship, IFF, and EWS** when trying to determine whether it was hostile or friendly.	According to your data, it looks as if you considered a track's **point of origin, IFF, and EWS** when trying to determine whether it was hostile or friendly.
Dismiss the cues that the trainee used that the expert did not	While the track's relative direction to ownship may contain information that could potentially be used to help you determine the intent of a track, the expert typically made this determination without paying much attention to that information.	While point of origin, IFF and EWS may contain information that could potentially be used to help you determine the intent of a track, the expert typically made this determination without paying much attention to that information.
Acknowledge the overlapping cues and discuss similarities and/or differences in how they cue was used	Both you and the expert agree that tracks are likely to have the same intent as their IFF signal. For example, tracks with a hostile IFF are likely to be hostile. While both you and the expert generally agree that tracks are likely to have the same intent as their EWS signal (for example, tracks with a hostile EWS, such as APS-115, are likely to be hostile), you rely more heavily on this cue than the expert.	NA
Introduce a cue that the expert used that the student didn't and HOW the expert uses that cue	The expert also takes speed and altitude into consideration when trying to identify the intent of unknown tracks. In particular, according to the expert, faster tracks are more likely to be hostile and lower tracks are more likely to be hostile.	The expert, on the other hand, used altitude when trying to identify the intent of unknown tracks. In particular, according to the expert, very low tracks are likely to be friendly, moderately low tracks are likely to be hostile, and all other tracks are likely to be friendly.
Discuss the constant (for regression equation only)	Finally, you have a tendency to start with the assumption that an unknown track is more likely to be hostile, whereas the expert starts with the assumption that an unknown track is somewhat more likely to be friendly.	NA
Outcome feedback	Throughout this task your primary activities include hooking tracks and trying to identify their type and intent. The feedback on this page refers to the characteristics of unknown tracks which may influence your decision to identify them as hostile or friendly. According to your data, you identified 61 unknown tracks and were accurate 59% of the time when trying to decide if a tracks was hostile or friendly. Because tracks can provide misleading information, it is not always possible to correctly determine the intent of the track you hooked; however, the expert identified 70 tracks and was accurate 94% of the time. A comparison of your data to the expert's suggests that you should be entering more intent identifications into the system, and you should be paying more attention to the relevant cues to help you determine whether a track is hostile or friendly.	

one participant were dropped from all remaining analyses when it was determined that the adjusted accuracy scores were outliers (pretest $z = -2.8$, posttest $z = 1.8$, difference $z = 4.6$).

Pretest scores were significantly correlated with posttest scores, $r = 0.71$, $p = 0.001$. In addition, it appeared that for at least two of the three decisions (intent and type), there were a number of participants who were performing at asymptote during the pretest and did not show any improvement on the posttest. Thus, for each of the three decisions, we applied a mean split on participants' standardized

Table 11.3. All possible regression feedback statements associated with the cue "speed"

B-Weight	Values	Feedback Statement
Absent		"The expert also takes speed into consideration when trying to identify the intent of unknown tracks. In particular, according to the expert, faster tracks are more likely to be hostile."
Below	−0.0019	"While both you and the expert generally agree that the faster the track the more likely it is to hostile, the expert waits until a track is going faster before labeling it hostile than you do."
Between	−0.0018 and 0.0002	"Both you and the expert agree that the faster the track, the more likely it is to be hostile."
Above	0.0003	"While both you and the expert generally agree that speed provides useful information when determining the intent of unknown tracks, you and the expert disagree about how this cue is used. Specifically, you are more likely to identify slower tracks as hostile. The expert, on the other hand, is more likely to identify faster tracks as hostile."

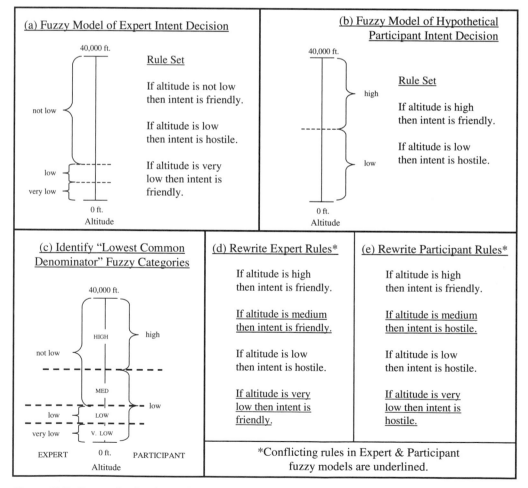

Figure 11.3. Process for developing fuzzy model–based feedback.

pretest scores, and conducted six separate analyses of covariance (ANCOVAs). In each ANCOVA, the between-subjects independent variable was feedback type (regression, fuzzy, and outcome), the covariate was pretest adjusted accuracy score, and the dependent variable was posttest adjusted accuracy score. Adjusted accuracy scores can be found in Table 11.4, and residualized gain scores for each decision, by feedback type, are shown in Figure 11.4.

Considering the hook and intent decisions, there were no significant main effects of feedback type for either the participants below the mean, $F(2,20) = 1.999$, $p = 0.168$ and $F(2,21) = 0.852$, $p = 0.444$ respectively, or the participants above the mean, $F(2,27) = 0.402$, $p = 0.674$ and $F(2,26) = 0.852$, $p = 0.440$ respectively.

Considering the type decision, for participants with pretest scores below the mean, the main effect of feedback type was significant, $F(2,21) = 4.315$, $p = 0.031$, est. $\eta^2 = 0.337$. Bonferroni tests revealed that after removing the variance accounted for by pretest performance, those participants who received fuzzy model-based feedback achieved significantly higher posttest scores than participants who received regression model-based feedback. However, there was no main effect of feedback type for participants above the mean, $F(2,26) = 1.071$, $p = 0.360$.

Conclusion

In this experiment, we tested the hypothesis that feedback based on a comparison of fuzzy models of student and expert data would lead to significantly more performance improvement during training than feedback based on a comparison of linear regression models of that data. This hypothesis was only partially supported. For the one decision (type) for which our expert model had a reasonably high predictive validity, and for the subset of participants who actually had room for improvement, our hypothesis was supported. In other words, among participants performing below the mean on the pretest, those who received fuzzy model–based feedback performed significantly better on the posttest for the type decision than those who received regression model–based feedback. Beyond that, there were no statistically significant differences in posttest performance that could be attributed to the type of feedback. Examination of the low predictive validity of the expert models for the hook and intent decisions suggests those models may not have captured strategies that would lead to good task performance. It should also be noted that consistent with the findings from Experiment 1, there were no statistically significant differences in the predictive validity of the different modeling techniques.

Table 11.4. Adjusted accuracy scores

Feedback Type	Below Mean		Above Mean	
	Average Pretest Score (SD)	Average Posttest Score (SD)	Average Pretest Score (SD)	Average Posttest Score (SD)
Hook decision				
Fuzzy	0.58 (0.09)	0.64 (0.16)	0.78 (0.08)	0.83 (0.11)
Regression	0.56 (0.07)	0.78 (0.09)	0.80 (0.07)	0.81 (0.16)
Control	0.51 (0.08)	0.67 (0.22)	0.79 (0.07)	0.84 (0.08)
Intent decision				
Fuzzy	0.42 (0.08)	0.63 (0.12)	0.58 (0.04)	0.71 (0.05)
Regression	0.41 (0.07)	0.60 (0.14)	0.57 (0.02)	0.67 (0.07)
Control	0.47 (0.03)	0.57 (0.19)	0.62 (0.06)	0.72 (0.06)
Type decision				
Fuzzy	0.48 (0.08)	0.72 (0.15)	0.86 (0.11)	0.82 (0.19)
Regression	0.51 (0.15)	0.60 (0.14)	0.89 (0.13)	0.87 (0.15)
Control	0.36 (0.16)	0.58 (0.19)	0.74 (0.05)	0.85 (0.11)

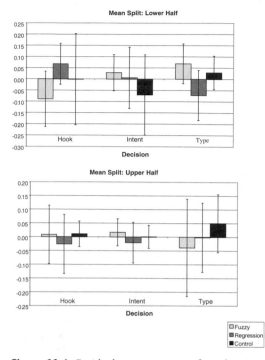

Figure 11.4. Residual posttest scores, after adjusting for pretest scores, for participants above and below the mean, averaged by decision and feedback type.

Discussion

Combining the Brunswik lens model with a mathematical modeling technique that is capable of identifying the actual proximal–distal relationships that form the basis of a person's judgment and behavior would produce a powerful tool for computer-based training systems. Although regression has been used successfully to model decision-making behavior in many domains, some of the assumptions of this mathematical technique may not be consistent with the nature of human reasoning across all domains. It has been proposed that fuzzy logic is a viable alternative technique for modeling human judgment data. Potential advantages of fuzzy logic are that it does not require the modeler to specify a functional form a priori, and it produces a representation that may be more consistent with human cognitive processes in some domains. This research was designed to compare regression and fuzzy modeling techniques in their capability to diagnose decision-making processes and facilitate the development of effective feedback to support training.

We had two hypotheses. First, we hypothesized that fuzzy logic would be significantly more predictive of human performance than regression. This hypothesis was not supported in either experiment. Our second hypothesis was that fuzzy model–based feedback would lead to significantly more improvement than regression-based feedback. We found only weak supporting evidence for this hypothesis. Significant results were in the hypothesized direction, however, they were only obtained for participants performing below the mean at pretest on one of the three decisions investigated. It should be noted that there was a large amount of variance in our participants' performance data, so the lack of significant results may have resulted in part from our relatively small sample sizes.

Some encouragement may be derived from the fact that significant results were obtained for the one decision for which we had a reasonably predictive expert model available to generate the feedback messages. In addition, for this case, the two types of models (regression and fuzzy) were equally predictive of expert performance. Thus the differential impact of the feedback derived from each type of model must be attributed to the fact that the two modeling techniques abstracted different strategies from the data, rather than to the relative abilities of the two techniques to capture variance in the data. In fact, we repeatedly found that when regression and fuzzy models were derived from the same human judgment data, they did not converge to the same underlying reasoning strategy. They often selected different cues, and the fuzzy models often incorporated interactions between cues to explain performance. (Though it is true that the addition of product and exponent terms to a regression equation allows for that modeling technique to identify nonlinear patterns such as interactions, we found that interpreting a significant product term was problematic. More specifically, a significant product term in a regression equation does not specify the exact nature of the interaction in the data, and thus does not readily support the qualitative interpretation necessary to generate feedback.) Thus, the two techniques would lead to the production of qualitatively different feedback in a training setting. Given these two outcomes, we believe that further research investigating the capability of alternative mathematical modeling techniques to support training goals is worthwhile.

An examination of our data suggests potential modifications for future experiments. First, the decision to provide each participant with feedback on all three decisions may have led to information overload and resulted in confusion among some participants as to which advice was meant for which decision. Second, although it was true that the predictive validity of the participant models increased when only the data from last three out of five scenarios was used to build the models, the opposite was true for the expert model. We decided to build the expert model from the exact same set of scenarios as the participant models and accept the lower predictive validity. Given that the only decision for which we found statistically significant results was the one in which the expert model was reasonably predictive, this may have been the wrong choice. Third, the control condition of providing outcome information (a comparison of the participant's and expert's scores) appears to have had a motivational effect on some participants. In future research, alternative control conditions should be considered.

Conducting these studies has brought to light several practical limitations on the application of mathematical modeling to generate effective training feedback. For example, not all domains are amenable to mathematical modeling. This type of modeling requires a large set of data, and thus is only appropriate for training contexts in which trainees routinely make many decisions within a relatively short amount of time. Our experiences with scenario design brought to light another issue: the tension between the tenets of Brunswik's representative design (Brunswik, 1952) and the modeler's needs. For example, modeling algorithms perform best when provided with a data set that includes multiple performance examples across all possible combinations of cues, which is not always consistent with collecting data under representative conditions. Unfortunately, when two cues are highly correlated in the operational context we are trying to simulate (and thus, in the data set), it is not possible to determine mathematically which cue a person was using when making decisions. More information on the modeling lessons learned from this research can be found in Campbell et al. (2001).

Finally, there are several other related research questions that could be pursued in the future. For example, other mathematical modeling techniques should also be evaluated for their ability to support diagnosis and feedback development in automated training systems. Second, some of the earlier research with regression-based feedback found that simply providing the expert regression model was as effective at improving performance as explicitly comparing the participant's model to the expert's model (Balzer et al., 1989). Our team has replicated these findings with fuzzy logic–based expert models (Buff & Campbell, 2002), and this comparison could be investigated with any other mathematical technique as well. Though there has been some research directly comparing linear regression and process tracing modeling techniques (Einhorn, Kleinmuntz, & Kleinmuntz, 1979), training effectiveness comparisons (e.g., Bolton, Buff, & Campbell, 2003) should be made between mathematical modeling techniques and the process tracing or cognitive modeling approaches typically used in Intelligent Tutoring Systems (for an introduction to Intelligent Tutoring Systems, see Shute & Psotka, 1996). Finally, although our particular domain did not appear to elicit reasoning that required fuzzy logic modeling, there may be other domains that do. In fact, a domain analysis technique (or a taxonomy of domains) that provides guidance for selecting the most appropriate modeling representation would be a very useful tool for the entire community.

In closing, although we did not find strong evidence in these two studies to advocate the use of fuzzy logic instead of regression to model decision making in our particular training domain, it may still prove advantageous in other domains. More important, we have illustrated an extension to the traditional application of the lens model, and our efforts demonstrate the powerful utility of this model as a general paradigm to support training and training research. By focusing on the nature of probabilistic relationships in operational environments, rather than committing to the modeling method du jour, Brunswik's paradigm will continue to provide a framework for trainers and researchers as new modeling techniques emerge over the years to come.

Acknowledgments. The views expressed here are those of the authors and do not reflect the official position of the organization with which they are affiliated. This work was supported by the Naval Air Systems Command In-House Laboratory Independent Research Program. We also thank David O.

Holness and Randy S. Astwood for their assistance in data collection.

References

Balzer, W. K., Doherty, M. E., & O'Connor, R. (1989). Effects of cognitive feedback on performance. *Psychological Bulletin, 106*(3), 410–433.

Balzer, W. K., Sulsky, L. M., Hammer, L. B., & Sumner, K. E. (1992). Task information, cognitive information, or functional validity information: Which components of cognitive feedback affect performance? *Organizational Behavior and Human Decision Processes, 53*, 35–54.

Bolton, A. E., Buff, W. L., & Campbell, G. E. (2003). Faster, cheaper, and just as good: A comparison of the instructional effectiveness of three human behavior representations that vary in development requirements. *Proceedings of the 12th Annual Conference on Behavior Representation in Modeling and Simulation* [CD-ROM].

Brunswik, E. (1952). *The conceptual framework of psychology*. Chicago: University of Chicago Press.

Buff, W. L., & Campbell, G. E. (2002). What to do or what not to do?: Identifying the content of effective feedback. *Proceedings of the Human Factors and Ergonomics Society 46th Annual Meeting, 46*(2), 2074–2078.

Campbell, G. E., Buff, W. L., & Bolton, A. E. (2000). The diagnostic utility of fuzzy system modeling for application in training systems. *Proceedings of the Human Factors and Ergonomics Society 44th Annual Meeting, 44*(2), 370–373.

Campbell, G. E., Buff, W. L., Bolton, A. E., & Holness, D. O. (2001). The application of mathematical techniques for modeling decision-making: Lessons learned from a preliminary study. In E. M. Altman, A. Cleermans, C. D. Schunn, & W. D. Gray (Eds.), *Proceedings of the Fourth International Conference on Cognitive Modeling* (pp. 49–54). Mahwah, N.J.: Lawrence Erlbaum.

Campbell, G. E., Rhodenizer, L. G., & Buff, W. L. (1999). A comparison of two mathematical modeling approaches to produce cognitive feedback. *Proceedings of the Human Factors and Ergonomics Society 43rd Annual Meeting, 43*(2), 1406.

Cohen, J., & Cohen, P. (1983). *Applied multiple regression/correlation analysis for the behavior sciences* (2nd ed.). Hillsdale, N.J.: Lawrence Erlbaum.

Dorsey, D. W., & Coovert, M. D. (2003). Mathematical modeling of decision making: A soft and fuzzy approach to capturing hard decisions. *Human Factors* [special issue], *45*(1), 117–135.

Einhorn, H. J., Kleinmuntz, D. N., & Kleinmuntz, B. (1979). Linear regression and process-tracing models of judgment. *Psychological Review, 86*(5), 465–485.

Gay, P., Phipps, D. A., Bisantz, A. M., Walker, N., Kirlik, A., & Fisk, A. D. (1997). Operator specific modeling of identification judgments in a complex dynamic task. *Proceedings of the Human Factors and Ergonomics Society 41st Annual Meeting, 41*(1), 225–229.

Math Works. (1996). MATLAB: The language of technical computing (Version 5) [Computer software].

Medin, D. L., & Smith, E. E. (1984). Concepts and concept formation. In M. R. Rosenzweig & L. W. Porter (Eds.), *Annual Review of Psychology, 35*, 113–118.

Newell, A. (1973). Production systems: Models of control structures. In W. G. Chase (Ed.), *Visual information processing* (pp. 463–526). New York: Academic Press.

Rogelberg, S. G., Ployhart, R. E., Balzer, W. K., & Yonker, R. D. (1999). Using policy-capturing to examine tipping decisions. *Journal of Applied Social Psychology, 29*(12), 2567–2590.

Rosch, E. (1978). Principles of categorization. In E. Rosch & B. B. Lloyd (Eds.), *Cognition and categorization* (pp. 27–48). Hillsdale, N.J.: Erlbaum.

Shute, V. J. & Psotka, J. (1996). Intelligent tutoring systems: Past, present and future. In D. H. Jonassen (Ed.), *Handbook of research for educational communications and technology: A project of the Association for Educational Communications and Technology* (pp. 570–600). New York: Macmillan.

Smithson, M. (1988). Possibility theory, fuzzy logic, and psychological explanation. In T. Zetenyi (Ed.), *Fuzzy sets in psychology* (pp. 1–50). Amsterdam: North Holland Elsevier Science.

Stewart, T. R. (1988). Judgment analysis: Procedures. In B. Brehmer & C.R.B. Joyce (Eds.), *Human judgment: The SJT view* (pp. 41–74). Amsterdam: North Holland Elsevier Science.

Zadeh, L. A. (1965). Fuzzy sets. Information and Control, 8, 338–353.

Kathleen L. Mosier and Shane T. McCauley

Achieving Coherence: Meeting New Cognitive Demands in Technological Systems

Introduction

Examinations of human judgment have historically been aligned with one of two theoretical perspectives on the nature of truth—the *correspondence* approach or the *coherence* perspective—each characterized by different models and methods for defining, testing, and assessing the quality of judgment processes. Many of the previous chapters demonstrate that valuable insights into cognition and performance can be gained by viewing them as geared toward adapting to the demands of technological ecologies; that is, in making judgments and decisions in correspondence with the environment. These studies, it must be noted, focus primarily on the correspondence mode of judgment, as originally described by Brunswik and subsequently elaborated by Hammond (e.g., 1966, 1996).

Within a correspondence framework, the goal of cognition is empirical, objective accuracy in human judgment; *correspondence competence* refers to an individual's ability to accurately perceive and respond to multiple fallible indicators in the environment (e.g., Brunswik, 1943; 1956; Hammond, 1996). Correspondence is a relatively natural, adaptive process; humans "exercise . . . correspondence judgments almost instantaneously without think-

ing, just as we correctly perceive the world around us without thinking, without making strong, conscious demands on memory" (Hammond, 2000, p. 35). Correspondence competence has evolved in response to the necessity of being accurate in our judgments of the current and future state of our environment. We live in a correspondence-driven world, a domain in which the actual state of the world imposes constraints on our interactions within it (e.g., Vicente, 1990). The measure of correspondence competence is the accuracy of the judgment, that is, how well it corresponds to fact.

Brunswik's lens model offers a classic description of the correspondence process (1943, 1956). According to this model, judgments of people and objects are based on "probabilistic cues," or attributes that can be perceived by an individual and are used to evaluate elements in the environment (e.g., Hammond, 2000; Hammond & Stewart, 2001). The degree of relatedness between cues and their criterion is referred to as ecological validity; and the accuracy of judgment is referred to as functional achievement. The model has been applied in a variety of contexts, including those described in this volume (see also Cooksey, 1996, for a review). The lens model, like other correspondence theories (e.g., social judgment theory, Hammond, 1966,

1996; and signal detection theory, Green & Swets, 1974; Swets, 1973), emphasizes the objective correctness of human judgment and the factors that influence it. The decision maker makes a judgment or prediction based on cues or indicators in the environment, all of which are fallible to some degree.

According to the correspondence framework, features of the environment and of the cues used will impact the accuracy of judgments. For example, cues that are highly ecologically valid, are concrete, and/or can be perceived clearly will facilitate accurate judgments. Cues that are ambiguous, are murkier because they are not as concrete in nature, or are obscured by factors in the environment will hinder accurate judgments. Correspondence judgments cannot be made without reference to the real world and are evaluated according to how well they represent, predict, or explain objective reality. Today, we practice correspondence competence whenever we use probabilistic cues to make judgments about other people, predict the stock market, or estimate whether our car will fit into a parking space. A pilot exercises correspondence competence when using cues outside the cockpit to figure out where he or she is or judging height and distance from an obstacle or a runway. A weather forecaster performs a correspondence judgment when predicting tomorrow's weather from today's weather patterns. A doctor strives for correspondence when diagnosing a patient's set of symptoms. The ultimate test of the correspondence process is the empirical accuracy of the resultant judgment—*regardless of the process by which that accuracy was achieved.*

Coherence theories, on the other hand, focus on the rationality of the judgment process—*coherence competence* refers to the ability to maintain logical consistency in judgments and decisions (Hammond, 1996). Coherence is not as natural a process as correspondence; rather, it is culturally determined. "Coherence competence, or the achievement of rationality . . . must come through participation in a culture that educates its members in coherence competence . . . [and] appears . . . at the encouragement, assistance, and demands of a culture" (Hammond, 2000, p. 35). Coherence competence must be acquired artificially. It entails training on what constitutes coherence and time to think when applying what has been learned, and it is more susceptible to time pressure, distraction, and stress. Moreover, achieving and maintaining coherence

involve rationality, logic, use of discrete data and processes (see chapter 13) and typically require the decision maker to move toward the analytical modes on the cognitive continuum (Hammond, 2000).

Coherence theorists place great emphasis on the logical consistency, or coherence, of the judgment process. In contrast to correspondence, *coherence competence* is not evaluated by empirical accuracy relative to the real world; instead, the sole evaluative criterion is the quality of the cognitive process used. We practice coherence when we assess the logic in a politician's argument. A juror exercises coherence competence when evaluating the body of evidence supporting a defendant's guilt or innocence. A pilot exercises coherence competence when he or she evaluates the information displayed inside the cockpit to ensure that system parameters, flight modes, and navigational displays are consistent with each other and with what should be present in a given situation.

Neither of these perspectives is sufficient in itself to describe or evaluate human judgment—coherence and correspondence are complementary cognitive goals. Judgment researchers such as Hammond (1996, 2000) have discussed the need for complementarity in approach and in assessment; within an extended framework, the "best" judgments would arguably be those that are not only correspondent (objectively accurate) but also coherent (rationally sound). Moreover, the introduction of technology into the decision-making environment has heightened the need for analytical coherence in diagnoses and judgments and has introduced new coherence requirements for the human as well as the technology in the decision system.

Is Coherence Really Necessary?

One could make the argument that coherence in judgment is of minor importance in a correspondence-driven world. People may prefer striving to be accurate in their judgments over being consistent and rational. After all, the achievement of coherence is not sufficient in itself to ensure good outcomes (e.g., Sunstein et al., 2001), but on the other hand, a judgment process that lacks coherence may nonetheless produce a judgment that is quite accurate. Gigerenzer, for example, has demonstrated that what he describes as "fast and frugal" heuristics, such as use of the one cue with the highest validity ("take the best"), result in judgments that are just as accurate as a more coherent multiple-regression model (Gigerenzer, Todd, & the ABC Research Group, 1999; Gigerenzer & Goldstein, 1996). Others have pointed out that the use of heuristics in general provides a quick and simple way to deal with information and is reasonably accurate most of the time (Lopes & Odin, 1991). Laboring under the assumption, then, that coherence is either too difficult for us to achieve (e.g., Kahneman, Slovic, & Tversky, 1982) or that it is really not that important (e.g., Gigerenzer & Goldstein, 1996), many technological interventions have focused almost exclusively on helping humans achieve correspondence by reducing uncertainty and increasing accuracy, while contributing little to the achievement and maintenance of coherence.

Coherence, however, is critically important in those decision environments in which correspondence simply cannot be accomplished without coherence. In the world characterized by advanced technology, the environment is more deterministic than probabilistic in that the uncertainty has, for most practical purposes, been engineered out through technical reliability. Technology brings proximal cues into exact alignment with the distal environment, and individuals in decision environments aided by technology can make judgments much more accurately than ever before. The potential for heightened accuracy, however, comes with a cost: The technological environment creates a discrete rather than continuous space, as described by Degani et al. (chapter 13), and as such demands more formal cognitive processes than does the continuous ecology of the physical world.

Ironically, then, the creation of technological decision aids to help correspondence has heightened the need for coherence in judgment, in terms of internal consistency and appropriate use of cues and information. Technology has introduced the requirement that information be evaluated analytically to ensure that information displayed on indicators forms a cohesive, coherent representation of what is going on. The ecological validity of technological information approaches 100%—*if* coherence among relevant indicators exists.

In the glass cockpit, for example, designers have facilitated correspondence by creating an electronic world in which accuracy of judgment is ensured as long as coherence is achieved—that is, system parameters, flight modes, and navigational displays must be consistent with each other and with what should be present in a given situation. The achievement of coherence is both a prerequisite for and the method by which the pilot accomplishes correspondence. Pilots can trust the empirical accuracy of the data used to achieve correspondence; in fact, they may not be able to verify accuracy because they do not always have access to either correspondence cues or to "objective reality." When flight crews achieve coherence in the cockpit—for instance, when they have ensured that *all* information inside the cockpit paints a consistent picture of the aircraft on the glide path—they have also achieved correspondence and can be confident that the aircraft *is* on the glide path. The pilots do not need to look out the window for airport cues to confirm it, and in fact, visibility conditions often do not allow them to do so.

A vivid example of both the need to assess information analytically and the cost of noncoherence in a technological environment can be found in the report of an incident that occurred in Strasbourg, France (Ministere de l'Equipement, des Transports et du Tourisme, 1993), when pilots of an Airbus 320 confused approach modes:

> It is believed that the pilots intended to make an automatic approach using a flight path angle of –3.3° from the final approach fix. . . . The pilots, however, appear to have executed the approach in heading/vertical speed mode instead of track/flight path angle mode. The Flight Control Unit setting of "–33" yields a vertical descent rate of –3300 ft/min in this mode, and this is almost precisely the rate of descent the airplane realized until it crashed into mountainous terrain several miles short of the airport. (Billings, 1996, p. 178)

It should be noted that coherence is an essential but not necessarily sufficient requirement in many technological environments. Both correspondence and coherence are important in any domain that exists within an objective, real-world context. Aviation, for example, is a correspondence-driven domain in that it exists in a physical and social world and is subject to rules and constraints of that world (Vicente, 1990). It does the pilot no good to make a perfect "coherence" landing with all systems in sync if a truck is stalled in the middle of the runway. Additionally, low-tech cues, such as smoke or sounds, can often provide critical input to the diagnosis of high-tech systems.

Diagnosing the *Columbia* Disaster: A Struggle for Coherence

On February 1, 2003, Mission Control engineers at the NASA Johnson Space Center, Houston, struggled to formulate a coherent picture of events aboard the space shuttle *Columbia* (Langewiesche, 2003). At Mission Control, automatically transmitted data gave the engineers exact information on the status of systems on the shuttle—but the information did not gel or point to a common root for the indications they were seeing. The first piece of information that was inconsistent with a normal, routine approach was a low tire pressure indicator for the left main landing gear. Other disparate indicators included a "strange failure of temperature transducers in a hydraulic return line. . . . All four of them . . . located in the aft part of the left wing" (p. 61). All of the telemetric indications were valid, but the combination of readings did not make sense. Phrases like "Okay, is there anything common to them?" and "All other indications for your hydraulic systems indications are good? . . . And the other temps are normal?" and "And there's no commonality between all these tire pressure instrumentations and the hydraulic return instrumentations?" (pp. 61, 62) illustrate the process of seeking coherence, of trying to construct a story that would encompass the information being transmitted to Mission Control.

Even though they had precise readings of system states, the engineers at Mission Control could not know precisely what was going on until they could fit seemingly contradictory indications together for a diagnosis. Frustration with the incoherence of indications, as well as an unwillingness to accept the unknown disaster they portended, is reflected in phrases such as "What in the world?," "Is it instrumentation? Gotta be," and "So I do believe it's instrumentation" (pp. 61, 62). Interestingly, at least one engineer in Houston had envisioned a scenario that could account for all the data they were receiving. NASA program managers had been aware that a chunk of solid foam had broken off during launch and smashed into the left wing at high speed and had dismissed the event as "essentially unthreatening" (Langewiesche, 2003,

p. 61). Engineer Jeff Kling, however, had discussed with his team possible ramifications of the foam hit and the telemetric indications they might expect if a hole had been created, allowing hot gases to enter the wing during reentry. His model was consistent with the data that were coming in and could have been used to achieve a coherent picture of what was happening.

Unfortunately, the possibility of this diagnosis was precluded because Kling's model was not even mentioned during the event—in part because "it had become a matter of faith within NASA that foam strikes—which were a known problem—could not cause mortal damage to the shuttle" (p. 73). This event dramatically illustrates not only the need for coherence in effective use of technological systems but also the requirement that data within the electronic environment be integrated in the context of an accurate correspondent world.

Approaches to the Measurement of Coherence

Much of the research on coherence in judgment and decision making has focused on human difficulty in maintaining coherence. Perhaps the best-known example of a coherence approach to judgment research can be found within the "heuristics and biases" research tradition (e.g., Kahneman et al., 1982). Tversky and Kahneman (1971, 1973, 1983), for example, have documented a host of judgment errors due to the use of heuristics such as *availability*, the judgment of the likelihood of events dependent on the ease of their recall; *representativeness*, the tendency to use the similarity of a past event to a present situation to judge the likelihood that the current event will have the same outcome; and the *conjunction fallacy*, the tendency to see a conjunction as more probable than one of its elements if the combination presents a more representative picture. The key issue in this research is not whether heuristics may result in accurate judgments, but rather the notion that they exemplify the flawed, noncoherent nature of the human judgment process. Researchers in this tradition compare human judgment, characterized by various heuristics (short-cuts) used by individuals use to speed up the decision-making process, against normative or mathematical models such as Bayes's (1958) theorem. Typically, they pit participants' responses against what a statistician would have responded according to Bayesian calculations. Using these criteria for rationality, they have found human judgment to be at best an approximate process and at worst irrational and subject to systematic biases.

Mathematical Coherence: The Best Metric?

Evaluation against mathematical models is not the only and may not even be the best way to gauge the coherence of an individual's judgment processes. Many judgments, such as those involving moral assessments or opinions, for example, are made without reference to a statistical standard. With other judgments, features of a particular case may make statistical probabilities across cases irrelevant or misleading. Moreover, early definitions of coherence were rooted in the gestaltist emphases on "good figure," "completeness," "wholes," and patterns (Hammond, 1996), rather than in mathematical models of probability. In a technological world, coherence requires thinking logically and analytically about data and information in the work environment. This involves knowing what data are relevant, integrating *all* relevant data to come up with a "story" of the situation, and ensuring that the story of the data is rational and appropriate. It also entails recognizing inconsistencies in data that signal lack of coherence, as well as understanding the limits of coherence-based systems and recognizing their strengths and inadequacies.

In many cases then, and certainly in technological environments, the incorporation of all relevant cues and information, appropriate discounting of irrelevant information, and the seeking and resolution of any information that might disconfirm one's judgment might be a better metric for coherence than normative mathematical models. Such a metric might, in fact, provide a more effective starting point for improving people's coherence competence, especially given people's demonstrated difficulty in using mathematical information in judgments. Examining coherence from this perspective demands insight as to what individuals are thinking as they formulate judgments. Coherent information searches and proper situation assessment processes would be defined by the extent to which decision makers seek out a complete, cohesive, and consistent picture prior to diagnosis. A

coherence strategy would entail an evaluation of how elements fit together or contradict each other, the handling of contradictory information, and appropriate and consistent use of cues and information. To evaluate coherence, we would need to know, more precisely than a retrospective mathematical policy-capturing method can tell us, what information or cues people use in a particular judgment situation, what they consider to be important, what they discount, and how they put information together to formulate a coherent judgment.

In concentrating on correspondence, technology has greatly increased the need for coherence in diagnosis and judgment. This means that workers in high-technology environments will be called on to assess the consistency—or coherence—of information rather than its correspondence or accuracy and to attain, maintain, and recover coherence as needed. Strategies to accomplish these requirements will be different than many of the kinds of strategies that have been discussed in this volume to this point and are likely to involve cognitive processes that are more analytical than intuitive. Metrics to evaluate coherence in high-technology environments will be different than those used to measure correspondence and will also be different from those used in the past. Moreover, to meet these new cognitive demands in technological environments, we will need to develop new ways of thinking about system and display design, especially to ensure that the design of automation and information displays elicits the mode of rationality most appropriate for meeting the demands of workers' tasks.

Factors Impacting Coherence in High-Technology Environments

Features of the High-Technology Environment

System Design

Given the importance of coherence competence in technological environments, it is important to understand what factors may facilitate or impede the utilization of coherent decision processes. The way information is presented, for example, may have a powerful impact on the judgment meta-strategy that will be educed and thus whether or not coherence will be elicited or facilitated. A match must exist between the cognitive tactics required to achieve coherence in the technological environment and the cognitive tactics elicited by it. In many cases, the design and display of technological systems elicit intuitive or quasi-analytical rather than analytical cognition. Within seemingly intuitive displays, however, may reside numerical data that signify different commands or values in different modes. When dealing with coherence disruptions, these data must be interpreted—even at the simplest levels of technology. (Why isn't the VCR recording my program?) More sophisticated technological systems, as mentioned by Degani et al. (chapter 13), may include thousands of possible states. Once interpreted, data must be compared with expected data to detect discrepancies, and if they exist, analysis is required to resolve them.

Moreover, before system data can be analyzed, they must first be located. This is often not an easy process, because in many cases the data that would allow for analytic assessment of a situation may not only not be obvious but might not be presented at all or may be buried below surface features. In a technological environment, what the worker may see is an apparently simple display that masks a highly complex combination of features, options, functions, and system couplings that may produce unanticipated, quickly propagating effects if not analyzed and taken into account (Woods, 1996).

Technological systems, then, typically analyze information and may present only what has been deemed necessary. Data are preprocessed, and presented in a format that allows, for the most part, only a surface view of system functioning and precludes analysis of the consistency or coherence of data. In their efforts to provide an easy-to-use display format, designers have often buried the data needed to retrace or follow system actions. Calculations and resultant actions often occur without the awareness of the human operator. This system opacity interferes with the capability to track processes analytically, a phenomenon that has often been documented and discussed with respect to the automated cockpit (e.g., Sarter, Woods, & Billings, 1997; Woods, 1996). The spontaneous generation of poor mental models of system functioning results in mistaken perceptions of coherence and/or faultily based attempts to achieve and restore it.

To be effective, technological innovations designed to enhance human judgment should be based on correct assumptions about human judgment processes. Many technological decision aids, however, are designed on the basis of incomplete or inaccurate suppositions about the nature of human judgment and the requirements for metacognitive awareness and sound judgment processes. Designers of these aids have concentrated on enhancing the judgment environments by providing decision aids and interventions designed to make judgment more accurate and have made assumptions about what individuals need to know and how this information should be displayed. These assumptions are often based on models of human judgment processes that emphasize accuracy (correspondence) rather than internal coherence and may in fact make coherence difficult to achieve. Defining correct assumptions entails an incorporation of both coherence and correspondence metatheoretical perspectives into the definition of sound human judgment.

A Case in Point: Automation Bias

In our aviation work, we have identified *automation bias*, a flawed decision process characterized by the use of automated information as a heuristic replacement for vigilant information seeking and processing, as a factor in decision errors in technological environments (e.g., Mosier et al., 1998, 2001; Mosier & Skitka, 1996; Skitka, Mosier, & Burdick, 1999). Studies of this phenomenon involved professional pilots flying event scenarios in a high-fidelity "part-task" simulator, that is, a computer-based flight simulator that incorporated the flight instrumentation and dynamics of a multi-engine glass-cockpit aircraft (Mosier et al., 1998, 2001), as well as student participants performing a low-fidelity flight analog task (Skitka et al., 1999, 2000).

In the diagnosis and decision-making scenarios in our studies, cues and information were present that were not consistent with automated indications—in other words, a disruption to the coherence of information existed. In all cases, correct information was available to cross-check indicators and formulate a coherent judgment, but in many cases, participants demonstrated a heuristic reliance on automation, and other information was not sought out or used. Results of these studies documented error rates of approximately 55% for both pilot and student samples and across one- and two-person crews. Moreover, higher levels of experience did not foster higher coherence in judgment; on the contrary, increased experience *decreased* the likelihood of detecting disruptions to coherence.

Susceptibility to automation bias may be exacerbated by the fact that automated information is typically displayed in a way that makes it more salient than other cues or information and is usually designed to be noticed quickly. The presence of automated information also diminishes the likelihood that decision makers will either make the cognitive effort to seek other diagnostic information or process all available information in cognitively complex, more coherent ways. This is particularly likely when high-tech displays give the impression that they are presenting the whole picture or when other information is hidden or not easily accessed, or displayed in a format that requires analytical processing for integration. In addition, automation increases the probability that decision makers will cut off the diagnosis phase of decision making prematurely when prompted to take a course of action by a computer or technological aid.

The design of technological systems, then, may hinder rather than facilitate the cognitive processing needed to maintain and coherence, and may encourage cognitive processing that is not internally consistent and therefore not rational. This has occurred because not enough attention has been paid to the cognitive processes elicited by inherent features of the judgment context, either as defined by display and presentation factors or by situational factors. Decision aids may actually make it very difficult for individuals to maintain coherence in judgment, for example, by burying relevant information below surface displays, by displaying information that has different meanings depending on the display mode, or by *not* cueing decision makers to check specific situational features and details that would erode coherence (Mosier, 2002; Woods, 1996; Woods & Sarter, 2000). Technological aids in many high-tech fields, such as medicine or nuclear power, may fall into the same trap as in aviation.

Time Pressure

Time pressure is often a characteristic of high-technology environments and may negatively impact coherence. Rothstein (1986), for example, found that time pressure decreased the consistency of judgments. In our automation bias research, students who were told to make judgments as quickly as possible checked less information and made

more errors than others (Skitka et al., 2000). Our most recent study was designed to track diagnosis and decision-making strategies for different types of problems as a function of time pressure and two other operational variables: source—automated or other—of the initial indication of a problem; and congruence versus inconsistency of available information. Ninety-three professional pilots responded to a series of scenarios on an interactive Web site by accessing relevant information until they could make a diagnosis and come to a decision about what to do. As predicted, pilots who were under time pressure took less time to come to a diagnosis, checked fewer pieces of information, and performed fewer double-checks of information than those who experienced no time pressure. As a consequence of this, they saved on average about 100 seconds in the diagnostic process—however, diagnoses were less accurate under time pressure, particularly when conflicting information was present (Mosier et al., 2003). (The difference in time between time pressure and no time pressure conditions, it should be noted, was very small, and was also inflated due to the nature of the Internet interface because pilots had to click on an instrument or display, and wait until the relevant information appeared in a pop-up box.) What seemed to be happening when pilots were pushed to make judgments quickly was that they checked only enough information to formulate an initial diagnosis and did not take time to verify it or to seek any disconfirming information. Time pressure, then, may exacerbate the erosion of coherence in technological environments by making it less likely that individuals will seek out and find all the information and cues required to assess a judgment situation.

Characteristics of the Human Decision Maker

Risk Assessment

The perceived level of risk in a diagnostic situation can also disrupt the search for information and impact the achievement of coherence. In particular, *attitude toward risk* is a factor that is known to constrain information search; the amount of information sought out by a decision maker can vary based on his or her perceived level of situational risk (Mann & Ball, 1994). This dispositional factor is broken into two facets: risk propensity (an individual's tendency to take or avoid risks) and risk perception (an individual's assessment of the riskiness of a situation), which interact with situational variables (Sitkin & Weingart, 1995). Empirical evidence suggests that the propensity–perception interaction affects decision behavior in that successful outcomes in past risky decisions will lead to an increased propensity to take future risk, which lowers an individual's level of perceived situational risk, which then may influence subsequent willingness to engage in risky decision-making behavior (Sitkin & Weingart, 1995).

Risk attitudes may have an effect at each stage of the decision process. The amount of information that is sought out during the information gathering process delineates the coherence of the judgment process and has a large impact on the quality of the eventual diagnosis and action. When people search information fully and use a complex strategy they will be more likely to create a correct representation of a situation (Mann & Ball, 1994). Research has shown that in the initial information gathering stage, a decision maker who has a tendency to take risks or perceives the situation as less risky is likely to seek out less information than an individual who exhibits risk avoiding tendencies (Lion & Meertens, 2001).

After the information-gathering and diagnostic phases, the decision maker must determine an action to take. The selection of action can depend both on individuals' risk perception (how risky is this option) and risk propensity (have they experienced success in the past in similar situations). As mentioned, these factors interact such that an individual who exhibits a tendency to take risk may see a particular option as less risky than would an individual who exhibits a tendency to avoid risk. Moreover, the impact of noncoherence in the diagnostic process extends to action selection, as decision makers that use random or single-attribute searches tend to make more risky decisions than those who seek more information (Mann & Ball, 1994). The extent to which individuals are willing to take and accept risks is also dependent on their perceived level of personal control in the management of contingencies that may arise (Forlani, 2002). The belief that one is in control of a given situation and has levers to pull that will lead to the desired outcome makes decision makers more willing to accept risk.

These tendencies have been documented in the behavior of commercial aviation pilots. The manner in which pilots respond to threats has been shown to depend on their perception of the safety risk. Additionally, the extent to which these pilots perceived a situation as more or less risky was dependent on their level of experience and varied based on the degree of controllability they perceived in the situation (Fischer, Davidson, & Orasanu, 2003). More experienced pilots perceived situations as less risky than more junior pilots, perhaps because they understood the dynamics of a situation more thoroughly than would someone with less experience. This is consistent with Sitkin and Weingart's (1995) decision-making model, in that past experience of successful risk taking can impact subsequent situational risk assessments. In technological environments, then, differences in risk attitudes and risk assessment may directly affect the maintenance of coherent diagnostic and judgment processes by impacting the extent of information search as well as the action taken.

Expertise

Differences between experts and novices on knowledge organization and the ability to identify domain relevant information have been repeatedly demonstrated (e.g., Chi, Glaser, & Farr, 1988; Einhorn, 1974; Klein, 1993; Murphy & Wright, 1984). It is intuitively compelling to assume that experts will make domain-related judgments in a more coherent fashion than novices. Research investigating expert judgment processes, however, has not always supported this hypothesis, and experts often prove to be no better at coherence than others. Eddy (1982), for example, compared expert physician diagnoses against mathematical models (the traditional test of coherence) and found that they made significant errors. Expert pilots proved to be highly susceptible to automation bias (Mosier et al., 1998, 2001) and time pressure (Mosier et al., 2003), and more likely to perceive risky situations as being controllable (Fischer et al., 2003). Kuipers, Moskowitz, and Kassirer (1988) found that physicians did not make decisions after checking all the facts but rather made an initial decision at an abstract level and then tailored their processes to further specify that decision more precisely. One result of this strategy was that information not consistent with initial diagnoses was not always weighted appropriately in the judgment. In short, although experts *should* be able to make more coherent judgments because they have more experience, more domain knowledge, and a better grasp of what is relevant and important in a judgment, they do not always do so.

In assessing the internal coherence of judgment processes in technological environments, then, it is important to differentiate between domain experts and nonexperts to determine similarities and differences in terms of accessing and using cues and information. One factor to be taken into account is that human experts make many decisions non-analytically, often intuitively (Dreyfus, 1997; Simon, 1983), using pattern matching as a judgment tactic. This ability to recognize patterns affords them with a heightened ability to make correspondence judgments. However, in a technological environment, this mode of processing may leave experts vulnerable to errors in coherence if recognition is accomplished before they have sought out and incorporated all relevant information into the pattern. Expertise does not offer the same advantages to the decision maker in the electronic world as in the naturalistic world. Experience may offer hints as to where to look for anomalies in technological ecologies, but it does not insulate even domain experts from the need to analyze their way back to coherence when anomalies occur.

Moreover, the sequential or layered presentation inherent in many technological systems may short-circuit coherence processing in experts because it encourages them to focus on the most salient, available cues and to make intuitive, heuristic judgments before they have taken into account a broader array of relevant cues and information. Novices, on the other hand, may be more likely to seek out all available information before making a judgment (because they are not as confident of their ability to intuitively recognize the situation or instance) but may be less able to find where the relevant information is buried or to put it all together to form a coherent judgment. The roots of non-coherence, then, and thus the kinds of interventions required for experts versus novices may be different. It is possible that for experts, achieving coherence is simply a matter of being reminded that they need to do so. For them, the way in which information is presented may not be as critical to coher-

ence in judgment as maintaining an awareness that coherence is necessary. Novices, on the other hand, may require more than meta-cognitive reminders—they may need assistance putting cues and information together in a coherent fashion. Processing characteristics such as this, once defined and recognized, have implications for the design of aids and interventions to enhance coherence in expert and novice judgment.

Putting It All Together: Achieving Coherence and Correspondence in High-Tech Environments

Technology should be able to help us achieve both coherence and correspondence in enhancing human judgment performance. Today, certainly, highly sophisticated decision aids ought to enable us to make judgments that are "good" from the standpoint of any theoretical perspective. Computers and high-tech aids can perform complex calculations, combine probabilistic information accurately and consistently, and accomplish complex data retrieval and analysis. One possibility suggested by Degani et al. (chapter 13) would be to gear system design toward reducing the need for "coherence-seeking, analytical cognition," and essentially assign "the task of ensuring the coherence of overall system operation to the designer." Although this sounds promising—*if* it is achievable—it has the drawback of removing operators a step further from system functioning, making it less likely that they will know and understand system logic or limitations and rendering them less able to restore coherence if it is disrupted.

Another possible solution to improve coherence in the human–automation system would be to provide support for the cognition it requires. Through appropriate design in the presentation of information and cues, technological aids should also be able to assist individuals in achieving coherence by prompting them to look at relevant cues and information before making a judgment, helping them determine whether all information is consistent with a particular diagnosis or judgment, and providing assistance in accounting for missing or contradictory information. Again, perhaps one of the most important tasks that technological aids can perform is the enhancement of individual meta-cognition—that is, helping people be aware of how they are thinking and making judgments and whether their process is appropriate, coherent, and accurate.

In our aviation research, for example, we have found that the perception of *accountability* for one's decision-making processes fosters more vigilant information seeking and processing, as well as more accurate judgments. Students who were made accountable for either overall performance or accuracy (which demanded checking several sources of information) displayed more vigilant information seeking compared with nonaccountable students (Skitka et al., 2000). Pilots who reported a higher internalized sense of accountability for their interactions with automation, regardless of assigned experimental condition, verified correct automation functioning more often and committed fewer errors than other pilots (Mosier et al., 1998). These results suggest that aiding the meta-cognitive monitoring of judgment processes may facilitate more thorough information search, more analytical cognition, and more coherent judgment strategies.

Meta-cognitive interventions, however, are important but not sufficient aids for judgment processes. To aid both coherence and correspondence in high-technology environments, we will need to know what variables are associated with the elicitation of each of these cognitive goals, what is at the root of noncoherence, and what is required to facilitate the achievement of both coherence and correspondence. An ideal strategy would seem to be one in which individuals alternate between coherence and correspondence, eventually making judgments that are both coherent and as accurate as possible. According to Hammond, for example, "Meteorologists can (and do) alternate between [weather] presentations, first calling for pattern (coherence) information, and then calling for indicator (correspondence) information or, when both types of information are offered on the same display, alternating between them" (1996, pp. 199–200). We also have evidence that pilot strategies will also shift depending on whether conditions permit the use of out-of-the-cockpit cues (Jacobson & Mosier, 2004).

The most effective way to present information so that both coherence and correspondence will be elicited, however, is unknown at this time. In fact, according to Hammond, "it has never been considered" (1996, p, 200). This may explain in part why technological systems and aids have been designed with only half the judgment process in mind. What has happened in technological ecologies is that correspondence has been greatly bolstered while the ability to achieve, maintain, and repair coherence has been eroded. Technology has created a shift in cognitive demands, and these demands cannot be met by strategies that have worked in the past. Designers in this era need to recognize this and to meet the challenge of not only providing the data required for correspondent, accurate judgment but also of presenting these data in a way that elicits and facilitates analytical coherence in judgment processes.

References

Bayes, T. (1958). Essay towards solving a problem in the doctrine of chances. *Biometrika, 45,* 293–315. (Reprinted from *Philosophical Transactions of the Royal Society, 1763, 53,* 370–418.)

Billings, C. E. (1996). *Human-centered aviation automation: Principles and guidelines.* NASA Technical Memorandum #110381. Moffett Field, Calif.: NASA Ames Research Center.

Brunswik, E. (1943). Organismic achievement and environmental probability. *Psychological Review, 50,* 255–272.

Brunswik, E. (1956). *Perception and the representative design of psychological experiments.* Berkeley: University of California Press.

Chi, M. T. H., Glaser, R., & Farr, M. J. (1988). *The nature of expertise.* New Jersey: Lawrence Erlbaum.

Cooksey, R. W. (1996). *Judgment analysis: Theory, methods, and applications.* San Diego, Calif.: Academic Press.

Dreyfus, H. L. (1997). Intuitive, deliberative, and calculative models of expert performance. In C. E. Zsambok & G. Klein (Eds.), *Naturalistic decision making* (pp. 17–28). New Jersey: Lawrence Erlbaum.

Eddy, D. M. (1982). Probabilistic reasoning in clinical medicine: Problems and opportunities. In D. Kahneman, P. Slovic, & A Tversky (Eds.), *Judgment under uncertainty: Heuristics and biases.* New York: Cambridge University Press.

Einhorn, H. J. (1974). Expert judgment: Some necessary conditions and an example. *Journal of Applied Psychology, 59*(5), 562–571.

Fischer, U., Davidson, J., & Orasanu, J. (2003). What makes flight situations risky? Examining commercial and general aviation pilots concepts of risk. *Proceedings of the 12th International*

Symposium on Aviation Psychology, April 14–17, Dayton, Ohio.

Forlani, D. (2002). Risk and rationality: The influence of decision domain and perceived outcome control on manages' high-risk decisions. *Journal of Behavioral Decision Making, 15*, 125–140.

Gigerenzer, G., & Goldstein, D. (1996). Reasoning the fast and frugal way: Models of bounded rationality. *Psychological Review, 103*, 650–699.

Gigerenzer, G., Todd, P. M., & the ABC Research Group (1999). *Simple heuristics that make us smart*. New York: Oxford University Press.

Green, D. M., & Swets, J. A. (1974). *Signal detection theory and psychophysics*. Huntington, N.Y.: Krieger.

Hammond, K. R. (Ed.). (1966). *The psychology of Egon Brunswik*. New York: Holt, Rinehart, & Winston.

Hammond, K. R. (1996). *Human judgment and social policy*. New York: Oxford University Press.

Hammond, K. R. (2000). *Judgments under stress*. New York: Oxford University Press.

Hammond, K. R., & Stewart, T. R. (Eds.). (2001). *The essential Brunswik: Beginnings, explications, applications*. New York. Oxford University Press.

Jacobson, C., & Mosier, K. L. (2004). Coherence and correspondence decision making in aviation: A study of pilot incident reports. *International Journal of Applied Aviation Studies. 4*(2), 123–134.

Kahneman, D., Slovic, P., & Tversky, A. (Eds.). (1982). *Judgment under uncertainty: Heuristics and biases*. Cambridge: Cambridge University Press.

Klein, G. A. (1993). A recognition primed decision (RPD) model of rapid decision making. In G. A. Klein, J. Orasanu, R. Calderwood, & C. E. Zsambok (Eds.), *Decision making in action: Models and methods* (pp. 138–147). Norwood, N.J.: Ablex.

Kuipers, B., Moskowitz, A. J., & Kassirer, J. P. (1988). Critical decisions under uncertainty: Representation and structure. *Cognitive Science, 12*, 177–210.

Langewiesche, W. (2003). *Columbia*'s last flight. *Atlantic Monthly, November*, 58–87.

Lion, R., & Meertens, R. (2001). Seeking information about a risky medicine: Effect of risk-taking tendency and accountability. *Journal of Applied Social Psychology, 31*(4), 778–795.

Lopes, L. L., & Odin, G. C. (1991). The rationality of intelligence. In E. Eells & T. Maruszewski (Eds.), *Probability and rationality: Studies on L. Jonathan Cohen's philosophy of science*. Amsterdam: Rodopi.

Mann, L., & Ball, C. (1994). The relationship between search strategy and risky choice. *Australian Journal of Psychology, 46*(3), 131–136.

Ministre de l'Equipement, des Transports et du Tourisme. (1993). *Rapport de la Commission d'Enquete sur l'Accident survenu le 20 Janvier 1992 pres du Mont Saite Odile a l/Airbus A320 Immatricule F-GGED Exploite par lay Compagnie Air Inter*. Paris: Ministre de l'Equipement, des Transports et du Tourisme.

Mosier, K. L. (2002). Automation and cognition: Maintaining coherence in the electronic cockpit. In E. Salas (Ed.), *Advances in human performance and cognitive engineering research, Volume 2* (pp. 93–121). Amsterdam: Elsevier Science.

Mosier, K., Lyall, E., Sethi, N., Wilson, J., McCauley, S., Harron, G., Khoo, L., Harron, G., Richards, J., Hecht, S., & Orasanu, J. (2003). Factors impacting coherence in the automated cockpit. *Proceedings of the 47th Annual Meeting of the Human Factors and Ergonomics Society*, October, Denver, Colo.

Mosier, K. L., & Skitka, L. J. (1996). Human decision makers and automated aids: Made for each other? In R. Parasuraman & M. Mouloua (Eds.), *Automation and human performance: Theory and applications* (pp. 201–220). New Jersey: Lawrence Erlbaum.

Mosier, K. L., Skitka, L. J., Dunbar, M., & McDonnell, L. (2001). Air crews and automation bias: The advantages of teamwork? *International Journal of Aviation Psychology, 11*, 1–14.

Mosier, K. L., Skitka, L. J., Heers, S., & Burdick, M. D. (1998). Automation bias: Decision making and performance in high-tech cockpits. *International Journal of Aviation Psychology, 8*, 47–63.

Murphy, G. L., & Wright, J. C. (1984). Changes in conceptual structure with expertise: Differences between real-world experts and novices. *Journal of Experimental Psychology: Learning, Memory, and Cognition, 10*, 144–155.

Rothstein, H. G. (1986). The effects of time pressure on judgment in multiple cue probability learning. *Organizational Behavior and Human Decision Processes, 37*, 83–92.

Sarter, N. B., Woods, D. D., & Billings, C. (1997). Automation surprises. In G. Savendy (Ed.), *Handbook of human factors/ergonomics* (2nd ed., pp. 1926–1943). New York: Wiley.

Simon, H. A. (1983). Alternative visions of rationality. In *Reason in human affairs*. Stanford, Calif.: Stanford University Press. (Reprinted in H. R. Arkes & K. R. Hammond [Eds.] [1986], *Judgment and decision making: An interdisciplinary reader*. Cambridge: Cambridge University Press.)

Sitkin, S., & Weingart, L. (1995). Determinants of risky decision-making behavior: A test of the mediating role of risk perceptions and propensity. *Academy of Management Journal, 38*(6), 1573–1592.

Skitka, L. J., Mosier, K. L., & Burdick, M. (1999). Does automation bias decision making? *Interna-*

tional Journal of Human-Computer Studies 50, 991–1006.

Skitka, L. J., Mosier, K. L., Burdick, M., & Rosenblatt, B. (2000). Automation bias and errors: Are crews better than individuals? *International Journal of Aviation Psychology, 10*(1), 83–95.

Sunstein, C. R., Kahneman, D., Schkade, D., & Ritov, I. (2001). Predictably incoherent judgments. John M. Olin Law & Economics Working Paper No. 131 (2nd series). University of Chicago Law School.

Swets, J. A. (1973). The relative operating characteristic in psychology. *Science, 182*, 990–1000.

Tversky, A., & Kahneman, D. (1971). Belief in the law of small numbers. *Psychological Bulletin, 76*, 105–110.

Tversky, A., & Kahneman, D. (1973). Availability: A heuristic for judging frequency and probability. *Cognitive Psychology, 5*, 207–232.

Tversky, A., & Kahneman, D. (1983). Existential vs. intuitive reasoning: The conjunction fallacy in probability judgment. *Psychological Review, 90*, 293–315.

Vicente, K. J. (1990). Coherence- and correspondence-driven work domains: Implications for systems design. *Behavior and Information Technology, 9*(6), 493–502.

Woods, D. D. (1996). Decomposing automation: Apparent simplicity, real complexity. In R. Parasuraman, & M. Mouloua (Eds.), *Automation and human performance: Theory and applications*. New Jersey: Lawrence Erlbaum Associates. (pp. 3–18)

Woods, D. D., & Sarter, N. B. (2000). Learning from automation surprises and "going sour" accidents. In N. B. Sarter & R. Amalberti (Eds.), *Cognitive engineering in the aviation domain* (pp. 327–353). Mahwah, N.J.: Lawrence Erlbaum.

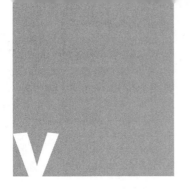

Into the Field:
Vicarious Functioning
in Action

Alex Kirlik

Introduction

To this point in the book, each empirical study has been either an instance of the use of Brunswik's methodology of representative design (see chapter 2) or else an instance of the use of hybrid, representative/systematic design. In the former case, tasks and simulations are constructed to preserve the psychologically relevant aspects of the target context or contexts to which findings, models, and interventions are intended to generalize. In the latter case, representative design is augmented by various experimental manipulations, such as time pressure, display design, aiding, and training to test a variety of hypotheses about adaptive behavior and cognition in these settings.

The three chapters in this section take matters a step further by moving out of the laboratory into actual technological work settings. Also in the spirit of representative design, the research presented in these pages did not stop there, instead illustrating the importance of abstracting the essential characteristics of observed behavior and the task environment into formal models and measures. In chapter 13, Degani and colleagues present the results of a study in which data on flight crew automation use was collected while aboard Boeing glass cockpit (757/767) aircraft during 60 actual revenue-generating flights. Canonical correlation

(also see chapter 6) was used to analyze data to discover a variety of informative relations linking patterns of environmental variables and patterns of automation use. Additionally, Degani et al. embark on a more encompassing theoretical inquiry using Brunswik's concept of vicarious functioning (see chapter 2) to understand what features of technological ecologies both promote and inhibit the development of robust and flexible goal-directed behavior. Their theoretical framework is illustrated using a variety of concrete examples, including pedestrian signal lights and automobile warning systems in addition to aviation.

In chapter 14, Casner also presents the results of an airline cockpit "jumpseat" observational study. He observed crew behavior and monitored crew–ATC communications during 16 revenue-generating commercial airline flights between San Francisco and Los Angeles, with a particular interest in how the temporal and probabilistic structure of clearances (instructions to flight crews provided by ATC) were reflected in pilots' strategies for using the cockpit flight control resources available to them. Casner used a variety of techniques to measure adaptive fit, resulting in a numerous interesting and practically relevant findings. For example, he found that pilots' use of the highest level of automation (the Flight

Management Computer, or FMC) was associated with the highest level of clearance predictability and that pilots use lower forms of automation as clearance predictability decreases. Although this finding suggests an adaptive use of flight control resources on the part of pilots, it also means that the current design of cockpit automation leaves pilots less supported in more uncertain (and therefore more challenging) situations than it does in more predictable ones.

In chapter 15, Kirlik presents a field study in a relatively low-technology work context and a model of observed behavior using a quantitative realization of the original, perception-action version of the lens model presented in 1935 by Tolman and Brunswik (see chapter 2). He notes that it may be possible to learn useful lessons for designing me-diating interface technology by improving our understanding of the factors leading to high levels of adaptive fit and fluent achievement in relatively unmediated interaction. In particular, Kirlik's observations and formal modeling highlight the intimate, dynamic interplay between perception, action, and the external world. With these results in hand, he discusses their implications for both interface design and cognitive modeling. In particular, he concludes that there is "little hope for specifying the demands made upon internal cognition during interactive behavior without a detailed, functional analysis of a performer's action repertoire. In particular, this analysis must consider how that repertoire is deployed, using whatever tools or technologies are at hand to shape the world in addition to passively adapting to it."

13

Asaf Degani, Michael Shafto, and Alex Kirlik

What Makes Vicarious Functioning Work? Exploring the Geometry of Human–Technology Interaction

The essence of modeling lies in establishing relations between *pairs* of system descriptions.
—Zeigler, Praehofer, & Kim, 2000, p. 295.

Introduction

In this chapter we provide a Brunswikian perspective on human interaction with everyday technologies, such as traffic lights, automotive devices (e.g., warning systems), and also advanced technologies, such as flight control systems in modern airliners. We apply this perspective toward suggesting a framework for evaluating interface designs and for ultimately improving the usability, robustness, and effectiveness of a range of interactive technologies.

Today's automated systems, such as modern commercial, "glass cockpit" aircraft, afford the user various levels, or modes, of interaction, ranging from fully manual to fully automatic. These modes provide the pilot with various control strategies to achieve a given goal. In all automated control systems, including those found in cars, ships, and aircraft, the control modes are discrete, whereas the behavior of the controlled system (e.g., the aircraft) is continuous. In commercial aviation, the pilots' task of coping with the mapping between discrete mode changes and dynamic, continuous changes such as altitude, heading, and speed is challenging. Incident and accident data show a strong relationship between environmental demands (e.g., air traffic control clearances), mode-selection strategies,

interface design, and operational problems (Degani, 2004).

We believe that a deeper understanding of the nature and implications of the relationships between the demands of the operational environment (e.g., air traffic control), the physical space in which performance occurs (e.g., the airspace), the technology that's employed (the automation and its interfaces), and finally human cognition are important for enhancing human interaction with the semi-automated systems of today and hopefully the autonomous systems (e.g., planetary rovers) of the future.

Vicarious Functioning, a.k.a. "Purposive Behavior"

"There is a variety of 'means' to each end, and this variety is changing, both variety and change being forms of vicarious functioning" (Brunswik, 1952, p. 18). In today's cognitive parlance, vicarious functioning might be glossed as flexible, goal-oriented behavior. Wolf (1999) elaborates on the central role of this type of adaptive behavior in Brunswik's work. Brunswik emphasized the adaptive relations between an organism and its environment. His analysis of the environment revealed it to be stochastic, dynamic, and nonrepeating, at once ambiguous and partially redundant. In response, adaptive behavior requires what Wolf calls a "virtuosity of replacement," or an ability to select from a wide repertoire of adaptations in response to the dynamic structure of the environment at each point in time.

As a synonym for *vicarious functioning*, Brunswik himself (1952, p. 16) used the more transparent phrase *purposive behavior*. He noted that without a goal or purpose, behavior itself is hard to define: He agreed with E. G. Boring that nothing would make a robot seem more human than "an ability to choose one means after another until the goal is reached" (Brunswik, 1952, p. 17). Wolf (1999) notes the similarity of Brunswik's concept of vicarious functioning to a currently popular approach in artificial intelligence (AI), i.e., "reactive" (incremental, least-commitment) planning:

> According to Brunswik, it is typical for humans to make use of alternatives, to commit only provisionally order to keep possibilities for revision open [cf. Connolly, 1999]. For human perception—or more generally cognition—as well as for human action, it is necessary to cope with inconsistent, unexpected, incomplete, and imperfect events.

This emphasis on incremental opportunism and robustness has connections with other distinctive characteristics of Brunswik's psychology: the entire program of probabilistic functionalism, the lens model, and the requirement to conduct research in representative environments (Brunswik, 1956). If dynamic and stochastic ecological processes are abstracted away, leaving only the bite board and the response key, then neither perception nor the control of action can exhibit their evolved relations. As Allen Newell memorably put it, "If you study simple systems, you will learn a lot about simple systems."

A Field Study of Human–Automation Interaction in Commercial Aviation

Degani (1996) made cockpit observations of pilots' interactions with the automatic flight control system of the Boeing 757/767 aircraft during 60 flights (cf. Casner 1994; chapter 14). During the flights, every observable change in the aircraft's control modes, either manually initiated (e.g., the pilot se-

lected a new mode) or automatically initiated (e.g., an automatic mode transition), was recorded, along with all the parameters relating to the flight control system status (e.g., waypoints and altitude values selected by the pilot). Likewise, every observable change in the operating environment (e.g., a new air traffic control [ATC] instruction, switching from one ATC facility to another) was recorded, along with other variables such as the aircraft's altitude, speed, and distance from the airport. In a way, it was like taking a snapshot of every change that took place in the cockpit. Overall, the data set consisted of 1,665 such snapshots. Each snapshot consisted of 18 categories describing the status of the automatic flight control system and 15 categories describing the operational environment. Data analysis and presentation are discussed next.

Analysis, Visualization, and Interpretation

Jha and Bisantz (2001; also see chapter 6) noted that the multivariate lens model can be extended to the analysis of categorical judgments. Methods for the analysis of multivariate categorical data were integrated and generalized during the 1980s and 1990s, by relating multivariate analysis to graphical algorithms (De Leeuw & Michailidis, 2000). This line of work unifies principal component analysis, canonical correlation analysis, and other types of multivariate analysis and extends their coverage to include categorical data.

To interpret the results of the field data described here, we used one version of this type of approach, canonical correlation analysis, to examine the relations between patterns of environmental variables and patterns of mode selections (see Degani, 1996; Shafto, Degani, & Kirlik, 1997, for details). We considered the environmental patterns to be the independent variables (X) and the automation mode selection patterns to be the dependent variables (Y). Conceptually speaking, this analysis correlates two multivariate patterns in the same way bivariate correlation measures the relationship between two single (X, Y) variables.

Due to the high dimensionality of our data set, we explored several graphical methods to help us understand and communicate the relationships between the two multidimensional patterns found by the canonical correlation. One of the most helpful suggestions we found was due to Cliff (1987) advocating presentation of structure correlations rather than weights. Structure correlations are the correlations of the *X* canonical variate with each of the original independent variables and of the *Y* canonical variate with each of the original dependent variables. In this way, the canonical variates can be interpreted in terms of observed variables.

To display the independent *X* (environmental) and dependent *Y* (technology use) patterns, we developed a visual display we termed a "heliograph." In this, sunburst-like display (see Figure 13.1), the

relative sizes of the structured correlations are indicated by the lengths of the bars extending outward (positive correlations) or inward (negative correlations), both indicating relations between features of the ecology and features of technology use.

Figure 13.1 shows two strong patterns between the demands of the operational environment (*X*), and mode selections (*Y*): The first pattern (positive correlations), shows that when aircraft altitude is above average (of 13,000 feet), during the "descent" (phase of flight), and while under "approach" (ATC

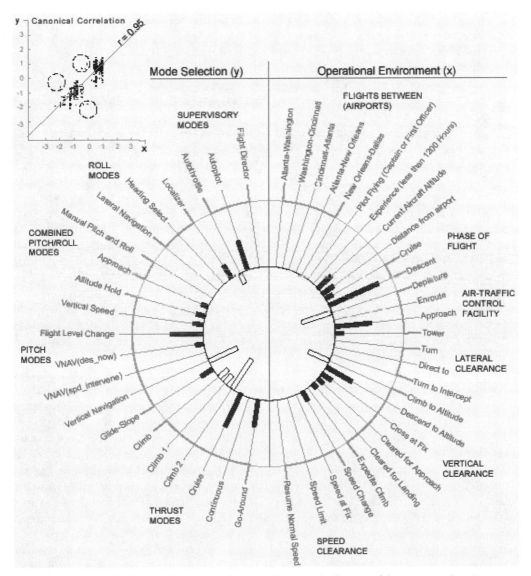

Figure 13.1. Heliograph showing the patterns (*r* = 0.95) between the features of the operational environment (*x*) and pilots' mode selections (*y*).

facility), and in response to a "descend to altitude" clearance—flight crews usually engage "Flight Level Change" (pitch) mode, cruise (thrust) mode, and engage the autopilot. The behaviors can all be classified as engaging "supervisory" modes of automation, in that automation has direct control over the aircraft, while the flight crew mainly supervises, monitors, and intervenes only when necessary (see Sheridan, 1997, on supervisory control).

The second pattern (negative correlations) shows that while under "departure" (ATC facility) control and in response to a "climb to altitude" clearance, flightcrews usually engage "Vertical Navigation" (pitch) mode, climb (thrust) mode, and the autothrottles. In addition to the engaged modes, it is also important to note in Figure 13.1 what is *not* engaged. In the first pattern (positive correlations), note that the "autothrottles" did not appear, meaning that many pilots do not engage the autothrottles during the descend/approach phase (rather, they manually move the throttles). As for the second pattern (negative correlations), note that the autopilot is not always used during departure and initial climbout and that many pilots prefer to hand-fly the aircraft during this phase of flight. Finally, the plot in the upper left corner of the graph is a conventional scatter diagram showing the relationship between the two composite variables (X and Y), plotted here in standard units, suggesting a strong overall relationship ($r = 0.95$) between the patterns displayed.

It is possible to use canonical correlation to identify additional patterns in data sets such as these, and readers can refer to Degani (1996) for three other heliographs based on the same data set demonstrating additional environmental-automation usage patterns with correlations of $r = 0.88$, $r = 0.81$, and $r = 0.72$. Overall, the canonical correlation analysis produced eight meaningful, consistent, and statistically independent patterns that were later corroborated by expert pilots. Two of the empirically derived patterns actually turned out to mirror standard operating procedures for the particular airline from which data was collected.

In addition to displaying any patterns existing in the data, canonical correlation can be used to help the analyst define, in a data-driven way, the most important environmental conditions and their corresponding patterns of judgment and action selection on the user's side (in this case, mode selection). Equally as important are deviations from any central tendencies in these patterns. Such de-

viations (outliers) from a standard pattern of human–automation interaction derived from data across many users can mean two things: either an unusual (yet safe) mode selection or a dangerous (and potentially unsafe) mode selection.

For example, one flight in our data set was an obvious outlier, falling seven standard deviations from the mean on one of the spatial dimensions. Inspection of the data revealed that the autothrottles were not used throughout the flight. The reason for this was that the aircraft had been dispatched with inoperative autothrottles. This situation was definitely unusual, but not unsafe, because the crew knew of the inoperative autothrottles well before the flight and planned accordingly.

As for unsafe outliers, two flights were observed falling three standard deviations from the mean. These flight crews used the "Flight Level Change" mode while making a final approach for landing during what is called a "back-course localizer" approach to a runway, without the typically present glideslope instrument system. This is a quite rare occurrence because most runways used by large aircraft do indeed have glideslope instrumentation. This mode selection in this particular situation is potentially dangerous during final approach. Indeed, its use at very low altitudes has contributed to several incidents and two accidents (Court of Inquiry, 1992; Ministry of Planning, Housing, Transport and Maritime Affairs, 1989). Usually, flight crews use the "Flight Level Change" mode during descent, and then switch to "Glide Slope" mode on final approach. But on these two occasions during the field study, because there was no glideslope instrument (and therefore no *continually available* indication to prompt crews to switch control modes), flight crews kept on descending using the "Flight Level Change" mode, which, as mentioned earlier, is not safe for making a final approach.

We believe that these examples of unsafe mode usage represent instances of a broader class of human–technology interaction problems associated with discretely mediated interaction with and control over variables that are highly dynamic. Presenting a system operator, such as a pilot, with an abstracted, discrete suite of action opportunities and an abstracted, solely discrete display of automation operation (e.g., mode settings) can lead to situations in which the controlled system drifts away into unsafe states where the fixed mode setting is no longer appropriate. This discrete approach to automation and interface design, we believe, short-circuits some of the naturally evolved psychological mechanisms supporting vicarious functioning in an ecology that is (or at least once was) inherently continuous. The result, we suggest, is undermining some of the basic mechanisms of adaptive behavior itself. We now turn to examining and elaborating this diagnosis and hypothesis in more detail.

What Kinds of Environments Support Vicarious Functioning?

Understanding and especially predicting human adaptation to dynamic environments is by no means simple nor straightforward (Bullock & Todd, 1999; Kirlik, in press). How, then, should we design digital and automated control systems to meet the computational requirements posed by various tasks in these environments (e.g., aircraft navigation) on the one hand, and also leverage, if not short-circuit, our evolutionarily acquired resources for flexible, goal-directed behavior on the other hand? One approach that we believe is promising is to distinguish between the physical space in which behavior occurs, the psychological space in which adaptive mechanisms operate, and the technological spaces that increasingly characterize today's ecology. Mapping out these spaces as well as the relations among them is what we allude to in our title as characterizing and analyzing the geometry of human–technology interaction.

Physical Space

Natural, physical space provides the strongest set of constraints on design, because we are well equipped to adapt to constraints imposed by inherently continuous physical space. Rarely do we try to walk through walls. Any discussion of physical space at the scale of the human ecology starts with the four-dimensional trajectories to which we are comfortably adapted. As long as four-dimensional Euclidean space is the only option, we can rely on the typically fluent and highly adaptive perception and action mechanisms that are keyed to getting around in this space; these are evolution's legacy.

Technological Space

In contrast, when we consider the computer-based artifacts increasingly present in our ecology, design options mainly span or sample discrete spaces (e.g., see chapter 17). The reason for this lies in the logic governing the behavior of any computer system rooted in the discrete, finite-state machine (FSM) formalism, the von Neumann architecture, and the Turing-inspired algorithmic approach to software specification. Additionally, in some automated control systems, we encounter hybrid spaces that harbor both discrete logic (modes) and continuous parameters (such as speed and flight path angle) that are based on laws of physics. We also encounter hybrid spaces in computer networks, in which continuous variables like task priority and processing time must also be considered to achieve robust communication and coordination (Lowe, 1992; Roscoe, 1998; Schneider, 2000). The geometry of the computational ecology is complex indeed. As we will suggest in the following, this complexity becomes mirrored in the cognitive activities necessary to adapt to and navigate through these discrete and hybrid ecologies.

Psychological Space

We now turn our attention to more distinctly psychological issues, relying on slightly more metaphorical notions of space and geometry. A large and growing literature supports the conclusion that psychological space also has both continuous and discrete dimensions. Continuous psychological processes and representations mirror the structure of physical space, in that they are have few dimensions, are strongly continuous, and are strongly metric. In contrast, symbolic processes based in language and logic, which serve as the basis for analytical cognition, are largely discrete, are weakly metric or nonmetric, and are typically discontinuous.

Kahneman (2003; see also Hammond, 1996; Hastie & Dawes, 2001, p. 4; Sun, 2000) contrasts between his notions of System 1 (our "continuous") and System 2 (our "discrete") psychological activities:

> The operations of System 1 are typically fast, automatic, effortless, associative, implicit (not available to introspection), and are often emotionally charged; they are also governed by habit and are therefore difficult to control or modify. The operations of System 2 are slower, serial, effortful, more likely to be consciously monitored and deliberately controlled; they are also relatively flexible and potentially tend to

disrupt each other, whereas effortless processes neither cause nor suffer much interference when combined with other tasks. (Kahnemann, 2003, p. 699)

In their analysis of dual-process theory (e.g., Kahneman's Systems 1 and 2), Norenzayan and colleagues (2002) suggest that intuitive cognition (our continuous, Kahneman's System 1) tends to dominate over formal cognition (our discrete, Kahneman's System 2), although both systems are typically active simultaneously:

> In recent years, a growing number of research programs in psychology have examined these two cognitive systems under the rubric of "dual process" theories of thinking. . . . These two cognitive systems coexist in individuals, interact with each other in interesting ways, and occasionally may be in conflict and produce contradictory inferences . . . intuitive reasoning [continuity] tends to dominate, but the relative dominance can be modulated by a variety of factors. (Norenzayan et al., 2002, pp. 654–655)

Current wisdom suggests that people can operate in either of these two contrasting modes of cognition. A pioneer in theory along these lines, Hammond (1996), motivated by Brunswik's (1956) initial observations on the distinctions between perceiving and thinking, has developed an even more sophisticated theory in which people can operate and even oscillate between various points along a "cognitive continuum" with both analytical and intuitive poles. Researchers such as Gigerenzer and Goldstein (1996), Kirlik (1995), Klein (1999), Norenzayan et al. (2002), Reason (1990), and Rouse (1983), among others, have all suggested that people tend to rely on intuitive as opposed to analytical cognition when possible, although this preference can be mitigated by a variety of factors (e.g., the demand for accountability or to justify one's actions, necessitating accessibility to the processes of thought, and thus more analytical cognition).

In short, we conceive of skilled, fluent, and robust adaptive behavior as relying heavily on relatively resource-unlimited, intuitive cognition, which is most naturally supported (as we will suggest in more detail in the following) by continuous ecologies. More resource-intensive analytical cognition, in contrast, functions mainly to monitor the on-going success of intuitive behavior and to intervene when necessary or demanded, given that time and cognitive resources are available to do so (Kahneman, 2003). We next discuss the crucial role played by continuity in supporting the intuitive, adaptive mode behavior Brunswik described as vicarious functioning.

Ecological Continuity: A Key Resource for Vicarious Functioning

The most obvious source of the dominance or preference for cognition that is based on continuous spaces and intuitive (or System 1) activities is their evolutionary priority. These activities are responsible for coordinating perception and action in the physical world, and as such, perception is adapted to the regularities of the physical environment (Barlow, 2001; see also Hubbard, 1999; Shepard, 1999). Experiments by Shepard and others have shown, for example, that the perceived trajectories of objects seen only in successive snapshots obey the kinematics of actual objects moving through physical space, as though physical laws had been internalized. Based on a sustained program of research in this tradition, Shepard (1999) concluded that "objects support optimal generalization and categorization when represented in an evolutionarily shaped space of possible objects as connected regions with associated weights determined by Bayesian revision of maximum-entropy priors [probabilities]."

The "connected regions" to which Shepard alludes echo our own emphasis on the importance of continuity to cognition and adaptive behavior generally. Shepard's mention of Bayesian revision of probabilities points to Brunswik's and our own observation that many environments often possess irreducible uncertainty. As such, the human is required to adapt to the world in a statistical, rather than a deterministic sense. James J. Gibson titled his 1957 *Contemporary Psychology* review of Brunswik's probabilistic functionalism "Survival in a World of Probable Objects" (Gibson 1957/2001; Cooksey, 2001; Kirlik, 2001). This title suggests that Gibson's gloss of Brunswik's approach to describing the demands of adapting to an uncertain world was very much in the spirit of Shepard's work, presented some 40 years later.

In the spirit of Shepard's research, Barlow (2001) has noted, for example, that there is widespread agreement that the perceived "trajectory of an object is a joint function of perceptually sampled data and of the bias that is intrinsic to psychological space." Perception can thus be regarded as a process at the intersection of internalized, environmental regularities (via evolution, development, and experience) and the information available from the external, currently present environment. Barlow pointed out that it was Brunswik who first suggested that

> The laws governing grouping and segregation of figure from ground were more than empirical facts about perception: they were rules for using statistical facts about images to draw valid inferences from the scene immediately before the eyes. [Brunswik] pointed out that two perceptual samples having similar local characteristics are likely to be derived from the same object in the external world. Therefore, it is adaptive to have a built-in heuristic bias that they are from the same object. (p. 603)

Barlow (2001) also reviewed recent neurophysiological results that further confirm that the natural ecology's reflection: a four-dimensional, strongly continuous, metric space is "wired into" the central nervous system at a fundamental level. This body of research lends support to the lens model's basis in principles of environmental-psychological symmetry.

Additionally, Barlow has noted the existence of "neurophysiological mechanisms that exploit the redundancy of sensory messages resulting from statistical regularities of the environment," lending additional support to Brunswik's view that vicarious functioning, exploiting these ecological redundancies, may very well play the role of the "backbone of stabilized achievement" (Brunswik, 1956, p. 142).

The question remains, however, as to why a preference for low-dimensional, continuous representations should extend beyond basic perception and action and also into the cognitive realm, "beyond the information given" (Bruner, 1973). The answer, we believe, lies in the advantages of continuous representations for supporting learning and efficient information processing, advantages to which Shepard (1999) alluded.

As demonstrated by the groundbreaking research of Landauer et al. (1997), discrete, symbolic representations such as natural language are not necessarily separable from Kahneman's System 1 or Hammond's intuititon. Rather, as Landauer and colleagues' work demonstrates, a ubiquitous learning process exists to convert the discrete to the continuous. This adaptive process automatically converts symbolic perceptual information, such as text, into continuous, spatial cognitive representations; tends to produce and strengthen constraints on inference; and tends to reduce the dimensionality of the discrete input space. By "strengthening constraints," we refer to a process of mapping discrete or categorical representations to continuous metric spaces and mapping weakly continuous spaces into strongly continuous ones.

To take a more concrete example, Landauer et al. (1997) have shown that a linear neural network, operating on a corpus of sequenced discrete tokens (words, for example), will induce a multidimensional continuous space summarizing the tokens and their associated contexts. The space is bootstrapped from the underlying continuity of time, which enforces the basic sequential ordering of the tokens. On the basis of the induced continuous space, a range of abstract, *symbolic* tasks can be performed at levels of achievement equal to or better than expert human performance. Examples include matching documents of similar meaning but with no shared words, while rejecting documents with shared words but having dissimilar meaning; choosing correct answers on standardized vocabulary tests; responding to semantic priming in laboratory experiments; learning from instructional texts; interpreting novel analogies and metaphors; and, in many instances, grading student essays as well as human graders. Along similar lines, McGreevy and Statler (1998), using a different but related algorithmic technique, have demonstrated that the interpretation and comparison of discrete and symbolic verbal accounts of aviation incident reports could be enhanced by translating these verbal data into continuous spatial representations.

The Unique Benefits of Continuous Spaces

At a high level we have already discussed some of the benefits that continuous, metric spaces confer on adaptation. The availability of convergent, recursive learning processes (Landauer et al., 1997) and the compression of information made possible by continuous, metric representations can, in many cases, offset the disadvantages of applying continuous operations to problems that could be more ideally addressed by discrete, logical, and symbolic activities. On the down side, Kahneman (2003) provides a thorough discussion of these potential disadvantages (see also Hastie & Dawes, 2001; Freed & Remington, 1998). On the upside, the recursive learning and information compression enabled by continuous representations point to the most obvious (and some might say, the only) information-processing capabilities of neural networks. This property of intrinsic, environmental, or automatically derived cognitive continuity, tacitly presumed in so many studies and models of learning and adaptation, is so ubiquitous that it is easily overlooked. Yet continuity confers an enormous range of functional advantages enabling purposive behavior and adaptation in an environment that is dynamic and unpredictable.

Most important, continuity supports *approximation* and *convergence*. These properties enable statistical or neural network–based learning and generalization. In contrast, discrete spaces, characteristic of the interfaces of many everyday technologies (e.g., VCRs, cell phones), do not support efficient learning and generalization, nor do they support flexible goal-directed behavior. Why? Simply put, because one discrete state is no more or less like any other discrete state. As such, unless an interface designer provides cues (e.g., proximity, color or shape coding, hierarchical menu structuring), to *explicitly* support inference, there is typically little support for generalizing what is known about any one discrete state (display or control) to any other.

In the natural ecology at the human scale, continuity as a resource for learning and generalization is crucial to guarantee the convergence of adaptive solutions to problems of many types. For example, if we are practicing our piano skills and our teacher tells us that we played a certain note too softly in one case and too loudly on our next attempt, we can infer that if we play the note at an intermediate level of force on our third try that we are at least likely to obtain a better outcome. Contrast this case with trying to adapt to a discrete space, such as the state space of a digital wristwatch. Given that you know the result of pushing two of the three buttons on the watch, what can you learn about what is likely to happen if you push the third? Nothing.

In some cases, of course, a continuous, multidimensional space simply cannot accurately represent all the necessary distinctions required to achieve perfect adaptation, as is sometimes the case in understanding natural language. Yet as Dawes (1979) has suggested in his classic article, "The robust beauty of improper linear models," the degree of "meaning" that is lost by moving from discrete and symbolic to continuous metric spaces (e.g., those spaces supporting simple cue weighting and averaging judgment strategies) is often minimal enough that this inaccuracy is tolerable (also see Goldberg, 1968). In short, the benefits of continuity-supported generalization, convergence, and robustness often outweigh the costs of losing discrete precision.

It is important to recognize the central role of the concept of robustness in the present context, due to its intimate relationship to vicarious functioning, Brunswik's term for the "backbone of stabilized achievement." Hammond (1996), in commenting on the pioneering work of Dawes and Corrigan (1974) on this issue, has aptly characterized the central insights:

> An interesting and highly important discovery, first introduced to judgment and decision making researchers by R. M. Dawes and B. Corrigan, is that organizing principles of this type [weighting and summing cues] are extremely robust in irreducibly uncertain environments. That is, if (1) the environmental task or situation is not perfectly predictable (uncertain), (2) there are several fallible cues, and (3) the cues are redundant (even slightly), then (4) these organizing principles (it doesn't matter which one) will provide the subject with a close approximation of the correct inference about the intangible state of the environment, no matter which organizing principle may actually exist therein—that is, even if the organism organizes the information incorrectly relative to the task conditions! (p. 171)

Thus, intuitive or System 1 cognitive strategies, which are dependent on ecological continuity to support simple weighted averaging, provide reasonable levels of adaptation even if a person has little or no a priori knowledge of the structure of the environment (Hammond's "organizing principle therein"). Also, by supporting generalization and convergence, ecological continuity supports the statistical or neural network learning underlying adaptive behavior.

If we take continuity-supported, intuitive (System 1) cognition as the "backbone of stabilized achievement," what, then, is the primary functional role of the analytical pole of the intuitive-analytical continuum (Hammond, 1996; Kahneman, 2003)? Current research on dual process theory suggests that discrete, analytical processes seem to be involved in noticing potential anomalies, in monitoring the effectiveness of intuitively driven behavior, in directing attention to novel events, and in resolving conflicts when multiple and competing intuitive judgments or decisions must be arbitrated (Barnden, 2001; Kahneman, 2003). Activities such as these each touch on the demand for cognition to achieve internal coherence (Hammond, 1996; Thagard, 2000), which is typically understood to be an analytical activity involving the use of discrete logical operations, or System 2 cognition. We should note, however, that Hammond (2000) has recently proposed the intriguing idea that both coherence and correspondence can each be achieved either intuitively or analytically. For the purposes of this chapter, however, our treatment remains more faithful to previous account offered by Hammond (1996/2000, p. 63), that "the central feature of the correspondence theory of judgment is its emphasis—inherited from Darwin—on the flexibility of the organism in its adaptive efforts, its multiple strategies, its ability to rely on various intersubstitutable features—what are called multiple fallible indicators [i.e., vicarious functioning]" (p. 63). As such, although possibly simplified, we will assume that the *essence* of correspondence-based achievement lies in the intuitive mechanisms underlying vicarious functioning, whereas the *essence* of coherence-competence lies in analytically dominated, System 2 cognition.

The logical and analytical operations underlying coherence-seeking activities stand in contrast to the demand for cognition to arrive at adaptive solutions corresponding with the facts, constraints, or demands of the external world (empirical accuracy). Understanding this latter, continuity-supported, intuitively gained, adaptive correspondence between the actual and the perceived was Brunswik's primary focus. It is our own focus as well, in the sense that we believe that computer and interface technology that short-circuits these adaptive mechanisms will lead to a variety of learning and performance problems in human–automation interaction. For more on this coherence versus correspondence (analytical/intuitive) distinction, see Mosier and McCauley (chapter 12), suggesting that

increasingly technological ecologies are indeed placing increased demands on discrete, symbolic, and analytical coherence-seeking (rather than correspondence-seeking) cognition. Note also that Mosier and McCauley's findings are consistent with what our analysis would expect: People are generally poor at attaining cognitive coherence in discrete, digital ecologies, quite possibly for the reasons we have already suggested.

Implications for the Design of Human–Automation Interaction

There is ample evidence that people have trouble interacting with discrete interfaces and navigating through their many modes, menus, submenus, and sub-submenus (Degani, 2004; Norman, 1999). The frustrations that people have setting up the VCR and using the menus of cell phones are popular examples. In more complex systems, it is well documented that digital interactive systems may embody design flaws tied to their discrete mode structures (Degani, 2004). These flaws lead to confusion and at times deadly mishaps (Degani & Heymann, 2002).

To better understand these problems, in the following we leverage the distinctions we have made between continuous and discrete ecologies, along with their attendant cognitive implications, with the goal of better supporting human–automation interaction through better interface design. To this point we have emphasized that humans often gravitate toward intuitive (System 1) strategies for making judgments and decisions. Additionally, we have suggested that these strategies are generally robust and reasonably effective but are best supported when the human is interacting with a continuous (rather than a solely discrete) ecology (or interface).

We have also pointed out that humans, especially in dynamic and uncertain contexts, often have limited cognitive resources available for effectively navigating the geometry of digital ecologies in an analytical fashion. We and the findings reported by Mosier and McCauley (chapter 12) suggest that everything possible should be done in design to reduce the demands for a system user or operator to rely on coherence-seeking, analytical cognition. If this goal is achieved, then the resources demanded by analytical cognition would be freed up for the monitoring, arbitrating, and attending-to-novelty activities to which it appears suited.

Like any cognitive system, a system made up of humans coupled with technology requires both internal coherence and correspondence with the external facts of the world. As already described, we have advocated leaving the attainment of correspondence to the adaptive, intuitive competence of the human operator or user. Regarding the goal of ensuring overall human–automation system coherence, we suggest that this task should fall largely on the designer, prior to a system being put into operation. With the task of achieving coherence (e.g., ensuring the integrity of the system with respect to efficiency and safety), offloaded to the design process, the human operator or user can then rely to the greatest extent possible on the intuitive mode of cognition known to underlie fluent, robust, and adaptive behavior.

Thus, one can view our solution to the problem of ensuring the goals of both maintaining correspondence with the facts of the world, as well as overall system coherence, in terms of a simple problem decomposition. We advocate assigning the first task to the human operator, or user, who we presume to rely heavily on robust and adaptive intuitive (System 1) cognition, and who is able to benefit by real-time access to timely information. In contrast, our solution assigns the task of ensuring the coherence of overall system operation to the designer, who is shielded from the time pressure and other stressors of real-time operations, and who thus has the cognitive resources available to rely on analytical tools and analytical (System 2) cognition.

As such, we advocate the use of formal analysis and design techniques to verify that the geometry of human–technology interaction is efficient and safe. This approach to design requires highly detailed, functional analyses of technological artifacts, their interfaces, their environments of use, and the tasks they support. We will first discuss these formal techniques at a general level and then demonstrate the approach using a variety of concrete examples.

Analytically Ensuring Coherence in System Design

One formal approach to ensuring the coherence of human–automation interaction in the design phase is a hybrid modeling technique known as Communicating Sequential Processes (CSP; see Hoare, 1985;

Schneider, 2000). Techniques such as CSP ensure the overall integrity or coherence of systems comprised of multiple computational elements to, for example, guard against deadlocking, the system entering dangerous or "illegal" states, and so on. Relatedly, a variety of discrete, finite-state machine models can also be used to create formal representations of human interaction with control systems. A basic element of such a description is a labeled, directed graph that captures system states, events, conditions, and transitions. For example, while an aircraft is in CRUISE mode (current state), and button x is pressed, and the descent profile is armed (two conditions that when TRUE trigger an event), the aircraft control system will transition to DESCENT mode (a new state).

Due to the lack of continuity in discrete space, human operators or users cannot always reliably anticipate the future mode configuration of a machine unless they have a detailed internal model of the machine's behavior, including its states, conditions, and transition logic (Degani, Shafto, & Kirlik, 1999). They must rely on a priori knowledge (e.g., an internal model), because, lacking a continuous, metric representation of the technology, they cannot deploy their robust, intuitive cognition in the sense discussed by Dawes, Hammond, and Kahneman.

Human interaction with automation is currently evaluated through extensive simulation. Smith et al. (1998) note the serious problems that can occur with solely simulation-based, (empirical) evaluation of complex human–automation interaction. Because of their combinatorial nature, discrete and hybrid systems have enormous state spaces, and empirical techniques that necessarily sample only a small subset of the entire state space are clearly insufficient as a basis for design verification. As such, predictive, model-based, formal methodologies for design verification are critical for identifying deficiencies early in the design phase. To verify system safety, a safety specification is initially represented as a restricted region of the state space in which the system should remain. On the basis of this functional analysis, the goal is to synthesize automation design that guarantees that the state of the system will remain within a safe region.

Using the same modeling formalisms used to describe machine behavior (the "machine model"), it is possible to also describe the information provided to the user. This "user model" of the system, which is based on the information provided to the user (e.g., pilot) via displays, manuals, procedures, training, and personal experience, may differ from the actual machine model of the system. With these two models in place, it becomes possible to systematically and comprehensively verify that the interfaces (and all other information provided to the user) are correct. This, in principle, is done by constructing a *composite* model where the user-model states and machine-model states are combined into state pairs. Next, the verification process simulates an activation of the composite model, where the user model and the machine model evolve concurrently in a synchronized manner (Heymann & Degani, 2002).

This verification process detects three types of user interface inadequacies that are based on the criteria set by Heymann and Degani (2002). The first inadequacy—the existence of error states—occurs when the user interface indicates that the machine is in one mode, when in fact it is in another. Interfaces with error states lead to faulty interaction and errors. The second inadequacy—the existence of restricting states—occurs when the user is unaware that certain user interactions can trigger additional mode changes in the machine. Interfaces with restricting states tend to surprise and confuse users. The third inadequacy—the existence of augmenting states—occurs when the user is informed that a certain mode is available, when in fact the machine does not have that mode or access to certain modes is disabled. Interfaces with augmenting states puzzle users.

Exploring the Geometry of Human–Technology Interaction: Concrete Examples

To illustrate our perspective on designing to enhance human–technology interaction, we now turn our attention to three everyday examples.

Pedestrian Crossing Signals

The first example consists of a pedestrian crossing signal found at many intersections with traffic lights. The most familiar ones have three states (or modes): a red hand for "don't walk," a walking-person symbol for "walk," and a flashing hand to indicate that the light is about to turn red and crossing is unsafe. Newer models, which now can be found in many intersections, provide, in addition to the flashing hand a digital countdown display (in seconds) indicating when crossing will become unsafe (and the "don't walk" symbol will appear).

The old interface is discrete: don't walk, walk, hurry up. The new interface also indicates the time remaining until crossing will become unsafe (the "don't walk" symbol appears). The new design is a hybrid interface, containing both discrete states and one (close approximation to a continuous variable), the countdown time. Most people prefer the new interface because it reduces their fear that the light will turn red while they are in the middle of an intersection. When the light begins to flash and the countdown is displayed, the walker can assess the situation and decide if he or she needs to run, walk, or perhaps turn back and wait for the next light. Note that by augmenting the interface with continuous information, better supporting the walker's intuitive judgment, the entire human–technology system gains a greater level of coherence (in this case, through an increased level of assurance that safety goals are met).

Traffic Signals

Consider the next scenario: You are in your car driving toward an intersection, and you can see a green traffic light in the distance. As you approach the intersection, the light turns yellow. What should you do? Brake or proceed through? Figure 13.2 shows a region in which braking is safe; that is, given any combination of speed and distance within the dark gray region, the car will stop before the intersection. This region is determined by calculating the stopping distance for every speed from 1 to 60 miles per hour based on a car's maximum braking performance. The yellow light is 4 seconds long, and we take into account that it takes the average driver 1.5 seconds to react and press on the brakes.

As for the other option, driving through the intersection, let us assume that the driver, once he or she observes the yellow light, simply maintains the current speed. Figure 13.3 depicts the safe drive-through region (while maintaining constant speed). Now that we know the consequences of either stopping before the intersection or driving through it, we can turn to the decision itself. So how do we know, when the yellow light appears, what to do? The truth is that in most cases we don't. We don't have the analytically derived graphs of Figures 13.2

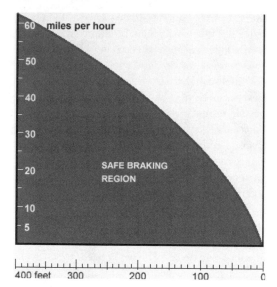

Figure 13.2. The safe braking region (*X*-axis is distance from intersection, *Y*-axis is speed).

and 13.3 available, and therefore our decision is based on our intuitive estimation of what Gibson and Crooks (1938) called "the field of safe travel." Most of the time our intuition works, but in some cases we either pass through a red light or try to brake but end up stopped in the intersection.

Now consider designing a dashboard interface to help the driver make this decision. To do so, we first need to map the physical space and the system behavior vis-à-vis the operational demands (stopping or proceeding through). We do this by considering the safe braking region and the safe proceed through region together. Figure 13.4 shows that the composition of the two graphs divides the physical space into four regions. The dark gray region is safe braking, the light gray is safe proceed through, and the black region is where these overlap (if you are in the black region, you can either brake or proceed through, and you'll still be safe and legal).

Unlike the three regions from which a safe control action can be taken, the fourth (hatched) region represents combinations of speed and distance from which you *cannot* safely brake or proceed safely. If you try to stop, even at maximum braking force, you will find yourself entering the intersection on red. If you proceed through, you will reach the white line with a red light above you. In other words, if you are in the hatched region when the light turns yellow, you *will* commit a violation, no matter what you do (and as for the tempting option of "gunning it" through, calculations show that acceleration only reduces the size of the hatched region but does not eliminate it). See Oishi, Tomlin, and Degani (2003) for the technical details of this kind of analysis.

This problematic region, which is well known to traffic engineers, is called the dilemma zone and exists in many intersections (Liu, Herman, & Gazis, 1996). From a design perspective, this implies that we need to display the brake or drive-through region, and also the dilemma zone. But if we think about it

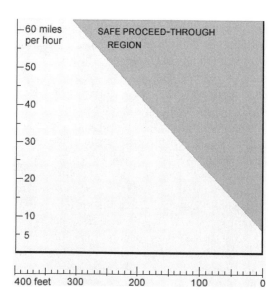

Figure 13.3. The safe proceed-through region.

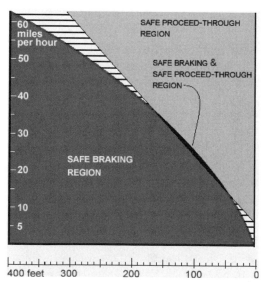

Figure 13.4. Composite of the safe breaking and safe proceed-through regions.

for a minute, just providing a discrete indication, "You are in a dilemma zone," is not enough. Why? Because it's too late! For the interface to ensure the coherent, safe operation of the entire human–technology system, it must provide a *continuous* indication of the proximity of the car to the dilemma zone, so that the driver can avoid entering it. Unlike the pedestrian light, where the countdown timer is a welcome, nice to have addition, in the yellow light case, it is an imperative. An interface that provides solely discrete indications (brake, drive through, in the dilemma zone) is unsafe!

Automatic Landing Systems

Our final example concerns one aspect of the automatic flight control system on board modern airliners designed to make a fully automatic landing. An automatic landing system, or "autoland," is commonly used in bad weather, specifically in a condition called zero-zero in pilot lingo, meaning visibility is zero and the clouds or fog reach all the way to the ground.

In these severe conditions, only the autoland system is permitted to make a landing. But there is one

option that is always available to the pilot—to discontinue the approach and abort the landing and then command the aircraft to climb out. Such aborted landings, or go-arounds, are well-practiced maneuvers, with the goal of taking the aircraft away from an unsafe situation such as an autoland component failure, electrical system failure, or any other malfunction making the approach and landing unsafe. In some cases, a go-around is requested by ATC. For example, an aircraft may come too close to another aircraft on approach, or there may be debris, a vehicle, or another aircraft on the runway on which the aircraft is to land.

We wish to consider the kind of information that must be provided to the pilot when the autoland system is making the approach and landing. In particular, our focus is on the critical, last 60 feet of the approach. Just as we did in the case of the yellow light, we first need to map out the physical space and the technological (control system) spaces. Then we need to relate them to the two control options available: either the airplane lands or attempts a go-around.

The funnel shape in Figure 13.5 depicts the region from which an autoland system can make a

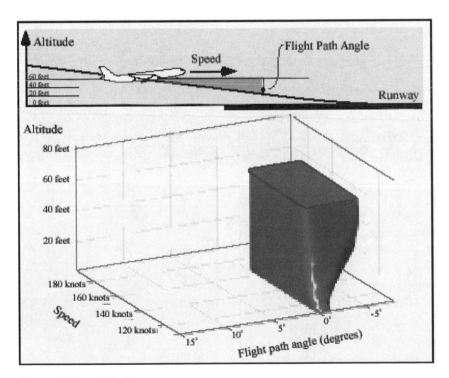

Figure 13.5. Safe landing.

safe landing. The three axes are the aircraft's altitude above the runway, speed, and flight path angle (which is the angle at which the airplane descends toward the ground—see top of Figure 13.5). In principle, the shape is computed in the same way as the (safe breaking and safe proceed through) regions in the yellow light example. We start from touchdown, where the flight path angle should be between 0° and −2° and work our way back. (If the angle is greater than 0°, the airplane will not be able to land; if the angle is less than −2°, the aircraft's tail will hit the ground). For each altitude from 0 to 60 feet we compute the speed and flight-path angle the autopilot needs to maintain, such that eventually the aircraft *will* make a safe landing.

As for the second option, the safe go-around, Figure 13.6 depicts a rather large region, because unlike the safe landing region that funnels down to the runway at a tightly constrained angle and speed, the go-around can be executed safely at a variety of flight path angles and speeds (see Oishi, Tomlin, & Degani, 2003 for the technical details of these computations).

We now combine the safe landing region and the safe go-around region (just as we did in the yellow light example). For the sake of illustration, consider what will happen when a go-around is commanded when the aircraft is 20 feet above the ground. Figure 13.7 is a slice of the safe landing region at this altitude. Figure 13.8 is a similar graph for the safe go-around region. The composite graph of Figure 13.9 shows three emerging regions: The gray region is the safe go-around region, the black region depicts where safe go-around overlaps with

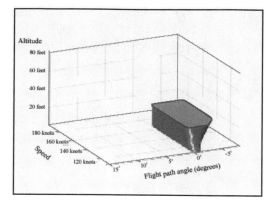

Figure 13.7. Safe landing region at 20 feet.

safe landing, and the hatched region is solely the safe landing region. Because a go-around is a situation that can occur at any time during landing (and there may be no advance warning of when the maneuver will be needed), the black region is where we *always* want to be: From here the autopilot can make a safe landing, and if a go-around is needed, it can be executed safely by the pilot.

The hatched area, however, is where we *don't* want to be. Under normal conditions, the autopilot will try to make the landing when the flight path angle is close to 0°, but under less than nominal conditions, such as gusts or a strong tailwind, the autopilot may be operating in the hatched region in which nevertheless a safe landing can be completed. Safe landing, however, is only *one* requirement. We also need to be in the safe go-around region, and herein lies the problem: If the autopilot is operating in the hatched region, the pilot will not be able to execute a safe go-around, either at

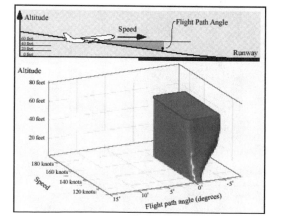

Figure 13.6. Safe go-around.

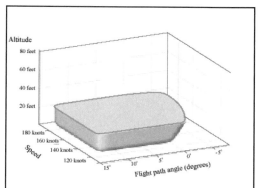

Figure 13.8. Safe go-around region at 20 feet.

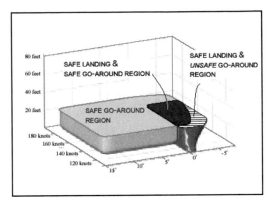

Figure 13.9. Composite graph at 20 feet.

this altitude of 20 feet or at any lower altitude. If the autopilot is operating in the hatched region and a go-around is attempted, the aircraft may stall!

Lesssons Learned

To summarize, the yellow light and autoland examples highlight several important issues in the design of automated control systems in general, and human–automation interaction in particular. One issue has to do with the complexity of the physical space and system behavior that produces the dilemma zone and the safe landing/unsafe go-around regions. Identifying these regions requires analysis, which can yield counterintuitive results (did you know that when you get a citation for a red light violation, in some cases it may be not your fault at all?). This analysis requires a perspective drawing on the discrete versus continuous ecology distinction and analytical tools for mapping out the geometry of human–technology interaction.

Another issue, centering on interface design, concerns a tendency many designers have to provide solely discrete indications. There are two problems with this. First, a driver using such a discrete alerting interface has no warning as to when the dilemma zone is being neared. The interface would just light up or alarm. If it does, it's too late, because the human–technology system is already in an unsafe region. Likewise, by providing the pilot with solely a discrete indication of the unsafe go-around region, we haven't solved the problem. In most automated control systems, the existence of unsafe regions is inevitable, so interfaces must also provide the user with *continual* guidance as to system's proximity to the unsafe region.

Finally, an important distinction should be made between the driving example and the aviation example. In the yellow light case, it is the driver who (manually) enters the unsafe region from which any action (brake or proceed through) will have dangerous consequences. In contrast, in the autoland case, it is the *automation* that takes the user into an unsafe region, from which recovery is difficult and at times impossible. This situation, arising from the complex and not yet well understood interaction between discrete modes and continuous processes is termed "automation lock." Such locks have lulled many pilots into dangerous situations, some unfortunately resulting in accidents (Federal Aviation Administration, 2004; Degani, 2004, chap. 17).

Conclusions

The title of this chapter is borrowed from Bryant (1985, p. 87), who asks, "What makes analysis work?" His answer is built around the concept of *continuity*. Continuity makes it possible to represent and reason about complex, dynamic, and nonrepeating phenomena. It makes available a range of tractable methods for interpolation, extrapolation, approximation, and the integration of fragmentary data. All are essential to vicarious functioning.

The products of the psychological processes of perception, cognition, and learning can be described in terms of cognitive representations, ranging from the continuous to the symbolic and discrete. Basic perceptual processes enforce assumptions about spatio-temporal continuity (Barlow, 2001; Shepard, 1999). And even in situations where discrete, symbolic representations are more precise, continuity is generated to support adaptive, heuristic reasoning and learning in abstract symbolic spaces (Hastie & Dawes, 2001; Kahneman, 2003; Landauer et al., 1997).

Digital control systems and their corresponding discrete (mode) interfaces disrupt continuity. In the extreme case, we are left with a step-by-step search through a space in which each move is equally capable of taking us into a familiar room or a blind alley. Furthermore, it is very difficult (and most of the time impossible) to design or learn to operate large and complex systems that are based on unrestricted, discrete spaces. Designers are overwhelmed by the large state spaces of technological systems (which may include thousands, if not millions, of possible states). Users are faced with the challenge that achieving an exact understanding of a system's behavior is impossible, yet reliable abstractions or approximations are unavailable.

Brunswik emphasized the role of pattern–pattern correlations in complex perception and action. This is the fundamental principle underlying the lens model. In natural environments, spatial cues and spatiotemporal trajectories rarely or never repeat themselves exactly. An underlying continuity must be assumed to enable inference and generalization from fragmentary, nonrepeating data to stable objects and predictable trajectories. Vicarious functioning, or purposive behavior, is essentially adaptive. Local adaptations involve corrections and alternate paths. Global adaptations involve learning converging to stable pattern–pattern relations, in that the patterns are more reliable and robust than single cues or individual, cue-object associations.

Early in this chapter, we described how canonical correlation analysis can be used to identify pattern–pattern correlations in the way pilots interact with automation and, more important, how to capitalize on the regularities of these patterns to identify unusual deviations and dangerous outliers. It may be appealing to think that because stochastic patterns repeat with some regularity even in digital systems that human users or operators can adapt to them just as they can adapt to the familiar, physical environment. This, however, is only true as long as the system remains in a restricted, familiar subspace of the overall state space. Problems arise from the fact that although approximations to continuous processes can have bounded errors, continuous approximations to discrete systems are not so well behaved. Outside the nominal, familiar subspace in which a system nominally operates, that is, in unusual situations and at unexpected times, underlying ecological discontinuities may suddenly manifest themselves, and the resulting consequences of the errors in a continuous approximation may be arbitrarily large.

Currently, a tendency exists among designers of both everyday devices and more complex systems to mimic the underlying, discrete nature of computer-based artifacts with a "simplified," all-discrete interface. Because many consumer devices and all automated control systems are hybrid (i.e., they contain both discrete and continuous process), discrete-only interfaces to automation (e.g., mode settings, alerts, alarms) may abstract away critical regions of the state space.

Due to the paucity of formal, rigorous, and systematic methods for supporting human–technology interaction design, the tasks of creating these abstractions and their attendant interface design simplifications are too often performed intuitively. The result in many cases is user frustration, confusion, and in the case of high-risk systems, the possibility of disaster. To this end, we hope that the insights we have offered here about the geometry of human–technology interaction will take at least a small step toward remedying this situation.

Acknowledgments. The work described in this chapter was conducted as part of NASA's Intelligent Systems program with the intent of supporting the development of future interfaces for controlling and managing semi-autonomous rovers. Asaf Degani would like to thank Yosi Amaram for a fruitful discussion that contributed to the writing of this chapter and Lisa Burnett for her essential teaching of flow and continuity.

References

Barlow, H. (2001). The exploitation of regularities in the environment by the brain. *Behavioral and Brain Sciences, 24*, 602–607.

Barnden, J. A. (2001). Uncertainty and conflict handling in the ATT-meta context-based system for metaphorical reasoning. In *Proceedings of CONTEXT'01: Third International Conference on Modeling and Using Context*. Dundee, Scotland.

Bruner, J. S. (1973). *Beyond the information given: Studies in the psychology of knowing.* New York: Norton.

Brunswik, E. (1952). *The conceptual framework of psychology.* Chicago: University of Chicago Press.

Brunswik, E. (1956). *Perception and the representative design of psychological experiments.* Berkeley: University of California Press.

Bryant, V. (1985). *Metric spaces: Iteration and application.* Cambridge: Cambridge University Press.

Bullock, S., & Todd, P. M. (1999). Made to measure: Ecological rationality in structured environments. *Minds and Machines, 9*, 497–541.

Casner, S. M. (1994). Understanding the determinants of problem-solving behavior in a complex environment. *Human Factors, 36*(4), 580–598.

Cliff, N. (1987). *Analyzing multivariate data.* San Diego: Harcourt Brace Jovanovich.

Connolly, T. (1999). Action as a fast and frugal heuristic. *Minds and Machines, 9*, 479–496.

Cooksey, R.W. (2001). On Gibson's review of Brunswik and Kirlik's review of Gibson. In K. R. Hammond & T. R. Stewart (Eds.), *The essential Brunswik: Beginnings, explications, applications.* New York: Oxford University Press.

Court of Inquiry. (1992). *Report on accident to Indian Airlines Airbus A-320 aircraft VT-EPN at Bangalore on 14th February 1990.* Indian Government.

Dawes, R., & Corrigan, B. (1974). Linear models in decision making. *Psychological Bulletin, 81,* 95–106.

Dawes, R. M. (1979). The robust beauty of improper linear models. *American Psychologist, 31,* 571–582.

Degani, A. (1996). Modeling human–machine systems: On modes, error, and patterns of interaction. Unpublished doctoral dissertation. Atlanta: Georgia Institute of Technology.

Degani, A. (2004). *Taming HAL: Designing interfaces beyond 2001.* New York: Palgrave Macmillan.

Degani, A., & Heymann, M. (2002). Formal verification of human–automation interaction. *Human Factors, 44*(1), 28–43.

Degani, A., Shafto, M., and Kirlik, A. (1999). Modes in human-machine systems. Constructs, representation, and classification. *International Journal of Aviation Psychology, 9*(2), 125–138

De Leeuw, J., & Michailidis, G. (2000). Graph layout techniques and multidimensional data analysis. In F. T. Bruss & L. Le Cam (Eds.), *Game theory, optimal stopping, probability and statistics. Papers in honor of Thomas S. Ferguson.* IMS Lecture Notes-Monograph Series, 219–248.

Federal Aviation Administration. (2004). *Advisory circular to supplement Federal Aviation Regulation 25.1329: Automatic pilot systems.* Washington, D.C.

Freed, M., & Remington, R.W. (1998). A conceptual framework for predicting errors in complex human-machine environments. In *Proceedings of the 1998 Conference of the Cognitive Science Society.* Madison: University of Wisconsin.

Gibson, J.J. (1957/2001). Survival in a world of probable objects. In K. R. Hammond & T. R. Stewart (Eds.), *The essential Brunswik: Beginnings, explications, applications.* New York: Oxford University Press.

Gibson, J. J., & Crooks, L.E. (1938). A theoretical field-analysis of automobile driving. *American Journal of Psychology, 51,* 453–471.

Gigerenzer, G., & Goldstein, D. G. (1996). Reasoning the fast and frugal way: Models of bounded rationality. *Psychological Review, 103,* 650–670.

Goldberg, L. R. (1968). Simple models or simple processes? Some research on clinical judgment. *American Psychologist, 23,* 483–496.

Hammond, K. R. (1996). *Human judgment and social policy.* New York: Oxford University Press.

Hammond, K. R. (1996/2000). Coherence and correspondence theories in judgment and decision making. In T. Connolly, H. R. Arkes, & K. R. Hammond (Eds.), *Judgment and decision making: An interdisciplinary reader* (2nd ed., pp. 54–65). Cambridge: Cambridge University Press. Originally appeared in Hammond (1996).

Hammond, K. R. (2000). *Judgments under stress.* New York: Oxford University Press.

Hastie, R., & Dawes, R.M. (2001). *Rational choice in an uncertain world: The psychology of judgment and decision making.* Thousand Oaks, Calif.: Sage.

Heymann, M., & Degani, A., (2002). *On abstractions and simplifications in the design of human–automation interfaces.* NASA Technical Memorandum 2002–21397. Moffett Field, Calif.

Hoare, C. A. R. (1985), *Communicating sequential processes.* New York: Prentice Hall.

Hubbard, T. L. (1999). How consequences of physical principles influence mental representation: The environmental invariants hypothesis. In P. R. Killeen & W. R. Uttal (Eds.), *Fechner Day 99: The end of 20th century psychophysics.* Proceedings of the Fifteenth Annual Meeting of the International Society for Psychophysics. Tempe, Ariz.: International Society for Psychophysics.

Jha, P., & Bisantz, A. M. (2001). Modeling fault diagnosis in a dynamic process control task using a multivariate lens model. *Proceedings of the HFES 45th Annual Meeting,* Minneapolis/St. Paul, Minn.

Kahneman, D. (2003). A perspective on judgment and choice: Mapping bounded rationality. *American Psychologist, 58*(9), 697–720.

Kirlik, A. (1995). Requirements for psychological models to support design: Towards ecological task analysis. In J. Flach, P. Hancock, J. Caird, & K. Vicente (Eds.), *Global perspectives on the ecology of human–machine systems* (pp. 68–120). Mahwah, N.J.: Erlbaum.

Kirlik, A. (2001). On Gibson's review of Brunswik. In K. R. Hammond & T. R. Stewart (Eds.), *The essential Brunswik: Beginnings, explications, applications.* New York: Oxford University Press.

Kirlik, A. (in press). Work in progress: Reinventing intelligence for an invented world. In R. J. Sternberg & D. Preiss (Eds.), *Intelligence and technology.* Mahwah, N.J.: Erlbaum.

Klein, G. A. (1999). *Sources of power: How people make decisions.* Cambridge, Mass.: MIT Press.

Landauer, T. K., Laham, D., Rehder, B., & Schreiner, M. E. (1997). How well can passage meaning be derived without using word order? A comparison of latent semantic analysis and humans. In M. G. Shafto & P. Langley (Eds.), *Proceedings of the 19th*

Annual Meeting of the Cognitive Science Society. Mahwah, N.J.: Erlbaum.

Liu, C., Herman, R., & Gazis, D. (1996). A review of the yellow interval dilemma. *Transportation Research A, 30*(5), 333–348.

Lowe, G. (1992). *Some extensions to the probabilistic, biased model of timed CSP.* Technical Report PRG-TR-9-92. Oxford University Computing Laboratory.

McGreevy, M. W., & Statler, I. C. (1998). *Rating the relevance of QUORUM-selected ASRS incident narratives to a "controlled flight into terrain" accident.* NASA Technical Memorandum 1998-208749. Moffett Field, Calif.: NASA-Ames Research Center.

Ministry of Planning, Housing, Transport and Maritime Affairs. (1989). *Investigation commission concerning the accident which occurred on June 26th 1988 at Mulhouse-Habsheim to Airbus A-320, registration number F-GKC.*

Norenzayan, A., Smith, E. E., Kim, B. J., & Nisbett, R. E. (2002). Cultural preferences for formal versus intuitive reasoning. *Cognitive Science, 26,* 653–684.

Norman, D. (1999). *The invisible computer.* Boston: MIT Press

Oishi, M., Tomlin, C., & Degani, A. (2003, Nov.). Discrete abstractions of hybrid systems: Verification of safety and application to user-interface design. NASA Technical Memorandum 2003-212803. Moffett Field, Calif.: NASA-Ames Research Center.

Reason, J. (1990). *Human error.* Cambridge: Cambridge University Press.

Roscoe, A. W. (1998). *The theory and practice of concurrency.* London: Prentice Hall.

Rouse, W. B. (1983). Models of human problem solving: Detection, diagnosis, and compensation for system failures. *Automatica, 9,* 613–625.

Schneider, S. (2000). *Concurrent and real-timesystems: The CSP approach.* Chichester, UK: John Wiley & Sons, LTD.

Shafto, M., Degani, A., & Kirlik, A. (1997). Canonical correlation analysis of data on human–automation interaction. *Proceedings of the 41st Annual Meeting of the Human Factors and Ergonomics Society.* Albuquerque, N.M.

Shepard, R. N. (1999). *Perception, imagery, and science.* Hitchcock Lecture, University of California, Santa Barbara.

Sheridan, T. (1997). Supervisory control. In G. Salvendy (Ed.), *Handbook of human factors.* New York: Wiley.

Smith, S., Duke, D. J., Marsh, T., Harrison, M. D., & Wright, P. C. (1998). *Modeling interaction in virtual environments.* UK-VRSIG '98. Exeter, U.K.

Sun, R. (2000). *The duality of mind: A bottom-up approach toward cognition.* Mahwah, N.J.: Lawrence Erlbaum.

Thagard, P. (2000). *Coherence in thought and action.* Cambridge, Mass.: MIT Press.

Wolf, B. (May, 1999). Vicarious functioning as a central process-characteristic of human behavior. In K. R. Fischer & F. Stadler (Eds.), *Wahrnehmung und Gegenstandswelt. Zum Lebenswerk von Egon Brunswik.* Wien: Springer. University of Landau, Center of Educational Research. Available online at www.brunswik.org/notes/essay4.html.

Zeigler, B. P., Praehofer, H., & Kim, T. G. (2000). *Theory of modeling and simulation: Integrating discrete event and continuous complex dynamic systems* (2nd ed.). San Diego: Academic Press.

14

Stephen M. Casner

Understanding the Determinants of Adaptive Behavior in a Modern Airline Cockpit

Introduction

In his classic work *The Sciences of the Artificial*, Herbert Simon offers an allegory about how adaptive behavior might be determined by internal and external influences: the goals of the problem solver and the features of the environment. The allegory stars an ant making "his laborious way across a wind and wave-molded beach. He moves ahead, angles to the right to ease his climb up a steep dunelet, detours around a pebble, stops for a moment to exchange information with a compatriot. Thus he makes his weaving, halting way back to his home" (Simon, 1981, p. 63). Because the path of the ant over the beach is determined as much by the features of the beach as by the goals of the ant, the allegory suggests that the study of problem-solving behavior has to include not only a detailed consideration of the nature of problem solvers but also of the environments in which they conduct their business.

Understanding how the features of a complex environment influence problem-solving behavior is difficult because it is generally not possible to enumerate all of the relevant features of a complex environment. However, I can test the extent to which problem-solving behavior is adapted to selected features by comparing a record of those features, measured directly in the environment, with a record of problem-solving behavior measured in that same environment. Statistical techniques can then be used to assess the extent to which the two records are related. As a simple example, the extent to which the ant's behavior is adapted to the topographical features of the beach can be tested by comparing a trace of the ant's path with a trace of the contour of the beach.

This research quantitatively explores the influences of a complex environment on pilots' problem-solving behavior when managing the flight path of a modern commercial airliner. The problem requires the flight crew to guide the aircraft along a planned flight route that consists of particular courses, altitudes, and airspeeds. During the flight, the flight crew must also deal with modifications to the planned flight route made by air traffic control (ATC). These modifications instruct the flight crew to follow assigned headings, altitudes, and airspeeds that differ from the original route. Characteristics of the routes and clearances issued to the flight crew represent one kind of environmental landscape that affects the way pilots do their job.

The flight crew must follow planned routes and comply with clearances by choosing among a collection of flight control resources found in the modern airline cockpit. These flight control resources represent a second kind of environmental landscape. Pilots may choose to operate the aircraft's manual flight controls or make use of several automated systems that can perform varying amounts of the work required to fly the aircraft. Manual control allows the flight crew to respond quickly but requires close and constant attention to details. The use of automated flight control systems requires time and effort to configure the systems but then allows the crew to monitor the systems as they do their work. Deciding which flight control resources to use creates its own system of costs and benefits that pilots must consider when deciding how to do their job.

The first step in understanding the influence of the problem-solving environment on pilots' behavior is to develop a detailed profile of the environment. This profile considers the flight routes and clearances received by the flight crew as well as the flight control resources from which pilots must choose when performing their duties. Toward this end, a record of ATC clearances issued during 16 commercial flights is explored for features of the clearances that might influence the way pilots decide to solve the problem. A similar analysis is performed on the flight control resources available to pilots when responding to the clearances. Two criteria were used to choose among the many possible dimensions along which the environment might be measured. First, each environmental dimension chosen offers some incentive to pilots in return for adapting their problem-solving behavior around that dimension. Second, each dimension exhibits patterns of regularities that pilots could detect through their experiences and exploit to formulate strategies that are adapted to that dimension.

The second step is to consider the environmental profile and hypothesize advantages and disadvantages of using each flight control resource to comply with each type of clearance with respect to each environmental dimension that was measured. Predictions are made about how the information provided by the environment might lead to adaptations in the way that pilots choose flight control resources when responding to clearances.

The final step is to examine a record of the flight control resources chosen in response to each of the clearances issued during the same 16 flights. Statistical methods are used to test the extent to which pilots' problem-solving behavior is adapted to the environmental dimensions that were examined. The results demonstrate that the measured features of the environment account for more than half of the variability in pilots' problem-solving behavior.

Previous Work

Although the idea of examining environmental influences on behavior is an old one (see chapter 2; Brunswik, 1943; Gibson, 1979; Tolman and Brunswik, 1935), perhaps the most detailed proposals for carrying it out can be found in the work of Hursch, Hammond, and Hursch (1964). Refining an idea first suggested by Brunswik in 1943, Hursch et al. (1964) proposed the lens model equation. The lens model equation makes use of multiple regression techniques to model the way a set of environmental cues might influence subjects' understanding of a target variable. The lens model equation goes beyond comparing subjects' responses and target variables by considering the environmental cues available to the subject when generating a response. Specifically, the lens model attempts to identify (1) statistical regularities in the environment by examining the correlation between the available environmental cues, and (2) the effects of the cues on subjects' responses using correlations between cues and responses.

Schooler and Anderson (1991) took a statistical approach to modeling human memory based on the notion that a detailed characterization of the environment in which human memory operates can inform the study of human memory. Their work focuses on discovering temporal and contextual patterns of variation in the way everyday life charges humans with the task of remembering things. Assuming that the goal of human memory is to remember the right things at the right time, memory should tune itself to the demands of the environment. By analyzing several corpuses of environmental data, Schooler and Anderson were able to reproduce in a natural setting a number of well-known memory results obtained in laboratory experiments.

Kirlik (1993) studied pilots' use of an automated flight control system in a simulated flight environment. His study aimed to demonstrate ways the particulars of the automated system, when inserted in a multitask environment, would determine pilots' use of the system. Six environmental features were examined pertaining to the immediate use or secondary consequences of using the automated system in the presence of other competing tasks. Because the data were collected in a controlled laboratory task, pilots' behavior was not given the opportunity to adapt to the patterns of variation that might reside in an actual aviation environment. As Kirlik points out, as we place other environmental pressures on pilots, it is likely that the automated system will begin to look attractive to pilots along a number of additional dimensions.

Measured Dimensions of the Environment: ATC Clearances

Prior to the departure of any airline flight, the flight crew is issued a detailed flight route between the airports of origin and destination. This route is comprised of an ordered sequence of route segments as shown in Figure 14.1. The job of the flight crew is to essentially play a game of connect the dots prescribed by the flight route, until instructed to do otherwise.

ATC follows the progress of every airline flight as it makes its way along the planned route. The airspace covering the United States is quite large and is divided up into smaller areas called sectors, so that the workload of following all flights can be divided among many air traffic controllers. Six sectors lie along the route from San Francisco (SFO) to Los Angeles (LAX) shown in Figure 14.1, seven from Los Angeles to San Francisco.

Even though every flight is issued a flight route prior to departure, there remains the task of ensuring that the flight paths of no two airplanes intersect. Air traffic controllers assigned to each sector are re-sponsible for monitoring the progress of all aircraft transitioning the sector and for devising modifications to the flight routes for each aircraft such that safe separation is guaranteed between them. Controllers make modifications in the individual flight plans by issuing *clearances*. A clearance issued to an aircraft instructs the pilot flying the aircraft to fly an assigned course, heading, altitude, or airspeed that is different from the original route. The task of the flight crew is to follow the flight route and to be prepared to accept and obey modifications to that flight route made by air traffic control.

Participants

Thirty-two pilots served as flight crew aboard 16 commercial carrier flights as part of their regular job duties. Federal Aviation Administration (FAA) air traffic controllers worked the sectors along the routes that the flights were conducted.

Apparatus

The aircraft used on each flight were one of two anonymous make and model automation-equipped commercial jetliners.

Procedure

The data were collected by a single experimenter while serving as a flight deck observer with the permission of the airline company and the FAA. The experimenter had roughly 125 hours of previous observer experience. The data were gathered through headphone monitoring of all ATC–cockpit communications transmitted over the same channel monitored by the flight crew. The data were recorded using a pen and notebook. The experimenter recorded all clearances issued to the aircraft by ATC during the course of the flight. Because it is required that the flight crew read back all issued clearances, an additional source of feedback was available to reduce the probability that a clearance was recorded in error. No interpretation or analysis of the clearances was attempted during the flights. A total of 16 flights were observed, 8 flights in each direction between San Francisco and Los Angeles. All flights in a given direction were initially issued the same flight route. Flights were chosen such that the departure times were distributed as evenly as possible between the hours of 12 noon and 10 p.m.

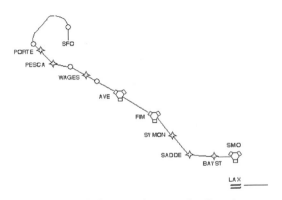

Figure 14.1. Flight routes between San Francisco and Los Angeles airports.

Results

The 287 clearances recorded on the 17 flights were analyzed along 5 dimensions. These dimensions were selected on the basis that they exhibit interesting patterns of regularities that pilots might learn about through their flying experiences, and use to their advantage.

Clearance Type

The first dimension along which the clearances were examined concerns the types of clearances that were issued. Table 14.1 lists each of the unique types of clearances issued during the 16 flights along the horizontal axis and the sectors within each flight route along the vertical axis. The cells of the table reflect the number of times each type of clearance was issued within each sector. Of an estimated 98 possible types of clearances that require responses, only 10 unique types of clearances were actually issued during the 16 flights between SFO and LAX (landing and takeoff clearances are omitted). Furthermore, the four most common types of clearances listed in Table 14.1 accounted for 88% of all clearances issued.

Clearance Predictability

The regularity observed in the type of clearances raises the question of how regular are the clearances received across flights. Asked another way, what is the probability that after studying the clearances issued during all flights traveling the same route (SFO–LAX or LAX–SFO), a pilot might correctly anticipate the clearances that will be issued on the next flight? Correctly anticipating a clearance requires a pilot to predict not only the type of the clearance but also the particular course, heading, altitude, airspeed, and so on that the clearance prescribes. The following measure, from Shannon and Weaver (1949), was used to estimate the uncertainty about future clearances for each sector along each route based on the records of clearances issued on previous flights. If C is the set of unique clearances issued at least one time across all same-route flights within a sector, and C_i is a particular clearance (e.g., "fly a heading of 160°"), then the uncertainty about future clearances is given by:

$$-\sum_{i=1}^{|C|} P(c_i)\log_2[P(c_i)],$$

where $P(c_i)$ is the probability that clearance c_i will be issued in that sector along that route. Measures

of predictability for the sectors can be obtained by taking the complement of the uncertainty measures normalized on the interval [0, 1]. Figure 14.2 shows the predictability measures for each of the sectors.

The information measure does not attempt to recover additional clues about future clearances that might be derived from dependencies that might exist among the individual clearances, from ordering among clearances, from a consideration of the clearances that were not issued, or from knowledge of conventions commonly used by air traffic controllers.

Time Constraints

Every clearance has associated with it a time frame in which the air traffic controller expects an initiation of response. Time frames associated with clearances vary as a function of two variables: (1) the type of clearance, and (2) the phase of flight. The 10 unique types of clearances observed are listed along the vertical axis of the grid in Table 14.2. The phase of flight dimension roughly categorizes a flight into those portions of the flight conducted at or below 18,000 feet (e.g., takeoff, departure, arrival, approach, and landing), and those portions conducted above 18,000 feet (e.g., en route cruise). These two categories are depicted along the horizontal dimension of the grid. The time constraints corresponding to each combination of clearance type and flight phase are recorded in the cells. The values appearing in the cells were obtained by consensus of three participating air traffic controllers. Three values were possible: normal (comply within 20 seconds), relaxed (comply within 1 minute), and pilot's discretion (comply when convenient).

Average Number of Clearances per Sector

A fourth dimension along which the clearances were examined is the average number of clearances that were issued in each sector. The mean number of clearances for each sector are shown in the rightmost column in Table 14.1. An analysis of variance shows that the number of clearances issued significantly differs from sector to sector within each route: F (5, 35) = 35.4, $p < 0.0001$ for SFO to LAX; and F (6, 42) = 7.3, $p < 0.0001$ for LAX to SFO. This result, together with the small variances associated with the means, suggests that each sector has its own characteristic number of clearances.

Table 14.1. Type, number, and average number of air traffic control clearances (by sector)

	Heading	Altitude	Speed	Heading Until Altitude	Altitude At Fix	Altitude Until Localizer	Speed At Fix	Speed Until Fix	Direct to Fix	Intercept Radial	Mean Clearances/Sector
SFO–LAX											
Bay Dep	7	1	0	1	0	0	0	0	4	4	2.1
Oak Ctr 1	0	7	9	0	0	0	0	0	8	0	3.0
Oak Ctr 2	0	10	0	0	0	0	0	0	0	0	1.3
LA Ctr 1	0	9	1	0	0	0	0	0	1	0	1.4
LA Ctr 2	2	4	8	0	1	0	2	0	0	1	2.3
LA App	19	22	13	0	0	3	0	3	1	0	7.6
LAX–SFO											
LA Dep	0	11	8	0	0	0	0	0	0	0	2.4
LA Ctr 1	0	10	8	0	0	0	0	0	8	0	3.3
LA Ctr 2	1	11	7	0	0	0	0	0	1	0	2.5
Oak Ctr 1	0	9	5	0	2	0	0	0	2	0	2.3
Oak Ctr 2	0	9	3	0	9	0	0	0	0	0	2.6
Bay App 1	2	6	3	0	0	0	0	0	0	0	1.4
Bay App 2	6	9	6	0	2	1	0	5	1	1	3.9
Total	37	118	71	1	14	4	2	8	26	6	

Total Clearances = 287

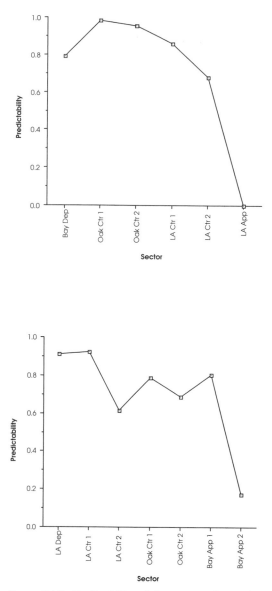

Figure 14.2. Predictability of clearances within each sector.

Number of Clearances Issued at Once

A fifth dimension along which the clearances were examined concerns the number of clearances that were issued at once. It is common for ATC to simultaneously issue several clearances to a single aircraft during the same radio transmission. When this occurs, no time extensions are given for complying with the clearances. For each of the individual clearances, responses must be initiated in the time frame listed in Table 14.2. Figure 14.3 shows

the probability that any given clearance issued in each sector will be accompanied by at least one other clearance.

The analyses profile those aspects of the task environment pertaining to the ATC clearances to which pilots are required to respond. I now turn my attention to an analogous study of the flight control resources that pilots must choose from when confronted with these clearances. Again, the point of these examinations is to produce concurrent profiles of the ATC and flight control resource environments. These profiles will later allow me to form detailed hypotheses about what combinations of clearances and flight control resources might look tempting to pilots trying to do their job.

Measured Dimensions of the Environment: Flight Control Resources

The problem of managing the flight path of an aircraft has three fundamental components (McRuer, Ashkenas, & Graham, 1973). *Control* refers to the problem of making small but continual adjustments necessary to maintain a single course, heading, altitude, or airspeed. *Guidance* refers to the problem of deciding what sequence of control inputs are necessary to achieve a new target course, heading, altitude, or airspeed. *Navigation* refers to the problem of formulating in advance a sequence of courses, altitudes, and airspeeds that make up a flight route and to track the position of the aircraft at all times throughout the flight.

The modern airline cockpit provides three basic categories of flight control resources that allow pilots to perform the tasks of control, guidance, and navigation.

1. Manual Flight Controls

The most basic way to manage the flight path of the aircraft is to manually perform all three of the control, guidance, and navigation tasks. Control is performed by manipulating a control yoke and throttles levers in response to indications shown on a set of flight instruments. Guidance is performed using a collection of instruments used to compare the current course, heading, altitude, and airspeed to that

Table 14.2. Time constraints associated with air traffic control clearances

Clearance	Below 18,000 Feet	Above 18,000 Feet
Heading	Normal	Normal
Altitude	Normal	Relaxed
Speed	Normal	Relaxed
Heading until altitude	Normal	Normal
Altitude at fix	Relaxed/pilot's discretion	Relaxed/pilot's discretion
Altitude until localizer	Relaxed/pilot's discretion	—
Speed at fix	Relaxed/pilot's discretion	Relaxed/pilot's discretion
Speed until fix	Normal	Relaxed
Direct to fix	Normal	Normal
Intercept radial	Normal	Normal

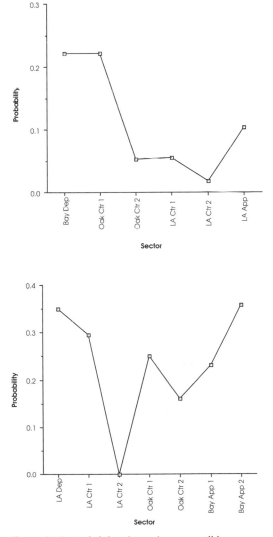

Figure 14.3. Probability that a clearance will be accompanied by at least one other clearance (by sector).

which is needed. Navigation is performed using a collection of position-finding instruments and displays and a paper map that details prescribed flight routes.

2a. Autopilot

An autopilot can assume responsibility for both the guidance and control tasks. By way of guidance, an autopilot has the capability to decide what control responses must be made to achieve a target course, heading, altitude, or airspeed. By way of control, an autopilot features servomechanisms capable of executing the control inputs prescribed by the autopilot.

The autopilot is invoked via a mode control panel (MCP) that offers the pilot several command features useful for complying with an ATC clearance. Figure 14.4 (top) shows a facsimile of the MCP from a commercial airliner.

The autopilot can be used to comply with a clearance in the following way. To fly an assigned course, heading, altitude, or speed, two steps are required. First, a pilot must move his or her hand to the appropriate dial on the MCP, marked COURSE, HEADING, ALTITUDE, or IAS/MACH (indicated airspeed) and dial in the desired value. Second, a button appearing on the MCP must be pushed to engage the autopilot function being selected, one of VOR/LOC, HDG SEL, LVL CHG, or SPEED.

The autopilot is not capable of performing the navigation task because it has no ability to track the current position of the aircraft or store multiple target courses, altitudes, or airspeeds that make up an entire flight route.

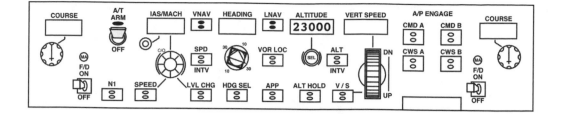

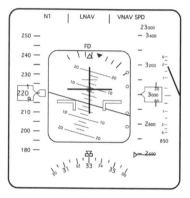

Figure 14.4. Mode control panel (MCP) and flight director.

2b. Autopilot (Flight Director)

The autopilot has a second mode of operation that allows the pilot to assume responsibility of the control task. That is, the autopilot can be instructed to issue the control inputs it prescribes directly to the pilot instead of the servomechanisms. Guidance instructions are presented to the pilot using an instrument called a *flight director*. Guidance information is presented on the flight director shown in Figure 14.4 (bottom) using symbols indicating which control inputs are required. The flight director in Figure 14.4 (bottom) is commanding a climbing left turn.

3a. FMC

The FMC allows the flight crew to preprogram a flight route prior to departure, and represents the highest level of automation found in the modern cockpit. Using the FMC together with the autopilot, the control, guidance, and navigation tasks are performed automatically. As each segment of the flight route is completed, the FMC will direct the autopilot to follow the next segment in the planned route. As long as the anticipated flight route is followed, little further interaction with the FMC is required once it is initially engaged. In the case that a clearance is issued requiring modification of the flight route, reprogramming the FMC is required. The FMC is programmed using the interface shown in Figure 14.5 called a *control display unit* (CDU).

Flight routes programmed into the FMC are distributed across a series of pages of the CDU that are accessed using the buttons appearing immediately below the screen of the CDU in Figure 14.5. Pushing a button causes the text associated with that page to appear on the CDU screen. This text description of the flight plan can then be modified using the alphanumeric keys located on the CDU.

3b. FMC (Flight Director)

The FMC also offers the pilot the option of assuming responsibility for the control task. In this mode of operation, the control task is performed by the pilot using the same flight director shown in Fig-

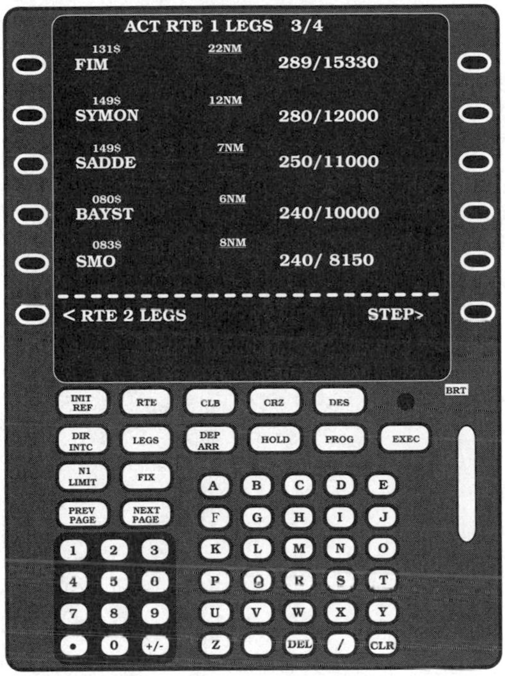

Figure 14.5. Control display unit (CDU).

ure 14.4 (bottom). The guidance and navigation tasks are performed by the FMC.

For each flight control resource and mode of operation, Table 14.3 summarizes which of the control, guidance, and navigation tasks are performed by the flight crew and which are performed by the automation.

Analysis of the Flight Control Resources

Clearance Type

The three basic flight control resources do not differ in the types of clearances for which they can be used to respond, with one exception: It is generally not possible to comply with a heading clearance using the FMC.

Predictability

The flight control resources do not vary in the minimum amount of information about future clearances required to use them. Only knowledge of the current course, heading, altitude, or airspeed to be flown is necessary. However, when information about future portions of a flight route is available, a pilot can type this information into the FMC, and the FMC can fly the programmed route with little need for further pilot intervention.

Time Constraints

The flight control resources do vary in the minimum time required to initiate a response to a clearance. To estimate the minimum time to respond using a flight control resource, I adopt a variation of the keystroke-level model proposed by Card, Moran, and Newell (1983). The keystroke-level model predicts the *minimum* time to execute a well-practiced, error-free procedure. When applied to highly practiced procedures, this model has produced accurate execution times (John, 1988) owing to the fact that such procedures rely on relatively few assumptions about what users are doing when executing the procedure.

A complete catalog of execution times was generated by constructing a grid in which the different types of clearances issued during the 16 flights were listed along the horizontal axis, and the possible flight control resources—manual, autopilot, and FMC—were listed on the vertical axis. For each cell in the grid, a procedure was generated that enumerates the sequence of steps required to use the control resource to execute the clearance (Bulfer, 1991; Casner, 2001). Following Card et al., these steps included keystrokes, dialing, movement of the hand between relevant devices, mental preparations, system response times, and initiations of motor actions. These steps are

Table 14.3. Delegation of control, guidance, and navigation tasks using each flight control resource

Flight Control Resource	Control	Guidance	Navigation
Manual	Pilot	Pilot	Pilot
Autopilot	Automation	Automation	Pilot
Autopilot with flight director	Pilot	Automation	Pilot
FMC	Automation	Automation	Automation
FMC with flight director	Pilot	Automation	Automation

captured by the following formula, which was used to calculate the execution times appearing in each cell of the grid:

$$Texecute = Tkeystroke + Tdialing + Thoming + Tmental + Tsystem + Tmotor.$$

Estimates for each of the parameters in the formula were generated by running timed trials with volunteer pilots working at the NASA Ames Research Center. Pilots were asked to use an MCP and CDU to comply with each type of clearance while their execution time was tracked using a stopwatch.

Figure 14.6 plots the minimum execution time for combinations of the flight control resources and the five most common clearances in Table 14.1. The clearances appear along the vertical axis. The horizontal axis reflects execution time and is subdivided into the three time constraint categories derived from the analysis of the ATC environment. The rectangles appearing in each row indicate the time constraint categories in which each clearance is typically issued. Three sorts of labeled points appear in the plot: M (manual), AP (autopilot), and FMC. The manual solution for any clearance is uniform and small because initiating a response requires only a manipulation of the control yoke or throttle levers in the appropriate direction. The times for the autopilot functions reflect the various dialing and button-pushing steps required to use them. Recall that for some clearances, the time to use the FMC varies depending on the extent to which a pilot is able to anticipate and preprogram the specifics of the clearance. Thus, the time to execute some clearances using the FMC is expressed as a range of possible times. The lower time in the range represents the case in which a clearance is fully anticipated and pre-

programmed, requiring little or no additional interaction to comply. The higher time estimate represents the case in which a pilot must program the clearance from scratch. Note that with respect to execution times, there is no difference between the two alternative modes of operation for the autopilot and FMC (i.e., manual or automated control).

Predicted Adaptations to the Measured Dimensions of the Environment

I have thus far created a profile of both the ATC clearances that are issued to pilots as well as the flight control resources that pilots must choose among to comply with them. The following formulates five hypotheses about how pilots' behavior when responding to ATC clearances might be adapted to each of the measured dimensions of the environment.

Clearance Type

A first dimension of the environment to which pilots might adapt their behavior is the variation in the type of clearances that are issued. If the type of clearance issued is a driving force behind pilots' choice among flight control resources, then I can expect pilots to follow rules that associate these resources with clearance types. This adaptation implies that there should be little variation among flight control resources chosen for each clearance type. The analyses of the ATC clearances and the flight control resources seem to suggest no incentives for this adaptation.

Predictability

A second dimension along which pilot behavior might be adapted is that of the predictability of clearances. Recall that the flight control resources each offer different advantages with respect to pilots' ability to anticipate upcoming clearances. All such resources allow pilots to respond when minimal information is available. However, the FMC allows future portions of the flight plan to be entered in advance. In the case that a flight plan is entered and few changes are required, the aircraft can literally fly itself. On the other hand, when a

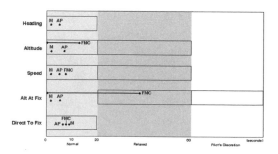

Figure 14.6. Time constraints for clearances versus minimum execution times using each flight control resource.

flight plan is entered and then later changed by ATC, a pilot is forced to make changes to the programmed flight plan or abandon the FMC. If clearance predictability is a driving force behind pilots' choice among flight control resources, then I can expect the predictability measures given in Figure 14.2 to correlate positively with the use of the FMC, in either of its two modes of operation.

Time Constraints

A third dimension along which pilots might attempt to adapt their use of the flight control resources is the time allowed to comply with a clearance. The plot in Figure 14.6 shows that the decision to use more automated flight control resources has the general effect of adding to the total time required to respond to a clearance. However, the manual and two autopilot modes fall comfortably within the time constraints presented by most clearances. Hence, I should expect time constraints to have little effect on how pilots choose between manual and autopilot operations. The decision about whether to work with the FMC might also depend on the extent to which pilots are able to anticipate clearances. In the case that a clearance has been anticipated and programmed in advance, using the FMC can be a rewarding alternative. However, in the case that additional FMC programming is required, the option of using the FMC becomes less plausible. For example, working at a pace approaching the limits of human perceptuomotor ability, pilots can reprogram the FMC to comply with an altitude clearance. However, the autopilot can be used to accomplish the same goal in roughly half the time. Pilots might opt for this more comfortable time frame to ensure that the procedure is performed correctly or to allow time for other activities.

If time pressure is important to pilots, then they should opt for flight control resources that allow them to obey the prevailing time constraints. That is, when responding to unanticipated clearances issued under demanding time constraints, pilots should opt for the more time-efficient manual and autopilot resources.

Number of Clearances per Sector

A fourth dimension of the environment to which pilots might adapt their behavior is the number of clearances that are issued in each sector. When many clearances are issued, less time is available, not only for initiating a response to a clearance but, more important, for any ongoing activities that the pilot must perform as a result of choosing a particular flight control resource. For example, some choices of flight control resources require continuous attention from the pilot. If the average number of clearances issued per sector is a driving force behind pilots' choices between flight control resources, one might expect pilots to opt for those resources that make use of the automation and free pilots attention when operating in sectors in which they expect high numbers of clearances to be issued. Similarly, one should expect pilots to favor the FMC in an effort to offload the effort of dealing with multiple clearances.

Number of Clearances Issued at Once

A fifth measured dimension of the environment was the number of clearances issued at once. Recall that when several clearances are issued during the same radio transmission, no relaxation of time constraints is provided. If pilots' choices between flight control resources is affected by the number of clearances issued at once, then one might expect them to opt for resources that can be quickly engaged, namely, the manual and autopilot resources, when multiple clearances are issued under demanding time constraints.

A Record of Pilots' Problem-Solving Behavior

Specific hypotheses were made about how pilots' problem-solving behavior might be adapted to the measured dimensions of the environment. The following discussion analyzes a record of pilots' actual use of the flight control resources on the same 16 flights on which the clearances were issued. Regression analysis is used to measure the extent to which pilots' problem-solving behavior can be accounted for by the variability observed in the measured dimensions of the environment.

Participants

The same 32 pilots were observed on board the same 16 flights on which the clearances were recorded.

Procedure

The data were gathered by the same observer through visual monitoring of pilots' actions and auditory monitoring of pilots' verbal behavior. Pilots' choices among flight control resources were recorded using the same pen and notebook as they responded to each ATC clearance issued. The flight control resource chosen by the pilot to respond to each clearance was available to the experimenter in three ways: (1) by observing actions, (2) by reading an alphanumeric display on the instrument panel that reflects the names of all resources engaged at the time, and (3) verbal reviews of pilots' behavior initiated by the experimenter. All three information sources were used redundantly to reduce the probability that a response was recorded in error. A response was recorded for each clearance issued from runway to runway on all 16 flights.

Results

Multiple regression was used to determine the extent to which the five measured dimensions could predict the flight control resource chosen to comply with each clearance. The predictor variables consisted of (1) the type of clearance (coded as a series of binary variables), (2) the predictability measure for the sector in which the clearance was issued, (3) the time constraint associated with the clearance, (4) the average number of clearances issued within that sector (measured across flights), and (5) the number of clearances that were issued at the same time as the clearance. All clearances that were instances of a clearance type that constituted less than 5% of the total number of clearances were discarded. The five most common clearances shown in Table 14.1 remained in the model: heading, altitude, speed, direct to fix, and altitude at fix. The five clearances types were coded using four binary variables. The three levels of the time constraints

predictor variable were ordinally coded (i.e., 1, 2, 3) because no specific time constraint is associated with pilot's discretion clearances. All predictor variables were converted to standard scores so that standardized beta coefficients would be produced. Reliable correlation coefficients were obtained between several of the predictor variables and are shown in Table 14.4. The high correlation between clearance predictability and the number of clearances is expected because the probability of correctly guessing future clearances generally decreases as the number of clearances to be guessed increases. Nonetheless, the high correlation complicates the problem of understanding the isolated roles of each dimension.

The outcome to be predicted, the flight control resource chosen to comply with the clearances, was coded as a series of three binary variables. These binary variables represent the control, guidance, and navigation tasks that each flight control resource either performs automatically, or leaves to the pilot. Because less than 5% of the 287 clearances were complied with using manual controls, these clearances were discarded. Furthermore, because pilots opted to use automation to perform the guidance task in all but two of the remaining cases, the outcome variable describing the guidance task was also eliminated from the analysis. The two remaining outcome variables, navigation and control, naturally map onto two independent features of the automation. The navigation variable reflects which of the two remaining flight control resources was used: autopilot or FMC. The control variable reflects whether the servomechanisms were turned on or off.

Because the correlation between the control and navigation outcome variables was small (-0.167, $p < 0.05$), the two outcome variables were considered in two separate regression models. The fit of the models (adjusted) was $R^2 = 0.246$ and $R^2 = 0.552$, respectively. The relationship between each

Table 14.4. Correlations between measured dimensions of the environment

	Clearance Type	Predictability	Time Constraints	Clearances/Sector
Clearance type				
Predictability	0.249**			
Time constraints	0.041	−0.416**		
Clearances/sector	0.215**	−0.901**	0.378**	
Clearances at once	0.078	−0.057	0.132*	−0.042

N = 245, * = p < 0.05; ** = p < 0.01.

predictor variable and the two outcome variables is discussed within the context of regression models that contained all five predictor variables.

Clearance Type

As predicted, the type of clearance had no reliable effect on either of the two outcome variables. The finding casts considerable doubt on the hypothesis that pilots make use of simple rules that associate clearance types with flight control resources. Thus, simple models that do not take into account the details of the environment are unlikely to provide good explanations of how pilots choose flight control resources.

Predictability

The predictability of future clearances produced the largest coefficients for both outcome variables: $\beta = 0.429$, $p < 0.0001$ for the control variable, and $\beta = 0.546$, $p < 0.0001$ for the navigation variable. This result suggests that among the measured dimensions of the environment considered here, the predictability of upcoming clearances is the principal determinant of how pilots choose between flight control resources. With respect to the control variable, pilots opted to perform the control task themselves when operating in sectors of low predictability. Because the analysis of the measured environmental dimensions did not suggest any incentive for this adaptation, any explanation of this result likely falls beyond the scope of the environmental dimensions considered here. With respect to the navigation variable, the result shows that pilots took advantage of the navigation capabilities of the FMC whenever possible. The mean proportion of clearances for which the FMC was used and for which no additional programming was performed was 0.87 with a standard deviation of 0.17. This result shows that pilots were indeed preprogramming the FMC when possible and exploiting the most efficient execution times for the FMC shown in the plot in Figure 14.6.

Time Constraints

The time constraints associated with the clearances reliably accounted for a small portion of pilots' choices with respect to both outcome variables: $\beta = 0.101$, $p < 0.0004$ for the control variable, and $\beta = 0.069$, $p < 0.002$ for the navigation variable. Because the time required to respond to a clearance was shown to be determined mainly by how pilots

choose to handle the navigation task, I fail to account for why pilots preferred to assume responsibility for the control task when operating under demanding time constraints. The unexpectedly small size of the effect on the navigation variable is perhaps best explained in terms of the predictability dimension. Recall from Figure 14.6 that the time required to use the FMC depends on whether pilots are able to reasonably anticipate upcoming clearances. When clearances have been programmed in advance, the time required to use the autopilot and FMC both fall comfortably within the time constraints. Only in less predictable sectors do the two resources begin to differ. However, perhaps due to the futility of preprogramming clearances into the FMC when they are unlikely to occur, I observed that the FMC is generally avoided in low-predictability sectors. Thus, a more parsimonious explanation is possible that makes no mention of time constraints: Pilots take advantage of the FMC in predictable sectors and resort to the autopilot in unpredictable sectors that preclude the use of the FMC.

Number of Clearances per Sector

The average number of clearances issued per sector reliably accounted for a sizable portion of the variation along both outcome variables: $\beta = 0.335$, $p < 0.0001$ for the control variable, and $\beta = 0.26$, $p < 0.0001$ for the navigation variable. When operating in the busiest sectors, pilots chose to turn the servomechanisms off and assume responsibility for the attention-demanding control task. Again, pilots' decisions about how to perform the control task is unexplained by the five environmental dimensions. With respect to the navigation variable, pilots opted to perform the navigation task manually, using the autopilot, in sectors associated with high numbers of clearances. Because high numbers of clearances were highly correlated with unpredictability, it is not clear whether pilots avoided the FMC because of the time-consuming interactions it requires, their own inability to anticipate future portions of the flight route, or a combination of these and/or other pressures not considered here.

Number of Clearances Issued at Once

The number of clearances issued at once did not reliably predict either of the control or navigation variables. Recall that when several clearances are issued at once, no special time provisions are given.

All clearances must be executed roughly in the time allotted for a single clearance. The results suggests that pilots' responses to clearances may not be sensitive to the single/multiple-clearance distinction. Rather, pilots may associate a general probability of being issued multiple clearances at once within a sector, and handle all clearances in the same way. Conversely, when a single clearance is issued in a sector characteristic of multiple clearances, offering pilots the opportunity to exploit a few free seconds, they generally do not bother with it.

Discussion

A number of generalizations about the way pilots choose to solve the flight path management problem are suggested by the results. With respect to the navigation task, the results suggest a scenario in which pilots prefer to delegate navigation responsibilities to the FMC whenever possible but are often faced with environmental conditions that are unfriendly toward its use. The observation that the FMC was consistently used when future clearances could be anticipated and when time constraints could be met (and was not used when they could not) casts a strong vote for such a scenario. It is an open question whether pilots' general preference for automating this higher level task stems from a more global plan about how to manage one's problem-solving efforts, convention, or factors yet to be identified.

With respect to the guidance task, the record of pilots' responses to the clearances shows that pilots unanimously opted to use automated flight control resources in almost every case. Even when pilots performed the control and navigation tasks themselves, an automation resource was almost always used to handle the guidance task. Consequently, few instances of strictly manual flight were observed.

With respect to the control task, although the five measured dimensions of the environment predicted modest portions of the variance, they seem to offer little explanation of why this occurred. In fact, the observation that pilots prefer to assume responsibility for the attention-demanding control task in the busiest sectors seems counterintuitive in some ways. One possible explanation is that manually performing the control task allows pilots to initiate a control response at the same time that they are assigning the guidance or navigation task to an automation resource. This allows the aircraft to move in the general direction prescribed by a

clearance a few seconds before the guidance commands appear on the flight director. A related explanation is that pilots may prefer to be closer to the control of the aircraft during crucial phases of flight, prepared to respond in the shortest time to any unexpected events that might transpire. A third explanation is that because the busy sectors are the most challenging phases of the flight, pilots exploit the opportunity to sharpen their control skills.

Conclusions

I have considered the question of how problem-solving behavior is influenced by the features of the environment in which the behavior is observed. Exploratory statistical methods were used to profile the features of a single complex environment: flight operations between two California cities. A number of hypotheses were made about how pilots' choices about how to manage the flight path of the aircraft might be adapted to the measured features of the environment. A record of pilots' behavior aboard 16 airline flights was compared to the profile of the environment to test the extent to which problem-solving behavior was adapted to the environment. The results suggest a process by which pilots repeatedly fly a particular flight route, extract a set of useful specifics about that flight route, and use this information to devise strategies that are tuned to the environmental demands. It is important to note that the statistical profiles of the two routes between San Francisco and Los Angeles are in no way claimed to be a general characterization of other flight routes. What we can speculate to be generalizable between environments is this: that each flight route has its own set of signature features, patterns, of regularities that manifest themselves in the particulars of the problems that pilots are asked to solve. As in the case of the California routes, pilots must certainly fly through them, learn their subtle lessons, and put them to use.

One potential benefit of the approach to studying behavior with respect to the details of the environment is that it may offer a quantitative basis for the design of task (and training) environments. For example, the statistical profiles of both the ATC and flight control resource environment can be used in a straightforward manner to arrive at a set of quantitative design specifications for a more attractive flight management computer. This is accomplished by considering the environmental dimensions that have been shown to influence pilots' decisions. For example, from the plot of time constraints and execution times shown in Figure 14.6, one can see that the FMC loses much of its appeal because of the lengthy interactions required when operating in unpredictable situations. I can hypothesize that if I shorten these interaction times to make them competitive with the interaction times offered by the autopilot, then the FMC might become a more likely candidate for choice.

Because pilots' behavior was demonstrated to be partly a product of the ATC environment, it follows that changes could also be instituted by manipulating the ATC environment itself. That is, changes could be made in the statistical patterns of variation in the clearances issued by ATC. A group at NASA has developed an algorithm that prescribes small but well-planned adjustments in the speeds of incoming aircraft before they reach the airport terminal area (Erzberger & Nedell, 1989). Better separation between aircraft once they arrive in the vicinity of the airport means that fewer heading and altitude clearances are needed to work the aircraft down to the ground. The net effect from the pilots' perspective is fewer clearances being issued and a greater regularity among clearances.

References

Brunswik, E. (1943). Organismic achievement and environmental probability. Psychological Review, 50(3), 255–272.

Bulfer, B. (1991). FMC user's guide. Kingwood, Tex.: Technical Publications.

Card, S. K., Moran, T. P., & Newell, A. (1983). *The psychology of human–computer interaction*. Hillsdale, N.J.: Erlbaum.

Casner, S. M. (2001). *The pilot's guide to the modern airline cockpit*. Ames: Iowa State University Press.

Erzberger, H., & Nedell, W. (1989). Design of automated system for management of arrival traffic. (Technical Memorandum 102201). Washington, D.C.: NASA.

Gibson, J. J. (1979). *The ecological approach to visual perception*. Boston: Houghton-Mifflin.

Hursch, C. J., Hammond, K. R., & Hursch, J. L. (1964). Some methodological considerations in multiple-cue probability studies. *Psychological Review, 71*, 42–60.

John, B. E. (1988). *Contributions to engineering models of human-computer interaction*. Unpublished doctoral dissertation. Department of Psychology, Carnegie Mellon University, Pittsburgh, Penn.

Kirlik, A. (1993). Modeling strategic behavior in human-automation interaction: Why an aid can (and should) go unused. *Human Factors, 35*, 221–242.

McRuer, D., Ashkenas, I., & Graham, D. (1973). *Aircraft dynamics and automatic control*. Princeton, N.J.: Princeton University Press.

Schooler, L. J., & Anderson, J. R. (1991). Does memory reflect statistical regularity in the environment? In *Proceedings of the 12th Annual Meeting of the Cognitive Science Society* (pp. 227–232). Chicago: Cognitive Science Society.

Shannon, C. E., & Weaver, W. (1949). *The mathematical theory of communication*. Urbana: University of Illinois Press.

Simon, H. A. (1981). *The sciences of the artificial* (2nd ed.). Cambridge, Mass.: MIT Press.

Tolman, E.C., & Brunswik, E. (1935). The organism and the causal texture of the environment. *Psychological Review, 42*, 43–77.

15

Alex Kirlik

Abstracting Situated Action: Implications for Cognitive Modeling and Interface Design

If perceptivity and curiosity are indeed critical for scientific progress, why don't we in the behavioral sciences teach our students to keep their eyes peeled?
—Frans de Waal, *The Ape and the Sushi Master* (2001, p. 186)

Introduction

Perhaps no event in the history of the social and behavioral sciences has prompted a greater interest in field-based observational studies of human cognition and behavior than the widespread introduction of information technology into the human ecology. Recall, for example, that the human–computer interaction (HCI) discipline was originally conceived by Card, Moran, & Newell (1983) as largely a laboratory science based on experimental psychology and cognitive modeling methods. It did not take long, however, before it became widely recognized that the psychological and design issues amenable to study with such techniques, although certainly important, where nevertheless relatively narrow in scope compared to the demands of understanding and supporting interaction with realistically complex computer applications, distributed networks, and the social, organizational and cultural factors surrounding their use (Carroll, 1991; Carroll & Campbell, 1989; Klein & Calderwood, 1991; Olson & Olson, 1991; Rasmussen, 1990; Suchman, 1987). In turn, these concerns have led to the development of diverse conceptual frameworks and methods focused on broadening the domain of inquiry in human–technology interaction,

largely eschewing the confines of the laboratory and instead promoting the importance of field research (e.g., Beyer & Holtzblatt, 1998; Cole, 1996; Dourish, 2001; Hollnagel, 2003; Hutchins, 1995; Kirsh, 2001; Militello & Hutton, 1998; Nardi, 1996; Suchman, 2000; Vicente, 1999; Woods, 2003).

Currently, however, a somewhat tenuous relationship remains between the largely descriptive, field-oriented perspectives and methods advocated by many of the authors just mentioned (e.g., activity theory, distributed cognition, situated cognition, cognitive task analysis, and ethnomethodology, among others) and the normative task of providing concrete prescriptions for design (e.g., Hughes, Randall, & Shapiro, 1992; Vicente, 1999). To take one illustrative example, in a previous review of Suchman's (1987) insightful field study of why a photocopier's "help" system was far from helpful, I commented that the design implications of that research were far from clear (Kirlik, 1998). Although Suchman's study clearly demonstrated that user interaction with the copier's "intelligent" help system was problematic, little in the way of concrete, normative guidance for how one might have improved the copier's design resulted from that work.

In reality, my observations were far from original: They merely echoed the reactions of many of the graduate students in my cognitive engineering and human factors courses over the years in response to analyzing Suchman's (1987) study. When asked by the engineering psychology and human factors majors in my classes if Suchman's work implied that user interaction could have been better enhanced by a revamping of the copier's interface (display and control) design according to accepted human factors principles (instead of by adding a computerized help system), I could only say "possibly." When asked by the computer science and engineering majors if the study instead implied that the intelligent help system was simply not intelligent enough, again, "possibly" was the best answer I could give. Of course, this should not be read in any way as an indictment of Suchman's study, which has been important in highlighting the intimate rather than abstracted nature of much (successful) human–technology interaction, a contribution providing some design guidance at a conceptual level. All I mean to emphasize here is that the high levels of descriptive richness or "thickness" (Geertz, 1973) to which many largely observational approaches to the study of technological work aspire provide no built-in guarantee that the resulting descriptions will provide prescriptive resources for informing design (see Anderson, Simon, & Reder, 1997, who have made a similar point in relation to the implications of the situated perspective for education).

Abstracting Fluent Practice

What might be the design implications of the realization that many if not most successful cases of adaptive cognition and behavior involve an intimate interplay between humans, technologies, and their environments of use? Because there are surely many answers to this question, my aim in this chapter is not to provide any single answer but instead a methodology for addressing this question in practically meaningful terms. In particular, I hope that the field study, functional analysis, and modeling presented will demonstrate a number of points:

1. Observational studies of behavior in relatively unmediated, low-technology settings have the ability to provide unique insights into design that may not be available from studying high-technology settings. In particular, the possible contributions to high

levels of adaptation and fluency provided by relatively direct perception–action access to the environment are not likely to be observable in situations where interaction is already highly mediated by information technology.

2. Formal, functional analysis and modeling can complement what is learned through purely qualitative research by providing potentially more generalizable insights into design than do purely context-bound approaches. Such modeling can show not only *that* context matters but also precisely *how* it matters.

3. The type of task analysis required for functional modeling of interactive cognition and behavior can inform cognitive theory and modeling by specifying how perception, central processes, action, and the environment itself can collectively share the overall burden for cognitive performance.

4. In interactive tasks, a performer may draw on both adaptation *to* the environment and adaptation *of* the environment in an integrated, seamless fashion to achieve task goals while keeping cognitive workload at manageable levels.

5. For technological interfaces mediating a performer's interaction with a task environment, it is possible, if not probable, that both display and control design should considered simultaneously and in a mutually informing way to promote the high levels of fluency often characteristic of unmediated interaction.

In the following, I first present the observational study that served as the empirical foundation for these claims. I then present an approach for abstracting and modeling the observed behavioral situation by creating a quantitative realization of the original lens model framework presented by Tolman & Brunswik (1935). This quantitative model can be considered an extension of Brunswik's traditional lens model (see Goldstein, chapter 2) to include resources for describing the ecology's proximal–distal means–ends relations in addition to its proximal–distal cue–criterion relations. These two classes of relations map directly onto, respectively, Norman's (1988) concepts of the "gulf of execution" (i.e., bridging the gap between an intended—distal—effect on the world and whatever actions are readily available) and the "gulf of evaluation" (i.e., bridging the gap between whatever perceptual information is directly available and covert—distal—states or properties of the world). As such, the approach allows adaptation to both forms of proximal–distal structure to be examined simultaneously and in a common framework. Historically, these phenomena have largely been dealt with in isolation (e.g., adaptation to cue–criterion relations in the study of judgment using Brunswik's lens model; adaptation to means–ends relations in the study of problem solving using such models as Newell and Simon's [1972] general problem solver).

Importantly, the approach developed in this chapter allows one to investigate how action may play an epistemic, or knowledge-granting role as well as a performatory role in the execution of interactive tasks. Although the interdependency of perception and action is a fundamental tenet of Gibson's (1962, 1966) ecological approach, this notion has arrived on the scene in cognitive science only more recently. Traditionally, most cognitive scientists have largely viewed the action system purely in its performatory light, as a mechanism devoted solely to moving the world toward desirable states (e.g., see Newell, 1992). Here, action makes no contribution to cognition other than to execute commands that are handed down by some sort of central executive.

More recently, however, a few cognitive scientists have begun to become interested in how people use action to structure their worlds to apparently simplify their cognitive tasks. For example, Kirsh & Maglio (1994) distinguished epistemic from "pragmatic" action. They illustrated this distinction by showing how one component of skill in the Tetris video game involved taking actions to gain more reliable perceptual information from the video display. Additionally, Kirsh (1995) described a number of everyday situations (e.g., grocery bagging, salad preparation) in which he observed people taking actions to simplify choice, perception, and reduce demands for internal computation through the effective use of spatial organization. Spatial structuring can also play a key role in intellectual development as well as in everyday activities. For example, Piaget (1974) observed that during mathematical learning children often arrange objects in rows or columns, demonstrating a "need to manipulate concrete things in order to understand structures which are otherwise too abstract" (p. 92). He introduced the phrase "pseudoempirical abstraction" to describe "a reading of the objects involved, but a reading which

is really concerned with properties due to the action of the subject himself" (p. 92). The following field investigation, which I originally conceived as a study of skilled (internal) memory, quickly turned instead into a study of "a reading of the objects" in an environment, where this reading "is really concerned with properties due to the action of the subject himself."

A Field Study of Short-Order Cooking

In fact, the animal does not merely adapt to the environment, but constantly adapts the environment to itself . . . turning "noise" into "information."
—Arthur Koestler, *The Act of Creation* (1964)

I made observations of the behavior of short-order cooks at a diner. In busy periods, these cooks may be responsible for preparing a large number of food orders, each with a large number of component items, simultaneously. Task demands are uncertain and arrive dynamically. Here I concentrate on the strategies I observed for how both relatively inexperienced and highly experienced cooks managed cooking meat (hamburger patties) on a grill.

At any time, the cook could have up to 10 or 15 pieces of meat on the grill: Each was to be cooked to a specified degree (e.g., rare, well done). I observed the following three strategies for performing this task. The latter, more sophisticated strategies were typically (though not always) associated with increasingly experienced cooks (the transmission of these strategies among cooks was evident but not a focus of the present study). Additionally, although some cooks used a single strategy regardless of workload, other cooks appeared to switch among strategies as a function of workload (an example of Brunswik's concept of vicarious functioning at work—see chapter 2).

- *Brute Force Strategy.* Place pieces of meat on the grill in apparently random locations. Attempt to remember how each piece of meat should be cooked. Periodically check and recheck the degree to which the underside of each piece of meat is cooked. Flip meats at the appropriate degree of doneness. Continue this process for the second side of each piece of meat. Take meat off the grill at the appropriate degree of doneness.
- *Position Control Strategy.* Place pieces of meat in an area of the grill associated with how

well each piece of meat should be cooked (left for rare, middle for medium, right for well done). Use location information to better implement a method closely corresponding to the Brute Force Strategy.

- *Position + Velocity Control Strategy.* Place meats in an area of the grill associated with how well each piece of meat should be cooked (the rear of the grill for well done, the middle of the grill for medium, the front of the grill for rare). In addition, within these horizontal slices of the grill, place meat to be cooked well done at the far right side of the grill, place meat to be cooked medium at the center of the grill, and place meat to be cooked rare toward the left side of the grill. Finally, as the meat is cooking, and interspersed with other food preparation tasks, intermittently slide all pieces of meat toward the left side of the grill to induce an approximately fixed velocity of meat movement toward the left. Flip meat at the midpoint of its journey across the grill. Remove meat when is reaches the left boundary of the grill.

These strategic behaviors are of course highly specific to this particular task environment. However, when viewed abstractly, they illustrate how action strategies, by exploiting sources of latent constraint in the behavior of the human–environment system, are capable of giving rise to information to support more efficient control of the environment. Note that all three strategies are (approximately) functionally equivalent: To the extent they are implemented satisfactorily, each cook will succeed at the task. Note, however, that the cognitive demands associated with implementing the various strategies are quite different. In the following section, I present a detailed functional analysis of this behavioral situation in terms of a mathematical formulation of Tolman and Brunswik's (1935) original, perception–action formulation of the lens model.

Modeling Situated Action: A Functional Approach

Any ecological analysis and modeling approach to understanding adaptive cognition and behavior, whether it be in the tradition of Brunswik, Gibson, or their followers, begins with a detailed analysis

of the "causal texture" of the environment (see chapter 2).

Constraint and Latent Constraint

What we typically consider to be normally available sources of perceptual information exist due to the presence of constraint between a perceptible variable and some other environmental variable whose value is specified to some degree by the perceptible variable. This is true whether we are considering natural environments (e.g., smoke likely means fire) or artificial ones (e.g., the sound of a smoke alarm likely means the presence of smoke and fire). Runeson (1977) has described such constraints as "grantors of information" in that constraint causes variables to covary and thus carry information about each other's values. Sources of information produced by epistemic action differ from these normally available sources only in their origin, not in their manner of functioning as information sources.

Specifically, I consider epistemic action to result from exploiting *latent constraint* in the human–environment system. This additional constraint grants additional information, in Runeson's (1977) sense of the term. For example, a child shaking a gift-wrapped birthday present to try to identify its contents takes actions causing variables relating to the contents of the package to covary with perceptible acoustic and kinesthetic variables. Prior to shaking, there is no active constraint between these hidden and overt variables causing them to carry information about each other. Shaking the package activates a constraint only previously latent between the contents of the package and its dynamical properties. Similarly, a driver often puts new car "through its paces" because the constraints active during normal, more reserved driving do not produce the perceptual information necessary to specify the dynamics of the automobile when driven under more severe conditions. In short, I view the role of epistemic action to be exploiting latent constraint in the behavior of a human–environment system, causing proximal perceptual variable values to covary with and thus carry information about the values of distal environmental variables.

Environmental Modeling Approach

To get more precise, this conceptualization suggests a functionalist modeling perspective and an environmental description in terms of dynamic variable values. In addition, a distinction is needed between variable values that can be directly perceptually obtained and variable values that cannot. In the history of psychology this distinction has been variously expressed in terms of the proximal versus the distal, the overt versus the covert, or the environmental surface versus the environmental depth. I do not intend to refine or contribute to an understanding of this distinction but instead use it heuristically. The purpose of a given modeling and analysis effort will determine what variables should be considered proximal and distal. A particular variable (e.g., the velocity of an automobile) could be described as proximal if the purpose of a study was to understand how a driver might use velocity to infer less readily available information relating to a vehicular control task (e.g., whether he or she can make a given turn safely). In other cases, velocity could be considered a distal variable if the goal of the effort was to understand how velocity itself was estimated on the basis of even more immediate perceptual information (e.g., optical flow patterns, speedometer readings, etc.). In short, environmental variables do not arrive to an analysis neatly sorted into proximal and distal categories but are always categorized in a relative fashion based on observing which variables seem to be used as the basis for inferring the values of other variables.

Brunswik (1956) used the proximal versus distal distinction in his functional representation of human perception and judgment known as the lens model (see chapter 2). The lens model provides a useful starting point for developing a modeling framework for situated action for a number of reasons. First, it distinguishes between directly available, proximal information and the distal objects, properties or events that must be inferred on the basis of this information. Second, it embodies the notion of information arising out of constraint—in this case, constraint existing between the values of proximal cues and distal objects, properties or events. Third, it reflects a functional orientation portraying an image of a performer as seeking to adapt to the environmental structure with which it is faced. Performance is deemed to be successful not when it meets some artificially stated criteria or task instruction but rather when it is adaptive to the goals and environmental structure it faces.

Beyond Passive Adaptation

One deficiency of the traditional lens model is that it portrays a view of the organism without any control over the environmental structure to which it must adapt. This is because there are no resources within that model to describe how an organism might use action to adapt the environment given its own needs and capacities for action. Adding such resources requires elaborating the lens model with resources describing the proximal–distal structure of action, in addition to the proximal–distal structure of perception (see Kirlik, 1995, for a more elaborate treatment of this issue). An action-based proximal versus distal distinction is directly analogous to its perceptual counterpart. I consider variables to be proximal from the perspective of action if the performer can directly manipulate their values. In contrast, I consider variables to be distal from the perspective of action if their values cannot be so changed but instead can be changed only by manipulating proximal variables over which the performer has more direct control. As was the case with the proximal versus distal distinction concerning perception, the distinction between proximal and distal action variables is here used heuristically and in a relative fashion. Only the purpose of a given study can determine which environmental variables should be considered proximal and distal from the perspective of action.

Elaborating the *environmental* components of lens model in this manner results in the framework for environmental description shown in Figure 15.1, which could be considered to be a generalization of the lens model to include resources to describe the action status of environmental variables. As discussed in Kirlik (1995), however, this so-called generalization is actually more faithful to Tolman and Brunswik's (1935) original conception of the lens model than is the more familiar version widely used in judgment and decision making research. As Hammond (2001) has discussed, Tolman and Brunswik were motivated to collaborate on their article by noting the symmetry between Brunswik's interest in the multiple, potentially fallible pathways between cues and a criterion in perception and Tolman's interest in the multiple, potentially fallible pathways between means and ends in goal-oriented action and learning. The fact that only "half" the original conceptual version of the lens

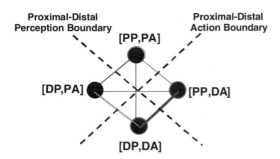

Figure 15.1. A functional model of the ecology for perception and action.

model became formalized as a tool for judgment and decision-making (J/DM) research reflected a strategic decision as to what constituted the proper domain of inquiry for the J/DM discipline. As such, the action side of Tolman and Brunswik's original conception of the lens model has not received nearly as much attention as the perceptual or judgment side. However, J/DM theorists with interests in interactive settings such as Connolly (1988) and Hogarth (1981) have more recently suggested that it may be necessary to bring action back into the J/DM picture, if not into the lens model proper.

Whereas the environmental component of the traditional lens model has two types of variables (proximal and distal) and one constraint relationship between them, the generalization shown in Figure 15.1 has four types of variables and six types of constraint relationships among these variables. The four new variable types are Type I [PP,PA]: a variable that is proximal from the perspective of both perception and action; Type II [PP,DA]: a variable that is proximal for perception but distal for action; Type III [DP,PA]: a variable that is distal for perception yet proximal for action; and Type IV [DP,DA]: a variable that is distal for both perception and action. Constraint relationships can potentially exist between any of these classes of variables, as indicated by the six lines connecting the four variable types in the figure. The fact that the elaborated environmental model depicted in Figure 15.1 is actually a direct generalization of the traditional lens model's environmental component is also apparent in the figure: the traditional lens model environmental component consists of the right [PP,DA] and bottom [DP,DA] variable types plus the single highlighted line joining them (i.e., the traditional model represents passive judgment).

An Ontology of Variable Types

The generalized framework provides an ontology for describing an environment of a performer engaged in interactive activity. In actuality the performer is surrounded by a world of surfaces, objects, events, and artifacts, but we can often describe the state of this world in terms of variable values. In addition, note that a variable value can be one of four types. Type I [PP,PA] variables are perhaps the most common to phenomenal experience as they best describe the here and now. The location of the book you are now reading can most likely be represented by variables of this type: Most of us can directly manipulate the values of these variables by hand and arm movements, and we can also perceive the location of the book directly. One can think of these variables as representing Gibson's (1979) directly perceptible affordances.

Type II [PP,DA] variables are directly available to perception but can only have their values changed by manipulating proximal variables that via constraints existing in the environment cause changes in the values of distal action variables. It may be easy for you to directly feel that it is cold in your room, but you cannot manipulate temperature directly. Instead, you must manipulate a proximal action variable, perhaps the knob on a thermostat, to eventually change room temperature.

Type III [DP,PA] variables can be directly manipulated but not directly perceived. These variables are experienced relatively infrequently because our perceptual world, considered spatiotemporally, normally envelops the portions of the world we can directly manipulate. When I am sitting at my desk, my perceptual world extends throughout the room, out the windows to the skyline, and to the nearby traffic that I cannot see but I can nonetheless hear. The world on which I can directly act, however, is limited at the present time to a portion of space within a meter or so of my desk. It is rare that my perceptual world does not envelop my world of action due the presence of distal senses such as vision and audition and an associated lack of distal action capacities. However, a great many of my actions change the values of environmental variables I cannot directly perceive. For example, when posing for a photograph I change the location of my image in the viewfinder of a camera without being able to perceive how it has been changed. I have to rely on the photographer for this information.

Type IV [DP,DA] variables can be neither directly perceived nor acted on. These variables are very common anytime our interaction with the world is mediated by technology. We infer the values of these variables from interface displays, and we change the values of these variables by using interface controls. Norman's (1988) concepts of the gulf of evaluation and gulf of execution were invented to describe the challenges we sometimes face in using the proximal perceptual and action variables we have immediately available to infer and alter the values of the distal variables which are typically the true target of our interaction.

Mathematical Model

A rigorous understanding of adaptive, situated behavior requires quantification of the degree of constraint between variables in a dynamic system. This is required to identify whether an environment supports epistemic action, and also to describe the functional role of epistemic action and how to measure its cognitive contribution in any particular case.

System Description

I conceive of a task environment or controlled system, as one can conceive of any system, as a set of variables $S = (X_1, X_2, \ldots X_n)$. A set-theoretic description of a system is this set of variables plus a relation defined over this set. For a dynamic system, one can view the system as the progression of X values over time. For my purposes, I would like to be able to find a way to measure the degree of constraint within a system; that is, the degree to which the system variables covary over time or the degree to which knowledge of a particular variable (or particular set of variables) is informative about the values of the remaining variables in the system. Measuring constraint relationships is important because the role of epistemic action has been conceived in terms of a performer taking action exploiting latent constraint among system variables to cause proximal variables to carry information about the values of distal variables.

The generalized lens model for environmental description suggests that perceptual variables can be decomposed into proximal or surface variables whose values can be directly observed, and distal or depth variables whose values must be inferred from the surface variables. Given a measure of constraint among system variables, one can then measure the various degrees to which surface variables specify depth variables as a function of the trajectories of those variables over time. In particular, I would like to measure the differing degrees to which surface variables provide information about depth variables as a function of the different action strategies used to control a dynamic system.

Entropy and Multidimensional Information

For this purpose, I employ N-dimensional information theory, or NDIT (Ashby, 1965; McGill, 1954). NDIT is a generalization of information theory to systems with multiple variables. In NDIT, one generalizes the common $H(x)$ information measure to $H(S)$, which is the uncertainty of system S conceiving S as a single vector variable. This is done straightforwardly by viewing s as a particular element (state) of S and viewing $p(s)$ as the probability distribution of the n-tuples of S. $H(S)$ is then a measure of the uncertainty within S or the entropy of S, or conversely, a measure of the degree of constraint within S.

Specifically, I would like to measure the degree to which a particular subsystem of S corresponding to the (observable) surface variables in S is informative about the complementary subsystem of S composed of the (unobservable) depth variables in S. To do this, I use the notion of *conditional entropy*. Any system S can be partitioned into arbitrary subsystems, $S_1, S_2, \ldots S_n$. In this case, I can partition S into two mutually exclusive and collectively exhaustive subsystems S_P and S_D, corresponding to the proximal perceptual and distal perceptual variables in S, respectively. The concept of conditional entropy allows me to measure the average amount of uncertainty about a particular subsystem of S that remains for one who knows the variable values of a complementary subsystem of S. In this case, I can write $S = (S_P, S_D)$ to indicate that the system S is made up of the subsystems S_P and S_D. I can also write $H_{S_P}(S_D)$ as the conditional entropy of S_D given S_P: that is, the average uncertainty about the variables in S_D given knowledge of the variables in S_P.

Conveniently, it is known that for any partitioning of S into subsystems S_1 and S_2,

$$H_{S1}(S_2) = H(S_1, S_2) - H(S_1)$$

$$= H(S) - H(S_1).$$

Thus, $H_{S1}(S_2) = 0$ if the variables in subsystem S_2 are completely determined by the variables in subsystem S_1. This result can be generalized to any number of subsystems for an arbitrary partitioning of S using an entropy chain rule. For my purposes, I am seeking to measure $H_{Sp}(S_D) = H(S) - H(S_P)$, which indicates, given a particular trajectory of the variables in the system S over time, the degree to which the surface variables are informative about the depth variables. Given actual streams of behavioral data corresponding to each of the system variables, and a particular partitioning of system variables into S_P and S_D, one can then readily compute a quantitative scalar measure of the degree to which proximal variables specify distal variables. Recall that for my purposes, I am especially interested in how this measure differs as a function of the action strategy used to control the system S.

Analysis and Modeling of the Cooking Case

Using x and y to indicate a Cartesian coordinate system for the rectangular grill (x measuring the left–right position, and y measuring the near–far position), one can model this behavioral situation in terms of the generalized lens model framework, as shown in Figure 15.2. The x and y positions (Meat(x, y) in Figure 15.2) of a particular piece of meat are Type I [PP,PA] variables because they can be both directly manipulated and perceived. In contrast, the doneness of the top side of a piece of meat (Meat (Dtop)) in the figure) is a Type II [PP, DA] variable because it can be directly perceived but not directly manipulated (one must flip the meat so the opposite side rests on the grill surface and wait a specified period of time to manipulate its doneness). Finally, two Type IV [DP,DA] variables present in the cook's task environment, indicated by Meat(Dbot, Dreq) in the figure, can neither be directly manipulated nor directly perceived. Dbot represents the doneness of a piece of meat's bottom side, whereas Dreq represents the required doneness of the meat specified by the customer's order (rare, medium, well done). Given this description, one can intuitively see that the different grilling strategies (associated with manipulating the proximal action variables Meat(x, y)) cause different amounts of constraint to exist between meat positions and the distal, criterion Meat(Dbot, Dreq) variables that the cook must know and control to successfully perform the task.

To make these intuitions more precise, the next step is to describe the three strategies in terms of the constraint induced by each strategy between the position of a piece of meat (the proximal variables) and the degree to which its underside has been cooked and the required doneness specified by the customer's order (the distal variables). In the following, x_0 and y_0 indicate initial conditions for the position of a piece of meat on the grill, and $xdot$ and $ydot$ indicate rates of change of position or velocity. $I(x)$ or $I(y)$ is used as a categorical indicator variable over x or y. For example, $I(x)$ might = 0, 1, or 2 to capture the left, center, or right side of the grill.

The entries in Table 15.1 describe each of the three strategies in terms of specified variable values for $x0$, $xdot$, $y0$, and $ydot$. For the Brute Force strategy, note the only constraint on these variables is that initial meat position must be on the grill and that no movements of the meats are made. The Position Control strategy is similar, except for the fact that the indicator function $I1$ constrains the initial x location of a piece of meat to be a function of "order," which is a variable indicating whether the meat is to be cooked rare, medium, or well done. For the Position + Velocity control strategy, the initial x location of the piece of meat is also a function of the meat order (but a different function, $I2$), the velocity of the meat is some constant movement toward the left side of the grill, and the initial y position of the meat is some other ($I3$) indicator function of meat order.

The reader should compare these variable values to the qualitative descriptions of the three strategies to verify that the table entries do indeed describe the behaviors observed. In addition, note

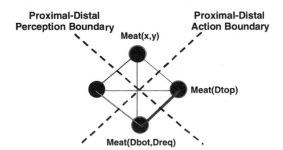

Figure 15.2. Variable types relevant to the cooking analysis and modeling.

Table 15.1. Mathematical description of the action variable constrained in the three cooking strategies

Variable	Cooking Strategy		
	Brute Force	Position Control	Post + Velocity Control
$x0$	$xmin < x0 < xmax$	$I1$(order)	$I2$(order)
$xdot$	0	0	$xdot$ = constant
$y0$	$ymin < y0 > ymax$	$ymin < y0 < ymax$	$I3$(order)
$ydot$	0	0	0

that no observed strategies involved manipulating $ydot$, and that in general, the observed strategies occupy a very small region of the space of possible strategies associated with just these four controlled variables. The reader is invited to invent novel strategies by trying out other possible sets of variable values (e.g., a commonly used strategy in home grilling is to place a piece of meat that is ready to come off the grill before other meats have been cooked sufficiently on top of the latter to keep the former from being overcooked yet warm; this would require adding a z or height dimension to the analysis).

I now consider how well the surface variable values (trajectories for x and y over time) inform the cook about the distal variable of interest in this case (the degree to which the underside of a piece of meat is cooked). If I had actual data at this fine grain of observation available from the diner observed, I could use NDIT and the concept of conditional entropy to quantitatively measure this quantity of information. However, such information was not available. I therefore created a computer simulation of this human–environment system, based on simple and plausible functional models of the cook, the grill, and the meats to generate streams of behavioral data to use for such an analysis.

Simulation and Entropy Analysis

I wrote a discrete event simulation of the cook–meat–grill system that modeled meat order arrival times according to the Poisson distribution. Meat order (rare, medium, well) was a uniformly distributed random variable. The meat was modeled by incrementing its cooked state (per side) as a simple linear function of time plus Gaussian noise. Each strategy was modeled according to the information in the table below, that is, as a dynamic system governed by difference equations.

For the Brute Force strategy, initial meat location was uniformly distributed in both x and y, and the meat did not move while cooking. For the Position Control strategy, it was assumed no errors were made in the initial x placement of the meat (left, middle, or right) as a function of the amount of cooking required (rare, medium, or well). In addition, for the Position Control strategy the initial y location of the meat was uniformly distributed on the grill surface, and no motion of the meat was produced while cooking. For the Position + Velocity control strategy, the initial x position was a simple function of desired cooking time (right, medium, left) plus a small amount of Gaussian noise used to mimic the inability of the cook to always perfectly place a meat at the exact location necessary. In addition, meat velocity was a constant plus a similarly small amount of Gaussian noise used to mimic the inability of the cook to move meats at a perfectly constant velocity across the grill.

Finally, the simulation contained a simple procedural model of the cook that flipped each piece of meat at the required time and removed each piece of meat from the grill at the required time. One hundred runs of the simulation were performed with different initial seeds for the random number generator. The simulation logged the x and y locations of each piece of meat, along with the degree to which each side of each piece of meat had been cooked at each time step.

The output of the simulation was a stream of variable values for both the surface variables (meat x and y locations) and depth variables (how well the underside of each meat had been cooked and how well cooked it had been ordered). On the basis of simulation output, I first calculated $H(S)$, the entropy of the entire system S containing both proximal perceptual variables S_P and distal variables S_D. I then calculated $H_{SP}(S_D)$, which is the conditional entropy of the distal subsystem of variables

S_D (the doneness levels of the meat undersides and the doneness level specified by the customer's orders) given knowledge of the proximal subsystem of variables S_P (the meat x and y positions). The latter measure indicates how much uncertainty about the doneness of a piece of meat underside and the required doneness specified by an order remains after one has knowledge of the meat's position on the grill.

Results

Figure 15.3 summarizes the total system and conditional entropies of the simulated human-environment system under the three observed cooking strategies. Considering first the entropies of the overall system composed of meat positions and doneness states, that is, $H(S)$, note that this value was highest for the system controlled by the most sophisticated (Position + Velocity) strategy. Although this may be surprising, on reflection the reason is clear. The two simpler (Brute Force and Position) strategies, by constraining meat motion to be zero, resulted in less overall system variability and thus less entropy than did the system controlled via the Position + Velocity strategy. This result is noteworthy in that it provides evidence of a case whereby a more skillfully controlled system has higher overall variability than does a less skillfully controlled system. This variability has been introduced to increase system observability.

Now consider the values of $H_{Sp}(S_D)$, the conditional entropies of the meat doneness variables given knowledge of the meat position variables. Here, I find that these entropies corresponding to the uncertainty the cook would have about meat

doneness progressively decreases as the strategies become more sophisticated (i.e., induce more constraint on system behavior). Thus the most sophisticated strategy, while creating the most variability in the total system, created this variability in the values of observable, proximal variables, which were highly informative about the values of the distal variables. As noted by Koestler (1964), the animal does not merely adapt to the environment, but adapts the environment to itself, "turning noise into information."

The modeling results showed that the cook using the most sophisticated Position + Velocity Control strategy used action to create an environment in which there was little uncertainty about the value of distal, criterion variable values. This cook effectively created a world in which he could work entirely at the surface by exploiting constraints that guaranteed that depth variables would take care of themselves, so to speak. Intuitively, a cook using this strategy would not need to have any internal model of the dynamics of meats cooking on the grill, because his proximal perceptual and action environment contained all the resources needed to effectively perform the task. In the following section I make this intuition more precise by applying a basic result from control theory.

Requisite Variety and External Models

Conant (1969) discussed the law of requisite variety as a way to describe the capabilities a regulating system must have to effectively control a dynamic system. In short, the law of requisite variety states that a controller of a system must model the disturbances being controlled against. Let R be a regulating system and let D be a system of disturbances. Collectively, R and D define a set of outcomes Z, via a function f: $R \times D \to Z$. Given this formulation, the objective of the regulator R is to choose values matched to those of the disturbance D so that outcomes fall in some desirable goal subset G of Z. Taking an everyday example, we could let R be a thermostat plus furnace, D be fluctuating ambient temperature, Z be the temperature of a room controlled by R, and G be the desirable temperature range.

The law of requisite variety states that

Variety of Z > (Variety of D)/(Variety of R).

That is, the regulator R must have sufficient variety (capability to generate a range of control actions)

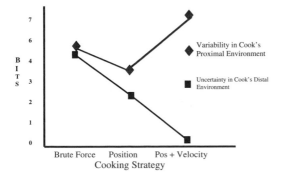

Figure 15.3. Analysis and modeling results from the short-order cook study.

to counteract the variety of the disturbances D. Put another way, the variability of the output of a controlled process can never be less than the ratio of the variety of the disturbances to the variety of the regulation. The furnace example provides an intuitive illustration. If the goal is to keep a room at a constant temperature, the required capabilities of the thermostat-plus-furnace (regulating) system are determined by the range of external temperatures (disturbances) the regulating system must counteract. Conant interpreted this result to demonstrate that the regulator or controller must in some sense model the disturbances.

Requisite Variety in the Cooking Case

Consider an application of the law of requisite variety to the grilling example. In this case a cook (with his control strategy) is the regulator R. The process of the grill cooking a piece of meat is the disturbance D. The dynamic meat doneness state is the output Z. The goal states G are the required doneness levels specified by the customer's order.

By the law of requisite variety, the cook as the regulator R must in some sense model the process of the grill cooking a piece of meat. Take the example of a cook using the Brute Force strategy who also does not use any actions to check the undersides of the meats as they are cooking. Also assume this cook is always successful in cooking meats to order, that is, to their goal states G. Clearly we have to assume in this case that the cook has developed and is using an internal model of the rate of meat cooking on the grill that he can use in lieu of perceptual information. Here, the cook as regulator is modeling the disturbances D in the form of an internal model.

Now consider a cook using the Position + Velocity Control strategy. By the law of requisite variety, this cook too must have a model of the rate of meat cooking on the grill. What kind of model has this cook developed? Figure 15.4 is a depiction of meat cooking on the grill as controlled by the Position + Velocity strategy. As the meats are cooked they are moved steadily leftward on the grill surface. As such, there is variability in the positions of the meat on the grill surface commensurate with the variability of the doneness states of the meat. It follows that we can therefore consider this cook's *grill area itself* to be a model of the dynamics of meat cooking on the grill. Creating this external, perceptible model obviates the need to rely on an internal

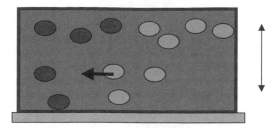

Figure 15.4. The grill as it appears when controlled by the Position + Velocity cooking strategy.

model with the same information content. This example demonstrates not only how situated action is capable of creating novel information sources but also how it may even aid in actually modeling the covert dynamics of a task environment.

Discussion

Yet another device for seeing differently would be to consider higher-status kinds of work with the insights gained through blue collar study.
  —Mike Rose, *The Mind at Work* (2004, p. 147)

This chapter began with a question posed by primatologist Frans de Waal, asking why behavioral scientists frequently fail to emphasize to their students the value of naturalistic observation. One answer to this question is that our conceptual and cultural categories are so constraining that one often has to first invent a way of literally "seeing differently" to observe or discover anything novel. The need to learn this lesson is hardly new to anthropologists, but it may present considerable barriers to those trained in other traditions or forms of inquiry. In the epigraph for this section, educational theorist Mike Rose offers one such tactic for breathing fresh air into the large and growing area of naturalistic and observational studies of technology-based work. One thing is certain about the hairstylists, waitresses, plumbers, welders, and carpenters who serve as the focus of Rose's (2004) book. Lacking symbolic information technologies mediating their direct interaction with the objects of work, these workers often spoke of the difficulty of mastering their tools and trades, but they rarely complained of suffering from the characteristic symptoms of today's knowledge worker or operator of a sociotechnical system (see Keller & Keller, 1996; Perrow, 1984; Zuboff, 1988).

But what can the tricks used by short-order cooks teach us about working with information and information technology? Recall that a central finding was that some cooks were able to dynamically structure the grill area to serve as a fully informative and perceptible external model of the otherwise covert dynamics of their work environment. How untrue would it be to make a similar claim about office-based work, or about Donald Norman's (1988) classic example of power plant workers who substituted beer tap handles for controls that were difficult to tell apart? Look around your own desktop, both actual and virtual, and note the many ways you have probably structured the proximal surface of that environment to be informative about the otherwise covert dynamics of your work (e.g., task priorities, deadlines, opportunities, progress, available resources, and so forth; see Kirsh, 2001). From a cognitive modeling perspective, one lesson learned from this study is that there is little hope for specifying the demands made on internal cognition during interactive behavior without a detailed functional analysis of a performer's action repertoire. In particular, this analysis must consider how that repertoire is deployed, using whatever tools or technologies are at hand to shape the world in addition to passively adapting to it.

From a design perspective, the cooking study demonstrated the importance of the intimate, closed-loop interdependency between perception and action as a resource for fluent and adaptive behavior. The grill in operation was simultaneously both display and control in one. Too few technological interfaces have this quality, thereby requiring performers to alternate back and forth (often many times) between discrete stages of perceiving and acting, short-circuiting the fluent and seamless engagement characteristic of high levels of adaptation and performance. The analysis and modeling approach presented in this chapter allows one to represent the closed-loop, mutually informing nature of perception and action without the mathematically convenient yet limiting assumptions of related techniques such as feedback control theory (e.g., Jagacinski & Flach, 2003) or dynamic systems modeling (e.g., Port & van Gelder, 1995). Instead, all that is required is streams of environmental variable values, their classification in terms of the taxonomy presented in Figure 15.1, and simple calculations of entropy and conditional dependency. Armed with a taxonomy of controls or input devices

such as the one presented in Card, Mackinlay, and Robertson (1992), one is then in a position to explore the space of input devices by using the modeling techniques presented here to find not only devices giving the user control but also those that give the user an ability to generate epistemic action through improvisation. Techniques of this type will hopefully prove useful for designing interface displays and controls in a mutually informing fashion rather than in isolation, as is typically the case today.

References

Anderson, J. R., Simon, H. A., & Reder, L. M. (1997). Rejoinder: Situative versus cognitive perspectives: Form versus substance. *Educational Researcher*, 26, 18–21.

Ashby, W. R. (1965). *Measuring the internal information exchange in a system. Cybernetica*, 8, 5–22.

Beyer, H., & Holtzblatt, K. (1998) *Contextual design: Defining customer-c entered systems*. San Francisco: Morgan Kaufman.

Brunswik, E. (1956). *Perception and the representative design of psychological experiments*. Berkeley. University of California Press.

Card, S. K., Mackinlay, J., & Robertson, G. G. (1992). The design space of input devices. In M. M. Blattner & R. B. Dannenberg (Eds.), *Multimedia interface design* (pp. 217–232). New York: ACM Press.

Card, S., Moran, T., & Newell, A. (1983). *The psychology of human–computer interaction*. Hillsdale, N.J.: Erlbaum.

Carroll, J. M. (1991). Introduction: The Kittle House manifesto. In J. M. Carroll (Ed.), *Designing interaction* (pp. 1–16). New York. Cambridge University Press.

Carroll, J. M., & Campbell, R. L. (1989). Artifacts as psychological theories: The case of human–computer interaction. *Behaviour and Information Technology*, 8, 247–256.

Cole, M. (1996). *Cultural psychology: A once and future discipline*. Cambridge, Mass.: Harvard University Press.

Conant, R. C. (1969). The information transfer required in regulatory processes. *IEEE Transactions on Systems Science and Cybernetics*, SSC-5, no. 4, 334–338.

Connolly, T. (1988). Hedge-clipping, tree-felling, and the management of ambiguity: The need for new images of decision-making. In L. R. Pondy, R. J. J. Boland, & H. Thomas (Eds.), *Managing ambiguity and change* (pp. 37–50). New York: Wiley.

de Waal, F. (2001). *The ape and the sushi master*. New York: Basic Books.

Dourish, P. (2001). *Where the action is: The foundations of embodied interaction*. Cambridge, Mass.: MIT Press.

Geertz, C. (1973). Thick description: Toward an interpretative theory of culture. Chapter 1 in his *The Interpretation of Cultures*. New York: Basic Books, 1973

Gibson, J. J. (1962). Observations on active touch. *Psychological Review, 69*, 477–491.

Gibson, J. J. (1966). *The senses considered as perceptual systems*. Boston: Houghton-Mifflin.

Gibson, J. J. (1979). *The ecological approach to visual perception*. Boston: Houghton Mifflin.

Hammond, K. R. (2001). A meeting of minds. In K. R. Hammond and T. R. Stewart (Eds.), *The essential Brunswik* (pp. 15–16). New York: Oxford University Press.

Hogarth, R. M. (1981). Beyond discrete biases: Functional and dysfunctional aspects of judgmental heuristics. *Psychological Bulletin, 90*, 197–217.

Hollnagel, E. (2003). *Handbook of cognitive task design*. Mahwah, N.J.: Erlbaum.

Hughes, J. A., Randall, D., & Shapiro, D. (1992). Faltering from ethnography to design. *Proceedings of the 1992 ACM Conference on Computer-Supported Cooperative Work* (pp. 115–122). New York: ACM Press.

Hutchins, E. (1995). *Cognition in the Wild*. Cambridge, Mass.: MIT Press.

Jagacinski, R. J., & Flach, J. M. (2003). *Control theory for humans*: Mahwah, N.J.: Erlbaum.

Keller, C. M., & Keller, J. D. (1996). *Cognition and tool use: The blacksmith at work*. Cambridge: Cambridge University Press.

Kirlik, A. (1995) Requirements for psychological models to support design: Towards ecological task analysis. In J. Flach, P. Hancock, J. Caird, & K. Vicente (Eds.), *Global perspectives on the ecology of human–machine systems, vol. 1* (pp. 68–120). Hillsdale, N.J.: Erlbaum.

Kirlik, A. (1998). The design of everyday life environments. In W. Bechtel & George Graham, (Eds.) *A Companion to cognitive science*. Oxford: Blackwell.

Kirsh, D. (1995). The intelligent use of space. *Artificial Intelligence, 73*, 31–68.

Kirsh, D. (2001). The context of work. *Human-Computer Interaction, 16*, 305–322.

Kirsh, D., & Maglio, P. (1994). On distinguishing epistemic from pragmatic action. *Cognitive Science, 18*, 513–549.

Klein, G. A., & Calderwood, R. (1991). Decision models: Some lessons from the field. *IEEE Transactions on Systems, Man, and Cybernetics, 21*, 1018–1026.

Koestler, Arthur (1964). *The Act of Creation* (p. 448). London: Penguin Books.

McGill, W. J. (1954). Multivariate information transmission. *Psychometrika 19*, 97–116.

Militello, L. G., & Hutton, R. J. B. (1998). Applied cognitive task analysis (ACTA): A practitioner's toolkit for understanding cognitive task demands. *Ergonomics, 41*(11), 1618–1641.

Nardi, B. A. (1996). *Context and consciousness: Activity theory and human–computer interaction*. Cambridge, Mass.: MIT Press.

Newell, A. (1992). Precis of unified theories of cognition. *Behavioral and Brain Sciences, 15*, 425–492.

Newell, A. & Simon, H. A. (1972). *Human Problem Solving*. Englewood Cliffs, N.J.: Prentice Hall.

Norman, D. A. (1988). *The design of everyday things*. Basic Books.

Olson, G. M., & Olson, J. S. (1991). User-centered design of collaboration technology. *Journal of Organizational Computing, 1*, 61–83.

Perrow, C. (1984). *Normal accidents: Living with high-risk technologies*. New York: Basic Books.

Piaget, J. (1974). *Adaptation and intelligence*. Chicago: University of Chicago Press.

Port, R., & van Gelder, T. (1995). *Mind as motion: Explorations in the dynamics of cognition*. Cambridge, Mass.: MIT Press

Rasmussen, J. (1990). Cognitive engineering, a new profession? In L. P. Goodstein, S. E. Olson, & H. B. Anderson (Eds.), *Tasks, errors, and mental models* (pp. 325–334). New York: Taylor & Francis.

Rose, M. (2004). *The mind at work: Valuing the intelligence of the American worker*. New York: Viking.

Runeson, S. (1977). On the possibility of "smart" perceptual mechanisms. *Scandanavian Journal of Psychology, 18*.

Suchman, L. A. (1987). *Plans and situated actions*. New York: Cambridge University Press.

Suchman, L. A. (2000). Embodied practices of engineering work. *Mind, Culture, and Activity, 7*(1/2), 4–18.

Tolman, E.C., & Brunswik, E. (1935). The organism and the causal texture of the environment. *Psychological Review, 42*, 43–77.

Vicente, K. J. (1999). *Cognitive work analysis: Toward safe, productive, and healthy computer-based work*. Mahwah, N.J.: Erlbaum.

Woods, D. D. (2003). Discovering how distributed cognitive systems work. In E. Hollnagel (Ed.), *Handbook of cognitive task design* (pp. 37–53). Mahwah, N.J.: Erlbaum.

Zuboff, S. (1988). *In the age of the smart machine: The future of work and power*. New York: Basic Books.

VI

Ecological Analysis Meets Computational Cognitive Modeling

Alex Kirlik

Introduction

We are impressed by the close correspondence between the rational analysis framework developed by Anderson and the "Lens" model for the analysis of judgment.
—Hastie & Hammond (1991, p. 498)

Hastie & Hammond comment on the similarities and differences between this program and that of Brunswik. I think the similarities are quite strong and am inclined to agree with Hastie & Hammond's assessment that rational analysis is quite in keeping with the spirit of Brunswik's work..
—John R. Anderson (1991b, p. 513)

In 1990, John Anderson, a highly accomplished cognitive scientist and creator of the ACT-R cognitive architecture, published a book signaling his appreciation for what an ecological perspective could contribute to the study of cognition (Anderson, 1990). Characterizing the mechanistic cognitive theories of the time as a "random set of postulates let loose on the world" (1990, p. 30), and as "bizarre and implausible" (Anderson, 1990, p. iii), he responded by presenting a research approach designed to take some of the arbitrariness out of cognitive modeling. He called this approach *rational analysis*: "an explanation of an aspect of human behavior based on the assumption that it is optimized somehow to the structure of the environment" (Anderson, 1991a, p. 471). In his *Behavioral and Brain Sciences* précis of his 1990 book (Anderson, 1991a), Anderson began by clearly indicating the ecological tradition in which he considered rational analysis to lie, citing books by both Brunswik (1956) and Gibson (1966, 1979) as related attempts to understand cognition as an adaptation to the environment. The epigraphs drawn from the dialogue spawned by that précis suggest that both Anderson and psychologists working from a Brunswikian orientation (Hastie and Hammond, 1991) recognized the relationship between rational analysis and Brunswik's probabilistic functionalism and apparently thought well of this confluence of ideas.

One motivation for the development of rational analysis was a concern that the mechanistic cognitive theories of the time were too empirically underconstrained, but Anderson also shared a second motivation: "I have always felt that something was lost when the cognitive revolution abandoned behaviorism, my work on rational analysis can be viewed as an attempt to recover that" (1991b, p. 513). Among post–cognitive revolution psychologists, Anderson is clearly not alone in this regard: Consider the distinctly ecological shifts represented by the differences between Neisser's *Cognitive Psychology* (1967) and *Cognition and Reality* (1976), and Donald Norman's transition from information processing theorist to author of the *The Design of Everyday Things* (1989). These individual responses to the perceived excesses of environmentally abstracted cognitivism have of course been reflected in more sweeping, ecologically enriched, conceptual frameworks and perspectives such as embodied cognition (e.g., Barsalou, 1999; Clark, 1997; Dourish, 2001), distributed cognition (e.g., Hutchins, 1995; Kirsh, 1996), and ecological rationality (Gigerenzer & Goldstein, 1996; Gigerenzer & Selten, 2001; Gigerenzer, Todd, & the ABC Research Group, 1999).

The three chapters in this section portray attempts to draw on both the conceptual resources of Anderson's ACT-R cognitive architecture and the types of detailed ecological analysis and modeling advocated by Brunswik as well as by some of those working in the traditions of embodied or distributed cognition and ecological rationality. In doing so, it is important to emphasize that the authors of these chapters are working at the intersection and boundaries of various psychological orientations that are in some cases portrayed to be in conflict. This is hardly surprising, as these authors have as goals not only to understand adaptive cognition and behavior in human–technology interaction but to improve it through design. In such situations it is common to find researchers adopting a problem-solving orientation, opportunistically drawing on whatever conceptual resources are found useful, instead of rigidly attempting to remain faithful to one paradigm or another. Application is indeed where rubber meets road in cognitive science. It would seem only adaptive for those concerned about the empirically underconstrained status of much cognitive theory to warmly welcome the additional empirical constraint brought about by application.

Additionally, in prefacing these chapters it is important to emphasize that time often has a way of transforming apparently conflicting viewpoints into complementary ones. The history of psychology is replete with theories whose proponents were largely on the mark with respect to one aspect of behavior or another but prematurely overgeneralized their positions. In the present context, for example, it is useful to highlight that although many of the mechanisms comprising ACT-R are based on constrained optimization using Bayesian analysis and cost-benefit maximization (i.e., rational analysis), and although the ecological rationality approach of Gigerenzer and Todd (Gigerenzer, 1991; Gigerenzer & Todd, 1999) eschews such constrained-optimization accounts in favor of purely ecological, empirical criteria for success, the authors of the chapters have been able to profitably draw on both ACT-R and ecological rationality notions in their modeling.

Instead of signaling any incoherence, however, this fact may indeed suggest important boundary conditions of both of the rational analysis and ecological rationality approaches, thus indicating how they may eventually come to be viewed as complementary rather than in conflict. For example, the fast and frugal heuristics comprising Gigerenzer and Todd's (1999) "adaptive toolbox" must surely be implemented in some sort of broader, resource-limited account of the real-time dynamics of cognition (ACT-R is one such example). And ACT-R has never really been presented as a serious theory of decision or action, but instead as a plausible repository for and engine for simulating whatever task-specific decision and action strategies seem appropriate to the task and ecology at hand (the adaptive toolbox is one such example). Only time will tell whether these speculations have merit. One can at least be hopeful that the chapters in this section will not be the final word on these issues.

References

Anderson, J. R. (1990). *The adaptive character of thought*. Cambridge, Mass.: Harvard University Press.

Anderson, J. R. (1991a). Is human cognition adaptive? *Behavioral and Brain Sciences, 14*(3), 471–485.

Anderson, J. R. (1991b). Author's response: More on rational analysis. *Behavioral and Brain Sciences, 14*(3), 508–517.

Barsalou, L. (1999). Perceptual symbol systems. *Behavioral and Brain Sciences, 22*, 577–609.

Brunswik, E. (1956). *Perception and the representative design of psychological experiments*. Berkeley: University of California Press.

Clark, A. (1997). *Being there: Putting brain, body and world together again*. Cambridge, Mass.: MIT Press.

Dourish, P. (2001). *Where the action is: The foundations of embodied interaction*. Cambridge, Mass.: MIT Press.

Gibson, J. J. (1966). *The senses considered as perceptual systems*. Boston: Houghton-Mifflin.

Gibson, J. J. (1979). *The ecological approach to visual perception*. Boston: Houghton Mifflin.

Gigerenzer, G. (1991). Does the environment have the same structure as Bayes theorem? *Behavioral and Brain Sciences, 14*(3), 495–496.

Gigerenzer, G., & Goldstein, D. G. (1996). Reasoning the fast and frugal way: Models of bounded rationality. *Psychological Review, 103*, 650–669.

Gigerenzer, G., & Selten, R. (Eds.). (2001). *Bounded rationality: The adaptive toolbox*. Cambridge, Mass.: MIT Press.

Gigerenzer, G., & Todd, P. M. (1999). Fast and frugal heuristics: The adaptive toolbox. In G. Gigerenzer, P. M. Todd, and the ABC Research Group (Eds.), *Simple heuristics that make us smart* (pp. 3–34). New York: Oxford University Press.

Gigerenzer, G., Todd, P. M., & the ABC Research Group (1999). *Simple heuristics that make us smart*. New York: Oxford University Press.

Hastie, R., & Hammond, R. (1991). Rational analysis and the lens model. *Behavioral and Brain Sciences, 14*(3), 498.

Hutchins, E. (1995). *Cognition in the wild*. Cambridge, Mass.: MIT Press.

Kirsh, D. (1996). Adapting the environment instead of oneself. *Adaptive Behavior, 4*(3/4), 415–452.

Neisser, U. (1967). *Cognitive psychology*. New York: Appleton

Neisser, U. (1976). *Cognition and reality*. New York: Freeman.

Norman, D. A. (1989). *The design of everyday things*. New York: Doubleday.

Wayne D. Gray

The Emerging Rapprochement between Cognitive and Ecological Analyses

The functional approach [Brunswik's] has its place mainly in the appraisal of the interplay and relative contribution or weight of factors in the adjustment to a given ecology, while the reductive approach [Experimental Psychology's] reveals the technological details of the machinery that brings about such adjustment.

—Brunswik (1955/2001, p. 148)

Now if an organism is confronted with the problem of behaving approximately rationally, or adaptively, in a particular environment, the kinds of simplifications that are suitable may depend not only on the characteristics—sensory, neural, and other—of the organism, but equally upon the structure of the environment. Hence, we might hope to discover, by a careful examination of some of the fundamental structural characteristics of the environment, some further clues as to the nature of the approximating mechanisms used in decision making.

—Simon (1956, pp. 129–130)

Introduction

As revealed by the epigraphs, nearly 50 years ago Brunswik and Simon agreed on the necessity of understanding the environment to understand cognition. They also agreed that the cost and benefit of environmental cues was an important piece of the ecological-cognitive puzzle. For example, in discussing the relationship between the ecological validity of a cue and its utilization, Brunswik (1955/2001) pointed out that "ideally, cues should be utilized in accordance with their validity. But here we must inject . . . the element of 'cost' to the organism, just as we must ask for the cost of an automobile along with its efficiency in budgeting our expenditures. Functional theory here takes on certain features of economic theory" (p. 147). In turn, Simon (1956), in amassing the arguments against classical economics that eventually led to his Nobel Prize (Leahey, 2003), complained that the models of rational be-

havior employed in economics postulated "a much greater complexity in the choice mechanisms, and a much larger capacity in the organism for obtaining information and performing computations" than was supported by the psychology of that day. Stating his problem as one of "behaving approximately rationally, or adaptively, in a particular environment" he went on to explore the "fundamental structural characteristics of the environment" to show that "we should be skeptical in postulating for humans, or other organisms, elaborate mechanisms for choosing among diverse needs" (p. 137).

Given the common emphasis on the environment and common skepticism regarding the need to postulate complex cognitive processes, someone who was new to cognitive science might be forgiven for thinking that in the past 50 years, the intellectual descendants of Brunswik and Simon have merged into one happy family. Although this has not happened yet, it is happening now.

Keys to the Emerging Rapprochement

Fifty years ago, neither side of what Brunswik called the "functional" versus "reductive" approach had a coherent story as to how the mechanisms of cognition meshed with the external environment to form integrated cognitive systems. Since then, major advances have been made in understanding the interplay between the internal psychological activities that Brunswik dismissed as mere process detail and the environment. Some of these advances have led to the realization that we do not store the mental equivalent of a 360°, high-definition, visual display of the world with surround sound in our heads, but rather we construct what we need when we need it. Although this construct may feel seamless to the perceiver it is, in fact, patchy and partial (Ballard et al., 1997; Simons & Levin, 1998).

In this section I introduce three of these advances, embodied cognition (Kieras & Meyer, 1997; Wilson, 2002) architectures of cognition (Newell, 1990), and soft constraints (Gray & Fu, 2004). In the following section, I turn to research from the CogWorks Laboratory at Rensselaer Polytechnic Institute that illustrates how these three advances yield an understanding of the *functional task environment* that is the key to the rapprochement between cognitive and ecological analyses.

Embodied Cognition

There are many senses of the term *embodied cognition* (Clark, in press; Kieras & Meyer, 1997; Wilson, 2002); however, simply put, embodied cognition implies that properties of functional cognition and of the perceived world are in a tight loop. Properties of our cognitive, perceptual, and action systems determine how much and what aspects of the world we perceive, whereas properties of the world determine the mixture of cognitive, perceptual, and action operations required for us to perceive it. Another way of saying this is that "the embodied view is that the environment and perceiver should not be separated but should be viewed as an integrated system" (Ballard, 2002, p. 56).

Embodied cognition has profound implications for how we view what it means to have an "ecological analysis." Surely, if we and the world form an integrated system, then an ecological analyses of our task environment cannot be separated from an analysis of functional cognition. By themselves, both ecological and cognitive analyses are incomplete. Advances in understanding one requires understanding how it is integrated with the other. Rapprochement is not simply an interesting new direction, it is vital for the continuing progress of our science.

We can get by with a patchy and partial mental representation of the world because we are able to perform "just-in-time" processing. This view implies that we must be as unaware of the construction processes (under normal circumstances) as we are with the patchy and partial nature of what they construct. Indeed, pundits as diverse as Neil Cassidy (Wolfe, 1968), John R. Anderson (1987), and Dana Ballard (Ballard, Hayhoe, & Pelz, 1995; Ballard et al., 1997) have proposed that there is a 1/3 to 1 second delay in our awareness of the world. We are aware of the end product of the processes that fill this gap but not the processes themselves. Ballard has labeled the mixture of cognitive, perceptual, and action operations that mediate between the world and our awareness of it the *embodiment level*.

Architectures of Cognition

Verbal descriptions of theoretical processes cannot suffice to capture the rapid and nondeliberate control of operations at the embodiment level. Serious theorizing demands the adoption of a suitable architecture of cognition.

Architectures of cognition (Newell, 1973, 1990, 1992) focus on the control of a central system. Issues of control for the central system include control of the central processor itself as well as the initiation of functional processes (such as visual search, action, and memory retrieval) and the harvesting of the results of those processes. Such control by the central system is conceptually distinct from the internal control required by individual functional processes. For example, the central controller may initiate a visual search for a given target, but once initiated, visual search (e.g., where to move the eyes next) is under the local control of the functional process. Hence, architectures incorporate two types of theories: type 1 theory denotes central control, whereas type 2 theories deal with control of the various functional processes. Type 1 provides a theory of central control that determines how the processing performed by the various functional processes are interleaved to produce an integrated cognitive system. Type 2 consists of theories of the internal control of functional processes as well as how and what they communicate to the controller.

Some of the work presented next includes models written in ACT-R 5.0 (Anderson et al., 2004). An full understanding of ACT-R 5.0 is not required to understand this chapter; however, ACT-R was chosen as it is an open architecture that incorporates type 1 and type 2 theories. For type 2, ACT-R 5.0 includes functional processes such as an activation-based memory, current focus of attention (often thought of as the current goal), movement of visual attention, a theory of eye movements (Salvucci, 2001), the Treisman theory of feature detection (Treisman & Gelade, 1980; Treisman & Sato, 1990), and the theory of motor movements used by EPIC (Kieras et al., 2000). The operation of these type 2 processes is viewed as largely subsymbolic.

Type 1, central control, is provided by three elements: production rules, functions that specify and initiate type 2 processes, and process-specific buffers that can cache the result of type 2 processes. A production rule is a symbolic component in the form of a condition–action pair. On each cycle any production rule whose condition side matches the current state of the system is eligible to fire. The matching process is massively parallel; however, only one production rule can fire on any given cycle. If the conditions for more than one production rule match, then the choice among production rules is based on a subsymbolic calculation of each rule's expected utility. After being selected, the action side of the condition–action pair is executed. The action side may initiate a type 2 process. Complementarily, the results of type 2 processes are cached in process-specific buffers. The contents of these buffers can be harvested or accessed by the condition side of production rules.

Soft Constraints in Interactive Behavior

The Soft Constraints approach (Gray & Fu, 2004) builds on the notions of bounded rationality (Simon, 1956, 1992) and rational analysis (Anderson, 1990, 1991) to apply the rational, expected utility framework to selecting the elementary activities that

occur at the embodiment level. It embraces methodological adaptationism (Godfrey-Smith, 2001) in that it assumes that interactive behavior at the < 1,000 millisecond time scale reflects an adaptation to the task environment. It does not, however, postulate that behavior reflects an optimal adaptation (Fu & Gray, 2004).

For any given task environment, a set of elementary activities (Gray & Boehm-Davis, 2000) can be defined for interactive behavior. For example, moving a mouse on the computer screen to a given interactive object consists of a network of cognitive, perceptual, and action operators such as shown in Figure 16.1. This network defines the elementary activity of move-cursor. The set of elementary activities available in a given task environment is de-

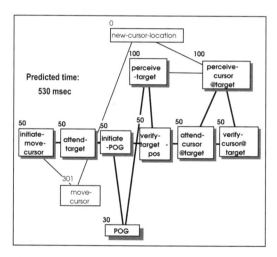

Figure 16.1. A CPM-GOMS model of the activity or routine required to move a mouse to a predetermined location on a computer screen. Total predicted time is 530 ms. CPM-GOMS is a network modeling technique (Schweickert, Fisher, & Proctor, 2003). In the middle row are cognitive operators with a default execution time of 50 milliseconds each. Above that line are the perceptual operators, and below it are the motor operators. The flow of operators is from left to right with connecting lines indicating dependencies. Within an operator type the dependencies are sequential. However, between operator types the dependencies may be parallel. The numbers above each operator indicate the time in milliseconds for that operator to execute. Time is accumulated from left to right along the critical path. (The critical path is indicated by bold lines connecting shadowed boxes.) loc = location; POG = point of gaze. See Gray & Boehm-Davis (2000) for more detailed information.

fined by the variety of ways the tools available to the agent can interact with the objects in the task environment. At their most basic, the tools available to an agent include hands and arms, eyes and ears, memory and attention. Tools may also include mouse and keyboard, hammer and nails, stethoscope and thermometer, mathematics and language.

As defined by Gray and Boehm-Davis (2000), elementary activities have properties similar to Ullman's (1984) visual routines; namely, they are computational primitives that can be composed (Ballard, 2002) into higher order units. For Gray and Boehm-Davis, activities are composed into microstrategies that accomplish a unit of meaningful activity.

As a type of control, soft constraints are positioned between bottom-up (or stimulus-driven) and top-down (or strategic) control of behavior. For example, take the case of searching a visual display for a target L hidden among distractor T's. To make the search task slightly easier, although the target L is always surrounded by distractor T's, it is always located in the center of one of four quadrants (see Figure 16.2) of the visual display (Myers & Gray, 2005).

In performing this task, people may deliberately adopt the top-down strategy of always starting their search at the upper left quadrant and moving clockwise until the target is found. Alternatively, if one of the quadrants contains a denser configuration of distracters than the other quadrants, bottom-up or stimulus-driven factors may attract the eye so that the dense quadrant is the one that is ini-

tially searched. This stimulus-driven capture effect may occur even though the dense quadrant is no more likely than the other quadrants to contain the target (see Wolfe, 1998, for a discussion of stimulus-driven factors that influence visual search). Finally, if the dense quadrant never contains the target, the subject may adapt to the task environment by searching the dense quadrant less frequently than would be expected by chance. This last case is an example of adaptation to the expected utility of a particular task environment and, as such, reflects the operation of soft constraints. (Whether people are aware of soft constraints and whether they apply them deliberately or not deliberately is not essential to the definition.)

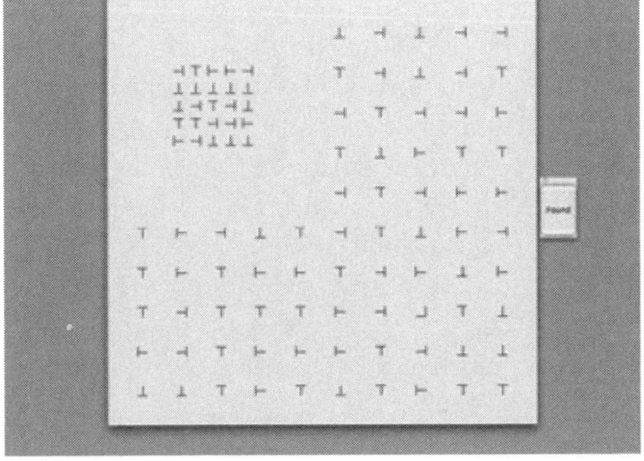

Although specifying the task environment appears in principle to be both objective and deterministic, the soft constraints approach implies that the *functional* task environment for a given activity always reflects a mixture of internal and external resources. For example, to obtain information it may be possible to move eyes and attention to a location on a computer screen, alternatively, the same information may be retrieved from memory. In such situations, the sets of elementary activities with the highest expected utility may not be defined simply by reference to the physical task environment but must incorporate the agent as well. Hence, despite the presence of perfect knowledge in the world, soft constraints may lead the agent to rely on imperfect knowledge in-the-head (Gray & Fu, 2004). In this example, the imperfect knowledge in-the-head becomes part of the functional task environment. (The supposition that the cognitive controller is indifferent to the source of resources is congruent with many contemporary accounts of cognition [for example, Anderson et al., 2004; Carlson, 2002; Clark, 2004] and obtains support from the Gray and Fu [2004] study discussed shortly.)

Soft constraints represent an adaptation to the cost-benefit structure of the task environment. The adaptation to costs may proceed at a different rate than the adaptation to benefits (Fu & Gray, in press). The adaptation may reflect experience in past task environments as well as in the current task environment. It is important to emphasize that stable adaptations may not be optimal adaptations. Indeed, there is considerable evidence that many adaptations result in stable, suboptimal performance (Fu & Gray, 2004, in press; Herrnstein, 1991; Yechiam et al., 2003).

Figure 16.2. Saccadic selectivity. L hidden among T's. The target is always presented in the center of one of the four quadrants. The upper left quadrant is an example of a dense stimulus configuration.

Defining the Functional Task Environment

The functional task environment emerges from the interaction of embodied cognition performing a given task in a given physical task environment. The functional task environment includes both less and more than the physical task environment. The physical task environment may well be a 360°, high-definition, visual display with surround sound. However, the functional task environment is not; it is partial and patchy.

The patches to the functional task environment are provided by various levels of cognitive control including bottom-up, top-down, and soft constraints. The work presented in this section emphasizes the role of soft constraints. I present three lines of research, each of which bears on the topic of the functional task environment and each of which draws on theories of embodied cognition, soft constraints, and the ACT-R architecture of cognition.

Soft Constraints in the Adoption of Interaction-Intensive versus Memory-Intensive Strategies

Hard constraints derive from the physical task environment to limit the variety of activities that are available to perform a task. Soft constraints define the functional task environment and determine the set(s) of elementary activities that are most likely to be used. Despite the fact that human behavior is variable and in many circumstances hard to predict, time and again we see people settling on one or a very few ways of accomplishing the same task. For example, in an empirical study (Gray, 2000), out of nine subjects who discovered how to program a simulated VCR, seven adopted the same procedural rule hierarchy and two adopted minor variants. In the work discussed here by Gray and Fu (2004), of the 80 subjects shown a depiction of that procedural rule hierarchy as the experimenter programmed the first show, all used it to program the next four shows. Although extreme variation was possible, little variation was found. Working within the hard constraints explicitly designed into the artifact, soft constraints determined how people attempted to use the VCR.

Soft constraints imply that the combination of resources brought to bear in performing a task is not fixed by either the physical task environment or the cognitive system but emerges from the interaction of the two. This section reviews two studies that explore the influence of the design of the task environment on how subprocesses required for task performance are composed.

Dynamic Decision Making

The landmark studies of Payne, Bettman, and Johnson (1993) showed that strategy selection in decision making trades off effectiveness for efficiency. For example, people are willing to adopt strategies that are, say, 85% as effective as the optimal strategies if they incur, say, 40% of the costs in terms of time to execute.

Three limits to this classic work are discussed in Gray, Schoelles, and Myers (2004). Here the focus is on one of those limits—confounding of the costs of steps in the decision-making algorithm with the costs of steps in a given task environment and its corollary assumption that time is the only cost worth considering.

The data discussed here were obtained by embedding a decision-making task (DMT) in a dynamic classification task that required subjects to rate the threat value of air targets on a radar display. Over the course of a 12-minute scenario, a good subject would classify approximately 70–85 targets using the algorithm they were taught for combining information. (The classification task is discussed in more detail later.) For the DMT the classification task was interrupted and subjects were presented with a set of four (DMT-4) or six (DMT-6) already classified targets and asked to pick the one with the highest threat value.

In two between-subject conditions, to obtain the threat value subjects had to locate the target's identification number (id#) on the radar screen and move the cursor to the number. In the 0-Lock condition, as soon as the cursor was above the id# the target's threat value would appear in a tool-tip windoid. In the 2-Lock condition, the threat value appeared after a lockout period of 2 seconds. A research question of interest was how this slight increase in cost would affect the process of information acquisition.

The results showed that the more targets in a decision-making set, the lower the percentage of threat values that were checked. For DMT-4, subjects checked approximately 72% of the targets compared to 62% of the DMT-6 targets. There were no significant differences between the 0-Lock and 2-Lock conditions on the number of targets checked.

A very different story was told by the data on the number of targets that were rechecked. As Figure 16.3 shows, for the 0-Lock condition over 50% of the checked alternatives were rechecked. In contrast, the 2-Lock group rechecked less than 7% of the checked alternatives. Relying on interaction-intensive strategies, the 0-Lock group was willing to recheck the targets before making their decision, presumably comparing a recently checked threat value with an earlier one. In contrast, during their initial check, the 2-Lock group spends about twice as long per target (even when the 2-second lockout time is subtracted) and apparently uses memory-intensive strategies that entail mentally encoding and comparing the current target's threat value with the highest-so-far threat value.

For this chapter, there are three take-away points from this research. First, a small difference in the cost structure between two otherwise physically identical task environments resulted in subjects adopting either an interactive-intensive or memory-intensive strategy for determining the alternative with the highest threat value. Second, as the small error bars in Figure 16.3 suggest, although there were no hard constraints forcing subjects in the two conditions to adopt two different approaches to this task, soft constraints operated to channel interactive behavior within each condition into common paths of greatest expected utility. Third, although the difference between the two physical task environments is small, the difference between the functional task environments is great. Compared to 2-Lock, the

0-Lock functional task environment incorporates many more perceptual and motor operations. Compared to 0-Lock, the 2-Lock functional task environment incorporates a large memory annex for storage and retrieval of threat values. These differences between the functional task environments emerge from the interaction of embodied cognition attempting to accomplish a given task in a given physical task environment.

Ignoring Perfect Knowledge In-the-World for Imperfect Knowledge In-the-Head

In a recent paper, Gray and Fu (2004) studied the use of alternative basic activities to obtain information required to do a simple task—program a VCR. In that study, subjects were presented with a VCR simulation on the computer screen with an information window displayed approximately five inches below (see Figure 16.4). The window contained the information required to program the current show: start time, end time, day of week, and channel.

Across three different conditions, the cost of acquiring information was varied to mimic the costs of acquiring information during routine interactions with a modern computer interface. For example, in the Free-Access condition, the information was clearly visible on the screen. The costs here mimic the case of working in one window but needing to obtain information in another visible window. In the Gray-Box condition the information fields were covered by gray boxes. To obtain information from these fields, subjects had to move their mouse and visual attention to the gray box (field names, such as "start time," were clearly visible) and click. This condition mimics the case where the information needed is on the screen but its window is obscured by another window. In this case, the user needs to move to and click on a portion of the window to bring it to the foreground. The third condition was Memory-Test. In this condition, the display was similar to that seen by the Gray-Box subjects. The main difference was that subjects had to memorize the show information before they were allowed to begin programming the VCR. This condition mimics the case where the information is in an obscured window, but it is information that is well learned.

In each of the three conditions, to obtain the information needed to program the VCR, subjects could either acquire information from the show information window or retrieve the information from memory. Based on estimates of times for perceptual-motor

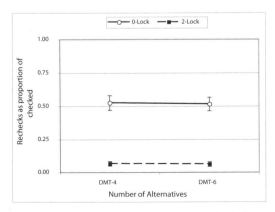

Figure 16.3. Proportion of alternatives rechecked per decision-making task (DMT) (error bars show the standard error).

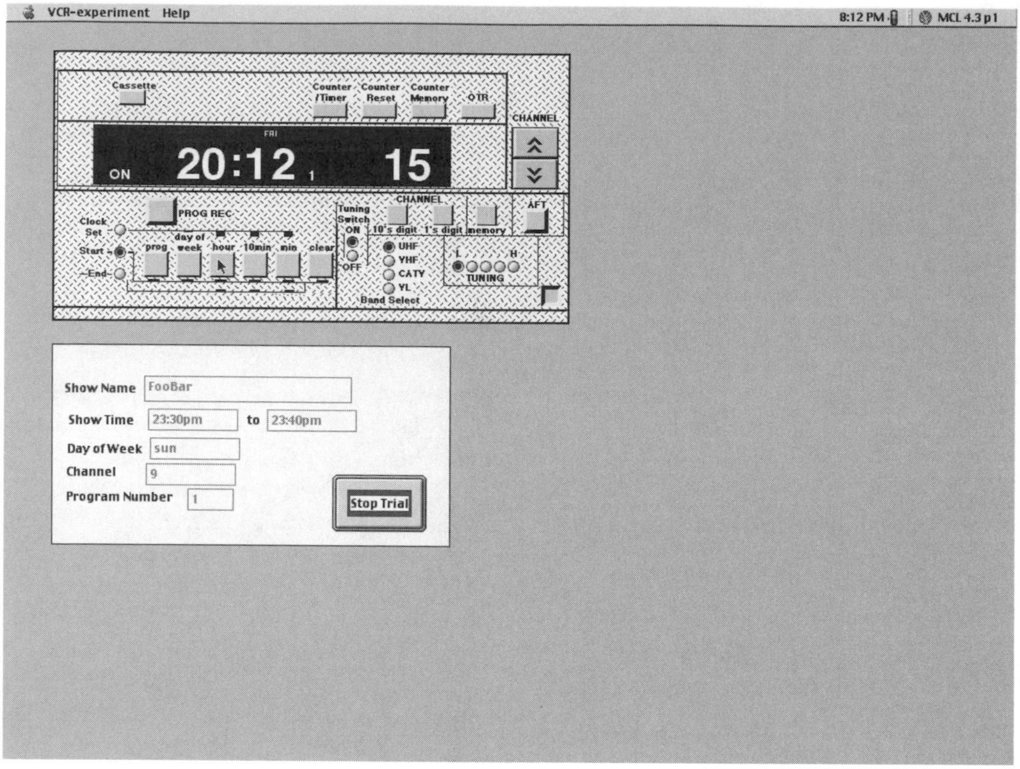

Figure 16.4. VCR 2.0 with Show Information window. The figure shows what the Free-Access condition would have seen. For both the Gray-Box and Memory-Test conditions the fields (but not their labels) would have been covered by gray boxes.

versus memory retrieval in each condition (see Table 16.1), the Soft Constraints perspective predicted that subjects in the Memory-Test condition would rely on strong memories in-the-head rather than retrieving information in-the-world. In the Gray-Box condition the estimated time to retrieve weak memories was competitive with the time required to move the mouse and attention to the show information window. Hence, at least sometimes when information was needed, subjects would rely on imperfect knowl-edge in-the-head rather than perfect knowledge in-the-world. In the Free-Access condition, the low cost of information access should lead subjects to rely on knowledge in-the-world. However, here too, soft constraints were expected to lead subjects to rely to some degree on imperfect knowledge in-the-head.

In line with these predictions, two independent measures of error showed that the Memory-Test group was best, followed by Free-Access, followed by Gray-Box. A third independent measure examined the timing of information accesses. For both the Gray-Box and Free-Access condition, if subjects accessed information in-the-world they tended to access it right before they needed it. For example, they would access the day-of-week field right before they programmed day-of-week. Subjects almost never interrupted their programming of, for example, day of week to check the day-of-week field. Similarly, they almost never double-checked a field after they had finished programming a setting. (In line with our expectations, the Memory-Test condition rarely accessed the show information window.)

Table 16.1. Estimates (in miliseconds) of perceptual-motor and memory retrieval effort by condition (rational and derivation of these estimates is provided in Gray & Fu, 2004)

Condition	Percpeutal-Motor Access	Memory Retrieval
Free-Access	500	500 to 1000 (weak)
Gray-Box	1000 to 1500	500 to 1000 (weak)
Memory-Test	1000 to 1500	100 to 300 (strong)

The data suggest that the Free-Access and Gray-Box subjects used a mix of interaction-intensive versus memory-intensive strategies. This mix probably does not reflect an extended deliberation on the part of the subject to use one strategy or the other. Rather, the mix reflects a horse race between two readily available strategies. On a case-by-case bases, subjects tended to rely on the process (retrieval of knowledge in-the-head versus in-the-world) that completed first.

The study supports the Soft Constraints perspective that milliseconds matter (Gray & Boehm-Davis, 2000). The functional task environment includes information in memory just as it includes information in the show information window. With all else equal (see Fu & Gray, 2004, for a discussion of factors other than time cost that may affect the expected utility of a basic activity), the cognitive system favored the basic activities that required the least effort in the functional task environment. The study also shows that the central controller is indifferent to the source of resources (in-the-head versus in-the-world) by showing that source selection is sensitive to least-effort costs of information acquisition. Finally, the data argue against Ballard's suggestion (Ballard, et al., 1997) that people are willing to incur higher perceptual–motor costs to avoid lower memory costs.

Probing the Paradox of the Active User: Asymmetric Transfer May Produce Stable Suboptimal Performance

The "paradox of the active user" (Carroll & Rosson, 1987) is the persistent use of inefficient procedures in interactive environments by experienced or even expert users when demonstrably more efficient procedures exist. The paradox is an instance of stable, suboptimal performance (Fu & Gray, 2004). This stability contrasts with the least-effort explanations adopted to explain the results already discussed. However, people do not exclusively use one tool or one piece of software. Rather, we work in multiple task environments, and our functional task environment seems cobbled together based on the statistical structure of these multiple environments. The two components of expected utility are an activity's cost and its history of success and failure. History is balanced against cost. This section explores the balance of the two by reporting an attempt to create the paradox of the active user under laboratory conditions (see Fu & Gray, 2004, for a more naturalistic approach).

Inducing the Paradox under Laboratory Conditions

In this work-in-progress (Gray, Veksler, & Fu, 2004), two minor variations to the same physical task environment were created (VCR 3.0 shown in Figure 16.5) and different groups of subjects were trained on each. One interface condition was nominally harder than the other. Two sets of issues were examined. First, do subjects trained on the hard interface develop different procedures than those trained on the easy one? Second, when subjects transfer from the hard to easy or from the easy to hard interface, do they keep the procedures they acquired during training or do they acquire new procedures?

The physical task environment for this study was provided by the VCR 3.0 simulation. To program a setting (e.g., channel), the subject first clicked on its radio button (one of the 12 small buttons located in the lower half of the display) and then used the up/down arrows (toward the upper right of the figure) to reach the target value. As shown in Figure 16.5, to set the start time the subjects must set start-hour, start-10min, and start-min. To set the end time, they must set end-hour, end-10min, and end-min. In the interface used here the three radio buttons to set start time are in one row, and the three buttons to set end time are in another row.

Two variations of the interface were created that varied the ease of selecting a radio button. For the hard condition (shown in Figure 16.5), subjects had to select a column button before they could choose a radio button. There were no column buttons in the easy condition; subjects could select any radio button at any time.

The difference between these easy and hard conditions was not particularly great. However, they were chosen to be representative of the differences in costs typically found in commercially produced interfaces. The first research question of interest was whether these small differences would suffice to induce subjects to adopt different procedures for programming the VCR.

Strategies Adopted across the First Four Shows

It was hypothesized that due to the role of prior knowledge, subjects in the easy condition would

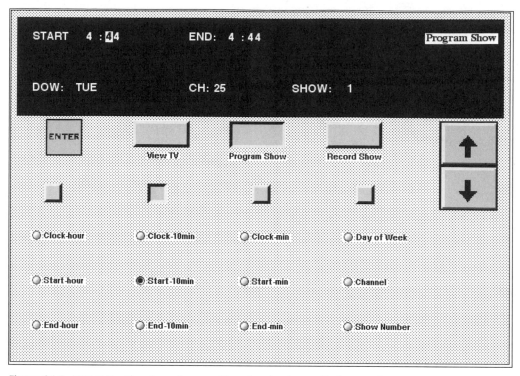

Figure 16.5. VCR 3.0 with column buttons. Note that the three radio buttons for setting start-time are in the middle row, and the three for setting end-time are in the bottom row.

adopt the by-row strategy. Specifically, once they began programming, say, start time they would complete it by programming start-hour, start-10min, and start-min (not necessarily in order) and would not interrupt themselves to program the day of week, channel, or any part of end time. The same prediction applies to programming all three parts of end time. In contrast, the hard condition increases the perceptual–motor cost of this knowledge-based strategy by requiring subjects to click column buttons on and off each time they wish to select a button in another column. Consequently, the hard interface would seem to encourage a by-column strategy that minimizes the cost of perceptual–motor activity, namely, setting parts of the start and end time in pairs (for example, start- and end-hour, start- and end-10min, and start- and end-min).

Each subject programmed eight shows to the criterion of two consecutive trials of correctly programmed shows. Half of the subjects (32) programmed the first four shows with the hard interface and half with easy interface. For the last four shows they switched interface conditions. The dependent variable in this study was the strategy

used by subjects to program start time and end time—either by row or by column.

For each show that each subject programmed, a measure of strategy use was derived based on the sequence in which radio buttons were selected. A positive score indicated a predominately by-row strategy and a negative score indicated a predominately by-column strategy.

As shown in Figure 16.6, on trial 4 subjects with the easy interface [easy(tr4)] programmed by row and those with the hard interface [hard(tr4)] programmed by column [$F(1, 62) = 55.02, p < 0.0001$, MSE = 17.15]. A very simple manipulation of the perceptual–motor cost of interacting with the environment changed the way that subjects programmed the VCR from a strategy that was congruent with prior knowledge (programming all of start-time and all of end-time) to a strategy that in some way ran contrary to prior knowledge. Congruent with the least-effort expectations of the Soft Constraints approach, these findings show that small changes in the cost of cognitive, perceptual, and action operations result in major changes in how the same step (programming the start-time or end-time) is implemented.

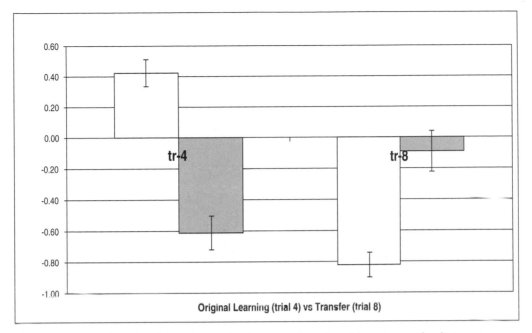

Figure 16.6. Use of row-based (positive numbers) versus column-based (negative numbers) strategies on trials 4 and 8 as a function of interface condition. Subjects trained on either the easy or hard interface for four trials and then transferred to the opposite condition for four more trials.

Strategies Adopted after Transfer

The easy–hard group trained with the easy interface before switching to the hard interface. However, the by-row strategies they used on easy(tr4) were completely dropped by hard(tr8); that is, they changed strategies when they switched to the hard interface. Indeed, on hard(tr8) (column three in Figure 16.6) the easy–hard group is statistically indistinguishable from the hard–easy group on hard(tr4) (column two in Figure 16.6), $p > 0.10$. The strategies adopted with the easy interface condition during training did not transfer to the hard interface.

In contrast, the group that transfers to the easy interface after experience using the hard interface [the hard(tr4)–easy(tr8) group] transfers the by-column strategies they acquired during training. Comparing column one with column four in Figure 16.6, it is apparent that unlike the nonsignificant difference between hard(tr4) and hard(tr8) there is a significant difference in strategy use between easy(tr4) and easy(tr8) [F (1, 62) = 10.55, $p = 0.002$, MSE = 4.24].

Although on easy(tr8) subjects could program by row without incurring an extra perceptual–motor cost, most of them did not. The paradox to

be explained is why the entire group did not switch to the intuitively simpler by-row strategy. Apparently, in transferring from a hard interface to an easy interface, the methods acquired with the hard interface persisted. Just as apparently, in going from an easy to a hard interface, subjects quickly adapted to the hard interface.

Summary and Conclusions

Prior experience changes the nature of the functional task environment. Rather than being driven by local considerations of least effort, prior experience brings in more global issues concerning what works well across the range of task environments that people use (Fu & Gray, 2004).

For the VCR study, the finding of asymmetric transfer seems surprising only from the perspective of an outside observer. From the perspective of subjects in the hard–easy condition, during the easy phase of the study (shows 5–8) the perceptual–motor cost of the by-column strategy greatly decreased and the memory cost stayed about the same. Hence, a strategy that worked well under the conditions of the hard task environment still worked and was easier to implement in the easy task environment.

In contrast, going from the easy to hard task environment greatly increased the perceptual–motor costs. Hence, during transfer, subjects in the easy–hard condition are motivated to reduce their workload. The expected utility calculations of soft constraints include not simply the local cost of a strategy but also its success and failure in other task environments in which it has been applied. Another way of saying this is that the functional task environment includes not just the physical task environment plus embodied cognition but a significant component of prior experience.

The asymmetric transfer suggests an extension of the Bayesian satisficing theory developed by Fu (2003; Fu & Gray, in press), which shows that people adapt more quickly to changes in costs than to changes in benefit. Increasing the cost of a strategy increases the probability that people will search for a new one. Paradoxically but predictably, decreasing the cost of a strategy prematurely terminates the search for a more efficient strategy, resulting in stable, but suboptimal performance.

Costs without Benefits: Distinguishing between Cognitive versus Ecological Limits to Optimal Performance

In an influential paper, Norman and Bobrow (1975) pointed out that human performance could fail to achieve its goals due to either limits in the design of the task environment (design limits) or limits in the available human resources (resource limits). Whatever the available resources, performance could not exceed design limits. (In the zeitgeist of the times, Norman and Bobrow conducted their study within an information processing paradigm and spoke about their results in terms of data limits and cognitive resource limits. However, their basic point extends to design limits as well as to limits on any aspects of embodied cognition.)

Simon warned us to be sure we consider the beach as well as the ant (Simon, 1996) when making inferences about human performance. This exhortation often is ignored by cognitive researchers who may interpret less than perfect performance in their paradigm as shedding light on cognitive theory. It also often is ignored by human factors professionals who may interpret less than perfect performance as indicating a training problem or the need for better compliance to standard operating procedures.

For example, in a recent study of errors that commercial airline pilots make when taxiing (i.e., the period between landing the plane and getting it to the right gate), Byrne and Kirlik (2005; see also chapter 18) discovered that the strategies reported by their experts worked differentially well at different U.S. airports. Hence, getting lost while trying to find your gate can be attributed in part to the application of a strategy that works well at most airports, just not the airport in which you are currently located. Infinite amounts of training and exhortations to get pilots to perfectly execute strategies that work well at, say, Denver, will not reduce the error rate at, say, O'Hare.

This section discusses two related questions, both of which ignore resource limits to focus on design limits. The first question asks, "regardless of human limits, what is the optimal performance in this task environment?" (Neth et al., 2004). The second asks, "regardless of the cost, if strategy X were consistently used, how successful would it be?" (Gray, Schoelles, & Myers, 2002).

TRACS: An Optimality Analysis of the Task Environment

TRACS is a Tool for Research on Adaptive Cognitive Strategies (Burns, 2004). As shown on the upper left of Figure 16.7, TRACS has three shapes—triangle, circle, and square—with eight cards per shape. Each shape has two types of cards—red and blue—and each card has two sides. The distribution of card types per shape varies; triangles start with six red and two blue; circles with four each, and squares with two red and six blue.

Straight TRACS is the simplest version of the TRACS family of games. In Straight TRACS three cards are dealt at a time (as shown in the main part of Figure 16.7). The center card is face-up showing its color and shape (in this case a blue triangle). The left and right cards are face down, showing their shape (triangle on the left and square on the right), but not their colors. The player's task is to pick the card, left or right, that is most likely to match the color of the center card.

Burns (2002) makes the counterintuitive claim that TRACS players exhibited a baseline bias. One game of TRACS consists of 11 turns. Over the course of these turns the proportion of red and blue cards played out varies. However, rather than picking cards based on the proportion of reds and blues remaining in each shape, players picked cards based

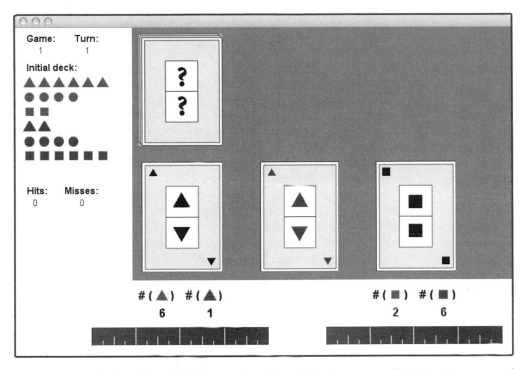

Figure 16.7. Screen shot of TRACS*. There are three shapes (triangle, square, and circle) with two types of cards per shape—red or blue. The color is revealed on the card's face (as shown by the middle card). The backs of the cards indicate the shape, but not the color (as shown by the left and right cards). See text for more details.

on the baseline distribution of red and blue cards. As it ran contrary to the well-known bias of baserate neglect (e g , see Gluck & Bower, 1988), this failure to update in a dynamic card game appeared to be a potentially interesting phenomenon.

Playing many games of TRACS confirmed our inability to perform better than baseline. However, it also raised a suspicion that perhaps updating memories for cards played did not benefit performance. A detailed task analyses of TRACS (Neth et al., 2004) confirmed this suspicion. Neth and colleagues followed up the task analysis with a simulation of 10,000 TRACS games played by each of four very different players. The Random player always selected the left or right card at random. The Baseline player always based the choices on the baseline distribution of red and blue cards in a shape. The Update player carefully updated its distribution of red and blue cards per shape as they were played. It based each choice on the number of red and blue cards remaining in each shape. Finally, the Omniscient player could see through the backs of the cards. If either the left or right card

matched the color of the middle card, the Omniscient player would choose it. (If both matched or if neither matched, it chose one at random.)

Across 10,000 games the Random agent scored a mean of 5.24 correct matches out of 11 turns per game with the Omniscient agent at 8.54 per game. The Baseline and Update agents were about equal at 6.57 and 6.79, respectively. The two-tenths of a point difference between Baseline and Update would be easily lost in the variance of real human performance.

Neth et al. (2004) provide a detailed task analysis of Straight TRACS, a fuller discussion of the simulation, and a detailed explanation of the results. They also report on a new version, TRACS*, that was designed so that the difference between a perfect Baseline and a perfect Update agent would be 8.22 versus 10.83. An experiment performed using TRACS* shows that on their first game humans averaged a score of 8.8, but by their 10th game they averaged 9.7. This improvement is significant. With experience in the task environment, humans perform better than the optimal Baseline agent but poorer than the optimal Update agent. To avoid drawing false inferences about the limits of boundedly rational cognition, it must be clear that performance is resource limited, not design limited.

Computational Cognitive Models in Search of Ecologically Optimal Strategies

Argus (Schoelles & Gray, 2001a, 2001b) requires participants to classify the threat value of multiple targets in a radar-like monitoring task. Having an effective target acquisition strategy for selecting the next target to classify is a key component of effective performance.

The Border and Scan strategies are two search strategies that seem reasonable, but which subjects use inconsistently if at all. For maximum performance, each target needs to be correctly classified before it leaves one sector and enters another (see Figure 16.8). A Border strategy would always select the target that was closest to the border. In

contrast, for the Scan strategy people pick one of the four radar sectors and methodically process targets from right to left (or reverse). This strategy requires subjects to keep track of their current sector and, minimally, something about the spatial location of the last target checked.

Of the two, the Border strategy was my personal favorite, because it seemed to be the most efficient. To explain its inconsistent use, I postulated that powerful bottom-up or stimulus-driven factors (such as configural properties of the visual displays) distracted subjects from the consistent application of this strategy. The supposition was that performance would be better if subjects ignored these distracters and consistently applied the Border strategy.

To test the effectiveness of the consistent application of both strategies (Gray et al., 2002), we took one computational cognitive model (Schoelles, 2002) and, holding all else constant, swapped in and out three strategies for target acquisition. In

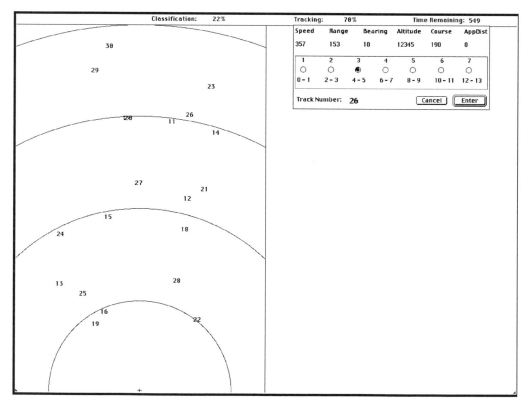

Figure 16.8. One version of the interface to Argus Prime. The left half shows the radar screen and status bar (top). Ownship is indicated by the small +at the bottom. Across the top is summative feedback for the classification and tracking tasks, as well as the time remaining in the scenario (in seconds). The top right half shows the target's attributes and the radio buttons used for entering the estimated threat value of the target on a 1–7 scale. The black dot in radio button 3 indicates the threat value assigned this target by the subject.

addition to the Border and Scan strategy a Random strategy was implemented that would always pick its target at random from the 18 on the screen. The model was then run many times on each strategy.

The original study varied two interface factors and one model factor. Although these details are very interesting, they varied the size of the difference between strategies but not their rank order. (Consequently, details of these strategies are not discussed here. Interested readers are referred to the original paper, Gray et al., 2002.) Across all interface and model factors, on the classification task the Scan strategy was consistently the best (71%), followed by the Random strategy (63%), with the Border strategy producing the worst performance (50%).

How do these findings relate to the stated theme of using computational cognitive models to determine a set of ecologically optimal strategies for the Argus task? First, I was surprised by how poorly the pure Border strategy did. Contrary to my intuitions, apparently hunting for the target that is just about to cross a border consumes time that could be better used elsewhere. In any case, the data are now in; even implemented correctly and consistently, the Border strategy is simply not an ecologically optimal model for the Argus Prime task.

Second, it was even more surprising to see how well the Random strategy did. The Random strategy was included to provide a baseline of performance and reveal how bad the human subjects would be if they did not adopt a systematic target acquisition strategy but simply selected targets at random. However, because the Random strategy was not intended to be cognitively plausibility the heart of the Random strategy was a piece of software code that picked one target at random from among all the targets currently on the screen. It is a reasonable certainty that (most of) the human subjects do not have an implanted random number generator. Although I know of no studies that have compared a truly random search strategy with a human attempt at a random search strategy, it is the case that humans are generally bad at attempts to generate random sequences (Towse & Neil, 1998). Hence, despite its high level of ecological optimality across interface conditions, a true Random strategy is one that humans are incapable of implementing.

Third, the relatively unsophisticated but systematic Scan strategy ranked higher than the Border strategy and the Random strategy in all interface conditions.

Summary of Costs without Benefits

It is obvious that even an agent with infinite resources could not perform better than the optimal allowed by the design of the task environment. This section has discussed two studies that investigated explanations that attributed lower than expected performance to limits of the agent.

In cases such as TRACS, optimal performance of a strategy can be evaluated without considering human limits of cognition, perception, and action. For TRACS the conclusion was that even an ideal agent would not benefit from a memory update strategy. The limit to performance was built into the design of the task environment and was not an issue for cognitive analysis.

For Argus Prime, two cognitively plausible search strategies were compared. It was hypothesized that the Border strategy was optimal and that the failure to find consistent use of this strategy reflected the operation of powerful bottom-up or stimulus-driven factors (such as configural properties of the visual displays) that distracted subjects from the consistent application of the optimal strategy. *A priori* beliefs have been forced to yield to hard data. In the Argus Prime simulated task environment, the Border strategy is not particularly good. Indeed, it is beaten by both the Scan strategy and the Random strategy. As the developers of Argus Prime, my colleagues and I are truly chagrined to admit our long-held belief that the Border strategy was the optimal strategy was inaccurate.

Summary of the Studies

As Simon (1992) said, to define optimal performance we must analyze the structure of the task environment along with the goals of the user. The work reported here suggests that ignoring the analysis of optimality may lead one to draw false conclusions about people's willingness or success at implementing different strategies in a given task environment.

The TRACS study used a cognitively implausible ideal agent to demonstrate that there was no benefit to implementing an effortful memory update strategy. Half of the soft constraints question is about benefit, and the other half is about costs. However, asking about costs without first asking about benefit is clearly a fruitless endeavor.

In the study comparing Border versus Scan strategies for target acquisition, two cognitively plausible strategies were implemented but run without considering soft constraints. That is, the model was forced to use a fixed strategy under circumstance in which an adaptive agent would not have. Hence, this research assessed the benefits of each search strategy regardless of its cost.

The study on the paradox of the active user drew attention to the multiple task environments in which human performance takes place. The investigation of transfer from an easy to a hard interface condition showed that differences in the costs of interaction across two varieties of a task environment produced asymmetrical differences in strategy transfer. Strategies adopted for a low-cost task environment were dropped when the costs of maintaining these strategies was increased. In contrast, strategies adopted in a high-cost task environment were transferred to a lower cost task environment. This transfer occurred even though the transferred by-column strategy was higher cost in the new task environment than the unused by-row strategy. This finding emphasizes the fact that soft constraints encompass a strategy's history of success and failures (i.e., its benefit), not simply its current cost.

When the benefits are about equal, the Soft Constraints framework suggests that different compositions of activities may be recruited based on considerations of local costs. This conclusion was found to be true in the dynamic decision-making study. In that study, different lockout costs led to the adoption of either an interaction-intensive or memory-intensive strategy. Likewise, the results of Gray and Fu's (2004) VCR study were interpreted as reflecting a least-effort competition between alternative implementations of the same step. Within each of three conditions, Gray-Box, Free-Access, and Memory-Test, the same step could be accomplished by retrieving knowledge from in-the-world or in-the-head. The pattern of results suggested that subjects at least sometimes ignored perfect knowledge in-the-world for imperfect knowledge in-the-head. This pattern was explained as the influence of soft constraints in selecting the least-effort basic activities in the functional task environment.

Conclusions

Advances in our study of embodied cognition have led to the realization that properties of functional cognition and of the world are in a tight loop. Prop-erties of our cognitive, perceptual, and action systems determine how much and what aspects of the world we perceive; whereas properties of the world determine the mixture of cognitive, perceptual, and action operations required for us to perceive it. If we and our world form an integrated system, then an ecological analyses of our task environment cannot be separated from an analysis of functional cognition. Indeed, rather than speaking of task environments in general, we need to distinguish between physical and functional task environments. The physical task environment consists of objects that can be interacted with by the human perceptual–motor system. The functional task environment encompasses both more and less than the physical task environment. First, the functional task environment only incorporates those physical features with which the embodied cognitive system interacts. Second, the methods for interaction are shaped by soft constraints. Third, cognitive resources such as long-term memory, working memory, and attention form an integral part of the functional task environment.

The more naive view of the trade-offs between knowledge in-the-head versus in-the-world views the task environment as providing an external memory that can be used to reduce the amount of in-the-head processing we need to do to get by. Recasting the physical task environment as a functional task environment results in viewing the mixture of in-the-head versus in-the-world resources as not fixed but fluid. The Soft Constraints approach shows how the mixture of external versus internal resources is driven by the nondeliberate calculation of benefits and costs. Understanding the resources that the cognitive controller can obtain from the task environment should be the bases of ecological analyses. Understanding the costs of retrieving and processing information and how these costs are realized in-the-head or driven by changes in the task environment should be the bases of cognitive analyses. Rapprochement of ecological and cognitive analyses is not simply an interesting new direction, it is vital for the continuing progress of our science.

Acknowledgments. Thanks to Michael Byrne, Christopher W. Myers, Hansjörg Neth, Peter Pirolli, Michael J. Schoelles, Chris R. Sims, and V. Daniel Veksler for their close reading and helpful comments on earlier versions of this chapter. The writing of this chapter was supported by a grants from the Air Force Office of Scientific Research AFOSR

#F49620-03-1-0143, as well as the Office of Naval Research ONR \#N000140310046.

References

Anderson, J. R. (1987). Methodologies for studying human knowledge. *Behavioral and Brain Sciences, 10*(3), 467–477.

Anderson, J. R. (1990). *The adaptive character of thought*. Hillsdale, N.J.: Lawrence Erlbaum.

Anderson, J. R. (1991). Is human cognition adaptive? *Behavioral and Brain Sciences, 14*(3), 471–517.

Anderson, J. R., Bothell, D., Byrne, M. D., Douglas, S., Lebiere, C., & Quin, Y. (2004). An integrated theory of the mind. *Psychological Review, 111*(4), 1036–1060.

Ballard, D. H. (2002). Our perception of the world has to be an illusion. *Journal of Consciousness Studies, 9*(5–6), 54–71.

Ballard, D. H., Hayhoe, M. M., & Pelz, J. B. (1995). Memory representations in natural tasks. *Journal of Cognitive Neuroscience, 7*(1), 66–80.

Ballard, D. H., Hayhoe, M. M., Pook, P. K., & Rao, R. P. N. (1997). Deictic codes for the embodiment of cognition. *Behavioral and Brain Sciences, 20*(4), 723–742.

Brunswik, E. (2001/1955). Representative design and probabilistic theory in a functional psychology. In K. R. Hammond & T. R. Stewart (Eds.), *The essential Brunswik* (pp. 135–155). New York: Oxford University Press.

Burns, K. (2002). On straight TRACS: A baseline bias from mental models. In W. D. Gray & C. D. Schunn (Eds.), *Twenty-fourth Annual Conference of the Cognitive Science Society* (pp. 154–159). Mahwah, N.J.: Erlbaum.

Burns, K. (2004). *TRACS: A tool for research on adaptive cognitive strategies: The game of confidence and consequences*. Online document available at www.tracsgame.com.

Byrne, M. D., & Kirlik, A. (2005). Using computational cognitive modeling to diagnose possible sources of aviation error. *International Journal of Aviation Psychology, 15,* 135–155.

Carlson, R. A. (2002). Conscious intentions in the control of skilled mental activity. In *Psychology of Learning and Motivation: Advances in Research and Theory, 41,* 191–228.

Carroll, J. M., & Rosson, M. B. (1987). Paradox of the active user. In J. M. Carroll (Ed.), *Interfacing thought: Cognitive aspects of human–computer interaction*. Cambridge, Mass.: MIT Press.

Clark, A. (2004). *Embodiment and ecological control*. Online document available at www.cognitivesciencesociety.org/colloquium/archive.html.

Clark, A. (in press). Re-inventing ourselves: The plasticity of embodiment, sensing, and mind. *Journal of Medicine and Philosophy.*

Fu, W.-T. (2003). *Adaptive planning in problem solving—cost-benefit tradeoffs in bounded rationality*. Unpublished doctoral dissertation, George Mason University, Fairfax, Va.

Fu, W.-T., & Gray, W. D. (2004). Resolving the paradox of the active user: Stable suboptimal performance in interactive tasks. *Cognitive Science, 28*(6), 901–935.

Fu, W.-T., & Gray, W. D. (in press). Suboptimal tradeoffs in information seeking. *Cognitive Psychology*

Gluck, M. A., & Bower, G. H. (1988). From conditioning to category learning: An adaptive netword model. *Journal of Experimental Psychology: General, 117,* 227–247.

Godfrey-Smith, P. (2001). Three kinds of adaptationism. In S. H. Orzack & E. Sober (Eds.), *Adaptationism and optimality* (pp. 335–357). New York: Cambridge University Press.

Gray, W. D. (2000). The nature and processing of errors in interactive behavior. *Cognitive Science, 24*(2), 205–248

Gray, W. D., & Boehm-Davis, D. A. (2000). Milliseconds matter: An introduction to microstrategies and to their use in describing and predicting interactive behavior. *Journal of Experimental Psychology. Applied, 6*(4), 322–335.

Gray, W. D., & Fu, W.-T. (2004). Soft constraints in interactive behavior: The case of ignoring perfect knowledge in-the-world for imperfect knowledge in-the-head. *Cognitive Science, 28*(3), 359–382.

Gray, W. D., Schoelles, M. J., & Myers, C. W. (2002). Computational cognitive models ISO ecologically optimal strategies, *46th Annual Conference of the Human Factors and Ergonomics Society* (pp. 492–496). Santa Monica, Calif.: Human Factors and Ergonomics Society.

Gray, W. D., Schoelles, M. J., & Myers, C. W. (2004). Strategy constancy amidst implementation differences: Interaction-intensive versus memory-intensive adaptations to information access in decision-making. In K. D. Forbus, D. Gentner, & T. Regier (Eds.), *26th Annual Meeting of the Cognitive Science Society, CogSci2004* (pp. 482–487). Hillsdale, N.J.: Lawrence Erlbaum.

Gray, W. D., Veksler, V. D., & Fu, W.-T. (2004). Probing the paradox of the active user: Asymmetrical transfer may produce stable, suboptimal performance. In K. D. Forbus, D. Gentner, & T. Regier (Eds.), *26th Annual Meeting of the*

Cognitive Science Society, CogSci2004 (pp. 1564). Hillsdale, N.J.: Lawrence Erlbaum.

Herrnstein, R. J. (1991). Experiments on stable suboptimality in individual behavior. *American Economic Review, 81*(2), 360–364.

Kieras, D. E., & Meyer, D. E. (1997). An overview of the EPIC architecture for cognition and performance with application to human-computer interaction. *Human-Computer Interaction, 12*(4), 391–438.

Kieras, D. E., Meyer, D. E., Ballas, J. A., & Lauber, E. J. (2000). Modern computational perspectives on executive mental processes and cognitive control: Where to from here? In S. Monsell & J. Driver (Eds.), *Control of cognitive processes: Attention and performance XVIII* (pp. 681–712). Cambridge, Mass.: MIT Press.

Leahey, T. H. (2003). Herbert A. Simon—Nobel Prize in economic sciences, 1978. *American Psychologist, 58*(9), 753–755.

Myers, C. W., & Gray, W. D. (2005). Affecting initial saccades through stimulus configuration and cognitive load: Capturing the competition between deliberate and unintentional processes. Manuscript submitted for publication.

Neth, H., Sims, C. R., Veksler, V. D., & Gray, W. D. (2004). You can't play straight TRACS and win: Memory updates in a dynamic task environment. In K. D. Forbus, D. Gentner, & T. Regier (Eds.), *26th Annual Meeting of the Cognitive Science Society, CogSci2004* (pp. 1017–1022). Hillsdale, N.J.: Lawrence Erlbaum.

Newell, A. (1973). You can't play 20 questions with nature and win: Projective comments on the papers of this symposium. In W. G. Chase (Ed.), *Visual information processing* (pp. 283–308). New York: Academic Press.

Newell, A. (1990). *Unified theories of cognition.* Cambridge, Mass.: Harvard University Press.

Newell, A. (1992). Precis of unified theories of cognition. *Behavioral and Brain Sciences, 15*(3), 425–437.

Norman, D. A., & Bobrow, D. G. (1975). On data-limited and resource-limited processes. *Cognitive Psychology, 7*, 44–64.

Payne, J. W., Bettman, J. R., & Johnson, E. J. (1993). *The adaptive decision maker.* New York: Cambridge University Press.

Salvucci, D. D. (2001). An integrated model of eye movements and visual encoding. *Cognitive Systems Research, 1*(4), 201–220.

Schoelles, M. J. (2002). *Simulating human users in dynamic environments.* Unpublished doctoral dissertation. George Mason University, Fairfax, Va.

Schoelles, M. J., & Gray, W. D. (2001a). Argus: A suite of tools for research in complex cognition. *Behavior Research Methods, Instruments, & Computers, 33*(2), 130–140.

Schoelles, M. J., & Gray, W. D. (2001b). Decomposing interactive behavior. In J. D. Moore & K. Stenning (Eds.), *Twenty-Third Annual Conference of the Cognitive Science Society* (pp. 898–903). Mahwah, N.J.: Lawrence Erlbaum.

Schweickert, R., Fisher, D. L., & Proctor, R. W. (2003). Steps toward building mathematical and computer models from cognitive task analyses. *Human Factors, 45*(1), 77–103.

Simon, H. A. (1956). Rational choice and the structure of the environment. *Psychological Review, 63*, 129–138.

Simon, H. A. (1992). What is an "explanation" of behavior? *Psychological Science, 3*(3), 150–161.

Simon, H. A. (1996). *The sciences of the artificial* (3rd ed.). Cambridge, Mass.: MIT Press.

Simons, D. J., & Levin, D. T. (1998). Failure to detect changes to people during a real-world interaction. *Psychonomic Bulletin & Review, 5*(4), 644–649.

Towse, J. N., & Neil, D. (1998). Analyzing human random generation behavior: A review of methods used and a computer program for describing performance. *Behavior Research Methods Instruments & Computers, 30*(4), 583–591.

Treisman, A. M., & Gelade, G. (1980). A feature integration theory of attention. *Cognitive Psychology, 12*, 97–136.

Treisman, A. M., & Sato, S. (1990). Conjunction search revisited. *Journal of Experimental Psychology: Human Perception and Performance, 16*, 459–478.

Ullman, S. (1984). Visual routines. *Cognition, 18*(1–3), 97–159.

Wilson, M. (2002). Six views of embodied cognition. *Psychonomic Bulletin & Review, 9*(4), 625–636.

Wolfe, J. M. (1998). Visual search. In H. Pashler (Ed.), *Attention* (pp. 13–73). East Sussex, UK: Psychology Press.

Wolfe, T. (1968). *The electric kool-aid acid test.* New York: Bantam Books.

Yechiam, E., Erev, I., Yehene, V., & Gopher, D. (2003). Melioration and the transition from touch-typing training to everyday use. *Human Factors, 45*(4), 671–684.

Peter Pirolli

The Use of Proximal Information Scent to Forage for Distal Content on the World Wide Web

The legacy of the Enlightenment is the belief that entirely on our own we can know, and in knowing, understand, and in understanding, choose wisely. . . . Thanks to science and technology, access to factual knowledge of all kinds is rising exponentially while dropping in unit cost. . . . We are drowning in information, while starving for wisdom.
—E. O. Wilson (1998)

Introduction

Information foraging theory addresses how people will adaptively shape their behavior to their information environments and how information environments can best be shaped to people. It is a psychological theory explicitly formulated to deal with the analysis of adaptation (good designs) and explicitly formulated to deal with how external content is used to gain valuable knowledge. This symmetrical focus on users and their information system environments has been inspired in many ways by methods and concepts championed in Brunswik's (1952) probabilistic functionalism. This chapter summarizes information foraging research on use of the World Wide Web (hereafter, the Web). This research involves concepts that are akin to ones developed by Brunswik, including the use of representative design, in which realistic Web tasks are studied, a variant of a lens model of how people judge the relevance of navigation cues on the Web, and the use of an idiographic-statistical approach to model aspects of human cognition.

The particular focus of this chapter will be on a psychological theory of *information scent* (Pirolli, 1997, 2003; Pirolli & Card, 1999) that is embedded in a broader model (Pirolli & Fu, 2003) of in-

formation foraging on the Web. The notion of information scent also has been used in developing models of people seeking information in document-clustering browsers (Pirolli, 1997) and highly interactive information visualizations (Pirolli, Card, & Van Der Wege, 2003). *Information scent* refers to the cues used by information foragers to make judgments related to the selection of information sources to pursue and consume. These cues include such items as Web links or bibliographic citations that provide users with concise information about content that is not immediately available. The information scent cues play an important role in guiding users to the information they seek; they also play a role in providing users with an overall sense of the contents of collections. The purpose of this chapter is to present a theoretical account of information scent that supports the development of models of navigation choice.

Information foraging theory is an example of a recent flourish of theories in adaptationist psychology that draw on evolutionary-ecological theory in biology (e.g., Anderson, 1990; Cosmides, Tooby, & Barow, 1992; Gigerenzer, 2000; Glimcher, 2003). The framework of adaptationist psychology involves the analysis of the structure of the environments faced by people and analysis of the design (or engineering) rationale of the psychological mechanisms and knowledge used by people to perform adaptively in those environments. Such theories are developed through methodological adaptationism that assumes that it is a good heuristic for scientists to presuppose that evolving, behaving systems are rational or well designed for fulfilling certain functions in certain environments. In other words, there is an assumption of *ecological rationality* regarding the behavior of the system being observed (Bechtel, 1985; Dennett, 1983, 1988, 1995; Todd & Gigerenzer, 2000). Many (e.g., Anderson, 1990; Dennett, 1995; Marr, 1982) have argued that to understand the cognitive mechanisms underlying behavior, one has to begin by defining its function in relation to the environment. The adaptationist approach involves a kind of reverse engineering in which the analyst asks (a) *what* environmental problem is solved, (b) *why* is a given system a good solution to the problem, and (c) *how* is that solution realized by mechanism. This simultaneous concern with environment and organism echoes the approach of Brunswik. Information foraging theory (Pirolli & Card, 1999) is an adaptationist theory that assumes that human information-seeking mechanisms and strategies adapt to the structure of the information environments in which they operate.

Next I present some aspects of the Web environment that will be relevant to developing a model of how people assess information scent cues to navigate.[1] Users' navigation in the Web environment can be seen as involving assessments of proximal information scent cues to make action choices that lead to distal information sources. This view is a variant of Brunswik's lens model (Brunswik, 1952). This lens model view is then used to frame the development of a stochastic model of individual utility judgment and choice that derives from a Bayesian analysis of the environment. This Bayesian analysis motivates a set of cognitive mechanisms based on spreading activation (Anderson, 1990; Anderson & Milson, 1989) and a decision model based on the random utility model (RUM; McFadden, 1974, 1978). The general argument is that information foragers operate in an ecologically rational manner to make choices based on their predictive judgments (under uncertainty) based on information scent. This information scent model (spreading activation plus RUM) of the navigation choice behavior of individuals can be seen as a variant of the idiographic-statistical approach advocated by

Brunswik (1952). Finally, I summarize a model of Web foraging (Pirolli & Fu, 2003) that addresses data (Card et al., 2001; Morrison, Pirolli, & Card, 2001) collected from Web users working on tasks in a study that attempted to follow Brunswik's tenets of representative design.

Aspects of the Structure of the Web

Task Environment and Information Environment

It is useful to think of two interrelated environments in which an information forager operates: the *task environment* and the *information environment*. The classical definition of the task environment is that it "refers to an environment coupled with a goal, problem or task—the one for which the motivation of the subject is assumed. It is the task that defines a point of view about the environment, and that, in fact allows an environment to be delimited" (Newell & Simon, 1972, p. 55). The task environment is the scientist's analysis of those aspects of the physical, social, virtual, and cognitive environments that drive human behavior.

The information environment is a tributary of knowledge that permits people to engage their task environments more adaptively. Most of the tasks that we identify as significant problems in our everyday life require that we get more knowledge— become better informed—before taking action. What we know or do not know affects how well we function in the important task environments we face in life. External content provides the means for expanding and improving our abilities. The information environment, in turn, structures our interactions with this content. Our particular analytic viewpoint on the information environment will be determined by the information needs that arise from the embedding task environment. From the standpoint of a psychological analysis, the information environment is delimited and defined in relation to the task environment.

When people interact with information through technology, those technological systems act as *cognitive prostheses*[2] that more or less help us intelligently find and use the right knowledge at the right time. People shape themselves and their cognitive prostheses to be more adaptive in reaction to their goals and the structure and constraints of their information environments. A useful abstract way of thinking about such adaptation is to say that human–information interaction systems will tend to maximize the value of external knowledge gained relative to the cost of interaction. Schematically, we may characterize this maximization tendency as

(17.1)   max[Expected value of knowledge gained/Cost of interaction]

This hypothesis is consistent with Resnikoff's (1989, p. 97) observation that natural and artificial information systems evolve toward stable states that maximize gains of valuable information per unit cost (when feasible). Cognitive systems engaged in information foraging will exhibit such adaptive tendencies.

It is important to note that the numerator in Equation 17.1 is not simply "amount of knowledge gained," rather than a measure of the value (utility) of the knowledge gained. If people simply maximized gain of knowledge, then the prediction would be that people would spend all of their time in the biggest library possible or all of their time on the Internet. The value of knowledge may be measured against improvements that the knowledge brings to the information forager. Discussion of the value of knowledge (or information) may be found in microeconomics (e.g., Stigler, 1961), artificial intelligence (e.g., Pearl, 1988, see esp. pp. 313–327), and cognitive science (Newell, 1990, sec. 2.7). It is also important to note that the numerator refers to the *expected value* of knowledge gained. An expected value is typically defined using probabilistic terms —for instance, the consideration of the possible values that might be attained by different courses of action weighted by the probability of taking each action and attaining those values. Thus Equation 17.1 is crucially dependent on probabilistic analysis because the information forager operates in a probabilistically textured information environment.

Probabilistic Texture

In contrast to application programs such as text editors and spreadsheets, in which actions have fairly determinate outcomes (barring bugs, of course), foraging through a large volume of information involves uncertainties—for a variety of reasons— about the location, quality, relevance, veracity, and so on, of the information sought and the effects of foraging actions. In other words, the information

forager must deal with a *probabilistically textured* information environment. The ecological rationality of information foraging behavior must be analyzed through the theoretical lens and tools appropriate to decision making under uncertainty. The determinate formalisms and determinate cognitive mechanisms that are characteristic of the traditional approach to cognitive models in human–computer interaction (e.g., Card, Moran, & Newell, 1983) are inadequate for the job of theorizing about information foraging in probabilistically textured environments. Models developed in information foraging theory draw on probabilistic models, especially Bayesian approaches, and bear similarity to economic models of decision making (rational choice) under uncertainty and engineering models.

A Lens Model Framework for Information Scent

Throughout the foraging literature, it is assumed that organisms base their foraging decisions on predictions about the typology and utility of habitat and the typology and utility of food items (e.g., species of prey or plants). I assume that the information forager must also base decisions on assessments of information habitats and information items and that these assessments are based on learned utility judgments. Information scent refers to those environmental cues that feed into the utility judgments made by information foragers.

Figure 17.1 presents some examples of information scent cues. Figure 17.1a is a typical page generated by a Web search engine in response to a user query. The page lists Web pages (search results) that are predicted to be relevant to the query. Each search result is represented by its title (in blue), phrases from the hit containing words from the query (in black), and a URL (in green). Figure 17.1b illustrates an alternative form of search result representation provided by *relevance enhanced thumbnails* (Woodruff et al., 2002), which combine thumbnail images of search results with highlighted text relevant to the user's query. Figure 17.1c is a hyperbolic tree browser (marketed by Inxight as the Star Tree) (Lamping & Rao, 1994; Lamping, Rao, & Pirolli, 1995). Each label on each node in the hyperbolic tree is the title for a Web page. Finally, Figure 17.1d presents the Microsoft Explorer browser with a typical file system view. Each label on a node represents a folder, file, or application.

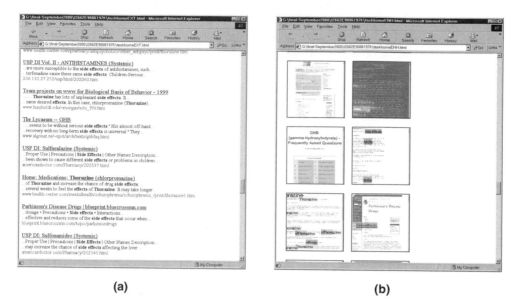

(a)   (b)

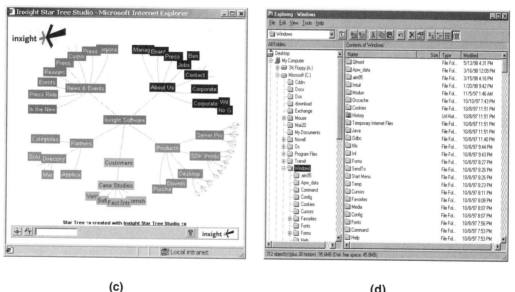

(c)   (d)

Figure 17.1. Examples of proximal information scent cues: (a) A standard list of results returned by a Web search engine, (b) relevance-enhanced thumbnails, (c) hyperbolic tee, and (c) the Explorer file browser.

Egon Brunswik's (1956) ecological lens model can be used to frame our thinking about examples of information scent, such as those in Figure 17.1. The lens model (Figure 17.2) characterizes the judgment problems facing organisms in probabilistically textured environments. In each example in Figure 17.1, the distal sources of information (e.g., Web articles) are represented by some set of mediating cues (link summaries; relevance enhanced thumbnails; node labels; bibliographic citations). On the

basis of these proximal cues, the user must make judgments about what is available and potential value of going after the distal content.[3] This distinction between proximal cues and distal objects is a well-known aspect of Brunswik's (1956) ecological theory of perception and judgment in a probabilistically textured environment. In Brunswik's lens model (Figure 17.2) the perception or judgment of a distal object or event is indirect and must be made on the basis of proximal cues. Brunswik (1956)

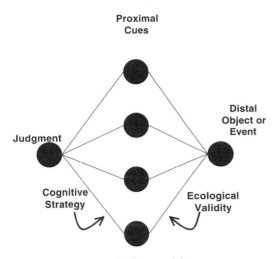

Figure 17.2. Brunswik's lens model.

advocated a detailed analysis of the probabilistic relationships between observer and proximal cues (cognitive strategy) and between proximal cues and distal object or events (ecological validity) This will be done using Bayesian analysis and a computational model— tools that were not in prevalent use during Brunswik's time.

Topical Patches and Diminishing Returns

Users often surf the Web seeking content related to some topic of interest, and the Web tends to be organized into topical localities. Davison (2000) analyzed the topical locality of the Web using 200,998 Web pages sampled from approximately 3 million pages crawled in 1999. Davison assessed the topical similarity of pairs of Web pages from this sample that were linked (had a link between them), siblings (linked from the same parent page), and random (selected at random). The similarities were computed by a normalized correlation or cosine measure,[4] r, on the vectors of the word frequencies in a pair of documents (Manning & Schuetze, 1999).[5] The linked pages showed greater textual similarity ($r = 0.23$) than sibling pages ($r = 0.20$), but both were substantially more similar than random pairs of pages ($r = 0.02$).

Figure 17.3 shows how topical similarity between pages diminishes with the link distance between them. To produce Figure 17.3 I used data collected from the Xerox.com Web site in May 1998 (used for another purpose in Pitkow & Pirolli, 1999) and I computed the page-to-page content similari-

ties for all pairs of pages at minimum distances of 1, 2, 3, 4, and 5 degrees of separation. The similarities were computed by comparing normalized correlations of vectors of the word frequencies in a pair of documents (Manning & Schuetze, 1999). Figure 17.3 shows that the similarity of the content of pages diminishes rapidly as a function of shortest link distance separating them. Figure 17.3 suggests that the Web has topically related information patches.

Of course, what users actually see as links on the Web are sets of proximal cues such as those in Figure 17.1. Davison (2000) compared elaborated anchor text (the anchor plus additional surrounding text, having a mean of 11.02 terms) to a paired document that was either linked (the page linked to the anchor) or random (a random page). The normalized correlation (cosine) similarities were linked $r = 0.16$ and random $r \approx 0$. Davison's analysis of the correlation of proximal cues to distal content confirms our intuition that the cues have ecological validity (Figure 17.2).

Information scent cues are expected to be useful to the information forager in at least two ways. First, information scent provides a way of judging the utility of following alternative paths (i.e., choosing a link from a set of links presented on a Web page). Second, information scent provides a way of detecting that one is moving out of a patch of topical relevance (i.e., by detecting that the quality of information scent is dwindling as in Figure 17.3).

The Theory of Information Scent

Anderson (Anderson, 1990; Anderson & Milson, 1989) presented a rational analysis of human memory that serves as an analogy for the theory of information scent presented here. Anderson and Milson (1989) proposed that human memory is designed to solve the problem of predicting what past experiences will be relevant in ongoing current proximal contexts and allocating resources for the storage and retrieval of past experiences based on those predictions. These authors developed a mathematical formulation that assumes that current proximal *context* factors and past *history* factors combine in forming those predictions about the relevance of past experience. Here I assume that stored past experiences are retrieved, based on proximal features of the current context, and then used to predict the

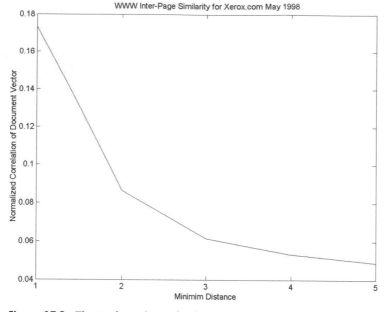

Figure 17.3. The similarity (normalized correlation of document word frequency vectors) of pairs of Web pages as a function of the minimum link distances separating the pairs. Data collected from the Xerox.com Web site, May 1998.

likelihood of distal features. Before delving into the derivation of equations to characterize information scent, it is important to note the ways in which this analysis differs from the analysis of memory. The analysis of memory assumes that there is some internal context (including a goal) that requires predictions about which internal memories might be relevant to achieving goals in that internal context. The analysis of information scent involves predictions about unobserved external content based on observed cues in the external information environment. The equations presented in the following can be viewed as a specification of a Bayesian analysis of how proximal cues are probabilistically related to distal objects. Furthermore, the Bayesian analysis of information scent prediction is a piece of a larger analysis of expected utility and choice. This is quite different than the analysis of memory presented by Anderson and Milson (1989).

Figure 17.4 presents an example for the purposes of discussion in this section. The figure assumes that a user has the goal of finding distal information about medical treatments for cancer, and encounters a hypertext link labeled with the text that includes cell, patient, dose, and beam. The user's cognitive task is to predict the likelihood of the desired distal information from the proximal cues available in the hypertext link labels. It should be noted that Brunswik quantified the linkages between proximal and distal information in the lens model (Figure 17.2) using regression models (i.e., each link in Figure 17.2 could be associated with a correlation coefficient). The extension presented here employs Bayesian likelihoods to quantify the linkages (Figure 17.4).

Bayesian Analysis of Memory-Based Prediction of Distal Features

Bayes's theorem can be applied to the information foraging problem posed by situations such as those in Figure 17.4. The probability of a distal structure of features, D, given a structure of proximal features, P, can be stated using Bayes's theorem as,

$$(17.2) \qquad \Pr(D|P) = \Pr(D) \bullet \Pr(P|D),$$

where $\Pr(D|P)$ is the posterior probability of distal structure D conditional on the occurrence of proximal structure P, $\Pr(D)$ is the prior probability (or base rate) of D, and $\Pr(P|D)$ is the likelihood of P occurring conditional on D. It is mathematically

Desired distal information | **Proximal cues**

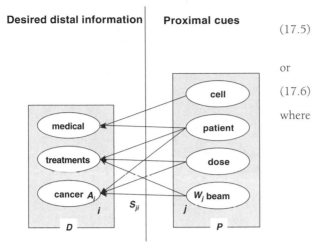

Figure 17.4.. Relations among chunks (the nodes) representing proximal cues (P) in the environment (e.g., a Web link) and the desired distal (D) information (e.g., a goal). Links represent associative strengths between chunks.

more tractable to conduct the analysis using *log odds*. The odds version of Bayes's theorem in Equation 17.2 is

$$(17.3) \quad \frac{\Pr(D|P)}{\Pr(D|\sim P)} = \frac{\Pr(D)}{\Pr(\sim D)} \cdot \frac{\Pr(P|D)}{\Pr(P|\sim D)}$$

where $\Pr(D|\sim P)$ is the probability of distal structure D conditional on a context in which proximal structure P does not occur, $\Pr(\sim D)$ is the prior probability of D not occurring, and $\Pr(P|\sim D)$ is the probability of P occurring given that D does not occur. With some simplifying assumptions and equation manipulation, I can specify an odds equation for each individual feature i of the distal structure D and each individual feature j of the proximal structure,

$$(17.4) \quad \frac{\Pr(i|P)}{\Pr(\sim i|P)} = \frac{\Pr(i)}{\Pr(\sim i)} \cdot \prod_{j \in P} \frac{\Pr(i|j)}{\Pr(i)}$$

where $\Pr(i|j)$ is the conditional probability of a distal feature i occurring given that a proximal feature j is present, $\Pr(\sim i|j)$ is the posterior probability of i not occurring when j is present, $\Pr(i)$ is the prior probability (base rate) of distal feature i occurring, $\Pr(\sim i)$ is the probability of i not occurring, and $\Pr(j|i)$ is the likelihood of proximal feature j occurring given distal feature i. Taking the logarithms of both sides of Equation 17.4 leads to an additive formula,

$$(17.5) \quad \log\left[\frac{\Pr(i|j)}{\Pr(\sim i|j)}\right] = \log\left[\frac{\Pr(i)}{\Pr(\sim i)}\right] + \sum_j \left[\frac{\Pr(j|i)}{\Pr(i)}\right]$$

or

$$(17.6) \quad A_i = B_i + \Sigma_j S_{ji},$$

where

$$A_i = \log\left[\frac{\Pr(i|j)}{\Pr(\sim i|j)}\right],$$

$$B_i = \log\left[\frac{\Pr(i)}{\Pr(\sim i)}\right],$$

$$S_{ji} = \log\left[\frac{\Pr(j|i)}{\Pr(i)}\right].$$

This Bayesian analysis specifies the prediction problem facing the information forager in a probabilistically textured environment. The argument is that a rational (adaptive) solution on the part of the information forager would be to develop mechanisms and strategies that implement an approximation to the solution in Equation 17.6.

Mapping the Bayesian Rational Analysis to Spreading Activation

Having specified a Bayesian analysis of information scent in an ecologically rational way, I can illustrate the proposed cognitive mechanisms for performing these computations. Pirolli (1997) proposed a spreading activation model of information scent. Spreading activation models are neurally inspired models that have been used for decades in simulations of human memory (e.g., Anderson, 1976; Anderson & Lebiere, 2000; Anderson & Pirolli, 1984; Quillan, 1966). In such models, activation may be interpreted metaphorically as a kind of mental energy that drives cognitive processing. Activation spreads from a set of cognitive structures that are the current focus of attention through associations among other cognitive structures in memory. These cognitive structures are called chunks (Anderson & Lebiere, 2000; Miller, 1956; Simon, 1974).

Figure 17.4 presents a scenario for a spreading activation analysis. The chunks representing proximal cues are presented on the right side of the figure. Figure 17.4 also shows that there are associations between the goal chunks (representing needed distal information) and proximal cues (the link summary chunks). The associations among chunks come from past experience. The strength of associations reflects the degree to which proximal cues predict the occurrence of unobserved features. For instance, the words *medical* and *patient* co-occur quite frequently, and they would have a high strength of association. The stronger the associations (reflecting greater predictive strength) the greater the amount of activation flow. These association strengths are reflections of the log likelihood odds developed in Equation 17.6.

Previous cognitive simulations (Pirolli, 1997); Pirolli & Card, 1999) used a spreading activation model derived from the ACT-R theory (Anderson & Lebiere, 2000). The activation of a chunk *i* is

$$(17.6) \qquad A_i = B_i + \Sigma_j W_j S_{ji},$$

where B_i is the base-level activation of *i*, S_{ji} is the association strength between an associated chunk *j* and chunk *i*, and W_j is reflects attention (*source activation*) on chunk *j*. Note that Equation 17.7 reflects the log odds Equation 17.6 but now includes a weighting factor *W* that characterizes capacity limitations of human attention. One may interpret Equation 17.7 as a reflection of a Bayesian prediction of the likelihood of one chunk in the context of other chunks. A_i in Equation 17.7 is interpreted as reflecting the log posterior odds that *i* is likely, B_i is the log prior odds of *i* being likely, and S_{ji} reflects the log likelihood ratios that *i* is likely given that it occurs in the context of chunk *j*. This version of spreading activation was used in the past (Pirolli, 1997; Pirolli & Card, 1999) to develop models of information scent. The basic idea is that information scent cues in the world activate cognitive structures. Activation spreads from these cognitive structures to related structures in the spreading activation network. The amount of activation accumulating on the information goal provides an indicator of the likelihood of the distal features based on the proximal scent cues.[6]

Learning the Strengths

As discussed in Pirolli and Card (1999), it is possible to automatically construct large spreading activation networks from online text corpora. In early research (Pirolli, 1997; Pirolli & Card, 1999), my colleagues and I derived these networks from the Tipster corpus (Harman, 1993). Unfortunately, the Tipster corpus does not contain many of the novel words that arise in popular media such as the Web. In the SNIF-ACT model (Pirolli & Fu, 2003) discussed later, we augmented the statistical database derived from Tipster by estimating word frequency and word co-occurrence statistics from the Web using a program that calls on the AltaVista search engine to provide data. Recently, Turney (2001) has shown that pointwise mutual information (PMI) scores computed from the Web can provide good fits to human word similarity judgments, and PMI turns out to be equal to the interchunk association strength S_{ji} in Equation 17.7. The spreading activation networks and mechanisms capture the probabilistic texture of the linguistic environment.

The Random Utility Model

From proximal information scent cues, the user predicts the utility of a distal information source and makes choices based on the utilities of alternatives. This is achieved by spreading activation from the proximal cues (e.g., cell, patient, dose, and beam in Figure 17.4) and assessing the amount of activation that is received by the desired features of the information goal (e.g., medical, treatments, and cancer in Figure 17.4). The information scent approach developed in Pirolli and Card (1999) is consistent in many ways with the RUM framework (McFadden, 1974, 1978). For my purposes, a RUM consists of assumptions about (a) the characteristics of the information foragers making decisions, including their goal(s); (b) the choice set of alternatives; (c) the proximal cues (attributes) of the alternatives; and (d) a choice rule. For current purposes, I will assume a homogenous set of users with the same goal *G* with features, $i \in G$ (and note that there is much interesting work on RUMs for cases with heterogeneous user goals). Each choice made by a user concerns a set *C* of alternatives, and each alternative *J* is an array of displayed proximal cues, $j \in J$, for some distal information content. Each proximal cue *j* emits a source activation *Wj*. These source activations spread through associations to features *i* that are part of the information goal *G*. The activation received by each goal feature *i* is A_i and the summed activation over all goal features is

$$\sum_{i \in G} A_i.$$

The predicted utility U_{JIG} of distal information content based on proximal cues *J* in the context of goal *G* is:

(17.8) $$U_{JIG} = V_{JIG} + \varepsilon_{JIG}$$

where

$$V_{JIG} = \sum_{i \in G} A_I$$

is the summed activation, and where ε_{JIQ} is a random variable error term reflecting a stochastic component of utility. Thus, the utility U_{JIQ} is composed of a deterministic component V_{JIQ} and a random component ε_{JIQ}. RUM assumes utility maximization where the information forager with goal G chooses J if and only if the utility of J is greater than all the other alternatives in the choice set, that is,

$$U_{JIG} > U_{KIG} \text{ for all } K \varepsilon C.$$

Stated as a choice probability, this gives

(17.9) $\Pr(J|G,C) = \Pr(U_{JIG} \geq U_{KIG}, \forall K \in C)$.

Because of the stochastic nature of the utilities U_{KIG} it is not the case that one alternative will always be chosen over another.

The specific form of the RUM depends on assumptions concerning the nature of the random component ε_i associated with each alternative i. If the distributions of the ε_i are independent identically distributed Gumbel (1958) distributions (double exponential),[7] then Equation 17.9 takes the form of a multinomial logit

(17.10) $$\Pr\left(J|G,C\right) = \frac{e^{\mu V_{JIQ}}}{\sum_{K \in C} e^{\mu V_{KIQ}}}$$

where μ is a scale parameter.[8] If there is only one alternative to choose (e.g., select J or do not select J) then Equation 17.9 takes the form of a binomial logit,

(17.11) $$\Pr\left(J|Q,C\right) = \frac{1}{1 + e^{\mu V_{JIQ}}}$$

Many off-the-shelf statistical packages (e.g., Systat, SPSS) include modules that can estimate the parameters of multinomial logistic models from discrete choice data.

Relating the Spread of Activation to Utility and Choice Probability

For a navigation judgment, I can now specify how the computation of spreading activation yields utilities by substituting Equation 17.7 into Equation 17.8:

(17.12) $$U_{JIQ} = V_{JIQ} + \varepsilon_{JIQ}$$

$$= \sum_{i \in Q} A_i + \varepsilon_{JIQ}$$

$$= \sum_{i \in Q} (B_i + \sum_{j \in J} W_j S_{ji}) + \varepsilon_{JIQ}$$

The RUM is grounded in classic microeconomic theory, and it has relations to psychological models of choice developed by Thurstone (1927) and Luce (1959). Its recent developments are associated with the work of McFadden (1974, 1978). So there are at least three reasons for casting information scent as a RUM.

1. There is prior empirical support for the applicability of the RUM to information scent (Pirolli & Card, 1999).
2. RUM provides a connection among models in psychology microeconomic models of consumer preferences and choice and human–information interaction models.
3. Because of its connections to microeconomics and econometrics, a considerable body of work exists on the statistical estimation of RUMs from choice and ratings data (e.g., Walker & Ben-Akiva, 2002), which could provide an influx of new measurement technology into cognitive science and human–computer interaction.

The study of human–computer interaction will require sophisticated tools, and the established literature and tools associated with RUMs could be useful in this regard.

In the next section I summarize a study (Card et al., 2001) that illustrates in a general way the manner in which information scent controls the behavior of Web users. Then, I present a model (Pirolli & Fu, 2003) that uses the information scent mechanisms outlined in this section to simulate those Web users.

A Laboratory Study of Web Users

Card et al. (2001) conducted a study of Web to develop a base protocol analysis methodology and to begin to understand behavior and cognition involved in basic information foraging on the Web. These analyses were the basis for developing the SNIF-ACT computational cognitive model presented next. The procedure for the experimental design was partly inspired by the notion of representative design championed by Brunswik (1952, 1956).

Brunswik (1952, 1956) developed the method of representative design to ensure that experimental results would be (in modern terminology) *ecologically valid*—that results would generalize from the laboratory to important tasks in the real world. The basic idea behind this method is to use experimental conditions (materials, tasks, etc.) that reflect conditions of the world. Others (notably, Gibson, 1979; Neisser, 1976) have argued strongly that human psychology is exquisitely adapted to its environment and consequently is best revealed through the study of tasks and stimuli representatively sampled from the environment. Brunswik (1944) presents the general argument for designing studies such that their results have situational generality and presents studies of size constancy that illustrate the method. More recently, Gigerenzer (2000) laments psychology's myopic focus on method and inferential statistics aimed at generalizing findings to populations of participants, but psychology's underdevelopment of complementary methodology and statistical machinery for generalizing findings to conditions of the world. Interestingly, a particular version of the methodological problem of using statistics that generalize over subjects but not environmental stimuli was recognized in psycholinguistics in Clark (1973). His specific solution (the use of quasi-F tests) has seen limited use outside of psycholinguistics (but see Pirolli et al., 2003).

To develop a representative set of Web tasks for laboratory study, my colleagues and I (Morrison et al., 2001) conducted a survey to collect and analyze real-world Web tasks. We inserted a survey question into the GVU Tenth WWW User Survey (Kehoe et al., 1999) conducted October–December 1998 by the Graphics, Visualization, and Usability Center at the Georgia Institute of Technology (henceforth called the GVU Survey). From 1994 to 1998 the GVU Survey collected information from online surveys on Internet demographics, culture, e-commerce, advertising, user attitudes, and usage patterns. The survey question (henceforth the Significance Question) we used was a variation on those used in the critical incident technique: "Please try to recall a recent instance in which you found important information on the World Wide Web; information that led to a significant action or decision. Please describe that incident in enough detail so that we can visualize the situation."

The critical incident technique originated in studies of aviation psychology conducted during World War II (Fitts & Jones, 1961), achieved wider recognition with the work of Flanagan (1954) and has evolved many variations in human factors (Shattuck & Woods, 1994), cognitive task analysis (Klein, Calderwood, & Macgregor, 1989), usability (Hartson & Castillo, 1998), and Web use in particular (Choo, Detlor, & Turnbull, 1998). The key idea in this technique is to ask users to report a *critical incident*, which is an event or task that is a significant indicator (either positive or negative) of some factor of interest in the study. The method and its variants provide a way of obtaining concrete descriptions of events or tasks that are identified as critical (important, significant) by typical people operating in real-world situations. It is not aimed at obtaining a random sample of tasks or events (which is a weak, general method of understanding the world), but rather a sample of tasks or events that are revealing of the domain. As noted by Nielsen (2001), the use of critical incident technique on the Web is also useful in identifying important value-added tasks for Web providers and for gaining insights for innovations on the Web.

A total of $N = 14$ Stanford students participated in the study and worked on the tasks in Table 17.1. Of those students in study, $N = 4$ were subject to detailed analysis. Participants performed their Web tasks using a standard desk top computer running Windows 98 and the Internet Explorer Web browser on a 1024×768 pixel color monitor. As participants worked on Web tasks, a video recorder captured their think-aloud protocols and the computer screen. A program called WebLogger (Reeder, Pirolli, & Card, 2001) collected and time-stamped all user interactions with the Web browser, including user keystrokes, mouse movements, scrolling, use of browser buttons, and all pages visited. WebLogger also collected and time-stamped all significant browser actions, including the retrieval and rendering of Web content.

Participants were given think aloud instructions and practice (Ericsson & Simon, 1984). Each question (in random order) was displayed on the computer screen to the left of Internet Explorer and remained in view throughout the task. If participants did not complete the task within 10 minutes, they were given a hint in the form of a set of search

Table 17.1. Tasks used in the Web study

Task Name	Task	Source Response to Significance Question
City	You are the Chair of Comedic events for Louisiana State University in Baton Rouge. Your computer has just crashed and you have lost several advertisements for upcoming events. You know that the Second City tour is coming to your theater in the spring, but you do not know the precise date. Find the date the comedy troupe is playing on your campus. Also find a photograph of the group to put on the advertisement.	Searched and found (Using Yahoo Canada) for a comedy troupe Web site to copy their photo for a poster to be printed and distributed locally for an upcoming community event.
Antz	After installing a state-of-the-art entertainment center in your den and replacing the furniture and carpeting, your redecorating is almost complete. All that remains to be done is to purchase a set of movie posters to hang on the walls. Find a site where you can purchase the set of four *Antz* movie posters depicting the princess, the hero, the best friend, and the general.	Doing a little research on my boyfriend's heritage and the history of the name Gatling. I knew his great-grandfather had invented the Gatling gun and the name had been passed down over generations. In a search engine, the word "Gatling" appeared as a movie. I looked up the movie, and went searching to purchase a movie poster from the movie *The Gatling Gun*. It was not a popular movie, therefore the poster was difficult to find. I finally purchased one from a poster company (with a Web site) located in Boulder, CO. He believes it is the only GG movie poster around.

terms that would help them find the target Web page. If participants did not complete the task within 15 minutes they were given the Web site where they could find the target information.

Results

Detailed protocol analyses were extremely time-consuming, and consequently my colleagues and I decided to focus our efforts on protocols collected from four participants working on the Antz and City tasks listed in Table 17.1. The participants were chosen because they had the most intact data on these two tasks.

The data collected from participants were merged into a coded Web protocol transcript. Data were drawn from transcriptions of the video recordings of the think-aloud protocol and the WebLogger recording of system and user actions with the browser (including the actual Web pages visited). Several initial passes were made over a subset of the protocols to develop a Web Protocol Coding Guide.[9] Sample protocols coded independently by two analysts yielded a 91% agreement in the partitioning of the protocol and a 93% agreement on the specific codings.

Problem Spaces

Excluding the eye movement data, the participants' protocols suggest that three problem spaces structure the bulk of their Web foraging behavior.[10] There are the following problem spaces.

1. A *link* problem space in which the states are information patches (typically Web pages) and the basic operators involve moving from one patch to another by clicking on links or the back button.
2. A *keyword* problem space in which the states are alternative legal queries to search engines, and the operators involve formulating and editing the search queries.
3. A *URL* problem space in which the states are legal URLs to be typed into the address bar of a Web browser and the operators involve formulating and editing the URB strings.

The participants' behavior in the Web Protocols can be visualized using a Web behavior graph (WBG; Card et al., 2001), which is an elaboration of the problem behavior graphs used in Newell and Simon (1972). Figure 17.5 presents a schematic explanation of the WBG graphical representation.

Web Behavior Graph Representation

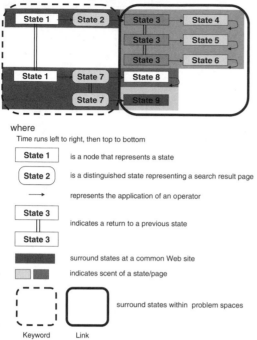

Figure 17.5. Schematic explanation of the components of a Web behavior graph.

Following Information Scent

Inspection of Figure 17.6 reveals several phenomena. The Antz task is more difficult than the City task. Only one-fourth of the participants found a solution to the Antz task as opposed to three-fourths of the participants who found solutions to the City task. The WBGs for the Antz task show more branches and backtracking than the WBGs for the City task, which is an indication of less informed search. The participants on the City task move very directly to the target information, whereas the participants on the Antz task follow unproductive paths. Antz task participants spend more time visiting search engines and in the keyword problem space. On the Antz task participants generated about 3.25 separate sets of search results each, whereas on the City task they generated about 1.25 sets of search results each.

Figure 17.6 presents the WBGs of the four participants' data on the Antz and City tasks.[11] Because the participants' protocols provide sparse data regarding their evaluations of the pages they visited, we had three independent judges rank the potential utility (information scent) of each page visited in the eight Web Protocols. Specifically the judges were asked to rate the relevance of Web pages to the City and Antz tasks in Table 17.1. The judges were presented with every page visited by participants in the Web study and were asked to rate the relevance of the pages (a) after a cursory skimming of the page (initial rating) and (b) after a more thorough examination of the page (final rating). The ratings were done on a 4-point scale: No Scent (0), Low Scent (1), Medium Scent (2), or High Scent (3). The geometric mean of the judges ratings were taken to reduce the effect of outlying ratings. These final ratings are plotted in the WBGs in Figure 17.6 on a scale of white (0), light gray (1), medium gray (2), and dark gray (3).

One reason for the greater difficulty of the Antz task could be the poverty of information scent of links leading to the desired target information. We asked $N = 10$ judges to rate the information scent of links on the search results pages visited by participants in both the Antz and City tasks. The links were rated on a 3-point scale of Not Relevant (0), Low Relevant (1), Medium Relevant (2), and Highly Relevant (3). To verify that the judges' ratings were a valid indicator of information scent, we first checked them against users' link choices. A median split analysis showed that higher rated links were more likely to have been the ones selected by the study participant, $\chi^2_{(1)} = 15.46$, $p < 0.0001$. The ratings data revealed that indeed, the information scent on Web pages in the Antz task was lower than on Web pages in the City task. The links followed by the study participants had a lower information scent average on the Antz task ($M = 1.56$) than on the City task ($M = 2.44$) although the links not followed where about the same for the Antz task ($M = 0.65$) and the City task ($M = 0.62$).

Difficulty of foraging on the Web appears to be related to the quality of information scent cues available to users. Under conditions of strong information scent, users move rather directly to the target information, as is characteristic of the City task WBGs in Figure 17.6. When the information scent is weak, there is a more undirected pattern of foraging paths, as characteristic of the Antz WBGs in Figure 17.6, and a greater reliance on search engines.

Foraging in Information Patches

Although multiple Web sites were visited by all participants on both tasks, it is apparent that they tended not to flit from one site to another. There

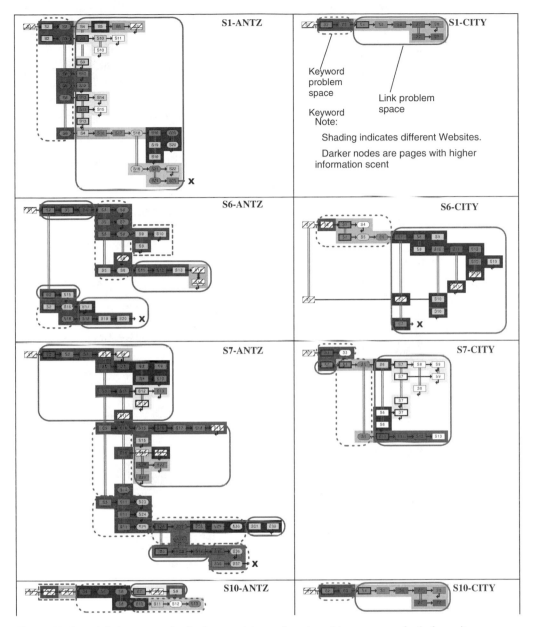

Figure 17.6. Web behavior graphs for four participants (rows) working on two tasks (columns).

were more transitions within a Web site than between sites. The ratio of within-site to between-site transitions was M = 2.1 for the Antz task and M = 5.2 for the City task. Inspection of Figure 17.7 suggests that as the information scent of encountered Web pages declines at a site that there is a tendency for participants to leave the site or return to some previously visited state. From the Web Protocols I identified segments where participants visited three or more pages at a Web site that was not a search

engine or Web portal. I found N = 3 three-page sequences, N = 5 five-page sequences, and N = 1 six-page sequence. The Web pages in these sequences were divided into the first page visited at the site, the last page visited at a site, and the pages visited between the first and last page (middle pages). Figure 17.7 presents the scent ratings (initial ratings, see previous description) of the pages in these sequences. Each point in the figure is based on the geometric mean of scent ratings of the visited

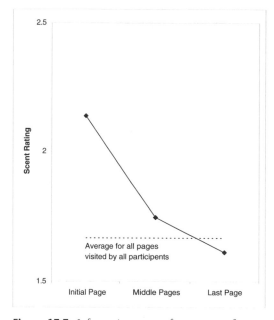

Figure 17.7. Information scent of sequences of pages visited at Web sites prior to going to another Web site.

pages produced by the independent panel of raters already discussed. Also plotted in Figure 17.7 is the average scent rating of all the Web pages visited by our participants. The figure shows that initially the information scent at a site is high and when that information scent falls below the average information scent users switch to another site or search engine.

There also appears to be a relation between the amount of information scent first encountered at a Web site and the length of the sequence (the *run*) of page visits at the Web site. I identified $N = 68$ sequences of page visits (one or greater) at Web sites, and split these runs two ways: (a) run length ≥ 3 versus run length ≤ 2, and (b) start page information scent $\geq$ median versus start page information scent < median. This median split analysis showed that starting with a high information scent was strongly associated with longer runs at a Web site, $\chi^2(1) = 8.69$, $p < 0.005$.

SNIF-ACT Architecture

A model called SNIF-ACT (Pirolli & Fu, 2003) was developed to simulate the participants in the Web study presented herein. SNIF-ACT extends the ACT-

R theory and simulation environment (Anderson & Lebiere, 2000). ACT-R is a hybrid production system architecture designed to model human psychology. ACT-R contains three kinds of assumptions about (1) knowledge representation, (2) knowledge deployment (performance), and (3) knowledge acquisition (learning). There are two major memory components in the ACT-R architecture: a *declarative knowledge* component and a *procedural knowledge* component. The distinction between these two kinds of knowledge is close to Ryle's (1949) distinction between *knowing that* and *knowing how*. One kind of knowledge (knowing that; declarative) is the kind that can be contemplated or reflected on, whereas the other kinds of knowledge (knowing how; procedural) is tacit and directly embodied in physical or cognitive activity.

Declarative knowledge in SNIF-ACT includes the task goal and the results of attending to the content of Web pages. Procedural knowledge is represented formally as condition-action pairs, or *production rules* (Figure 17.5). For instance, the SNIF-ACT simulations contain the production rule (summarized in English):

> Use-Search-Engine:
> IF   the goal is Goal*Start-Next-Patch
>   & there is a task description
>   & there is a browser
>   & the browser is not at a search engine
> THEN
>   Set a subgoal Goal*Use-search-engine

The production (titled Use-search-engine) applies in situations where the user has a goal to go to a Web site (represented by the tag Goal*Start-Next-Patch), has processed a task description, and has a browser in front of them. The production rule specifies that a subgoal will be set to use a search engine. The condition (IF) side of the production rule is matched to the current goal and the active chunks in declarative memory, and when a match is found, the action (THEN) side of the production rule will be executed. Roughly, the idea is that each elemental step of cognition corresponds to a production. At any point in time, a single production fires. When there is more than one match, the matching rules form a *conflict set*, and a mechanism called *conflict resolution* is used to decide which production to execute. The conflict resolution mechanism is based on a utility function. The expected utility of each matching production is calculated based on this utility function, and the one with the highest expected utility will be picked. In modeling Web users, the utility function is provided by information scent.

Utility and Choice: The Role of Information Scent

In a SNIF-ACT simulation, information scent cues on a computer display activate chunks and spread through the declarative network of chunks. The amount of activation accumulating on the chunks matched by a production is used to evaluate and select productions. The activation of chunks matched by production rules is used to determine the utility of selecting those production rules. This is the most significant difference between SNIF-ACT and ACT-R, which does not have an activation-based model of utility.

For instance, the following Click-link production rule matches when a Web link description has been read,

Click-link:
  IF   the goal is Goal*Process-element
       & there is a task description
       & there is a browser
       & there is a link that has been read
       & the link has a link description
  THEN
       Click on the link

If selected, the rule will execute the action of clicking on the link. The chunks associated with the task description and the link description will have a certain amount of activation. That combined activation will be used to evaluate the rule. If there are two Click-link productions matching against chunks for two different links, then the production with more highly activated chunks will be selected.

It is important to note that the SNIF-ACT simulation is not an omniscient optimizer. Production rules are selected based on utilities (activation values) that come from the information that is matched on the production conditions. Productions have no information about other productions, what those productions match to, or the consequences of actions beyond those specified by the production rule itself. The computation of expected information value is myopic (Pearl, 1988). For instance, productions that select particular links "know" only about

the links that they match and the spreading activation emitting from those links.

The predictions made by the SNIF-ACT model were tested against the log files of the data sets summarized in Figure 17.6. The major controlling variable in the model is the measure of information scent, which predicts two major kinds of actions: (1) which links on a Web page people will click on, and (2) when people decide to leave a site. These kinds of actions were therefore extracted from the log files and compared to the predictions made by the model. I call the first kind of actions *link-following* actions, which were logged whenever a participant clicked on a link on a Web page. The second kind of actions was called *site-leaving* actions, which were logged whenever a participant left a Web site (and went to a different search engine or Web site). The two kinds of actions made up 72% (48% for link-following and 24% for site-leaving actions) of all the 189 actions extracted from the log files.

Link-Following Actions

The SNIF-ACT model was matched to the link-following actions extracted from the data sets. Each action from each participant was compared to the action chosen by the simulation model. Whenever a link-following action occurred in the user data, I examined how the SNIF-ACT model ranked (using information scent) all the links on the Web page where the action was observed. My colleagues and I then compared the links chosen by the participants to the predicted link rankings of the SNIF-ACT model. If there were a purely deterministic relationship between predicted information scent and link choice, then all users would be predicted to choose the highest ranked link. However, we assume that the scent-based utilities are stochastic (McFadden, 1974, 1978) and subject to some amount of variability due to users and context (which is also consistent with ACT-R; Anderson & Lebiere, 2000). Consequently I expect the probability of link choice to be highest for the links ranked with the greatest amount of scent-based utility, and that link choice probability is expected to decrease for links ranked lower on the basis of their scent-based utility values.

Figure 17.8 shows that link choice is strongly related to scent-based utility values. Links ranked higher on scent-based utilities tend to get chosen over links ranked lower (note that there are many

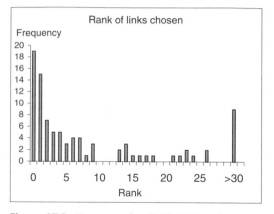

Figure 17.8. Frequency that SNIF-ACT productions match link-following actions. The SNIF-ACT production rankings are computed at each simulation cycle over all links on the same Web page and all productions that match.

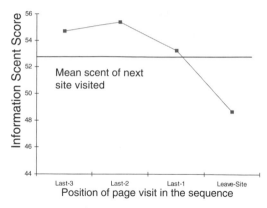

Figure 17.9. Information scent computed by SNIF-ACT on the last four pages visited at a Web site (extracted from sequences of four or longer).

links in the > 30 class that are being summed). There are a total of 91 link-following actions in Figure 17.8. The distribution of the predicted link selection was significantly different from random selection χ^2 (30) = 18,589, $p < 0.0001$. This result replicates a similar analysis made by Pirolli and Card (1999) concerning the ACT-IF model prediction of cluster selection in the Scatter/Gather browser.

Site-Leaving Actions

To test how well information scent is able to predict when people will leave a site, site-leaving actions were extracted from the log files and analyzed. Site-leaving actions are defined as actions that led to a different site (e.g., when the participants used a different search engine, typed in a different URL to go to a different web site, etc.) These data are presented in Figure 17.9. Each data point is the average of $N = 12$ site-leaving actions observed in the data set. The x-axis indexes the four steps made prior to leaving a site (Last-3, Last-2, Last-1, Leave-Site). The y-axis in Figure 17.7 corresponds to the average information scent value computed by the SNIF-ACT spreading activation mechanisms. The horizontal dotted line indicates the average information scent value of the page visited by users after they left a Web site.

Figure 17.9 suggests that users essentially assess the expected utility of continuing on at an information patch (i.e., a Web site) against the expected utility of switching their foraging to a new informa-

tion patch. This is consistent with the predictions of information foraging theory and with previous findings on information patch foraging (Pirolli & Card, 1999). Figure 17.9 also suggests that spreading activation mechanisms compute activation values from information scent cues to reflect expected utilities associated with navigation choices. It is worth emphasizing that the formulation of the spreading activation networks employed in the information scent model were motivated by a lens model analysis of the environmental problem faced by the forager. Furthermore, the actual parameters of the spreading activation networks (the strengths) were set by an automated analysis of the statistical properties of the environment. The spreading activation networks used in the cognitive model reflect the probabilistic texture of the environment.

General Discussion

The notion of information scent has played a role in understanding other areas of human–information interaction and in practical application. Information scent was originally developed as part of information foraging models of a document clustering and browsing systems called scatter/gather (Pirolli & Card, 1999). A computational cognitive model called ACT-IF, very similar to the one presented here, modeled the navigation choices and patch foraging behavior in scatter/gather using information scent. Information scent was also used as an explanatory concept in understanding how users visually scan and interact with novel information visualization systems such as the hyperbolic browser (Pirolli et al., 2003) and relevance enhanced thumbnails (Woodruff et al., 2002). The most significant current problem for the future development of the models concerns the analysis of nontext information scent cues, such as graphical icons, animations, and so on, and the relation of proximal information scent cues to nontext distal content such as video and music.

Another line of future theoretical development concerns learning. To date, cognitive models of information foraging, such as ACT-IF and SNIF-ACT, are built on spreading activation networks that represent associations among words. As already discussed, network strengths are estimated directly from statistics obtained from large corpora of language. The match of proximal cues to the desired information goal in Equations 17.10 through 17.12 can be viewed as implementing a kind of exemplar-based category match model. In fact, I derived the original equations presented in Pirolli and Card (1999) from consideration of the examplar-based categorization models of Medin and Schaffer (1978) and Kruschke (1992). It seems unquestionable that people develop richer category representations of the world of information around them, and all large repositories (e.g., libraries or the Web) attempt to index into that category structure. Pirolli (2003) summarizes a nascent model called InfoCLASS that builds on Anderson's (1991) rational model of categorization. The goal of that model is to capture the observation that different kinds of information browsers and different histories of information foraging lead to different individual conceptions of what is out there. Pirolli (2004) discusses how to measure conceptual consensus (Romney, Weller, & Batchelder, 1986) using InfoCLASS and the relation of conceptual consensus to the effectiveness of information foraging by groups.

Information scent has become a design concept in Web site design and usability (Nielsen, 2003; Spool et al., 1998; User Interface Engineering, 1999). Computational models of information scent have been used in the development of Bloodhound (Chi et al., 2001, 2003; Chi, Pirolli, & Pitkow, 2000), which is a system that performs automated Web site usability analysis. A similar Web site usability system based on latent semantic analysis (Landauer & Dumais, 1997) rather than spreading activation networks has also been developed (Blackmon et al., 2002). These automated usability systems basically take a hypothetical user goal (input as a set of words), compute the probability of navigation choice of links emanating from each page given that goal, flow simulated users through the Web site, and perform usability analyses such as estimates of the number of steps it would take on average to reach desired information from a given start page.

Particularly intriguing is the inverse problem of inferring user goals from observed navigation behavior. The RUM model in Equation 17.10 predicts choices given a goal and a set of alternative choices. Economists also attempt to infer goals given the observed choices made by people from set of alternatives (called *revealed preferences*). The lumberjack system (Chi, Rosien, & Heer, 2002) is an attempt to use the theory of information scent to perform such goal inference. It may be possible to develop information environments that automatically tailor themselves to optimize the foraging behavior of users.

Acknowledgments. I thank Mike Byrne and Wayne Gray for their helpful comments on earlier drafts of this chapter. This research has been funded in part by an Office of Naval Research Contract no. N00014-96-C-0097 to Peter Pirolli and Stuart K. Card, and an Advanced Research and Development Activity contract no. MDA904-03-C-0404 to S. Card and P. Pirolli.

Notes

1. Others (e.g., Baldi, Frasconi, & Smyth, 2003; Barabàsi, 2002) provide additional analyses of the regularities in the structure and growth of the Web.

2. See *International Journal of Man-Machine Studies*, 27, nos. 5–6, 1987.

3. Furnas (1997) developed a theory of user interface navigation that uses notion of residue, which is very similar to the notion of proximal cues. Furnas develops a formal theory for the analysis of different kinds of user interaction techniques largely based on discrete mathematics.

4. Manning and Schuetze (1999) show a mapping between the normalized correlation and a Bayesian analysis of the log likelihood odds of a document being relevant given a set of word cues representing the interest of a user.

5. Davison used two additional measures that yielded similar results.

6. It should be noted that this is different than the formulation of spreading activation used to model

memory in ACT-R, where activation spreads from a goal to structures to be retrieved from memory. Information scent flows activation from external cues to the goal.

7. This is also the assumption in ACT-R (Anderson & Lebiere, 2000).

8. Note that in both Information Foraging Theory (Pirolli & Card, 1999) and ACT-R (Anderson & Lebiere, 2000) this equation was specified as a Boltzman equation with the substitution of $1/T$ for μ, where T is the "temperature" of the system.

9. The detailed Web Protocol Coding Guide is available on request.

10. Other problem spaces are evident the protocols, for instance, for navigating through the history list, but are much rarer than the ones discussed here. Other problem spaces could easily be added to the analysis.

11. WBGs can be automatically generated from WebLogger data.

References

Anderson, J. R. (1976). *Language, memory, and thought*. Hillsdale, N.J.: Lawrence Erlbaum.

Anderson, J. R. (1990). *The adaptive character of thought*. Hillsdale, N.J.: Lawrence Erlbaum.

Anderson, J. R. (1991). The adaptive nature of human categorization. *Psychological Review, 98*, 409–429.

Anderson, J. R., & Lebiere, C. (2000). *The atomic components of thought*. Mahwah, N.J.: Lawrence Erlbaum.

Anderson, J. R., & Milson, R. (1989). Human memory: An adaptive perspective. *Psychological Review, 96*, 703–719.

Anderson, J. R., & Pirolli, P. L. (1984). Spread of activation. *Journal of Experimental Psychology: Learning, Memory, and Cognition, 10*, 791–798.

Baldi, P., Frasconi, P., & Smyth, P. (2003). *Modeling the Internet and the Web*. Chichester: Wiley.

Barabàsi, A.-L. (2002). *Linked: The new science of networks*. Cambridge, Mass.: Perseus.

Bechtel, W. (1985). Realism, instrumentalism, and the intentional stance. *Cognitive Science, 9*, 473–497.

Blackmon, M. H., Polson, P. G., Kitajima, M., & Lewis, C. (2002). Cognitive walkthrough for the Web. *CHI 2002, ACM Conference on Human Factors in Computing Systems, CHI Letters, 4*(1).

Brunswik, E. (1944). Distal focusing of perception: Size constancy in a representative sample of situations. *Psychological Monographs, 56*(254), 1–49.

Brunswik, E. (1952). *The conceptual framework of psychology*. Chicago: University of Chicago Press.

Brunswik, E. (1956). *Perception and the representative design of psychological experiments*. Berkeley: University of California Press.

Card, S. K., Moran, T. P., & Newell, A. (1983). *The psychology of human-computer interaction*. Hillsdale, N.J.: Lawrence Erlbaum.

Card, S., Pirolli, P., Van Der Wege, M., Morrison, J., Reeder, R., Schraedley, P., & Boshart, J. (2001). Information scent as a driver of Web behavior graphs: Results of a protocol analysis method for Web usability. *CHI 2001, ACM Conference on Human Factors in Computing Systems, CHI Letters, 3*(1), 498–505.

Chi, E., Pirolli, P., Chen, K., & Pitkow, J. E. (2001). Using information scent to model user needs and actions on the web. *CHI 2001, Human Factors in Computing Systems, CHI Letters, 3*(1), 490–497.

Chi, E., Pirolli, P., & Pitkow, J. (2000). The scent of a site: A system for analyzing and predicting information scent, usage, and usability of a Web site. *CHI 2000, ACM Conference on Human Factors in Computing Systems, CHI Letters, 2*(1), 161–168.

Chi, E. H., Rosien, A., & Heer, J. (2002). *Lumberjack: Intelligent discovery and analysis of Web user traffic composition*. Paper presented at the ACM-SIGKIDD Workshop on Web mining for usage patterns and user profiles. WebKDD 2002, Edmonton, Canada.

Chi, E. H., Rosien, A., Suppattanasiri, G., Williams, A., Royer, C., Chow, C., Robles, E., Dalal, B., Chen, J., & Cousins, S. (2003). The Bloodhound project: Automating discovery of Web usability issues using the InfoScent simulator. *CHI 2003, ACM Conference on Human Factors in Computing Systems, 5*(1), 505–512.

Choo, C. W., Detlor, B., & Turnbull, D. (1998). *A behavioral model of information seeking on the Web: Preliminary results of a study of how managers and IT specialists use the Web*. Paper presented at the 61st Annual Meeting of the American Society for Information Science. Pittsburgh, Pa.

Clark, H. H. (1973). The language-as-fixed-effect fallacy: A critique of language statistics in psychological research. *Journal of Verbal Learning and Verbal Behavior, 12*, 335–359.

Cosmides, L., Tooby, J., & Barow, J. H. (1992). Introduction: evolutionary psychology and conceptual integration. In J. H. Barkow, L. Cosmides, & J. Tooby (Eds.), *The adapted mind: Evolutionary psychology and the generation of culture* (pp. 3–15). New York: Oxford University Press.

Davison, B. (2000). *Topical locality in the Web*. Paper presented at the Proceedings of the 23rd Annual International Conference on Information Retrieval. Athens.

Dennett, D. C. (1983). Intentional systems in cognitive ethology: The "Panglossian Paradigm" revisited. *The Behavioral and Brain Sciences, 6*, 343–390.

Dennett, D. C. (1988). *The intentional stance.* Cambridge, Mass.: Bradford Books, MIT Press.

Dennett, D. C. (1995). *Darwin's dangerous idea.* New York: Simon and Schuster.

Ericsson, K. A., & Simon, H. A. (1984). *Protocol analysis: Verbal reports as data.* Cambridge, Mass.: MIT Press.

Fitts, P. M., & Jones, R. E. (1961). Psychological aspects of instrument display: Analysis of factors contributing to 460 "pilot error" experiences in operating aircraft controls (1947). Reprinted in *Selected papers on human factors in the design and use of control systems* (pp. 332–358). New York: Dover.

Flanagan, J. C. (1954). The critical incident technique. *Psychological Bulletin, 51,* 327–358.

Furnas, G. W. (1997). *Effective view navigation.* Paper presented at the Human Factors in Computing Systems, CHI 97. Atlanta, GA.

Gibson, J. J. (1979). *The ecological approach to visual perception.* Boston: Houghton Mifflin.

Gigerenzer, G. (2000). *Adaptive thinking: Rationality in the real world.* Oxford: Oxford University Press.

Glimcher, P. W. (2003). *Decisions, uncertainty, and the brain: The science of neuroeconomics.* Cambridge, Mass.: MIT Press.

Gumbel, E. J. (1950). *Statistics of extremes.* New York: Columbia University Press.

Harman, D. (1993). *Overview of the first text retrieval conference.* Paper presented at the 16th Annuam International ACM/SIGIR Conference. Pittsburgh, PA

Hartson, H. R., & Castillo, J. C. (1998). *Remote evaluation for post-deployment usability improvement.* Paper presented at the Working Conference on Advanced Visual Interfaces, AVI 98. L'Aquila, Italy.

Kehoe, C., Pitkow, J., Sutton, K., & Aggarwal, G. (1999, May). *Results of the Tenth World Wide Web User Survey* [URL]. Available online at www.gvu .gatech.edu/user_surveys/survey-1998–10/ tenthreport.html.

Klein, G. A., Calderwood, R., & Macgregor, D. (1989). Critical decision method for eliciting knowledge. *IEEE Transactions on Systems, Man, and Cybernetics, 19*(3).

Kruschke, J. K. (1992). ALCOVE: An exemplar-based connectionist model of category learning. *Psychological Review, 99,* 22–44.

Lamping, J., & Rao, R. (1994). *Laying out and visualizing large trees using a hyperbolic space.* Paper presented at the UIST 94. Marina del Rey.

Lamping, J., Rao, R., & Pirolli, P. (1995). A focus + context technique based on hyperbolic geometry for visualizing large hierarchies. *Proceedings of the Conference on Human Factors in Computing Systems, CHI 95* (pp. 401–408). New York: ACM.

Landauer, T. K., & Dumais, S. T. (1997). A solution to Plato's problem: The latent semantic analysis theory of acquisition, induction, and representation of knowledge. *Psychological Review, 104,* 211–240.

Luce, R. D. (1959). *Individual choice behavior.* New York: Wiley.

Manning, C. D., & Schuetze, H. (1999). *Foundations of statistical natural language processing.* Cambridge, Mass.: MIT Press.

Marr, D. (1982). *Vision.* San Francisco: Freedman.

McFadden, D. (1974). Conditional logit analysis of qualitative choice behavior. In P. Zarembka (Ed.), *Frontiers of econometrics.* New York: Academic Press.

McFadden, D. (1978). Modelling the choice of residential location. In A. Karlqvist & L. Lundqvist, F. Snickars, & J. Weibull (Eds.), *Spatial interaction theory and planning models.* Cambridge, Mass.: Harvard University Press.

Medin, D. L., & Schaffer, M. M. (1978). A context theory of classification learning. *Psychological Review, 85,* 207–238.

Miller, G. A. (1956). The magical number seven plus or minus two: Some limits on our capacity for processing information. *Psychological Review, 63,* 81–97.

Morrison, J. B., Pirolli, P., & Card, S. K. (2001). A taxonomic analysis of what World Wide Web activities significantly impact people's decisions and actions. *Proceedings of the Conference on Human Factors in Computing Systems, CHI 2001,* 163–164.

Neisser, U. (1976). *Cognition and reality.* San Francisco: Freeman.

Newell, A. (1990). *Unified theories of cognition.* Cambridge, Mass.: Harvard University Press.

Newell, A., & Simon, H. A. (1972). *Human problem solving.* Englewood Cliffs, N.J.: Prentice Hall.

Nielsen, J. (2001, April). *The 3Cs of critical Web use: Collect, compare, choose.* Nielsen Norman Group. Available online at www.useit.com.

Nielsen, J. (2003, June). *Information foraging: Why Google makes people leave your site faster.* Available online at useit.com.

Pearl, J. (1988). *Probabilistic reasoning in intelligent systems: Networks of plausible inference.* Los Altos, Calif.: Morgan Kaufman.

Pirolli, P. (1997). *Computational models of information scent-following in a very large browsable text collection.* Paper presented at the Conference on Human Factors in Computing Systems, CHI 97. Atlanta, GA.

Pirolli, P. (2003). A theory of information scent. In J. Jacko & C. Stephanidis (Eds.), *Human-computer interaction* (vol. 1, pp. 213–217). Mahwah, N.J.: Lawrence Erlbaum.

Pirolli, P. (2004). The InfoCLASS model: Conceptual richness and inter-person conceptual consensus about information collections. *Cognitive Studies: Bulletin of the Japanese Cognitive Science Society,* 11(3), 197–213.

Pirolli, P., & Card, S. K. (1999). Information foraging. *Psychological Review, 106,* 643–675.

Pirolli, P., Card, S. K., & Van Der Wege, M. M. (2003). The effects of information scent on visual search in the hyperbolic tree browser. *ACM Transactions on Computer-Human Interaction,* 10(1), 20–53.

Pirolli, P., & Fu, W. (2003). SNIF-ACT: A model of information foraging on the World Wide Web. In P. Brusilovsky, A. Corbett, & F. de Rosis (Eds.), *User modeling 2003, 9th International Conference, UM 2003* (vol. 2702, pp. 45–54). Johnstown, Pa.: Springer-Verlag.

Pitkow, J. E., & Pirolli, P. (1999). *Mining longest repeated subsequences to predict World Wide Web suring.* Paper presented at the Second USENIX Symposium on Internet Technologies and Systems.

Quillan, M. R. (1966). *Semantic memory.* Cambridge, Mass.: Bolt, Bernak, and Newman.

Reeder, R. W., Pirolli, P., & Card, S. K. (2001). Web-Eye Mapper and WebLogger: Tools for analyzing eye tracking data collected in web-use studies. *Proceedings of the Human Factors in Computing Systems, CHI 2001,* 19–20.

Resnikoff, H. L. (1989). *The illusion of reality.* New York: Springer-Verlag.

Romney, A. K., Weller, S. C., & Batchelder, W. H. (1986). Culture as consensus: A theory of culture and informant accuracy. *American Anthropologist, 88,* 313–338.

Ryle, G. (1949). *The concept of mind.* London: Hutchinson.

Shattuck, L. W., & Woods, D. D. (1994). *The critical incident technique: 40 years later.* Paper presented at the 38th Annual Meeting of the Human Factors Society.

Simon, H. A. (1974). How big is a chunk? *Science, 183,* 482–488.

Spool, J. M., Scanlon, T., Snyder, C., & Schroeder, W. (1998). *Measuring Website usability.* Paper presented at the Conference on Human Factors and Computing Systems, CHI 98. Los Angeles, Calif.

Stigler, G. J. (1961). The economics of information. *Journal of Political Economy, 69,* 213–225.

Thurstone, L. (1927). A law of comparative judgment. *Psychological Review, 34,* 273–286.

Todd, P. M., & Gigerenzer, G. (2000). Précis of simple heuristics that make us smart. *Behavioral and Brain Sciences, 23,* 727–741.

Turney, P. D. (2001). Mining the Web for synonyms: PMI-IR versus LSA on TOEFL. Paper presented at the 12th European Conference on Machine Learning, ECML 2001. Freiburg, Germany.

User Interface Engineering. (1999). *Designing information-rich Web sites.* Cambridge, Mass.: Author.

Walker, J., & Ben-Akiva, M. (2002). Generalized random utility model. *Mathematical Social Sciences, 43,* 303–343.

Wilson, E. O. (1998). *Consilience.* New York: Knopf.

Woodruff, A., Rosenholtz, R., Morrison, J. B., Faulring, A., & Pirolli, P. (2002). A comparison of the use of text summaries, plain thumbnails, and enhanced thumbnails for Web search tasks. *Journal of the American Society for Information Science and Technology, 53,* 172–185.

18

Michael D. Byrne, Alex Kirlik, and Chris S. Fick

Kilograms Matter: Rational Analysis, Ecological Rationality, and Closed-Loop Modeling of Interactive Cognition and Behavior

It should be noted that from now on "the system" means not the nervous system but the whole complex of the organism and the environment. Thus, if it should be shown that 'the system' has some property, it must not be assumed that this property is attributed to the nervous system: it belongs to the whole, and detailed examination may be necessary to ascertain the contributions of the separate parts.

W. Ross Ashby, *Design for a Brain* (1952, p. 34)

Introduction

More than 50 years have passed since cybernetics pioneer Ross Ashby so clearly articulated the nature and difficulty of the challenge imposed in making correct causal attributions to the multiple human and environmental components participating in closed-loop interaction with the world. In psychology, it has been more than 100 years since John Dewey tried to caution psychologists about the dangers inherent in the tendency, however seductive, of basing a theory of human behavior on a causality of stimulus–response relations, in his classic (1896) article "The Reflex Arc Concept in Psychology." Dewey emphasized that such a framing was to a large extent arbitrary because behavior itself nearly always plays a role in creating the available environmental stimulation, with the result that there is no clear logical, conceptual, or epistemological basis for drawing the S–R causal arrow in either direction and that perhaps it should be drawn in both directions simultaneously. These ideas have always found resonance in the study of perception and action, where the intimacy and interdependency between the human and external world are most obvious. Perhaps the best examples

of such closed-loop thinking are Powers (1973), the field of manual control modeling (Jagacinski & Flach, 2002), Gibson's studies of active touch (1962), and dynamical systems approaches to modeling human–environment interaction (e.g., Beer, 1995).

Although Kirlik (chapter 1) has noted that creating integrated, closed-loop models of both the human and the task environment has a long tradition in the field of human–machine systems (albeit perhaps with overly primitive models of the human), the computational cognitive modeling community appears to be learning this lesson only somewhat recently. Why? There are almost certainly many factors involved. Among them, as Bently (1954) put it, is that people have a pronounced tendency to identify their own boundaries physically, even though adaptive behavior is often best understood in terms of a functional interaction between a person and the external world (see Clark, 2003, for a more recent treatment of this same point in the context of cognitive prostheses and "embodiment"). Viewing cognition and behavior in this functional light, implying that the organism–environment system should be the appropriate unit of analysis in psychology, provided the common foundation for both

Brunswik's and Gibson's ecological theorizing (see Kirlik, 2001). We also suggest that the adoption of a functionally oriented modeling perspective provided Ashby's (1952) motivation for his precautionary note on the subtle challenges associated with making correct causal attributions to the various (internal and external) entities participating in adaptive behavior.

The two preceding chapters in this section, both suggesting intriguing marriages of ecological and cognitive analysis and modeling, represent to us the exact style of detailed examination Ashby advocated as necessary for meeting these challenges. Gray (chapter 16) presents a body of research demonstrating just how acutely sensitive adaptive behavior is to finely grained temporal details at the intersection of cognition and design, or, as he puts it, "milliseconds matter" (also see Gray & Boehm-Davis, 2000). Pirolli (chapter 17) presents a body of research analogously demonstrating that sophisticated modeling of the probabilistic (chance) features or "causal texture" (Brunswik, 1956) of a technological ecology, in his case the World Wide Web, is necessary to understand "how people adaptively shape their behavior to their information environments, and how information environments can best be shaped to people." Our chapter, too, presents work in the spirit of a "rapprochement" (chapter 16) between cognitive and ecological analyses, viewing them, as did Brunswik, to be most fruitfully framed in symmetrical terms.

Theoretical Background and Approach

There are, of course, many possible ways in which a rapprochement between cognitive and ecological analyses could occur, and we believe that it is quite possible, if not likely, that some of these ways are more useful for shedding light on different areas of psychology than others (for a diverse collection of analyses in support of this view, see Gigerenzer & Selten, 2002; Oaksford & Chater, 1998). As background for the presentation of our own particular cognitive modeling research in human–technology interaction, we provide sketches of what we believe to be both weak and strong senses in which rapprochement can be viewed. We do so to clarify the relationship between the approach we have taken in our own modeling research and related themes

within Brunswik's (1956) probabilistic functionalism, Anderson's (1990) rational analysis, Gigerenzer's (2002) and Todd's (2002) ecological rationality, Gray's (chapter 16) soft constraints approach, and Pirolli's (chapter 17) theory of information foraging.

Weak versus Strong Rapprochement in Modeling Adaptive Behavior

We believe it is especially important for those interested in human–technology interaction to make a distinction between what we call weak versus strong readings of rapprochement, that is, theoretical integration across ecological/cognitive lines. In what we take to be the strong reading, ecological analysis and modeling does not merely *inform* internal (cognitive) modeling, it may also become *constitutive* of the resulting psychological theory, model and scientific explanation.

That is, following Brunswik (1956), the strong reading of rapprochement assumes that human interaction with the environment is the appropriate unit of analysis, and modeling in psychology and cognition is not merely what goes on between the eye and hand, so to speak. Under this reading, rapprochement may often require developing theories and models representing the union of both cognition and the ecology. This view stands in contrast to merely using ecological analysis to inform cognitive theory or merely using cognitive analysis to inform ecological theory.

By the union of cognitive and ecological analyses, we mean nothing less than how that union is conceptually portrayed in Brunswik's lens model: that is, that a *psychological* model of adaptive behavior should be comprised of a pair of joined submodels, one representing internal cognition, the other representing the external ecology. Put more strongly, for describing the types of adaptive, interactive behaviors that are the focus of this book, we suggest that the ecological submodel *participates* in the functional description of adaptive behavior itself, and as such, it may be found to play an equally important role in the explanation of adaptive behavior as do the activities or content represented in the submodel of internal cognition. Importantly, under this strong reading, causal attributions to actual ecological variables themselves as influencing behavior are warranted, in addition to the consequences they entail for internal cognition.

Note that this is a stronger reading of rapprochement than is proposed by rational analysis, ACT-R, or the many interesting studies that have recently been performed under the broad umbrella of rational analysis (e.g., Oaksford & Chater, 1998). All of these studies could be described as falling within the adaptationist tradition (for a discussion, see chapter 17), which is frequently framed as owing to the pioneering work of Marr (1982) on vision. The general notion in that tradition is to first study the structure of the task environment in light of the task to be performed to inform a "functional specification" for the design of the cognitive mechanisms that will perform that task adaptively (Anderson, 1990; Marr, 1982; Newell & Simon, 1972).

But note that under this latter, weaker reading of rapprochement, once the ecological analysis phase is completed, it no longer serves any purpose in the cognitive explanation of behavior as it happens, even though real-time behavioral achievement may in fact be partially determined by environmental structure, contingencies, and so on. But if levels of human achievement are only determined after passing through such an environmental filter, then predicting or supporting achievement will require psychological modeling to include elements representing these same environmental filters. It is exactly for this reason that the ACT-R model that we used in the study that follows had to be supplemented with additional components for actually simulating the external environment with which our performers were interacting.

Analogously, or so we believe, it was for this same reason that Pirolli (chapter 17) had to provide his SNIF-ACT model access to actual to the Web itself to make predictions about the behavior of human users. The rationale behind these extensions to the ACT-R architecture should perhaps not be surprising. Anderson (1991, p. 508) has noted that rational analysis and ACT-R were primarily created to shed light on the cognitive phenomena that most interested him, namely, learning, memory, and problem solving. Note that these activities are neither inherently technology-related, nor are they usually viewed to be particularly interactive (but see Anderson's own concerns on this matter in his discussion of the apparently interactive type of problem solving inherent in repairing a clothesline: Anderson, 1990; also see Kurz & Tweny, 1998, on this point). To be clear, we view what we propose here as a strong view of rapprochement as nothing more nor less than cumulative science at work, despite augmenting rational analysis, ACT-R, and ecological rationality (Gigerenzer, 2002; Todd, 2002) as they currently exist.

As will be seen in the following, we indeed performed analyses of our task environment to inform the design of our cognitive submodel, resulting in the identification of some "fast and frugal heuristics" (Gigerenzer & Goldstein, 1996), which we subsequently embedded in ACT-R.

As such, our work benefited from the activities we have described as falling within a weak reading of rapprochement. However, we also used additional ecological analysis and modeling as the basis for constructing an environmental submodel that when linked with the cognitive model, jointly provided a model of adaptive, interactive cognition behavior. So although the heuristic discovery component of our research was an illustration of what we have described as weak rapprochement, the latter ecological modeling and integration represented strong rapprochement.

We suggest that not only weak but also strong rapprochement will be especially valuable when attempting to model what Gray (chapter 16) and others have called embodied or distributed cognition (Hutchins, 1995). In fact, an appreciation of exactly this point is what we believe inspired Gray (chapter 16) to describe his soft constraints approach as implying "that the functional task environment for a given activity always reflects a mixture of internal and external resources." A similar appreciation, we believe, underlies the scientific legitimacy of Pirolli's (chapter 17) many causal attributions in the examination of Web users to features of the proximal and distal properties of the Web itself, and not solely to the (internal) cognitive consequences they entailed (i.e., that both the proximal and distal features of the design of the Web, and its causal texture, actually mattered).

The Interactive Behavior Triad

Our approach toward conceptualizing ecological-cognitive rapprochement useful for guiding computational cognitive is presented in terms of Figure 18.1, which we refer to as the interactive behavior triad (IBT). The IBT can be considered to be a broader variant of a perspective first sketched elsewhere (Byrne, 2001; Gray, 2000; Gray & Altmann, 1999).

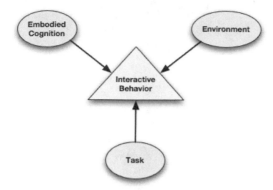

Figure 18.1. The interactive behavior triad (IBT).

Under this view, we consider interactive behavior, such as a pilot interacting with a cockpit, as jointly constrained by three factors: embodied cognition, the environment, and the task. We take *embodied cognition* to mean the capabilities and limitations of the integrated human perceptual-cognitive-motor system (see also Gray's discussion, chapter 16). We take the environment to include the constraints and affordances available to the human (in our case, a pilot) from his or her environment. This includes the various artifacts in that environment, the properties of any system being controlled directly or indirectly (e.g., an aircraft), and the broader environment in which that behavior is embedded (e.g., airports in general). Finally, we take the task to mean the goal, or more often, the set of goals the operator is trying to accomplish and the knowledge required to fulfill these goals, per the description in Card, Moran, and Newell (1983).

As Gray and Altmann noted, traditional disciplines have generally considered these three entities singly or pairwise rather than as a triad. The experimental psychology community has generally been concerned with properties of the human, but often with either artificial tasks or in contexts that minimize or eliminate the role of the environment. Ethnographic or ecological analysis typically focuses on the environmental context and often the tasks but often overlooks issues rooted in the capabilities and limitations of the human element of the system. Engineers and computer scientists have traditionally considered the design of artifacts (an aspect of the environment), but often with incomplete understanding of the true tasks at hand and/or constraints imposed by the capabilities and limitations of the human users. Indeed, there are likely

to be some situations, even in aviation, in which all three need not be simultaneously considered to obtain insight into interactive and adaptive cognition and behavior (e.g., Casner, 1994). However, we believe that to understand and predict human performance in many practical situations, all three sources of constraint must be jointly considered and ideally incorporated into quantitative or computational modeling formalisms (see Byrne & Gray, 2003, for more on formalism).

As an example of the application of this perspective, we will now describe the results of a study in which dynamic and integrated, computational cognitive modeling—or more specifically, pilot-aircraft-scene-taxiway modeling—was performed to shed light on the possible sources of error in aviation surface operations, more specifically, taxi navigation. Modeling consisted of integrating a pilot model developed within the ACT-R cognitive architecture (Anderson et al., 2004), a model of aircraft taxi dynamics, and models of both the visible and navigable airport surface, including signage and taxiways. This modeling effort was motivated by experiments performed in NASA Ames Advanced Concept Flight Simulator.

Adaptive Behavior and Error in Airline Taxiing

Figure 18.2 depicts the out-the-window view provided to a pilot of a modern commercial airliner navigating the taxiways of Chicago O'Hare Airport who is trying to obey a set of directions called clearances provided just prior to landing. These directions are not unlike the driving directions a host might provide to a party: "go right on X, go left at Y, proceed to Z," and so on. Except in this case the party host has a malevolent streak and omits the "left" and "right" instructions and simply provides a list of road names, assuming partygoers will work out the turn directions on their own based on a map. Each of the yellow lines in the figure indicates a potential route of travel, or an option from which the pilot can choose to bring the aircraft successfully to its destination gate despite the dense fog and associated limited field of view.

Errors made during navigating on an airport surface have potentially serious consequences, but this is not always the case. Many such errors are detected and remedied by flight crews themselves,

Figure 18.2. An out-the-window view in NASA's Chicago O'Hare Taxi Simulation (used by permission of NASA Ames Research Center).

others are detected and remedied by controllers, and even many uncorrected errors still fail to result in serious negative consequences due to the sometimes forgiving nature of the overall, multiagent space that constitutes the modern taxi surface. However, some errors in taxi navigation can result in drastic consequences.

A particularly pernicious type of error is the runway incursion, which is any occurrence involving an aircraft or other object creating a collision hazard with another aircraft taking off or landing or intending to take off or land. Since 1972, runway incursion accidents have claimed 719 lives and resulted in the destruction of 20 aircraft (Jones, 2000). The problem of runway incursion accidents continues to only get worse, despite acknowledgment of the importance of the problem by both the Federal Aviation Administration (FAA) and the National Transportation Safety Board (NTSB), and plans to remedy the problem with technologies such as the Airport Movement Area Safety System (*NTSB Reporter*, 2003). For example, the number of U.S. runway incursions in 1996, 1997, and 1998, totaled 287, 315, and 325, respectively. In 1999, a KAL airliner with 362 passengers swerved during takeoff at Chicago O'Hare (ORD) to avoid hitting a jet that entered the runway, and an Iceland Air passenger jet at JFK came within 65 meters of a cargo jet that mistakenly entered the runway (Jones, 2000).

These problems show no immediate sign of going away. There were a total of 337 U.S. runway incursions in 2002, more than 1.5 times the number reported a decade earlier. The *NTSB Reporter* (2003) noted that "despite FAA programs to reduce

incursions, there were 23 reported in January, 2003, compared with only 14 in January 2002" (p. 15). Due in part to the inability to deal with incursion problems to date, NASA established an Aviation System-Wide Safety Program to address this and other challenges to aviation safety. The NASA simulation and technology evaluation study described in the following section represented one attempt to use aviation psychology and human factors research techniques to address critical challenges to aviation safety.

Not surprisingly given the scene depicted in Figure 18.2, aviation incident and accident investigations often find both cognitive and environmental contributing factors to these events. Environmental sources include such factors as flawed interface design (e.g., Degani, Shafto, & Kirlik, 1999; chapter 13), confusing automation (e.g., Olson & Sarter, 2000), and unexpected weather conditions (Wiegmann & Goh, 2001). Cognitive sources include poor situation awareness (Endsley & Smolensky, 1998), procedural noncompliance (chapter 7), and poor crew coordination (Foushee & Helmreich, 1988) among others.

Many (if not most) significant incidents and accidents result from some combination of both cognitive and environmental factors. In fact, in a highly proceduralized domain such as aviation, with highly trained and motivated crews, accidents rarely result from either environmental or cognitive causes alone. Training and experience are often sufficient to overcome even the most confusing interface designs, and the environment is often sufficiently redundant, reversible, and forgiving (Connolly, 1999) that most slips and errors have few serious consequences. Most significant incidents and accidents result when cognitive, environmental, and perhaps even other (e.g., organizational) factors collectively conspire to produce disaster (Reason, 1990).

For this reason, an increasing number of human factors and aviation psychology researchers have realized that the common phrases "human error" and "pilot error" often paint a misleading picture of error etiology (e.g., Hollnagel, 1998; Woods et al., 1994). By their nature, these terms predicate error as a property of a human or pilot, in contrast to what has been learned about the systemic, multiply caused nature of many operational errors. These often misleading terms only contribute to the "train and blame" mindset still at work in many operational settings and perhaps contribute to the failure of such interventions to improve the safety landscape in settings from commercial aviation to military operations to medicine.

The Challenge Posed by the Systems View of Error

Although advances in theory may well present a more enlightened, systemic view of error, in our opinion one of the most significant barriers to the development of human factors interventions based on the systems view is the lack of techniques and models capable of simultaneously representing the many potential factors contributing to an ultimate error, and how these factors interact in typically dynamic, often complex, and usually probabilistic ways. To say that multiple contributing factors "conspire together" to produce error is one thing. To provide techniques capable of representing these multiple factors and the precise manner in which they conspire is quite another. This problem is difficult enough in the realm of accident investigation, where at least some evidence trail is available (Rasmussen, 1980; Wiegmann & Shappell, 1997). It is significantly more challenging, and arguably even more important, in the case of error prediction and mitigation (e.g., Hollnagel, 2000).

Motivated by this problem, we used *dynamic* and *integrated,* computational cognitive modeling—or more specifically, pilot-aircraft-scene-taxiway modeling—to shed light on the possible sources of error in taxi navigation. Modeling consisted of integrating a pilot model developed within the ACT-R cognitive architecture (Anderson & Lebiere, 1998; Anderson et al., 2004), a model of aircraft taxi dynamics, and models of both the visible and navigable airport surface, including signage and taxiways. This modeling effort was motivated by experiments performed in NASA Ames Advanced Concepts Flight Simulator (for more detail, see Hooey & Foyle, 2001; Hooey, Foyle, & Andre, 2000). The purpose of the NASA experimentation was both to attempt to better understand the sources of error in aviation surface operations and also to evaluate the potential of emerging display and communication technologies for lowering the incidence of error (Foyle et al., 1996). The purpose of our cognitive system modeling research was to evaluate and extend the state-of-the-art in computational cognitive modeling as a resource for human performance and error prediction.

Simulation, Experimentation, and Data Collection

Called T-NASA2 (for more detail, see Hooey & Foyle, 2001; Hooey, Foyle, & Andre, 2000) throughout this chapter, the experimental scenario required 18 flight crews, consisting of active pilots from 6 commercial airlines, to approach, land, and taxi to gate at Chicago O'Hare International Airport (ORD). The flight crews had varying levels of experience with the ORD surface configuration. Experimentation used baseline conditions (current paper-chart technology only), as well as conditions in which pilots were provided with various new display and communication technologies, including a moving-map and head-up displays with virtual signage (e.g., a superimposed stop sign at a hold point). The modeling performed in this research was focused solely on performance in the baseline (current technology) conditions.

The T-NASA2 Data Set

Nine different taxiway routes were used in the baseline trials of the T-NASA2 simulation. Each of the 18 crews were tested over a balanced subset of 3 different routes for a total of 54 trials. Each trial began approximately 12 nautical miles out on a level approach into ORD. Pilots performed an autoland, and the first officer (FO) notified the captain of their location with respect to the runway exit on the basis of clearance information obtained during the final stages of flight and the paper airport diagram. As the aircraft cleared the runway, the crew tuned the radio to ground controller frequency, and the controller provided a taxi clearance (set of intersections and directions) from the current location to the destination gate. Crews were then required to taxi to the gate in simulated, visually impoverished conditions (RVR 1000 feet). Further details can be found in Hooey and Foyle (2001). It should be noted that the simulation did not represent all standard operating procedures (after landing checklists, log, and company paperwork), nor all communication activities (with the cabin crew, dispatch, and gate). As a result, the level of crew workload was somewhat lower than they might experience in operational conditions, lending support to the idea that the experimental situation with respect to error was closer to best-case rather than worst-case conditions (other than low visibility).

Across the 54 baseline T-NASA2 trials, a total of 12 off-route navigation major errors were committed. Major errors were defined as deviation of 50 feet or more from the centerline of the cleared taxi route. These major errors were used for the modeling effort because they were objectively determined using simulation data and did not require subjective interpretation for classification. On each, crews proceeded down an incorrect route without any evidence of immediate awareness or else required correction by ground control. The T-NASA2 research team designated these 12 major errors. Additionally, 14 other deviations were observed but were detected and corrected by the crews. These latter 14 deviations were thus classified as minor errors by the NASA team, and we were instructed that the modeling effort should focus solely on the major errors. NASA provided our modeling team with descriptions of each major error, in terms of intersection complexity, turn severity, and their own classification of each in terms of planning, decision making, or execution (Hooey & Foyle, 2001; Goodman, 2001)

Two aspects of the T-NASA2 data set provided the primary motivation for the present modeling effort. First, it was believed that modeling might shed light on the underlying causes of the errors observed in the experimental simulations. A second motivation was the fact that the suite of situation awareness and navigation aids used in the new technology conditions of the T-NASA2 experiments were observed to eliminate navigation errors almost entirely (Hooey & Foyle, 2001). Our research therefore had as its goal to provide a systemic explanation for the errors that were observed in a fashion that was consistent with the finding that no errors were observed when the quality of information available to support navigating was improved.

Constructing an ACT-R Model of Taxi Performance

Taxiing a commercial jetliner is obviously a complex task, and the construction of an ACT-R model of a pilot performing this task was similarly complex along multiple dimensions.

Model Scope

One of the first decisions that had to be made regarded scope. In one sense, there are clearly multiple humans in the taxi loop, even in the somewhat simplified NASA simulation. These include the captain, who is actually head up looking out the window and actually controlling the aircraft, the FO, who looks primarily head down and assisting both the captain and the ground-based controller. To limit the scope of the project, we chose to model only the captain in ACT-R and treated both the ground controller and the FO as items in the environment. We thought this decision was a good balance between tractability and relevance, because the captain made the final decisions and also controlled the aircraft.

A second, important aspect of scoping model coverage was to select the psychological activities on which we would focus our efforts. Our research team was one of many also creating cognitive models of the same data (e.g., see Deutsch & Pew, 2002; Gore & Corker, 2002; Lebiere, et al., 2002; and McCarley et al., 2002). In this light, we considered both the strengths and weaknesses of our ACT-R approach with the alternative approaches taken by other research teams, with the goal of providing a unique contribution to the overall research effort. For example, we ruled out focusing on multitasking, because ACT-R is less mature in this area than some other models, and we ruled out focusing on situation awareness issues (losing track of one's location on the airport surface), because this was less mature in this area than some other models. All things considered, including our own previous experience in ecologically oriented, closed-loop human performance modeling (e.g., Kirlik, 1998; Kirlik, Miller, & Jagacinski, 1993), we decided to focus on the interactive, dynamic decision-making aspects of the task in its closed-loop context.

As a result, we focused on those contributions to error that may result from the interaction of the structure of a task environment and the need to make often rapid decisions on the basis of imperfect information, resulting from decay of clearance information from memory, low visibility, and sluggish aircraft dynamics due to the fact that the aircraft in question weighed approximately 60,000 kilograms. Our focus on dynamic decision making, which assumed pilots had accurate knowledge of their current location, was complemented by another modeling team's focus on situation awareness errors associated with losing track of one's location on the airport surface (McCarley et al., 2002).

The Model's Environment

Thus we created an ACT-R model of one human pilot, but this pilot model still had to be situated in an accurate environment. In this research, three external entities were modeled to describe the environment: the simulated aircraft controlled by the pilot model, the simulated visual information available to the pilot model, and the simulated runway and taxiway environment through which the simulated aircraft traveled. Each of these three environmental entities was computationally modeled and integrated with the cognitive components of the pilot model to create an overall representation of the interactive human–aircraft–environment system.

Code for the vehicle dynamics that was used to drive the actual NASA flight simulator in which behavioral data was collected was unfortunately unavailable. We therefore had to create a simplified vehicle model with which the pilot model could interact. Given vehicle size, mass, and dynamics, however, we still required a somewhat reasonable approximation to the actual aircraft dynamics used in the experiments to be able to get a handle on timing issues. Although we were not interested in control issues per se, the dynamics of the aircraft played an important role in determining decision time horizons, a key factor in the cognitive representation of the pilot's activities. The aircraft model we constructed assumed that the pilot controlled the vehicle in three ways: applying engine power, braking, and steering. For the purposes of modeling an aircraft during taxiing, these three forms of control are sufficient. Based on Cheng, Sharma, and Foyle's (2001) analysis of the NASA simulated aircraft dynamics, we proceeded with a model in which it was reasonable to assume that throttle and braking inputs generated applied forces that were linearly related with aircraft speed. A dynamic model related these applied forces to their effects on aircraft speed, and naturally this model was highly sensitive to aircraft weight (60,000 kg).

Steering, however, was another matter. After consideration of the functional role that steering inputs played in the T-NASA2 scenario, we decided that we could finesse the problem of steering dynamics by assuming that the manual control aspects of the steering problem did not play a significant role in the navigation errors that were observed. That is, we assumed that making an appropriate turn was purely a decision-making problem and that no turn errors resulted from correct turn decisions that were erroneously executed. Note that this assumption does not completely decouple the manual and cognitive aspects of the modeling, however. It was still the case that manual control of the acceleration and braking aspects of the model did play a role in determining the aircraft's position relative to an impending turn, and importantly, placed a hard constraint on the aircraft's maximum speed of approach to each turn.

The maximum aircraft speeds for the various types of turns required in the NASA simulation were calculated under the constraint that lateral acceleration be limited to 0.25 g for passenger comfort (Cheng et al., 2001) and also the field data reported in Cassell, Smith, and Hicok (1999). For our model, these speeds were found to be 20 knots for a soft (veer) turn, 16 knots for a right turn, and 14 knots for a U-turn and were based on actual turn radius measurements from the ORD taxiway layout (all turns made in these scenarios could be classified according to this scheme). Although due to airport layout constraints taxiing would not always occur at the maximum possible speed, these maximum speeds partially determined the time available to make a turn decision, and in our model, because this time is reduced there was a greater probability of an incorrect turn decision. Our simplification regarding steering merely boiled down to the fact that once the model had made its decision about which turn to take, that turn was then executed without error.

To implement this aspect of the model, we decided to model the ORD airport taxiway as a set of interconnected rails on which travel of the simulated aircraft was constrained. Taxiway decision making in this scheme, then, boiled down to the selection of the appropriate rail to take at each taxiway intersection. In this manner, we did not have to model the dynamics of the aircraft while turning: We simply moved the aircraft along each turn rail at the specified, turn radius–specific speed.

The model used to represent the visual information available to our ACT-R pilot model was obtained from the actual NASA flight simulator in the form of a software database. This database consisted of location-coded objects (e.g., taxiways, signage) present on the ORD surface or at least those objects presented to flight crews during NASA experimentation. Distant objects became visible to the pilot model at similar distances to which these same objects became visible to human pilots in T-NASA2 experimentation.

Modeling Pilot Background Knowledge

Obviously, the environment and its dynamic properties are critically important in understanding pilot performance in this domain, but of course they do not completely determine pilot behavior; thus the use of a knowledge-based performance model such as ACT-R. As mentioned earlier, the ACT-R model must be supplied with the knowledge of how to do this task. This part of the model-building process is often referred to as knowledge engineering because the demands of gathering and structuring the knowledge necessary to perform the tasks in such domains are significant. We focused our efforts on the identification of procedures and problem-solving strategies used by pilots in this domain as well as the cost benefit structure of those procedures and strategies.

Task Analysis and Knowledge Engineering

The task-specific information required to construct the model was obtained by studying various task analyses of taxiing (e.g., Cassell, Smith, & Hicok, 1999) and through extensive consultation with two subject matter experts (SMEs) who were experienced airline pilots. We first discovered that in many cases, pilots have multiple tasks in which to engage while taxiing. Based on this finding, our ACT-R model only concerned itself with navigation decision making when such a decision was pending. In the interim, the model iterated through four tasks deemed central to the safety of the aircraft.

These four tasks included monitoring the visual scene for incursions, particularly objects like ground vehicles, which are difficult to detect in poor visibility; maintaining the speed of the aircraft, because the dynamics of a commercial jetliner require relatively frequent adjustments of throttle and/or brake to maintain a constant speed; listening for hold instructions from the ground-based controller; and maintaining an updated representation of the current position of the aircraft on the taxi surface and the location of the destination. Although these tasks often have little direct impact on navigation, they do take time to execute, and time is the key limited

resource in making navigation decisions in our integrated pilot–aircraft–environment system model.

With respect to navigation decisions, we found that decision making is highly local. That is, the planning horizon is very short; flight crews are quite busy in the time after landing and thus, in situations like ORD in poor visibility, report they do not have the time to plan ahead and consider turns or intersections other than the immediately pending one. Second, the decision process tends to be hierarchical: Pilots first decide if the next intersection requires a turn, and if it does, then decide which turn to make. We found that in the error corpus available to us, errors in the first decision (whether to turn) were rare (which was also consistent with our SME reports), so we concentrated our efforts on understanding how pilots made the second decision.

The first issue to be addressed was: What kinds of knowledge and strategies are actually brought to bear by actual pilots in the kinds of conditions experienced by the pilots in the NASA study? Largely though interviews with SMEs, we discovered a number of key strategies employed by pilots and also that some of these strategies would not have been available to our model. Many of these strategies involved the open communications between ground-based controllers and other aircraft. For example, if Qantas flight 1132 has just been given a clearance that overlaps with the clearance given to United flight 302, one viable strategy for the United pilot is to simply follow the Qantas aircraft for the overlapping portion of the clearance.

Similarly, pilots can use dissimilar clearances to rule out certain decision alternatives. For example, when faced with an intersection that forces the pilot to choose between taxiways A10 and D, if the pilot has just heard another flight given a clearance that involves A10, then D is the more likely choice, because the ground controller is unlikely to assign two aircraft to be on the same taxiway approached from different directions. It is unclear the extent to which these strategies were available to the pilots in the T-NASA2 study, because details of what clearances were given to the (simulated) other aircraft and when such clearances were given were not available to us. Thus we had no choice but to exclude these strategies from the model.

At the end of both our task analyses and SME interviews, we had identified five primary decision strategies available for making turn decisions.

1. Remember the correct clearance. Though fast, this strategy is increasingly inaccurate as time lapses between obtaining the list of turns described in the clearance and the time at which turn execution is actually required.
2. Make turns toward the gate. Somewhat slower than the first strategy, but this option has a reasonable level of accuracy at many airports.
3. Turn in the direction that reduces the larger of the X or Y (cockpit-oriented) distance between the aircraft and the gate. We deemed this strategy to be moderately fast, like strategy 2, but with a potentially higher accuracy than strategy 2, because more information is taken into account.
4. Derive from map/spatial knowledge. This is the slowest strategy available, with high accuracy possible only from a highly experienced (at a given airport) flight crew.
5. Guess randomly. This is a very fast strategy, although it is unlikely to be very accurate, especially at multiturn intersections. However, we did include it as a possible heuristic in the model for two reasons: (a) It may be the only strategy available given the decision time available in some cases; and (b) it provides insights into chance performance levels.

The next modeling issue to be dealt with was how to choose between strategies when faced with a time constrained decision horizon.

This type of meta-decision is well modeled by the conflict resolution mechanism ACT-R uses to arbitrate between multiple productions matching the current situation. The accuracy of strategies 1 (recall the clearance) and 4 (derive from map knowledge) is primarily a function of the accuracy of the primitive cognitive operations required of these tasks, moderated by factors such as ACT-R's memory decay and constrained working memory. However, the accuracy of strategies 2, 3, and 5 is less cognitively constrained and instead critically dependent on the geometry of actual clearances and taxiways. As such, we thus employed an SME as a participant in a study to provide data for an analysis of the heuristic decision strategies 2 and 3 (the accuracy of strategy 5, random guessing, was determined by the taxiway geometry itself).

For this study, Jeppesen charts for all major U.S. airports were made available to the SME, a working B-767 pilot for a major U.S. carrier. He was asked to select charts for those airports for which he had significant experience of typical taxi routes, and he was asked to draw, using a highlighter on the charts themselves, the likely or expected actual taxi routes at each airport from touchdown to his company's gate area. We would have perhaps never thought of performing this study had the ACT-R model not required us to provide it with high-level (i.e., airport-neutral) strategies pilots might use in deciding what turns to make during taxi operations, along with their associated costs (times required) and benefits (accuracy).

Ecological Analysis: Identifying Taxi Decision Heuristics

To obtain this information, which was required to inform modeling, we provided our SME Jeppesen charts for all major U.S. airports and then asked him to select charts for those airports for which he had significant experience of typical taxi routes and clearances. He selected nine airports (DFW, LAX, SFO, ATL, JFK, DEN, SEA, MIA, ORD). The SME was asked to draw, using a highlighter on the charts themselves, the likely or expected taxi routes at each airport from touchdown to his company's gate area. A total of 284 routes were generated in this way.

Our goal at this point was to identify whether any of the heuristic strategies identified during task analysis and knowledge engineering would be likely to yield acceptable levels of decision accuracy. We obtained an estimate of the accuracy of heuristic strategies 2 (turn toward the company's gates) and 3 (turn in the direction that minimizes the largest of the X or Y distance between the current location and the gates) by comparing the predictions these heuristics would make with the data provided by the SME for the airports studied. We recognize that these accuracy estimates may be specific to the (major) carrier for whom the SME flew, because other carriers' gates may be located in areas at these nine airports such that their pilots are provided more or less complex (or geometrically intuitive) clearances than those providing the basis of our SME's experience. However, we do believe that this study resulted in enlightening results regarding the surprisingly high level of accuracy of simple, fast and frugal decision heuristics (Gigerenzer & Goldstein, 1996) in this complex, operational environment.

Figure 18.3 presents the results of an analysis of the effectiveness of these two heuristic strategies. Note that the *XY* heuristic is quite good across the board, and the even simpler toward terminal heuristic is reasonably accurate at many major U.S. airports. As such, we created the turn decision-making components of the pilot model to make decisions according to the set of strategies described previously, including the two surprisingly frugal and robust toward terminal and *XY* heuristics portrayed in Figure 18.3. One can think of these five strategies as being hierarchically organized in terms of their costs (time requirements) and benefits (accuracies). The decision components of the cognitive model worked by choosing the strategy that achieved the highest accuracy given the decision time available.

Detailed Description of Dynamic Decision Modeling

From a time-horizon (cost) perspective, the selection of decision strategies was informed by a procedure for estimating the time remaining before a decision had to be made. Time remaining was based on the aircraft's distance to an intersection and the amount of slowing necessary to make whatever turns were available, which was thus dependent on aircraft dynamics. Recall that we had an algorithm available to calculate the maximum speed with which a turn of a given type could be negotiated. Thus the computation of time remaining assumed a worst-case scenario for each specific intersection. That is, the time horizon for decision making was determined by the intersection distance combined with knowledge of aircraft dynamics, used to determine whether breaking could slow the aircraft sufficiently to negotiate an intersection's sharpest turn.

This time remaining calculation was not implemented in ACT-R (i.e., we did not create a cognitive model of how the pilot estimated this time), but rather was made by a call from ACT-R to an external algorithm, so that the model could determine which of the decision strategies were available in any particular instance. Because we believed pilots' abilities to estimate these times were imperfect, noise was added to the result of the computations based on the aircraft model such that the result returned was anywhere from 80% to 120% of the true time remaining.

Each turn-related decision strategy was one production rule, which was allowed to enter conflict resolution only if the average time it would take the model to execute the procedure was less than 0.5 second less than the decision horizon. This somewhat conservative approach was used to compensate for the fact that both the time estimation and strategy execution times were noisy. Those productions

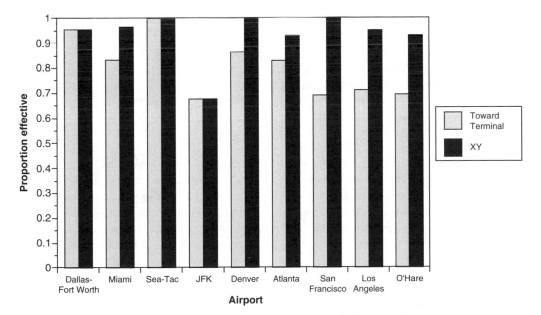

Figure 18.3. Accuracy of "toward terminal" and "minimize greater of *XY* distance" heuristics.

meeting these criteria competed in a slightly modified version of ACT-R's standard conflict resolution procedure. In the default ACT-R procedure, the utility of each production is estimated by the quantity $PG - C$, where P is the probability of success if that production is selected, G is a time constant (20 seconds is the default), and C is the time taken until an outcome is reached if that production fires. Because time cost was irrelevant in this application as long as the cost was less than the time remaining, this term was removed, though there was a 1-second penalty applied to productions whose time cost was within 0.5 second of the remaining time, again a conservative move to ensure that a decision strategy likely to be completed will be selected (one of our SMEs indicated a conservative bias in this direction). The utility of each production is also assumed in ACT-R to be a noisy quantity, so the system was not always guaranteed to select the strategy with the highest utility as computed by the $PG - C$ measure. (Amount of noise in this computation is a free parameter in ACT-R and a value of 1 was used as the s parameter in the logistic noise distribution. This yields a standard deviation of about 1.8, which was not varied to fit the data.) Thus there were two sources of noise in this situation: estimation of time remaining, and the utilities of the strategies themselves.

In the pilot model, the P for each production was estimated according to the actual probability of success of each of the decision strategies. Thus, P for the production initiating the "turn toward the gate" production was 80.7% because that was the success rate for that strategy as determined by the SME study. P-values for the other two decision heuristics (3 and 5) were calculated in an analogous fashion, and p-values for strategies 1 (recall the actual clearance) and 4 (derive from the map) were determined by the boundedly rational cognitive mechanisms inherent in the ACT-R cognitive architecture.

It should be noted that we did make some modifications to the standard conflict resolution mechanism in ACT-R, namely, that only productions that met the time horizon were considered, and when they did so, cost was factored out. We believe this was justified on ecological grounds and does describe the selection process in other contexts, as per Payne and Bettman (2001). Additionally, we are not the first to modify the conflict resolution equation to suit a particular task; Pirolli and Card (1999) replaced ACT-R's default conflict resolution behav-

ior with one based on ecological foraging models (also see chapter 17).

With the entire model in place, we then ran a Monte Carlo simulation (300 repetitions at each of 50 time horizons) to determine the probability of selection for each strategy as a function of decision time available. These simulation results are presented in Figure 18.4.

As is clear from Figure 18.4, in the time window from about 2.5 to about 8 seconds, the fast and frugal heuristics derived from ecological analysis dominate alternative strategies. An examination of videotapes from the simulation indicated that these decision time horizons were not uncharacteristic of the taxi scenarios. In addition, this finding can be viewed as adaptive because an economical strategy that can run to completion can frequently outperform an analytically superior decision strategy that must be truncated due to time constraints (Gigerenzer & Goldstein, 1996). As such, these results are not necessarily surprising but do suggest that error reduction efforts requiring new decision strategies will have to be evaluated in light of the availability of potentially more frugal heuristics that may yield relatively robust performance, yet fail in situations where the environmental regularities embodied in these heuristics are not satisfied (Reason, 1990). For example, modeling indicated that the turn toward gate heuristic takes approximately 2.5 seconds to compute with 80% accuracy. A rational pilot would likely not favor a new strategy or technology over this heuristic unless the increased benefit/cost ratio of a novel decision strategy was significantly superior to this quick and dirty method.

Empirical Adequacy

Appropriate techniques for the verification and validation of human performance models based on computational, cognitive modeling is an issue of great current interest (see, e.g., Leiden, Laughery, & Corker, 2001), and it is fair to say that there are no unanimously agreed on criteria in this area. In the following, we present two sources of empirical evidence in support of our dynamic, integrated, computational model of this pilot–aircraft–visual scene–taxiway system. The first source of support is a global analysis of the frequency of taxi navigation errors as a function of intersection type. The

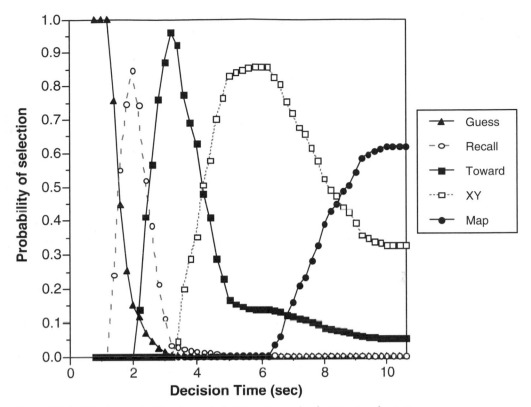

Figure 18.4. Selection probability for each decision strategy by decision time horizon.

second is a more finely grained analysis at an er ror-by-error level.

Global Evidence for Decision Heuristic Reliance

Nine different taxiway routes were used in the T-NASA2 baseline scenarios, covering a total of 97 separate intersection crossings. Because each route was run six times, a total of 582 intersection crossings occurred in the baseline trials. As mentioned earlier, in only 12 instances were crews observed to make significant departures from the cleared route, resulting in an error rate (per intersection, rather than per trial) of approximately 2% (Goodman, 2001).

As Goodman (2001) reported, of the 582 in- tersection crossed, the clearance indicated that crews should proceed in a direction toward the destination gate in 534 cases (91.8%), whereas the clearance directed crews in directions away from the gate in only 48 cases (or 8.2%). On examin- ing this information with respect to the predictions

of both the toward terminal and *XY* heuristics em- bodied in our model, we discovered that at *every* one of the 97 intersection crossings in T-NASA2 scenarios at which the cleared route conflicted with both these two heuristics, at least one taxi error was made. These accounted for 7 of the 12 taxi errors observed.

In addition, and as will be discussed in the fol- lowing section, 4 of the 12 taxi errors were attrib- uted not to decision making, but rather to a loss of situation awareness or situation awareness (i.e., losing track of one's position on the airport sur- face, see Goodman, 2001; Hooey & Foyle, 2001), a cognitive phenomenon beyond the scope of the present modeling. Our modeling approach assumed that location knowledge (loss of situation aware- ness) was not the primary factor in contributing to taxi error but instead time-stressed decision making combined with what might be called counter- intuitive intersection and clearance pairs; that is, those at which both the toward terminal and *XY* heuristics failed due to either atypical geometry or clearances.

Local Evidence of Decision Heuristic Reliance

The Goodman (2001) report provided a detailed analysis of each of the 12 taxi errors observed in the baseline conditions of T-NASA2 experimentation. In the following, we briefly consider each error in turn. When we use the term *classification*, we refer to the terms adopted by Hooey and Foyle (2001), and we have put in boldface errors we believe to provide evidence for our model, especially for the fast and frugal decision heuristics it used to make decisions under time stress. We have used italics to indicate errors due to loss of situation awareness, which are beyond the purview of our research, thus providing neither support for or against our model, given our initial modeling focus. In the following, all quotations are from Goodman (2001).

Error 1: This error was classified as a decision (as opposed to planning or execution) error, and it confirms our modeling as the crew turned toward the gate when the clearance indicated a turn away from the gate.

Error 2: This error was also classified as a decision error associated with lack of awareness of airport layout and concourse location. We thus consider this error due to a loss of situation awareness.

Error 3: This error was classified as a planning error in which the crew verbalized that Tango didn't seem to make sense because it was a turn away from the concourse. They thus turned in a direction toward the destination gate.

Error 4: This error was classified as an execution error due to perceptual confusion over center lines; the crew nonetheless prematurely turned in the direction of the concourse.

Error 5: This error was classified as an execution error as vocalizations indicated the crew was aware of the proper clearance. However, they made a premature turn toward the gate.

Error 6: This error was classified as an execution error because the captain stated that the lines were confusing but made a premature turn into the ramp area near the destination gate.

Error 7: This error was classified as a planning error as the FO verbally omitted an intermediate turn in the clearance to Foxtrot. However "the turn to Foxtrot would have led pilots away from concourse— Instead, FO suggested turning toward concourse on Alpha."

Error 8: This error was classified as a decision error because the crew immediately made a turn toward the gate after exiting the runway, whereas the clearance prescribed a turn away from gate.

Error 9: This error was classified as an execution error, because the FO voiced confusion over center lines. Crews made a (one-gate) premature turn into the concourse area while the clearance indicated they should proceed ahead further prior to turning into the concourse.

Errors 10, 11, and 12: Each of these errors was classified as a due to a loss of situation awareness, due to the FO being "head down with Jepp chart, [and] didn't realize where they were on the airport surface" (Error 10), the crew "demonstrated lack of awareness of airport layout" (Error 11), and "FO lacked awareness of their location on the airport surface" (Error 12).

Although several of these errors were not classified as decision errors by NASA, we think it is revealing to note that every one of the errors classified as planning, decision, and execution errors are consistent with the fast and frugal decision decision-making heuristics discovered during ecological analysis.

Summary

Errors in the T-NASA2 experimentation arose due to both poor situation awareness as well as to turn-related decision making (Goodman, 2001). As described in an early section of this chapter, we decided to focus our modeling efforts on decision-related errors, thus complementing other modeling efforts that took situation awareness–related errors to be the focus of their efforts. In summary, given the empirical results provided, we conclude that there is reasonably good empirical support for our model.

Conclusions

We are encouraged by the results of this research to continue to pursue computational, cognitive modeling of human performance in dynamic, interactive contexts. We believe that the errors observed in the T-NASA2 scenario were consistent with the results of our ecological analysis of this information-impoverished, dynamic decision-making environment and also the mechanisms by which the results of the ecological analysis were embedded in the ACT-R modeling architecture. We believe this marriage of the ecological rationality approach (i.e., the discovery and evaluation of the various decision heuristics—Gigerenzer, 2002; Todd, 2002) and the rational analysis–based mechanisms comprising the design of ACT-R provided an illustration of the weak version of cognitive-ecological rapprochement, as we have described previously. Actually coupling the internal cognitive model with computational models of the visual scene, taxiways, and aircraft dynamics additionally provided an illustration of what we have described as strong rapprochement. Finally, the general portrayal of adaptive behavior as constrained adaptation to the statistical and cost-benefit structure of the previously experienced task environment also achieves some level of support from this research. We believe that perhaps the strongest source of empirical evidence in favor of this interpretation was that both our model and the pilots studied *failed* to perform adaptively in a specified class of ecologically atypical situations.

The crux of the interpretation of taxi errors in T-NASA2 is that pilots had multiple methods for handling individual turn decisions and used the most accurate strategy possible given the time available (compare Payne & Bettman, 2001). These findings are in accord with Todd's (2002) observation that "the most important factors shaping cognitive (and physical) evolution came from the external environment—and one of the most pressing concerns facing a variety of organisms in a variety of dynamic environmental situations is simply the passage of time" (p. 53). In sum, our modeling and validation demonstrated that pilots tended to rely on cognitively cheaper, but less specific information gained from experience when time was short, and in a manner reasonably well (but not perfectly) adapted to decision horizons collectively determined by both visibility conditions and the problem of coping with the dynamics of a vehicle the size of a modern airliner. Furthermore, we take our results as evidence for success of the IBT-based approach. We believe it was necessary to include constraints and information from all three sources in the triad to achieve a successful model of performance in the task studied here; any pairwise approach would have lacked important sources of constraint. Kilograms can indeed matter.

Discussion

We are encouraged by our modeling results and have gone on to model additional operational scenarios associated with the approach and landing phases of flight (Byrne et al., 2004; Byrne & Kirlik, in press). We see many prospects for cognitive modeling in the spirit of a strong sense of rapprochement between cognitive and ecological analyses, as described in the introduction to this chapter.

We consider the studies presented by Gray (chapter 16), Pirolli (chapter 17), many of the studies influenced by rational analysis (e.g., Oaksford & Chater, 1998) and ecological rationality (e.g., Gigerenzer & Selten, 2002) to be among the most interesting exemplars of exactly the type of detailed examination of adaptive behavior and cognition Ashby (1952) recommended. To the extent that we view our own research in a related light and to be a rapprochement, we see it as furthering the goals of both ecological and cognitive discovery. We believe that our strong interpretation of rapprochement remains true to both Brunswik's goal of providing an ever more faithful and extensive mapping of the cognitive ecology, and Newell's (1990) goal of providing ever more coherent accounts of internal cognition. These goals are of equal importance and practical relevance in both understanding and supporting adaptive behavior in human–technology interaction. Future psychological and human factors research should strive to achieve both.

Acknowledgments.   This research was supported by NASA Ames grants NCC2-1219 and NDD2-1321 to Rice University and NAG 2-1609 to the University of Illinois. We thank Captains Bill Jones and Robert Norris, who served as SMEs, and Brian Webster and Michael Fleetwood for their contributions to this research.

References

Anderson, J. R. (1990). *The adaptive character of thought*. Hillsdale, N.J.: Lawrence Erlbaum.

Anderson, J. R. (1991). Author's response: More on rational analysis. *Behavioral and Brain Sciences, 14*(3).

Anderson, J. R., Bothell, D., Byrne, M. D., Douglass, S., Lebiere, C., & Quin, Y. (2004). An integrated theory of the mind. *Psychological Review, 111,* 1036–1060.

Anderson, J. R., & Lebiere, C. (1998) *The atomic components of thought*. Mahwah, N.J.: Lawrence Erlbaum.

Ashby, W. R. (1952). *Design for a brain*. London: Chapman & Hall.

Beer, R. D. (1995). A dynamical systems perspective on agent-environment interaction. *Artificial Intelligence, 72*(1–2), 173–215.

Bently, A. F. (1954). The human skin: Philosophy's last line of defense. In S. Ratner (Ed.), *Inquiry into inquiries*. Boston: Beacon Press.

Brunswik, E. (1956). *Perception and the representative design of psychological experiments*. Berkeley: University of California Press.

Byrne, M. D. (2001). ACT-R/PM and menu selection: Applying a cognitive architecture to HCI. *International Journal of Human-Computer Studies, 55*(1), 41–84.

Byrne, M. D., & Gray, W. D. (2003). Returning human factors to an engineering discipline: Expanding the science base through a new generation of quantitative methods—preface to the special section. *Human Factors, 45,* 1–4.

Byrne, M. D., Kirlik, A., & Fleetwood, M. D. (in press). Closing the loop on computational cognitive modeling: Describing the dynamics of interactive decision making and attention allocation. In D. C. Foyle & B. L. Hooey (Eds.) *Human performance modeling in aviation: Surface operations and synthetic vision systems*. Mahwah, NJ: Lawrence Erlbaum.

Byrne, M. D., Kirlik, A., Fleetwood, M. D., Huss, D. G., Kosorukoff, A., Lin, R., & Fick, C. S. (2004). A closed-loop, ACT-R approach to modeling approach and landing with and without synthetic vision system (SVS) technology. *Proceedings of the Human Factors and Ergonomics Society 48th Annual Meeting* (pp. 2111–2115). Santa Monica, Calif.: Human Factors and Ergonomics Society.

Card, S. K., Moran, T. P., & Newell, A. (1983). *The psychology of human-computer interaction*. Hillsdale, NJ: Lawrence Erlbaum Associates.

Casner, S. M. (1994). Understanding the determinants of problem-solving behavior in a complex environment. *Human Factors, 36,* 580–596.

Cassell, R., Smith, A., & Hicok, D. (1999). Development of airport surface required navigation performance (RNP). NASA/CR-1999–209109.

Cheng, V. H. L., Sharma, V., & Foyle, D. C. (2001). A study of aircraft taxi performance for enhancing airport surface traffic control. *IEEE Transactions on Intelligent Transportation Systems, 2*(2), 39–54.

Clark, A. (2003). *Natural-born cyborgs*. New York: Cambridge University Press.

Connolly, T. (1999). Action as a fast and frugal heuristic. *Minds and Machines, 9,* 479–496.

Degani, A., Shafto, M., & Kirlik, A. (1999). Modes in human-machine systems: Review, classification, and application. *International Journal of Aviation Psychology, 9*(2), 125–138.

Deutsch, S., & Pew, R. (2002). Modeling human error in a real-world teamwork environment. In *Proceedings of the Twenty-fourth Annual Conference of the Cognitive Science Society* (pp. 274–279). Mahwah, N.J.: Erlbaum.

Dewey, J. (1896). The reflex arc concept in psychology. *Psychological Review 3,* 357–370.

Endsley, M. R., & Smolensky, M. W. (1998). Situation awareness is air traffic control: The big picture. In M. W. Smolensky & E. S. Stein (Eds.), *Human factors in air traffic control*. San Diego: Academic Press.

Foushee, H. C., & Helmreich, R. L. (1988). Group interaction and flight crew performance. In E. L. Wiener & D. C. Nagel (Eds.), *Human factors in aviation*. San Diego: Academic Press.

Foyle, D. C., Andre, A. D., McCann, R. S., Wenzel, E., Begault, D., & Battiste, V. (1996). Taxiway navigation and situation awareness (T-NASA) system. Problem, design, philosophy, and description of an integrated display suite for low visibility airport surface operations. *SAE Transactions: Journal of Aerospace, 105,* 1511–1418.

Gibson, J. J. (1962). Observations on active touch. *Psychological Review, 69,* 477–491.

Gigerenzer, G. (2002). The adaptive toolbox. In G. Gigerenzer & R. Selten (Eds.), *Bounded rationality: The adaptive toolbox* (pp. 37–50). Cambridge, Mass.: MIT Press.

Gigerenzer, G., & Goldstein, D. G. (1996). Reasoning the fast and frugal way: Models of bounded rationality. *Psychological Review, 103,* 650–669.

Gigerenzer, G., & Selten, R. (2002). *Bounded rationality: The adaptive toolbox*. Cambridge, Mass.: MIT Press.

Goodman, A. (2001). Enhanced descriptions of off-route navigation errors in T-NASA2. NASA Ames Research Center, Moffet Field, Calif.

Gore, B., & Corker, K. M. (2002). Increasing aviation safety using human performance modeling tools: An air man-machine design and analysis system application. In M. J. Chinni (Ed.), *2002 Military, government and aerospace simulation, 34*(3), 183–188. San Diego: Society for Modeling and Simulation International.

Gray, W. D. (2000). The nature and processing of errors in interactive behavior. *Cognitive Science, 24,* 205–248.

Gray, W. D., & Altman, E. M. (1999). Cognitive modeling and human–computer interaction. In W. Karwowski (Ed.), *International encyclopedia of ergonomics and human factors.* New York: Taylor & Francis.

Gray, W. D., & Boehm-Davis, D. A. (2000). Milliseconds matter: An introduction to microstrategies and to their use in describing and predicting interactive behavior. *Journal of Experimental Psychology: Applied, 6,* 322–335.

Hollnagel, E. (1998). *Cognitive reliability and error analysis method.* Oxford: Elsevier.

Hollnagel, E. (2000). Looking for errors of omission and comission or *The Hunting of the Snark* revisited. *Reliability Engineering and System Safety, 68,* 135–145.

Hooey, B. L., & Foyle, D. C. (2001). A post-hoc analysis of navigation errors during surface operations. Identification of contributing factors and mitigating strategies. *Proceeedings of the 11th Symposium on Aviation Psychology.* Columbus: Ohio State University.

Hooey, B. L., Foyle, D. C., & Andre, A. D. (2000). Integration of cockpit displays for surface operations: The final stage of a human-centered design approach. *SAE Transactions: Journal of Aerospace, 109,* 1053–1065.

Hutchins, E. (1995). *Cognition in the wild.* Cambridge, Mass.: MIT Press.

Jagacinski, R. J., & Flach, J. M. (2002). *Control theory for humans.* Mawwah, N.J.: Erlbaum.

Jones, D. (2000). Runway incursion prevention system (RIPS). Presentation to the SVS CONOPS Workshop, NASA Langley Research Center, February 23, 2003.

Kirlik, A. (1998). The ecological expert: Acting to create information to guide action. *Fourth Symposium on Human Interaction with Complex Systems.* Dayton, OH: IEEE Computer Society Press. Available online at www.computer.org/proceedings/hics/8341/83410015abs.htm.

Kirlik, A. (2001). On Gibson's review of Brunswik. In K. R. Hammond & T. R. Stewart (Eds.), *The*

essential Brunswik: Beginnings, explications, applications* (pp. 238–241). New York: Oxford University Press.

Kirlik, A., Miller, R. A., & Jagacinski, R. J. (1993). Supervisory control in a dynamic uncertain environment: A process model of skilled human-environment interaction. *IEEE Transactions on Systems, Man, and Cybernetics, 23*(4), 929–952.

Kurz, E. M., & Tweny, R. D. (1998). The practice of mathematics and science: From calculus to the clothesline problem. In M. Oaksford & N. Chater (Eds.), *Rational models of cognition* (pp. 415–438). New York: Oxford University Press.

Lebiere, C., Bielfeld, E., Archer, R., Archer, S., Allender, L., & Kelly, T. D. (2002). Imprint/ACT-R: Integration of a task network modeling architecture with a cognitive architecture and its application to human error modeling. In M. J. Chinni (Ed.), *2002 Military, government and aerospace simulation, 34*(3), 13–19. San Diego: Society for Modeling and Simulation International.

Leiden, K., Laughery, R., & Corker, K. (2001). Verification and validation of simulations. Online report available at https://postdoc.arc.nasa.gov/postdoc/t/folder/main.ehtml?url_id=90738.

Marr, D. (1982). *Vision.* San Francisco: W. H. Freeman.

McCarley, J. S., Wickens, C. D., Goh, J., & Horrey, W. J. (2002). A computational model of attention/situation awareness. *Proceedings of the 46th Annual Meeting of the Human Factors and Ergonomics Society* (pp. 1669–1673). Santa Monica, Calif.

Newell, A. (1990). *Unified theories of cognition.* Cambridge, Mass.: Harvard University Press.

Newell, A. & Simon, H. A. (1972). *Human problem solving.* Englewood Cliffs, N.J.: Prentice Hall.

NTSB Reporter (2003). Runway incursions. Special issue, *21*(3).

Oaksford, M. & Chater, N. (1998). *Rational models of cognition.* New York: Oxford University Press.

Olson, W. A., & Sarter, N. B. (2000). Automation management strategies: Pilot preferences and operational experiences. *International Journal of Aviation Psychology, 10*(4), 327–341.

Payne, J. W., & Bettman, J. (2001). Preferential choice and adaptive strategy use. In G. Gigerenzer & R. Selten (Eds.), *Bounded rationality: The adaptive toolbox* (pp. 123–146). Cambridge, Mass.: MIT Press.

Pirolli, P., & Card, S. (1999). Information foraging. *Psychological Review, 106,* 643–675.

Powers, W. T. (1973). *Behavior: The control of perception.* New York: Aldine DeGruyter.

Rasmussen, J. (1980). What can be learned from human error reports? In K. D. Duncan, M. M. Gruneberg, & D. Wallis (Eds.), *Changes in working life* (pp. 97–113). Chichester: Wiley.

Reason, J. (1990). *Human error*. Cambridge: Cambridge University Press.

Todd, P. M. (2002). Fast and frugal heuristics for environmentally bounded minds. In G. Gigerenzer & R. Selten (Eds.), *Bounded rationality: The adaptive toolbox* (pp. 51–70). Cambridge, Mass.: MIT Press.

Wiegmann, D. A. & Goh, J. (2001). Pilots' decisions to continue visual flight rules (VFR) flight into adverse weather: Effects of distance draveled and flight experience. University of Ilinois, Aviation Research Laboratory Tech Rept ARL-01-11/FAA-01-3.

Wiegmann, D. A., & Shappell, S. A. (1997). Human factors analysis of post-accident data: Applying theoretical taxonomies of human error. *International Journal of Aviation Psychology, 7*(1), 67–81.

Woods, D. D., Johannesen, L. J., Cook, R. I., & Sarter, N. B. (1994). *Behind human error: Cognitive systems, computers and hindsight*. Columbus, Ohio: CSERIAC.

VII

Reflections and Future Directions

19

Terry Connolly

Reflections from a Judgment
and Decision Making Perspective

Among the more irreverent Northwestern graduate students of my day there was active debate as to whether Egon Brunswik's reputation as a deep thinker had been achieved in spite of or because of the opacity of his prose. It was only the firm hand of Donald T. Campbell (once, I believe, Brunswik's teaching assistant at Berkeley, but at that time the guru of the Northwestern psychology department) that drove us through the thickets of dense German and imperfect translation. A first reaction to the present volume is to conclude that Brunswik's reputation is secure. Here is a body of first-class work inspired by, informed by, or otherwise tied to central Brunswikian ideas of half a century or more ago. The prose, it turns out, was worth the struggle. If only we had had Goldstein's lucid introductory essay (chapter 2) to guide our earlier studies!

The second reaction, at least to this judgment and decision making (JDM) researcher, is a certain envy. Most of our studies, defying Brunswikian rules, rely on super-simple, artificial tasks—one-sentence scenarios, transparent gambling games, unfamiliar hypotheticals. Not uncommonly our data matrix is $N \times 1$, a single response from N different subjects. If nothing else, such data leave a considerable burden on the investigator to explain just why anyone should care what these subjects did

in this task. It is not an impossible task to explain that this is, we think, the way (a way?) to theory, but it is a burden nonetheless. One assumes that the authors of the chapters collected in this volume rarely face such a demand for explanation. When one addresses tasks such as aircraft collision avoidance, battlefield threat assessment, chemical plant fault diagnosis, or identification of radar images as friendly or hostile aircraft, it seems self-evident that understanding and improving the judgment and decision processes involved will be matters that the relevant practitioners care about.

It is self-evident that JDM researchers would also like to have something useful to say in the world of significant decisions—to medical doctors forming diagnoses, to investors planning a retirement strategy, to faculty selecting graduate students. Here, I think, JDM researchers have set themselves a more difficult task than have the human–technology interaction (HTI) researchers represented in this volume. At least the latter start with one domain of application, the one in which the original research was conducted. The JDM researcher, in contrast, having started with a highly simplified, thin task must undertake a tricky extrapolation before reaching even the first domain of potentially useful application.

The work of extrapolation is not always done well. The simplest and nearly always the most misleading approach is simply to assert that the extrapolation works. "We have discovered in our lab that human beings display the following capability/bias/error. You should therefore be ready to deal with this capability/bias/error in your application problem." The simplistic assertion of universalism across subjects, tasks, settings, and times is too obviously dubious to be made explicitly but can be accomplished less obtrusively. Often a simple shift of verb tense does the trick. The results section reports what *these* subjects *did* (specific past tense); the discussion section moves to what humans *do* (continuing nonspecific present tense), a claim on which the author has essentially no evidence. What a good empirical study establishes is an existence theorem: There exists at least one population, task, setting, and time for which some effect has been observed. Replication with other subjects, and so on, is a matter for demonstration, not assertion. Very often, the demonstrations fail.

HTI/JDM Collaboration

So what *does* JDM research bring to the cognitive engineering, HTI table? One possible division of labor was suggested by Brunswik: "The functional approach has its place mainly in the appraisal of the interplay and relative contribution or weight of factors in the adjustment to a given ecology, while the reductive approach reveals the technological details of the machinery that brings about such adjustment" (Brunswik, 1955; also see chapter 16).

The functionalists (HTI?) establish which sound and visible cues contribute to a given achievement, the reductionists (JDM?) caution that sounds should be in the range 20–20k Hertz, light in the range 4,000–7,000 nanometers, and so on. Even in parody this won't work. As JDM researchers have repeatedly found, the cue is not simply a matter of psychophysics but of meaning. "Making sense of the problem" is surely more a matter of functional achievement than it is of "technological machinery."

A more plausible division of labor between cognitive engineering and JDM research might be based on their relative cost. Part of the JDM researcher's envy of the work reported in this volume is the extraordinary richness of the task environments, whether studying real pilots in real planes or trainee pilots in flight simulators. These planes and simulators do not come free, and it is not surprising that virtually all the chapters acknowledge substantial grant support, often from branches of the military. By comparison, JDM research is virtually free: volunteer student subjects, paper and pencil tasks, little special equipment. With this huge cost advantage, the JDM researcher can afford to run 100 studies for every 1 the cognitive engineer mounts. We should exploit this advantage as part of our collaboration.

An example might clarify the sort of complementarity I have in mind. Consider the phenomenon of judgmental overconfidence, the tendency to assign higher probabilities to the correctness of predictions than is justified by track records (see, for example, Juslin, 1994; O'Connor, 1989). The JDM literature on overconfidence is now extensive, and there is at least a modest understanding of the situational factors that exacerbate and ameliorate the effect. However, I know that few JDM researchers would be bold enough to predict whether the effect would be found in a specified setting or how large it would be.

Suppose now that a cognitive engineer consults with a JDM researcher on the possibility of human overconfidence in a threat assessment task such as that studied by Horrey and colleagues (chapter 5). Information displayed in that task was labeled as being of high, medium, and low reliability. Perhaps it would be prudent for the interface designer to label information received from a highly confident human observer with a discounted level of trust to reflect the concern about observer overconfidence. Or perhaps the user should be trained to apply such a discount. This seems to me a poor solution. I am not an overconfidence researcher, but I do know that various studies have found larger or smaller effects; that incentives and training matter; that not all JDM researchers are convinced that the effect exists at all; and that there are populations (weather forecasters are the commonly cited example) where excellent calibration has been found.

When the cognitive engineer asks, "Should I expect overconfidence in these reports?" the JDM researcher would be well advised to answer, "Good question; let's find out. There are good grounds for your concern but no sufficiently well-established theory to allow a confident prediction. We do, however, have excellent instruments, clear hypotheses, well-developed statistical routines and lots of experience running studies like this. Furthermore we can run it on the loose change from your main grant." Such collaboration offers payoffs for both parties. The engineer garners the design information she needs, and the JDM researcher establishes one more point in the range of settings to which overconfidence effects do or do not generalize. As in so many engineering disciplines, the flow of information can be as strong from application to theory as it is in the reverse direction. Numerous authors have noted that for many years, thermodynamics learned more from steam engine makers than the reverse. Interface design may offer similar two-way flows for cognitive engineers and JDM researchers.

Theory Building

Even a cursory sampling of the studies in this book suggests that leading researchers are increasingly concerned at the absence of general and testable theory, a concern shared with such related fields as naturalistic decision making and dynamic decision making. The concern, of course, is that without such theory there is little to tie one study to another, so that each new study must be undertaken more or less de novo. Bisantz and colleagues (chapter 3) offer some initial steps to address the problem and identify other potentially promising ideas scattered throughout the book. These encouraging hints notwithstanding, it is difficult for an outsider to see very much cross-fertilization even between the various efforts reported here. Nor is it a surprise to read Degani and colleagues (chapter 13) worrying that "interface design simplifications are too often performed intuitively, and in an ad hoc way . . . [often resulting in] . . . user frustration, confusion and, in the case of high-risk systems, the possibility of disaster." Everyday experience exposes us to a vast range of interfaces, ranging from the superb to the essentially unusable, and it is very difficult for a user to distinguish the features that drive the design one way or the other. The studies in this book remind us of the huge effects on user behavior of apparently trifling design changes—a momentary delay before a window opens, one frame highlighted to contrast with another. Clearly, the development of integrating theory that will allow cross-study generalization, even of a tentative sort, is both the most pressing and the most difficult facing the field right now. As Rothrock and Kirlik warn (chapter 10), "If

we do not continue to pursue the path toward abstraction and formalization, we are destined to a future in which it will be impossible to educate competent professionals in cognitive engineering, human factors, and related fields."

Representative Design and Time Constants

Given how deeply Brunswikian thinking is woven into the texture of these chapters, it is interesting to examine just what has happened to the notion of representative design as we move from a natural to a built information environment. Brunswik famously urged sampling of "stimulus situations from well-defined natural-cultural 'ecologies'; only by such representative design of experiments can the ecological generalizability of functional regularities of behavior and adaptation be ascertained" (Brunswik, 1956, p. 159). This is a reasonably clear goal in a JDM study of distance perception (forbidding, for example, the use of artificial stimuli deprived of the natural covariation among the various cues). By analogy it helps the researcher select stimuli in studying a more cognitive judgment, such as diagnosis of a specific class of medical patients (where the same prohibition would forbid presenting imaginary patients with, say, normal respiration and zero pulse). But how is the spirit of representative design to be preserved when the informational environment is built de novo, where no "well-defined natural-cultural ecologies" exist, as in the design of a new power plant control room? What if the informational environment is being consciously manipulated to deceive, as when an enemy attempts to cloak hostile intentions by flying a warplane at a speed and altitude that suggests a civilian airliner?

In one sense the answer to these vexing questions is to remember that this is engineering, not science: The primary question is "What works?" Given that one has just created an interface, as in the power plant example, it is obviously unrealistic to suppose that a new operator arrives preadapted to it. This is a built, not a natural, environment. Normal training and achievement testing will be required—using, of course, a representative sample of the sorts of operating and malfunction incidents that might arise in the plant and allowing the interface to represent these incidents in the way it normally would. An interface that proves hard to learn or operate will be modified and the same testing repeated. Similarly, interfaces designed to allow the possibility of enemy deception would be tested over a (representative?) range of warfare conditions, presumably with interfaces designed to highlight inconsistencies that might signal deceptive intent. Where Brunswik (1955) in the passage quoted earlier relegated to the second rank the elucidation of nature's "technological details" that bound the distal target to the central response, in engineered systems those technological details are fixed by the engineer herself. The primary focus, as before, is on achievement, and for this representative design is still required.

A somewhat subtler puzzle arises when both the human and the ecological subsystems are evolving over time, perhaps at different rates. Suppose, for example, one were interested in the judgmental skills of the world's leading diagnostician of some rare but deadly cancer. The diagnostician agrees to cooperate and gives you access to his entire collection of the medical records of every patient he has seen in his professional lifetime. Which cases would you sample to represent his diagnostic ecology (and thus, one hopes, to capture his diagnostic expertise)? A moment's reflection suggests that there may be many different ecologies represented in these files: the patients he saw as a beginning oncologist using the diagnostic technology of 30 years ago; those seen before and after important changes in diagnostic and treatment techniques, such as new drugs or new tests; changing symptom sets reflecting a lifetime of societal and lifestyle changes; and finally, the increasingly bizarre and baffling symptom sets of the patients he saw as his reputation grew and he became the consultant to whom lesser doctors referred their most difficult cases.

Distinguishing these ecologies will clearly be a complex empirical and conceptual problem, as will selecting the one that best matches your investigative purpose (perhaps the early patients, if one is building a physician replacement program for a third-world country; the most recent cases for a model of his fully evolved capabilities). But the core issue the example illustrates is the common observation that both ecology and responder change over time, and that a two-system match at one moment may switch to a glaring mismatch at another. We may, as Brunswik urges, be prepared to adopt a

"laissez-faire policy for the ecology" (Brunswik, 1955, p. 198) and be careful "not to interfere with naturally established mediation patterns" that allow vicarious functioning (Brunswik, 1952, p. 26). This is not the same as ignoring the fact that ecologies change, as do the organisms that interact with them. The time constants of these changes is a problem begging for more systematic attention. As a recent thoughtful commentator (Wolf, 2005, p. 6) notes, even after all these years of discussing the idea, "The establishment of representative procedures must be a priority task for our future research in the tradition of Brunswik's probabilistic functionalism."

Action

Brunswik's (1956) object constancy studies are usually discussed in terms of their use of everyday situations that preserve the redundancy among cues and that thus allowed vicarious functioning. What is less often noted is the fact that the subject in these experiments was allowed to move about—to *act*—in the environment. Without such freedom the subject is deprived of important distance cues, such as parallax and changes of relative size. Moving out of the lab does more than eliminate factorial design. It also eliminates the bite bar that immobilizes the subject's head—a restraint essential to the demonstration of any number of depth-related visual illusions.

The single-pass study predominant in JDM has also relied on immobilizing the subject for many of its effects. For example, in a now famous experiment, Tversky and Kahneman (1983) showed that a conjunction of two descriptive elements may be judged more probable than the less likely element alone. Linda, a woman described by a three-line thumbnail sketch, is judged as more likely to be both a bank teller *and* a feminist than she is to be a feminist alone, in clear violation of probabilistic canons. The effect has been extensively discussed, but the example itself seems unlikely to pose a serious practical problem. "How's life at the bank?" we ask as we are introduced. "Whatever makes you think I work in a bank?" she replies. The error disappears, at the price of a moment's embarrassment—and, importantly, as a result of taking an action based on our error. Such action–feedback loops are presumably an important part of our cognitive strategies in general and may help overcome the defects and biases thought to result from the heuristics that occupied so much of JDM research in the 1980s and 1990s (see, e.g., Hogarth, 1981; Connolly, 1999). The contributions of Kirlik (chapter 15) and Gray (chapter 16) in the present volume suggest how quickly cognitive engineering is moving beyond merely recognizing such loops and is developing higher level formalisms by which they can be treated in complex practical settings. The extraordinarily difficult challenges posed by Tolman and Brunswik (1935) of treating simultaneously distal–central linkages in both perception and action are finally being met in such efforts.

Conclusion

An invitation to comment on the work of others, apart from its worrying signal that one is too old for useful work oneself, is an opportunity to visit and reflect in areas removed from the familiar pastures. To this JDM researcher, the world of HTI looks like one of great excitement and challenging, important problems. It is a world to which the JDM community can and should make a richer connection. There are problems here to which we can contribute and from which we can learn. By stretching our comfortable range to connect with these new issues, we will understand better the meanings and limits of our familiar world. Here, in short, is a collaboration with potential payoffs for all concerned. I hope this book will be the stimulus to bring it about.

References

Brunswik, E. (1952). The conceptual framework of psychology. *International encyclopedia of unified science, volume 1, no. 10.* Chicago: University of Chicago Press.

Brunswik, E. (1955). Representative design and probabilistic theory in a functional psychology. *Psychological Review, 62,* 193–217.

Brunswik, E. (1956). Historical and thematic relations of psychology to other sciences. *Scientific Monthly, 83,* 151–161.

Connolly, T. (1999). Action as a fast and frugal heuristic. *Minds and Machines, 9,* 479–496.

Hogarth, R. M. (1981). Beyond discrete biases: Functional and dysfunctional aspects of judgmental heuristics. *Psychological Bulletin, 90,* 197–217.

Juslin, P. (1994). The overconfidence phenomenon as a consequence of informal experimenter-guided selection of almanac items. *Organizational Behavior and Human Decision Processes, 57,* 226–246.

O'Connor, M. (1989). Models of human behavior and confidence in judgment: A review. *International Journal of Forecasting, 5,* 159–169.

Tolman, E. C., & Brunswik, E. (1935). The organism and the causal texture of the environment. *Psychological Review, 42,* 43–77.

Tversky, A., & Kahneman, D. (1983). Extensional versus intuitive reasoning: The conjunction fallacy in probability judgment. *Psychological Review, 90,* 293–315.

Wolf, B. (2005). Fundamental principles of Brunswik's representative design. Posted to the Brunswik Society Web site, February. Available at: http://www.brunswik.org/notes/WolfRepDesign2005.pdf.

20

Kim J. Vicente

Reflections from a Cognitive Engineering and Human Factors Perspective

Both organism and environment will have to be seen as systems, each with properties of its own, yet both hewn from basically the same block.

—Brunswik (1957, p. 5)

What psychology needs is the kind of thinking that is beginning to be attempted in what is loosely called systems theory.

—Gibson (1979, p. 2)

By adopting a systems approach that focuses on the organism–environment interaction, Egon Brunswik and James Gibson developed a version of psychology that dovetails seamlessly with the practical aims of systems design. Nevertheless, it took decades before this connection was noticed and explored by human factors and cognitive engineering researchers and practitioners. The design relevance of Gibsonian psychology was marked a decade ago by the publication of a pair of companion monographs (Flach et al., 1995; Hancock et al., 1995). With the publication of this long overdue volume, we now begin to see how Brunswikian psychology can also impact critical issues in the design of human–technology interaction.

The research compiled here exhibits a number of positive features. Many of the chapters begin with a practical problem and use its characteristics to dictate the choice of theory and methods. To take but one example, Bisantz et al. (chapter 3) describe the demands faced by Anti-Air Warfare Coordinators and then go on to argue how the lens model equation (LME) provides a suitable means for studying that phenomenon. This problem-driven approach contrasts with much psychological and human factors research that has the tail wagging the dog by letting methodology take primacy over phenomena (Vicente, 2000). Many of the chapters

also focus on developing insights that have important implications for systems design. In fact, the number of design interventions that are addressed—displays, alerts, decision aids, training, and evaluation —is impressive and shows the breadth of applicability of a Brunswikian approach to human factors and cognitive engineering. The complexity of the tasks investigated in this volume is also laudable, including sophisticated laboratory simulations and even naturalistic operational environments. The inclusion of dynamic tasks—a comparatively infrequently investigated aspect of judgment and decision making (Hogarth, 1981)—is particularly important for reasons that I will address later. The diversity of methods adopted is also important.

Traditionally, Brunswikian research has been equated with lens model research (Vicente, 2003), and although many of the chapters still adopt the LME, they also illustrate creative and sophisticated variations on that theme, variations that begin to reflect the complexity of the practical problems being investigated (e.g., by taking multiple time slices, by adopting an n-dimensional approach, by adopting a multilevel approach, and by adopting a hybrid hierarchical/n-system approach).

Other researchers bring in a breath of fresh air by dropping the LME altogether and adopting other methods that are consistent with the Brunswikian systems approach (e.g., ACT-R, Bayesian statistics, information theory, genetic algorithms). An important next step in this evolution would be to follow the lead of Campbell et al. (chapter 11) and conduct comparative analyses of the LME and other methodologies, in their case, fuzzy set theory. These comparative studies would broaden the arsenal of tools in the Brunswikian toolbox and elucidate the boundary conditions, and thus the comparative merits and weaknesses, of various methods.

These are all important achievements, and it would be unreasonable to expect more from this volume, given the current state of the field. However, in writing a summative reflective chapter, the criterion of reasonableness can be relaxed so that we can take a blue-sky look toward the future. There is one issue in particular—time—that I would like to explore in more detail with the aim of identifying future research directions. As I mentioned earlier, judgment and decision making research has traditionally focused on static, one-shot decisions (for exceptions, see Brehmer, 1992). Brunswikian research has been no exception; the LME is exquisitely tailored to static, multiattribute judgment tasks. There are no dynamics, no continuities, and no feedback loops. All of this becomes a problem when one considers two additional facts: Almost half of the empirical chapters in this volume still use the LME, and virtually all of the tasks with which human factors and cognitive engineers are concerned are dynamic.

Several authors try to address this thorn by taking multiple time slices using the LME (e.g., chapters 3, 6). There is no doubt that this represents an improvement on the traditional application of the LME, and the authors should be applauded for this innovation. However, the limitations of this approach are strong and should not be overlooked. The time-slice approach is still static because it freezes time by taking a series of snapshots. The continuity in the dynamics that is clearly present in the environmental simulations is not fully exploited theoretically or methodologically. The implications of this fact were pointed out by Hogarth (1981) several decades ago: "Theories of judgment and choice that lack a continuous perspective exclude one of the most important determinants of the behavior they purport to explain" (p. 213).

To be fair, these limitations are acknowledged. For example, Jha and Bisantz (chapter 6) clearly state that "this [time-slice] approach does not capture information that judges may have relied on concerning dynamic aspects of the cue values. . . . Future research regarding lens models of judgment behavior should similarly expand the use of dynamic cue information." The weighty implications of these limitations are also recognized. Campbell and others (chapter 11) recognize that "there are a number of characteristics and assumptions inherent in regression that make it unlikely that regression equations are capable of capturing the entire range of reasoning processes that humans employ across all domains." Similarly, Rothrock and Kirlik (chapter 10) observed that "linear regression approaches for inferring these [noncompensatory] strategies from behavioral data in these contexts may be inappropriate and may lead to misleading accounts of the behavior of these performers."

So the limitations and implications of not fully accommodating the highly dynamic nature of human–technology interaction are recognized. But where do we go from here? A few chapters in this volume have a dynamic component (e.g., chapters 15, 18), but ideally we would like to have a systematic conceptual framework that puts time front and center where it deserves to be rather than incorporating it implicitly, on an ad hoc, case-by-case basis or not at all.

I believe dynamical systems theory (DST)—an area of pure and applied mathematics that has been gaining attention in cognitive science (Port & van Gelder, 1995; van Gelder, 1998)—can achieve this aim. Like the LME, DST provides a mathematical language that can be used to model and measure human performance in complex dynamic systems, but its modeling capability is considerably wider. State variables provide a continuous, quantitative description of the behavior of the system over time. Time plays a central role because sequences of behavior are described as trajectories in a state space. The latter represents the set of constraints that are acting on the system. A state space can be conceptualized geometrically as a field that describes the entire range of possible system trajectories, much like a magnetic field describes the possible paths that a charged particle can follow. Fields for different systems can exhibit recurring patterns of dynamic behavior, such as attractors, repellors, limit cycles, and chaos.

DST has a number of important features that distinguish it from the LME. First, it has a tremendous range of applicability: "Dynamics is arguably the most widely used and powerful explanatory framework in science. An extraordinary range of phenomena have turned out to be best described as . . . a matter of interdependent variables. It would hardly be surprising if dynamics found application in the study of cognition as well" (van Gelder, 1998, p. 622). Second, it represents time explicitly and continuously, so it can capture continuous sequences of behavior (rather than a single snapshot or multiple snapshots), such as feedback loops and dynamic coupling between variables.

By replacing the mechanical view embedded in the LME with a field theoretic view, DST has a number of additional benefits (Einstein & Infeld, 1938/1966). For example, it captures action possibilities rather than just actions, lending itself nicely to the modeling of affordances (Gibson, 1979). In addition, all of our knowledge of the constraints acting on the system is captured in the construction of a single field, providing an element of conciseness and power. Just as important, the field description used in DST provides a basis for integrating seemingly different influences into a common representation, giving insight into the functional equivalence of otherwise disparate forces. This capability for functional equivalence leads to an elegance and parsimony in modeling because "the properties of the field alone appear to be essential for the description of phenomena; the differences in source do not matter" (Einstein & Infeld, 1938/1966, p. 134). Port and van Gelder (1995) describe additional advantages of DST compared to traditional ways of conceiving human cognition.

But is DST compatible with Brunswik's view of psychology? If we equate Brunswikian research with the LME, then DST is incompatible because it offers a different modeling framework. However, if we go beyond the LME and view Brunswikian psychology as a commitment to understanding human behavior—not just judgment and decision making—by focusing on adaptation to functionally significant environmental regularities (Vicente, 2003), then not only is DST compatible with Brunswik's vision but it can be seen as a twenty-first-century means for furthering that vision. To illustrate this claim, I will briefly review what I believe to be the most sophisticated and creative attempt in the cognitive engineering literature to use DST to model human behavior in a Brunswikian fashion.

Kirlik, Miller, and Jagacinski (1993) developed a process model of skilled human–technology–environment interaction in a dynamic and uncertain task environment. Participants piloted one scout craft and had supervisory control over four additional semi-autonomous craft that navigated in a simulated landscape consisting of irregularly shaped regions of forest. The operator's aims were to search the landscape for enemy aircraft to be destroyed and to find and load valuable cargo that was to be taken to a home base. In achieving these goals, participants also had to manage a limited set of resources (i.e., cargo capacity, fuel, and missiles). Actions were input using a joystick, push buttons, and a keyboard.

Following Brunswikian tenets, Kirlik and colleagues (1993) developed a model of the environment, a model of the human, and a model of their dynamic interaction, but they did not use the LME. In fact, the most innovative feature of this work is the ecologically inspired application of DST. More specifically, Kirlik et al. described the simulation environment as a set of quantitative, dynamic affordance distributions, creating a field-theoretic description of the action possibilities available to operators. Just as a charged particle would move according to the contours of a magnetic field that defines a set of attractive forces, skilled operators in this simulation are influenced by the gradients defined by the dynamic affordance distributions, as if there was an invisible attractive force operating on each aircraft. Moreover, the affordance distributions were nested to illustrate the hierarchical nature of action. As an example, the searching affordance distribution could be decomposed into a locomotion affordance and a sighting affordance. The peaks in the higher order searching affordance distribution thereby represent a compromise between the conflicting demands of, on the one hand, sighting objects in forested regions, and on the other hand, flying through open regions.

This modeling technique was used to describe regions of the simulated world from the perspective of various action possibilities, including searching, locomotion, loading, and refueling. Affordance values were used in a continuous fashion to represent the degree of match between state of the environment and the capability of each aircraft at every point in time. Action possibilities were based on critical points, which represented the current peak in the affordance distributions, suggesting that that action is the most appropriate one to take. Note, however, that the model does not fall into the trap of environmental determinism. In addition to the affordance distributions described suggesting which behaviors are possible at any point in time, the model also has a cognitive-action component that represents the current priorities based on task goals. This operator model contains a hierarchical planning mechanism that acts as a scheduler to generate routes defined by an ordered sequence of way points. There is also a hierarchical action mechanism that acts as a coordinator of the many types of actions that are required to control aircraft in the simulated world. Thus, behavioral trajectories emerge from the confluence of what is possible (the environmental component) with what is desirable (the human component).

The behavior of this model was compared with that generated by several human crews, and good agreement was found between the two, thereby showing the promise of this innovative application of DST to cognitive engineering.

Indeed, this application of DST within the umbrella of an ecological approach has several critical features. First, time is modeled explicitly and continuously, both in the environmental and human models. Rather than representing behavior at a frozen point in time, this research takes up the challenging task of accounting for changes in behavior over time. Second, the uniform field-theoretic modeling approach represents the action possibilities in the environment, thereby capturing not just what happens but also what can happen. In this way, the field concept provides a concise but powerful description of the world. Third, the field-theoretic approach also provides a basis for determining functional equivalence by integrating and coordinating multiple functions (e.g., locomotion and sighting) that would otherwise be incommensurate and therefore treated in isolation. From the perspective of DST, what is most important is not so much the objects in the world but their functional properties as captured by the field description (Einstein & Infeld, 1938/1966). Fourth, all of these benefits are captured, not in a lone ad hoc model developed solely and specifically for one idiosyncratic simulated environment but in a generalizable conceptual framework that can conceivably be transferred to many different environments. For instance, the concept of affordance distributions can, in principle, be instan-

tiated in any environment. Finally, by using DST, Kirlik et al. (1993) place their results in the context of the many applications of DST in other areas of science and engineering, providing the potential to borrow from and build on findings from a wide variety of disciplines (see also Hajdukiewicz & Vicente, 2004).

Despite all of these advantages, however, the potential of this line of research has not been fully realized, so there is still much to be gained by following and exploring the creative example set by Kirlik et al. (1993).

Given what we know about the highly stratified nature of citation rates in science in general (Hamilton, 1991) and in human factors and cognitive engineering in particular (Lee, Cassano, & Vicente, in press), many of us would be very happy to generate an experimental finding that is deemed to be noteworthy by our research community. Perhaps even more rewarding is the discovery of a novel method with a wide scope of applicability that can be used to generate many noteworthy experimental findings. At least as important is the discovery of a novel theory that can make sense of many existing experimental findings in a concise and coherent fashion, as well as making important untested predictions. Contributions at these last two levels in particular would be highlights of a successful scientific career, simply because noteworthy methodological and theoretical breakthroughs are so difficult to achieve.

But both Brunswik and Gibson did much more than this. Even though Brunswik is known primarily for his lens model theory and Gibson is known primarily for his theory of direct perception, their contributions to psychology are more vast and more important than these solitary contributions (Vicente, 2003) because what they did was create a qualitatively different type of psychology, one that is based on a systems approach and thus deals with the human–environment system rather than with the human alone. This new systems view, which Brunswik labeled ecological psychology, is based on several meta-theoretical commitments, including (a) a distinction between distal structure (i.e., "thing") and proximal structure (i.e., "medium"), (b) commensurate descriptions of the organism and environment, and (c) understanding human behavior by focusing on adaptation to functionally significant environmental regularities (Vicente, 2003).

These commitments can lead to many different theories and methods, not just the lens model and direct perception. The research of Kirlik et al. (1993) shows the power and the flexibility of these commitments when combined with the mathematical and conceptual arsenal provided by DST.

In this volume, the promise of ecological psychology for the human factors and cognitive engineering communities is beginning to be realized. We see examples of existing methods and theories to new problems, of innovations to existing methods and theories, and perhaps most important of all, of new methods and theories inspired by the tenets of ecological psychology. I believe that the future of human factors and cognitive engineering lies in continuing to explore this path defined by Brunswik and Gibson, broadly defined. The chapters in this volume represent a vital step forward.

Acknowledgments. The writing of this chapter was sponsored by a discovery grant and an E. W. R. Steacie Memorial Fellowship from the Natural Sciences and Engineering Research Council of Canada. I thank Olivier St.-Cyr for his helpful comments.

References

Brehmer, B. (1992). Dynamic decision making: Human control of complex systems. *Acta Psychologica, 81,* 211–241.

Brunswik, E. (1957). Scope and aspects of the cognitive problem. In H. E. Gruber, R. Jessor, & K. Hammond (Eds.), *Contemporary approaches to cognition* (pp. 5–31). Cambridge, Mass.: Harvard University Press.

Einstein, A., & Infeld, L. (1938/1966). *The evolution of physics: From early concepts to relativity and quanta.* New York: Simon & Schuster.

Flach, J., Hancock, P., Caird, J., & Vicente, K. J. (1995). *Global perspectives on the ecology of human–machine systems.* Hillsdale, N.J.: Erlbaum.

Gibson, J. J. (1979). *The ecological approach to visual perception.* Boston: Houghton-Mifflin.

Hajdukiewicz, J. R., & Vicente, K. J. (2004). What does computer-mediated control of a thermal-hydraulic system have to do with moving your jaw to speak? Evidence for synergies in process control. *Ecological Psychology, 16,* 255–285.

Hamilton, D. P. (1991). Research papers: Who's uncited now? *Science, 251,* 25.

Hancock, P., Flach, J., Caird, J., & Vicente, K. J. (1995). *Local applications of the ecological approach to human-machine systems.* Hillsdale, N.J.: Erlbaum.

Hogarth, R. M. (1981). Beyond discrete biases: Functional and dysfunctional aspects of judgmental heuristics. *Psychological Bulletin, 90,* 197–217.

Kirlik, A., Miller, R. A., & Jagacinski, R. J. (1993). Supervisory control in a dynamic and uncertain environment: A process model of skilled human-environment interaction. *IEEE Transactions on Systems, Man, & Cynernetics, SMC-23,* 929–952.

Lee, J. D., Cassano, A., & Vicente, K. J. (in press). Bibliometric analysis of *Human Factors* (1970–2000): Scientific impact, stratification, predictability, and trends. *Human Factors.*

Port, R. F., & van Gelder, T. (1995). *Mind as motion: Explorations in the dynamics of cognition.* Cambridge, Mass.: MIT Press.

van Gelder, T. (1998). The dynamical hypothesis in cognitive science. *Behavioral and Brain Sciences, 21,* 615–665.

Vicente, K. J. (2000). Toward Jeffersonian research programmes in ergonomics science. *Theoretical Issues in Ergonomics Science, 1,* 93–113.

Vicente, K. J. (2003). Beyond the lens model and direct perception: Toward a broader ecological psychology. *Ecological Psychology, 15,* 241–267.

Name Index

Subject Index

Boldface page numbers indicate that the topic is mentioned in a table or figure.